The Mahābhārata

The Mahābhārata

An Inquiry in the Human Condition

Chaturvedi Badrinath

Orient BlackSwan

THE MAHĀBHĀRATA

ORIENT BLACKSWAN PRIVATE LIMITED

Registered Office
3-6-752 Himayatnagar, Hyderabad 500 029 (A.P.), INDIA
e-mail: centraloffice@orientblackswan.com

Other Offices
Bangalore, Bhopal, Bhubaneshwar, Chennai, Ernakulam, Guwahati, Hyderabad, Jaipur, Kolkata, Lucknow, Mumbai, New Delhi, Noida, Patna

First Published in Hardback by Orient BlackSwan Private Limited 2006
First published in Paperback 2007
This Orient BlackSwan impression 2013

ISBN 978-81-250-3238-0

Typeset in 11.5/14pt, New Times Roman

Typeset by
i Links 'n' Grafix Pvt. Ltd.
New Delhi

Printed in India at
B.B. Press
Noida

Published by
Orient Blackswan Private Limited
1/24 Asaf Ali Road
New Delhi 110 002
e-mail: delhi@orientblackswan.com

Contents

Acknowledgements

My studies in the *Mahābhārata* began systematically in 1971 with the award of a Homi Bhabha Fellowship to me (1971–73), to write on dharma as the key to understanding the history of the Western encounter with Indian civilisation. That encounter took place in the form of Western Christianity, Liberalism, Modern Science and Marxism, each of these forces trying to change India from its own perspective. My journeys in that history showed that each one of them had perceived the foundations of Indian civilisation wrongly. That led me to dharma, upon which those foundations were laid, and dharma led me to the *Mahābhārata*, opening an entirely new universe of the knowledge of the self and of the other in relationship, individually and collectively. My journey changed from studying a history that was limited, anyway mostly negative in being a history of wrong understandings and misunderstandings, to studying the *Mahābhārata*'s inquiry into those universal questions of human existence that every human being asks practically at every turn of his or her life.

In writing this work I have come to owe a debt of gratitude to many.

To Jyotirmaya Sharma, most of all. For his unwavering faith in my work on the *Mahābhārata*; reading several chapters of it as they were being written and then the entire text; taking upon himself from the beginning, and that in the midst of his own taxing work, the task of finding a publisher for a book of this size; and for mostly freeing me from the burden of anxieties that arise in the process of having a work of this kind published, taking that burden upon himself instead, and bearing it with patience and grace.

To each of those many institutes and universities, in India and in Europe, who during the last three decades invited me to speak on the various dimensions of dharma in modern contexts or on the *Mahābhārata* as an inquiry in the human condition. Equally to those men and women, in India and in Europe, with whom, at different times, at different places, in different circumstances, I have been having continuing conversations on the *Mahābhārata*'s contribution to the knowledge of man and the world. For it is through those conversations that my own understanding of the foundations of relationships, of the self with the self and of the self with the other, deepened. If I do not name those institutes and persons individually here, it is only because their list is long, virtually covering my history of the last three decades of seeking.

To Vishnu Bhagwat, for his abiding faith in this work and its relevance to the India of today; for his continuing concern, even charming impatience, that it be published as early as possible and reach the people. To his wife Niloufer Bhagwat, for setting up, for the women of the diplomatic community in New Delhi, my talk on 'The Women of the *Mahābhārata*', at the Navy House, on 11 March 1998, and for her graciousness to me always. The response of the women of different nationalities assembled at that talk was a proof that the women of the *Mahābhārata* are universally incarnate—as teachers of mankind.

To O.P. Jain; Abdul Rehman Antulay; to Harsh Sethi and to his wife, Vimala Ramachandran; and to Mahesh Buch; for their faith in the relevance of this work and for their support.

To Seeta Badrinath, for her paying the entire expenses of having the Sanskrit shloka-s cited in this book typed into the manuscript.

To Mohini Mullick, for preparing the first draft of the Index and Concordance, in itself considerable work. For its present form and contents, and for any error(s) in them, the responsibility is mine.

To Punam Kumar, for reading the first eight chapters of the book and suggesting some editorial changes which were very helpful in removing errors and improving at places the text.

To Saradamani Devi, I owe a special debt of deep gratitude.

There are two different recensions of the *Mahābhārata*, the Southern and the Northern, with different editions in each. In the Southern recension, the Kumbakonam edition is best known; in the Northern, the Gita Press Gorakhpur and the Pune editions. The difference between the two recensions is not only in their size, the Southern omitting in some cases the material that exists in the Northern, and the Northern adding some material that does not exist in the Southern, but also in the numbering of chapters in each of the eighteen *parva*-s of the *Mahābhārata*, which can vary quite erratically. A substantial part of the present book was written when I lived in Madras (now Chennai) and even though I had 'Gorakhpur' with me then, I had used 'Kumbakonam', all references to chapter and verse being to that edition. The remaining and the major part of it, was written during the last six years in Gurgaon where I lived; all references to chapter and verse now being to 'Gorakhpur', for I didn't have with me 'Kumbakonam'. To avoid what undoubtedly would have been maddening confusion, and to make the references uniform, I had to change from 'Kumbakonam' to 'Gorakhpur'. That journey turned out to be more painful and draining than

I imagined it would be, especially because I could not find 'Kumbakonam' in any of the libraries of Delhi, not even in those where I had hoped I would. For that matter, even in Madras the Kumbakonam edition, out of print for decades, can be seen only in the library of the Kuppuswami Sastri Research Institute.

It was during my maddening journey from 'Kumbakonam' to 'Gorakhpur' (via Gurgaon) that I was led to Saradamani Devi, a Sanskritist. On hearing my tale of woe, she brought out her eighteen volumes of the *Mahābhārata*. They were not 'Kumbakonam' but yet another edition of the Southern recension, the one compiled by P.P.S. Sastri (1935) from the manuscripts at the Tanjore Palace Library (with his variations even in that!). It was clear they would be no help, for the numbering of chapter and verse in them varied from 'Kumbakonam' as much as it did from 'Kumbakonam' to 'Gorakhpur'. Noticing the look of desolation on my face, Saradamani Devi said, 'Even so, take them. They may be of some use to you in your work.' She told me that those books had belonged to her late mother, Ratnamayi Devi, also a Sanskritist. To one totally unknown to her, Saradamani Devi gave away what was to her a family treasure; for her mother would have turned the pages of that edition of the *Mahābhārata* numerous times, leaving upon them the invisible traces of her hand. Saradamani Devi's generosity to me could easily be a story from the *Mahābhārata* itself—of spontaneous, selfless giving.

To Lance Dane, I owe a debt of gratitude for his passionate support to this work from the moments he read it in manuscript; for his sage counsel as regards the aesthetics of its final production; and for joyfully offering for the cover his photograph of a rare painting depicting Ganesha taking down Vyasa's dictated composition of the *Mahābhārata*, most appropriate for this book, for it begins with the story of Vyasa and his divine stenographer, Ganesha.

And, finally, to Hemlata Shankar of Orient Longman, I owe my profound thanks for the great care and enjoyment she has taken in the editing and production of this book.

Should this work on the *Mahābhārata* be of any value to anyone reading it, and help bring in his or her life the joy of relationships in truth and freedom, my debts of gratitude would have been repaid—in some measure at least.

Pondicherry.
March 2006 CHATURVEDI BADRINATH

A Note on the Diacritical Marks and Translations

In providing the customary diacritical marks for Sanskrit names and words, I have kept the standard usage, except in one respect. There are two different *sh*-s in the Devanagari script in which Sanskrit is written: श and ष. The first is generally indicated by ś, as for example in the word deśa; and the other by ṣ, as in the name 'Bhīṣma'. I've removed this distinction, without any injury to the script. Thus, I've kept them as *'desha'* and 'Bhīṣma'. For that is exactly how they are pronounced as far as *sh* is concerned. Likewise, I've made it as dharmashāstra instead of *dharmaśāstra.* (Where I've quoted P.V. Kane's *History of Dharmaśāstra*, it is as he wrote it. Likewise in the case of other authors, the diacritical marks are as they have used them.) Instead of Kṛṣṇa, with three standard diacritical marks, I keep it as *Krishna, smriti* instead of *smṛti*, *prakriti* instead of *prakṛti,* for that is exactly how they are pronounced.

All translations of the Sanksrit verses from the *Mahābhārata* are mine (except where they are expressly indicated as being by someone else.) The original text is followed by my translation. They are not literal translations of every word in the verse, but of its substance. For their accuracy, I take full responsibility. I am not a Sanskrit pandit; should there remain some errors in my translations, despite my taking great care to ensure their accuracy, I seek forgiveness from Sanskrit scholars.

Dramatis Personæ of the *Mahābhārata*

The self and the *other*

The Eighteen Main *Parva-s* of the *Mahābhārata*

(in the following sequence)

1 *Ādi-parva*

2 *Sabhā-parva*

3 *Vana-parva*

4 *Viratā-parva*

5 *Udyoga-parva*

6 *Bhīṣma-parva*

7 *Droṇa-parva*

8 *Karṇa-parva*

9 *Shalya-parva*

10 *Sauptika-parva*

11 *Strī-parva*

12 *Shānti-parva*

13 *Anushāsana-parva*

14 *Āshvamedhika-parva*

15 *Āshramavāsika-parva*

16 *Mausala-parva*

17 *Mahāprasthana-parva*

18 *Svargārohana-parva*

CHAPTER ONE

Introduction to the Mahābhārata

- The subjects of the inquiry and their universality
- The method in the inquiry

When Krishna-Dvaipāyana Vyāsa set out to write the *Mahābhārata* he looked for a stenographer, an intelligent one, to find whom was as difficult an undertaking then as it is now. He approached Gaṇesha, who graciously agreed but not without imposing a condition, that during working hours the dictation would have to be continuous and his pen must not be kept idle even for a moment.[1] In an act of reckless courage the author agreed. But, somewhat cunningly, with a smile on his lips, he imposed a counter-condition: that Gaṇesha would take nothing down until he had understood the real import of what was said.[2] What was said had so many levels of meaning that he often took time to understand the essence of a statement, which was the time Vyāsa gained to compose further.[3]

The author and the stenographer of the *Mahābhārata* made a remarkable team. Vyāsa has left us a portrait of himself. He was of dusky dark colour; hence *Krishna* as a part of his name. His mother, *Satya*vatī, a fisherwoman in the earlier part of her life, known then also as Matsyagandhā, 'the one who smelt of fish', gave birth to him on an island in the river Yamunā; hence *Dvaipāyana* as the other part of his name. The sage Parāshara was his father. On seeing young Satyavatī, Parāshara was greatly roused by her beauty, and she was so awed by his fame and authority, that, while ferrying him across the river in her boat one day, she reluctantly submitted to his desire for her, and Vyāsa was born of that most unlikely union.[4] At the same time she was miraculously cured of her disagreeable smell of fish, and acquired an exquisite fragrance in its place, and would thereafter be known also as Divyagandhā, 'the one with a divine smell'. Vyāsa grew to be frighteningly ugly, his visage so fierce, besides his matted hair, that women, when they looked at him, would close their eyes from shock. The story of his birth was later narrated also by his mother,[5] Satyavatī, now a young woman, when this time she captured the heart of a king, Shāntanu, who proposed marriage to her, even though she was of a lower social level, and she became his queen. Vyāsa had promised his mother that should she ever want him to be of service to her, she had only to think of him, and he would be with her instantly. That promise he kept.

The stenographer looked even more remarkable. He carried on his human body the head of an elephant. His legs were stubby and short. And he had a huge stomach, so grotesquely out of proportion with the rest of his body that, at the sight of him, one day some gods and sages laughed at him. Roused to great anger by that act of gross disrespect, Gaṇesha broke his right tusk into two, and with the broken end in his right hand he threatened to destroy them and their universe. Knowing that he was perfectly capable of doing so, they apologised abjectly, and took a vow that whenever they would begin a work they would do so by seeking his blessings first, a practice kept up to the present day even by ordinary mortals.

Vyāsa and Gaṇesha together produced what became a vast and a most systematic inquiry ever undertaken into the foundations of human relationships, a journey towards understanding the human condition: the *Mahābhārata*. Let me begin this work by offering to them my salutations, again, again, and yet again.

The subjects of the inquiry and their universality

The concerns of the *Mahābhārata* are the concerns of everyday life everywhere. In its inquiry into the human condition it raises those very questions the answers to which we all seek in the diverse circumstances of our lives. What is happiness? What is unhappiness? What is health? What is sickness? In what relation does the mind exist with the body? What is pleasure? What is pain? What is the nature of sexual pleasure? What kind of energy is sex? What are the conditions in which it flourishes, and what are the conditions in which it dies? What is wealth? What is poverty? What is truth? What is untruth? Are they absolutes? And also, *whose* truth? What is violence? From where does violence arise? What kind of relation is there between what one does and thinks and what one becomes? What is freedom? What is bondage? Who is wise? And who is a fool? What is it to be a saint? What is purity? What is pilgrimage? Why did a thing happen the way it happened? And, conversely, why did a thing not happen when there was every reason to believe that it would happen? Is one free to make oneself what one is? Or is one determined by some other force: Fate, or God, or History? What is the right ordering of one's relationship with one's self and with the *other*? What relation does it have with time and place? What is governance? What are its foundations? What is order? And what is disorder? What relation do they have with time and place? What is death? And what is that which is deathless? These and related questions are the substance of the *Mahābhārata*; as, indeed, they are the substance of human life.

In its opening chapter, the *Ādi-parva*, the *Mahābhārata* provides us with a very detailed table of contents. Stated in its brief outline, the inquiry is into the four ends of human life. Related at all times intimately with each other, they are: *dharma*, or the foundations of all relationships, personal and social; *artha*, or the material conditions of life; *kāma*, sexual happiness, or, used in a wider sense, fulfilment of desire; and *mokṣha*, freedom, liberation.[6] No one of them would have meaning without the other three. And all of them give rise to very many questions, which all of us ask, with varying degrees of intensity, at one turn or the other of our circumstances. And they are the questions the *Mahābhārata* takes up in their concrete expressions.

What is *dharma*? What are those foundations upon which all human relationships everywhere are based? Who determines what those foundations shall be? Are they given as inherent in human life itself? Are they subject to the varying conditions and circumstances of a person's life, so that there is one *dharma* for normal conditions, and another in times of distress, for example? Is there one *dharma* for the scholar devoted to learning and teaching; another *dharma* for the householder; a different *dharma* for the king; and a separate *dharma* for one who would maintain services? Is *dharma* a self-determining reality that gives direction to a person's life, and is it to be discovered in a process of self-discovery as to what one is meant to be? And since self-discovery cannot ever be a finished product, is *dharma* a state of *becoming*, changing with the different perceptions one has of oneself at different times? Or is it determined collectively by each society, determined differently by different societies at different times, so that it is history that will determine what an individual person is meant to be? If *dharma* be the order of life, without which life could not be, what are the universally unchanging elements of *dharma*, and what is in it that will necessarily be open to change, which is unpredictable besides? How is this tension between the eternal and the transient to be resolved, when both form parts of the same reality? This question will apply to *dharma* as the foundation of law and governance most of all. The question of *satya*, truth, is inseparable from the question of *dharma*. What *is* truth, and what is untruth? The same questions that apply to *dharma* apply simultaneously to truth as well. From the beginning to the end, all these questions occupy, in specific contexts, a very considerable part of the *Mahābhārata*'s inquiry into the human condition. These questions are discussed, in different circumstances of different people, in the *Ādi-parva*, in the *Sabhā-parva*, in the *Vana-parva*, in the *Anushāsana-parva*, in the *Āshvamedhika-parva*, and more especially in the *Shānti-parva*.

What amount of material resources, *artha*, is essential to human happiness and dignity? In what way does the lack of *artha*, and the unending greed for more, both affect one's relationship with one's self and with the *other*? Is wealth necessarily a value? In what measure is *artha*, or material well-being, itself a foundation of *dharma*? In order that there be a sane society, and freedom from the violence of acquisition, to what abiding principles as *dharma* must the acquisition of wealth and its consumption be at all times everywhere subordinate? What must a just and rational economic system be like? Of the four ends of life, is not *artha*, or the acquisition of material resources, of the greatest importance, the quality of the other three depending upon it? By what principles must the king, now the state, be governed in relation to wealth? What shall be the just principles of taxation as the main resource of state revenues? And in what ways must those revenues be spent to create the welfare and the good of the people? In case there is a conflict between *dharma*, as the ethical foundation of relationships, and *artha*, which of the two shall have, in principle, precedence over the other? In what kind of life will material concerns cease to have the hold over the mind which they indisputably have? These questions are raised and discussed in great detail in the *Mahābhārata*, some of them in the *Udyoga-parva*, most of them in the *Shānti-parva*, and some in the *Anushāsana-parva*.

Since prudence, or *nīti*, is intimately associated with the acquisition of wealth and with the keeping of it, as it is with the art of governance, indeed with most situations of life, there is in the *Mahābhārata* a good amount of prudence-literature, or the *nīti*-maxims. They all focus on *svārtha,* self-interest, as the spring of all human actions. Many of them focus on *vāṇī*, speech, to which everything in the functional world is tied. They discuss the probable conflict between the need to speak pleasantly and the greater need to speak truthfully. In case there is a straight conflict between the two, how is it to be reconciled? Many of the *nīti*-maxims focus on *trust and trusting* which is so very central to all relationships, personal and social, and on the problems connected with them. They discuss the danger that arises when trust is wrongly placed; and they discuss the even greater danger when nobody trusts anybody. Some other *nīti*-maxims focus on the relationship between the strong and the weak: on the attitude the weak should have towards the strong as a means of self-preservation, and the attitude which the strong must have, equally in their own interest, towards the weak and the poor. There is the problem, besides, that something that is inherently right and, in many circumstances, also a prudent thing to do, that the same thing, in certain other circumstances, may not at all be a prudent thing to do, even though it may be on principle a right thing to do. How is it to be ensured that the element of expediency, present in human situations at all times, does not turn into unprincipled opportunism, which it so very easily can, and often does? Once expediency is allowed as a defensible principle of conduct in *abnormal times*, *āpadkāla*, what is the mechanism by which it can be held in check and not used in bad faith at other times, when the presence of bad faith will be impossible to establish? How is *tension between prudence and truth*, between *nīti* and *dharma*, to be resolved? How is a *dilemma* to be resolved when there is a straight conflict between what is right and what is also right, and both inviolable duties besides? These questions are discussed in the *Mahābhārata* in great detail and in different circumstances, more especially in the area of governance, in the *Udyoga-parva*, in the *Sabhā-parva*, in the *Anushāsana-parva*, and in the *Shānti-parva*.

Of the four ends of life, which one has primacy in actual reality? In one answer to this question, it is maintained that it is sexual impulse, *kāma*, which governs most human conduct. Primacy is assigned to human sexuality, to which everything else in actual practice is shown to be subordinate. But this is only one of the positions taken in the *Mahābhārata*, although a dominant one. Sexual energy, *kāma*, and its varied manifestations, are explored in great depth, and from different angles. What is also examined is the question: between the man and the woman, who derives the greater sexual pleasure? Assigning primacy to the sexual impulse and to its workings, the bounds within which it is to be kept nevertheless, if it can be kept within any prescribed bounds at all, are explored systematically. What is explored in the main is the question whether *kāma* is just physical appetite, as hunger and thirst are, or is it, even in its physicality, a state of togetherness between a man and a woman in the first place? If it is a state of togetherness, then it must also lead to the question of its *disha*, direction. What are the conditions of sexual fulfilment? In other words, what is the relation between *dharma* and *kāma* above all? What does it mean to say that sexuality should be subject to *dharma*? These questions are discussed in the *Mahābhārata*, in great detail, in the *Ādi-parva*, in the *Anushāsana-parva*, and in the *Shānti-parva*, and indeed throughout that work.

In the context of human sexuality, but not in that context alone, what is examined is *desire* and its workings. Desire, in being a human attribute, and therefore to be acknowledged with respect, can also lead to its tyranny and violence—the tyranny of desire. The *Mahābhārata* acknowledges the evident psychological force of desire, *kāma*, that permeates all life; but at the same time it examines the greater need for its disciplining, if desire is not to become self-destructive, and become destructive also of the *other*, which it so easily can. Does *self-discipline* mean self-denial? The *Mahābhārata* examines them as two different paths; the latter, if turned into a principle, being quite as destructive as self-indulgence.

Desire for *sukha*, pleasure, and avoidance of *duhkha*, pain, being the two main driving forces of human life, the *Mahābhārata* explores in a most thoroughgoing manner these twin realities, and man's blinding subjection to them. '*Pleasure*' and '*pain*' are discussed in some forty chapters spread over different *parva*-s. Connected with this subject is the analysis of human faculties, of the body and the mind, and their workings either in harmony with each other or out of joint. What emerge are reflections on human freedom.

The question of *mokṣha*, human freedom, forms a substantial part of the *Mahābhārata*. It is only *in* freedom that one can be fully human. But what *is* freedom? In the first place, freedom is freedom *from*. So what is *mokṣha* freedom *from*? That freedom once gained, what still remains to be gained is freedom *into*. What is the state of *mokṣha* like? How is *mokṣha* to be gained? What are the paths to *mokṣha*? What is *mokṣha* in its relation to *dharma*, *artha*, and *kāma*? In that state of freedom, are those three dissolved as any further concerns of one's life? Or, are they, in that state, only the more heightened as to their meaning to life? What kind of person, in relationship with the *other*, is he, or she, who has achieved freedom? Or is *mokṣha* a going beyond *all* relationships, beyond all ties and human bonds? Or, in that state, are they actually not repudiated but only perceived differently, away from the narrowness of their limits? These questions are raised in the *Mahābhārata* again and again, in different contexts, in the process of reflecting upon *mokṣha* as human freedom, the ultimate end of life. They are to be found in the *Vana-parva*, in the *Anushāsana-parva*, in the *Shānti-parva*, and in the *Āshvamedhika-parva*.

The question of human freedom is seen in yet another light. Most of human drama takes place between *the opposites* of every kind—birth and death, pleasure and pain, attraction and repulsion, happiness and suffering, prosperity and adversity, confusion and clarity, gain and loss, laughter and tears, joy and sorrow, success and failure, praise and condemnation, coming together and parting. If man is not to be a dangling man between one and the other, dangling perpetually, then he must seek freedom from the workings of the opposites. It is a necessity for ordinary human sanity as well. The *Mahābhārata* takes up this question in its concrete expressions in human living in the afore-mentioned *parva*-s.

But *is* man truly free? Is a person free to determine what he, or she, shall be? Or does some other force, over and above the individual, govern a person's destiny? Why do things happen the way they happen, or why do they not happen the way they *should* happen, given the appropriate conditions of their happening? This raises the familiar question concerning *free will* vs *determinism*, which, in its essence, is the question of causality. And this is not some question of abstract philosophy, but is intimately related to every person's life. The *Mahābhārata* throughout has this as one of its fundamental concerns: *karma* or *daiva*? Human endeavour *or* fate? Reflections on *kāla*, time, as the force which determines a person's changing fortunes, and the attitude that one can accordingly adopt towards the events of one's life, form another substantial part of the *Mahābhārata*. The problem of causality remains unresolved, as it must, by its very nature; but, the *Mahābhārata* suggests, it need not lead to moral paralysis of the will. This subject is spread throughout the *Mahābhārata*, in the context of one human situation or another, but is discussed in a more concentrated form in the *Ādi-parva*, in the *Udyoga-parva*, in the *Vana-parva*, in the *Anushāsana-parva*, and in the *Shānti-parva*.

Even if predeterminism was to be acknowledged, in whatever degree, as that which conditions human life, the question would still remain: *who*, or *what*, determines in advance how things shall be? Is it Time that is the cause of every event, the changing Time explaining the changing circumstances of one's life? Or is it human effort, individual and collective? In any case, on what basis is there predeterminism? Does it have rationality, the human mind can grasp and come to terms with it thereby, or is it capricious and arbitrary, wrapped up in a mystery beyond human reach? Predeterminism may still be *self-determinism*, which the *Mahābhārata* explores systematically, in its application to the individual and collective life. For the question of *responsibility* is at all times inseparably connected with one's own acts, *karma*, as being ultimately the determining factor in what one makes of oneself. The question of *the causality of karma*, which in essence is self-determinism, remains throughout a central concern of the *Mahābhārata*, and is examined from very many different angles in the afore-mentioned *parva*-s.

Belief in *rebirth* arises from the mechanism of *karma*; for not all 'acts' fructify during one lifetime, although a great many acts do. Even among the latter, some take longer to come to fruition than do others. Every *karma*, individual or collective, starts its own logic; and once set up the logic of *karma* must work itself out. This gives rise to very many other questions: the relation between divine grace and the inexorable logic of *karma*, for example; or the relation between compassion and another's *karma*, as another example. In the domain of *karma*, is there place for grace? Is there in it any reprieve? Or is there in the logic of *karma* neither grace nor reprieve, and does one stand totally alone? Besides, there is the universally seen puzzle that those who are good suffer and those who are wicked flourish. If all that about *karma* is true, how is *this* disparity to be explained? These questions occupy the *Mahābhārata* from the beginning to the end.

There is, moreover, *the question of history and meaning*. This is explored in the *Mahābhārata* at many different levels. *Kāla*, 'time', in which everything originates and is destroyed, the determining factor of one's destiny, is not the historical 'time'. Neither is it the 'time' that is physically measured. It is a force, say, akin to God, in which originate all that *is* and also all that *is not*. It is the ultimate cause of all happenings. At another level, *kāla*, 'time', is a measure of appropriateness. It is combined with *desha* and *pātra*, 'place' and 'the person concerned'. These three, *desha*, *kāla* and *pātra*, that is, 'the proper place', 'the proper time', and 'the proper person', determine the appropriateness of an act, and thus its *meaning*. In other words, they determine the *context*, in which a person lives and has his, or her, being; and meaning lies in context. At still another level, 'time' as *history* is examined as giving substance to one's life. The three attributes of history, the 'past', the 'present' and the 'future', and one's relationship with them as one's relationship with one's self, constitutes one of the subjects of the inquiry into the human condition. At the same time, acknowledging the power of *kāla* in different forms, the *Mahābhārata* raises the question: *am I my history alone*? Is 'context' all that there is to 'meaning'? And with that, the inquiry moves on to a different plane—that of the relationship between history and its transcending, between the eternal and the transient, *nitya* and *anitya*, as the substance of life and relationships. All these questions are to be found throughout the *Mahābhārata*.

A very large part of the *Mahābhārata* is concerned with *danda*, 'governance'; in other words, with *rāja-dharma*, or with the duties of the State towards the people. 'What is governance? What is it like? What are its forms? What is it based on? What is its purpose? What is its origin? What is its structure?' In the course of this inquiry, very many other questions naturally arise, for example, the question concerning *nyāya*, justice, which has the meaning both of *law* and *justice*. The other question is, to take another example, about the relationship between *ends* and *means*. Can the ends justify the means? All these questions are taken up in a thoroughgoing discussion on *dharma* as the foundation of law and governance, which are instruments of regulating human relationships, one's relationships with the *other*. But governance is not by an external force, the State, alone, but by one's self in the first place. Self-governance is the best, in the absence of which even the force of the State will eventually not be able to govern. *Dharma* as law is self-regulation, in relation both to one's self and to the *other*. These questions make up the main part of the *Shānti-parva*, but are to be found no less in the *Ādi-parva*, the *Udyoga-parva*, the *Vana-parva*, and the *Anushāsana-parva*.

The method in the inquiry

If we cast a quick look at the history of thought, especially in the West, we can see that, when systematised into an *ism*, the various explanations of the human condition had fiercely rejected each other. The rationalism of eighteenth-century Enlightenment rejected faith and tradition, and therefore all religions, not just Christianity. Romanticism rejected the Enlightenment. Utilitarianism and psycho-analysis rejected romanticism. Existentialism rejected them all, although there were two or three Christian existentialists, like Kierkegaard and Gabriel Marcel and Jaspers. Marxism, a child of the Enlightenment, rejected romanticism, liberal individualism, nationalism, and much of existentialism as well. There has been, in the history of Western philosophy, a continuing war between rationalism and empiricism, and between idealism and realism, other *isms* aligning themselves with the one or the other. Positivism rejected moral statements as subjectivism and also most of metaphysics as nonsense in a literal sense. Science rejected the mystical; and mysticism rejected science. Objectivism despises all forms of relativism; and relativism has tried to show that objectivism, especially in science, is an intellectual myth. Materialism rejected spiritualism as emotional froth; and spiritualism looked upon materialism as base and ignoble. The universal has been defined in such a way as to remove all particularities from it: there has been, therefore, a war between the assumed universalism of the Enlightenment idea of history and the visible particularities of human life. That soon gave rise to the claims of regionalism and of nationalism. And then, in turn, it became regionalism vs nationalism, and nationalism vs universalism. And Man has been set against Nature.

But, although fiercely rejecting each other, all these *isms* have one thing in common—a logic which fragments human attributes into irreconcilable polarities, and then assumes that *either* the one *or* the other is *the* reality, and constructs its world view wholly on that, or the logic of *either/or*.

What distinguishes the *Mahābhārata* is the method it follows in exploring these human questions. The answers to them in other traditions, religious or philosophical, come from either the divine revelation, or from the definitions that are set up, and from the presuppositions that surround them and are held true *a priori*. But that also means that if one's critical faculties remain unconvinced by what the divine revelation, different anyway in different religions, says about the human condition, then one has to seek answers to them somewhere else. And by now it is undeniable that the answers to them, when they came from the arbitrary definitions and presuppositions of philosophical systems, or from what is called scientific method, were so fragmented that, true in some measure, they falsified human reality in its totality. The definitions of *history*, and the presuppositions about it, offer one example. When human material would not respond to those definitions, then that material would either be dismissed, or would be forced somehow into the mould of those definitions, both leading to untruth. The utilitarian definitions of *pleasure* and *pain* offer yet another example, which, open always to serious questions as ethical or psychological theory, had very nearly devastated the lives of a great many people.

The *Upanishad*-s had, in a most revolutionary shift, moved the human mind away from the fearful worship of many 'gods', which were the elements of Nature. The focus of their inquiry became, instead, that one reality, *Brahman*, which pervades the universe and is manifest also in one's self, the *ātman*. The emphasis now was on what is within and its unity with the outside world. The *Mahābhārata* took another great leap forward; it became an inquiry into the nature of 'self' in relation with the *other*. Since life is evidently a system of relationships, personal and social, it became an inquiry into what sustains them, their order, or *dharma*, and what destroys them, their *a-dharma*, disorder. Human living, vastly varied and infinitely complex, was the natural material of that inquiry.

The inquiry revolves around the self and the *other*. It begins with the evident fact that, in the first place, one has a relationship with one's self, with one's physical body, desires, hopes, fears, and search for meaning. And one has at the same time a relationship with the *other*. The two constitute the indivisible unity of life. Thus, one's relationship with one's self and with the *other* is the central concern of the *Mahābhārata*. It is around this issue that every parable in it revolves, with which every discussion begins and ends, and it is in it that the philosophical and the political find their ultimate ethical ground.

The *Mahābhārata* shows that it is not until one's relationship with one's self is right that one's relationship with the *other* can be right, and the two being inseparable, it is by achieving a right relationship with the *other* that one comes to one's self, fulfilled. Disturbed in my relationship with myself, I will be disturbed in my relationship with everyone else. Therefore, self-understanding is an essential condition of understanding the *other*. The two are inseparable.

But what is the *right* ordering of one's life and relationships? What criteria will determine what a 'right relationship' is? And who will decide what those criteria are? How are these questions to be answered without either taking them into the bottomless pit of philosophic abstractions or dispersing them into empty moralising? The *Mahābhārata* shows that the answers lie in the rhythms of man's own being. Any view of the ordering of life and relationships, if it is to have a universal meaning, must be derived from life itself, from the rhythms of life, and not be something in which the proof of what you want to prove is already provided. Hence, the method it follows is inherent in life itself; it is not an artificial construct of the mind. This puts the *Mahābhārata* above every school of philosophical and political theory. In this respect, as in many others, the *Mahābhārata* stands distinctly apart from all systems of philosophy. What distinguishes it is its *method* of reflecting upon life and relationships. The following are the main characteristics of that method. They are manifest throughout that work as:

1. Every philosophical school in India had first developed its particular view of *ātman*, Self, or the denial, as in Buddhism, that any such entity exists. Their distinct ethical and spiritual disciplines were based primarily on

that. But their metaphysical positions hardly related to the everyday life and its puzzling complexities. Neither did they throw any great light on how one can understand who one is in his, or her, specific individuality; placed in his, or her, specific situation; with specific relationships; each with his, or her, specific temperament, inclination, desires, fears, and joys. The big *'self' of Indian philosophy swallowed the small 'self' of the individual*. The understanding of the 'Self' did not necessarily lead to self-understanding. Therefore, the *Mahābhārata* takes up self-understanding, or self-knowledge, not in the shadow of the big 'Self' but in relation to concrete situations and contexts through which one lives one's life. However, while the small 'self' must not be swallowed by the big 'Self', the *Mahābhārata* shows, too, that the particularity of the former can be understood only in terms that go beyond the particular. The personal is best understood by understanding the human issues that go beyond the personal.

2. There is in the *Mahābhārata* no dichotomy between the particular and the universal. There is only the demonstration that just as there can be the tyranny of the particular and the specific when separated from the universal, there is also the tyranny of the universal when it is removed from its domain the particular altogether. The tyranny of the transcendent can be as much as the tyranny of the given.

3. The *Mahābhārata* does not base its understanding of human life on divine revelation or on philosophic presuppositions *a priori*. Neither does it ask for the definitions of things but for their *lakṣaṇa*, attributes, by which a thing is known, is recognised. That is how the discussions concerning *dharma* and truth proceed, enumerating their *lakṣaṇa*-s, their attributes, by which they are known, or by which they become manifest. However complex the discussion about them, they invariably are connected with the simple question as to how they are reflected in one's relationship with one's self and with the *other*. Likewise the question is not of the definition, say, of 'happiness', but: what is a happy person like, or what is an unhappy person like, in relation to himself, or herself, and in relation to the *other*? Similarly, not the definition of 'love', but the *lakṣaṇa*-s of love manifest in one's life by which a loving person is recognised. This applies in the *Mahābhārata* equally to that most prized state, *moksha*, supreme freedom. In other systems of philosophy, *mokṣha* is squeezed to death by all kinds of intricacies

and speculations; the *Mahābhārata* only asks: what is a free person like in his, or her, relationships? What are his, or her, attributes by which he, or she, can be recognised? To define a thing is to set its boundary, which is the definition of 'definition'. But boundaries are set arbitrarily, which explains how empirical facts often upset definitions completely. Life is so diverse and complex that no aspect of it can be limited to the boundaries of definitions without leading to untruth. However, this does *not* mean that there are no boundaries or limits whatsoever, and that all things can mean everything, in which case nothing will mean anything in particular. What the *Mahābhārata* suggests is that these boundaries and limits cannot be conceptual, for life is not limited to concepts, nor is it bound by them. Thus, for example, 'truth' is not a *concept*. It is the foundation of life and relationships; and *they* would suggest, and not some arbitrary definition of it, what truth is.

4. Human life, from the beginning to the end, being demonstrably a system of relations, whatever naturally binds them is to be understood *relationally*. Thus, throughout the *Mahābhārata*, '*dharma*', 'truth', 'justice', 'law', 'governance', 'wealth', 'sexual happiness', 'freedom', and everything else, even the meaning of 'death', are shown to be naturally relational. They are that in the sense that none of them can breathe except in relation with the rest. They are relational in the sense that they do not stand alone as 'ideas' or 'concepts'; they are woven intimately with the relation of the self with the self and of the self with the *other.* Self-understanding and understanding the *other* will have no meaning without them, and they will be empty without *them*.

5. The *Mahābhārata* demonstrates the interrelated nature of the attributes of human personality. In that, it carries forward the method in the *Upanishad*-s by exploring the workings of the body and the mind and of the desire that permeates them. It demonstrates that each human attribute has its own place and value, but that each can be meaningful only in its relation with the rest. Fragment one from the rest and assign it an overriding value—to the pursuit of pleasure, for example—and it soon turns, as it must, into its own negation, which is a state of violence to one's self. The violence in the outside world is a natural extension of it.

6. The *Mahābhārata* shows that human attributes form a natural unity, their wholeness. Perceiving them wrongly, to fragment any one of them from the rest, and place upon it either too great a value or too little, is to invite disorder, *adharma*, and do violence to one's self, from which arises the violence to the *other*. The *Mahābhārata* demonstrates this in a systematic manner. To disrespect self-interest, sexual energy, desire for material prosperity, or the more fundamental desire for pleasure, is to invite violence to one's self. But their idolatry invites even greater violence. In one case, the violence is to the individual and to his relationships; in the other case, because it enters economic and political thought and becomes an ideology, the violence is collective and extensive. The question is one of knowing the true place of everything in the scheme of human life. To value too greatly or too little a particular human attribute in its relation to the rest is to disintegrate the natural wholeness of human personality. To value the material over the spiritual, or the spiritual over the material, the transient over the eternal, or the eternal over the transient, the body over the mind, or the mind over the body, the individual over the society, or the society over the individual, the self over the *other*, or the *other* over the self, is to create conflicts both within one's self and between one's self and the rest of the world.

7. The direction the *Mahābhārata* takes is a continuation of the one that the *Upanishad*-s had taken. The latter had broken away from vedic ritualism and its belief in the magical efficacy of 'acts', and had turned human attention to the *inwardness* of the self instead. The *Mahābhārata* is even more steadfast on that path. The vedic idea of *ṛta*, the cosmic order out there, is replaced with the idea of *dharma* as the foundation of life. The *yajña* or sacrificial act is replaced with self-understanding. Gaining *puṇya*, merit, is replaced with giving and sharing with no eye on 'reward'. *Tapas* or austerity is given an inward, ethical meaning. *Tīrtha* or pilgrimage is not to some geographical place but to one's inner self in relation with the *other*. Thus *dayā* or kindness, or compassion is a *tīrtha*. The focus radically shifts from 'acts' to relationships. The *Mahābhārata* radically changes the meaning of *yajña*, *tapas*, *karma*, and *tīrtha*; and in making them relational, it gives them a deeply ethical meaning. The word *ṛta* is heard only rarely, and *dharma* becomes the dominant sound. The chanting of *mantra*s is replaced with the sound of *inquiry* into the foundations of the relationships of the self with the self and of the self with the other.

8. One of the most significant contributions of the *Upanishad*-s had been that in the search for the knowledge of reality, no one proposition about reality could ever be a complete statement about it. Hence their suggestion that, to every statement concerning the nature of reality, the word *neti* should be added—and repeated twice. Hence the famous upanishadic discipline—*neti neti*. Unfortunately, the word '*neti*' has *always* been translated wrongly as '*not this, not this*,' which completely misses its proper meaning. Composed of two words *na+iti*, it clearly means '*not yet the end*', '*not yet complete*'. *Neti* does *not* mean '*not this*', but 'not this *alone*'. *Something more remains to be said*. In its inquiry into the human condition, the *Mahābhārata* applies this discipline of *neti neti*, 'it is not this *alone*: it is not this *alone'*, even more rigorously. The discipline of *neti neti* is quite as much an ethical discipline in the service of truth as it is an intellectual discipline in the service of knowledge.

9. The *Mahābhārata* further shows, as an integral part of its method, that life is to be understood, and lived, paradoxically; for human life is paradoxical. Reality is composed of opposites; and they are related in a way that to assert the one is to assert its opposite as well. The paradox of *having* is that the more one has the greater is one's discontent. The paradox of *pleasure* is that self-control is the very first condition of pleasure; the pleasure that is unrestrained kills itself. The paradox of *intimacy* is that distance is the first condition of intimacy; the intimacy in which there is no distance turns very soon either into resentment or even into hatred. The paradox of *sexual pleasure* is that all those factors which create sexual pleasure and sexual happiness lie outside sexuality. The paradox of *self-interest* is that the only way of serving one's interest is to serve the interest of the *other*, that is to say, the pleasure and the happiness of the other is an essential condition of one's own pleasure and happiness. The paradox of the *self* is that without the *other*, the self will be inconceivable. The paradox of *language* is that silence is its highest function. And there is the paradox of *limits*, which consists in the fact that *one becomes aware of one's limits only by transgressing them*; there is no known way by which one can know one's limits in advance. Above all, there is the paradox of *life* itself, which consists in the fact, even biological, but emotional and spiritual equally, that it is by *dying* that life is. One is impossible without the other.

10. Therefore, the *Mahābhārata* systematically confronts one reality with another, one truth with another, when one is clearly the opposite of the other, but both are manifest in life simultaneously. For example, the necessity of *kshmā*, forgiveness and reconciliation, is shown to be fundamental to human relationships, and is spoken of in the highest terms, which are also lyrical. But the opposite truth is also brought up at the same time: that forgiveness is almost always interpreted as a sign of one's weakness. To forgive *always* is to invite further offence and disrespect. And this is demonstrated in as forceful a language as the necessity of forgiveness is. Similarly, the necessity of *ahiṁsā*, not-violence, as another foundation of life is discussed side by side with the opposite truth, that 'life feeds on life', and that there are situations, moreover, where violence is quite as necessary. This may appear to be confusing, especially when the opposing truths are stated equally forcefully, and there is no denying either of them. But to state only the necessity of forgiveness, or of not-violence, is to turn it into empty moralising, however noble it may sound, and will leave one still confused in the face of situations where forgiveness doesn't help, and violence may be a just necessity, to take only two examples. It is when the opposing truth has also been taken into account that a discourse will keep close to human realities. To state only one side of the truth may create a sense of clarity, but that clarity would have been achieved at the expense of truth.

11. Towards self-understanding, what has simultaneously to be taken into account is the contrary nature of human desires, leading to self-division and conflicts within one's self. Nobody is wholly a coherent being. The *Mahābhārata* consistently portrays the conflicts within oneself, between the contrary desires which constitute the unending incoherent drama of human relationships, of the self with the self and of the self with the *other.* And although the contrary elements in man's being is a universal theme of life, the way that drama unfolds, and the way in which one resolves conflicts within one's self, or does not resolve them, is the story of every specific character. There is the conflict, to take only one example, between the desire for home, and for all that home means, and also for homelessness, and for its freedom. Both have their force. It is by describing the incoherence of what is contrary, and its disquiet, that the *Mahābhārata* shows how to achieve inner coherence and its quiet.

12. There are conflicts generated within one's self not by contrary desires alone. There are familiar conflicts, besides, between what is right and what is wrong, 'right' and 'wrong' being understood not just in conventional terms of conventional morality; and one makes a choice between the two. I know what is 'right', but I may choose to do what is 'wrong'. But there is yet another area of conflict, which is a conflict not between 'right' and 'wrong' but between 'right' and 'right'. *That* produces moral *dilemma*, of having to make a choice between two equally inviolable duties when they are also in serious conflict with each other. Some moral dilemmas may be mild, some others deeply agonising. By what criteria of conduct can one resolve a dilemma between right and right? The *Mahābhārata* does not pretend that there can be any final answer to the problem of moral dilemma; for every answer would have presupposed what is in question. Then how does one act in the face of a moral dilemma?

13. Every question concerning the human condition begins with a personal question, of a specific person, who seeks to understand his, or her, specific situation, in which he, or she, is. That is because the human condition can be experienced and felt only *in* one's person. For example, injustice, untruth, and violence are experienced by a person. They are not mere concepts; they are experiential. In the process of answering a question that relates to a specific individual, the inquiry then points to a ground that goes beyond the individual and the personal, from which injustice, untruth, and violence arise universally. It is in that light that a person's individual situation is understood. The light spreads over a still larger area as one question naturally leads to another question. The inquiry into the personal leads to the impersonal; but at the end, it returns to the individual, as it began with him, or her.

14. The *Mahābhārata* shows, what is evident everywhere, that human life is lived, not so much on the basis of *thoughts* and *ideas*, but on the basis of *feelings*. *Rāga* and *dvesha*, attraction and repulsion, which dominate human life throughout, are feelings. Love is a feeling, and so is hatred. Some say that hatred is even a stronger feeling than love; hatred occupies a person's inner space far more strongly than love. Friendship and compassion are feelings, just as hostility and cruelty are feelings. Trust is a feeling; distrust is a feeling. Joy is a feeling; sorrow is a feeling, too. Contentment is a feeling, and so is greed. Bondage of every kind creates feelings. Freedom of every variety is a feeling. Fear is a feeling; freedom from fear is a feeling. Forgiveness is a feeling, as are anger and revenge. Reconciliation is a feeling; continued enmity is a feeling, too. The calm of the one and the burning fire of the other are feelings equally. The quality of one's life will depend on the quality of *feelings* one has towards one's self and towards the *other*. Thus, most questions in the *Mahābhārata*, which lead to a realm that is universal and not confined to the world of an individual, begin nonetheless with the expressions of a person's feelings as regards his, or her, particular situation, even the question concerning truth. The attributes of truth, in being relational, are a matter of feeling as well. And so are the fruits of untruth. The *Mahābhārata* does not, on principle, separate *subject* and *object* into two mutually exclusive domains. Therefore, it shows that *feeling* is not of less importance because it is something *subjective*, and what is subjective is then assumed, *a priori*, to be also confused and muddled. It may be so; but that is not because it is subjective. The 'objective' discussions about objective reality have been no less confused and muddled. There is in the *Mahābhārata* no idolatry of the objective as an *ism*; but neither is there in it the worship of the subjective, as another *ism*. The *Mahābhārata* only repeats, at every turn: the quality of one's life will depend on the quality of *feelings* one has towards one's self and towards the *other*.

15. The *Mahābhārata*'s inquiry is entirely conversational, as it had been in the *Upanishad*-s. The main difference between the two is that whereas, in the *Upanishad*-s, the conversation begins, and ends, mostly with an abstract problem of knowledge, seeking to know the nature of reality, in the *Mahābhārata*, it begins, and ends, with concrete human living in all its complexities. The inquiry into the human questions listed briefly in the preceding chapter proceeds by means of conversations. Some of them are between two scholars. Some of them are between a sage and a king, often in a royal assembly. Some of them are between a housewife and a scholar, or between a scholar and a shopkeeper. At least one of them is between a young boy and a scholar of great repute, in the form of a debate between the two, in the presence of a king. Some of them are between father and son, and between father and daughter, or mother and son, or between brother and brother. Some of them are between friends; and some between those who have nothing but hatred for each other but address each other nevertheless. Some of them are between the conqueror and the defeated. And many of the conversations are between husband and wife. Some of them are between a man and a woman seeking pleasure. Some of them are between a human and a god, or even between a man and a bird, or between a man and a beast. Some conversations are brief, some long, some are extended over very many days. The longest of all conversations is between the dying Bhishma, lying on his bed of arrows, and Yudhishṭhira, who would now be king. Conversations take place in every conceivable human situation. They take place as much in a language charged with emotion as in a language calm and detached.

16. A unique characteristic of the *Mahābhārata* is the intellectual and spiritual presence of women. In a great many conversations exploring the human condition, women are present throughout the *Mahābhārata* not as listeners but equally as teachers. They are portrayed, with utmost respect, as teachers of mankind, and in that, there is no self-consciousness, nor is there a trace of condescending concession. Women challenge kings as easily as they challenge scholars, when they feel that they must, to correct either the arrogance of power or the arrogance of learning. One of the most engaging of all conversations in the *Mahābhārata* is between a woman and the Lord of Death, which is as endearing as it is brilliant.

17. The *Mahābhārata* demonstrates that the understanding of order and truth, and of their negation, revolves around 'speech', *vāṇī*. The *Upanishad*-s had done likewise, in showing the interrelation between the mind and speech, *vāc*. What the *Mahābhārata* does, unlike the *Upanishad*-s, is to show in a concrete way, with reference always to concrete situations, how in all relationships *vāc*, speech, is central. More than any other school of philosophy, it shows how the ordering of language is an essential part of the language of order.

18. Another aspect of the method in the *Mahābhārata* is concerned itself with the evident fact that all forms of relationships, personal and social, are rooted in history. *Desha* and *kāla*, 'place' and 'time', are the two coordinates of history. These keep changing with the flow of time. Self-understanding and the knowledge of the other are thus linked with history, *desha* and *kāla*. This is emphasised at every turn. The *Mahābhārata* then takes another step. It is to show that undoubtedly while every person is located within history, he, or she, is not his, or her, history *alone*. In every act of relating, it is given to man to transcend history—not as any ethical 'ought', but as a spiritual necessity, indeed as an emotional necessity of living. People achieve it all the time; they go beyond given contexts and their histories. And that is how the sanity of human living is possible. And that is how friendship and love are still possible. Hence there is in the *Mahābhārata* the simultaneous presence of two languages: *the language of experience* and *the language of transcendence*. They flow into each other. There is neither the idolatry of *history*, nor the empty abstraction of transcendence. Each when separated from the other leads to *anṛta*, untruth, and to its violence, as it always has.

CHAPTER TWO

Food, Water and Life

- Food and water in the Upanishad-s
- Food and water in the *Mahābhārata*
- Giving and sharing not ritual 'acts'
- The always-full cooking pot
- A portion for the unknown guest

In a culture where attention was paid to the body in as great a measure as to the mind and to the *ātman*, it was natural that *anna*, food, and *āpas,* water or *jala*, should have occupied a basic place. Side by side the exalted interest in the nature of the ultimate reality, and not in opposition to it, the *Upanishad*-s looked upon food as the primary condition of all life and thought. At no time did they disregard the material basis of life. In fact, they regarded food as an inseparable aspect of the ultimate reality. The *Mahābhārata* likewise placed the greatest emphasis on food as the foundation of everything.[1] Naturally, the production of food, and the knowledge of the factors involved in it, were highly regarded throughout. Food and water were considered as the highest gifts that one could give to others. *Āyurveda*, the ancient science of medicine, comprised an astonishingly detailed knowledge of the effect that various kinds of food and drinks produced on the human body and mind, and regarded the use of wholesome food and drink as primary factors in physical and intellectual well-being. The *Arthashāstra* state was the biggest agency for clearing vast areas of land and bringing it under the plough. The *Arthashāstra* sounds almost modern in its methods of supervision of agriculture and irrigation.

Food and water in the *Upanishad*-s

According to the *Taittirīya Upanishad*, from the uncreated Brahman came *ākāśa* space; from space, *vāyu* wind; from wind, *agni* fire; from fire, *āpas* water; from water, *prithvi* earth; from earth, *oshadha* herbs and plants; from plants, *anna* food; from food, *purusha* human body.[2] Whatever lives on this earth, is born of food, is sustained by food, and at the end reverts to the earth which itself is born of food; of all the material things, food is thus the most superior; whoever worships Brahman in the aspect of food, obtains food always.[3] The material body, made up of the nature of food and its *anna-maya*, sap, is suffused with *prāna*, vital breath, by virtue of which all beings, gods and men and beasts, live (*prāna-maya*).[4] Distinct from these two, there is a subtler substance, the mind, with which the material body and vital breath are completely suffused (*mano-maya*).[5] Distinct from these three, there is a subtler substance, intelligence, with which the material body and vital breath and mind are completely suffused (*vijnāna-maya*).[6] Distinct from the previous four, there is a subtler substance, pure bliss, with which the material body and vital breath and mind and intelligence are completely suffused (*ananda-maya*).[7] And distinct from these five, but suffusing them completely, is the *ātman*, the Self, which is the same as Brahman.[8] And Brahman is the ultimate reality.[9] Thus, according to the *Taittirīya*, the material body in the aspect of food and sap is an integral part of the ultimate reality. It did not say that food and sap are all that there is to the ultimate reality. It proceeded to show that neither food, nor vital breath, nor mind, nor intelligence, is by itself the ultimate reality, but that each is an inseparable aspect of it.[10] The *Taittirîya* then emphasises, by means of simple and brief exhortations, the utmost importance of food and water in which life originates and in which it is sustained.[11]

> अन्नं न निन्द्यात् । तद्व्रतम् । प्राणो वा अन्नम् । शरीरमन्नादम् । प्राणे शरीरं प्रतिष्ठितम् । शरीरे प्राणः प्रतिष्ठितः । तदेतदन्नमन्ने प्रतिष्ठितम् । स य एतदन्नमन्ने प्रतिष्ठितं वेद प्रतितिष्ठति । अन्नवानन्नादो भवति । महान् भवति प्रजया पशुभिर्ब्रह्मवर्चसेन । महान् कीर्त्या ।
>
> *Do not denigrate food. Let that be the resolve. Life is because of food. The body consumes food. Life is established in the body. The body is established in life. Thus food is established in food. He who knows this, becomes established in that knowledge. And then he becomes full with food, with offspring, with cattle, with glory and with fame.*[12]

> अन्नं न परिचक्षीत । तद् व्रतम् । आपो वा अन्नम् । ज्योतिरन्नादम् । अप्सु ज्योतिः प्रतिष्ठितम् । ज्योतिष्यापः प्रतिष्ठिताः । तदेतदन्नमन्ने प्रतिष्ठितम् । स य एतदन्नमन्ने प्रतिष्ठितं वेद प्रतितिष्ठति । अन्नवानन्नादो भवति । महान्भवति प्रजया पशुभिर्ब्रह्मवर्चसेन । महान्कीतर्या ।
>
> *Do not show indifference to food. Let that be the resolve. Water is food. Heat consumes water. Water is established in heat. Heat is established in water. Thus food is established in food. He who knows this, becomes established in that knowledge. And then he becomes full with food, with offspring, with cattle, with glory and with fame.*[13]

> अन्नं बहु कुर्वीत । तद् व्रतम् । पशथिवी वा अन्नम् । आकाशोऽन्नादः । पृथिव्यामाकाशः प्रतिष्ठितः । आकाशे पृथिवी प्रतिष्ठिता । तदेतदन्नमन्ने प्रतिष्ठितम् । स य एतदन्नमन्ने प्रतिष्ठितं वेद प्रतितिष्ठति । अन्नवान्नादो भवति । महान्भवति प्रजया पशुभिर्ब्रह्मवर्चसेन । महान्कीर्त्या ।

Grow more food. Let that be the resolve. Earth is food. Space is food. Earth is established in space. Space is established in earth. Thus food is established in food. He who knows this, becomes established in that knowledge. And then he becomes full with food, with offspring, with cattle, with glory and with fame.[14]

न कंचन वसतौ प्रत्याचक्षीत। तद् व्रतम्। तस्माद्यया कया च विधया बह्वन्नं प्राप्नुयात्। आराध्यस्मा अन्नमित्याचक्षते। एतद्वै मुखतोऽन्नँराद्धम्। मुखतोऽस्मा अन्नँराध्यते। एतदै मध्यतोऽअन्नँराद्धम। मध्यतोऽस्मा अन्नतताऽस्मा। एतद्वा अन्ततोऽन्नँराद्धम्। अन्ततोऽस्मा अन्नँराध्यते। य एवं वेद।

Do not treat a guest with indifference. Let that be the resolve. For that reason gather plenty of food by all means. Say to the guest, 'Food is ready.' The food that is prepared with the utmost attention and respect is requited in the same manner. The food that is prepared with little attention and respect is requited in the same manner. He who knows in this manner.[15]

Not only was a knowledge of material elements as sources of food considered essential, but the effort to multiply food, and the habit of sharing it with others with an attitude of attention and respect was also considered important. Hence the exalted status accorded to a guest. According to the *Taittirīya*, just as 'mother is god', 'father is god', 'teacher is god', so also 'a guest is god' अतिथि देवो भव.[16]

There is in the *Chāndogya Upanishad* a series of discussions on the material basis of life, which are at once empirical and symbolical. The chief concern of this Upanishad was to demonstrate, from different angles, that the ultimate reality is a composite of material and spiritual elements in such a way that neither is comprehensible without the other. So, far from any gulf existing between the body and the mind, and between the mind and the spirit, they form a totality in which nothing can be separated from the rest and still remain intelligible.

The central concern of various discussions was the question, what is *that* in which everything else is established? The method was to point to a hierarchy of substances, one more general than the other, of which the ultimate basis was shown to be Brahman, which was inherent in them all, which was them all. This involved a close analysis of material reality. First of all, through the parable of Ushasti and the three priests[17] it was maintained that, in a *yajña*, the god that is actually invoked is prāna life;

the god to whom the hymn is sung is the (*sûrya*) sun; and the god that is propitiated is *anna* food. For all beings originate in life; and life is sustained by heat and food; in their turn sustained by the other elements of Nature. Next, attention was turned from sacrificial rituals to the totality of Nature, to its gross as well as its subtle forms, such as earth, fire, space, sun, clouds, rain, water, the seasons, the four directions, animals, speech. It is these that must be worshipped with chants and songs.[18] Next, in a higher movement, the outward *yajña*, sacrificial act, was replaced with inner meditation on the unity of nature and life.[19] The meditation was to be on life, on the physical world, on man, on the sense organs, and on the mind, all in their relatedness. They were seen as enfolded within Brahman as the cosmic reality.

Next, in a movement of still higher refinement, the attempt was to prove that everything is permeated with an ultimate substance, on knowing which everything else becomes known.[20] Brahman, which is the same as the *ātman*, the Self, is that ultimate in which everything is established.[21] Next, although everything is established in Brahman, everything was shown to be only of relative value in a hierarchy of generality.[22] Each of the following was shown to be more general than the previous one and therefore 'superior'. The various forms of learning were collectively designated as *nāma*, 'name', *vāc*, speech, *manas*, mind, *samkalpa*, will, *chitta*, consciousness, *dhyāna*, meditation, *vijnāna*, understanding, *bala*, force, *anna*, food, *āpas*, water, *tejas*, heat, *ākāsha*, space, *smara*, memory, *āshā*, desire, *prāña*, life. Life as the most general substance was to be worshipped as Brahman. However, while Brahman is the Truth, the place of food as a constituent of the mind is not to be neglected. Uddalaka, in the course of instructing his son, Shvetaketu, as regards Brahman, did not neglect to tell him that the finest part of the food forms the mind; the middle part forms the flesh; and the grossest part is eliminated.[23] To demonstrate that the powers of the mind and its processes depend upon food, he asked his son to go without food for fifteen days, during which he could still sustain his life with water. At the end of that period, Shvetaketu was asked to recite the Veda, which he could not; for all his mental powers had become feeble. He was then asked to eat food, after which his mental strength slowly returned.[24] The same exercise was repeated in relation to water. According to the *Chāndogya*, the mind is a material substance and is nourished with food.

The *Brihad-āranyaka Upanishad*, even before it entered upon a discussion as to the nature of the one most general reality of which every material and mental thing is only a transformation, emphasised the central importance of life, and therefore of food.[25] And it is with that theme that it ends.[26] Here, as in the *Chāndogya*, the method was:

a. to demonstrate the unity of all forms of life, because all beings, the gods, the humans, and the beasts, are suffused with life and the essence of food;
b. to demonstrate the unity of body and mind, with life as their common support.

Looking upon life and food as practically synonymous, this *Upanishad* speaks of food as being of seven kinds.[27] The first kind is common food all living beings consume. The second and third kinds of food are meant for the gods, by way of sacrificial offerings. The next three are in the nature of speech, mind, and life. Milk as the seventh kind of food is reserved for animals as their very first and most tender food, which is the reason why, in their infancy, humans and animals are sustained by milk.[28] The living universe is permeated with speech, mind, and life.[29] That in all human perceptions, the mind is the central agency is proved by the common expression, 'My mind was elsewhere, therefore I did not see; my mind was elsewhere, therefore I did not hear'.[30] Actually, desire, will, doubt, faith, lack of faith, comprehension, lack of comprehension, intelligence, and fear are the results of the workings of the mind.[31] Similarly, all sound is speech, and it is speech that expresses what is unexpressed.[32] Expression, however, is not speech; rather, speech is that expression which makes expression possible.[33] And all movement is life.[34]

The *Brihad-āraṇyaka Upanishad* divides all forms of existence into three primary categories of speech, mind, and life.[35] The physical world is assigned to *speech*, the space to the *mind*, and the heavens to *life*. Speech is the *Ṛg-Veda*; the mind is the *Yajur-Veda*; and life is the *Sama-Veda*. Speech is the gods; the mind is the manes; and life is humanity. Speech is mother, the mind is father, and life is offspring. Whatever is knowledge, is speech; whatever is the subject of inquiry, is mind; and whatever is mystery, is life. For life is mystery.[36]

The *Kaushītaki Upanishad* was given almost entirely to demonstrating the pre-eminence of life (*prāña*) and to equating it with Brahman. This was sought to be achieved by establishing, as in the *Chāndogya* and the *Bṛihad-āranyaka*, a hierarchy of generality within which the sense organs, the faculties, the will and the mind, make up the complex of the physical body and the personality, with life as the most general substance permeating them all. Towards that end some evident facts were stated first.[37] Smell is sensed by the nose: form is sensed by the eyes: sound is heard by the ears: food is tasted by the tongue: physical acts are done by the hands: pleasure and pain are experienced by the body; sexual union is achieved by the sexual organs: walking is done by the two feet: all the objects of the senses and of knowledge and of desire are experienced by the faculty of comprehension (*prajñā*). The relative generality of various faculties was established next.[38] Seeing is more general than speech, hearing is more general than seeing, the mind is more general than hearing, and life is more general than the mind. These propositions were stated to be a matter of empirical experience. That the faculty of seeing is more general than speech is demonstrated by the fact that seeing is the proof of what is spoken. That hearing is more general than seeing is illustrated by the fact that whereas the seeing can be often illusory, the hearing is only of the sound that actually is. That the mind is more general than hearing is proved by the fact that the perception of sound is possible only when the mind is attentive. That life is more general than the mind is demonstrated by the fact that where there is no life, there is no mind. The next step was to show that physical life is not a thing qualitatively apart from mental life and that there is no gulf between them that is unbridgeable.[39] The method by which this was demonstrated was empirical as well as deductive. The conclusions were:

a. that which is life, is also *prajñā*, comprehension; what is called comprehension, that is also life: the two inseparably reside in the body;[40]
b. it is only in conjunction with *prajñā* that the faculties and the sense organs make the material world sensible;[41]
c. the material world, the world that is sensed, and the mental world form a composite whole;[42] and
d. *prāṇa* is the final ground of them all. That is the *ātman*, and that is the Brahman.[43]

The *Aitareya* further illustrates the fact that in all these earlier *Upanishad*-s the concept of Brahman as the ultimate reality arose from a close reflection on the material world. One cannot be understood without the other. Beginning with a picturesque account of creation, this Upanishad spoke of hunger and thirst being created along with the gods and man. Each god was assigned a place in the human body. Fire, in the mouth as the faculty of speech; wind, in the nostrils as the vital breath; the sun, in the eyes as the faculty of sight; the four directions, in the ears as the faculty of hearing; vegetation, in the skin as the faculty of touch; the moon, in the heart; water, in the sexual organs; and death, in the navel.[44] Hunger and thirst were similarly connected with the body.[45] To sustain Creation and to appease hunger and thirst, food was created out of the five primary elements.[46] Food is the substance that can be consumed neither by speech, nor by the nose, nor by the eyes, nor by the ears, nor by the skin, nor by the mind, nor by the sexual organs.[47] If food could be so consumed by any of these sense organs, then man would appease his hunger by talking about food, or by smelling it, or by looking at it, or by hearing about it, or by touching it, or by thinking about it.[48] It is only through the mouth that food is taken, and life is sustained through food.[49] Life is Brahman. This Upanishad also states: *hṛdaya*, the heart; *manas,* mind; *samjñā,* awareness; *ajñānam*, the capacity to order, and *vijñānam*, to analyse, and *prajñānam*, to comprehend; *medhā*, memory; *drishti*, insight; *dhriti*, preservance; *manishā*, reflection; *jûti*, impulse; *samkalpa*, the will; *kratu*, purpose; *asu*, life; *kāma*, desire; and *vasha*, control; all are permeated with Brahman, the ultimate reality in which everything is upheld.[50]

The upanishadic emphasis on prāṇa is the emphasis on energy. And energy, while it flows in many channels, is indivisible. The control of the mind is not something distinct from the control of the physical body. And the physical body, like the mind, is to be nourished with wholesome food.

Food and water in the Mahābhārata

The *Mahābhārata* likewise attaches the utmost importance to food and to its sharing.[51]

अन्नं वै प्रथमं द्रव्यमन्नं श्रीश्च परा मता।
अन्नात् प्राण: प्रभवति तेजो वीर्य बलं तथा।। अनुशासन ६६.५९।
Food is the primary substance. Food is considered as the manifestation of all well-being. It is through food that the life force and its radiance and its strength are nourished.[52]

अन्नं ह्यमृतमित्याह पुराकल्पे प्रजापति:।
अन्नं भुवं दिवं खं च सर्वमन्ने प्रतिष्ठितम्।।

The universe with all that lives and moves in it is sustained by food. The Primeval Being has described food as nectar.[53]

अन्नमूर्जस्करं लोके प्राणाश्चान्ने प्रतिष्ठिता: ।
अन्नेन धार्यते सर्वं विश्वं जगदिदं प्रभो ।। अनुशासन ६३.७ ।।
अन्नाद् भवन्ति वै प्राणा: प्रत्यक्षं नात्र संशय: ।। अनुशासन ६३.८ ।।

Life is possible only through food, and it is food that sustains the whole world.[54] *That life is possible only through food is evident and there is no doubting it.*[55]

अन्नं प्रजापते रूपमन्नं प्रजननं स्मृतम् ।
सर्वभूतमयं चान्नं जीवश्चान्नमय: स्मृत: ।। आश्वमेधिक पृ. ६३२७ ।।

Food is a manifestation of the Primeval Being. Food is the source of creation. Food is suffused with all creation; and all living beings are suffused with food.[56]

अन्नाद्धि प्रसवं यान्ति रतिरन्नाद्धि भारत ।
धर्मार्थावन्नतो विद्धि रोगनाशं तथान्नत: ।। अनुशासन ६३.३० ।।

Offspring is born through food; sexual pleasure is possible because of food; social and material prosperity are achieved through food; and it is through food that disease is overcome.[57]

अन्नप्रणाशे भिद्यन्ते शरीरं पञ्च धातव: ।
बलं बलवतोऽपीह प्रणश्यत्यन्नहानित: ।। अनुशासन ६३.३२ ।।

The absence of food makes the five principal elements of the body disintegrate; and with the loss of food, the strength of even the strongest is lost.[58]

प्राणा ह्यन्नं मनुष्याणां तस्माज्जन्तुश्च जायते ।
अन्ने प्रतिष्ठितो लोकस्तस्मादन्नं प्रशस्यते ।। अनुशासन ११२.११ ।।

Food is man's life; and it is through food that the living beings are born. The whole world is based upon food. And, therefore, food is regarded as the highest.[59]

The *Mahābhārata* simultaneously speaks of *jala*, water, as an essential basis of life; and generally the two are spoken together, *anna* and *jala*, food and water.[60] Therefore, *anna-dāna* and *jala-dāna*, the giving of food and water alike, are regarded as the greatest of all sharing in life, *dāna*.[61] The *Mahābhārata* dwells upon this throughout. Stated in brief, its teaching is:

> अन्नं प्राणा नराणां हि सर्वमन्ने प्रतिष्ठितम्।
> अन्नदः पशुमान् पुत्रो धनवान् भोगवानपि।। अनुशासन ६३.२५।।
> प्राणवांश्चापि भवति रूपवांश्च तथा नृप।
> अन्नदः प्राणदो लोके सर्वदः प्रोच्यते तु सः।। अनुशासन ६३.२६।।
> *Because life is sustained by food, and food is life, to give food to others is like giving life to them; and whoever gives food is known verily as the giver of life'.*[62]

Therefore:

> अन्नेन सदृशं दानं न भूतं न भविष्यति।
> तस्मादन्नं विशेषेण दातुमिच्छन्ति मानवाः।। अनुशासन ६३.६।।
> *There was not in the past, nor will there be in the future, a sharing comparable to the sharing of food. Therefore, mostly it is the gift of food that people wish to give.*[63]

> प्रत्यक्षं प्रीतिजननं भोक्तुर्दातुर्भवत्युत।
> सर्वाण्यन्यानि दानानि परोक्षफलवन्त्युत।। अनुशासन ६३.२९।।
> *The giving of food is one giving that brings visible satisfaction both to the giver and the one to whom it is given. The results of all other giving are invisible.*[64]

> अध्वश्रान्ताय विप्राय क्षुधितायान्नकाङ्क्षिणे।
> देशकालाभियाताय दीयते पाण्डुनन्दन।। आश्वमेधिक पृ. ६३२८।।
> *According to time and place, food should be offered to the one who is tired after a long journey and is hungry and thirsty.*[65]

> यस्तु पांसुलपादश्च दूराध्वश्रमकर्शितः।
> क्षुत्पिपासाश्रमश्रान्त आर्तः खिन्नगतिर्दिजः।।
> पृच्छन् वै ह्यन्नदातारं गृहमभ्येत्य याचयेत्।
> तं पूजयेत् तु यत्नेन सोऽतिथिः स्वर्गसंक्रमः।।
> तस्मिंस्तुष्टे नरश्रेष्ठ तुष्टाः स्युः सर्वदेवताः।। आश्वमेधिक पृ. ६३२८।।
> *Should a brāhmana, who is weak with hunger and thirst, his feet tired from a long journey, come to one's home and ask for food, he should*

be honoured. Such a guest is an occasion for heaven, and all gods are satisfied when he is satisfied.[66]

The same is the case with *jala-dāna*, sharing water.[67] Because it is evident that:

पानीयं परमं लोके जीवानां जीवनं स्मृतम् ।। आश्वमेधिक पृ. ६३२७ ।।
अभ्दिः सर्वाणि भूतानि जीवन्ति प्रभवन्ति च ।। आश्वमेधिक पृ. ६३२७ ।।
Water is considered in the world as the very life of the living beings.[68] *All living beings can live because of water and are sustained by it.*[69]

प्रणश्यत्यम्बुपानेन बुभुक्षा च युधिष्ठिर ।
तृषितस्य न चान्नेन पिपासाभिप्रणश्यति ।। आश्वमेधिक पृ. ६३२७ ।।
Yudhishthira, hunger can be assuaged by drinking water, but thirst cannot be assuaged by eating food.[70]

Therefore:

तस्मात् सर्वेषु दानेषु तोयदानं विशिष्यते ।। आश्वमेधिक पृ. ६३२७ ।।
Of all givings, the giving of water is a thing apart.[71]

पानीयस्य प्रदानेन तृपतिर्भवति पाण्डव ।। आश्वमेधिक पृ. ६३२७ ।।
When water is offered, there comes complete satisfaction.[72]

तस्मात् तोयं सदा देयं तृषितेभ्यो विजानता ।। आश्वमेधिक पृ. ६३२७ ।।
For that reason, knowing this, one should always offer water to the thirsty.[73]

चाण्डालोऽप्यतिथिः प्राप्तो देशकालेऽन्नकाङ्क्षया ।
अभ्युद्नम्यो गृहस्थेन पूजनीयश्च सर्वदा ।। आश्वमेधिक पृ. ६३२९ ।।
In accordance with time and place, if the lowliest of low arrives as a guest, the householder should welcome him too.[74]

अभ्यागतं श्रान्तमनुव्रजन्ति
देवाश्च सर्वे पितरोऽग्नयश्च ।
तस्मिन् द्विजे पूजिते पूजिताः स्यु-
र्गते निराशाः पितरो व्रजन्ति ।। आश्वमेधिक पृ. ६३२९ ।।
With a guest come all the gods and the manes. If a guest is honoured, so are they; if he goes away disappointed, they go away disappointed too.[75]

The *Mahābhārata* elaborates on how the blessings of this life and of the next attend upon the person who, according to time and place and his own capacity, readily gifts food to others.[76] Even more detailed are the injunctions as regards the gift of water, chiefly by constructing ponds, wells and reservoirs.[77]

Earth and trees being inseparable from food and water, the *Mahābhārata* finally enjoins upon the people, *bhumi-dana* and *vrksa-dana*, the giving of fertile land and the planting of trees, as steps towards sustenance and plenty for all.[78]

भूमौ जायन्ति पुरुषा भूमौ निष्ठां व्रजन्ति च।
चतुर्विधो हि लोकोऽयं योऽयं भूमिगुणात्मकः।। अनुशासन ६२.४९।।
Human beings are born on the earth, and to the Earth they return. All species of life are suffused with the attributes and energy of the Earth.[79]

एषा माता पिता चैव जगतः पृथिवीपते।
नानया सदृशं भूतं किंचिदस्ति जनाधिप।। अनुशासन ६२.५०।।
To the world, the Earth is like mother and father. There is no other material reality like the Earth.[80]

Neither is there a greater sharing and giving than the sharing and giving of land, with its resources—food, water and vegetation.

न हि भूमिप्रदानेन दानमन्यद् विशिष्यते।। अनुशासन ६२.६५।।

The Mahābhārata[81] says this repeatedly.

In the voice of Krishna, the *Mahābhārata* therefore says:

दानान्यन्यानि हीयन्ते कालेन कुरुपुङ्गव।
भूमिदानस्य पुण्यस्य क्षयो नैवोपपद्यते।। आश्वमेधिक पृ. ६३३१।।
The merit earned by other kinds of giving exhausts itself by the passage of time; but the merit earned by giving and sharing land is ever inexhaustible.[82]

न हि भूमिप्रदानाद् वै दानमन्यद् विशिष्यते।
न चापि भूमिहरणात् पापमन्यद् विशिष्यते।। आश्वमेधिक पृ. ६३३१।।
There is no greater giving than the giving of land; and there is no greater wrong than possessing land by force.[83]

आश्रुत्य भूमिदानं तु दत्त्वा यो वा हरेत् पुनः ।
स बद्धो वारुणैः पाशैः क्षिप्यते पूयशोणिते ।। आश्वमेधिक पृ. ६३३२ ।।
Whoever possesses by force the land gifted either by him or by another, is destined for the darkest of all hells.[84]

The meanings here are clear and straightforward. 'Heaven' and 'hell' are not *places* one goes to after death, depending upon one's acts. They are what one creates for one's self and for the other on *this* earth, and lives *in* heaven or hell, or both.

In all that Krishna pronounces upon the inexhaustible *punya*, merit, earned by giving and sharing, food and water and fertile land, the brāhmaṇa is a most favoured person.[85] It is very easy to misinterpret this, although not altogether without reason; especially in the light of the social history of Indian society. The subject of the *Mahābhārata*'s clearest position on social arrangements and social wealth is examined later in this book.[86] Here it will suffice to say that brāhmaṇa as a social calling within the fourfold division of labour was to devote himself to the pursuit of knowledge and teaching, and was excluded from making money; and, therefore, persons of that calling were to be especially supported by the king and the people. That support was the only means of their sustenance. Therefore, it had to be respectful, not grudging. Hence the very great emphasis upon giving to a brāhmaṇa, and earning thereby a special merit. But that emphasis was neither ever absolute nor unrelated to what a brāhmaṇa as a person was expected to be.

Giving and sharing not ritual 'acts'

What is of utmost importance is the fact that the *Mahābhārata* gives a radically different meaning to dāna, not as 'alms giving' or 'charity' as ritual acts, but sharing what one has been given, in the awareness that one's life is connected with other beings.[87] Hospitality is an expression of that awareness, and not just 'a rule of etiquette'. If the awareness of one's human bond with others is absent in one's actual conduct, then everything one may possess is *vritha*, useless. In the voice of Krishna, the *Mahābhārata* strongly says:

साङ्गोपाङ्गास्तु यो वेदान् पठतीह दिने दिने ।
न चातिथिं पूजयति वृथा भवति स द्विजः ।। आश्वमेधिक पृ. ६३२९ ।।
If he diligently, day after day, keeps studying the Veda but does not show utmost respect to the guest, then the life of such a brāhmaṇa is in vain.[88]

पाकयज्ञमहायज्ञैः सोमसंस्थाभिरेव च।
ये यजन्ति न चार्चन्ति गृहेष्वतिथिमागतम्।।
तेषां यशोऽभिकामानां दत्तमिष्टं च यद् भवेत्।
वृथा भवति तत् सर्वमाशया हि तया हतम्।। आश्वमेधिक पृ. ६३२९।।
Those who perform various sacrificial-rites, but do not with respect and care attend upon the guest who comes to their homes, then that which they do to earn a good name goes in vain. The guest's disappointment destroys it all.[89]

Therefore:

देशं कालं च पात्रं च स्वशक्तिं च निरीक्ष्य च।।
अल्पं समं महद् वापि कुर्यादातिथ्यमाप्तवान्।। आश्वमेधिक पृ. ६३३०।।
Considering 'time', 'place', 'the person concerned', and 'one's capacity', one should give to the guest in ways small, or middling, or generous.[90]

Lest the mention of the word pātra, or 'the person concerned', in this context, was interpreted as the freedom to weigh a guest in the scale of 'deservedness', and then decide the scale of one's welcome to him or her, the *Mahābhārata* quickly dispelled that notion by saying:

हितः प्रियो वा द्वेष्यो वा मूर्खः पण्डित एव वा।
प्राप्तो यो वैश्वदेवान्ते सोऽतिथिः स्वर्गसंक्रमः।। आश्वमेधिक पृ. ६३३०।।
Whether he wishes one good or ill, whether he is learned or a fool, the guest who comes is verily a way to heaven.[91]

क्षुत्पिपासाश्रमार्ताय देशकालागताय च।
सत्कृत्यान्नं प्रदातव्यं यज्ञस्य फलमिच्छता।। आश्वमेधिक पृ. ६३३०।।
If one wishes to reap the fruits of ritual rites, then let one attend upon a guest who arrives hungry, thirsty and tired, and offer him food with the utmost respect.[92]

Through another story,[93] the *Mahābhārata* teaches that:

अरावप्युचितं कार्यमातिथ्यं गृहमागते।
छेत्तुमप्यागते छायां नोपसंहरते द्रुमः।।शान्ति १४६.५।।
Should one's enemy arrive at one's doorstep, one should, and with respect too, attend upon him. A tree does not withdraw its cooling shade even from the one who has come to cut it.[94]

The always-full cooking pot

The *Mahābhārata* shows that where there is concern for the sustenance of others, and not for one's own alone, and where there is love in giving, there, the cooking pot is never empty, however adverse the circumstances.[95]

On losing the game of dice to the Kauravas, their first cousins, a game that was played fraudulently, Yudhishthira and his four younger brothers and their wife Draupadi are exiled from the realm for thirteen years as a pre-condition of losing the game. Suddenly they are bereft even of the means of sustenance. A great many brāhmaṇas express their desire to follow them into exile. Deeply touched, Yudhishthira dissuades them from doing so. 'Now I have no means of sustaining even my family, much less of offering the least hospitality to you who will be my guests', he says to them. And he speaks of his deepest anxiety on that account. 'No, you do not have to worry. We will take care of our needs ourselves, and will come with you, and will engage you in conversations that will delight you', they say to him. 'Yes, I always take delight in the company of scholars', Yudhishthira replies; 'but even so, being reduced so very greatly in my circumstances is for me a matter of shame.' And he recalls the obligations of a householder in offering food to those who come to him.

> संविभागो हि भूतानां सर्वेषामेव दृश्यते ।
> तथैवापचमानेभ्यः प्रदेयं गृहमेधिना ।। वन २.५३ ।।
> *In the food eaten by a householder, there is a share each for the gods of the universe, for one's ancestors, and for all living beings.*[96]
>
> तृणानि भूमिरुदकं वाक् चतुर्थी च सूनृता ।
> सतामेतानि गेहेषु नोच्छिद्यन्ते कदाचन ।। वन २.५४ ।।
>
> देयमार्तस्य शयनं स्थितश्रान्तस्य चासनम् ।
> तशषितस्य च पानीयं क्षुधितस्य च भोजनम् ।। वन २.५५ ।।
> *In the house of a good human being, four things are never absent: a proper seat, a place to sit, water to drink, and courteous speech. A bed for the ill; a seat for the tired; water for the thirsty; and food for the hungry.*[97]
>
> चक्षुर्दद्यान्मनोदद्याद् वाचं दद्यात् सुभाषिताम् ।
> उत्थाय चासनं दद्यादेष धर्मः सनातनः ।
> प्रत्युत्थायाभिगमनं कुर्यान्न्यायेन चार्चनम् ।। वन २.५६ ।।

Receive the visitor with courtesy; and with equal courtesy bid him farewell: look at him with kindly eyes; have for him kind thoughts; greet him with pleasant speech, and offer him a place to sit—these are the abiding dharma *of a householder.*[98]

The worry that he will not be able to fulfill these obligations, is the anxiety and sorrow of Yudhishthira, which he now mentions to his preceptor, the sage Dhaumya; that he can neither leave them nor does he have the means to offer them his hospitality: 'What do I do in these circumstances?'[99]

After giving his deep thought to Yudhishthira's situation, Dhaumya offers the following advice. 'At the beginning of creation, when the living beings suffered from hunger, the Sun-god *Sûrya* drew with his heat the water on earth, which the Moon converted through the clouds into the rains, which in turn produced on earth, vegetation, and from vegetation, food. Combined with the rays of the Moon, the Sun created six different kinds of *rasa*, sap, in the plants, which is food for the living beings.[100]

एवं भानुमयं ह्यन्नं भूतानां प्राणधारणम्।
पितैष सर्वभूतानां तस्मात् तं शरणं व्रज।। वन ३.१।।

The food that sustains life is thus in the aspect of the Sun, who is father to all beings. Appeal to the Sun for help therefore.'[101]

And that is what Yudhishthira did. Invoking the Sun[102], he ends with this prayer:

त्वं ममापन्नकामस्य सर्वातिथ्यं चिकीर्षतः।
अन्नमन्नपते दातुमभितः श्रद्धयार्हसि।। वन ३.६७।।

So that I may be able to offer food to all those who come to me, grant me the gift of food.'[103]

The Sun appears in the human form and gives him a copper cooking-pot; which, the Sun grants a boon, will never remain empty during the coming days of adversity and trial. Yudhishthira would eat only after he had fed others; and Draupadi would eat the last; and no sooner would she finish eating than the cooking-pot would be full again.[104]

A portion for the unknown guest

Equally important with the act of giving, is the *attitude*, the *feeling*, with which the food and water are offered. The word *dāna* does not mean 'charity' or 'alms-giving'. Its meanings are: '*sharing*', '*communicating*', '*imparting*', '*paying back*' (as in a debt), '*restoring*', '*adding to*'. The *Mahābhārata* places equal emphasis the attitude of respect, and on the feeling of affection, with which food and water are to be offered. The feelings of affection, and not just the materiality of the food, 'add' and 'restore'.

> अमृतं मनसः प्रीतिं सद्यस्तृप्तिं ददाति च ।
> मनो ग्लपयते तीव्रं विषं गन्धेन सर्वशः ।। अनुशासन ९८.१८ ।।
> *What creates feelings of friendship, affection, and a deep mental satisfaction, is nectar, amritam: what creates in the mind strong repulsion, is poison,* visha.'[105]

The Āyurveda speaks of four *dosha*, defects, in the cooked food. The *kāla-dosha*, the food that has been kept for too long, and has turned stale, the *rasa-dosha*, the food that has lost its flavour and taste, the *saṃsarga-dosha*, the food that has been touched with unclean hands, or in which some insect has fallen. But the worst defect is *bhava-dosha*, the food that is offered will ill grace, without feelings of affection. Such food is not food; it is poison.

It has been assumed, despite all the evidence to the contrary, that the main concerns of Indian culture were otherworldly.[106] To the *Upanishad*-s, and to the *Mahābhārata*, there was no conflict between material facts and spiritual perspectives. The joy of philosophy was never considered incompatible with the pleasures of culinary art. It is true that there grew up also taboos and practices as regards eating food, which became enormously complicated, often to the point of insanity. But they are not to be found either in the *Upanishad*-s or in the *Mahābhārata*. But however complicated they grew to be, and however ludicrous the forms that they took, many of the practices displayed nevertheless the belief that the act of eating is not a solitary affair; one's life is linked with the life of others. Eating is not complete until the food that one eats has been shared with others. One portion of the food one eats is to be set apart, if only symbolically, for the gods of the universe, which are the elements of Nature. Another portion is to be set apart for one's forefathers. And one portion of the food one eats is to be kept—for the *unknown guest*.[107]

CHAPTER THREE

The Spiritual and the Material in the Mahābhārata

- Perceptions of the self
- The manifest self: the unmanifest self
- Radical shift in the *Mahābhārata*
- Self, energy, and relationships

The spiritual and the material are not two states that are related only in their mutual antagonism. They are parts of the same reality in which human life is rooted. Separate them, and in separating them, build a philosophy that regards either the one or the other as the ultimate reality; you will have either material*ism* or spiritual*ism*. In turning into an *ism*, one is then as false as the other, and both equally dangerous, in individual and social terms alike. That is the concern of the *Mahābhārata*.

On this subject there have been two opposite misunderstandings. Debiprasad Chattopadhya, the Marxist philosopher, maintains that Indian civilisation is essentially materialistic. Sarvepalli Radhakrishnan, the Idealist philosopher, maintains that it is essentially spiritualistic. To maintain that it is essentially the one, or essentially the other, is essentially all wrong. At no time in its very long history did Indian thought posit any polarity between the material and the spiritual, much less an irreconcilable polarity. For example, the main aim of all the major *Upanishad*-s is to show the one as the expression of the other. Therefore, even before they examine what the true nature of reality is, the *Taittirīya*, the *Chāndogya*, the *Bṛihad-āraṇyaka*, and the *Kaushītaki* show how fundamental food and water are to life. Some of them show how human attributes, including sexuality, are to be worshipped as Brahman, the general name for the reality that pervades the universe. Then they show how, in separating the material from the spiritual, when they are inseparable, and then insisting that either the one or the other is the ultimate reality, we go into darkness—and death. The *Mahābhārata* demonstrates this in infinitely greater detail and, what the *Upanishad*-s do only rarely, it does so by taking up the concrete events of everyday human living.

The relation between the spirit, the *ātman*, and the body; between the body and the mind; between them and emotions and feelings; between emotions and perceptions; between perceptions and acts; and between acts and motives—all these have been central questions in the actual living of human life. In one form or another they appear in the principles of economics, politics, law, and governance. Modern psychology is rooted in them. The varied forms of the arts show them. The quality of relationships is decided by the quality of our understanding of them, which is self-knowledge and knowledge of the *other*.

The Sanskrit word *adhyātma* is mostly translated as 'spiritual' or 'spirituality'. However, in the various traditions of Indian thought, the word *adhyātma* is to be found only infrequently. In the *Upanishad*-s, only a few times; in the *Bhagvad-Gītā*, perhaps only twice; in the *Mahābhārata*, not many times either. On the face of it, this may appear to be astonishing because they are seen as 'spiritual' works. Since, however, the root meaning of *adhyātma* is 'inquiry into the nature of the self', and knowledge of the self is the main subject of all Indian thought, that word itself did not have to be used much. The inquiry '*who am I*?' involved naturally an inquiry into the material conditions of life in the first place. The questions concerning the big Self had to be at the same time also questions concerning the small self, the body with its faculties as its base.

The *Taittirīya-Upanishad* states this clearly. There the word *adhyātma*, or 'spiritual', relates to the human body and its attributes. For example, it says:

पृथिव्यन्तरिक्षं द्यौर्दिशोऽवान्तरदिशः अग्निर्वायुरादित्यश्चन्द्रमा नक्षत्राणि। आप ओषधयो वनस्पतय आकाश आत्मा। इत्यधिभूतम्। अथाध्यात्मम्। प्राणो व्यानोऽपान उदानः समानः। चक्षुः श्रोत्रं मनो वाक् त्वक्। चर्म माँसँस्नावास्थि मज्जा। एतदधिविधाय ऋषिरवोचत्। पाङ्क्तं वा इदँ सर्वम्। पाङ्क्तेनैव पाङ्क्तँस्पृणोतीति।

'One group of reality consists of the earth, the sky, the invisible, and the four directions. Another group consists of the fire, the wind, the sun, the moon, and the planets. Another group consists of water, vegetation and herbs, the space, and the body. They are the material groups. The spiritual group of reality exists in the human body and its faculties: the eyes, the ears, the mind, the speech, and the touch. Although these three groups are distinct, they are intimately connected with each other and form an unbroken unity. Whatever is, is unity; the outer completing the inner, and the inner completing the outer.'[1]

'All *Upanishad*-s are saying to us, in the clearest language, that by understanding the material, human beings develop their spiritual faculties; and by understanding the spiritual, they develop their material existence. In that, there is self-increasing, happiness, good health, love, fulfilment of desire, prosperity and peace.'[2]

The *Yoga-sūtra* of Patanjali demonstrates the innate unity of the body and the mind, of the physical and the spiritual, as the foundation of good health. Neglect the one, and the other is harmed. *Sāṃkhya* philosophy, the more theoretical part of the *Yoga*, and the earliest among the philosophical schools, demonstrates that truth through a somewhat different path. The *Mahābhārata* incorporates them; but, unlike any other work, before or since, it takes up the questions mentioned earlier, with the complexities of human life and relationships as their natural material. The inseparable relation between the material and the spiritual, between the body and the mind, is taken up again, but always through the stories of human situations where the body and the mind are together at work. In the *Mahābhārata*, as in life, neither 'the body' nor 'the mind' remains an abstract subject for the philosophers to weave intricate theories *of* and *around*. The *Mahābhārata* is concerned with their workings, one affecting the other; as all human beings are, everywhere, if not always self-consciously.

Then how did the wrong notion arise, even at the time of the *Mahābhārata*, that spirituality consists in negating and renouncing the material? That the spiritual is an exalted domain far away from the coarseness of the material is the notion of spirituality that most people have. Where does it come from? Here it will be sufficient to say that it was the *vairāgya* literature, or its equivalents in the other traditions of the world, that had brought it about in the main, although there were other factors as well. That was the literature of 'disgust', 'aversion', 'distaste for, and loathing of, the world', for that is what the word *vairāgya* means. The human body was its main object of disgust. And women, it hated the most. Both were despised and denounced.[3] The *Mahābhārata* recounts that thinking, from its mildest to its harshest expressions, that had taken possession of the human mind. Consistent with its method, it recounts that thinking faithfully;[4] to the degree that if, on reading the *Mahābhārata*, one lands on those parts, and remains only there, one can quite easily be misled into thinking that disgust from the world was its main teaching.

Having separated spirituality from the material conditions of life, *vairāgya* next separated it from the ethical; that is to say, from the relational. It concentrated upon one's self. That meant wrenching spirituality from social concerns. A general impression was created that those belonged to a lower level of consciousness. Justice and equality are no concerns of spirituality. This view followed from the theory of *vairāgya*; where, moreover, 'spirituality' itself came to be limited to the ritualistic. What also followed, mostly in practice, is that I can be 'spiritual' in one part and a liar and a cheat in another part, and be oppressive as well; and see no connection between the two. The *Mahābhārata*, in the voice of many different people, men and women, rejects it all; for the negation of life is the negation of truth.

The *Mahābhārata* shows the unity of the material and the spiritual; and furthermore shows both to be relational. *Artha,* material prosperity, is sacred. *Kāma*, sexual fulfilment, is sacred. *Sukha*, joy, is sacred. *Nyāya* and *samatā*, justice and equality, are not separate from the spiritual; and the spiritual is suffused with law and governance, *daṇḍa*, of which self-governance is the best. The *ātman*, self, is not an isolated entity; nor is *mokṣha*, freedom, a solitary state; the return of the self to the self. The greatest of the truly spiritual personalities of the world, men and women, showed in their whole being one concern above all—with the confusion, the dilemmas, the pain, and the suffering of others, from which they never separated themselves.

True spirituality has elegance as one of its many attributes. Elegance of speech: elegance of attitudes and conduct; elegance of dress; elegance of taste. They are expressions of the sacred. *Satyam*, truth, is also *shivam*, the good, and the good is also *sundaram,* the beautiful. Separate wealth and power and sexual pleasure from the spiritual, and they become the source of disease and ugliness. The truth of this is visible everywhere. Visible everywhere is also the truth that: separate the spiritual from the natural attributes of life, and such 'spirituality' turns into violence to life. For what is suffused with *prāṇa-maya*, life, is suffused also with *ānanda-maya*, joy.

Neither has spirituality anything to do with any particular form of dress and its colour. Nor is spirituality some profession, like that of law and medicine, to be practised and promoted by some special people called 'spiritual leaders'. Two of the most profound discussions in the *Mahābhārata* as regards the ordering of life are attributed to a meatseller in one case and to a grocer in the second case. Through them, and through so many other ordinary people, men and women, the *Mahābhārata* is saying that true spirituality is to be found in the ordinary.

Perceptions of the self

The idea of the *ātman*, the Self, as the abiding essence of all living beings was arrived at in the *Upanishad*-s by identifying it, in stages, first with the gross physical body; then with vital life force; then with will; then with the mind; then with the ego; and since each of these steps was found to be unsatisfactory, finally by declaring that there is something else besides, independent of them all—the *ātman*. It is neither born; nor does it die; it is eternal. There is nothing from which it emanates; and there is nothing that emanates from it. It is neither the cause nor the effect of anything. It is complete in itself. Its essence is pure being, pure knowledge, and pure bliss. It is called the *ātman* in reference to an individual; and *brahman*, as the reality behind the universe; but they are the same: *brahman* = *ātman*.

That there is an eternal entity, distinct from the body and the mind, indeed distinct from everything phenomenal, was the view of the other philosophical schools also, excepting the materialists and the Buddhists. But there the agreement stopped. As to the nature of the *ātman* there were such divergent views that they did not seem to be talking of the same thing. The divergence became still more pronounced on the question of the relation between the Self and the physical apparatus of perception, on the one hand, and between the Self and the will, on the other.

The Buddha would discard altogether the Upanishadic idea of a permanent substance called the *ātman* or the Self, distinct from the psychophysical self and beyond decay and death.[5] He maintained, on the contrary, that what we call the *ātman*, is only a conglomerate of the physical, the mental, the feeling, the conscious attributes of man, all of them moreover in a flux. 'Nowhere is a *Self* to be found', is the Buddha's doctrine of *anattā*, 'no-Self'.

The Jaina philosophers examined the concept of the *ātman* as put forth in other systems; and argued that each one of them was self-contradictory in certain respects, and erroneous in certain others.[6] In the Jaina view, whatever exists is either *jīva*, soul, or its opposite, *ajīva*, matter. There is plurality of souls, different in different bodies. The attributes of a *jīva* are: consciousness; knowledge; the capacity to feel, develop, and grow; to be affected by emotions; to be in bondage; and the capacity to be free. The Jain philosophers assumed that there is a person, a self.

The philosophy of the 'Self', the *ātman* or the *jīva*, or the *jīva-ātman*, in the *Mahābhārata* is manifestly on the lines of the *Sāṃkhya* philosophy. Propounded with great clarity, it is also entirely free from the burden of texts, commentaries upon those texts, and commentaries upon those commentaries, which in the succeeding centuries will come to dominate practically every school of philosophy, and very nearly kill philosophy. The philosophical perceptions of the Self in the *Mahābhārata* may be arranged around their three main aspects:

1. that the Self is a wholly distinct entity, not to be confused with the body and its faculties, and does not die when physical life comes to an end;[7]
2. that the Self is not perceived by any of the sense organs and its faculties, touch, hearing, seeing, tasting. It is experienced directly, for it is the Self that is the ground of all perceptions;[8] and
3. that the Self has to free itself from the entanglements with nature, and return to its own essence.[9]

A remarkable feature of the *Mahābhārata* is that the doubt whether there *is* any such entity as the Self, independent of the physical body and its apparatus, is stated quite as strongly, with its clear reasoning. Moreover, the doubt is expressed, almost always, in the voice of one venerable sage or another. Scepticism about the Self must have been deep and honest.

A doubt was raised in the *Mahābhārata* itself, as the Buddha would do later, whether there is any such entity as a permanent Self, by whatever name you call it, *ātman*, or *purusha*, or *jīva*, distinct from the five elements of Nature that constitute all living beings?[10] In their long conversation, spread over several days, Yudhishṭhira asks Bhīshma:

कुत: सृष्टमिदं विश्वं जगत् स्थावरजगंमम् ।
प्रलये च कमभ्येति तन्मे ब्रूहि पितामह ।। शान्ति १८२.१ ।।
How was this universe created? Where will it go at the end of time?

ससागर: सगगन: सशैल: सबलाहक: ।
सभूमि: साग्निपवनो लोकोऽयं केन निर्मित: ।। शान्ति १८२.२ ।।
Who has created the oceans, the sky, the hills, the clouds, the earth, the fire, and the wind?

कथं सृष्टानि भूतानि कथं वर्णविभक्तय: ।
शौचाशौचं कथं तेषां धर्माधर्मविधि: कथम् ।। शान्ति १८२.३ ।।
How were the living beings created? And how were they divided in different callings? What is purity, and what is impurity? How was that ordained? What is dharma, *and what is* adharma*? How was that ordained?*

कीदृशो जीवतां जीवः क्वा वा गच्छन्ति ये मृताः।
अस्माल्लोकादमुं लोकं सर्वं शंसतु नो भवान्।। शान्ति १८२.४।।

Of the living, what is their self? On dying, where do the dead go? What is the sequence of their going from this world to the next?[11]

Bhīshma then recounts the conversation that two sages, Bharadvāj and Bhrigu, had on this subject,[12] during which Bharadvāj had asked the same questions in the very same words.[13]

With astonishing self-confidence, as if he had watched the whole process of creation and its sequence, the sage Bhrigu offers a description of it. That need not hold us here. From the very serious doubts that Bharadvāj raised as to the existence of a Self *apart* from the five elements of Nature that constitute life, themselves created in a sequence, we can easily imagine the outline of Bhrigu's description of creation.

यदि प्राणयते वायुर्वायुरेव विचेष्टते।
श्वसित्याभाषते चैव तस्माज्जीवो निरर्थकः।। शान्ति १८६.१।।

If the wind is the vital life force, and the wind makes the living beings move; if it is the wind that breathes, and it is the wind that speaks, then it is meaningless to believe in the existence of a Self besides.[14]

यद्यूष्मभाव आग्नेयो वह्निना पच्यते यदि।
अग्निर्जरयते चैतत् तस्माज्जीवो निरर्थकः।। शान्ति १८६.२।।

If the warmth of life is from the fire; and it is the fire that digests the food eaten, and it is the fire that decays the body, then it is meaningless to believe in the existence of a Self besides.[15]

जन्तोः प्रमीयमाणस्य जीवो नैवोपलभ्यते।
वायुरेव जहात्येनमूष्मभावश्च नश्यति।। शान्ति १८६.३।।

When a living being dies, the Self is not to be had. It is the wind of life that leaves the body; and the fire leaving, the body turns cold.[16]

यदि वायुमयो जीवः संश्लेषो यदि वायुनाः।
वायुमण्डलवद् दृश्यो गच्छेत् सह मरुद्गणैः।। शान्ति १८६.४।।

If the Self of a living individual is suffused with the wind of life, then, like the wind, it should be susceptible of being sensed directly as the wind is. On the wind leaving the body, it should be seen going with the wind.[17]

कूपे वा सलिलं दद्यात् प्रदीपं वा हुताशने।
क्षिप्रं प्रविश्य नश्येत यथा नश्यत्यसौ तथा।। शान्ति १८६.६।।

पञ्चधारणके ह्यस्मिन् शरीरे जीवितं कुतः।
तेषामन्यतराभावाच्चतुर्णां नास्ति संशयः।। शान्ति १८६.७।।

नश्यन्त्यापो ह्यनाहाराद् वायुरुच्छ्वासनिग्रहात्।
नश्यते कोष्ठभेदात् खमग्निर्नश्यत्यभोजनात्।। शान्ति १८६.८।।
व्याधिव्रणपरिक्लेशैर्मेदिनी चैव शीर्यते।
पीडितेऽन्यतरे ह्येषां संघातो याति पञ्चधा।। शान्ति १८६.९।।

Just as the water thrown into a well loses its separate identity, and so does a burning lamp thrown into the fire, the Self can no longer remain distinct from the five elements of Nature when they separate. This should prove that, independent of them, there is no Self. For in the absence of any one of them, the others cannot remain as a unity.[18]

तस्मिन् पञ्चत्वमापन्ने जीवः किमनुधावति।
किं वेदयति वा जीवः किं शृणोति ब्रवीति च।। शान्ति १८६.१०।।

If there is a Self apart from the five elements; then their unity broken on death, after whom does the Self run, what does it experience, what does it hear, what does it speak?[19]

एषा गौः परलोकस्थं तारयिष्यति मामिति।
यो दत्त्वा म्रियते जन्तुः सा गौः कं तारयिष्यति।। शान्ति १८६.११।।

गौश्च प्रतिग्रहीता च दाता चैव समं यदा।
इहैव विलयं यान्ति कुतस्तेषां समागमः।। शान्ति १८६.१२।।

At the time of death, people give a cow in charity, hoping that the cow thus donated would save them. But when the individual dies after gifting the cow, whom will the cow save?[20]

विहगैरुपभुक्तस्य शैलाग्रात् पतितस्य च।
अग्निना चोपयुक्तस्य कुतः संजीवनं पुनः।। शान्ति पर्व १८६.१३।।

When dead, a person is either devoured by vultures, or breaks into pieces on being thrown from a hill, or is burnt by fire. How can then a Self be born again?[21]

छिन्नस्य यदि वृक्षस्य न मूलं प्रतिरोहति।
बीजान्यस्य प्रवर्तन्ते मृतः क्व पुनरेष्यति।। शान्ति १८६.१४।।

बीजमात्रं पुरा सृष्टं यदेतत् परिवर्तते।
मृतामृता: प्रणश्यन्ति बीजाद् बीजं प्रवर्तते।। शान्ति १८६.१५ ।।

Just as a tree cut from the roots has no roots, from where will the Self rise again? Creation is perpetuated from seed to seed, but the Self dies with death.[22]

Bhrigu (to Bharadvāj)

No, the Self is not destroyed, nor his acts. What is destroyed is the body he leaves behind; but the Self transmigrates to another body.

Even with the destruction of its host, the body, the Self does not die. Just as the fire itself can be seen when the fuel is burnt up; the Self can be experienced likewise.[23]

Bharadvāj ***(to Bhrigu)***

When the fuel is burnt up, the fire ends too, and cannot be had. The same is true of the Self as well. The fire without the fuel, I consider as good as extinguished. What does not have movement, or measure, or place, can only be described as non-existent.[24]

Bhrigu ***(to Bharadvāj)***

The fire, on the fuel being burnt up, cannot be had, for it then remains in its unseen form in the space; and it is true that without a host the fire cannot be had; but the fire itself is not destroyed.

In the same way, after death, the Self exists in its unseen form in the space. Being a subtle substance, it cannot be perceived, anymore than the fire can be perceived on being extinguished. But the Self continues to exist, of that there is no doubt.

The fire sustains life. Consider the Self likewise. The wind keeps that fire within the body; breathing stops when the wind leaves and, with it, the fire.

The fire in the body extinguished, the body falls on the earth dead, and the earth claims the physical. The wind goes to the space, and the fire likewise. The space, the wind, and the fire: these three come together; and the earth and the water remain on the earth.

The wind is where there is space, and the fire is where there is wind. Although formless, they acquire a form in the body.[25]

Bharadvāj ***(to Bhrigu)***

If the living beings have in their bodies as their constituents only the fire, the wind, the earth, the space, and the water, then what are the attributes of the Self inhabiting bodies?

The bodies of the living beings are made of those five elements; feel attracted towards their five objects; have, with consciousness, five faculties of sensing and experiencing. Of what form is the Self?

Where in the body is it anyway? On dissecting the body, one finds flesh, and blood, and bones, and nerves, and fat, but not the Self.

However, the question then will be, if the existence of the Self is disputed, *who* or *what* feels and experiences the pain of the body and the pain of the mind?

Plainly it is the mind that perceives. One may hear something from both ears; and yet, if the mind is not there, does not hear what the ears hear. It is meaningless, therefore, to posit the Self as yet another entity.

What can be seen, is seen only when the mind is united with the eyes. If the mind is disturbed, even on seeing one does not see.

While sleeping, one does not see, nor hears, nor smells, nor speaks, nor touches, nor tastes.

The question then is: *who* or *what* within the body is happy, or is angry? *Who* feels agitation, *who* feels sorrow? *Who* desires, *who* feels repulsed, and *who* engages in a conversation?[26]

Bhrigu *(to Bharadvāj)*

Even the mind has the five elements of Nature as its constituents; it is nothing distinct from them.[27] Only the Self is conscious of the body. Only the Self senses and experiences form, taste, smell, touch, sound, and the other attributes of life.

Pervading the physicality of life, every part of it, the Self, experiencing pleasure and pain, is the witness of the mind as well. When its relation to the body comes to an end, the body and, with it, the mind, can sense neither pleasure nor pain.

When the body made of the five elements of Nature senses neither form, nor touch, nor warmth, and the fire within dies, the Self, on leaving the body, does not itself die.

The entire creation is suffused with water, and so is the physical body. Within it, the mind is suffused with the Self; and it is the Self, pervading the universe, that is known as Brahma.[28]

When the Self acquires the attributes of Nature, it is called 'the person', 'the active agent'; when it gets free of them, dissociated from the attributes of life, it is called 'the cosmic spirit'.

But consider 'the person' to be the Self, the goodness in all beings. Inhabiting the physical body, it remains untouched by it, even as the water drops on lotus leaves do.

Consider the person to be the Self, the goodness in all beings. *Sattva*, *rajas*, and *tamas*, the three forms of energy, the energy of consciousness, the energy of action, and the energy that suffocates and depresses, are the main attributes of the Self as person.

In association with the Self as pure consciousness, those three attributes are also endowed with consciousness. The Self itself moves and acts; and the Self makes all others act. Those who have the knowledge of the true substance of things, regard, however, the Self in its cosmic form higher than the Self as person.

With the death of the physical, the Self does not die. Those who say that it does, are mistaken; and what they say is false. When the five elements of Nature separate from each other, the physical body dies; but the Self takes on another body.

The Self remains in the innermost of all beings, and can be perceived by the penetrating intelligence of those with knowledge.[29]

At another place in the *Mahābhārata*,[30] another conversation is narrated in which Pañchashikha, a *Sāṃkhya* philosopher, advocates the view of the Self that Bhrigu had. Pañchashikha arrives one day in the court of King Janaka. This king had a great taste for philosophy and an even greater curiosity. He had assembled in his court one hundred philosophers, whom he would engage in conversations that revolved around his question whether after death the Self exists or not. He was, however, not particularly satisfied with the different answers that he would get.[31] Janaka feels so greatly drawn towards Pañchashikha as to leave the company of the philosophers in his court and follow him.[32] Pañchashikha looks the very incarnation of the sage Kapilā, in whose teachings the philosophy of *Sāṃkhya* had originated.[33] He had grown up in the love and affection of his mother Kapilā; in grateful acknowledgement of what his mother meant to him, Pañchashikha came to be known as Kāpileya, 'the son of Kapilā'.[34] Persuaded that the king was genuinely interested in his inquiry as regards the Self, he plunges into a long discussion with him.

But Pañchashikha feels obliged to address an invisible audience in the first place. It consists of those who disputed that there is any such thing as a permanent Self, independent of the body – mind apparatus. He does not abuse them. He does not caricature their argument and its reasoning. He states both with perfect honesty. That is to say, the *Mahābhārata* states both with perfect honesty.

Pañchashikha *(to King Janaka)*

दृष्यमाने विनाशे च प्रत्यक्षे लोकसाक्षिके ।
आगमात् परमस्तीति ब्रुवन्नपि पराजित: ।। २१८.२३ ।।

They say that the decay and death of the Self as physical body can be seen directly, the whole world a witness to it. Despite that, quoting some scriptures, if its contrary is maintained, then those who do are defeated already.[35]

अनात्मा ह्यात्मनो मृत्यु: क्लेशो मृत्युर्जरामय: ।
आत्मानं मन्यते मोहात् तदसम्यक् परं मतम् ।। २१८.२४ ।।

The death of the body as the Self is the death of the Self. Likewise, old age, disease, and other pains constitute the death of the Self. The belief in the existence of any other Self is wholly mistaken, an illusion.[36]

अथ चेदेवमप्यस्ति यल्लोके नोपपद्यते ।
अजरोऽयममृत्युश्च राजासौ मन्यते यथा ।। २१८.२५ ।।

Against all evidence, should the existence of the Self that is independent of the body be accepted, which of course is not possible, it would be so only in a manner of speaking, just as those in prison call the king immortal.[37]

अस्ति नास्तीति चाप्येतत् तस्मिन्नसति लक्षणे ।
किमधिष्ठाय तद् ब्रूयाल्लोकयात्राविनिश्चयम् ।। शान्ति २१८.२६ ।।

Should inference be used to decide whether there is, or there is not, the Self, there exists no method of drawing inference that is free from error. What inference could then decide this question?[38]

प्रत्यक्षं ह्येतयोर्मूलं कृतान्तैतिह्ययोरपि ।
प्रत्यक्षेणागमो भिन्न: कृतान्तो वा न किञ्चन ।। शान्ति २१८.२७ ।।

Inference and the authority of scriptures, both these depend for their validity upon direct evidence. If they go against direct experience, then neither of them can be accepted as valid proof.[39]

यत्र यत्रानुमानेऽस्मिन् कृतं भावयतोऽपि च।
नान्यो जीवः शरीरस्य नास्तिकानां मते स्थितः।। शान्ति २१८.२८।।
Wherever inference is employed to prove the existence of God, or of the Unseen, or of the eternal Self, there the notion of purpose-and-means will be of no help either. Thus, in the view of the agnostics, the non-existence of the Self, independent of the body, is established.[40]

Furthermore, Pañchashikha continues:

नन्वेते हेतवः सन्ति ये केचिन्मूर्तिसंस्थिताः।
अमूर्तस्य हि मूर्तेन सामान्यं नोपपद्यते।। शान्ति २१८.३१।।
The examples in the agnostic reasoning are of the embodied objects. Consciousness is disembodied. One cannot give rise to the other.[41]

जरयाभिपरीतस्य मृत्युना च विनाशिना।
दुर्बलं दुर्बलं पूर्वं गृहस्येव विनश्यति।। शान्ति २१८.४०।।
Just as the weakest parts of a house crumble first, in the same way, assailed by old age and death, the weakest parts of the body crumble, and then the whole edifice.[42]

इन्द्रियाणि मनो वायुः शोणितं मांसमस्थि च।
आनुपूर्व्या विनश्यन्ति स्वं धातुमुपयान्ति च।। शान्ति २१८.४१।।
The sense organs, the mind, the breath, the blood, the flesh, and the bones—these are successively destroyed, and return to the five elements of Nature.[43]

लोकयात्राविघातश्च दानधर्मफलागमे।
तदर्थं वेदशब्दाश्च व्यवहाराश्च लौकिकाः।। शान्ति २१८.४२।।
At the same time, were the existence of the Self not admitted, then there would be no faith in sharing, giving, and other attributes of dharma *either; in other words, there would be no faith in the recompense of acts. For, done for the sake of social progress, they are done primarily for the sake of the Self.*[44]

King Janaka (*to Pañchashikha*)

भगवन् यदि न प्रेत्य संज्ञा भवति कस्यचित्।
एवं सति किमज्ञानं वा किं करिष्यति।। शान्ति २१९.२।।

After death, if no one has any distinct identity, then what meaning do knowledge and ignorance have?[45]

सर्वमुच्छेदनिष्ठं स्यात् पश्चाचैतद् द्विजोत्तम।
अप्रमत्त: प्रमत्तो वा किं विशेषं करिष्यति।। शान्ति २१९.३।।

After death, when man anyway loses consciousness and its instruments, then what does it matter if he was vigilant or careless before death.[46]

असंसर्गो हि भूतेषु संसर्गो वा विनाशिषु।
कस्मै क्रियेत कल्प्येत निश्चय: कोऽत्र तत्त्वत:।। शान्ति २१९.४।।

After death, does the Self retain, or does it not, any connection with the five elements of Nature? If it does, what is the purpose? Could anything be said on this subject that would be conclusive and definite?[47]

In answer to these questions, in the voice of Pañchashikha, the *Sāṃkhya* philosopher, the *Mahābhārata* draws a picture of the physical and the psychological apparatus of human personality.[48] The physical aspect of the human self, as indeed of all living beings, is made up of the five elements of Nature: space, wind, fire, water, and earth. By their *svabhāva*, inherent disposition, they combine and then separate. Consciousness, heat, and breath—from a combination of these three arise the sense organs, the mind, the life force, awareness, the inherent disposition, and the various changing forms they take, leading to all acts.[49] The ears, the skin, the tongue, the eyes, and the nose are the five *karma-indriya*, organs of physical sensation. Suffused with consciousness, and when combined with the mind, they become both the means and the subject of cognition. The *jñāna-indriya*, organs of cognition, are correspondingly five: sound, touch, taste, form, and smell. With external material object as the sixth element, they remain the organs of cognition till the very end of a person's life.[50] Each one of them is the natural object of its corresponding physical organ of sensation, towards which it rushes, or from which it recoils. The ears towards sound; the skin towards touch; the tongue towards taste; the eyes towards form; and the nose towards smell.[51] Although each has its corresponding sensation, they can all be sensed together. In all physical acts and in cognition, before they can take place, the five organs of physical sensation; the five organs of cognition; *manas*, the mind, as the eleventh; and the faculty of differentiating, *buddhi*, as the twelfth element, have to combine.[52] *Ahaṃkāra*, 'the individual will', and above all consciousness, *citta*, as the ground of all sensing and experience, complete the psychophysical apparatus of the empirical self. It is *this* self that has a beginning when it is born, and has an end when it dies; all its psychophysical elements disintegrate and separate, each returning to its inherent ground—*ākāsa*, 'the space'. It is to *this* psycho-physical self that feelings attach. It is *this* self that touches and is touched by the world.

Pañchashikha then talks about the three primordial *energies* with which, in their different measures, the whole creation is suffused: *sattva*, *rajas*, and *tamas*.[53] The distinct individuality of a person, the diversity of character and temperament, are the product of the many different combinations of these three energies.

प्रहर्षः प्रीतिरानन्दः सुखं संशन्तचित्तता।
अकुतश्चित् कुतश्चिद् वा चिन्तिः सात्त्विकोगुणः।। शान्ति २१९.२६।।
Feelings of delight, love, joy, happiness, and peace of mind, whether they arise with or without cause, are known as the energy of sattva.[54]

अतुष्टिः परितापश्चशोको लोभस्तथाक्षमा।
लिङ्गांनि रजसत्तानि दृश्यन्ते हेत्वहेतुतः।। शान्ति २१९.२७।।
Feelings of discontent, regret, sorrow, greed, and intolerance are the signs of the energy of rajas.[55]

अविवेकस्तथा मोहः प्रमादः स्वप्नतन्द्रिता।
कथंचिदपि वर्तन्ते विविधास्तामसा गुणाः।। शान्ति २१९.२८।।
Lack of judgement, blinding confusion of perceptions, carelessness, dreams, and laziness, no matter how they arise, are the different forms of the energy of tamas.[56]

अत्र यत् प्रीतिसंयुक्तं काये मनसि वा भवेत्।
वर्तते सात्त्विको भाव इत्यपेक्षेत तत् तथा।। शान्ति २१९.२९।।
The feelings arising from love in the mind and in the body are sattvic, *enhancing the energy of* sattva.[57]

यत् त्वसंतोषसंयुक्तमप्रीतिकरमात्मनः।
प्रवृत्तं रज इत्येवं ततस्तदपि चिन्तयेत्।। शान्ति २१९.३०।।

> *Whatever is unsatisfactory and unpleasant to one's self is to be interpreted as the outcome of the energy of* rajas.[58]
>
> अथ यन्मोहसंयुक्तं काये मनसि वा भवेत्।
> अप्रतर्क्यमविज्ञेयं तमस्तदुपधारयेत्।। शान्ति २१९.३१।।
>
> *And whatever produces, in the mind and in the body, blinding confusion of perceptions, a sense of meaninglessness, in which nothing makes any sense, is to be seen as coming from the energy of* tamas.[59]

It is the psychophysical self, the empirical self, of which there are as many as there are living beings, that is suffused with these three energies, existing together but in many different proportions. The predominance of one over the other two gives an individual his and her *sva-bhāva*, his and her specific disposition, distinct tendency, which may remain constant or may change. It is the psychophysical self that is subject to birth, dissolution, and death. Distinct from it, is the *ātman*, the Self, that is only 'housed' in the psychophysical self; but unlike that self, is not subject to birth and death. It is the confusion of one for the other that produces every other kind of ignorance: pain and sorrow, *duhkha*, above all.

However, without offering any lazy comfort on the question whether there is or there is not any other entity apart from the psychophysical self; in the voice of Pañchashikha the *Mahābhārata* says:

> इति सम्यङ्मनस्येते बहवः सन्ति हेतवः।
> एतदस्तीदमस्तीति न किष्चत्प्रतिदश्यते।। शान्ति २१८.४३।।
>
> *Thus many arguments arise in the mind. It does not seem that the question regarding the existence, or the non-existence, of the Self could be settled in that way.*[60]

The manifest self: the unmanifest self

The author of the *Mahābhārata*, Vyāsa, in his own voice, adds very substantially to the discussion concerning the self and the universe and the relation between the two. That he does in a long conversation with his son, Shukadeva, who had sought from his father knowledge on many intricate questions that were quite as difficult to answer. They ranged from the genesis of the universe to the reasoning for the path of a complete withdrawal from the world.[61] Vyāsa clearly says that he would be answering his son's questions from the knowledge he had from the philosophies of *Sāṃkhya* and *Yoga*. They generally go together as *Sāṃ khya-Yoga*: the *Sāṃkhya* being the more metaphysical, and the *Yoga* concerned mostly with the mind — body ethical discipline that followed from that metaphysics. 'Dear son! What I have said so far concerning the subjects in your questions come from the philosophy of *Sāṃkhya*.'[62]

पृच्छतस्तव सत्पुत्र यथावदिह तत्त्वत: ।
सांख्यज्ञानेन संयुक्तं यदेतत् कीर्तितं मया ।। शान्ति २४०.१ ।।

Touching most of the ground traversed already by the sages Bhrigu and Pañchashikha, as in the foregoing paragraphs, *Vyāsa* does it in greater detail, and says furthermore:

महाभूतानि पञ्चैव सर्वभूतेषु भूतकृत ।
अकरोत् तात वैषम्यं यस्मिन् यदनुपश्यति ।। शान्ति २४७.६ ।।
Although earth, water, fire, wind, and space constitute the physical self of all living beings alike, the reason for the evident dissimilarities is that those five elements combine in different beings in different proportions.[63]

There is the self that is manifest and differentiated, the psychophysical and the empirical self; and there is the self that is unmanifest and undifferentiated.

प्रोक्तं तद् व्यक्तमित्येव जायते वर्धते च यत् ।
जीर्यते म्रियते चैव चतुर्भिर्लक्षणैर्युतम ।। शान्ति २३६.३० ।।
What has the four attributes of a beginning with birth; a maturing; age and a progressive dissolution; and an end with death—is vyakta, *or that which is manifest.*[64]

विपरीतमतो यत् तु तदव्यक्तमुदाहृतम् ।
द्वावात्मानौ च वेदेषु सिद्धान्तेष्वप्युदाहृतौ ।। शान्ति २३६.३१ ।।
The reality that is its opposite is avyakta, *or that which is unmanifest: the Self; of which there are two: the individual Self and the Greater Self.*[65]

चतुर्लक्षणजं त्वाद्यं चतुर्वर्गं प्रचक्षते ।
व्यक्तमव्यक्तजं चैव तथा बुद्धमथेतरत्

सत्त्वं क्षेत्रज्ञ इत्येतद् द्वयमप्यनुदर्शितम् ।। शान्ति २३६.३२ ।।
द्वावात्मानौ च वेदेषु विषयेष्वनुरज्यतः ।
विषयात् प्रतिसंहारः सांख्यानां सिद्धिलक्षणम् ।। शान्ति २३६.३३ ।।

In its essence, although unmanifest, the individual self on coming in relation to the manifest self seems to acquire the four attributes of the manifest: birth, maturing, dissolution, and death. But the Greater Self, the unmanifest, remains beyond. The manifest originates from the unmanifest. What is manifest is called 'the field of acts', kshetra, *and the unmanifest Self 'the acting agent', 'the doer',* kshetrajna. *When the Self comes into awareness of its mistaken identity with the psychophysical self, it becomes free, according to the philosophy of Sāṃkhya.*[66]

Vyāsa, too, like Pañchashikha, feels obliged to answer those,[67] by no means a small number, who disputed the existence of consciousness as any reality apart from matter that is sensed directly. No such entity can be seen apart from physical life that comes into being by a conglomeration, a combining, of the five elements of Nature from their *svabhāva*, innate disposition, and ends when, out of the same natural disposition, they disintegrate.[68]

Vyāsa's answer in its main outline is as follows. If it were true that everything happens because it is in the nature of things to happen, then no conscious effort would be required for anything to happen, which demonstrably it is. The five physical senses, like their corresponding five elements of Nature, are in themselves immovable *jaḍa*, and can act only when they are brought into a purposeful unity by *chetanā*, a conscious element, apart from them. Similarly, the organs of cognition require that conscious element to make cognition a coherent unity. Perception is a function of *manas*, the mind. To bring the chaotic diversity of facts into order so as to have 'knowledge', 'understanding', or *jñāna*, is the function of the discriminating intelligence, or *buddhi*, through which all purposeful acts are done.[69] One should consider, besides, the evident fact that, in creation, there are four forms of life: one life giving birth to another life, as in humans and animals; arising from an egg; germinating as in a plant; and from heat and moisture as in insects. This part of creation, because it moves and lives, is superior to that part of creation which is fixed and immovable. Because he is endowed with discriminating intelligence, man is superior to all other living beings.[70] As regards the element of intelligence, or *buddhi*, in the psychophysical self of man, Vyāsa further says:

मनो बुद्धिः स्वभावश्च त्रय एते स्वयोनिजाः।
न गुणानतिवर्तन्ते गुणेभ्यः परमागताः।। शान्ति २४७.१३।।
यथा कूर्म इहागांनि प्रसार्य विनियच्छति।
एवमेवेन्द्रियग्रामं बुद्धिः सृष्टा नियच्छति।। शान्ति २४७.१४।।

The mind, the intelligence, and the will, these three although in their essence independent of the organs of sensing and cognition; they are connected with them all the same, and cannot go beyond them. But just as a tortoise opens its limbs outward and then withdraws them into itself, intelligence spreads the organs of sensing towards the corresponding objects, and then withdraws them from them.[71]

यदूर्ध्वं पादतलयोरवाङ्मूर्ध्नश्च पश्यति।
एतस्मिन्नेव कृत्ये तु वर्तते बुद्धिरुत्तमा।। शान्ति २४७.१५।।

The act of the individual perceiving his self as a distinct self, from his feet upwards and from his head downwards, is only another form of intelligence.[72]

गुणान् नेनीयते बुद्धिर्बुद्धिरेवेन्द्रियाण्यपि।
मनःषष्ठानि सर्वाणि बुद्ध्यभावे कुतो गुणाः।। शान्ति २४७.१६।।

In all acts of sensing and perceiving, intelligence unites that which senses and the mind with what is sensed. Or else how can the sound, the touch, the form, the smell, the taste, be sensed at all?[73]

इन्द्रियाणि नरे पञ्च षष्ठं तु मन उच्यते।
सप्तमीं बुद्धिमेवाहुः क्षेत्रज्ञं पुनरष्टमम्।। शान्ति २४७.१७।।

There are in man's body five organs of sensing; the mind, the sixth; intelligence, the seventh; and 'the active agent', 'the doer', is the eighth.[74]

चक्षुरालोचनायैव संशयं कुरुते मनः।
बुद्धिरध्यवसानाय साक्षी क्षेत्रज्ञ उच्यते।। शान्ति २४७.१८।।

For example, the eyes 'see'. The mind doubts and questions. The intelligence judges and evaluates. And the Self is a Witness to it all.[75]

इन्द्रियेभ्यः परे ह्यर्था अर्थेभ्यः परमं मनः।
मनसस्तु परा बुद्धिर्बुद्धेरात्मा महान् परः।। शान्ति २४६.३।।

The subjects that are sensed are stronger than the organs of sensing. Stronger than what is sensed is the mind. Stronger than the mind is the discriminating intelligence. And stronger than that is the Self.[76]

In the voice of Vyāsa, and in numerous other voices, the *Mahābhārata* dwells on the characteristics of the mind and of intelligence in a language that is as clear.[77]

धैर्योपपत्तिर्व्यक्तिश्च विसर्गः कल्पना क्षमा ।
सदसच्चाशुता चैव मनसौ नव वै गुणाः ।। शान्ति २५५.९ ।।
Steadiness; the skill of argument; memory; confusion; imagination; reconciliation; good or ill resolution; and fickleness—are the nine characteristics of the mind.[78]

इष्टानिष्टविपत्तिश्च व्यवसायः समाधिता ।
संशयः प्रतिपकत्तिश्च बुद्धेः पञ्चगुणान् विदु ।। शान्ति २५५.१० ।।
To discriminate between what is good and what is ill; to judge and differentiate; to evaluate; to resolve doubts; and to decide—are the five characteristics of the intelligence, buddhi.[79]

Furthermore:

बुद्धिरात्मा मनुष्यस्य बुद्धिरेवात्मनाऽऽत्मनि ।
यदा विकुरुते भावं तदा भवति सा मनः ।। शान्ति २४८.३ ।।
Governing the organs of sensing and of cognition, the intelligence is akin to their self. In experiencing them, it takes many forms of emotions and feelings, and then makes the mind likewise.[80]

इन्द्रियाणां पृथग्भावाद् बुद्धिर्विक्रियते ह्यतः
शृण्वती भवति श्रोत्रं स्पृशती स्पर्श उच्यते ।। शान्ति २४८.४ ।।
The organs of sensing are different from each other, and each has a different function. To enable them to function, the intelligence transforms itself into each of those organs. In hearing, it becomes the ears; in touching, it becomes the skin.[81]

पश्यती भवते दृष्टी रसती रसनं भवेत् ।
जिघ्रती भवति घ्राणं बुद्धिर्विक्रियते पृथक् ।। शान्ति २४८.५ ।।
In seeing, it becomes the eyes; in tasting, it becomes the tongue; in smelling, it becomes the nose. Thus, the intelligence de-forms *itself in as many ways.*[82]

इन्द्रियाणि तु तान्याहुस्तेष्वदृश्योऽधितिष्ठति।
तिष्ठती पुरुषे बुद्धिस्त्रिषु भावेषु वर्तते।। शान्ति २४८.६।।

Indeed, it turns into the organs of sensing themselves. The unseen individual self has a dwelling in them; and the intelligence has a dwelling in the self, flowing at all times in the three different forms of energy and the feelings and emotions they create.[83]

कदाचिल्लभते प्रीतिं कदाचिदपि शोचति।
न सुखेन न दुःखेन कदाचिदिह युज्यते।। शान्ति २४८.७।।

In that flow, the intelligence sometimes feels love and joy, sometimes pain and sorrow. And there are times when it feels neither the one nor the other.[84]

ये चैव भावा वर्तन्ते सर्व एष्वेव ते त्रिषु।
अन्वर्थाः सम्प्रवर्तन्ते रथनेमिमरा इव।। शान्ति २४८.११।।

The varied human emotions and feelings arise from the three energies of sattva, rajas, *and* tamas.[85]

What the *Mahābhārata* is saying here is that sensing is not merely sensation; it has to be intelligent sensing at the same time. Thus, the eyes do not 'see' merely in a physiological sense; no 'seeing' is merely ophthalmological; there is a natural ordering in 'seeing', a natural relating. Similarly, there is a natural ordering, a relating, in 'hearing', in 'touching', in 'smelling', in 'tasting'. In being physiological functions, they are not merely physiological. The ordering and relating in all physiological functions is the work of *buddhi*, in the psychophysical self. At the same time, in ordering physical sensations so as to make a meaningful image of what is sensed, the intelligence does a 'selection' as well, in accordance with the inclinations of sense organs, in a manner of speaking. With that, my eyes 'see' what I want them to see; and my ears 'hear' what I want them to hear; and so with the rest. The 'selection' done, my intelligence brings my mind into its service; that service being, the mind with its instruments of intellect and argument justifying 'the selection' I have made. Thereafter my eyes do not 'see' what my *buddhi* does not want them to see; and what I do not see, does not exist. Thus the natural ordering in all physiological functions becomes imperceptibly also an ordering that falsifies reality, including one's own. The *Mahābhārata* keeps reiterating that the physical organs by themselves are lifeless, *jaḍa*. It is consciousness in the living beings that breathes life into them; and only then can they function as living organs.

सत्त्वमात्मा प्रसरति गुणान् वापि कदाचन ।
न गुणा विदुरात्मानं गुणान् वेद स सर्वदा ।। शान्ति २४८.२० ।।
परिद्रष्टा गुणानां च परिस्रष्टा यथातथम् ।
सत्त्वक्षेत्रज्ञयोरेतदन्तरं विद्धि सूक्ष्मयो: ।। शान्ति २४८.२१ ।।

The Self, Puruṣa, *moves sometimes towards the senses and their objects enveloped in the three energies, and sometimes towards the intelligence. The organs of sensing and their energies do not know the Self, because they cannot; but the Self knows them, because it is their Witness, and is in a sense also their creator. The three energies and the Self are both subtle entities, but are different; the difference being that the one is the subject of cognition and the other is unseen.*[86]

सृजतेऽत्र गुणानेक एको न सृजते गुणान् ।
पृथग्भूतौ प्रकृत्या तौ सम्प्रयुक्तौ च सर्वदा ।। शान्ति २४८.२२ ।।

Prakriti, *Nature, in being the active reality, creates, so to say, the three energies; the* Puruṣa, *in essence passive, does not. In their essence separate from each other, they however become united.*[87]

Not only do the *Purusha* and *Prakriti* become united but the *Purusha* also loses awareness of its distinct identity as pure consciousness without objects to be conscious of; pure existence without forms of existence; complete in itself, shining in its own light, unmanifest. Identifying itself with Nature, the *Purusha*, the Self, takes all the colours of Nature and, flowing in its three energies, dances the dance of Nature, the dance of love and joy, the dance of greed and aggression, and also the dance that suffocates and chokes. Sound, touch, form, taste, smell, and the material object are the six steps in the dance of Nature. Consciousness acquires three different characteristics: the one that is beyond pain and pleasure; or feels both pleasure and pain; or feels neither clearly pain nor clearly pleasure, but is just confused.[88]

The ultimate human aim is for the *Purusha* to become aware of its true identity, cease dancing the dances of sound, touch, form, taste, smell, and the dance of the manifest, the dance of Nature. And return to its own—the return of the Self from the self, free from the sports of Nature. That is *mokṣha*, the ultimate freedom of the Self. This is the substance of *Sāṃkhya* philosophy as expressed in the voices of Bhrigu, Pañchashikha, and Vyāsa in the *Mahābhārata*. The return of the Self is to be achieved step by step, first by disciplining the body and the mind. *Yoga*, the other part of *Sāṃkhya*, has that disciplining as its subject. In his conversation about man and the world with his son Shukadeva, Vyāsa next moves to the disciplining of the physical senses and of the mind, and bringing thereby eventually a complete cessation of their workings.[89] Shukadeva is quick to ask what happens to Nature, *Prakriti*, subsequent to the *Puruṣa*, the Self, becoming free from its entanglements. Vyāsa's answer is a characteristic feature of the *Mahābhārata*.

> प्रध्वस्ता न निवर्तन्ते प्रवृत्तिर्नोपलभ्यते।
> एवमेके व्यवस्यन्ति निवृत्तिरिति चापरे।। शान्ति २४९.३।।
> उभयं सम्प्रधार्यैतदध्यवस्येद् यथामति।
> अनेनैव विधानेन भवेद् गर्भशयो महान्।। शान्ति २४९.४।।
>
> *According to some, Nature continues to exist, but without relation to the free Self. Some others believe that, with the return of the Self, Nature has no existence anymore.*

One should reflect deeply upon both these views and then decide.[90]

There are two questions that are necessarily connected with all discussions on the self and the world: *one*, the question of causality and, inherent in it, *two*, the question concerning *kāla*, Time. Both these come up in Vyāsa's conversation with his son as well,[91] and form a fundamental part of the *Mahābhārata*'s inquiry into the human condition, which we will examine later in this book.[92]

Directing the intelligence and the mind towards gaining self-knowledge and the disciplining of the physical senses presuppose freedom of will. I should be ontologically free of any other causal agent outside my self. Whether I let my physical senses run riot, letting my organs of sound, sight, taste, smell, and touch have their unchecked away – because that is what 'pleasure' is, and I equate pleasure with life – should be determined by my own free will. Likewise, my will should be free to will that I take the path of self-knowledge and self-control and direct my intelligence to see that, even on its own terms, to equate pleasure with life is false. In brief, my will should be free to will what I will. If it is not, then there is no meaning in any talk about self-discipline. Freedom of self-effort, self-endeavour, *purushartha*, is then presupposed. Just as the rest of the psychophysical apparatus of the self is given, the freedom of the self, undetermined, much less determined by any outside force, should also be *given* necessarily as an inherent part of that apparatus, whatever view one has of the self or the Self. On this question, Vyāsa honestly says:

केचित् पुरुषकारं तु प्राहुः कर्मसु मानवाः ।
देवमित्यपरे विप्राः स्वाभावं भूतचिन्तकाः ।। २३२.१९ ।।

Some people hold self-effort as leading to success in all acts. Some others hold fate or providence to be its cause. And those who perceive everything in terms of material reality hold the given disposition of things to be the cause.[93]

पौरुषं कर्म दैवं च फलवृत्तिः स्वभावतः ।
त्रय एतेऽपृथग्भूता न विवेकं तु केचन ।। २३२.२० ।।

Some others believe that self-effort, providence and the innate disposition of things, these three together are the cause. None of them by itself can be the cause of fulfilling acts.[94]

एतमेव च नैवं च न चोभे नानुभे न च ।
कर्मस्था विषयं ब्रूयुः सत्त्वस्थाः समदर्शिनः ।। २३२.२१ ।।

Then there are those who do not maintain that self-effort alone *is the determining cause of success in endeavour; but neither do they maintain that fate or providence* alone *is its determining cause. They do not say that the two together are the cause; but neither do they say that the two together are* not *the cause. In brief, they are unable to take any definite position on this subject. Regardless, they perceive all things with the eye of equality.*[95]

As we will see later in this book, Vyāsa's own position on the question of causality is quite definite: that *kāla*, and not human will, is the determining cause of all that *is*, and of all that is *not*.[96] But here he is propounding to his son the path of self-discipline suggested by *Yoga*, which undoubtedly presupposes freedom of will. 'Acting in the light of knowledge is the unfailing means to fulfilling acts.'[97]

In a picturesque language of images and metaphors, Vyāsa however describes to his son the self and the world.

ज्ञानागमेन कर्माणि कुर्वन् कर्मसु सिध्यति ।
पञ्चेन्द्रियजलां घोरां लोभकूलां सुदुस्तराम् ।। २३५.११ ।।

मन्युपकांमनाधृष्यां नदीं तरति बुद्धिमान् ।
कालमभ्युद्यतं पश्येन्नित्यमत्यन्तमोहनम् ।। २३५.१२ ।।

Life in the world is like a mighty river. The five sense organs are its water. Greed its banks. Anger its sludge. It is exceedingly difficult to cross it. Yet those endowed with knowledge do. Time is assailing in the form of confusion and it is blinding. Keep that in mind.[98]

महता विधिदृष्टेन बलेनाप्रतिघातिना ।
स्वभावस्त्रोतसा वृत्तमुह्यते सततं जगत् ।। २३५.१३ ।।

In that mighty flow of the innate nature of things, its power invincible, is the world flowing, in a flow limitless, unending.[99]

Employing some more images, some more metaphors:

कालोदकेन महता वर्षावर्तेन संततम् ।
मासोर्मिणर्तुवेगेन पक्षोलपतृणेन च ।। २३५.१४ ।।
निमेषोन्मेषफेनेन अहोरात्रजलेन च ।
कामग्राहेण धोरेण वेदयज्ञप्लवेन च ।। २३५.१५ ।।
धर्मद्वीपेन भूतानां चार्थकामजलेन च ।
ऋतवाङ्भोक्षतीरेण विहिंसातरुवाहिना ।। २३५.१६ ।।
युगह्रदौघमध्येन ब्रह्मप्रायभवेन च ।
धात्रा सृष्टानि भूतानि कृष्यन्ते यमसादनम् ।। २३५.१७ ।।

The mighty river of Time is flowing. The night and the day its flow. The years its whirls, the months its impetuous waves, the change of seasons its force. The fortnights are the creepers and the straw floating on it. The hours and the moments are its foam. The successive Ages are its centre. The erotic in it captivates, seizes, and swallows. Material prosperity and desire are its water. Truth and freedom are its two banks. Knowledge and sacrifice the two boats; dharma *the island of refuge.*[100]

With the trees of violence floating on it, in that river of Time are flowing all created beings, towards their end.

But the human self is not wholly helpless. In the voice of Vyāsa, the *Mahābhārata* offers strength and hope, both strength and hope being inherent qualities, *guna*, of the created self. Side by side the weakness of being human, the strength of being human is within one's self. And the hope of crossing the mighty river of Time, and not just being carried in its ceaseless flow, is in bringing one's self in harmony, and not at war, with one's self and with the *other*. This is what the *Mahābhārata* is saying to us throughout in the clearest of words.

Radical shift in the *Mahābhārata*

In the perceptions of the self, and what followed from them, there was a radical shift in the *Mahābhārata*. That shift has remained radical ever since. Just as it had distinguished it from the perceptions of the self then, distinguishes it from other perceptions concerning the self now—the ontology, the cosmology, the phenomenology, the teleology, the psychology, the physiology, and the political ideology of the self. If we examine that shift in the *Mahābhārata* with care, it may prove to be of great importance for human living today, in its collective forms as much as in the personal. Its main features are as follows:

a. After narrating the different views of the human self, the *Mahābhārata* then suggests that no final decision is required as to the validity of one metaphysical position or the other concerning the self, or the Self, the *ātman*. Of greater importance is the ordering of our physical and mental and emotional energies in order to live in the fullest worth of being human. This will remain independent of any metaphysics of the self. In that ordering of energies within, belief in the unmanifest *ātman* that is only 'housed' in the manifest psychophysical self will be of no particular help; nor will disbelief in any such entity be any particular hindrance.

   As we heard in the conversations of the sages Bhrigu, Pañchashikha, and Vyāsa, the rejection of the *ātman* as some permanent eternal entity was in the air in the domain of thought even before the Buddha. However, there was a new energy, and heat, in the debate that followed the Buddha's rejection of the *ātman*. But it should have been clear from the beginning that that energy was somewhat misdirected. The main concern of the Buddha was with the palpable, directly sensed, experienced, human suffering, *duḥkha*. Suffering has a cause, an origin *in*. That cause can be comprehended. And its origin seen, there is a way to overcoming suffering. Hence the Buddha's teaching as regards the 'twelve-fold chain of causation' of suffering, or *bhava-chakra*. That chain of causation will remain indisputable even if one rejects the Buddha's rejection of the *ātman*. Neither was his own rejection of the *ātman* as a permanent entity any part of his perception of the causal chain of human suffering. Whether one believes, or one does not, in the Self as *a permanent entity*, with a capital 'S', is hardly of any capital importance in man's encounter with pain and suffering. Hence also the Buddha's consistent refusal to fall into the bottomless pit of metaphysical questions and the wrangling over them.

Centuries earlier, the *Mahābhārata* had marked a radical shift from the *ātman* to *dharma*, and the one was no prerequisite for the other.

It was a shift from the abstract concepts of the *ātman* to human experience—the feelings of attraction, repulsion, or indifference and the conflicts generated thereby, both within the self and with others; the attitudes, and what one makes of oneself. In other words, it was a shift to *relationships*—with one's self and with the *other*. Thus, to take one example, whatever theory one may have of the Self, independent of it the necessity of self-control will remain indisputable. Since desire is the starting point of all acts, and the sense organs naturally rush towards objects that are pleasurable, and withdraw from the ones that are disagreeable, the variety of human acts and experiences arising from inclination and aversion, the sense organs must be kept under control. This is because they, and under their influence the will, tend to run riot if not disciplined, and become destructive of the self, and destructive of the *other* at the same time. Hence, the *Mahābhārata* keeps stressing, the need for self-discipline in relation to one's self. This will remain true independent of the *ātman*.

The favourite metaphor employed by the *Mahābhārata* in this regard is that of a chariot drawn by five horses: the body is the chariot, the five sense organs are its horses, the mind is the charioteer.[101] The person who holds firmly the reins of the five sense organs is a happy charioteer. And there is no heaven and there is no hell apart from what the sense organs, disciplined or left wild, create for one's self.[102] Acts being also of the mind and of speech, these are to be disciplined as well. This much will remain indisputable whether one is, or one is not, the *ātman* that is beyond decay and death but somehow gets related with that which is subject to both.

b. That radical shift is to be seen also in the meaning that the *Mahābhārata* gives to *ātma-jñāna,* 'self-knowledge'.

It is said again and again that 'greater than self-knowledge there is no knowledge'.[103] And self-knowledge is the abiding light on the path of life. This 'self-knowledge' in the *Mahābhārata* is not limited to the knowledge of the *ātman* being the eternal reality of all living beings, rationally reached after excluding all that the self could not be identified with. Neither was that knowledge ever considered sufficient, or even necessary, to enable us to live life in the full worth of being human. If it were, then nothing more would really be required, because nothing more would then really be left 'to know', 'to understand', 'to relate'. Through the complexities of relationships, through every human story it narrates, the *Mahābhārata* shows how much is still left to know and to understand, to know one's self above all. In the story of the humbling of an arrogant scholar and ascetic, the ordinary housewife and the meatseller were not reminding him that he was the *ātman* that is eternal but curing him of his notion that because he had mastered knowledge he had mastered also his self.[104] Being the eternal *ātman* is still no prevention of arrogance.

'Pleasure' and 'pain'; the workings of desire; self-interest; the attitudes towards *having* and *not having*; sexuality; the appetites and their range; the relations between the body and the mind and the will, feelings and emotions, health and sickness; the logic of *acts* and their recompense; the life-in-family or the life-alone; the dilemmas; social arrangements and social wealth; foundations of law and governance; the question of memory and the past, and freedom from history; the question of truth and untruth; the question of causality; the relation between the transient and the abiding; the meaning of life and the meaning of death; the foundations of life inherent in life, *dharma*, and their uprooting, *adharma*: the *Mahābhārata* seeks knowledge of all these towards self-knowledge. Self-knowledge is not a solitary exercise. And in none of them, as we will see in the following pages of this book, is the eternal *ātman* a first and fundamental requisite.

Self-knowledge is through contexts and situations in which one finds oneself, and also which one creates for oneself. It is through *the given* and *the self-created* that, understanding one's self in the distinctive character of one's self as a person, one begins to have also the knowledge of one's self as a fragment of a larger common human reality. That is the journey of understanding the self and the world on which the *Mahābhārata* takes us; and on that journey, it whispers into our ears, without making a metaphysics of it, belief in the *ātman* is of no particular help, nor is disbelief in any such entity any particular hindrance.

c. By that radical shift in the knowing of the self, the *Mahābhārata* demonstrates the commonly experienced truth that the whole conscious creation, and thus also the self, is a complex field of energy. This is first stated as an essential part of the *Sāṃkhya* metaphysics, as we heard in the conversations of the sages Bhrigu, Pañchashikha, and Vyāsa. Then, in its own radical shift, the *Mahābhārata* quietly disconnects the two. Set aside as 'fanciful', which the Nyāya-Vaisesika metaphysics would, the *Sāṃkhya* doctrine of *Purusha* and *Prakriti*, the Self and Nature, as two absolutely distinct and separate entities, *Purusha* somehow getting entangled in the games of *Prakriti*. But the *Sāṃkhya* view of the three forms of energy flowing through life will remain experientially true. There is the energy in the self that brings love and joy and clarity and *sattva*, inner peace. There is the energy that brings dissatisfaction, discontent, aggression, and greed, *rajas*. And there is the energy that depresses, disturbs, suffocates, and chokes, *tamas*. Even without its metaphysics, it will remain experientially true that the self is a field of these three energies.[105] Independent of the *Sāṃkhya* metaphysics, it will remain experientially true that, with self-knowledge and self-discipline, the self can channel the energies within. That is what the *Mahābhārata* is mainly concerned with—not the knowledge of the *ātman* but the living in *dharma*. The one is not a presupposition of the other.

Self, energy, and relationships

That life is a complex system of energy is evident. It is equally evident that *prāṇa*, life-energy, flows in many channels. It assumes many forms: the energy in earth and in water, and the energy of the human mind and of the human heart. Some forms of energy are of immeasurable beauty, some ugly and grotesque. Energy takes many names: love is energy; hatred is energy, too. What is also true, although not evident, is that there exists, at its very heart, a profound paradox. The highest form of energy arises from complete inner stillness—the paradox of energy. It completes itself in the truth that inner stillness is the natural goal of all energy, even as it is its origin. When energy moves away both from its origin and its goal, it turns upon itself, as it always has, and destroys everything, the self and the *other*, in their individual and collective sense.

Nowhere has the life energy, and its manifold workings, been investigated in greater detail and with greater thoroughness than in the

Mahābhārata.[106] It is mostly in the *Mahābhārata* that the inquiry proceeds through the complexity of concrete human relationships in the very many diverse situations of life. Given the fact that life is energy, and that life is a complex system of relationships, it follows that it is in relationships that the workings of energy are most manifest. That is, in one's relationship with one's self and with the *other*.

Let us now see how very central in the Indian inquiry into the human condition are the questions concerning *prāṇa*, the life energy. What follows is not a summary of the philosophical literature on that subject, but just a brief indication of the centrality of these questions.

All the major *Upanishad*-s revolve around the nature of *prāṇa*. One of the six questions in the *Prashno-Upanishad* that was put to the sage Pippalāda by six other sages, all of them of great eminence, is asked by Āsvalāyana. He wants to know: 'If all forms of life are suffused with *prāṇa*, or life energy, then what is the origin of *prāṇa* itself? How does it enter the human body? And how does it then divide itself into its varied expressions? How does it leave one's body, so that when it does, one is dead? How does life energy hold the outside material world? How does it hold the inner world of man's mind?'[107]

The two longest *Upanishads*, the *Cḥāndogya* and the *Brihad-āraṇyaka*, inquire into the intimate relation of the energy that flows in the elements of Nature and the energy manifest in the attributes of human personality. They inquire into the interrelatedness of man's various energies, physical and mental and emotional. They inquire into the unity of the material and the spiritual. And it is through *these* that they inquire into the nature of the Self, the *ātman*.

Sāṃkhya philosophy is certainly prior to the *Mahābhārata* and to Buddhism and Jainism. As one of its main views regarding creation, the *Sāṃkhya* speaks of the energy of love and joy, or *sattva*; the energy of discontent, greed, and of aggression, or *rajas*; and the energy that suffocates and chokes, or *tamas*, as being the three constituents of Nature, of all living beings. The word *tamas* has been mostly translated as 'darkness'; but it is that only in a metaphorical sense. Derived from the root word *tam*, it really means 'to suffocate; choke; to gasp for breath, be exhausted, be distressed, or disturbed'. The varying proportions in which the three energies combine, one predominating over the other two, account for the diverse characters of individuals, and account also for the character of the relationships which they form. Their proportions relative to each other keep changing with the passage of time; but even then one is more dominant than the other two. *Yoga* expands upon it further. It shows that the energies of the body and of the mind are inseparable in a way that one determines the other. It suggests ways of disciplining them so that they flow without being obstructed by the wrong attitudes and passions that we ourselves create. *Yoga*, properly understood, takes us, by disciplining our energies, towards simple human happiness, and towards beatitude.

The *Mahābhārata*, undoubtedly the largest and the most systematic inquiry into the human condition, has the ordering of energy, individual and social, as its main concern. It demonstrates how we misdirect, misuse, and abuse our personal and collective energies, doing violence to ourselves and to others thereby, the energy of *adharma*. The *Mahābhārata* then takes us, step by step, from the confines of the energy that does violence to human worth towards that freedom of which every human person is a natural heir.

The paradox of energy comprises, firstly, the paradox of *kāla*, as primordial energy or force. It is stated in the very first chapter of the *Mahābhārata*.

कालः सृजति भूतानि कालः संहरते प्रजा।
संहरन्तं प्रजाः कालं कालः शमयते पुनः।। आदि १.२४८।।

कालो हि कुरुते भवान् सर्वलोके शुभशुभान्।
कालः संक्षिपते सर्वाः प्रजा विसृजते पुनः।। आदि १.२४९।।

कालः सुप्तेषु जागर्ति कालो हि दुरतिक्रमः।
कालः सर्वेषु भूतेषु चरत्यविधृतः समः।। आदि १.२५०।।

अतीतानागता भावा ये च वर्तन्ति साम्प्रतम्।
तान् कालनिर्मितान् बुद्ध्वा न संज्ञां हातुमर्हसि।। आदि १.२५१।।

Time creates all beings; and Time destroys what is created. Destroying what is created, Time is then pacified by Time.

Time is the doer of all that happens in the universe: of the good and the bad alike. Time contracts and limits what is created; and then expands and sets free what is limited.

Time sleeps, and Time alone is forever awake; no one can transgress Time. Time moves in all beings equally.

What was in the past, what will come in the future, and what is now, are the creations of Time. Knowing this, do not lose your faculty of discrimination.[108]

'Time is the root of all that is; and all that is not; of happiness and suffering alike.'

This is the view of the author of the *Mahābhārata*, Vyāsa; and he maintains it throughout, from the beginning to the end of that work. Vyāsa perceives all human relationships as being determined by Time: the coming together, the parting; the loving, the hating, being indifferent; being gentle and tender, being nasty and brutal; going to war, and reconciling in the attitude of peace. Bhīshma, a dominant figure in the *Mahābhārata*, rejects that view. He maintains on the contrary that 'Time is no force; it is only a mental construct to explain sequence. The real force, the primary human energy, lies in the human mind and in the human heart, from which arise all human acts, *karma*.'

The *Yoga-Vāsishṭha* goes many steps further. Its main thesis is that, like the material world, time is wholly a creation of the mind, and has no existence independent of the mind. *Manas*, the mind, is the moving energy. That is to say, perception is everything. These two radically opposed conceptions of energy, one of Vyāsa and the other of Bhīshma and, many centuries later, of the *Yoga-Vāsishṭha*, have vastly different ethical implications as regards the question of responsibility. Both have existed everywhere side by side, as they do today, and can be seen in the common language of the peasant and the learned alike. 'I am passing through a bad time'; *or* 'These are good times for me', and expressions of this kind. We say also: 'I am responsible for what has happened.' And we say these things alternately, sometimes even in the same breath. One of them suggests that time, a force outside me, is against me; whereas the other suggests that I am against my self.

However, whether one believes time to be the font of all forms of energy, or believes the mind to be that source, or believes in both simultaneously, the paradox of energy remains. It takes the form of the paradox of memory.

Memory is a faculty without which human life will be impossible, even in its biological sense. Memory, as recollection and remembering, is a faculty of the mind, with the brain as its physiological basis. No human activity is possible without memory. And mind is energy. The paradox is that memory, which sustains life, must also destroy life, which we know that it does. Memory is history, or rather memory is *of* history—of the history of the individual person, of a family, of a society, indeed of a whole civilisation. It is what makes us what we are. Thus, when two persons meet, even if they are from birth located in the same society, it is actually two different *histories* that encounter one another. The same is true collectively of two different cultures, which may nevertheless contain persons with quite the same history—in a deeper sense. The paradox of memory is seen through the complexity of human possibilities. That very faculty without which a person is nothing, and a society is no society, also builds a prison in which there is, however, the illusion of freedom. Locked up in that prison, the collective memories of a society, of a people, have been throughout history a most fertile ground for hatred and violence. This is true of the memories of a person, too. In that prison, I live only in the past, and hear the menacing sounds of self-isolation. In brief, memory carries within itself an immense charge of energy that is quite as destructive as it is sustaining.

Let us return to the three forms of primordial energy the *Sāṃkhya* philosophy speaks of, namely, *sattva*, *rajas*, and *tamas*. *Sattva* creates a feeling of joy and peace of mind, arising from love, or *prīti*. Discontent, greed, intolerance, sorrow, and remorse are the natural products of *rajas*. And *tamas* brings a lack of judgement, confusion, inattentiveness, and laziness. None of the three exists without the other two. All human relationships are a combination of these three in proportions that are virtually countless; different energies, now in harmony and then colliding with each other, determining the quality as well as the course of the self with the self and of the self with the *other*.

Every self has a past, with its memories that bring joy and happiness and give to human life its worth. Every self has also a past with memories that are *tāmasic*. That is to say, they disturb, distress, exhaust, and suffocate. Memory has an enormous influence on the present, to a degree that the present becomes only an extension of the past. The paradox of memory is now transferred to the present. The paradox of the present is that the present can be lived only by transcending it.

The paradox of memory can neither be resolved, nor can it be dissolved; for it characterises reality in a way that to assert one part of it is to assert at the same time also its opposite, and the two are inseparable. Paradox can only be transcended. Even without knowing that word, most human beings do it all the time anyway. Or else, locked up in his, or her, memories, every self will be a stranger to every other self. Transcending our histories, personal and collective, we reach out to others, as the others reach out to us, in love and friendship—beyond the tyranny of memory. But like the tyranny of the past, there is also the tyranny of the present. The *Mahābhārata* discusses man's relation with history. In the form of my *sanchita karma*, the inheritance of acts, am I my past alone? Am I only what I am in the present? '*Rooted in my history, am I my history alone*?'

ज्ञानाधिष्ठानमज्ञानं त्रीँल्लोकानधितिष्ठति ।
विज्ञानानुगतं ज्ञानमज्ञानेनापकृष्यते ।। शान्ति २१५.२५ ।।
पृथक्त्वात् सम्प्रयोगाश्च नासू युर्वेद शाश्वतम् ।
स तयोरपवर्गज्ञो वीतरागो विमुच्यते ।। शान्ति २१५.२६ ।।

One finds in philosophical treatises sometimes statements that advocate separateness, and at other times statements that advocate identity, of the Self with the ultimate reality. Acknowledging this contradiction, but not in the spirit of argument, one should go beyond them.[109]

CHAPTER FOUR

Dharma—The Foundation of Life and Relationships

- The radical shift in the *Mahābhārata*: the universality of *dharma*
- *Dharma* and the question of relativism
- Another radical shift in the *Mahābhārata*
- *Dharma* as relationship of the self with the self and of the self with the *other*

There is in the history of mankind no other word like *dharma*, a word into which so much has been poured, and yet which is so restricted; which is so clear, yet so vague; so straight, yet so tortuous; so much like a rock, yet so wax-like. This had troubled even Yudhishṭhira, depicted in the *Mahābhārata* as being the very embodiment of *dharma*. At one place he announces almost in despair:

> विद्म चैवं न वा विद्मे शक्यं वा वेदितुं न वा।
> अणीयान् क्षुरधाराया गरीयानपि पर्वतात्।। शान्ति २६०.१२।।
>
> गन्धर्वनगराकार: प्रथमं सम्प्रदृश्यते।
> अन्वीक्ष्यमाण: कविभि: पुनर्गच्छत्यदर्शनम्।। शान्ति २६०.१३।।
>
> *Whether we know or do not know* dharma, *whether it is knowable or not,* dharma *is finer than the finest edge of a sword and more substantial than a mountain. On first sight, it appears clear and solid like a town; on a close logical look, it vanishes from the view.*[1]

Since *dharma* was defined also as *shreya*, 'the good', it gave rise to fresh problems with that definition; for there were many different opinions on what 'the good' is, each claiming '*this* is the good', '*this* is the good. Greatly perplexed, the sage Gālava puts this to the sage Nārada.[2]

> शास्त्रं यदि भवेदेकं श्रेयो व्यक्तं भवेत् तदा।
> शास्त्रैश्च बहुभिर्भूय: श्रेयो गुह्यं प्रवेशितम्।। शान्ति २८७.१०।।
>
> *Were there only one shāstra, and only one means of gaining the Good, the situation would be clear; but there are many shāstra-s, and by describing 'the Good' in different ways, they have hidden its meaning.*[3]

In order to see this, and then come into the clearest light of *dharma* as the *universal foundation of life and relationships*, it is necessary for us first to take a brief tour into the history of the meaning of the word *dharma*. It will be a tedious and tiresome tour but necessary nevertheless.

On the assumption that there is in the universe an impersonal order, *ṛta*, a kind of spiritual law that sustains it, the vedic gods Mitra and Varuṇa its guardians, an analogous order was believed to exist in the affairs of human beings as well. The latter was called *dharma*. It was believed to bind human beings in a way similar to the universe of gods being bound by *ṛta*. In the *Atharva-veda* (18.3.1), *dharma* means 'the old customary order', perhaps the oldest meaning of the word.[4] According to Surendranath Dasgupta, *dharma* and *dharman* are the regular words, the latter in the *Ṛg-veda*, for 'law' and 'custom'.[5] The pandits have not found it easy to say what precisely *dharma* meant in the earliest period of vedic history. In most cases, however, the meaning of *dharman*, according to Pandurang Vaman Kane (1880–1972), is 'religious ordinance' or 'rites' as, for example, in the *Ṛg-veda* I.22.18, V.26.6, VIII.43.24, and IX.64.1. We have in the *Ṛg-veda*, III.17.1, the words *prathama dharma*, which mean 'the very first ordinances'; and in III.3.1 *sanata dharmāṇī*, which mean 'ancient ordinances'.[6] Kane argued that in the places where this meaning would not fit the context, as in IV.53.3, V.63.7, VI.70.1, and VI.89.5, the meaning of the word *dharma* could be taken to be 'fixed principles' or 'rules of conduct'.[7] After giving a brief history of the meanings which *dharma* passed through, Kane concluded that its most prominent meaning came to be: 'the privileges, duties and obligations of a man, his standard of conduct as a member of the Aryan community, as a member of one of the castes, as a person in a particular stage of life'.[8] That is, the *varṇa-āshrama-dharma*. It is in this sense, he argued, that the word *dharma* is used in the *Taittirīya-Upanishad* (I.11), in the *Bhagvad-Gītā* (III.35), in the *Manu-smriti* (I.2), in the *Yājñavalkya-smriti* (I.1), in the *Tantra-vārttika* (p.237), and, of course, in the whole of the *dharmashāstra* literature.[9] The place given to an individual as of a caste, the *varṇa-dharma*, and the schemata of conduct appropriate to one of the four stages of life, the *āshrama-dharma*, secured that social order in which is to be lived the life of the dharmic man.

Mention should be made of certain other meanings given by tradition to *dharma*, each no less intricate, but all reducible in the end to the *varṇa-āshrama* meaning of it. That is to say, synonymous with a certain social structure and its codes. An account of these different meanings can be found in Dasgupta,[10] in Kane,[11] and in the fortieth special number of *Kalyāṇa*, devoted exclusively to discussing *dharma*.[12] When used in an abstract sense, as for example in the *Aitareya-Brāhmaṇa* (VII.17), the word *dharma* simply means 'the whole body of religious duties'. In some of the philosophical texts, *dharma* is used as a category of explanation. The Mimamsa, with its aim of establishing the self-validity of the Veda, regarded *dharma* as a desirable end reached by obeying *vidhi*, the vedic commands. Needing no justification beyond their own authority, the latter were assumed to be self-evident in the sense that, if obeyed, they were certain to give pleasurable experience. The force of whatever was vedicly prohibited, *adharma*, was equally self-evident; for it was bound to lead to unpleasant experience. *Dharma* and *adharma* were thus the direct results of following, or not following, the self-evident commands of the Veda. *Dharma* could be called 'virtue'; but in being motivated by something external, it had little to do with the 'ethical'; neither did *adharma* have the meaning of 'unethical'.[13] There were further refinements to the mimamsic definition of *dharma*, into which we need not go. A distinction was made between 'the good' obtained by following the commands of the Veda, the *acts*, and 'the good' obtained by rational means, *knowledge*. The latter is not *dharma*; only the automatic observance of the vedic ritual is. Whatever action is based on the Veda, according to the *Bhāgvata-purāṇa*, is *dharma*; whatever is not, is *adharma*.[14] According to Medhātithi (ninth century A.D.), any custom or practice that is not based on the teachings of the Veda is to be discarded as *not-dharma*.[15]

The *Mahābhārata* will completely discard this ritualistic, narrow, and sectarian perception of *dharma*. But let us continue our tour.

In the twin philosophical schools of Nyāya-Vaisheshika, *dharma* is that which leads one to *abhyudaya*, happiness, and to *niḥshreyasa*, beatitude. One is not told, though, what 'happiness' and 'beatitude' mean. In the Nyāya school of philosophy, *dharma*, an attribute of 'substance', is used as a category to explain happiness; *adharma* naturally makes for its opposite. 'What leads one to happiness, and what to unhappiness?' is a question on which Nyāya takes the same stand as the Yoga ethics does. Faith, non-injury, kindness, truthfulness, non-stealing, control of the senses, adherence to scriptural duties and to the duties assigned to each caste, make for *dharma*: their opposite make for *adharma*. All these meanings, often technical and narrow, eventually wound their way up to the *varṇa-āshrama* meaning of *dharma*. For, it was believed, it is only through a life lived in that social order that man could fulfil his destiny.

Of equal importance were some of those other meanings the *smriti*-s and the *dharmashāstra*-s gave to *dharma*, having used that word to mean generally the social order founded upon *varṇa* and archetypal conduct. According to Manu, the most influential among the ancient Indian lawgivers,[16] and—if the Manu of mythology is distinguished from the

Manu to whom is attributed the *Manu-smriti*—also one among the earliest,[17] *dharma* is that[18] which is practised by the learned, or by the men free from hatred and partiality, or by those who follow the assent of their heart, *ātmanas-tushṭih*.[19] This was only one of the several, and often conflicting, definitions that Manu himself gave to *dharma*. Sensing the danger perhaps of so open a dictum as *dharma* being that to which one's heart gives assent, some of the latter commentators, Medhātithi the most prominent among them, rejected that particular meaning of *dharma*. But there were others, like Govindarāja, Nārāyaṇa, and Rāmānanda, who supported the liberal interpretation of Manu's dictum that *dharma* is also what satisfies one's heart. Many interpretations of Manu's dictum were naturally possible—from the spiritual to the libertine. However, Dasgupta maintained, even those commentators eventually interpreted 'the slight concession that Manu had seemed to make to right character and self-contentment or conscience as the constituent element of *dharma*, more or less on Medhātithi's line, as meaning nothing more than loyalty to scriptural injunctions'.[20] Manu had left one in no doubt that he regarded the Veda and the *dharma-shāstra* as the two chief sources of *dharma*.[21] Although he mentioned in the same breath *sadāchāra*, 'good conduct', and self-satisfaction as the other two sources, they were shown themselves to have been derived from adherence to vedic rituals.[22]

Then there was the *pravritti-dharma*, meaning 'the works that are of this world', and the *nivritti-dharma*, meaning 'the works that are not of this world'.[23] These were more or less on the same lines as the *abhyudaya* and *niḥshreyasa* of the Vaisheshika school of philosophy. Also you hear the sound of *kula-dharma*, or 'the specific character of a family'; of *rāshṭra-dharma*, that is 'the specific character of a nation'; as also the sound of *yuga-dharma*, 'the specific character of an age, a particular time in history'. The authors of the *Amarakosha*, the famous dictionary, mentioned several meanings of *dharma*. *Puṇya*, 'the merit that comes of virtuous deeds'; vedic-*vidhi*, 'the vedic ritual sacrifices or commands'; *nyāya*, or 'law, justice';[24] *svabhāva*, or 'one's specific nature'; *āchāra*, 'social conduct'; and so forth—but all of them subsumed again in the *varṇa-āshrama* meaning. That is, *dharma* as a particular social structure, with its institutions. It was certainly not universal, for elsewhere in the human world there were different social structures founded upon different beliefs about human life.

That, that is how *dharma* was being perceived in the times the *Mahābhārata* was being composed, is recounted with its full force in the

Mahābhārata itself.[25] That is a part of its clear method: state the prevalent presuppositions, beliefs, conflicting opinions, and then subject them to a searching inquiry. That applies to the use of the word *sva-dharma* as well. This word has become a part of what may be called Hindu consciousness; and there have been in modern times a great many discussions about it. We may leave it out of our tour. It will suffice to see quickly that, like the word *dharma*, the word *sva-dharma*, was being clearly used in the times of the *Mahābhārata* as meaning 'one's caste duties assigned by birth'. The *Mahābhārata* honestly recounts that, too.[26] And with that, two more words were added to the already large and confusing vocabulary of *dharma*: *viśesa-dharma*, meaning 'the specific duties of a particular social group or the caste'; and *sādhāraṇa-dharma*, meaning 'the ethical obligations common to all'. In the event of a conflict between the two, which one was to have the greater weight? This became a stock controversy in any discussion on *dharma*, but had long been settled.[27] The evidence on this point is that the ethical was to be subordinate to the functional. The *varṇa-āshrama-dharma* as a social structure gave the fullest expression to this idea.

The present tour into what might appear to be tiresome variations of the use of a word is intended for us to see the following clearly before we breathe in the liberating air of the *Mahābhārata*'s teaching on *dharma* as the universal foundation of all relationships: of the self with the self, and of the self with the *other*. The use of the same word, for the most part clearly, but also to connote things dissimilar,[28] in contexts very different from one another,[29] gave rise in India to a tradition that was in sharp contrast to philosophic care in the use of words. Now meanings were blurred; in that twilight one thing was taken for another; the need for interpretation arose, but one interpretation was as good as the other, and no interpretation being decisive, the pandits and the commentators flourished, and the common man grew stupefied. In the practice of it, an idea seemed to its adherents clear; in the theory of it, it vanished into mystery, or into unending arguments. One result was that there was no definite meaning to anything. If a thing meant everything, and then at will, then nothing meant any one thing. Whatever else is involved in defining the meaning of a word, giving it a boundary is the least that is. It is the refusal in theory to give *dharma* boundary, when it had acquired in social practice a clear boundary all the time, that is common to the modern apologists of *dharma*.[30]

After using the word *dharma* in all sorts of manner, maintaining that no one meaning could be given to it, when it came to defending *dharma* upon which by common consent is founded the whole of Indian culture, the defence has always been of the social order, mainly *varṇa-āshrama-dharma*.[31]

A nineteenth-century Calcutta weekly even maintained that it was only 'by the power of *dharma*' that the English had conquered India, and not by military power, or by the power of wealth, neither of which they had with them when they came to India.

> So there remains only the power of dharma and it is by that power that Englishmen have conquered India. Now dharma is a very pervading thing and may be said to extend over every part of one's life. It includes such virtues as promptness, courage, endurance, secrecy in counsel, and the power of combining. It is these virtues which enable a people to make conquests, and it is precisely these virtues which Englishmen possess in a greater degree than the people of this country.[32]

Englishmen having conquered India 'by the power of *dharma*', let us conclude our tour into the brief history of the diverse uses of the word '*dharma*' by seeing the completely incorrect understanding created when the word '*dharma*' was translated into the English language as '*religion*'. Of all the erroneous understandings of *dharma*, translating it as 'religion' has been the greatest.

It will be an erroneous understanding, too, *if the exercise undertaken here is seen as an exercise in the semantics of a word. Dharma* is of course a word. But, beyond itself, it also points to the universal foundations of human living and their complexities. It has been a paradox that it is mostly through incorrect understandings that the truth of a thing is reached. Therefore, as for example in the *Upanishad*-s, before we could say what a thing *is*, it is often necessary first to say what *it is not*. But the knowledge of what 'it is not' implies already a knowledge of what 'it is'. And about that there can be different perceptions, and the consequent need to reconcile them somehow, often at the expense of truth.

Dharma is not 'religion'.[33] There has been no misunderstanding greater than the supposition that Indian culture was fundamentally 'religious' in the sense in which 'religion' and 'religious' have been used in the West for centuries. 'Religion' presupposes belief in God as the creator of the universe; in a central revelation of God; in a messenger of that revelation; and in a central book containing the revelation, and the life and the sayings of that messenger of God. 'Religion' implies a central code of commandments, a corpus of ecclesiastical laws to regulate thought and relationships in the light of these, and a hierarchy of priesthood to supervise that regulation and control. Though in their specific contents they vastly differ from each other, these are the common elements of what are described as the historical religions of the world. *Dharma* has none of these elements as any essential part of its meaning. It does not require as a presupposition even 'belief in the existence of God', which all religions do. Thus, *dharma* is not yet another 'religious faith' among many mutually conflicting 'religious faiths'. But neither is *dharma* antagonistic to any religious faith. Rather, *dharma* is the foundation of 'religion' itself, if we understand 'religion' also in its original Latin meaning, *relegio*, that is, 'to bind together'. And the questions will then be: bind *whom* together? Bind together *in what*? Bind together *with what*? These are the questions that the *Mahābhārata* explores as the perennial questions of all human relationships.

There have been two wrong understandings of what *dharma* is: one traditional, the other modern. The traditional wrong understanding of *dharma* consisted mostly in perceiving it as synonymous with *varṇa*, a given social structure, and *āshrama*, a certain scheme of the stages of life. The *Mahābhārata* disentangles *dharma* from them, pointing out at the same time that *varṇa* and *āshrama* have themselves been wrongly understood as to their foundations, and liberates them as well from the oppressive results of that wrong understanding.[34] *Dharma* is the natural foundation of all social arrangements everywhere. It cannot be reduced to being synonymous with the social structures developed in India, with caste as its basic feature, simply because the word *dharma* is added to *varṇa*.

The modern wrong understanding of *dharma* consists in its translation as 'religion'. Religion in its institutional form is divisive; *dharma* unites. A religion excludes all that it is not; *dharma* includes every form of life. Religion must be separated from the state and governance, as it has been in the modern West, for a sane world. Every shade of political thought and practice, and every act of governance, must necessarily have their foundations in *dharma* for us to have a sane world.[35] The problem has been that of conveying a fundamental insight of one culture to another, during which loss of meaning must necessarily occur.

Marco Pallis says:

> The word dharma which the Indian traditions have rendered familiar has no really adequate counterpart in the terminology of European

> languages; if the range of ideas this word stands for must needs be found, at least implicitly, in the substance of every religion, absence of a readily intelligible term to cover that range in all manner of contexts remains a sad drawback as far as communication is concerned. Today, one is feeling this lack more than ever, because the truths to which dharma corresponds in the field of metaphysical ideas and spiritual and even social applicability are among the ones which, by the questions they raise, are troubling people's mind most acutely at this moment.[36]

Let us now, at the end of this tour, place ourselves in the hands of the *Mahābhārata* as our guide on another journey that unites us with our self and with the self of the *other*, a journey that is at once healing and exciting.

The radical shift in the *Mahābhārata*: the universality of *dharma*

While *dharma* and its negation *adharma* are throughout the main concerns of the *Mahābhārata*, as they are the main concerns of human living in all its expressions everywhere, the following clearly give the substance of what the *Mahābhārata* says *dharma* is. They mark, equally clearly, a radical shift in the meaning of *dharma* that had become prevalent, and is prevalent even now.

> प्रभवार्थाय भूतानां धर्मप्रवचनं कृतम् ।
> यः स्यात् प्रभवसंयुक्तः स धर्म इति निश्चयः ।। शान्ति १०९.१० ।।
> *All the sayings of* dharma *are with a view to nurturing, cherishing, providing more amply, enriching, increasing, enhancing, all living beings: in one word, securing their* prabhava. *Therefore, whatever has the characteristic of bringing that about is* dharma. *This is certain.*[37]

> धारणाद् धर्ममित्याहुधर्मेण विधृताः प्रजाः ।
> यः स्याद् धारणसंयुक्तः स धर्म इति निश्चयः ।। शान्ति १०९.११ ।।
> *All the sayings of* dharma *are with a view to supporting, sustaining, bringing together, and in their togetherness upholding, all living beings, securing, in one word, their* dharana. *Therefore, whatever has the characteristic of doing that, is* dharma. *This is certain.*[38]

अहिंसार्थाय भूतानां धर्मप्रवचनं कृतम् ।
यः स्यादहिंसासम्पृक्तः स धर्म इति निश्चयः ।। शान्ति १०९.१२ ।।

All the sayings of dharma *are with a view to securing for all living beings freedom from violence, ahimsā. Therefore, whatever has the characteristic of not doing violence is* dharma. *This is certain.*[39]

Conversely, whatever has the characteristic of depriving, starving, diminishing, separating, uprooting, hurting, doing violence, debasing, and degrading is *the negation of dharma*. *Whatever* brings that about is, in one word, *adharma*.

Furthermore:

आरम्भो न्याययुक्तो यः स हि धर्म इति स्मृतः ।
अनाचारस्त्वधर्मेति एतच्छिष्टानुशासनम् ।। वन २०७.७७ ।।

Whatever has its beginning in justice, that alone is called dharma; *whatever is unjust and oppressive is* adharma. *This is the rule settled by those who can be respected.*[40]

And *nyāya*, 'justice', is *dharma*. But this is *not* a circular definition of the either. It is not a circular definition, which is so very irritating, and says nothing: 'What is *dharma*? Justice. And what is 'justice'? *Dharma*.' Justice is that which has the characteristics of: nurturing, cherishing, providing amply, enriching, increasing, enhancing all living beings; supporting, sustaining, bringing together, and in their togetherness, upholding all living beings; and securing for all living beings freedom from violence, freedom from fear.

Whatever is *anāchāra*, unjust and oppressive, is *adharma*, having the characteristic of depriving, starving, diminishing, separating, uprooting, hurting, doing violence, debasing, and degrading, that is, *the negation of dharma*.

In the voice of the sage Brihaspati, the *Mahābhārata* says:

अन्ये साम प्रशंसन्ति व्यायाममपरे जनाः ।
नैकं न चापरं केचिदुभयं च तथापरे ।। शान्ति २१.७ ।।

Some people praise conciliation and friendliness. Some others praise strenuous effort. Some praise neither the one nor the other exclusively. And there are others who praise both.[41]

यज्ञमेव प्रशंसन्ति संन्यासमपरे जनाः।
दानमेके प्रशंसन्ति केचिच्चैव प्रतिग्रहम्।। शान्ति २१.८।।

Some people praise sacrificial rites; and some praise total withdrawal from the world. There are those who praise only 'giving'; and there are those who praise only 'receiving'.[42]

केचित् सर्वं परित्यज्य तूष्णींध्यायन्ते आसते।
राज्यमेके प्रशंसन्ति प्रजानां परिपालनम्।। शान्ति २१.९।।
हत्वाछित्त्वा च भित्त्वा च केचिदेकान्तशीलिनः

Some people, leaving everything, are given to silence and meditation. Some others praise obtaining a kingdom after much fight and destruction, though with the aim of protecting the people. And there are those who do self-reflection in solitude.[43]

एतत् सर्वं समालोक्य बुधानामेष निश्चयः।। शान्ति २१.१०।।
अद्रोहेणैव भूतानां यो धर्मः स सतां मतः।

However, after observing this variety and reflecting deeply, the learned and the wise have concluded that not to be aggressive towards other beings is dharma *in the eyes of the good and the saintly.*[44]

It follows that:

धर्मं यो बाधते धर्मो न स धर्मः कुधर्म तत्।
अविरोधात् तु यो धर्मः स धर्मः सत्यविक्रम।। वन १३१.११।।

If one dharma *is destructive of another* dharma, *then it is wickedness in the garb of* dharma, *and not* dharma. *Only that is* dharma *truly that is established without denigrating and opposing another* dharma.[45]

विरोधिषु महीपाल निश्चित्य गुरुलाघवम्।
न बाधा विद्यते यत्र तं धर्मं समुपाचरेत्।। वन १३१.१२।।

गुरुलाघवमादाय धर्माधर्मविनिश्चये।
यतो भूयांस्ततो राजन् कुरुष्व धर्मनिश्चयम्।। वन १३१.१३।।

In case there is conflict between one dharma *and another, one should reflect on their relative weight, and then act accordingly; what does not denigrate and obstruct the others is* dharma.[46]

Here, in a coherent next step, the *Mahābhārata* teaches that human relationships, personal and collective, are to be independent of beliefs. Beliefs there are many, and the choices in believing are equally diverse. But the foundations of relationships, of one's self with one's self, and of one's self with the *other*, are universal. Thus, *dharma* is not a *doctrine* among other doctrines, nor yet another 'system of belief' among the many existing systems of belief, one contending with another. It is, to put it differently, the very flow of life in which all are united, and which the *Mahābhārata* set out to understand.

> मानसं सर्वभूतानां धर्ममाहुर्मनीषिण: ।
> तस्मात् सर्वेषु भूतेषु मनसा शिवमाचरेत् ।। शान्ति १९३.३१ ।।
> *Those who have thought deeply are of the view that* dharma *is what is done for all beings with one's heart and mind. Therefore, let one do, with one's heart and mind, what is good for all beings.*[47]

To those who may legitimately want to know as to how 'what is good for all beings' is to be decided, the *Mahābhārata* suggests, to begin with:

> यदन्यैर्विहितं नेच्छदात्मन: कर्म पूरुष: ।
> त तत् परेषु कुर्वीत जानन्नप्रियमात्मन: ।। शान्ति २५९.२० ।।
> *What he does not find agreeable when done by the others unto him, that he should not do unto others. He must know that what is unhappy for him cannot be happy for others.*[48]

> न तत् परस्य संदध्यात् प्रतिकूलं यदात्मन: ।
> एष संक्षेपतो धर्म: कामादन्य: प्रवर्तते ।। अनुशासन ११३.८ ।।
> *Whatever is not agreeable to him, that he should not do unto others. This, in brief, is* dharma; *all else is only selfishness.*[49]

On the journey on which the *Mahābhārata* takes us, we are invited to stay for a considerable time in each of the areas that constitute human life in order to understand its workings in relation to one's self and to the *other*. It takes us through *artha*, material prosperity and *having*,[50] through *kāma*, the fulfilment of desires and human sexuality,[51] through *danda*, law and governance,[52] and through *varna*, social arrangements.[53] In each of these areas, which cover so intimate a part of human life everywhere, *dharma* is shown to be the natural sovereign, to whom each one of them must be subject if human existence is to come into its full worth. What does that really mean?

Acknowledging the importance of material prosperity, individual and collective, the *Mahābhārata* is at the same time saying, in the clearest of voices, that wealth should be earned through *dharma* and never through *adharma*. It is saying that the pursuit of material prosperity of the one, or of a few, should never have the effect of depriving, starving, diminishing, separating, uprooting, hurting, doing violence, debasing, and degrading the *other*. When it does, it becomes self-destructive in the first place. True wealth, individual and social, is that wealth which creates: nurturing, cherishing, providing amply, enriching, increasing, enhancing all living beings; which supports, sustains, brings together, and in bringing together, upholds all living beings; and secures for all living beings freedom from violence, freedom from fear. These are the three foundations of *artha*, true material prosperity; and they are the main attributes of *dharma*.

Acknowledging, in the clearest of voices, the force of sexual impulse, the *Mahābhārata* is saying, in a voice even stronger, that *kāma* be subject to *dharma*. In saying that, it is saying that the sexual impulse is not to remain only an appetite of the body and of the mind alike, but that its physicality can find rest only in the togetherness of relationships. That *kāma* be subject to *dharma* clearly means that sexuality should never have the effect of depriving, starving, diminishing, separating, uprooting, hurting, doing violence, debasing and degrading, the *other*. When it does, it becomes self-destructive in the first place. True sexual pleasure is that which, in fulfilling itself: *one*, nurtures, cherishes, enriches, increases, and enhances the *other*; *two*, supports, sustains, brings together, and in bringing together upholds, the *other*; and *three*, secures for the *other* freedom from violence, freedom from fear. These are the three foundations of a fulfilling sexual pleasure, *kāma*; and they are the three attributes of *dharma*.

The *Mahābhārata* is saying, in the clearest and the strongest of voices, that all authority in all its acts be subject to *dharma*, and that *dharma* is the sovereign and not the king or the state. In saying that, it is saying that *daṇḍa*, whatever systems of law and governance there be, they shall never have the effect of depriving, starving, diminishing, separating, uprooting, hurting, doing violence, debasing, and degrading the *other*. When they do, they become self-destructive in the first place. The natural foundations of law and governance everywhere *are* in *dharma*. In nurturing, cherishing, providing amply, enriching, increasing, enhancing all living beings; In supporting, sustaining, bringing together, and in bringing together, upholding all living beings; and in securing for all living beings freedom from violence, securing freedom from fear. These are the foundations of *daṇḍa*, law and governance, and they are the attributes of *dharma*.

It is in *this* sense, clearly and unambiguously, that the *Mahābhārata* talks of *dharma* and *adharma* in all its meditations concerning human life, excepting when, consistent with its method, it is recounting the other perceptions of them as well, from which it is a clear break.

Dharma and the question of relativism

The most striking feature of the *Mahābhārata* is its honest observation of the human condition. It is a self-evident fact that what is 'right' in one context becomes 'wrong' in another context. What is beautiful and pleasing at one time becomes at another time ugly and offensive. There are familiar occasions of conflict between two sets of duties, both inviolable. There are situations of conflict between right and right. The value of an act, the *Mahābhārata* shows, depends not only upon one's motives wholly, but also upon *desha* and *kāla*, 'the given place' and 'the given time'.

एतौ धर्मार्थशास्त्रेषु मोक्षशास्त्रेषु चर्षिभि: ।
प्रधानाविति निर्दिष्टौ कामे चाभिमतौ नृणाम् ।। शान्ति १३७.२३ ।।
The sages have in the treaties relating to dharma, *wealth and material prosperity, and ultimate human freedom, too, considered 'time' and 'place' to be the prime factors in human achievements.*[54]

परीक्ष्यकारी युक्तश्च स यम्यगुपपादयेत् ।
देशकालवभिप्रेतौ ताभ्यां फलमवाप्नुयात् ।। शान्ति १३७.२४ ।।
The one who, after examining their true import, uses 'place' and 'time' in a way that is harmonious gains the fruits of his aspirations.[55]

पृथिवी देश इत्युक्त: काल स च न दृश्यते ।
अभिप्रेतार्थसिद्ध्यर्थे ध्यायते यच्च तत्तथा ।। शान्ति १३७.२२ ।।
'Place' can be seen, but not 'time'.[56]

It is within these two coordinates, one seen and the other unseen, that the drama of human life is endlessly enacted. In the light of the relativity of situations, the *Mahābhārata* subjects every human attribute, *satya* and *dharma*, 'truth' and 'order', most of all, to an intense examination.

In describing Yudhishṭhira's doubts regarding *dharma* and *adharma*,[57] the *Mahābhārata* is honestly raising a question as regards their relativity, given the evident complexities of human situations through which they become manifest. It would likewise raise an honest question regarding the relativity of 'truth' and 'untruth'.[58]

A typical statement of relativism is contained in that verse from the *Mahābhārata*, that says:

त्यजेत् कुलार्थे पुरुषं ग्रामस्यार्थे कुलं त्यजेत्।
ग्रामं जनपदस्यार्थे आत्मार्थे पृथिवीं त्यजेत्।। उद्योग ३७.१७ ।।

Sacrifice the individual for the sake of the family; the family, for the sake of the village; the village, for the sake of the region; and sacrifice the world for the sake of the soul.[59]

That is to say, the value of a thing is relative. The value of acts is relative to *desha* and *kāla*, 'place' and 'time'.[60] However, since no two authorities agreed on how to judge their relative importance, there are numerous occasions when, anxious to do the right thing but not mindlessly, people find themselves in a dilemma. They burden *their* lives as often as they lived the lives of the characters in the *Mahābhārata*. Can there ever be any principle, or scruple, or guide, offered as the way out of them? Given the relativistic nature of life, if there could still be a general principle on the basis of which to decide what, in a dilemma, would constitute one's *dharma*, the problem could of course be resolved—at least in principle. But the problem of the relativity of standards does not vanish at any point of human history.[61]

The three main authorities for *dharma* were said to be: the Veda, or *shruti*; 'the remembered tradition', or *smṛti*; and the custom, or the example of cultured people, or *sadāchāra*. A fourth source was also recognised. It was *artha*, wealth and commerce, according to some; *rāja-shāsana*, royal decree, according to others; and self-satisfaction according to some others. But the question of 'source' or 'authority' apart, *dharma* itself came to be seen as synonymous with the social structure that comprised a system of interdependent functional duties, *varṇa-dharma*, and a system of personal duties corresponding to the four stages in a man's life, *āshrama-dharma*. To secure the orderly progress of society and of the individual person had been the aim of that social order. To say that 'everything is upheld in *dharma*' was interpreted, wrongly, as asserting that order to be the essential ground of human living. In its general form, the theory underlying that social order made this at least clear, although it was erroneous to confuse *dharma* with any particular kind of social arrangement even at its best. *Dharma* was the foundation of the *varṇa* order, not the other way round. But no sooner did one go into the practical contents even of the *varṇa-āshrama-dharma* than several problems concerning it came to the surface, arising mostly as a result of confusing *dharma* with the latter.

But the apparent coherence of *dharma* was not free from doubt either. In the words of Yudhishṭhira:

> *Whether we know or we do not know* dharma*, whether it is knowable or not,* dharma *is finer than the finest edge of a sword and more substantial than a mountain. On first sight, it appears clear and solid like a town; on a close logical look, it vanishes from the view.*[62]

He then unfolds the problem of relativism as follows:

> पुनरस्य प्रमाणं हि निर्दिष्टं शास्त्रकोविदैः ।
> वेदवादाश्चानुयुगं ह्रसन्तीतीह नः श्रुतम् ।। शान्ति २६०.७ ।।
>
> अन्ये कृतयुगे धर्मास्त्रेतायां द्वापरे परे ।
> अन्ये कलियुगे धर्मा यथाशक्ति कृता इव ।। शान्ति २६०.८ ।।
>
> *The learned declare the Veda to be the basis of* dharma. *But the Veda change according to each cycle of Time: the* dharma *of* satya-yuga *is different; it is different in* treta; *in* dvāpara *it is different again; and in* kali-yuga *it is still different—different* dharma *according to different capacities.*[63]
>
> न धर्मः परिपाठेन शक्यो भारत वेदितुम् ।। शान्ति २६०.३ ।।
> *Neither can one ascertain* dharma *by a mere reading of the vedic texts.*[64]
>
> अन्यो धर्मः समस्थस्य विषमस्थस्य चापरः ।
> आपदस्तु कथं शक्याः परिपाठेन वेदितुम् ।। शान्ति २६०.४ ।।
> *There is one kind of* dharma *for a person in an equable situation, and of another kind for one in distress; how can a reading of the Veda alone decide what the* dharma *in a distress situation shall be?*[65]

आम्नायवचनं सत्यमित्ययं लोकसंग्रहः ।
आम्नायेभ्यः पुनर्वेदाः प्रसृताः सर्वतोमुखाः ।। शान्ति २६०.९ ।।

ते चेत् सर्वप्रमाणं वै प्रमाणं ह्यत्र विद्यते ।
प्रमाणेऽप्यप्रमाणेन विरुद्धे शास्त्रता कुतः ।। शान्ति २६०.१० ।।

As regards the smṛti, *they were derived from the Veda, and could be authoritative only if the Veda were so; but when the Veda were not free from ambiguity, nor authoritative for every situation, how could the* smṛti *be so? Often conflicting with each other, where was the force in either?*[66]

सदाचारो मतो धर्मः सन्तस्त्वाचारलक्षणाः ।
साध्यासाध्यं कथं शक्यं सदाचारो ह्यलक्षणः ।। शान्ति २६०.५ ।।

As for the cultured conduct being the standard of dharma, *it suffered from the fallacy of the circularity of definition; the conduct of good men is called* dharma, *and good men are those whose conduct reflects* dharma. *With this fallacy in its definition, 'cultured conduct' could not be a proof of* dharma.[67]

दृश्यते हि धर्मरूपेणाधर्मं प्राकृतचरन् ।
धर्मं चाधर्मरूपेण कश्चिदप्राकृतचरन् ।। शान्ति २६०.६ ।।

What is more, one could see the crude and the unsophisticated doing what looked like dharma, *but in fact was* adharma; *the reverse being often the case with the actions of the sophisticated and the cultured.*[68]

तेनैवान्यः प्रभवति सोऽपरं बाधते पुनः ।
दृश्यते चैव स पुनस्तुल्यरूपो यदृच्छया ।। शान्ति २६०.१८ ।।

येनैवान्यः प्रभवति सोऽपरानपि बाधते ।
आचाराणामनैकाग्रयं सर्वेषामुपलक्षयेत् ।। शान्ति २६०.१९ ।।

Furthermore, there was no one code of conduct beneficial to all in equal measure, or applicable to all in all circumstances. To the contrary, the very thing that helped some rise higher acted as an obstruction in the case of others.[69]

महाजना ह्युपावृत्ता राजधर्मं समाश्रिताः ।
न हि सर्वहितः कश्चिदाचारः सम्प्रवर्तते ।। शान्ति २६०.१७ ।।

None could see anywhere conduct that would be uniformly good for all.[70]

यत्राधर्मो धर्मरूपाणि धत्ते
धर्मः कृत्स्नो दृश्यतेऽधर्मरूपः ।
बिभ्रद् धर्मो धर्मरूपं तथा च
विद्वांसस्तं सम्प्रपश्यन्ति बुद्ध्या ।।उद्योग २८.२ ।।

Sometimes adharma *looked like* dharma, *at other times the established* dharma *turned seemingly into* adharma, *and there was no distinguishing the two.*[71]

स एव धर्मः सोऽधर्मस्तं तं प्रति नरं भवेत् ।
पात्रकर्मविशेषेण देशकालाववेक्ष्य च ।। शान्ति ३०९.१६ ।।

The same act is dharma *or* adharma *for different people, depending on 'time', 'place', and 'the person concerned'.*[72]

In the voice of Yudhishṭhira, the *Mahābhārata* expressed the problem by asking:

महानयं धर्मपथो बहुशाखश्च भारत ।
किंस्विदेवेह धर्माणामनुष्ठेय तमं मतम् ।। शान्ति १०८.१ ।।

The path of dharma *is a grand path from which several paths branch off; which of them must one follow?*[73]

सत्यं चैवानृतं चोभे लोकानावृत्य तिष्ठतः ।
तवोः किमाचरेद् राजन् पुरुषो धर्मनिश्चितः ।। शान्ति १०९.२ ।।
किंस्वित् सत्यं किमनृतं किंस्विद् धर्म्यं सनातनम् ।
कस्मिन् काले वदेत् सत्यं कस्मिन् कालेऽनृतं वदेत् ।। शान्ति १०९.३ ।।

All things of this world are shot through with truth and untruth; how does one distinguish one from the other? What is truth? What is untruth? At what time shall one speak the truth, and at what time may one speak the untruth?[74]

These agonising questions come up again and again in human living. They are concerned as much with the practice as they are concerned with the philosophy of *dharma*. For example, *santosha*, contentment, as an indisputable check on greed and its restlessness, to which the *Mahābhārata* attaches great importance, is in conflict with manly effort, discontentment with the existing conditions as its moving force, to which also the *Mahābhārata* attaches great importance throughout. The question is not merely one of finding a way out; but whatever criterion one might adopt with a view to resolving the dilemma, it would still be relativistic, and must therefore form part of the dilemma. The *Mahābhārata* is perhaps the only inquiry into the human condition that confronts us with this truth.

Another radical shift in the Mahābhārata

Without dispersing the problem of relativity inherent in life, the *Mahābhārata* then demonstrates, from very many different sides, how that problem must not paralyse us either. It is only when it is *dispersed*, and it is made out that relativism is the enemy of objective truth, that we are paralysed; because by refusing to acknowledge what goes against our arbitrary definitions, we remain within a self-defeating logic of *either — or* and its illusory comfort of clarity. That never happens in the philosophy of the *Mahābhārata*. Therefore, it is so challenging, for it does not offer us the lazy comfort of clarity at the expense of truth.

But it was seen clearly, too, that the relativity of ethical standards could quite easily degenerate into unprincipled conduct. The paradoxical problem was one of great danger inherent in a position that was in all respects realistic and sound. Could opportunism be avoided in the face of the evident relativity of ethical norms? Moreover, because truth and *dharma* are conditional to *desha* and *kāla*, 'time' and 'place', there has always been the problem as to how one might choose between two equally inviolable duties that were, however, incompatible. More than even a cynical misuse of relativism in ethics, the problem was one of genuine doubt. That was sought to be resolved in a perfectly honest fashion. In order to prevent what was palpably wrong and untruthful from being justified as expedient, the *Mahābhārata* places the conditionality of ethical norms and social functions in a larger context where *dharma* is said to be the order that sustains the people and secures the good of all living beings. It is with that innate order that every individual is to harmonise his, or her, life. But even this left the question open: 'Who decides what is good for the people?' Or rather, with reference to *what*, can 'the good of the people' be determined? On this question, avoiding dogmatism, and without pretending that the problem of relativism can ever be resolved at the level of logic, the *Mahābhārata* suggests two different positions:

One. In answer to the question: 'What is the way?', Yudhishthira says:

तर्कोऽप्रतिष्ठ: श्रुतयो विभिन्ना
नैको ऋषिर्यस्य मतं प्रमाणम्।
धर्मस्य तत्त्वं निहितं गुहायां
महाजनो येन गत: स पन्था:।। वन ३१३.११७।।

Reasoning is not stable; various are the sruti-s; *there is no one sage whose opinion can be taken as proof; the substance of* dharma *is as deep as a cave. Where the masses, the people, have trodden, that is the way.*[75]

This solution was really no solution. For not only had the masses, the people, in all times taken divergent paths, but even assuming that they had taken one path, that fact alone could be no proof of its being also the Good, unless 'the Good' was defined explicitly in that way, which it was not.

The following is the other position, stated in the sage voice of Bhīshma:

तस्मात् कौन्तेय विदुषा धर्माधर्मविनिश्चये।
बुद्धिमास्थाय लोकेऽस्मिन् वर्तितव्यं कृतात्मना।। शान्ति १४१.१०२।।

One should depend upon one's intelligence to decide between dharma *and* adharma, *and act accordingly.*[76]

ज्ञानमप्यपदिश्यं हि यथा नास्ति तथैव तत्।
तं तथा छिन्नमूलेन सन्नोदयितुमर्हसि।। शान्ति १४२.२३।।

Any knowledge that is covered with doubt can hardly be called knowledge; it is necessary to remove one's doubts with its very roots.[77]

अद्वैधज्ञ: पथि द्वैधे संशयं प्राप्तुमर्हति।
बुद्धिद्वैधं वेदितव्यं पुरस्तादेव भारत।। शान्ति १४२.८।।

The same act, depending upon circumstances, is now dharma *and then* adharma. *Not understanding their essential relativity, one is naturally assailed with doubt; and the only way to remove the doubt is to understand through intelligence their relative nature.*[78]

बुद्धिसंजननो धर्म आचारश्च सतां सदा।
ज्ञेयो भवति कौरव्य सदा तद् विद्धि मे वच:।। शान्ति १४२.५।।

Dharma *and cultured conduct arise from intelligence; and it is from intelligence that they are known.*[79]

बह्व्य: प्रतिविधातव्या: प्रज्ञा ततस्तत: ।
नैकशाखेन धर्मेण यत्रैषा सम्प्रवर्तते ।। शान्ति १४२.४ ।।
It is by recourse to intelligence, learning different things from different people, and not depending only upon one branch of dharma*, that one should illumine one's path.*[80]

शास्त्रं यदि भवेदेकं श्रेयो व्यक्तं भवेत् तदा।
शास्त्रैश्च बहुभिर्भूय: श्रेयो गुह्यं प्रवेशितम् ।। शान्ति २८७.१० ।।
Were there only one shāstra*, and only one means of gaining the good, the situation would be clear; but there are many* shāstra-s*, and by describing 'the Good' in many different ways, they have taken it into a labyrinth.*[81]

यत् तु निश्श्रेयसं सम्यक् तच्चैवासंशयात्मकम् ।। शान्ति २८७.१५ ।।
But the Good must also be free from doubt, which indeed it is.[82]

This was perhaps the only rational stand that could be taken on the dilemmas arising from the relativity of ethical standards.

There is no question that any knowledge that is covered with doubt could be called knowledge, and that the Good must be free from doubt. But that one should depend on one's intelligence to decide between *dharma* and *adharma*, or between truth and untruth, still did not free them from ambiguity. And, like ecstasy, certainty was what the *dharmic* man sought most, despite his awareness that certainty in knowledge is nowhere to be obtained. The need for certainty remained embedded in *dharmic* consciousness as deeply as did the scepticism about obtaining it.

Now, if nothing that had passed as 'knowledge' could be shown to be certain, independent of the perceiving mind and its limits, and free from doubt, one is still free to seek certainty in a region beyond the domains of knowledge and logic. There has been, moreover, always a logical ground for seeking that freedom. It was provided by the fact that the kind of certainty that logic had claimed is no more than formal. All analytical propositions are tautologies; the 'certainty' that they carry is already built into their structure; a tautology asserts nothing about the world, and therefore no fact of the world can either confirm it or refute it. Hence, the Upanishadic view that logic and reasoning, by *themselves*, are incapable of leading to knowledge that is certain.[83]

But neither did the *Mahābhārata* accept relativity as the ultimate condition of life that must paralyse understanding and decision.[84] The

Mahābhārata does not pretend that relativity as a natural attribute of human life can ever be set aside without falling into its opposite, absolutism, '*this is so, and that is all*', inviting thereby the greater danger of excluding any doubt that, seen from a different perspective, or seen from the same perspective *but* at a different time, 'this may *not* be so.' But neither does the *Mahābhārata* justify relativity of perceptions as a door to opportunism. It shows that everything in life is relational, the self in relation with the self, and the self in relation with the *other*, and the worth of anything is to be decided by what is created in human terms thereby, and not by scriptural authority, nor by the limited logic of argument in isolation. This was another radical shift in the teachings of the *Mahābhārata.*

Exploring the true meaning of *dharma*, Yudhishṭhira asks Bhīshma:

प्रत्यक्षमागमो वेति किं तयोः कारणं भवेत् ।। अनुशासन १६२.२ ।।
Of direct perception and scriptural authority, which is the test for deciding on dharma?[85]

And Bhīshma answers by saying:

नास्त्यत्र संशयः कश्चिदिति मे वर्तते मतिः ।
शृणु वक्ष्यामि ते प्राज्ञ सम्यक् त्वं मेऽनुपृच्छसि ।। अनुशासन १६२.३ ।।
You have asked a legitimate question. And I will answer it. In my view there can be no doubt whatsoever in regard to this matter.[86]

संशयः सुगमस्तत्र दुर्गमस्तस्य निर्णयः ।
दृष्टं श्रुतमनन्तं हि यत्र संशयदर्शनम् ।। अनुशासन १६२.४ ।।
To create doubt about dharma *is easy; but to resolve it is exceedingly difficult. There is no end to what can be seen by direct perception or to scriptural authority, and both create doubts.*[87]

प्रत्यक्षं कारणं दृष्ट्वा हैतुकाः प्राज्ञमानिनः ।
नास्तीत्येवं व्यवस्यन्ति सत्यं संशयमेव च ।। अनुशासन १६२.५ ।।
Those considering themselves endowed with true knowledge consider sense perception to be the test, and would not admit what cannot be seen but exists, thus creating doubt about reality.[88]

तदयुक्तं व्यवस्यन्ति बालाः पण्डितमानिनः ।
अथ चेन्मन्यसे चैकं कारणं किं भवेदिति ।। अनुशासन १६२.६ ।।

शक्यं दीर्घेण कालेन युक्तेनातन्द्रितेन च।
प्राणयात्रामनेकां च कल्पमानेन भारत।। अनुशासन १६२.७।।
तत्परेणैव नान्येन शक्यं ह्येतस्य दर्शनम्।

Thinking they are learned, they are however like children, in the reasoning that there is only one test—that of direct sense perception. It is only by long practice, and living one's life in its many expressions, that one can have insight into reality; there is no other way.[89]

हेतूनामन्तमासाद्य विपुलं ज्ञानमुत्तमम्।। अनुशासन १६२.२।।
ज्योतिः सर्वस्य लोकस्य विपुलं प्रतिपद्यते।
न त्वेव गमनं राजन् हेतुतो गमनं तथा।
अग्राह्यमनिबद्धं च वाचा सम्परिवर्जयेत्।। अनुशासन १६२.२।।

It is when the logic of argument comes to an end that one gains knowledge of a superior order. And it is in the fullness of the light of that knowledge that the world is lighted. Give up trying to limit within speech and the logic of argument what cannot be grasped.[90]

Still not convinced, Yudhishṭhira continues with his questioning. In fact, he repeats his question, now with the addition of *shishṭāchāra*, the nobility of conduct, the actual conduct of those who are good, as yet another test to decide on *dharma*.[91] Bhīshma answers that all the three *in their unity*, direct perception and inference, *and* scriptural authority *and* the conduct of those who are noble and good, are valid tests.[92]

Yudhishṭhira (*to Bhīshma*)

पुनरेव हि मे बुद्धिः संशये परिमुह्यति।
अपारे मार्गमाणस्य परं तीरमपश्यतः।। अनुशासन १६२.१७।।

वेदः प्रत्यक्षमाचारः प्रमाणं तत्त्रयं यदि।
पृथक्त्वं लभ्यते चैषां धर्मश्चैकस्त्रयं कथम्।। अनुशासन १६२.१८।।

Once again my mind is covered with doubt; I want to cross over, but I just do not see its end.

If scriptural authority and direct sense perception and goodness of conduct, all these three together are the tests, it is also evident that each of them points to different things whereas dharma *is a unity. In that case, how can they be tests for* dharma *alike?*[93]

Bhīshma (*to Yudhishṭhira*)

धर्मस्य ह्रियमाणस्य बलवद्भिर्दुरात्मभिः ।
यद्येवं मन्यसे राजंस्त्रिधा धर्मविचारणा ।। अनुशासन १६२.१९ ।।

एक एवेति जानीहि त्रिधा धर्मस्य दर्शनम् ।
पृथक्त्वे च न मे बुद्धिस्त्रयाणामपि वै तथा ।। अनुशासन १६२.२० ।।

उक्तो मार्गस्त्रयाणां च तत्तथैव समाचर ।
जिज्ञासा न तु कर्तव्या धर्मस्य परितर्कणात् ।। अनुशासन १६२.२१ ।।

अहिंसा सत्यमक्रोधो दानमेतच्चतुष्टयम् ।
अजातशत्रो सेवस्य धर्म एष सनातनः ।। अनुशासन १६२.२३ ।।

Know this that dharma *is a unity; and all the three proofs, tests, show that unity. My mind does not accept that they show different, separate,* dharma-s.[94]
The path that they show, walk on it. The inquiry concerning dharma *is not to be through the logic of argument.*[95]
Not to do violence to others; truth; conquest of anger and aggression; and giving and sharing—live in these. This is the abiding dharma.[96]

मानसं सर्वभूतानां धर्ममाहुर्मनीषिणः ।
तस्मात् सर्वाणि भूतानि धर्ममेव समासते ।। अनुशासन १६२.६० ।।

एक एव चरेद् धर्मं न धर्मध्वजिको भवेत् ।
धर्मवाणिजका ह्येते ये धर्ममुपभुञ्जते ।। अनुशासन १६२.६१ ।।

The wise maintain that dharma *is the heart of all living beings. Therefore, all beings should take recourse to* dharma.[97]
Living one's life in dharma, *let one not wave the flag of* dharma, *though. Those who turn* dharma *into a means of their livelihood are only merchants of* dharma.[98]

At the same time, by faithfully narrating the stories of human relationships, the *Mahābhārata* is showing, too, that the relationship of the self with the self remains mostly incoherent, and the relationship of the self with the *other*, the problematic. *Dharma* is the journey towards the coherence of life, which comes from life itself and not from logical argument or from scriptural authority alone.

सर्वे प्रियाभ्युपगतं धर्ममाहुर्मनीषिणः ।
पश्यैतं लक्षणोद्देशं धर्माधर्मे युधिष्ठिर ।। शान्ति २५९.२५ ।।

What is obtained by love and friendship, all that is dharma; *its opposite, all that is* adharma. *Consider this to be the distinguishing sign of* dharma *and* adharma.[99]

Dharma as relationship of the self with the self and with the _other_

The *Mahābhārata* is concerned first of all, even as the *Upanishad*-s are, with demonstrating the interrelated nature of all human attributes, each with its own place and value, but meaningful only in their relatedness with each other. Fragment one from the rest, and assign it an overriding place, to the pursuit of pleasure and wealth for example, and it will soon turn into its own negation, as it must, which is a state of violence to one's self. But to assign any human attribute altogether a low value is, too, a state of violence to one's self. The violence in the outside world is a natural extension,of both.

In the parable of Prahlāda, the Asura emperor, and Indra, the lord of the gods, the *Mahābhārata* illustrates the natural unity of human attributes.[100] Prahlāda had achieved so great a coherence within himself that he had come to possess the immense power of benevolence. Through that very power he had conquered the three worlds, including that of the gods, replacing Shakra in the celestial office of Indra. One day, disguised as a mendicant, Indra appeared before him, and said that he had come to learn from him what *shreya*, the Good, truly is. The emperor said that he was very busy with the administration of the three worlds and had not a moment to spare so as to teach him. The mendicant stayed in his palace nevertheless; attended on the emperor; and pleased him so much with his devotion to him that one day the emperor said to him: 'Ask for whatever you wish, and it shall be given.' Hearing the unsuspecting Prahlāda say this, the crafty god knew that to be the moment he was waiting for. Yet he wanted to make certain. 'You have already given me so much,' the mendicant replied. Pleased even more, the emperor said: 'Even so, ask.' And Indra struck.

'If you are pleased with me, and wish to do me good, grant me that I have your Śīla,' the mendicant said, bowing to the emperor most respectfully. Prahlāda was pleased, of course, that *that* is what was being sought from him; but he was seized also with a vague fear. Nevertheless, he pronounced the words, 'Be it so', and the mendicant left.

After he was gone, Prahlāda felt an inner disquiet without quite knowing why. Just then a column of light in human form emerged from his body. Astonished, he asked: 'Who are you?' The answer came: 'I am *Śīla*, who until now was inseparable from you, but you have given me away, and I am leaving you.' And the light vanished.[101]

Soon thereafter emerged another column of light from his body, whereupon Prahlāda asked: 'Who are you?' 'I am *Dharma*,' was the answer. 'I, too, am leaving you, for I live where *Śīla* lives.'[102]

There emerged from his body, in quick succession, three more columns of light: Truth, who said he followed Dharma; *Good Conduct*, who said he followed Truth; and *Strength*, who said he followed Good Conduct. One after another they all left him.[103]

The last to emerge from his body was a column of light that was the most effulgent of them all, and in the form of a woman. 'And who are *you*?', Prahlāda asked her. 'I am *Śrī*, all that which is desirable in human life. I lived in you, but you have abandoned me; and I, too, am leaving you, for I live where Strength is.'[104] Paralysed with fear, he asked her again: 'Who was that mendicant, that brāhmaṇa? I want to know the truth.' 'He was Shakra, *the* Indra, who robbed you of that effulgence of yours that had covered the three worlds,' *Śrī* said to Prahlāda. 'It was through *śīla* that you became what you were, and had conquered whatever there is to conquer. And it is that which you gave away yourself.' Before leaving him, his inner being now emptied, *Śrī* said to him:

धर्मः सत्यं तथा वृत्तं बलं चैव तथाप्यहम् ।
शीलमूला महाप्राज्ञ सदा नास्त्यत्र संशयः ।। शान्ति १२४.६२ ।।
Dharma, Truth, Wealth, Strength, and I—all of us are rooted in Śīla. Of that, there is no doubt.[105]

And what is *Śīla*, which abandoned takes away with it all that is of human worth? The same parable provides the answer:

अद्रोहः सर्वभूतेषु कर्मणा मनसा गिरा ।
अनुग्रहश्च दानं च शीलमेतत् प्रशस्यते ।। शान्ति १२४.६६ ।।
Freedom from malice towards any being, in act, thought, and speech; benevolence towards all; and sharing—this is śīla.[106]

The story narrated above is not to be read literally. For *śīla* is not some material object which, on being given away, one will be left without. It is a dramatic way of the *Mahābhārata* to bring into awareness what is manifestly true but is often ignored—the interrelatedness of human attributes. And that awareness is the very first step of ordering one's life, which is to say, of having a right relationship with one's self in one's inner coherence.

At another place, in answer to a question from Yudhishṭhira, whether there is anything that could deliver human beings from the fear of sorrow and death, in the voice of Bhīshma the *Mahābhārata* says:

न बान्धवा न च वित्तं न कौल्यं
न च श्रुतं न च मन्त्रा न वीर्यम्।
दुःखात् त्रातुं सर्व एवोत्सहन्ते
परत्रशीलेन तु यान्ति शान्तिम्।। शान्ति २८६.१५ ।।

Neither friends nor relatives, nor wealth, nor superior lineage, nor learning, nor the chanting of some mantra *nor one's strength, put together, can deliver a man from sorrow. It is only* śīla *that brings peace.*[107]

न विक्रमो न चाप्यर्थो न मित्रं न सुहृज्जनः।
तथोन्मोचयते दुःखाद् यथाऽऽत्मा स्थिरसंयमः।। स्त्री ७.२२ ।।

It is neither bravery, nor wealth, nor friends, nor relatives, that can free one from suffering, but only one's self, stable and self-controlled.[108]

In the voice of Vidura, the detached observer in the main story of the *Mahābhārata*, during his many long conversations with his half-brother Dhritarāshṭra, the king, the *Mahābhārata* says:

शीलं प्रधानं पुरुषे तद् यस्येह प्रणश्यति।
न तस्य जीवितेनार्थो न धनेन न बन्धुभिः।। उद्योग ३४.४८ ।।

In human beings, it is śīla *that has the chief place. If that is lost, a person's life, wealth, and friends, all are meaningless.*[109]

And the meaning of *śīla* consists in the right relationship with the other, as seen above, even as the attributes of being human are interrelated within the self. The *Mahābhārata* returns to the self in the following conversation which Bhīma, one of the five Pāṇdava brothers, has with his eldest brother Yudhishṭhira. The latter's exclusive concern with *dharma*, to the neglect of everything else, had begun to irritate his family, even though they all had the greatest respect for him. Bhīma says to him:

यस्य धर्मो हि धर्मार्थे क्लेशभाङ् न स पण्डितः ।
न स धर्मस्य वेदार्थं सूर्यस्यान्धः प्रभामिव ।। वन ३३.२३ ।।

Fragmented, whose dharma *is limited to* dharma *alone, is not a perceptive person, creating for himself only strife, and gratuitously. He does not know the meaning of* dharma, *just as a person who is blind cannot know the brightness of the sun.*[110]

यस्य चार्थार्थमेवार्थः स च नार्थस्य कोविदः ।
रक्षेत भृतकोऽरण्ये यथा गास्तादृगेव सः ।। वन ३३.२४ ।।

Fragmented, whose pursuit of wealth is for the sake of wealth alone does not know the substance of wealth. He is only its keeper, just as a shepherd is the keeper of the cattle in the woods.[111]

सततं यश्च कामार्थी नेतरावनुतिष्ठति ।
मित्राणि तस्य नश्यन्ति धर्मार्थाभ्यां च हीयते ।। वन ३३.२६ ।।

Similarly, he who is occupied with pleasures alone loses his friends, and remains deprived of dharma *and material prosperity as well.*[112]

तस्माद् धर्मार्थयोर्नित्यं न प्रमाद्यन्ति पण्डिताः ।
प्रकृतिः सा हि कामस्य पावकस्यारणिर्यथा ।। वन ३३.२८ ।।

Therefore, those who are wise are never careless in matters concerning either dharma *or material prosperity; for it is from them, together, that the pleasures come.*[113]

एवमेव पृथग् दृष्ट्वा धर्मार्थौ काममेव च ।। वन ३३.३८ ।।
न धर्मपर एव स्यान्न चार्थपरमो नरः ।
न कामपरमो वा स्यात् सर्वान् सेवेत सर्वदा ।। वन ३३.३९ ।।

Fragmenting dharma *from desire for material prosperity, and them from the desire for sexual pleasure, one should not pursue only one of them. One should enjoy them always without separating one from the other.*[114]

In order to demonstrate further how human attributes are interrelated in a way that any one of them invariably leads to another, and that any discussion about one of them must include the rest, *dharma*, the innate human order in which every being is sustained, is personified. Dharma has thirteen wives who are, in their English names: Faith, Intellect, Intelligence, Strength, Action, Wealth, Resoluteness, Satisfaction, Splendour, Success, Fame, Modesty, and Peace.[115] They have fifteen sons. From Faith, Desire. From Intellect, Learning. From Intelligence, Awareness. From Strength, Desire-for-more. From Action, Governance and Worldly Wisdom and Discipline. From Wealth, Arrogance. From Resoluteness, Rule. From Satisfaction, Contentment. From Splendour, Commerce. From Success, Happiness. From Fame, Recognition. From Modesty, Good Breeding, and from Peace, Comfort.[116]

Adharma, the human disorder, is personified as well. Violence is his wife, and they have Untruth as their son, and Dishonesty as their daughter. In their turn, they give birth to Fear, Hell, Illusion, Pain, and Death.[117]

In both *dharma* and *adharma*, there is a clear chain of psychological causation: '*Given this, that must arise.*' The *Mahābhārata* traces with manifest realism many such chains, the chain of greed, for example. No sooner do I grasp that chain than I am on the path of self-destruction and the destruction of the *other*, the words 'self' and 'the *other*' to be understood throughout in their individual and collective meaning.

पापस्य यदाधिष्ठानं तच्छृणुष्व नराधिप।
एको लोभो महाग्राहो लोभात् पापं प्रवर्तते।। शान्ति १५८.२।।

अत: पापमधर्मश्चतथा दु:खमनुत्तमम्।
निकृत्या कूलमेतद्धि येन पापकृतो जना:।। शान्ति १५८.३।।

From greed arises every conceivable act of harm to oneself and to others, and to great pain and suffering thereby.[118]

लोभात् क्रोध: प्रभवति लोभात् काम: प्रवर्तते।
लोभान्मोहश्च माया च मान: स्तम्भ: परासुता।। शान्ति १५८.४।।

अक्षमा ह्रीपरित्याग: श्रीनाशो धर्मसंक्षय:।
अभिध्याप्रख्यता चैव सर्वं लोभात् प्रवर्तते।। शान्ति १५८.५।।

From greed arise anger; confusion; egoism; and intolerance;[119] *shamelessness; loss of prosperity; worry; and ill-reputation.*[120]

अत्यागश्चातितर्षश्च विकर्मसु च या: क्रिया:।
कुलविद्यामदश्चैव रूपैश्वर्यमदस्तथा।। शान्ति १५८.६।।

सर्वभूतेष्वभिद्रोह: सर्वभूतेष्वसत्कृति:।
सर्वभूतेष्वविश्वास: सर्वभूतेष्वनार्जवम्।। शान्ति १५८.७।।

From greed arise miserliness; excessive 'thirst' arrogance of one's high family; arrogance of learning; arrogance of beauty; and arrogance of plentiful wealth; aggression; disrespect; distrust and deviousness towards all beings.[121]

हरणं परवित्तानां परदाराभिमर्शनम् ।
वाग्वेगो मनसो वेगो निन्दावेगस्तथैव च ।। शान्ति १५८.८ ।।

उपस्थोदरयोर्वेगो मृत्युवेगश्च दारुणः ।
ईर्ष्यावेगश्च बलवान् मिथ्यावेगश्च दुर्जयः ।। शान्ति १५८.९ ।।
रसवेगश्च दुर्वार्यः श्रोत्रवेगश्च दुःसहः ।
कुत्सा विकत्था मात्सर्यं पापं दुष्करकारिता ।। शान्ति १५८.१० ।।
साहसानां च सर्वेषामकार्याणां क्रियास्तथा ।

Forceful possession of the wealth of others, and rudeness to their women; onslaught of forceful speech and will; onslaught of the tendency to speak ill of others; hatred; self-praise; dangerous acts; and doing what ought not to be done—all these arise from greed. In greed arises the mighty onslaught of envy and jealousy; and in greed, the mighty onslaught of falsehood and lies. Then follows the onslaught of physical illness; and then the dreadful onslaught of death.[122]

यो न पूरयितुं शक्यो लोभः प्राप्त्या कुरुद्वह ।। शान्ति १५८.१२ ।।
नित्यं गम्भीरतोयाभिरापगाभिरिवोदधिः ।

Should one get all that one wants, one's greed would remain unfulfilled still, even as the sea does not get filled with all the rivers flowing into it.[123]

तस्याज्ञानाद्धि लोभो हि लोभादज्ञानमेव च ।
सर्वदोषास्तथा लोभात् तस्माल्लोभं विवर्जयेत् ।। शान्ति १५९.१२ ।।

मूलं लोभस्य मोहो वै कालात्मगतिरेव च ।। शान्ति १५९.११ ।।
लोभप्रभवमज्ञानं वृद्धं भूयः प्रवर्धते ।। शान्ति १५९.१० ।।

Ignorance is the root cause of greed; and greed feeds ignorance. So long as the one exists, the other must exist too.[124]

उभावेतौ समफलौ समदोषौ च भारत ।
अज्ञानं चातिलोभश्चाप्येकं जानीहि पार्थिव ।। शान्ति १५९.१ ।।

Indeed, in regard to their consequences and disorder, consider ignorance and excessive greed to be the same.[125]

Greed, *lobha*, as the main cause of all human disorder comes up in the *Mahābhārata* repeatedly. For the disorder of greed is pervasive. There is the greed for money and wealth; the greed for pleasure; the greed for political power; the greed for power over others in the name of religion. Therefore, this disorder of greed, that is the *adharma* of greed, is necessarily a large part of the *Mahābhārata*'s inquiry into wealth and material prosperity, *artha*; into sexual desire, *kāma*; and the foundations of law and governance, *rāja-dharma*.

The psychological causal chain of self-discipline, *dama*, an attribute of *dharma*, is shown to Yudhishṭhira by Bhīshma, when Yudhishṭhira asks him a question which will be our question as well:

बहुधा दर्शने लोके श्रेयो यदिह मन्यसे।
अस्मिंल्लोके परे चैव तन्मे ब्रूहि पितामह।। शान्ति १६०.२।।

महानयं धर्मपथो बहुशाखश्च भारत।
किंस्विदेवेह धर्माणामनुष्ठेयतमं मतम्।। शान्ति १६०.३।।
धर्मस्य महतो राजन् बहुशाखस्य तत्त्वत:।
यन्मूलं परमं तात तत् सर्वं ब्रूह्यशेषत:।। शान्ति १६०.४।।
There are in this world many philosophies of the Good. Which of them do you consider the best. Tell me about that.
The path of dharma *is a grand path from which many other paths branch off. Of them, which one do you consider the best?*
What is the origin of dharma *itself from which so many paths branch off?*[126]

In the voice of Bhīshma, the *Mahābhārata* gives a clear and straightforward answer to that equally clear and straightforward question.

धर्मस्य विधयो नैके ये वै प्रोक्ता महर्षिभि:।
स्वं स्वं विज्ञानमाश्रित्य दमस्तेषां परायणम्।। शान्ति १६०.६।।
According to their understanding, different sages and thinkers have given not one but many different answers to this question. However, self-discipline, dama, *remains the basis of them all.*[127]

दमेन सदृशं धर्मं नान्यं लोकेषु शुश्रुम।
दमो हि परमो लोके प्रशस्त: सर्वधर्मिणाम्।। शान्ति १६०.१०।।
There is in this world no dharma *greater than the conquest of the self.*[128]

As to everything else, to this statement as well, the *Mahābhārata* attaches its rationality. For why must the conquest of the self be considered the highest good? To begin with, for some simple reasons:

सुखं दान्तः प्रस्वपिति सुखं च प्रतिबुध्यते ।
सुखं पर्येति लोकांश्च मनश्चास्य प्रसीदति ।। शान्ति १६०.१२ ।।

The one who has brought his self under control sleeps a peaceful sleep, and awakes with a sense of peace. He walks with a feeling of happiness, and in his heart is always joyful.[129]

In contrast,

अदान्तः पुरुषः क्लेशमभीक्ष्णं प्रतिपद्यते ।
अनार्थांश्च बहूनन्यान् प्रसृजत्यात्मदोषजान् ।। शान्ति १६०.१३ ।।

The one who has not brought his self under control is full of agitation always. Besides, he keeps creating more disorders from the ones that exist in him already.[130]

क्षमा धृतिरहिंसा च समता सत्यमार्जवम् ।
इन्द्रियाभिजयो दाक्ष्यं मार्दवं ह्रीरचापलम् ।। शान्ति १६०.१५ ।।

अकार्पण्यमसंरम्भः संतोषः प्रियवादिता ।
अविहिंसानसूया चाप्येषां समुदयो दमः ।। शान्ति १६०.१६ ।।

The conquest of the self leads to: forgiveness and reconciliation; to patience; not-violence; an attitude of equality; to truth; to simplicity of character; control over one's physical senses; gentleness; modesty; generosity; to freedom from anger; to a feeling of contentment; pleasant speech; and not seeking fault in others. These are the manifestations of the conquest of the self.[131]

मैत्रोऽथ शीलसम्पन्नः प्रसन्नात्माऽऽत्मविच्च यः ।
मुक्तस्य विविधैः सङ्गैस्तस्य प्रेत्य फलं महत् ।। शान्ति १६०.२२ ।।

सुवृत्तःशीलसम्पन्नः प्रसन्नात्माऽऽत्मविद् बुधः ।
प्राप्येह लोके सत्कारं सुगतिं प्रतिपद्यते ।। शान्ति १६०.२३ ।।

Who has conquered his self has feelings of friendship towards all; dignity of conduct; cheerfulness; and self-knowledge.[132]

अभयं यस्य भूतेभ्यो भूतानामभयं यतः ।
तस्य देहाद् विमुक्तस्य भयं नास्ति कुतश्चन ।। शान्ति १६०.२६ ।।
समः सर्वेषु भूतेषु मैत्रायणगतिश्चरेत् ।। शान्ति १६०.२७ ।।

Himself free from fear, above all, he brings for others freedom from fear. Having an attitude of equality towards all beings, he has feelings of friendship for all.[133]

ज्ञानारामस्य बुद्धस्य सर्वभूताविरोधिनः।
नावृत्तिभयमस्तीह परलोकभयं कुतः।। शान्ति १६०.३३।।
Floating in self-knowledge; having no conflict with any other being; he has fear neither of this world nor of the next world.[134]

असाधुभ्योऽस्य न भयं न चौरेभ्यो न राजतः।
अकिंचित् कस्यचित् कुर्वन् निर्भयः शुचिरावसेत्।। शान्ति २५९.१५।।
Who has in him no wickedness fears neither those who are wicked, nor thieves, nor the king. Who has gained true purity, and acts accordingly, is forever fearless.[135]

मुदितः शुचिरभ्येति सर्वतो निर्भयः सदा।। शान्ति २५९.१७।।
Forever full of joy, he is also forever fearless.[136]

As regards the question, 'What is *shaucha*, or purity, truly?', the *Mahābhārata* clearly turns away from the outward ritual 'purity', and instead teaches us the purity of the heart and the mind as true purity.[137] *Dharma* is a journey from ritual *acts* to *relationships*. And on that path, self-discipline is the first requirement.

दान्तस्य किमरण्येन तथादान्तस्य भारत।
यत्रैव निवसेद् दान्तस्तदरण्यं स चाश्रमः।। शान्ति १६०.३६।।
Who has conquered his self, what need has he to take to the forest? And what good will the forest do to the one with no control over his self? Who has conquered his self, wherever he lives, that is for him the forest and the hermitage.[138]

The *Mahābhārata* dwells throughout upon *lakṣaṇa*, the attributes, by which *dharma* is to be recognised. Evenly divided, they relate with the self and the *other*. In relation to one's self, those attributes are: *satya*, truth; *dama*, self-control; *shaucha*, purity; *ārjava*, lack of deviousness; *hri*, endurance; *achapalam*, resoluteness of character; *dāna*, giving and sharing. And *tapas* and *brahmacharya*, which are not, as generally translated, 'austerity' and 'sexual continence', but, as we shall see later, the other names of truth and self-control.

In relation to the *other*, the attributes of *dharma* are: *ahiṃsā*, or not to violate the *other*'s being; *samatā*, the attitude of equality; *shāntih*, peace or tranquillity; *anraśanṣyam*, lack of aggression and cruelty; and *amātsara*, absence of envy.

They flow into each other. *Dharma*, like truth, is a state of being—in relation with oneself and with the *other*. This is the substance of the teaching of the *Mahābhārata*.

After all the complexities of human life have been taken into account, the answer to the question, *what is dharma*?, repeatedly raised in the *Mahābhārata*, is simple, straightforward, and universal. Bhīshma says to Yudhishṭhira:

सर्वं प्रियाभ्युपगतं धर्ममाहुर्मनीषिण: ।
पश्यैतं लक्षणोद्देशं धर्माधर्मे युधिष्ठिर ।। शान्ति २५९.२५ ।।

Whatever one obtains from being agreeable and loving to all is, in the opinion of those who know the true nature of things, the distinguishing mark of dharma *from what is* adharma.[139]

Elsewhere, in the voice of an ordinary grocer, Tulādhāra, instructing a vain ascetic, Jājali, who had wrong notions of *dharma*, the *Mahābhārata* says:

सर्वेषां य: सुहृन्नित्यं सर्वेषां च हिते रत: ।
कर्मणा मनसा वाचा स धर्मं वेद जाजले ।। शान्ति २६२.९ ।।

Who has in his heart always the well-being of others, and is wholly given, in acts, thoughts, and in speech, to the good of others, he alone knows what dharma *is.*[140]

In the voice of Shiva, in conversation with his wife Umā, the *Mahābhārata* teaches:[141]

सर्वभूतेषु य: सम्यग् ददात्यभयदक्षिणाम् ।
हिंसादोषविमुक्तात्मा स वै धर्मेण युज्यते ।। अनुशासन १४२.२७ ।।

Freeing himself from the disorder of violence, who offers to all beings freedom from fear is alone in unity with dharma.[142]

सर्वभूतानुकम्पी य: सर्वभूतार्जवव्रत: ।
सर्वभूतात्मभूतश्च स वै धर्मेण युज्यते ।। अनुशासन १४२.२८ ।।

Who has for all beings kindness and compassion, and who has the sense of unity with all beings, he alone is in unity with dharma.[143]

सर्ववेदेषु वा स्नानं सर्वभूतेषु चार्जवम्।
उभे एते समे स्यातामार्जवं वा विशिष्यते।। अनुशासन १४२.२९।।
To have acquired all knowledge, and to be simple and straightforward to all beings, are of equal value. Indeed, to be simple and straightforward is even more important.[144]

आर्जवं धर्ममित्याहुरधर्मो जिह्म उच्यते।
आर्जवेनेह संयुक्तो नरो धर्मेण युज्यते।। अनुशासन १४२.३०।।
Simplicity is dharma, *deviousness* adharma. *Who has united himself with simplicity and straightforwardness of character is in unity with* dharma *as well.*[145]

आर्जवे तु रतो नित्यं वसत्यमरसंनिधौ।
तस्मादार्जवयुक्तः स्याद् य इच्छेद् धर्ममात्मनः।। अनुशासन १४२.३१।।
Who is given to simplicity and straightforwardness of character lives in the nearness of that which is beyond death. Therefore, he who aspires to dharma, *should cultivate simplicity and straightforwardness of character.*[146]

क्षान्तो दान्तो जितक्रोधो धर्मभूतो विहिंसकः।
धर्म रतमना नित्यं नरो धर्मेण युज्यते।। अनुशासन १४२.३२।।
Forgiving, self-disciplined, conquering anger, not violating others, such a person is in unity with dharma.[147]

In the voice of a sage and philosopher, or of a grocer, or of a meat seller, or in the voice of the great god Shiva, and in many other voices, the *Mahābhārata*'s teachings on the true meaning of *dharma* as the foundation of a happy relationship of the self with the self, and of the self with the *other*, are so simple and straightforward, with their clear rationality, that no elaboration, or *ṭīkā*, is required.

And as for truth, its essence is this:

सत्यस्य वचनं श्रेयः सत्यज्ञानं तु दुष्करम्।
यद् भूतहितमत्यन्तमेतत् सत्यं ब्रवीम्यहम्।। शान्ति २८७.२०।।
Speech that has truth is the greatest good; but what truth really is, that knowledge is exceedingly difficult. I call truth only that which secures the utmost good of all.[148]

Once again, this time in the voice of a meat seller instructing another arrogant ascetic and scholar:

सत्यस्य वचनं श्रेय: सत्यं ज्ञानं हितं भवेत् ।
यद् भूतहितमत्यन्तं तद् वै सत्यं परं मतम् ।। वन २१३.३१ ।।
To be truthful is the Good; and the knowledge of truth of greatest benefit.
What secures the utmost good of all, verily that is truth.[149]

सर्वं प्रियाभ्युपगतं धर्ममाहुर्मनीषिण: ।
पश्यैतं लक्षणोद्देशं धर्माधर्मे युधिष्ठिर ।। शान्ति २५९.२५ ।।
Whatever one obtains from being agreeable and loving to all is, in the opinion of those who know the true nature of things, the distinguishing mark of dharma *from what is* adharma.

लोकसंग्रहसंयुक्तं विधात्रा विहितं पुरा ।
सूक्ष्मधर्मार्थनियतं सतां चरितमुत्तमम् ।। शान्ति २५९.२६ ।।

धर्मलक्षणमाख्यातमेतत् ते कुरुसत्तम ।
तस्मादनार्जवे बुद्धिर्न ते कार्या कथंचन ।। शान्ति २५९.२७ ।।
What has been established in times past to secure a happy existence for mankind, and is in unity with the good of all, you have in that the best attributes of dharma *and material prosperity.*
Thus I have described to you the attributes of dharma. *Let deviousness not ever find place in your mind or in what you do.*[150]

मानसं सर्वभूतानां धर्ममाहुर्मनीषिण: ।
तस्मात् सर्वेषु भूतेषु मनसा शिवमाचरेत् ।। शान्ति १९३.३१ ।।
Those who have reflected on life deeply perceive that to be dharma *which is done for all beings with one's heart. Therefore, with your heart, act for the good of all beings.*[151]

The utmost good of all is in what sustains, enhances, ennobles, brings together, creates happiness and joy, is just and fair, degrading and debasing no one, nor uprooting, securing for everyone freedom from fear.

CHAPTER FIVE

Ahiṃsā—Not-violence, the Foundation of Life

- Not-violence: the foundation of life and relationships
- The opposite reality: '*life lives upon life*'
- The rationality of *not-violence*
- Justification of anger on being wronged
- The rationality of forgiveness and its limits
- The argument against enmity and war
- Violence in speech and words
- Violence to one's self
- Freedom from fear: freedom from the violence of history

The three powerful words, *ahiṃsā paramo dharmo*, 'Not to do violence is the highest *dharma*', resound in the *Mahābhārata* throughout. They are spoken numerous times, in different voices, in different contexts. Later they would become the cardinal foundation of Jainism.

Yet the whole of the *Mahābhārata* is about violence—to one's self and to the *other*. And thus the whole of the *Mahābhārata* is about freedom from violence, about *abhaya-dāna*, 'the gift of freedom from fear', being the greatest gift of all. At first sight it would appear very strange that not-violence in human relationships should be the central concern of a work that describes in the greatest detail the Great War between the two sets of first cousins, the Kaurava-s and the Pāṇḍava-s, fought over their claims to the Kuru Kingdom. The daily happenings on the battlefield are narrated in such great detail that the *Mahābhārata* is known as the story mostly of a horrible war between them, with a few other stories here and there.

In this, however, the *Mahābhārata* is throughout following its own *method* of systematic inquiry into the human condition.[1] Nothing is discussed in the abstract. Since the *Mahābhārata* shows that everything in life is relational, everything concerning man is discussed relationally, and, in that, in the pair of opposites.

To legislate against an offence, or a crime, presupposes its existence. When a great emphasis is placed upon *ahiṃsā*, or not to do violence, and upon *satya*, or truth, it can safely be concluded, *from that emphasis alone*, that both violence and falsehood must be widespread in human relationships. Advocacy of compassion implies its general absence. Impassioned talk of justice shows that there is very little of it. And when people claim, at every turn, that happiness in life is their aim, and that whatever they do is directed towards it, one can be fairly certain that the very reverse is the truth.

And that is how it is in the *Mahābhārata*. Not-violence is discussed with every kind of violence around. Truth is discussed when there is a great deal of falsehood and lies. The need for control over one's tongue is discussed at the same time as practically everyone, the very best among the humans, are trading with each other wounding and nasty words. Freedom from fear is discussed when fear takes possession of human minds and hearts and stalks everywhere.

The *Mahābhārata* traces the main root of violence to ignorance. Violence comes from my ignorance about my relationship with my self and with the *other*. Who *am* I? And who is the *other*?

एकः शत्रुर्न द्वितीयोऽस्ति शत्रुरज्ञानतुल्यः पुरुषस्य राजन्।
येनावृतः कुरुते सम्प्रयुक्तो घोराणि कर्माणि सुदारुणानि।। शान्ति २९७.२८।।

There is only one enemy of man; there is no other enemy such as ignorance, clouded by which man acts in ways most cruel.[2]

But it is also a profound truth about man, the *Mahābhārata* says, that:

ज्योतिरात्मनि नान्यत्र सर्वजन्तुषु तत् समम्।
स्वयं च शक्यते द्रष्टुं सुसमाहितचेतसा।। शान्ति ३२६.३२।।

The light of the self is within, and nowhere else. It is in all human beings in the same measure. He who has united his consciousness with all that is, can see that light himself.[3]

Not-violence: the foundation of life and relationships

The *Mahābhārata* maintains in words of the utmost emphasis:

अहिंसा परमो धर्मस्तथाहिंसा परो दमः।
अहिंसा परमं दानमहिंसा परमं तपः।। अनुशासन ११६.२८।।

Ahiṃsā *is the highest* dharma*;* ahiṃsā *is the highest form of self-control;* ahiṃsā *is the highest offering;* ahiṃsā *is the highest austerity.*

अहिंसा परमो यज्ञस्तथाहिंसा परं फलम्।
अहिंसा परमं मित्रमहिंसा परमं सुखम्।। अनुशासन ११६.२९।।

Ahiṃsā *is the highest* yajña*;* ahiṃsā *is the best fruition;* ahiṃsā *is the best friend; and* ahiṃsā *is the greatest happiness.*

सर्वयज्ञेषु वा दानं सर्वतीर्थेषु वाऽऽप्लुतम्।
सर्वदानफलं वापि नैतत्तुल्यमहिंसया।। अनुशासन ११६.३०।।

Not all the sacrificial rituals, nor all the giving as charity, nor all the bathing in the holy waters, together, will ever be equal to not-violence.[4]

अहिंसा परमो धर्मस्तथाहिंसा परं तप: ।
अहिंसा परमं सत्यं यतो धर्म: प्रवर्तते ।। अनुशासन ११५.२३ ।।
Ahimsā *is the highest* dharma; ahiṃsā *is the highest austerity;* ahiṃsā *is the highest truth; and it is through them,* ahiṃsā *and truth, that* dharma *is advanced.*[5]

Ahiṃsā and truthfulness secure the highest good of all beings.

अहिंसा सत्यवचनं सर्वभूतहितं परम् ।
अहिंसा परमो धर्म: स च सत्ये प्रतिष्ठित:
सत्ये कृत्वा प्रतिष्ठां तु प्रवर्तन्ते प्रवृत्तय: ।। वन पर्व २०७.७४ ।।
Ahiṃsā *is the highest* dharma*, and it is rooted in truth. And it is on the basis of truth that whatever is done ought to be done.*[6]

Ahiṃsā is not just 'not killing'. *Ahiṃsā* is to do no violence to one's own being or to the being of the *other*. As an inviolable condition of fulfilling relationships, personal and social, the *Mahābhārata*, outwardly the story of a dreadful war, places the greatest emphasis on *ahiṃsā*. In a long conversation about the human condition with his wife Uma, Shiva declares:

अहिंसा परमो धर्मो ह्यहिंसा परमं सुखम् ।
अहिंसा धर्मशास्त्रेषु सर्वेषु परमं पदम् ।। अनुशासन २१३.५ ।।
Ahiṃsā *is the highest* dharma; ahiṃsā *is the greatest happiness.* Ahiṃsā *is the highest point of all the texts pertaining to* dharma.[7]

देवतातिथिशुश्रूषा सततं धर्मशीलता ।
वेदाध्ययनयज्ञाश्च तपो दानं दमस्तथा ।।
आचार्यगुरुशुश्रूषा तीर्थाभिगमनं तथा ।
अहिंसाया वरारोहे कलां नार्हन्ति षोडशीम् ।।
एतत् ते परमं गुह्यमाख्यातं परमार्चितम् ।। अनुशासन २१३.६ ।।
Service to gods and guests; steadfastness in dharma; *study of the Veda-s; performing* yajña-s; *austerity; giving; self-control; service to teachers; pilgrimage—all these together are not equal even to a sixteenth part of* ahiṃsā. *Thus I have conveyed to you the deepest mystical meaning of all.*[8]

In a conversation between two seekers, one of them says:

अहिंसा सर्वधर्माणामिति वश्द्धानुशासनम् ।
यदहिंस्त्रं भवेत् कर्म तत् कार्यमिति विद्महे ।। आश्वमेधिक २८.१६ ।।

The old and the wise say that, of all dharma-s, ahiṃsā *is the highest discipline. In my view, too, only that should be done which is free from violence.*[9]

अहिंसेति प्रतिज्ञेयं यदि वक्ष्याम्यतः परम् ।
शक्यं बहुविधं कर्तुं भवता कार्यदूषणम् ।। आश्वमेधिक २८.१७ ।।

Could I say more than that, then I would say, 'Vow not to do violence'; or else, whatever one does in whatever manner would have in it only defects.[10]

अहिंसा सर्वभूतानां नित्यमस्मासु रोचते ।
प्रत्यक्षतः साधयामो न परोक्ष्मुपास्महे ।। आश्वमेधिक २८.१८ ।।

Not to do violence to anyone is what is dear to me. That has direct results, and I am concerned with what can be seen. I do not worship the unseen.[11]

In the voice of the sage Parāshara, the *Mahābhārata* says:

तस्मादहं ब्रवीमि त्वां राजन् संचिन्त्य शास्त्रतः ।
संसिद्धाधिगमं कुर्यात् कर्म हिंसात्मकं त्यजेत् ।। शान्ति २९४.२४ ।।

After thinking well, I say to you: by all means strive for prosperity, but give up violence in your acts.[12]

Again:

अहिंसा सकलो धर्मो हिंसाधर्मस्तथाहितः ।
सत्यं तेऽहं प्रवक्ष्यामि यो धर्मः सत्यवादिनाम् ।। शान्ति २७२.२० ।।

Ahiṃsā *is a complete* dharma. *To do violence is* adharma; *and* adharma *does no good.*[13]

Of the three main attributes of *dharma*, from which all others follow, 'not to do violence', *ahiṃsā*, is one. Thus, in the voice of the dying Bhīshma, the *Mahābhārata* declares:

अहिंसार्थाय भूतानां धर्मप्रवचनं कृतम्।
यः स्यादहिंसाम्पृक्तः स धर्म इति निश्चयः।। शान्ति १०९.१२।।
All the sayings of dharma *are with the aim that no violence is done to any being. Whatever has the characteristic of doing no violence, is* dharma—*this is certain.*[14]

यत् स्यादहिंसासंयुक्तं स धर्म इति निश्चयः।
अहिंसार्थाय भूतानां धर्मप्रवचनं कृतम्।। कर्ण ६९.५७।।
Whatever is joined with not-violence is dharma—*this is certain. All the sayings of* dharma *are with the aim that no violence is done to any being.*[15]

In the same voice, it is said that:

अहिंस्रस्य तपोऽक्षय्यमहिंस्रो यजते सदा।
अहिंस्रः सर्वभूतानां यथा माता यथा पिता।। अनुशासन ११६.३१।।
The one who does not violate another's being is to all beings like father and mother.[16]

एतत् फलमहिंसाया भूयश्च कुरुपुगंव।
न हि शक्या गुणा वक्तुमपि वर्षशतैरपि।। अनुशासन ११६.३२।।
The benefits one gains from not-violence cannot fully be stated even over a hundred years.[17]

Furthermore, it is said that:

यत्र वेदाश्च यज्ञाश्च तपः सत्यं दमस्तथा।। शान्ति ३४०.८८।।
अहिंसाधर्मसंयुक्ताः प्रचरेयुः सुरोत्तमाः।
स वो देशः सेवितव्यो मा वोऽधर्मः पदा स्पृशेत्।।
Live in a place where there are together knowledge, yajña, *austerity, truth, self-control, and—*ahiṃsā, *not-violence. Then* adharma *could not touch you even remotely.*[18]

The *Mahābhārata* condemns in clear words the early vedic practice of the killing of animals as sacrificial offering in a *yajña*. This it does in the voice of King Vichakhnu, who once saw at a *yajña* site the head of a killed bull rolling on the ground, and the other cows waiting to be sacrificed, wailing.[19] Saying a prayer for the welfare of all the animals of the world,[20] he turned to the priests and said to them:

अव्यवस्थितमर्यादैर्विमूढैर्नास्तिकैर्नरैः ।
संशयात्मभिरव्यक्तैर्हिंसा समनुवर्णिता ।। शान्ति २६५.४ ।।

Only those will approve of violence that are disordered, are fools, are men of no faith, are doubtful about the self, and are not highly regarded either.[21]

सर्वकर्मस्वहिंसा हि धर्मात्मा मनुरब्रवीत् ।
कामकाराद् विहिंसन्ति बहिर्वेद्यां पशून् नराः ।। शान्ति २६५.५ ।।

Manu has propagated only ahiṃsā *in all human acts. It is some humans alone who kill animals as a sacrificial offering in a* yajña.[22]

तस्मात् प्रमाणतः कार्यो धर्मः सूक्ष्मो विजानता ।
अहिंसा सर्वभूतेभ्यो धर्मेभ्यो ज्यायसी मता ।। शान्ति २६५.६ ।।

It is proper therefore that one carefully examines the authority on which dharma *is based. For in all* dharma-*s for all living beings,* ahiṃsā *is regarded as the very first of all.*[23]

Through yet another story, the *Mahābhārata* conveys its condemnation of animal sacrifice as a ritual of vedic *yajña*, and speaks of *ahiṃsā* as the foundation of life, 'a complete *dharma*'.[24]

The opposite reality: 'Life lives upon life'

Relativity of ethics, like relativity of knowledge, is logically distinct from the problem of plurality of faith, opinion, and social custom. But the two generally become indistinguishable. That side by side the problem of relativity, the plurality of faith and opinion, had become highly confusing, even for the wisest of sages, was acknowledged by the *Mahābhārata* with much candidness.[25] The seven sages, weary and tired and confused, go to Brahmā himself, the Primeval Being, and without ceremony ask: 'What *is* truth?' 'What *is* evil?' 'What paths lead to the Good, *shreya*,[26] in the light of which one might order one's life?' In answer, Brahmā gives a somewhat long discourse breaking no new grounds and is not very coherent either.[27] Apparently unimpressed by Brahmā's rehash of the Sāṃkhya doctrines, the sages put before Brahmā, in seventeen clear verses,[28] the bewildering variety of philosophic positions on the fundamental questions that they had raised. They conclude with the lament: *ida shreya, ida shreya*, '*This* is the Good, *this* is the Good'—hearing this from all sides, men feel harassed, and so respect only that in which they have hitherto believed.[29] Because of the plurality of *dharma* and their contradictoriness, we are confused and unable to reach any certainty about them.[30] 'You should tell us about this great mystery,' they request Brahmā. 'What really is the Good?'[31] Brahmā answers them by saying:

समस्तमिह तच्छ्रुत्वा सम्यगेवावधार्यताम् ।
अहिंसा सर्वभूतानामेतत् कृत्यतमं मतम् ।। आश्वमेधिक ५०.२ ।।
एतत् पदमनुद्विग्नं वरिष्ठं धर्मलक्षणम् ।
Not-violence towards all beings is the path on which there is no inner disquiet; is superior to all others; and is the most superior characteristic of dharma.[32]

ज्ञानं निःश्रये इत्याहुर्वृद्धा निश्चितदर्शिनः ।
तस्माज्ज्ञानेन शुद्धेन मुच्यते सर्वकिल्बिषैः ।। आश्वमेधिक ५०.३ ।।
Those having insight into what is certain regard knowledge as the way to the Good and the Beatitude. For it is knowledge that brings freedom from blemish and disorder.[33]

In saying this, Brahmā is making the question of the right ordering of relationships, *dharma*, independent of philosophical opinions. *Dharma* is at all times experiential, relational. But his answer still left the question unresolved; for it is known, too, that there are occasions on which resorting to violence is inevitable, indeed a duty.

In practical terms, the problem of relativism takes the form of a straight conflict between two equally inviolable duties. For example, no *dharma* is considered greater than truth, and no evil greater than untruth.[34] But should speaking the truth endanger the lives of others, and it being one's duty to protect those in danger, must one at all times speak the truth?[35] The highest emphasis on not-violence, *ahiṃsā*, is in evident conflict not only with the *dharma* of a *kṣhattriya* which might involve hurting and killing as part of his social function to protect, but also it is in conflict with the *dharma* of every person when, for instance, somebody tries to kill the members of his family and it is his duty at once to protect them and not do violence to any living being.[36] The high value placed on forgiveness at all times is compromised by the shrewd awareness that if the enemy is left unfinished, later he will be sure to endanger one's life, and to save one's life by all means is also at all times one's primary duty to oneself. Forgiveness is in danger, moreover, of being interpreted as weakness of character, inviting disrespect and aggression.

The question of relativity apart, there are the two opposing realities that are together parts of human life. In the voice of Dharmavyādha the meatseller, the *Mahābhārata* acknowledges what is evident: that violence is inherent in life: 'life lives upon life', and places its discussion on not-violence side by side with that fact. The *Mahābhārata* confronts one reality with another. On the question of violence and not-violence, Dharmavyādha says to Kaushika:

कृषिं साध्विति मन्यन्ते तत्र हिंसा परा स्मृता।
कर्षन्तोलाङ्गलैः पुंसोघ्नन्ति भूमिशयान् बहून्।
जीवानन्याश्च बहुशस्तत्र किं प्रतिभाति ते।। वन २०८.१४ ।।

Some people regard the profession of agriculture as good; but violence is seen there, too. In ploughing the field, many living beings living in the folds of the earth are killed. Besides, many other lives are destroyed as well. What do you think about that?[37]

धान्यबीजानि यान्याहुर्व्रीह्यादीनि द्विजोत्तम।।
सर्वाण्येतानि जीवानि तत्र किं प्रतिभाति ते।। वन २०८.१५ ।।

The grains we eat as food have life in them, too. What do you think about that?[38]

अध्याक्रम्य पशूंश्चापि घ्नन्ति वै भक्षयन्ति च।
वृक्षांस्तथौषधीश्चापि छिन्दन्ति पुरुषा द्विज।। वन २०८.१६ ।।

Many people kill animals and have them as their food. They eat vegetables and fruits, which have in them living beings. What do you think about that?[39]

सत्त्वैः सत्त्वानि जीवन्ति बहुधा द्विजसत्तम।
प्राणिनोऽन्योन्यभक्षाश्च तत्र किं प्रतिभाति ते।। वन २०८.१९ ।।

Mostly living beings live upon other living beings, and also make each other their food. What do you think about that?[40]

सर्वं व्याप्तमिदं ब्रह्मन् प्राणिभिः प्राणिजीवनैः।
मत्स्यान् ग्रसन्ते मत्स्याश्च तत्र किं प्रतिभाति ते।। वन २०८.१८ ।।

Life lives upon life. The big fish eat the small fish. What do you think about that?[41]

Human beings, while walking, crush under their feet many living beings. What do you think about that?

Even men of knowledge, awake or sleeping, unintentionally kill many living beings. What do you think about that?

जीवैर्ग्रस्तमिदं सर्वमाकाशं पृथिवी तथा।
अविज्ञानाच्च हिंसन्ति तत्र किं प्रतिभाति ते।। वन २०८.२२।।

From the sky to the earth, this world is full of living beings. Many human beings, if only unintentionally, kill other beings. What do you think about that?[42]

अहिंसेति यदुक्तं हि पुरुषैर्विस्मितैः पुरा।
के न हिंसन्ति जीवान् वै लोकेऽस्मिन् द्विजसत्तम।
बहु संचित्य इति वै नास्ति कश्चिदहिंसकः।। वन २०८.२३।।

From the earliest times, men of learning and wisdom have advocated not-violence. But who in this world does not commit violence? After thinking well, I have reached the conclusion that there is no man in this world who is without violence.[43]

Arjuna, the great victor of the war, also questions the view that not-violence is the foundation of life by showing that life does not support any such conclusion.

न हि पश्यामि जीवन्तं लोके कञ्चिदहिंसया।
सत्त्वैः सत्त्वा हि जीवन्ति दुर्बलैर्बलवत्तराः।। शान्ति १५.२०।।

I do not see a single person in this world who lives by not-violence. The strong live on the weak.[44]

One can see, he points out, that:

नकुलो मूषिकानत्ति बिडालो नकुलं तथा।
बिडालमत्ति श्वा राजञ्श्वानं व्यालमृगस्तथा।। शान्ति १५.२१।।

तानत्ति पुरुषः सर्वान् पश्य कालो यथागतः।
प्राणस्यान्नमिदं सर्वं जगंम स्थावरं च यत्।। शान्ति १५.२२।।

Mongoose eats rat, cat eats mongoose, dog eats cat, and tiger eats dog, and man eats them all. Life is the food of life.[45]

विनीतक्रोधहर्षा हि मन्दा वनमुपाश्रिताः।
विना वधं न कुर्वन्ति तापसाः प्राणयापनम् ।। शान्ति १५.२४ ।।
Even those who have renounced the world and have taken to the forest cannot survive without doing violence in one form or another.[46]

उदके बहवः प्राणाः पृथिव्यां च फलेषु च।
न च कश्चिन्न तान् हन्ति किमन्यत् प्राणयापनात् ।। शान्ति १५.२५ ।।
There are numerous living beings in the water and on the earth, and very many in fruits, too. There is no one who does not kill any of those at any time in order to live himself. Men dig up the earth, and use its roots, trees, and kill birds and animals.[47]

नाघ्नतः कीर्तिरस्तीह न वित्तं न पुनः प्रजाः।
इन्द्रो वृत्रवधेनैव महेन्द्रः समपद्यत ।। शान्ति १५.१५ ।।
The truth is that he who refrains from violence can have neither wealth, nor recognition, nor a kingdom.[48]

All this is summed up at another place in the statement: '*Life preys upon life.*'

That is to say, violence is inherent in life as its natural condition. However, this is to be distinguished from the question of relativity. For if violence is inherent in life, and life cannot *be* without violence in one form or another, in one measure or another, then to say that not-violence is relative to 'time' and 'place' and 'the persons concerned' will be to say that violence is likewise conditional. What is evident is that violence is not conditional but inherent in life. In that case, what meaning can the teaching 'ahiṃsā *is the highest* dharma *and the greatest happiness*' have beyond its noble sound?

The rationality of not-violence

Let us next consider the rationality of not-violence that the *Mahābhārata* develops at the same time as it is making the statements, brought together above, about life living upon life. As mentioned at the beginning of this chapter, the rationality of *ahiṃsā* offered by the *Mahābhārata* is not a product of some notions held true *a priori*. It is manifest in life itself, from which it is derived. The *Mahābhārata* knows the human impulse to violence only too well. But it is pointing to the evident truth that there is manifest in man's being also the reality of not-violence with every shade of its meaning. If it is true that without violence in one form or another life cannot be, then it is equally true that life cannot *be* if there is only violence. The *Mahābhārata* talks about not-violence as the foundation of life by stating the simultaneously evident fact that:

न हि प्राणात् प्रियतरं लोके किंचन विद्यते ।
तस्माद् दयां नरः कुर्याद् यथाऽऽत्मनि तथापरे ।। अनुशासन ११६.८ ।।
Nothing does one love in this world more than one's life. Therefore, desiring kindness to oneself, one should be kind to others.[49]

नात्मनोऽस्ति प्रियतरः पृथिवीमनुसृत्य ह ।
तस्मात् प्राणिषु सर्वेषु दयावानात्मवान् भवेत् ।। अनुशासन ११६.२२ ।।
One should be kind to others, seeing in the other one's own self, for nothing on this earth is dearer than one's self.[50]

अनिष्ठं सर्वभूतानां मरणं नाम भारत ।
मृत्युकाले हि भूतानां सद्यो जायति वेपथुः ।। अनुशासन ११६.१७ ।।
To every living being, death is a disaster; at the time of death all living beings shake fearfully.[51]

एवं वै परमं धर्मं प्रशंसन्ति मनीषिणः ।
प्राण यथाऽऽत्मनोऽभीष्टा भूतानामपि वै तथा ।। अनुशासन ११५.१९ ।।
It is for this reason that men of intelligence praise not-violence as the highest dharma. *For just as one desires one's life, the others desire their life likewise.*[52]

सर्वस्य दयिताः प्राणाः सर्वः स्नेहं च विन्दति ।
तिर्यग्योनिष्वपि सतां स्नेहं पश्यत यादृशम् ।। शान्ति १५३.२९ ।।
Everyone loves one's life, and everyone receives affection from others. Even birds and beasts look at their children with eyes of affection.[53]

प्राणदानात् परं दानं न भूतं न भविष्यति ।
न ह्यात्मनः प्रियतरं किंचिदस्तीह निश्चितम् ।। अनुशासन ११६.१६ ।।
There has been no greater gift in the past, nor will there be in the future, than the gift of life, for doubtless there is nothing dearer to one than one's self.[54]

नात्मनोऽस्ति प्रियतरः पृथिवीमनुसृत्य ह ।
तस्मात् प्राणिषु सर्वेषु दयावानात्मवान् भवेत् ।। अनुशासन ११६.२२ ।।

In this world nothing is more dearly loved than one's self. For that reason one should be kind to all beings.[55]

The essence of the rationality of *ahiṃsā*, briefly stated, is *this*: To every man, since his own life is the most precious, how can he then take the life of another? That is to say:

न तत् परस्य संदध्यात् प्रतिकूलं यदात्मनः।
एष संक्षेपतो धर्मः कामादन्यः प्रवर्तते।। अनुशासन ११३.८।।
Whatever is not agreeable to him, that he should not do unto others. This, in brief, is dharma; *all else is only selfishness.*[56]

यदन्यैर्विहितं नेच्छेदात्मनः कर्म पूरुषः।
न तत् परेषु कुर्वीत जानन्नप्रियमात्मनः।। शान्ति २५९.२०।।
What one does not find agreeable when done by others to him, that he should not do to others. He must know what is unhappy for him, cannot be happy for others.[57]

जीवितुं यः स्वयं चेच्छेत् कथं सोऽन्यं प्रघातयेत्।
यद् यदात्मनि चेच्छेत् तत् परस्यापि चिन्तयेत्।। शान्ति २५९.२२।।
He who wishes himself to live, how can he take the life of another? The good one seeks for one's self, he should seek for others as well.[58]

It follows that:

सर्वभूतेषु यो विद्वान् ददात्यभयदक्षिणाम्।
दाता भवति लोके स प्राणानां नात्र संशयः।। अनुशासन ११५.१८।।

अहिंसालक्षणो धर्म इति धर्मविदो विदुः।
यदहिंसात्मकं कर्म तत् कुर्यादात्मवान् नरः।। अनुशासन ११६.१२।।
There has never been, nor will ever be, a gift greater than the gift of life. For nothing is more desired than one's own life. Of this there is no doubt.[59]
That not-violence is an attribute of dharma *is known to those who know the meaning of* dharma. *One should only do what is without violence.*[60]

In brief:

तस्माद् धर्मप्रधानेन भवितव्यं यतात्मना।
तथा च सर्वभूतेषु वर्तितव्यं यथात्मनि।। शान्ति १६७.९।।

> *Therefore, disciplining one's self,* dharma *should be given the main place; and we should behave towards others in the same manner as we want for ourselves.*[61]

However, a person may say: 'I don't love my life. So, on your argument, there is no reason for me to care for the life of anyone else, either in its physicality, or emotionally. Why should I not kill, or hurt, if that is a sport that I enjoy, which includes the possibility that I myself may be killed or hurt?' Or, in a refined version of the same argument, one may say: 'I certainly love my life, for it brings me the exhilaration of controlling others, and bending them to my will, which can be had only by violating their being. In that sense, I need the *other*; for without the *other* I cannot have the exhilaration I desire. Maybe someone or the other has the same project towards me, and it would be *I* who would be controlled, and it is *my* being that would be violated. But that would bring me, I suspect, even greater exhilaration.'

The *Mahābhārata* shows through several parables that not only is it conceivable that such an argument is brought forth, but also that, in one measure or another, in ways crude or refined, that is what a great many people do anyway, relationships its ceaseless theatre. It is a state of being at war with oneself. But since no one can perpetually be at war with himself, or herself, this argument can never have the force of a principle. Moreover, to live this argument consistently, one would doubtless require an extraordinary coherence of character, which is rare. In the same context, where malice and hatred are shown as knowing no bounds, and force is the decisive factor, the *Mahābhārata* shows, too, that reconciliation is as fundamental to life as conflict is. And just as violence to the *other* is violence also to one's self, reconciliation with the *other* requires one's reconciliation with one's self first.

To sum up, in one verse:

> एको धर्मः परं श्रेयः क्षमैका शान्तिरुत्तमा ।
> विद्यैका परमा तृप्तिरहिंसैका सुखावहा ।। उद्योग ३३.५२ ।।
> Dharma *is the highest good: forgiveness, the best means to peace: knowledge brings most satisfaction: and not-violence alone brings the greatest happiness.*[62]

Justification of anger on being wronged

Let us next trace in some detail, by taking up the question of forgiveness as one instance, the *Mahābhārata*'s view that:

> *Nothing is ever absolutely good nor anything ever absolutely bad, and that the same act is good or harmful depending on place, time, and the character of the person involved.*[63]
>
> नात्यन्तं गुणवत् किंचिन्न चाप्यत्यन्तनिर्गुणम् ।
> उभयं सर्वकार्येषु दृश्यते साध्वसाधु वा ।। शान्ति १५.५० ।।
>
> *There is nothing that has only qualities. Neither is there anything that is devoid of qualities altogether. In all acts, both good and bad can be seen together.*[64]

What follows is the *Mahābhārata*'s perception of the question of relativity; and nowhere has the relational aspect of that question been discussed with greater thoroughness than in the *Mahābhārata*.

There are two conflicting truths, and both are woven into every kind of human relationship, personal as well as social. *Bala*, or force, for self-protection and justice; *kshmā*, or forgiveness, for freedom from hatred and revenge. Both have their own indisputable rationality. Are there not in life occasions when anger is justified, and to avenge a wrong, just? Honest to human feelings, the *Mahābhārata* raises this question, and through numerous characters, men and women and children, who have grievously been wronged, answers it honestly. At the same time it raises the question: '*Of forgiveness and force, which is the superior*?'[65] It takes us through the logic both of anger and revenge *and* of forgiveness and reconciliation.

At the very beginning of its inquiry into the human condition, in the *Ādi-parva*, the *Mahābhārata* narrates the story of Aurva,[66] with a view to acknowledging that there *are* occasions in human life when anger is justified, and revenge as justice equally so. It does not dismiss those feelings in the shadow of the noble-sounding ideal of forgiveness and reconciliation. For that reason, when it advocates the necessity of forgiveness nevertheless as itself a force in which the human world is 'held together', it is that much more persuasive.

While the story of Aurva will be narrated more fully in a later chapter of this book, in the context of the *Mahābhārata* examining the antagonism between the king and the thinker, the *kṣhattriya* and the *brāhmaṇa*, in its brief outline it is as follows. Along with many other *brāhmaṇa*-s, Aurva's father was killed by some money-hungry princes who had their eyes on the very considerable wealth gifted by their father, the king, to them. When the princes found that they were tricked, and their intelligence insulted, they began killing all the *brāhmaṇa*-s on whom they could lay their hands. In their anger, they began killing even the pregnant *brāhmaṇa* women. Aurva's mother somehow survived, and protected the child she was then carrying. When Aurva heard from his mother what the princes had done, he began a revengeful killing of *all* the *kṣhattriya*-s, to rid the earth of cruel and unjust men. Appealed to by his ancestors to be peaceful, he justified his anger:

Aurva ***(to his forefathers)***

If my anger remains unfulfilled, it will turn upon *me*, and will destroy me as fire does a piece of wood.[67]

Whoever controls his just anger can protect nothing.[68]

Anger is to be employed at the right time to destroy the wicked and protect those who are good.[69]

Still in my mother's womb, I could hear the helpless cries of the women, my mothers, who were pregnant and were being killed by the wicked *kshattriya*-s. In terror, they looked for refuge everywhere, but did not find any.[70]

It is only so long as there is someone to prevent the cruel deeds of the wicked that the wicked will be restrained. Having strength, if he still does not restrain them, then surely he participates, too, in their wicked acts. I am fearful I will do likewise if I do not punish them for what they did to my fathers and to my mothers, and witness it without concern.[71]

In this world everyone loves his life. But no other king protected my fathers when they could have, and ought to have. Hence my anger. Forgive me, but I would not hear your words of appeasement.[72]

If I do, then this fire of anger raging within me, wanting to destroy a world that is unjust and cruel, would destroy me.[73]

Yet I know that you have in your heart the greater good of the world. Suggest a way, therefore, that the world is not destroyed, but nor am I destroyed by the fire of a just anger suddenly quietened?[74]

Aurva's forefathers *do* suggest a way. 'Release into the sea the fire of your anger. Water supports all life; and the waters of the sea will contain the fire of your anger.'[75] It would require a deep psychological analysis to understand this symbolism in relation to one's feelings and emotions; but that is to be done elsewhere. What is clear here is that, through the story of Aurva, the *Mahābhārata* suggests that anger is not always insanity, although the logic of anger is always destructive of the self. Hence, the conquest of anger is the greatest conquest of all.

In the person of an angry Ashvatthāmā, the grieving son of guru Dro*ṇ*a, the *Mahābhārata* honestly explores the question whether acts of revenge would be ethically wrong. And whether it would not be just and right to avenge a wrong *in the same manner* in which that wrong was done in the first place.[76] If these questions are not explored honestly, then whatever may be said about forgiveness and reconciliation would remain empty words. A careful reading of the *Mahābhārata* will show that, in all that it says about the foundations of human relationships, nothing remains empty words.

The killing of the great archer, guru Droṇa, was described in the previous chapter.[77] Ashvatthāmā's burning anger was not that his father was killed on the battlefield but rather *at the manner in which he was killed by the* Pāṇḍava-*s*:[78] not in a straight combat between two warriors, but by means of a despicable lie announced to him that '*Ashvatthāmā* is killed'. It was from Yudhishṭhira that Droṇa wanted to know the truth; for he had faith that Yudhishṭhira would not lie even to gain all the kingdoms in the world. The man said to him: '*Ashvatthāmā is killed*' in a loud voice, and the postscript '*It was Ashvatthāmā the war elephant that was killed*' in a whisper that Droṇa could not have heard. Believing that it was his son Ashvatthāmā, his only child, who was killed, Droṇa lost heart in the battle. He withdrew from it, putting aside his arms. He sat in his chariot, his head bent low, in deep grief. It was at that moment that Dhrishṭadyumna, the son of the Pāñchāla King Drupada, for whom Droṇa had much bitterness, rushed at him. He seized Droṇa by his hair, insulting him, and with one quick blow of his sword cut off his head. Droṇa died a death by ignoble means. Ashvatthāmā resolved to avenge his father's death, for that was 'a debt that he owed him.'[79]

His moment comes at the end of the war, in which only three are left alive from the side of the Kaurava-s: he, Kripāchārya, and Kritavarmā. The Pāṇḍava-s are victorious. Everybody of the Pāñchāla contingent of the winning army, the war having ended, has gone to sleep, so exhausted as almost like dead. The Pāṇḍava-s are not there, but are camping separately in a nearby village. Dhrishṭadyumna is sleeping in his own war tent. And there are also the five sons of the Pāṇḍava-s from Draupadī, Dhrishṭadyumna's sister. It is the dead of night, and a perfect moment for revenge. Moments earlier, Ashvatthāmā had seen a wild hawk attack some sleeping crows on a tree, killing them all, and he knew what he had to do.[80] 'This bird has taught me what I should do. I think this is the moment for me to destroy my enemies in the same manner.'[81] He was planning to attack and kill the killer of his father, Dhrishṭadyumna, and others while they were sleeping. He unfolded to Kripāchārya and Kritavarmā his purpose and the means. On hearing what he said, they felt deeply ashamed.[82] The following conversation then takes place between them.[83]

Kripāchārya

My brave warrior! I heard what you said. Now you listen to what *I* say.

Without first disciplining his own impulses, the man who does things driven by greed, excessive attachments, and anger, and who ignores others, is surely destroyed by his own self.

Duryodhana was always greedy and thoughtless. In whatever he did, he neither sought the approval of others nor did he think well himself. Ignoring those who had his welfare at hearts, and against the most sage counsel, he took the path of enmity with the Pāṇḍava-s.

Always wicked, knowing no patience, he ignored the counsel of friends; and now, when things have turned too bad for him, regrets that he didn't. We, too, following his misdeeds, are now in this grievous trouble.

I am unable to think very clearly in these moments. Therefore, I suggest that we seek advice from Dhritarāshṭra, Gāndhāri, and Vidura. When confused as to what is to one's good, and what is to one's ill, one should seek advice from those who are friends.[84]

Ashvatthāmā ***(Greatly upset by what Kripāchārya had said, although it was to his good; he hardens his heart.)***

Everyone justifies his own opinions. Everyone thinks himself to be wise, and praises his own perceptions, and his intelligence even more.

Everyone thinks his judgement alone worthy of being applauded and of a high order. Everyone thinks little of the judgement of the others, and again and again is self-congratulatory about his own. Should owing to a combination of other reasons, people in a group share the same opinion, they show great respect for each other. But when the time turns, the same opinions become different, too. Among human beings, opinions are as strange as they are different. Situations changing, and the mind troubled, judgements change as well.

Everyone acts according to his judgement.

In his youth, a man's judgement is of one kind; in his middle age, of another kind; and when he is old, of still another kind.

Tonight, deeply troubled, the resolve that has arisen in my mind, I'll tell you; for what I now judge that I should do, will pacify my sorrow.[85]

Kripāchārya

Dear son! I'm happy that you are so resolute in revenge as duty. And I can see that not even god Indra could obstruct you in your resolve. But tonight go to sleep, and tomorrow morning we two will follow you for the last battle.

It is late in the night, and you've been awake for long. Take a good sleep tonight. Engage your enemy in the morning tomorrow, and we will be with you.

If you sleep well through the night, you'll feel fresh, and your mind will be healthier.

You are a great warrior. Not even Indra with his deadly weapons could defeat you. With Kritavarmā and Kripāchārya with him, when Ashvatthāmā will set forth for the last battle, who among our enemies will dare face him? But take a good sleep tonight.

With you as the invincible warrior, our victory in tomorrow's battle with the Pāñchāla-s is certain, and we will then rejoice. But have a good sleep tonight.[86]

Ashvatthāmā ***(No fool, he rightly thinks his resolve to attack and kill Dhrishṭadyumna and other Pāñchāla-s when they were sleeping is being weakened by Kripāchārya, who undoubtedly is of the mind that to attack another warrior while he is asleep would be quite as much a despicable act; which Ashvatthāmā himself knows that it would be, but quickly quotes to himself a***

self-serving contrary opinion.[87] ***His mind still alert, he refuses to be taken in by Kripā's flattery as to his prowess, but ending each time with: 'Take a good sleep tonight'.***)

The man who is impatient is full of the passion of anger, has many things on his mind, and wanting something desperately, how can he sleep? I have today all these four things.

Anger, just the one-fourth of what is assailing me, is itself sufficient to destroy my sleep. On recalling my father's death, what sorrow is there in the world I do not feel? Burning my heart day and night, the fire of that anguish still burns.

You were a witness to *the way* in which these wicked people had killed my father. Its memory keeps piercing my heart. How can I live, much less sleep?

Tonight my mind is set upon one purpose alone. How can I then sleep?

The anger that is in my heart I'm unable to control. Neither do I know another person in this world who can.

Thus, in my judgement, the resolve I've made seems good to me. It is only after I've destroyed my enemies while they are asleep that I can myself rest and sleep.[88]

Kripāchārya ***(Tries again to dissuade Ashvatthāmā from what he proposes to do.)***

It seems to me that the man whose judgement is clouded by bad feelings, and has no control over himself, will understand nothing about material prosperity or *dharma* even if he would wish to.

Not even with a bright intellect if it is without discipline.

Whoever has someone to keep him from wrongdoing is of good fortune.

Just as a man with an unstable mind is helped, so do friends, by reasoning and by hard words as well, try to discipline one close to them. The one who lets himself be disciplined, gains happiness; the one who doesn't, invites misery.

Men of good will try always to keep a loved one from the wrong path.

Dear son! Control your mind for your own good, and be persuaded by what I say to you, so that you may later not regret that you didn't.

Those who are asleep, have given up their arms, and their horses unsaddled, have sought protection, saying: 'I'm in your

hands now'—must never be killed. To kill such men will be a*dharma*.
Hitherto your life has been without a blemish, not a blemish that anyone can speak of. And you are known as a great warrior.
Fight, therefore, in the *daylight*. That by doing something that is low you'll stain your life, as a white cloth is stained with a drop of red—is beyond my expectations from you.[89]

Ashvatthāmā (*Looks at Kripāchārya with eyes still red with anger*)
What you say is true, yes. But please do not read me a lesson in *dharma* and a*dharma*. The Pāṇḍava-s had on the battlefield already shattered *dharma* into a hundred pieces. Why don't you condemn *them*?
(***Here he lists the killings, besides that of his father Droṇāchārya, of Karṇa, Bhīshma, Bhurīshrava, and lastly of Duryodhana, by the Pāṇḍava-s. Each of those, by recourse to means that were foul and a negation of dharma, in complete negation of the very code of conduct that Kripā had just quoted, which was required to be respected by both sides in a battle.***)
For killing, while he is asleep, the murderer of my father, if I'm born in my next life as an insect, that is acceptable to me. So be it.
What I've resolved to do, that I must do, and I'm restless. Where is happiness for me? And where is for me sleep?
There was not born in this world any man who can alter my resolve.[90]

Saying this, Ashvatthāmā proceeds to saddle his horse and prepare his chariot—*for a journey*. 'Where are you going?', Kripāchārya and Kritavarmā ask him. 'You must never doubt that we are with you. We are with you in your suffering and joy alike.'[91] He tells them once again what his purpose now is.

While he is asleep, I'll kill Dhrishṭadyumna, the despicable murderer of my father, with my bare hands on his throat, killing him as if he was an animal.

I'll not let him have the dignity of dying with a weapon, the dignity of a warrior's death.[92]

He asks them to follow him. Soon they reach the gate of the unsuspecting and sleeping Pāñchāla army camp. For some moments, Ashvatthāmā stands there—alone. He is shining with a mysterious energy—of burning hatred and revenge.

He is astonished to find the entrance to the Pāñchāla camp being protected by a huge powerful mysterious human figure. His figure and what he is wearing are beyond description except to say that by looking at him even a mountain could break from terror.[93] But feeling no fear, Ashvatthāmā began aiming at that figure his deadly arrows, which were quickly swallowed by him. The still more powerful arrows shot at him met with the same fate. Ashvatthāmā's sword, used with great force, just disappeared in his body. The mace he threw at him broke into pieces. Soon Ashvatthāmā had no more weapons left with which to strike that mysterious figure, and he stood there, incredulous, helpless and forlorn.[94]

The *Mahābhārata* suggests that, it is not ghosts and demons but often our own a*dharma*, our own fears, which materialise in outer physical forms. We then see these as disaster willed by a cruel fate but in actual fact they are the shadows of our a*dharma*. This is what Ashvatthāmā now thinks.

न चैतदभिजानामि चिन्तयन्नपि सर्वथा ।
ध्रुवं येयमधर्मे मे प्रवृत्ता कलुषा मतिः ।। सौप्तिकपर्व ६.३० ।।

तस्याः फलमिदं घोरं प्रतिघाताय कल्पते ।
तदिदं दैवविहितं मम संख्ये निवर्तनम् ।। सौप्तिकपर्व ६.३१ ।।

I'm just not able to make out who this mysterious figure really is. It seems certain that it is my own wicked mind that I see before me in that form.[95]

Furthermore, he quickly acknowledges to himself his fear that:

ब्रुवतामप्रियं पथ्यं सुहृदां न शृणोति यः ।
स शोचत्यापदं प्राप्य यथाहमतिवर्त्य तौ ।। सौप्तिकपर्व ६.१९ ।।

शास्त्रदृष्टानविद्वान् यः समतीत्य जिघांसति ।
स पथः प्रच्युतो धर्मात् कुपथे प्रतिहन्यते ।। सौप्तिकपर्व ६.२० ।।

Whoever spurns what the kind-hearted and the caring say to him, unpleasant though it be, but is to his good, surely faces the kind of trouble I'm now in. The fool who wants to do violence to another, against every sage admonition, does violence to himself by his own hands.[96]

Pathetically powerless, and obstructed at the very beginning of his mission of revenge as duty, Ashvatthāmā sings a desperate prayer to Lord Shiva, and offers his life as an oblation to the great god.[97]

Shiva appears and smilingly holds Ashvatthāmā by his hand. 'Krishna is dear to me. Therefore, to show my respect to him I was protecting the Pāñchāla-s from you. Moreover, I wanted to test the strength of your Resolve. In protecting the Pāñchāla-s I have only honoured Krishna. But defeated by kāla, Time, their lives have now come to an end.'[98] Saying this, the great god Shiva offers a perfect sword, and enters his body.[99]

This is the most difficult part of the story to comprehend. For here human energy is seen as being united with divine energy towards revenge as duty. At the same time it is to Shiva, among others, including a meatseller, that the *Mahābhārata* attributes *ahiṃsā paramo dharmo*, 'not to do violence is the highest *dharma*', as a manifest foundation of all life and relationships.[100] Besides, in his saying that the Pāñchāla-s were already killed by kāla, there was a perfect parallel to Krishna saying to Arjuna, in the very first moments of that war, that he need not feel morally troubled, for he would only be destroying who are already dead by their *adharma*.[101] Here was offered an argument for the release from moral accountability, and from a moral dilemma, 'to fight or not to fight'. We will return to this later.

Feeling within himself a rush of new energy and force, Ashvatthāmā moves towards the place where he would find Dhrishṭadyumna sleeping in his luxurious bed. Kripāchārya and Kritavarmā had meanwhile reached the entrance to the army camp, unnoticed by anybody. Happy to see them there, Ashvatthāmā said to them in a whisper: 'If you are careful, the two of you can destroy a whole army, leave aside this one, unsuspecting, tired, and asleep. While I'll go inside, you make sure that not a single soldier escapes retribution.'[102] Kripāchārya, after giving a lecture to Ashvatthāmā on how it would be an ignoble act, an act of a*dharma*, for one warrior to attack another warrior while the latter was disarmed and asleep, had, in false loyalty, quickly abandoned that scruple, and was now himself ready for ignoble killings. And he was counted as among the venerable figures of the realm. But, on the first day of the war, he had candidly acknowledged to Yudhishṭhira, and probably for the first time to himself, that it was his *svārtha*, the bonds of self-interest, that had kept him tied to the Kaurava-s despite his knowledge of what they were.[103]

Ashvatthāmā found Dhrishṭadyumna, and striking him with his foot, woke him up. Dhrishṭadyumna, of course, recognised the son of the man he had killed. And, in the next moment, while he tried to get up from his bed, Ashvatthāmā had seized him by his hair, as Dhrishṭadyumna had seized Droṇa. Then began his slow killing. 'Enough! Kill me swiftly with a weapon,' he said in great agony to Ashvatthāmā. 'No, a murderer of your guru, you do not deserve the dignity of the death of a warrior, by a weapon. You are to be killed like an animal, which you are.' And, in the last act, Ashvatthāmā wrung his throat with his hands, and Dhrishṭadyumna died.[104]

Ashvatthāmā then looked for, and found, the five sons of the Pāṇḍava-s from Draupadī: Prativindhya, Sutasoma, Shatānika, Shrutakarmā, and Shrutakīrti, and killed them one by one, however valiantly they defended themselves.[105] Ashvatthāmā had blood flowing on his hands and the rest of his body.[106] But, even more, he had blood on his mind. With his hungry sword in his hand, Ashvatthāmā was dancing the dance of death.[107] The night seemed even more dreadful because it was so dark.[108]

Many there then remembered a dream they had at the beginning of the war, a recurring dream. They had dreamt of the Night of Death, the Kāla-rātri, dancing in her diverse forms, singing the Song of Death. Her tongue dripping with blood, her eyes red, wearing a garland of red flowers, and herself draped in a garment coloured red, claiming men and animals of the battlefield. And they dreamt that there was always Ashvatthāmā with the Night of Death. Remembering that dream, they said: 'That dream is being enacted in reality tonight.'[109]

The fierce killings were being done not wholly in the dark of night. In order greatly to please Ashvatthāmā, the other two, Kripā and Kritavarmā, had meanwhile torched the camp from three sides, so that many died in the fire thus started, and those who tried to escape from the fourth side found those two there, killing everyone mercilessly. And in the light of that fire, Ashvatthāmā was wreaking death in revenge as duty.[110] In the next moments, there was silence—the silence of death.[111]

Ashvatthāmā had entered that camp in the silence of warriors sleeping. He now left the camp in the silence of warriors dead. He had repaid the debt he owed to his slain father.[112]

The news of Ashvatthāmā killing all their five sons, and killing Dhrishṭadyumna, and the entire Pāñchāla army, is conveyed to the Pāṇḍava-s the following morning, by the driver of Dhrishṭadyumna's chariot who had somehow survived the massacre.[113] Draupadī was staying elsewhere with the women of the royal family. There was among the

Pāṇḍava-s first the complete disbelief that one person could have wrought that scale of destruction. Then Yudhishṭhira began to lament. Through the lament of Yudhishṭhira the *Mahābhārata* teaches that no victory in war is ever a complete victory, and that it turns into defeat in one way or another.

Yudhishṭhira

There are those who are victorious in their defeat. But we are defeated in our victory. Often a disaster is a blessing, but quite often what appears to be a blessing is only a disaster. Victorious, we are defeated.[114]

By having to kill the near ones in quest of victory, the victorious may for a while rejoice in their victory. But in the end they are destined to be defeated by the ever vigilant enemy.[115]

(***He laments the Pāṇḍava-s killing on the battlefield Droṇ-āchārya, Bhīshma, and Karṇa, the greatest of warriors all.***)[116]

There is for human beings no death greater than thoughtlessness. The thoughtless lose all; disasters come to them uninvited.[117]

I'm now exceedingly worried about Krishna (*another name of Draupadī*). Already she is very weak from anxiety: now, on hearing of the killings of her sons and her brother, she will be drowned in grief that will kill her.[118]

Nakula, one of Draupadī's five husbands, is sent to fetch her. In grief and misery she falls on the ground, 'looking like the sun totally eclipsed'.[119] It is Bhīma, always so tender, so gentle with her, who lifts her in his arms and tries to console her.[120] Always impatient with Yudhishṭhira, who like an unfeeling philosopher would engage her in long conversations about the virtues of forgiveness, in her deep sorrow, crying bitterly, she now mockingly addresses him thus:

Draupadī

Congratulations! Sacrificing your sons to Lord Death, in accordance with a *kshattriya* obligation, you have conquered a whole world. Enjoy it now well![121]

Congratulations! Yourself safe, you have gained a whole world. Now you will not even remember your nephew, Abhimanyu.[122]

Fortunate, too, that after the killings of your sons, you will still

> live with me, and will not remember them at all.[123]
> My grief at their death by that evil son of Droṇāchārya is now burning me as a fire would burn dry wood.[124]
> But you had better now pay heed to *my* resolve. If, in retribution of his evil deed, that wicked and evil Ashvatthāmā is not killed, I will end my life.[125]

Yudhishṭhira tries to console his wife. But by saying what he did, he deepened her sorrow only the more. 'Dear one, don't grieve for your sons and for your brother. Fighting as *dharma* would enjoin, they have attained a death *dharma* would celebrate.'[126]

Draupadī turns to Bhīma, recalls the many times in the past when he had protected her and saved her, and says to him: 'Bhīma! Only you can save me again. Find that evil son of Droṇāchārya and kill him for what he did.'[127] Unable to bear her pathetic crying, Bhīma prepares his chariot—*for his journey of revenge and retribution.* Nakula goes with him, and tracing the prints left behind by the chariot of Ashvatthāmā the previous night they were certain they would find him. They do.

Meanwhile, Sri Krishna says to Yudhishṭhira: 'Bhīma is a beloved brother of yours. In his grief, he has gone to find Ashvatthāmā, engage him in a battle, and to kill him. Why didn't you go with Bhīma? For engaging Ashvatthāmā, Bhīma will be in trouble, in very great trouble indeed.'[128] He reveals how Ashvatthāmā had in his possession a weapon of the greatest force, a weapon that could truly destroy the whole world, and how he had acquired the knowledge of it from his father Droṇāchārya, the great archery guru,[129] a weapon called *Brahmā-shiri*. Thereupon, they all go to protect Bhīma.

The rest of the events that took place may be narrated here only briefly.[130] Bhīma found Ashvatthāmā and challenged him to a duel. Meanwhile, Krishna, Yudhishṭhira and Arjuna had arrived there; on seeing them, Ashvatthāmā was struck with terror. He picked up *a piece of straw*, invested it with the power of the destructive weapon he invoked, and threw it into the air: 'May this destroy all the Pāṇḍava-s.' The awesome fire it produced would have destroyed the whole world, not just the Pāṇḍava-s. In response, on the urging of Krishna, Arjuna fired a weapon of equal force, but only after he had said a prayer for the good of the son of his guru Droṇa, for his own family, and after saying, 'May this weapon pacify the weapon of the enemy.'[131] The two weapons collided in the sky, filling the universe with their frightening light and sound, and the earth with the hills and the trees began to shake, and human hearts were filled with terror.[132] Some sages appeared on the scene, and said to them:

In your hatred and anger you have done something that has endangered all life. There have been in the past great warriors, having knowledge of weapons of many kinds. But none ever used them against mankind. Why did you do that? Withdraw your respective weapons.[133]

Arjuna did, because he *could*, having in him the greater power of self-control. But Ashvatthāmā could not:

Ashvatthāmā

Not having the power of self-control, I do not have the power of withdrawing this destructive force I've created. It must fulfil its purpose.[134]

It is aimed at destroying the Pāṇḍava-s at their very roots.[135]

There is no doubt that, in doing so, in hatred and anger, I have committed a great sin.[136] I'm protecting myself from Bhīma, who had on the battlefield killed Duryodhana by means that were low and foul.[137]

The sage Vyāsa suggests to Ashvatthāmā that he offer to the Pāṇḍava-s, in exchange for his life, the charmed jewel he had worn on his head from his very birth, and withdraw the weapon he had fired.[138]

Ashvatthāmā

The charmed jewel I carry on my head is of greater value than all the riches the Kaurava-s and the Pāṇḍava-s ever had. The happy powers of this charmed jewel are immeasurable. I must never give it up. But you are a venerable sage. My respect for you is boundless. I shall obey you.

Here I am, and here is my charmed jewel.

But I have no power to withdraw my destructive weapon. It must fulfil its aim. I am directing it at the Pāṇḍava wombs.[139]

Vyāsa

Do so. And be pacified.[140]

Krishna (*to Ashvatthāmā*)

Days ago, when Arjuna's daughter-in-law, Uttarā, was staying in the town of Uppalavya, an ascetic, on looking at her, had said to her, 'When the whole Kuru clan would have been destroyed, you would be blessed with a son, who would be called Parikṣhit, because he would be the last in the Kuru line, the words of that ascetic shall come true.[141]

Ashvatthāmā (*in great anger, to Krishna*)

Keshava! You were always partial to the Pāṇḍava-s, as you are now. But what you have just said would never happen.

My weapon would destroy the child Uttarā is carrying that you are trying to protect.[142]

Krishna (*to Ashvatthāmā*)

Son of Droṇa! The weapon you have directed at Uttarā's womb would have its effect, no doubt. Her child would be born still—and would then live long. I will bring him back to life. And you will see him being a great king, ruling for sixty years in the light of *dharma*, protecting the world.[143]

Krishna then pronounces a curse upon Ashvatthāmā.

But, in all civilised opinion, you are considered a coward; given to evil deeds again and again; a child-murderer. You are cursed. For three thousand years from now, you will drift on this earth, with no one to talk with, and live in places lonely and abandoned.

Your body will have the foul smell of flowing pus, wracked with every disease known. You will live in places where no human beings live. Go.[144]

There was here no forgiveness, no compassion, only hatred and curse.

With the speed of wind they all return to where Draupadī is, drowned in grief and sorrow. Bhīma places in her hands the charmed jewel surrendered by Ashvatthāmā in his total and humbling defeat.

Bhīma (*to Draupadī*)

Krishne! Here is the charmed jewel of Ashvatthāmā, the killer of your sons.

When Krishna on a peace mission was going to the Kaurava-s, do you remember what you had said to him then?

On hearing that, Yudhishṭhira was, for the sake of peace, keen on agreement with the Kaurava-s, you had spoken to Krishna these very hard words. 'Govinda! Neither do I have husband, nor son, neither brother, nor even you.'

The usurper of our kingdom, Duryodhana, is killed. I drank the blood of Duhshāsana, who had insulted you. Enmity has been fully avenged.

We let Ashvatthāmā go alive because he is the son of our guru and is also a Brāhmana. His renown reduced to dust, he has with him only his physical body left. His charmed jewel taken from him, he has been completely disarmed.[145]

Draupadī (*to Bhīmasena*)

In my eyes, too, the son of a guru is like the guru himself. I only wanted the killings of my sons avenged, and that has been achieved. Let this magic jewel taken from Ashvatthāmā adorn Yudhishṭhira.[146]

This story of *the endless cycle of hurt-revenge-another hurt-another revenge* has been saying many different things together, which the reader could easily read for himself or herself. The story itself is such that is being enacted everywhere, perhaps at the very time, when these lines are being written—in different forms but in substance the same. Through its last part, the *Mahābhārata* is saying, furthermore, in the language of symbols:

Hatred and the spirit of revenge are the weapons that destroy the world.

The power of physical weapons is increased beyond description by the power of anger and hatred and revenge breathed into them.

Even a piece of straw becomes a weapon of the greatest force when touched with great hatred and the greater resolve to revenge.

Once fired, the weapons of hatred and revenge cannot be withdrawn—except by those who have the greater power of self-control, forgiveness, and reconciliation.

Therefore, the physical weapons of most destructive power shall never be in the hands of those with no control over their mind and over their judgement even less.

No matter how great the danger to you, never use the weapon of ultimate force, especially never over human lives.[147]

The rationality of forgiveness and its limits

Aurva and Ashvatthāmā are only two among the many others wronged whose stories the *Mahābhārata* narrates, though not all are as grievous and extreme as theirs. And it is with the stories of men and women and children wronged, and their desire for revenge, as the familiar human material, that the *Mahābhārata* dwells on the necessity of *kṣhmā*, forgiveness and reconciliation, at the same time. It is in the voices mainly of Yudhishṭhira and his wife Draupadī, grievously wronged themselves, that the *Mahābhārata* develops the rationality of *kṣhmā*, forgiveness. Only those who have been wronged and hurt have a moral right to talk of forgiveness. It is a perfect method, a perfect device, that is rooted in life itself.

Draupadī was insulted and humiliated when Duḥshāsana had tried to disrobe her in the royal assembly, into which she was brought, being dragged by her hair. She had resisted when she was told that she was now a slave, having been put at stake by her eldest husband, Yudhishṭhira, in that game of dice which he was fraudulently made to lose. Her inner space was wholly occupied by the memory of that event ever since. What she had in mind, she expressed clearly when Krishna visited them after they were, having lost, banished from the realm.

Greatly reassured by that visit of Krishna, they discussed with him their altered situation, and he blames himself for his absence for those earlier events. Draupadī engaged his attention the most when she said: 'Because I love you, it is to you that I shall speak of my sorrow.'[148] She recounted that event in the assembly, but recalled also how, trembling with fear, she had been mortified even more by the silence of her five Pāạdava husbands, who were themselves, one by one, put at stake, and lost. 'It is an established *dharma* that even a weak husband protects his wife. For, the wife protected, one's children are protected; and the children protected, one is protected oneself. But, seeing me being treated in a way that was beastly, my husbands didn't protect me, while Karṇa was laughing at that cruel spectacle, and Duryodhana had made an obscene gesture. Why? Why did the Pāṇḍava-s, none possessed of greater strength than they, disregard my suffering?'[149] She began to cry bitterly and said:

ये मां विप्रकृतां क्षुद्रैरुपेक्षध्वं विशोकवत् ।
न च मे शाम्यते दुःखं कर्णो यत् प्राहसत् तदा ।। वन पर्व १२.१२६ ।।

नैव मे पतय: सन्ति न पुत्रा न च बान्धवा: ।
न भ्रातरो न च पिता नैव त्वं मधुसूदन ।। वन पर्व १२.१२५ ।।

All of you make light of the insult I suffered at the hands of those low men, as if it did not hurt you. The pain caused to me by Karṇa's mocking laughter never leaves me.[150]

For me, there is neither husband, nor son, nor friend, nor brother, nor father—not even you, Krishna![151]

Thirteen years passed. When out of greed, the Kaurava-s broke the condition that, after the period of banishment was over, the Pāṇḍava-s would have their share of the kingdom restored to them, a war seemed inevitable, Yudhishṭhira suggested one last attempt at reconciliation, and Krishna agreed to be the ambassador of reason and peace.[152] Draupadī argued against any such move, for it would be taken by the Kaurava-s as yet another sign of weakness. A war would doubtless have to be fought to wrench from the unjust what is justly one's inheritance. In that case, this mission of peace would receive not respect but insult, invited gratuitously. Her reasoning was disregarded, this time even by Bhīma, the mighty one, who at all times would be ready to indulge every fancy of hers, once with the knowledge that he was risking his life in doing so. Krishna shall go to the royal court at Hastināpura, and ask the Kaurava-s to behave justly and honourably.

Draupadī (***to Krishna. Her husbands listening—now with awe***)

Shame on Arjuna's skill in archery, shame on Bhīma's strength, Krishna, when Duryodhana is alive even for one moment.[153]
If I am worthy of your grace, and if you are kind to me, Krishna, keep your anger always against those sons of Dhritarāshṭra.
In all that you do towards peace, Krishna, remember these locks of my hair with which Duḥshāsana had dragged me.
If I cannot see that arm of Duḥshāsana cut into pieces, and lying in the dust, what peace can there be in my heart?
Keeping this anger in my heart like a burning fire, I have spent these thirteen years, waiting for that moment.
What pierces my heart today, like arrows, are the words of Bhīma. Disregarding me, he now sees only *dharma*.[154]

This was a most authentic setting for the *Mahābhārata* to develop *kṣhmā*, the rationality of forgiveness, with its limits.

Draupadī is arguing most forcefully for regaining through war what they had dishonestly been deprived of by their cousins, the Kaurava-s. Yudhishṭhira resists her arguments, and instead places emphasis on reconciliation, as the foundation of life. He maintains this in response to his wife's charge, that had become increasingly sharp in its expression, that there seems to be in his heart neither pain at their altered situation, nor anger against those who had brought it about. Her build-up to what is clearly an accusation, not entirely unjust, has in it emotional fire, but intellectually it is skillful even more. The purpose of both is to rouse him to anger and force.

Draupadī (*to Yudhishṭhira*)

When we set off on this life of misery and deprivation, clothed in garments mean and coarse, there were tears in the eyes of all excepting those four, wicked and evil, Duryodhana, Karṇa, Shakuni, and Duḥshāsana. They had mocking smiles on their lips, and not a tear in their eyes.[155]

Seeing what we are reduced to, and its injustice, how can you *not* be angry?

How *can* you have feelings of forgiveness towards your enemies?

A *kṣhattriya* who does not use force when time demands it, invites from everybody contempt alone. No, not for a moment must you entertain towards our enemies this feeling of reconciliation, for this is the time for force.[156]

Yudhishṭhira (*to Draupadī*)

Draupadī, if your appeal to anger and force were accepted as just principles of conduct, what kind of world would this be? There would never be peace among men, for anger is the root of all conflicts.[157]

If there were not men willing to forgive, and to subdue their anger, there would be no peace among men, for anger is the origin of all discord.[158]

If everybody is angry, then anger is returned with anger. Hurt, he hurts; violated, he violates. Fathers would kill sons, and sons would kill fathers; husbands would kill wives, and wives would kill husbands.[159]

In a world where there is only anger, Krishne, there can be no peace. For you must know, dear one, that reconciliation is the root of peace among people.[160]

It is forgiveness that keeps the world together.[161]

The opposite of forgiveness is anger and intolerance. And anger, uncontrolled, destroys men.[162]

That anger destroys human beings, this can be observed.[163]

It brings destruction all around because a man in anger does not know what should be said and what should not be said. To him, there is then nothing that must not be done, nor anything that must not be said.[164]

Driven by anger, a man can commit any offence, can kill the respected elders, by his offensive speech, insult men who are noble, or can kill even himself.[165] That is because he is not able to see a thing in its proper light and is unable to see the limits.[166]

Answering a probable question, '*Why* forgiveness*? Why not* revenge?', in the voice of Yudhishṭhira, the *Mahābhārata* says: प्रजानां संधिमूलं हि शमं विद्धि ।[167]

In that case, people will return aggression with aggression, hurt with hurt, violence with violence.[168]

In this way there will be no peace anywhere, and peace is based on reconciliation. प्रजानां संधिमूलं हि शमं विद्धि ।[169]

Therefore, a man who is wise controls his anger at all times and is ready to forgive the transgressions of others.[170]

In this world, reconciliation is the best.[171]

For, just as a man attacks another, that man attacks him in turn at the opportune moment.[172]

This is the rationality of *kṣhmā*.

Through Yudhishṭhira, the *Mahābhārata* places, therefore, the utmost emphasis on forgiveness and reconciliation.[173] The following words are as lyrical as they are profound:

क्षमा धर्मः क्षमा यज्ञः वेदाः क्षमा श्रुतम् ।
य एतदेवं जानाति स सर्वं क्षन्तुमर्हति ।। वन पर्व २९.३६ ।।

क्षमा ब्रह्म क्षमा सत्यं क्षमा भूतं च भावि च ।
क्षमा तपः क्षमा शौचं क्षमयेदं धृतं जगत् ।। वन पर्व २९.३७ ।।

क्षमा तेजस्विनां तेजः क्षमा ब्रह्म तपस्विनाम् ।
क्षमा सत्यं सत्यवतां क्षमा यज्ञः क्षमा शमः ।। वन पर्व २९.४० ।।

Forgiveness is dharma: *forgiveness is sacrifice: forgiveness is Veda: forgiveness is* sruti: *he who knows this, can forgive everything.*
Forgiveness is Brahmā, forgiveness is truth, forgiveness is the past and the future, forgiveness is austerity, forgiveness is purity. It is in reconciliation alone that the world is sustained.
Forgiveness is the force of the forceful, the Brahmā of the ascetics, the truth of the truthful, the discipline of the mind.[174]

In the *Āshvamedhika-parva*, the *Mahābhārata* narrates a long conversation between Yudhishṭhira and Sri Krishna, in which Yudhishṭhira asks him many questions about many different things. At one point, he begins to sing a most lyrical adoration of Sri Krishna.[175] Somewhat embarrassed, Krishna says to him: 'What is *this*, Yudhishṭhira? Stop it, and continue with your questions.'[176] This time, Yudhishṭhira asks what *is* true *tīrtha*, pilgrimage? Krishna describes *kṣhmā*, 'forgiveness and reconciliation', as the highest pilgrimage of all.

क्षमा तु परमं तीर्थं सर्वतीर्थेषु पाण्डव।
क्षमावतामयं लोक: परश्चैव क्षमावताम्।। आश्वमेधिक पृ. ६३७५।।
Of all the places of pilgrimage, forgiveness is the highest. The one who is forgiving secures happiness in this world and in the next world, too.[177]

क्षमा यश: क्षमा दानं क्षमा यज्ञ: क्षमा दम:।
क्षमा अहिंसा क्षमा धर्म: क्षमा चेन्द्रियनिग्रह:।। आश्वमेधिक पश. ६३७५।।
Forgiveness is true fame. Forgiveness, true giving. Forgiveness is the true yajña. *Forgiveness is the true self-control. Forgiveness is the true not-violence. Forgiveness, the true* dharma. *And forgiveness is the true discipline of one's self.*[178]

क्षमा दया क्षमा यज्ञ: क्षमयैव धृतं जगत्।। आश्वमेधिक पश. ६३७५।।
Forgiveness is the true compassion. It is forgiveness that holds the world together.[179]

But Draupadī had never disputed any of this. Neither had she ever advocated anger and force as the decisive factors in relationships *always*. She was a woman of intelligence that was as luminous as her beauty. She had moments earlier argued that to fragment reconciliation, or forgiveness, from *desha* and *kāla*, 'time and place', and the character of the person concerned, *pātra*, and then place upon it an absolute value, is to invite disrespect, not peace.

She gives numerous examples of it from daily life. She recounts a parable which, she said, she had heard as a little girl on the knees of her father. It was about a question that Bali had put to his grandfather, Prahlāda, and the latter's answer. The question was: '*Between force and reconciliation, which is superior?*' The answer was: '*Neither force nor reconciliation is good always.*'

The man who is gentle is disregarded by everybody; and the man who is harsh keeps hurting people. He who knows the occasion to be one or the other is truly a great king.[180]

Without disputing that *kshmā*, forgiveness, is a good quality, and reconciliation may be the best, Draupadī argued, on the other hand, that it would be a great mistake to think that they are so *always*.[181] Neither force nor reconciliation is good *always*: न श्रेय: सततं तेजो न नित्यं श्रेयसी क्षमा।[182]

योनित्यं क्षमते तात बहून् दोषान् स विन्दति।
भृत्या: परिभवन्त्येनमुदासीनास्तथारय: ।। वन पर्व २८.७ ।।

सर्वभूतानि चाप्यस्य न नमन्ति कदाचन।
तस्मान्नित्यं क्षमा तात पण्डितैरपि वर्जिता।। वन पर्व २८.८ ।।

He who is always forgiving invites several defects. His relatives, his subordinates, his enemies, and even those who are neutral to him, behave towards him with disrespect; nor does anybody ever show him courtesy, because forgiveness is seen as weakness, and weakness invites disrespect. Therefore, to forgive always is unwise even for the wise.[183]

But the man who uses force *always*, and never forgives, also invites many wrong things.[184] Without regard to place and occasion, full of anger and force, he keeps punishing people. He alienates friends and becomes an object of hatred to his own people; because he insults others, he suffers losses, and in turn is treated with reproach and disrespect; all around he generates anguish, hostility, and agitation, and in the process loses everything, often his life.[185]

Draupadī admonishes her husband, Yudhishṭhira, that for these reasons one should neither be always gentle nor be always forceful; rather, according to the different contexts, *desha* and *kāla*, one should be now gentle and then forceful.[186]

There is a time for forgiveness; and there is a time for force.[187]

If a person has done in the past a good turn to one, then, remembering that, even a serious offence on his part is to be forgiven.[188]

Likewise, he who has offended out of ignorance must be forgiven, for it is not possible for anybody to be wise everywhere.[189]

Just one offence is to be forgiven to everybody; the second offence, or if having knowingly committed an offence a person pretends innocence, however small the offence, then it must be punished.[190]

After careful examination, if it were found that the offence was a result of ignorance, then it is to be forgiven surely.[191]

The principle to be relied upon in these matters is this, she says. 'Whereas truly nothing is difficult with gentleness, and gentleness can conquer harshness, whether force should be applied or reconciliation, must depend on a rational grasp of *desha* and *kāla*, "time" and "place"; of one's own relative strength and weakness; and of the nature of the given situation and its cause.'[192]

> *"Gentleness achieves nothing if practised in a wrong place and at a wrong time and to a wrong person.*[193]
> *If he is always gentle, the people ignore him; if he uses force always, they become agitated. He should be gentle when it is time for gentleness, and be forceful when it is time for force."*[194]

Bhīshma expresses the same view metaphorically.

> *"In the same way as the autumn sun gives neither too great heat nor is too cold, the king should be neither too gentle nor too forceful.*[195]
> *You should not be forgiving always and everywhere. For, in being like a gentle elephant, such a king creates conditions only of* adharma.[196]
> *A gentle and forgiving king is ignored; the one who is severe and harsh always, hurts and agitates people. Therefore, according to the circumstances, take recourse to gentleness and firmness."*[197]

The argument against enmity and war

The sage Vāmadeva suggests to King Yayāti:

> अयुद्धेनैव विजयं बर्धयेद् वसुधाधिपः ।
> जघन्यमाहुर्विजयं युद्धेन च नराधिप।। शान्ति ९४.१।।
> *The victory obtained in a war is said to be only of a low quality. A king should therefore seek victory without recourse to war.*[198]

Yudhishṭhira reasons with Krishna that, first of all,

न चापि वैरं वैरेण केशव व्युपशाम्यति।
हविषाग्निर्यथा कृष्ण भूय एवाभिवर्धते।। उद्योग ७२.६३।।
Just as a fire only increases with fuel added to it, so is the fire of enmity not pacified by enmity, but increases even more.[199]

न हि वैराणि शाम्यन्ति दीर्घकालधृतान्यपि।
आख्यातारश्च विद्यन्ते पुमांश्चेद् विद्यते कुले।। उद्योग ७२.६२।।
Though suppressed for long, the fire of enmity does not die altogether. Should even one in the family remain, many would be found to narrate to him the incidents that had created the enmity.[200]

अतोऽन्यथा नास्ति शान्तिर्नित्यमन्तरमन्ततः।
अन्तरं लिप्समानानामयं दोषो निरन्तरः।। उद्योग ७२.६४।।
The other antagonist still remaining, there could be no complete peace ever. The other looking for an opportune moment, the fear of it would remain, too.[201]

Furthermore,

अन्ततो दयितं घ्नन्ति केचिदप्यपरे जनाः।
तस्याग बलहीनस्य पुत्रान् भ्रातृङ्गनपश्यतः।। उद्योग ७२.५५।।
निर्वेदो जीविते कृष्ण सर्वतश्चोपजायते।
By the time the war ends, the defeated army would have killed the loved ones of many a soldier among the victorious. Thus, though the victorious, they are left with no strength. On seeing their sons and brothers killed, they lose concern with their own lives, withdrawn from everything.[202]

अनुबन्धश्च पापोऽत्र शेषश्चाप्यवशिष्यते।
शेषो हि बलमासाद्य न शेषमनुशेषयेत्।। उद्योग ७२.५८।।
सर्वोच्छेदे च यतते वैरस्यान्तविधित्सया।
Pursuing a fleeing enemy is considered binding, but is a low act. Someone or the other among the defeated and killed would remain alive still. And the remaining enemy, gathering strength again, would aim to destroy the victorious by the roots.[203]

In saying this, Yudhishṭhira was being prophetic, without his knowing it. Though victorious at the end of the war, and regaining with his brothers their kingdom, he would live to see all his sons by Draupadī killed most cruelly by Ashvatthāmā avenging the despicable killing of his father Droṇa.[204]

The *Mahābhārata*'s argument against war above all is as follows:

Yudhishṭhira continues:

जयो नैवोभयोर्दृष्टो नोभयोश्च पराजयः।
तथैवापचयो दृष्टो व्यपयाने क्षयव्ययौ।। उद्योग ७२.५२।।

Neither of the two sides are seen anywhere to be victorious; nor are both sides seen to be defeated. What is seen, though, is the destruction of their prosperity alike.[205]

सर्वथा वृजिनं युद्धं को घ्नन् न प्रतिहन्यते।
हतस्य च हृषीकेश समौ जयपराजयौ।। उद्योग ७२.५३।।

War always is deceitful and wicked. In killing another, who is not himself killed also? And to the one killed in the war, victory and defeat are just the same.[206]

पराजयश्च मरणान्मन्ये नैव विशिष्यते।
यस्य स्याद् विजयः कृष्ण तस्याप्यपचयो ध्रुवम्।। उद्योग ७२.५४।।

I believe that death is no worse than defeat. But the victorious suffer as well.[207]

प्रतिघातेन सान्त्वस्य दारुणं सम्प्रवर्तते।
तच्छुनामिव सम्पाते पण्डितैरुपलक्षितम्।। उद्योग ७२.७०।।

Peace obstructed, war starts. The learned and the wise think it to be akin to a fight between two dogs.[208]

लाङ्गूलचालनं क्ष्वेडा प्रतिवाचो विवर्तनम्।
दन्तदर्शनमारावस्ततो युद्धं प्रवर्तते।। उद्योग ७२.७१।।

First they wag their tails, then bark, then approach each other. Then they show their teeth, and bark even louder. Then they begin to fight.[209]

तत्र यो बलवान् कृष्ण जित्वा सोऽत्ति तदामिषम्।
एवमेव मनुष्येषु विशेषो नास्ति कश्चन।। उद्योग ७२.७२।।

The stronger of the two gets the piece of meat over which they fought. The same is true about human beings. There is no difference.[210]

In another distressing context, the bird Pujanīya says to King Brahmadatta:

न हि वैराग्निरुद्भूत: कर्म चाप्यपराधजम्।
शाम्यत्यदग्ध्वा नृपते विना ह्येकतरक्षयात्।। शान्ति १३९.४६।।

Once lighted, the fire of enmity is extinguished not until one of the two sides to it is destroyed. Neither is an offensive act avenged until one of the two is destroyed.[211]

न हि वैराणि शाम्यन्ति कुले दु:खगतानि च।
आख्यातारश्च विद्यन्ते कुले बै ध्रियते पुमान्।। शान्ति १३९.७२।।

When enmity that can produce only suffering starts in a family, it is never pacified. There are always those who keep stoking its memory. Thus, so long as even one person is alive in that family, the enmity does not end.[212]

उपगृह्य तु वैराणि सान्त्वयन्ति नराधिप।
अथैनं प्रतिपिषन्ति पूर्णं घटमिवाश्मनि।। शान्ति १३९.७३।।

Harbouring enmity in their hearts, the wicked speak reassuring words though; but no sooner is the moment right than they destroy the other, as one would a clay pot with a stone.[213]

Every reason points to this. Therefore, as suggested by Bhīshma to Yudhishṭhira who had asked: 'By what means should a king conquer his enemies?'[214]

वर्जनीयं सदा युद्धं राज्यकामेन धीमता।। शान्ति ६९.२३।।

The king wanting the welfare of his kingdom should avoid war always.[215]

आत्मा जेय: सदा राज्ञा ततो जेयाश्च शत्रव:।
अजितात्मा नरपतिर्विजयेत कथं रिपून्।। शान्ति ६९.४।।

The king should always conquer himself first; for only then could he conquer his enemy. How would the king who has not conquered his own self conquer the enemy ever?[216]

नाधर्मेण महीं जेतुं लिप्सत जगतीपति:।
अधर्मविजयं लब्ध्वा को नु मन्येत भूमिप:।। शान्ति ९६.१।।

No king should ever wish to be the lord of the earth through adharma. *Achieving victory, but through* adharma, *which king can hope to gain respect too?*[217]

And violence, *hiṃsā*, in thought and in speech and in act, is the embodiment of *adharma*.

In the voice of a mother trying to reason with her son, Gāndhāri to Duryodhana, the *Mahābhārata* concludes:

न युद्धे तात कल्याणं न धर्माथौ कुतः सुखम् ।
न चापि विजयो नित्यं मा युद्धे चे आधिथाः ।। उद्योग १२९.४० ।।

There is no good in war, dear son, nor any holding together in the foundations of life. Where can there be in war any happiness? Nor is there any certainty of victory in every war. Therefore, do not put in it your thoughts and expectations.[218]

At the same time, the *Mahābhārata* dwells at length, and with great care, on what should be done for internal security in times of war, should war become inevitable, and at the battlefield to win the battle.

However, through it all, the foundations, the *dharma*, are repeatedly emphasised. Because war achieves no permanent good, only begins a long chain of pain and suffering, war should be avoided by all means. If it cannot be avoided, then there is a *dharma*, too, of how a war is to be conducted in human terms. Thus, beside the maxim that '*A debt left unpaid, an illness ignored, a fire not wholly extinguished, and a defeated enemy left alive, would be a cause of great fear always; none of them should therefore be left unfinished*',[219] immediately there is also this injunction, repeated numerous times:

The enemy who is exhausted; is fearful; has laid down his arms; is crying; or is running away; has no weapons left to fight with, or has given up the fight; is sick; is pleading for his life; is young or is old, must never be killed.[220]
Whoever is in such a state must indeed be protected:[221]

भग्नशस्त्रो विपन्नश्च कृत्तज्यो हतवाहनः ।
चिकित्स्यः स्यात् स्वविषये प्राप्यो वा स्वगृहे भवेत् ।। शान्ति ९५.१३ ।।

Whose weapons are broken; who finds himself in trouble; the string of whose bow is snapped; whose battle horse is killed—he should never be attacked. Such an enemy falling into one's hands, his wounds should be tended, and he should be taken to his home.[222]

The *Mahābhārata* is saying that there is honour even among thieves.[223]

यथा सद्भिः परादानमहिंसा दस्युभिः कृता।
अनुरज्यन्ति भूतानि समर्यादिषु दस्युषु।। शान्ति १३३.१५ ।।
Even among robbers there is a sense of limits. They will rob but will not cause physical violence. Why, many persons have a feeling even of affection for them, for the robbers also do some good to some.[224]

अयुद्ध्यमानस्य वधो दारामर्षः कृतघ्नता।
ब्रह्मवित्तस्य चादानं निःशेषकरणं तथा।। शान्ति १३३.१६ ।।
स्त्रियामोषः पतिस्थानं दस्युष्वेतद् विगर्हितम्।
संश्लेषं च परस्त्रीभिर्दस्युरेतानि वर्जयेत्।। शान्ति १३३.१७ ।।
To kill someone not in combat; to rape a woman, or misbehave with her; ingratitude; to rob one devoted to learning and knowledge; to deprive another of all he has—these are considered very low acts even among robbers.[225]

In this context, the *Mahābhārata* narrates the story of Kāyavya.[226] An elderly man, Kāyavya had been a robber by profession, a kindly robber, though. He now lived a disciplined life in relation with his self.[227] One day, assembling together, a thousand other robbers, who knew no limits and were cruel in their deeds, proposed to him that he become their leader. 'You have the knowledge of "time", "place", and "the appropriate moment". You are wise and brave and resolute in your promises. By our common consent we propose that you be our leader. We will follow your commands, and you take care of us as one's parents would.'[228]

'Very well, but on certain promises,' Kāyavya said to those robbers.

मा वधीस्त्वं स्त्रियं भीरुं मा शिशुं मा तपस्विनम्।
नायुद्ध्यमानो हन्तव्यो न च ग्राह्या बलात् स्त्रियः।। शान्ति १३५.१३ ।।
You shall never kill a woman, a child, or an ascetic. Nor kill any one not in combat with you. You shall never hold a woman by force.[229]

सर्वथा स्त्री न हन्तव्या सर्वसत्त्वेषु केनचित्।
नित्यं तु ब्राह्मणे स्वस्ति योद्धव्यं च तदर्थतः।। शान्ति १३५.१४ ।।
No one among you shall ever kill a woman. And you shall look to the welfare especially of those devoted to learning and knowledge. You would, should it become necessary, even fight for their sake.[230]

शस्यं च नापि हर्तव्यं सारविघ्नं च मा कृथाः ।
पूज्यन्ते यत्र देवाश्च पितरोऽतिथयस्तथा ।। शान्ति १३५.१५ ।।

You shall not destroy a harvest in the field; nor obstruct a marriage ceremony; nor create trouble where the gods, the ancestors, and guests are respected.[231]

इहैव फलमासीनः प्रत्याकाङ्क्षेत सर्वशः ।
ये ये नो न प्रदास्यन्ति तांस्तांस्तेनोभियास्यसि ।। शान्ति १३५.१९ ।।

You shall confine your robbing only to those who do not give you voluntarily some money.[232]

शिष्ट्यर्थेविहितो दण्डो न वृद्ध्यर्थं विनिश्चयः ।
ये च शिष्टान् प्रबाधन्ते दण्डस्तेषां वधः स्मृतः ।। शान्ति १३५.२० ।।

And you shall always remember that force is meant to be used against the wicked, not to harass those who are good.[233]

ये पुनर्धर्मशास्त्रेण वर्तेरन्निह दस्यवः ।
अपि ते दस्यवो भूत्वा क्षिप्रं सिद्धिमवाप्नुयुः ।। शान्ति १३५.२२ ।।

In their conduct towards others thus, even the robbers acquire a higher state of being.[234]

On hearing this, they said to him in one voice: 'To that we give you our pledge.' What Kāyavya was saying to them was: 'If a robber you must be, be a caring robber. The rest will follow.' The rest *did* follow. They gradually gave up the violence of robbing others altogether. Kāyavya had shown them a better way of living.[235] That he did, not by giving them a long lecture on not-violence, but first by showing them that even in violence there are limits one should never transgress.

Violence in speech and words

The *Mahābhārata* says: '*All functions of the world are tied with speech.*' वाक् प्रबद्धो हि संसारो.[236] Just as *vāni*, speech, expresses love, affection and friendship, it is an instrument also of violence. The larger number of prudence maxims centre on the evident necessity of self-control, of which the most essential is control over one's tongue. Hence, the general maxim:

विवक्षता च सद्वाक्यं धर्मं सूक्ष्ममवेक्षता।
सत्यां वाचमहिंस्त्रां च वदेदनपवादिनीम्।। शान्ति २१५.१०।।
He who can see the subtlety of dharma, *and wishes to cultivate proper speech, should speak in a way that what he says is true as well as free from violence and denunciation of others.*[237]

The *Mahābhārata* evokes the effects that hurtful and dry words must necessarily produce in the *other*.[238]

वाक्सायका वदनान्निष्पतन्ति
यैराहतः शोचति रात्र्यहानि।
परस्य नामर्मसु ते पतन्ति
तान् पण्डितो नावसृजेत् परेभ्यः।। उद्योग ३४.८०।।
They are like arrows that burn the bones and the heart and the life of their victim, who day and night is pained by them. The wise man should therefore forever give up hurtful speech.[239]

रोहते सायकैर्विद्धं वनं परशुना हतम्।
वाचा दुरुक्तं बीभत्सं न सरोहति वाक्क्षतम्।। अनुशासन १०४.३३।।
The trees pierced by arrows or cut by the axe grow again, but the dreadful wound by nasty words does not ever heal.[240]

कर्णिनालीकनाराचान् निर्हरन्ति शरीरतः।
वाक्शल्यस्तु न निर्हर्तुं शक्यो हृदिशयो हि सः।। अनुशासन १०४.३४।।
The ear-shaped arrow, or the spear, or the arrow made of iron, can still be removed from the body, but it is impossible to remove the arrow of hurting words, for it gets embedded in the heart.[241]

नारुन्तुदः स्यान्न सृशंसवादी
न हीनतः परमभ्याददीत।
ययास्य वाचा पर उद्विजेत
न तां वदेद् रुषतीं पापलोक्याम्।। अनुशासन १०४.३१।।
One should not therefore hurt where it is most vulnerable. Do not speak cruelly and lower others, or speak in a manner that agitates others.[242]

अरुन्तुदं परुषं रूक्षवाचं
वाक्कण्टकैर्वितुदन्तं मनुष्यान्।

विद्यादलक्ष्मीकतमं जनानां
मुखे निबद्धां निर्ऋतिं वै वहन्तम् ।। उद्योग ३६.८ ।।
He whose speech is dry and whose heart hard, who by his speech hurts and causes pain to others, should among men be regarded as the poorest of all, carrying in his mouth poverty and death.[243]

The *Shukranīti* says:

तीक्ष्णवाक्यान्मित्रमपि तत्कालं याति शत्रुतां
वक्रोक्तिशल्यमुद्धर्तु न शक्यं मानसं यतः ।। शुक्रनीति ३.२३३ ।।
Harsh words make instant enemies of friends, even those of long standing and the ones who are honoured, for the sting of sharp words cannot be removed from the mind.[244]

न भूषयत्यलंकारो न राज्यं न च पौरुषं ।
न विद्या न धनं तादृग्यादृक् सौजन्यभूषणम् ।। शुक्रनीति ३.२३६ ।।
Neither the splendour of ornaments, nor a kingdom, neither bravery, nor learning, nor wealth, is comparable to courtesy and gentleness.[245]

The *Pañchatantra* says:

रोहति सायकैविद्धं छिन्नं रोहति चासिना ।
वचो दुरुक्तं बीभत्सं न प्ररोहति वाक्क्षतम् ।। पन्चतंत्र ३.११२ ।।
The wound caused by an arrow is healed, and so is healed the wound caused by a sword, but the wound of hurtful speech is never healed.[246]

अदेशकालज्ञमनायतिक्षमं यदप्रियं लाधवकारि चात्मनः ।
योऽत्राब्रतीत्कारणवर्जित वचो न तद्वचः स्याद्विषमेव तद्वचः ।। पन्चतंत्र ३.११३ ।।
What is spoken without regard to place and time, is bitter in result, is unpleasant, displays one's meanness, and is spoken without cause—that is not speech but poison.[247]

वैरं पञ्चसमुत्थानं तच्च बुध्यन्ति पण्डिताः ।
स्त्रीकृतं वास्तुजं वाग्जं ससापत्नापराधजम् ।। शान्ति १३९.४२ ।।
Of the five causes of enmity, hard speech is one, woman, property, natural conflict, and previous offence comprising the rest.[248]

Hence the repeated warnings against harshness of speech, not in its form alone but in its content as well. Hence also the repeated injunction in the *Mahābhārata*, and in the other *nīti* literature, that one speak gently and pleasantly.

वात्सल्यात्सर्वभूतेभ्यो वाच्याः श्रोत्रसुखागिरः।
परितापोपघातश्च पारुष्यं चात्र गर्हितम्।। शान्ति १९१.१४।।

One's speech should be marked with affection towards all human beings and with pleasantness to the ears. To hurt others with wounding words is a low act.[249]

अभ्यावहति कल्याणं विविधं वाक् सुभाषिता।
सैव दुर्भाषिता राजन्ननर्थायोपपद्यते।। उद्योग ३४.७७।।

Spoken pleasantly, speech brings happiness in many ways; spoken harshly, it causes disaster.[250]

मार्दवं सर्वभूतेषु व्यवहारेषु चार्जवम्।
वाक् चैव मधुरा प्रोक्ता श्रेय एतदसंशयम्।। शान्ति २८७.१८।।

To be gentle to others, to be simple and straightforward in one's conduct, and to speak sweetly and kindly, are without doubt the way to the Good.[251]

There is the corresponding teaching against speaking ill of others, which pollutes one's own mind and does injury to others.[252] The *Shānti-parva* in the *Mahābhārata*, more than any other work, analysed this problem with objectivity and understanding and severely condemned the habit of speaking ill of others in their absence.

न वाच्यः परिवादोऽयं न श्रोतव्यः कथञ्चन।
कर्णावथ पिधातव्यौ प्रस्थेयं चान्यतो भवेत्।। शान्ति १३२.१२।।

One should not denigrate another, nor hear the other being denigrated. On hearing another being denigrated, one should either close one's ears or leave that place.[253]

असतां शीलमेतद् वै परिवादोऽथ पैशुनम्।
गुणानामेव वक्तारः सन्तः सत्सु नराधिप।। शान्ति १३२.१३।।

To speak ill of others is in the nature of those who are low. The good and the saintly speak of what is good in others.[254]

आत्मोत्कर्षं न मार्गेत परेषां परिनिन्दिया।
स्वगुणैरेव मार्गेत विप्रकर्षं पृथग्जनात्।। शान्ति २८७.२५।।

To denigrate others is not the way of raising oneself. To show one's superiority is to prove it by one's qualities.

निर्गुणास्त्वेव भूयिष्ठमात्मसम्भाविता नराः।
दोषैरन्यान् गुणवतः क्षिपन्त्यात्मगुणक्षयात्।। शान्ति २८७.२६।।

Only those without qualities denigrate others. Aware of their own lack of excellence, they criticise persons of quality.[255]

अनूच्यमानास्तु पुनस्ते मन्यन्तु महाजनात्।
गुणवत्तरमात्मानं स्वेन मानेन दर्पिताः।। शान्ति २८७.२७।।

If they are engaged in return, they in their pride regard themselves even greater than the great.[256]

अब्रुवन् कस्यचिन्निन्दामात्मपूजामवर्णयन्।
विपश्चिद् गुणसम्पन्नः प्राप्नोत्येव महद् यशः।। शान्ति २८७.२८।।

But the one who does not denigrate another, neither recites self-praise, such a person of quality gains high acclaim.[257]

अब्रुवन् वाति सुरभिर्गन्धः सुमनसां शुचिः।
तथैवाव्याहरन् भाति विमलो भानुरम्बरे।। शान्ति २८७.२९।।

Flowers do not proclaim themselves before giving their pure fragrance. Neither does the sun announce itself before shining in the sky.[258]

एवमादीनि चान्यानि परित्यक्तानि मेधया।
ज्वलन्ति यशसा लोके यानि न व्याहरन्ति च।। शान्ति २८७.३०।।

There are many things in the world that likewise shine without self-praise.[259]

न लोके दीप्यते मूर्खः केवलात्मप्रशंसया।
अपि चापिहितः श्वभ्रे कृतविद्यः प्रकाशते।। शान्ति २८७.३१।।

The fools cannot by self-praise alone shine in the world. But, assuredly, a person of excellence, be he hidden somewhere, will come into light.[260]

असदुच्चैरपि प्रोक्तः शब्दः समुपशाम्यति।
दीप्यते त्वेव लोकेषु शनैरपि सुभाषितम्।। शान्ति २८७.३२।।

Untruth, even if spoken loudly, vanishes into emptiness; the true and the good, even if spoken in a whisper, shines in the world.[261]

The *Mahābhārata* finds no conflict between strength and gentleness,[262] or between pleasant speech and truth. The central point of dharmic prudence has been:

परपरिवादः परिषदि न कथञ्चित्पण्डितेन वक्तव्यः।
सत्यमपि तन्न वाच्यं यदुक्तमसुखावहं भवति।। पंचतन्त्र III.११५।।

The wise should not denigrate another in the assembly of men, indeed, not even speak the truth if it is hurtful.
Speak the truth, speak pleasantly, but do not speak the truth if it is unpleasant.[263]

The perceptions of 'truth' in the *Mahābhārata*, as we saw in the previous chapter, are thoroughly secular, being in relationship with one's self and with the *other* in ways that sustain, enhance, bring together, and do no violence to one's self and to the *other*.

सत्यस्य वचनं श्रेयः सत्यज्ञानं तु दुष्करम्।
यद् भूतहितमत्यन्तमेतत् सत्यं ब्रवीम्यहम्।। शान्ति २८७.२०।।

It is best to speak the truth, but what really is truth is exceedingly difficult to know. I call only that truth that serves universal good. '[264]

That includes, of course, self-interest. This, too, is clearly stated, and the harmony between the two is made the very source of fulfilment of all endeavour.[265]

The prudence literature in the *Mahābhārata* displays at the same time the awareness that, understanding neither self-interest nor the importance of time and place with which it is connected, most people might as easily misinterpret the maxims of prudence. In order to prevent prudence from turning into a lack of principles, and the talk of 'time' and 'place' into a lack of scruple, every prudence maxim is balanced by its opposite. But self-interest is still kept as the basis of that balance.

For example, the advice against speaking unpleasant truth, if taken too literally, or pressed too far, may turn against one's own best interest, for there *are* occasions when the unpleasant truth must be spoken. In the voice of Vidura, the *Mahābhārata* says:

सुलभा पुरुषा राजन् सततं प्रियवादिनः।
अप्रियस्य तु पथ्यस्य वक्ता श्रोता च दुर्लभः।। उद्योग ३७.१५।।

Men who always speak pleasantly are easily met; rare are the people who speak, and listen to, words that are unpleasant but to one's good.[266]

यो हि धर्मं समाश्रित्य हित्वा भर्तुः प्रियाप्रिये।
आप्रियाण्याह पथ्यानि तेन राजा सहायवान्।। उद्योग ३७.१६।।
Based on dharma, *and regardless of pleasant or unpleasant, he who speaks for the good of the other, even if what is spoken be unpleasant, is a true friend to the king.*[267]

अव्याहृतं व्याहृताच्छ्रेय आहुः
सत्यं वदेद् व्याहृतं तद् द्वितीयम्।
प्रियं वदेद् व्याहृतं तत् तृतीयं
धर्मं वदेद् व्याहृतं तश्चतुर्थम्।। उद्योग ३६.१२।।
Silence is the first quality of speech; speaking the truth, the second; speaking pleasantly, the third; and speaking according to dharma, *the fourth.*[268]

It is accepted that '*One should not speak unpleasant truth.*' But it is added: '*One should not speak pleasant falsehood either.*'[269]

'Trust' and 'distrust' are related with *ahiṃsā* and violence. They are undoubtedly related with prudence and self-interest as well. The *Mahābhārata* suggests that:

न श्रद्दधाति कल्याणं परेभ्योऽप्यात्मशङ्कितः।
निराकरोति मित्राणि यो वै सोऽधमपूरुषः।। उद्योग ३६.१९।।
The one who, distrustful of himself, never expects any good to come from others, and does not make friends, is verily a low man.[270]

न तन्मित्रं यस्य कोपाद् बिभेति
यद् वा मित्रं शङ्कितेनोपचर्यम्।
यस्मिन् मित्रे पितरीवाश्वसीत
तद् वै मित्रं सङ्गतानीतराणि।। उद्योग ३६.३७।।
He whose anger one must fear, and in whose company one must remain distrustful, is not a friend; a friend is one who can be trusted like a father. Others are mere companions.[271]

Violence to one's self

Whereas in the West, pain and suffering were cultivated as the conscious means to self-experience and maximum feeling, in a considerable part of Indian thought, pain was sought for the very opposite reason—to gain freedom from experience, and from feelings, too. Through a great part of Indian thought there runs a definite fear of happiness, for happiness is seen as transitory, and what is transitory is perceived as of little value, for it is productive eventually of pain.

From that arose the sweeping conclusion that pleasure and happiness are only concealed *duḥkha*, pain. From that point onwards, through incalculable mutations of ideas and perceptions, there arose the love of self-inflicted suffering, and from that the love of violence, both to one's self and to the *other*. First came the notion that if *duḥkha* is to be avoided, pleasure and happiness are to be spurned as well. Then came the oppressive harangue of '*detachment*', '*renunciation*', '*denial*', 'abstinence'. All these, removed from their proper meaning, twisted and wrongly arranged, turned into a rich vocabulary of negation. From that arose aggression against joy, against happiness. Thus, a personality was formed, individual and collective, that was rooted in the philosophy of the fear of happiness, and grew in the mutated love of pain and violence to one's self, its expressions manifold. It had already taken shape in the vedic times, and the *Upanishad*-s were a decided moving away from it. After stating faithfully the argument for self-denial and its logic, the *Mahābhārata* then demonstrates how, wrenched from its proper context, it must turn into violence to one's self.

That *sannyāsa* is not 'renunciation' of the world and its joys, and that *saṃyama*, or self-control, is neither 'denial' nor 'abstinence', becomes perfectly clear if we just look at the root meaning of the word *sam*, which is a prefix to a great many words, including these two. *Sam* means 'holding together'. When it is used in the word *sam-nyāsa*, and the word *nyāsa* means '*to lay down*', '*to place*', as in a foundation, the composite word then means '*holding together the foundations*', or '*to know the proper place of everything*'. Thus, the state of *sam-nyāsa* is not a state of withdrawal or renunciation but a state of knowing the true place of human attributes in their natural unity. Similarly, the word *sama-yama* was wrongly perceived as meaning 'abstinence from sexual intercourse', when actually it means '*to hold together*', '*govern*', '*guide*'. These two examples will show how, completely misread, those states of the mind that affirm the proper place of everything that is human, and thus invoke the joy of life, are turned into negativity and its gratuitous violence, to one's self most of all.

Dharmic thought had never maintained that to inflict pain and suffering on one's body are prerequisites of finding one's self. The *Upanishad*-s, the *Mahābhārata*, the Jaina philosophy, the *Yoga-Vāsishṭha*, rather make us aware of those very many wrong perceptions as regards human personality that prevent us from experiencing the joy and happiness which is rightfully ours as human beings.

A person may easily conceal in a philosophy of revolutionary violence his, or her, personal delight in the acts of violence, and the ideology of revolution becomes a metaphysical justification of organised murder.[272] In the same way, in the philosophy of renunciation a person may easily conceal his, or her, incapacity for love. These have to be distinguished clearly and sharply, which the *Mahābhārata* does. In talking about the attributes of a free person, the *Mahābhārata* speaks of his 'love for all beings' and 'ever working for the happiness and the good of others' as the visible attributes by which a free person is recognised. 'Love for others' and 'working for the happiness and the good of others' are *feelings*. They are not meant to remain *concepts*. *Mokṣha* is always spoken of as a state of *ānanda*, which includes the feelings of simple human happiness, in the simple human acts of relating one's self with the self of the *other* in a way that each is enhanced.

There is another source of violence to one's self, and to the other thereby—the widespread notion that happiness is unexciting, boring. There is in happiness neither excitement nor exhilaration, and it is with them that we equate life. We then equate suffering with self-awareness, or self-knowledge. Just as we become acutely aware of our 'body' in a state of fever, it is in a state of suffering that we become aware of our deeper self. In this logic we soon make a reverse movement, in which sensitive intelligence is now equated with unhappiness. Only a fool can be happy. There is no literature in happiness, and that is why happiness has no literature. We then seek, cultivate, and spread *duḥkha*, unhappiness and violence, as the means both to a greater thrill and a greater awareness of the mystery of life. To say that we often mature through suffering is one thing, but to court pain and suffering as means to self-understanding and self-awareness is something altogether different. It is the latter which is false and dangerous. For it leads to the notion that there is in violence, inflicted upon one's self and others, so much more of life than there is in *ahiṃsā*. Hatred seems far more occupying than love, and, it is freely admitted, a bond stronger than the bonds of love and affection.

There are in the *Mahābhārata* a great many more stories of anger and hatred and revenge and war than of friendship and tenderness and love. There is not much laughter in it either, although there is plenty of irony. From this it will be easy to conclude that the *Mahābhārata* is more about the love of violence than about freedom from violence, more about *hiṃ sā* than about *ahiṃsā*. But if we constantly keep in mind the method it follows, it will also remain clear why.

Human passions that assail the mind are also called *kashāya*. The literal meaning of this word is '*to injure*', '*to hurt*', '*to destroy, kill*'. The *kashāya*-s of which the *Mahābhārata* constantly speaks, in every context, at every turn, are 'greed', 'anger', 'vanity and pride', 'falsehood and insincerity'. These injure and hurt one's self even before they hurt and injure the *other*. They certainly destroy and kill. That they do even in medical terms, there being an intimate relatedness between psyche and soma, the mind and the body. Violence to the one is also violence to the other. Hence, playing upon two similar sounding words, the other *kashāya* meaning 'ochre colour', the traditional colour of a renouncer's dress, King Janaka's wife says to him:

अनिष्कषाये काषायमीहार्थमिति विद्धि तम् ।
धर्मध्वजानां मुण्डानां वृत्त्यर्थमिति मे मिति: ।। शान्ति १८.३४ ।।
If one has not removed one's passions of the mind, kashāya, *it is no good wearing an ochre robe,* kashāya, *only a means to serving one's selfish ends.*[273]

Freedom from fear: Freedom from the violence of history

Freedom from fear is akin to the gift of life. Therefore:

सर्वभूतेषु यो विद्वान् ददात्यभयदक्षिणाम् ।
दाता भवति लोके स प्राणानां नात्र संशय: ।। अनुशासन ११५.१८ ।।
The man with wisdom securing for others freedom from fear becomes a giver of life—this is beyond doubt.[274]

एवं वै परमं धर्मं प्रशंसन्ति मनीषिण: ।
प्राणा यथाऽऽत्मनोऽभीष्टा भूतानामपि वै तथा ।। अनुशासन ११५.१९ ।।

It is for this reason that men of intelligence praise not-violence as the highest dharma. *For just as one desires one's life, the others desire their life likewise.*[275]

अभयं सर्वभूतेभ्यो यो ददाति दयापर: ।
अभयं तस्य भूतानि ददतीत्यनुशुश्रुम ।। अनुशासन ११६.१३ ।।

The man who, suffused with the spirit of kindness, offers to all beings freedom from fear, is himself offered by them freedom from fear. This is what I have heard.[276]

On this subject, Tulādhāra the grocer says to Jājali the ascetic:

तपोभिर्यज्ञदानैश्च वाक्यै: प्रज्ञाश्रितैस्तथा ।
प्राप्नोत्यभयदानस्य यद् यत् फलमिहाश्नुते ।। शान्ति २६२.२८ ।।

Whatever one could gain from austerity, from performing yajña, *from giving gifts, and from learning and knowledge—that he would gain alone by giving others freedom from fear.*[277]

लोके य: सर्वभूतेभ्यो ददात्यभयदक्षिणाम् ।
स सर्वयज्ञैरीजान: प्राप्नोत्यभयदक्षिणाम् ।। शान्ति २६२.२९ ।।

Whoever in this world gives to all beings freedom from fear, gains all that he would have by performing all the yajña-s, *and receive himself freedom from fear.*[278]

न भूतानामहिंसाया ज्यायान् धर्मोऽस्ति कश्चन ।
यस्मान्नोद्विजते भूतं जातु किंचित् कथंचन ।
सोऽभयं सर्वभूतेभ्य: सम्प्राप्नोति महामुने ।। शान्ति २६२.३० ।।

The dharma *one achieves by doing no violence to any being, greater than that there is no* dharma. *Who causes in others neither disquiet nor agitation, he becomes free himself from fear.*[279]

दानं भूताभयस्याहु: सर्वदानेभ्य उत्तमम् ।
ब्रवीमि ते सत्यमिदं श्रद्दधस्व च जाजले ।। शान्ति २६२.३३ ।।

Believe in what I'm saying to you, for it is true: there is no greater gift in life than the gift of freedom from fear.[280]

सर्वभूतात्मभूतस्य सर्वभूतानि पश्यतः ।
देवाऽपि मार्गे मुह्यन्ति अपदस्य पदैषिणः ।। शान्ति २६२.३२ ।।
Who sees his self in the others, and the others in his self, achieves a state of being where not even the gods of the universe could trace his footsteps.[281]

In their long conversation about the great questions of life, Shiva says to his wife Umā:

सर्वभूतेषु यः सम्यग् ददात्यभयदक्षिणाम् ।
हिंसादोषविमुक्तात्मा स वै धर्मेण युज्यते ।। अनुशासन १४२.२७ ।।
Freeing himself from violence, who offers to other beings the gift of freedom from fear, only he is in unity with dharma.[282]

सर्वभूतानुकम्पी यः सर्वभूतार्जवव्रतः ।
सर्वभूतात्मभूतश्च स वै धर्मेण युज्यते ।। अनुशासन १४२.२८ ।।
He alone is in unity with dharma *who has compassion towards all beings, is open and straightforward in his relations with others, and looks upon all beings as his own.*[283]

We will see in a later chapter of this book on *dharma* as the foundation of law and governance, how one of the chief obligations of the state is to create social conditions for the people to live without fear and its violence.[284] The *Mahābhārata* binds the king to his duty that he shall:

स्वतश्च परतश्चैव परस्परभयादपि ।
अमानुषभयेभ्यश्च स्वाः प्रजाः पालयेन्नृपः ।। अनुशासन पश. ५९५० ।।
Protect his subjects from their fear of him, from their fear of others, from their fear of each other, and from their fear of things that are not human.[285]

In that chapter we will see also the *Mahābhārata*'s simultaneous perceptions of the human material being such, though, that it mostly responds not to the language of love but to the language of fear. Hence the necessity of the fear of law and governance, *daṇḍa*, as a basis of social order at the same time as freedom from fear.[286]

Furthermore, violence in the present is quite as often, indeed mostly, an outcome of memory. That is to say, violence is an outcome of history, as can be seen everywhere. As one of its central concerns, the *Mahābhārata* is concerned with the evident paradox of history, which is the paradox of memory. Without memory we are nothing, human existence rooted in history; at the same time, *that* without which we are nothing, becomes our prison, in which we keep hearing, day and night, the fearful menacing sounds of the past. The *Mahābhārata* teaches, in the language of a reasoned and passionate concern, freedom from history, freedom from memory, freedom from what is past, as the final freedom from fear and its violence.[287]

In the voice of the sage Nārada to the young Shukadeva, the substance of the rationality of freedom from the violence of the memory of the past is as follows. It begins with what is universally true about human existence.

शोकस्थानसहस्राणि भयस्थानशतानि च ।
दिवसे दिवसे मूढमाविशन्ति न पण्डितम् ।। शान्ति ३३०.२ ।।
There are a hundred occasions for fear, and a thousand occasions for sorrow. They touch only the one who does not understand, and not the one who does.[288]

Seen from one perspective, there is no doubt that:

सुखाद् बहुतरं दुःखं जीविते नात्र संशयः ।
स्निग्धत्वं चेन्द्रियार्थेषु मोहान्मरणमप्रियम् ।। शान्ति ३३०.१६ ।।
In life there is more unhappiness than happiness. Everyone feels drawn towards the pleasures, and unhappy when they die.[289]

But it is also true that the memory of past unhappiness is unhappiness twice over, for now it is transferred to the present. To grieve for the past is to do violence to one's self.

मृतं वा यदि वा नष्टं योऽतीतमनुशोचति ।
दुःखेन लभते दुःख द्वावनर्थौ प्रपद्यते ।। शान्ति ३३०.९ ।।
Thinking of what has come to an end, and of what has been destroyed, who is drowned in thinking of the past hurts himself twice.[290]

भैषज्यमेतद् दुःखस्य यदेतन्नानुचिन्तयेत् ।
चिन्त्यमानं हि न व्येति भूयश्चापि प्रवर्धते ।। शान्ति ३३०.१२ ।।
The best cure for unhappiness is not to think of it too much. By thinking of one's unhappiness too much, it will not go away but will only increase.[291]

It is futile to brood over one's sufferings. For not only does pain not become less thereby, but one loses also one's capacity to discriminate and act, thus giving rise to suffering twice over.[292]

> दुःखोपघाते शारीरे मानसे चाप्युपस्थिते।
> यस्मिन् न शक्यते कर्तुं यत्नस्तन्नानुचिन्तयेत्।। शान्ति ३३०.११।।
> *If unhappiness is caused by physical or mental reasons, and nothing can be done about it, or what was done was not fruitful, then do not dwell upon it.*[293]

Through many stories, the stories of human situations everywhere, your story, my story, the *Mahābhārata* teaches how the memory of the past brings violence to one's self and to the *other*, quite as much in collective relationships as in the personal. And the memory is mostly of a hurt. Its consequences are deep and touch many lives beyond one's own.

At another level, the *Mahābhārata* shows that we do violence to our self when we fragment its attributes from their natural unity and turn any one of them into the sole end of life *or* value it so little that, in either case, we are separated from our self, and separated thereby from the *other*. The entire *Mahābhārata* is about freedom from that violence.

To conclude, the *Mahābhārata*'s teachings on not-violence to one's self and to the *other*:

> यथा नागपदेऽन्यानि पदानि पदगामिनाम्।
> सर्वाण्येवापिधीयन्ते पदजातानि कौञ्जरे।। शान्ति २४५.१८।।
> एवं सर्वमहिंसायां धर्मार्थमपिधीयते।
> अमृतः स नित्यं वसति यो हिंसा न प्रपद्यते।। शान्ति २४५.१९।।
> *Just as the signs of human footsteps get merged into the signs of an elephant's footsteps, so do the signs of* dharma *and material prosperity become inherent in not-violence. Who does no violence, lives in freedom from death.*[294]

> अहिंसकः समः सत्यो धृतिमान् नियतेन्द्रियः।
> शरण्यः सर्वभूतानां गतिमाप्नोत्यनुत्तमाम्।। शान्ति २४५.२०।।
> *Who is free from violence, has equality towards all, is given to truth, is self-disciplined, is protective of all beings, to all beings a refuge—obtains a state most splendid.*[295]

एवं प्रज्ञानतृप्तस्य निर्भयस्य निराशिष: ।
न मृत्युरतिगो भाव: स मृत्युमधिगच्छति ।। शान्ति २४५.२१ ।।
Who lives in a knowledge such as this, free from fear, from expectations, on him death has no force, for he has gone beyond all that death is.[296]

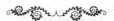

CHAPTER SIX

What is 'Death'? The Origin of *Mrityu*

Beyond all theories, all interpretations, all arguments, the essence of the *Mahābhārata* is this, which is also the essence of human life. Each person has a relationship with his, or her, self; with the particularities of one's body and one's mind, and with their specific workings together, in the form of desires, motives, acts, and emotions. Each person has a relationship also with the *other*, with his, or her, particularities. This *other* is a collective entity, too: group, society, nation. The *other* is not necessarily the human *other*. The *other* is also nature: earth, sky, fire, wind, water, trees, plants, rivers, lakes, hills, mountains. The *Mahābhārata* makes us aware of the plain truth that it is not until one's relationship with one's self is right that one's relationship with the *other* can be right. At the same time, it is by achieving a right relationship with the *other* that one achieves a right relationship with one's self. The two are inseparably linked. Life is relational.

And just as life is relational in all its attributes, so is death. The *Mahābhārata* narrates a story that begins with a question: '*What is death*?'

Abhimanyu, the son of Arjuna, has just been killed in that day's battle. The six great warriors of the other side had crafted a strategic circle, which the young Abhimanyu knew how to enter but did not know how to get out of. Overcome with grief, Yudhishṭhira surveys, moreover, the devastating scene of the battlefield: blood, mangled flesh, twisted or broken arms and legs of hundreds of soldiers killed. He is inconsolable at the treacherous killing of his nephew, a handsome youth of many qualities. And seeing the mangled bodies of so many others who had died in that day's battle, he is exceedingly sad. Vyāsa, the author of the *Mahābhārata*, and also a patriarch of the common family of the warring royal cousins, appears miraculously on the scene, and tries to console him. But Yudhishṭhira is inconsolable on seeing Abhimanyu killed. 'Neither victory in this war, nor the kingdom, nor the heavens, nor even immortality, can now please me.'[1] He asks Vyāsa:

इमे वै पृथिवीपाला: शेरते पृथिवीतले।
निहता: पृतनामध्ये मृतसंज्ञा महाबला:।। द्रोण ५२.१२।।

These kings and warriors are lying on the earth, with 'dead' as their identity.

मृता इति च शब्दोऽयं वर्तते च ततोऽर्थवत् ।
इमे मृता महीपालाः प्रायशो भीमविक्रमाः ।। द्रोण ५२.१६ ।।

Many of them were great warriors and men of great qualities as well. And now they are known by the adjective 'dead'.[2]

अत्र मे संशयः प्राप्तः कुतः संज्ञा मृता इति ।
कस्य मृत्युः कुतो मृत्युः केन मृत्युरिमाः प्रजाः ।। द्रोण ५२.१८ ।।

I wonder why they are now known as 'dead'? Who *dies?* What *causes death?* Why *does death claim the living?*[3]

Vyāsa then narrates the story of the creation of Death, Mrityu, in the form of a woman, by Brahmā. She asks him: 'Why am I created?' He tells her that the purpose of her creation is to relieve the Earth of the intolerable burden of the ever growing population of living beings, and she is meant to devour them, the uncultivated and the learned alike. On hearing the purpose for which she has been created, Mrityu begins to cry, and Brahmā takes her tears in the palms of both his hands, but some of them fall on the earth.[4] She demands an explanation from him.

त्वया सृष्टा कथं नारी ईदृशी वदतां वर ।
क्रूरं कर्माहितं कुर्यां तदेव किमु जानती ।। द्रोण ५४.२ ।।

Why did you create me in this *form, that of a woman? Why should I knowingly engage in the malevolent and cruel act of devouring living beings?*

She gives several reasons why she must not be appointed as the killer. 'When I will take the life of the sons, the brothers, the mothers, and the fathers, and the husbands, and the friends, their relatives will grieve on the death of their loved ones. And I will be the object of their hatred and their fear, but I will fear their tears of sorrow the most, as I fear *adharma*.'[5] Mrityu tells Brahmā firmly:

न हि शक्ष्यामि देवेश प्राणान् प्राणभृतां प्रियान् ।
हर्तुं विलपमानानामधर्मादभिरक्ष माम् ।। द्रोण ५४.९ ।।

No, I will not be able to extinguish life in living beings, to whom life is dear but who are fearful of death and are distressed. Save me from that adharma.[6]

Mrityu puts up against her creator, Brahmā, a resolute battle of wills, against the task for which Brahmā had created her. 'Confer upon me this boon instead that I do not have to cause death of living beings. This is the only thing I ask from you. I fear *adharma* the most. Relieve me of that fear.'[7]

Brahmā reasons with her. Now keeping her sadness to herself, she leaves his presence, for it would be impertinent to argue too much with one's creator. Finally, she submits. But she says to him:

यद्येवमेतत् कर्तव्यं मया न स्याद् विना प्रभो।। द्रोण ५४.३७।।
तवाज्ञा मूर्ध्नि मन्यस्ता यत् त वक्ष्यामि तच्छृणु।
If the task can be accomplished by no one else but me, I shall obey you. But you listen carefully to what I now say:

लोभः क्रोधोऽभ्यसूयेर्ष्या द्रोहो मोहश्च देहिनाम्।। द्रोण ५४.३८।।
अह्रीश्चान्योन्यपरुषा देहं भिन्द्युः पृथग्विधाः।
Greed; anger; talking ill of others; envy and jealousy; ill-will; confusion of perceptions; shamelessness; and harsh words spoken to each other— these *will devour the bodies of those who are embodied.*[8]

The conclusion, then, is:

मृत्युस्त्वेषां व्याधयस्तत्प्रसूता
व्याधी रोगो रुज्यते येन जन्तुः।
सर्वेषां च प्राणिनां प्रायणान्ते
तस्माच्छोकं मा कृथा निष्फलं त्वम्।। द्रोण ५४.४५।।
This is death, from which arise all kinds of diseases. Illness is the name of diseases which afflict man. All living beings die at the end of their lifespan Do not grieve, for that will do no good.[9]

आत्मानं वै प्राणिनो घ्नन्ति सर्वे
नैतान् मृत्युर्दण्डपाणिर्हिनस्ति।
तस्मान्मृतान् नानुशोचन्ति धीरा
मृत्युं ज्ञात्वा निश्चयं ब्रह्मसृष्टम्।

इत्थं सृष्टिं देवक्लृप्तां विदित्वा
पुत्रान्नाष्टाच्छोकमाशु त्यजस्व।। द्रोण ५४.५०।।

All living beings cause their own death. Death does not kill them with a stick in her hand.[10]

The creator of Death, Brahmā, had said to her, besides:

यान्यश्रुबिन्दूनि करे ममासं-
स्ते व्याधयः प्राणिनामात्मजाताः।
ते मारयिष्यन्ति नरान् गतासून्
नाधर्मस्ते भविता मा स्म भैषीः।। द्रोण ५४.४०।।

Your tears I took in my hands, but some fell on the earth. They will become the diseases born from the bodies of the living beings, who will cause their own death, not you. Don't fear. You will be doing no adharma.[11]

सर्वेषां वै प्राणिनां कामरोषौ
संत्यज्य त्वं संहरस्वेह जीवान्।
एवं धर्मस्त्वां भविष्यत्यनन्तो
मिथ्यावृत्तान् मारयिष्यत्यधर्मः।। द्रोण ५४.४२।।

With no partiality that comes with attraction and hostility, you destroy the living. Those given to untruth will cause their death by their own adharma, *not you.*[12]

In the voice of Vidura, the *Mahābhārata* says:

अतिमानोऽतिवादश्च तथात्यागो नराधिप।
क्रोधश्चात्मविधित्सा च मित्रदोहश्च तानि षट्।। उद्योग ३७.१०।।

There are six deadly swords. Too much pride and arrogance; too much of vain talk; absence of self-sacrifice; anger; to seek only one's own ends; and betrayal of a friend. These kill human beings, not death.[13]

Furthermore, again in his voice the *Mahābhārata* says,[14] the form of the argument being, as in everything else, 'This being indisputably so, *then why*?'

यदा प्राज्ञाश्च मूर्खाश्च धनवन्तश्च निर्धनाः।
कुलीनाश्चाकुलीनाश्च मानिनोऽथाप्यमानिनः।। स्त्री ४.१५।।

सर्वे पितृवनं प्राप्ताः स्वपन्ति विगतत्वचः।
निर्मांसैरस्थिभूयिष्टैर्गात्रैः स्नायुनिबन्धनैः।। स्त्री ४.१६।।

विशेषं न प्रपश्यन्ति तत्र तेषां परे जनाः ।
येन प्रत्यवगच्छेयुः कुलरूपविशेषणम् ।। स्त्री ४.१७ ।।

यदा सर्वे समं न्यस्ताः स्वपन्ति धरणीतले ।
कस्मादन्योन्यमिच्छन्ति प्रलब्धुमिह दुर्बुधाः ।। स्त्री ४.१८ ।।

The learned and the fools, the rich and the poor, the ones born in families of quality and those not so fortunate, the honoured and the disregarded, all alike find their place in the place of the dead.
All that can be seen of them, and what is seen is without distinction, is their nakedness in death. And in their common nakedness in death, there is nothing to mark the one as more distinguished than the other.
In the equality of death, when all sleep on the earth alike, then why do the mortal fools on this earth wish to cheat each other.[15]

The conquest of the fear of death consists in one's right relationship with one's self and with the *other*. In this context, the *Mahābhārata* narrates a conversation which a sage, Arishṭanemi, has with a group of kings. He says to them:

कारणं वः प्रवक्ष्यामि हेतुयोगसमासतः ।
(मश्त्युः प्रभवने येन नास्माकं नृपसत्तमाः ।
शुद्धाचारा अनलसाः संध्योपासनतत्पराः ।।
शुद्धान्न शुद्धसुधनाब्रह्मचर्यव्रतान्विताः ।)
सत्यमेवाभिजानीमो नानृते कुर्महे मनः ।
स्वधर्ममनुतिष्ठामस्तस्मान्मृत्युभयं न नः ।। वन १८४.१८ ।।

I will tell you why death has no power over us. We live our lives in truth, and do not take to untruth ever. We are free of sloth and laziness, are diligent in our duties. We earn money for our maintenance by proper means. Therefore, we have no fear of death.[16]

यद् ब्राह्मणानां कुशलं तदेषां कथयामहे ।
नैषां दुश्चरितं ब्रूमस्तस्मान्मृत्युभयं न नः ।। वन १८४.१९ ।।

अतिथीनन्नपानेन भृत्यानत्यशनेन च ।
सम्भोज्य शेषमश्नीमस्तस्मान्मृत्युभयं न नः ।। वन १८४.२० ।।

We speak only of what is good in teachers and thinkers, and not of their defects. Therefore, we have no fear of death. Those who visit us, we receive with the offerings of food and water. Those who depend on us, we feed them well; and it is only after they *have eaten that we ourselves eat from what is left. Therefore, we have no fear of death.*[17]

शान्ता दान्ताः क्षमाशीलास्तीर्थदानपरायणाः ।
पुण्यदेशनिवासाच्च तस्मान्मृत्युभयं न नः ।
तेजस्विदेशवासाच्च तस्मान्मृत्युभयं न नः ।। वन १८४.२१ ।।

At peace with ourselves; self-controlled and patient; forgiveness and giving and sila *being our pilgrimage; we live in places where there is goodness and nobility. And therefore we have no fear of death. And we live, besides, in places where those live who have in them the light of goodness. Therefore, we have no fear of death.*[18]

There is another conversation, between the sage Sanatsujāta, who had once said 'There is no death', and King Dhritarāshtra, which explores even the question whether there is, or there is not, death.[19]

Sanatsujāta

अमृत्युः कर्मणा केचिन्मृत्युर्नास्तीति चापरे ।
शृणु मे ब्रुवतो राजन् यथैतन्मा विशङ्किथाः ।। उद्योग ४२.३ ।।

Some people say, 'There is death'; some others say, 'There is no death.' The way it is, I shall say something on that. Do not doubt it.[20]

उभे सत्ये क्षत्रियैतस्य विद्धि
मोहान्मृत्युः सम्मतोऽयं कवीनाम् ।
प्रमादं वै मृत्युमहं ब्रवीमि
तथाप्रमादममृतत्वं ब्रवीमि ।। उद्योग ४२.४ ।।

Both are true. Some learned people accept the existence of death. They do so out of confusion of perceptions. But I say that pramada, *both drunkenness and stupour of the mind are death; freedom from them is freedom from death.*[21]

प्रमादाद् वै असुराः पराभव-
न्नप्रमादाद् ब्रह्मभूताः सुराश्च ।
नैव मृत्युर्व्याघ्र इवात्ति जन्तून्
न ह्यस्य रूपमुपलभ्यते हि ।। उद्योग ४२.५ ।।

Death does not devour living beings like a tiger, for it has no visible form.[22]

अस्यादेशान्नि:सरते नराणां
क्रोध: प्रमादो लोभरूपश्च मृत्यु: ।
अहंगतेनैव चरन् विमार्गान्
न चात्मनो योगमुपैति कश्चित् ।। उद्योग ४२.७ ।।

Death takes the forms of hatred and anger, greed, and the drunkenness of the mind. They arise from egotism, which keeps man from self-knowledge.[23]

अभिध्या वै प्रथमं हन्ति लोकान्
कामक्रोधावनुगृह्याशु पश्चात् ।
एते बालान् कृत्यवे प्रापयन्ति
धीरास्तु धैर्येण तरन्ति मृत्युम् ।। उद्योग ४२.११ ।।

Longing and desire destroy people first. Then hatred and anger take possession of them, and with them, death. Those able to reflect and think, swim across death.[24]

स क्रोधलोभौ मोहवानन्तरात्मा
स वै मृत्युस्त्वच्छरीरे य एष: ।
एवं मृत्युं जायमानं विदित्वा
ज्ञाने तिष्ठन् न बिभेतीह मृत्यो:
विनश्यते विषये तस्य मृत्यु-
र्मृत्योर्यथा विषयं प्राप्य मर्त्य: ।। उद्योग ४२.१६ ।।

This self within you, under the confusion of perceptions, is assailed by death taking the forms of hatred and anger and greed. But the one, recognising that death comes from the confusion of perceptions, no longer fears death, now firm in the true knowledge of things. Approaching him, death dies, in the same way as die all mortals.[25]

In their very long inquiry into the human condition, Yudhishṭhira asks Bhīshma: 'In view of *kāla*, Time, reducing all living beings, how, and by doing what, may man then obtain the Good?'[26] Bhīshma answers this question by narrating a conversation that a son once had with his father. The father was given to learning and knowledge, and the son had reflected deeply on the ordering of life.

The son

धीर: किंस्वित् तात कुर्यात् प्रजानन्
क्षिपं ह्यायुर्भ्रश्यते मानवानाम् ।

पितस्तदाचक्ष्वयथार्थयोगं
ममानुपूर्व्या येन धर्मं चरेयम् ।। शान्ति १७५.५ ।।

Dear father! The life of humans is passing quickly. In that case, how should a person order his life? Instruct me, so that I may do likewise.[27]

The father

वेदानधीत्य ब्रह्मचर्येण पुत्र
पुत्रानिच्छेत् पावनार्थं पितृणाम् ।
अग्नीनाधाय विधिवच्चेष्टयज्ञो
वनं प्रविश्याथ मुनिर्बुभूषेत् ।। शान्ति १७५.६ ।।

A brahmana *should first study the Veda*: second, *marry and raise a family, to discharge his debt to the ancestors*: third, *retire from the cares of the life-in-family*: *and* fourth, *renounce the world.*[28]

The son, whose name was Medhāvī, meaning 'the one endowed with bright intellect', had *not* asked, 'How should a *brahmana* order his life?' He had asked 'How should a *person* order his life, in view of his, or her, life passing quickly?' The father had only repeated the familiar formula of the four stages of life, and that was of no help, for the son knew it quite well. His inquiry was different. It concerned *all* human beings.

The son

एवमभ्याहते लोके समन्तात् परिवारिते ।
अमोघासु पतन्तीषु किं धीन इव भाषसे ।। शान्ति १७५.७ ।।

When this world is being struck, surrounded on all sides, everywhere, unfailingly going down, how can you talk with such confidence?[29]

The father

कथमभ्याहतो लोकः केन वा परिवारितः ।
अमोधाः काः पतन्तीह किं नु भीषयसीव माम् ।। शान्ति १७५.८ ।।

You frighten me, my son! What *is striking this world?* What *is surrounding it from all sides?* What *is unfailingly taking it down?*[30]

The son

मृत्युनाभ्याहतो लोको जरया परिवारितः ।
अहोरात्राः पतन्त्येते ननु कस्मान्न बुध्यसे ।। शान्ति १७५.९ ।।

By Death it is being struck: old age is surrounding it from all sides: 'the day' and 'the night'—these two are unfailingly taking it down. Why don't you understand this?[31]

Then in a tone at once hurried and tranquil, Medhāvī speaks of biological death, and asks, '*Given death, why don't people learn to live?*'

Given the complete uncertainty about the time that death would claim a person, he questions the notion that life can be ordered into a confidently planned sequence. Do *this*, when a boy; do *that*, when young; do *this*, when past middle age; and do *that*, when old. Rather, he says:

श्वः कार्यमद्य कुर्वीत पूर्वाह्ने चापराह्निकम् ।
न हि प्रतीक्षते मृत्युः कृतमस्य न वाकृतम् ।। शान्ति १७५.१५ ।।
What may be done tomorrow, do it today. What may be done in the evening, do it in the morning. For Death doesn't ask you whether your work has been completed or not.[32]

अद्यैव कुरु यच्छ्रेयो मा त्वां कालोऽत्यगादयम् ।
अकृतेष्वेव कार्येषु मृत्युर्वै सम्प्रकर्षति ।। शान्ति १७५.१४ ।।
Therefore, engage yourself in the Good today. *Let Time not slip away. For all your work will remain incomplete, and Death will carry you away.*[33]

Now, in a voice that seems to be coming from far away, he begins to address himself more than his father. He is first of all reminding himself of the absolute certainty of death and the equally absolute uncertainty of the time of its visit.

को हि जानाति कस्याद्य मृत्युकालो भविष्यति ।
(न मृत्युरामन्त्रयते हर्तुकामो जगत्प्रभुः ।
अबुद्ध एवाक्रमते मीनान् मीनग्रहो यथा ।।) शान्ति १७५.१५ ।।
Who knows who will die when? The controller of the world, Death, does not send an invitation in advance. Just as a fisherman gathers the fish without their knowing, Death does likewise.[34]

He uses several other metaphors to emphasise that uncertainty: 'the tiger pouncing upon the unsuspecting sheep grazing happily';[35] 'the lion carrying away the sleeping antelope';[36] or 'the fish in shallow water'.[37] And Death is no respecter of persons either.

दूर्बलं बलवन्तं च शूरं भीरु जडं कविम्।
अप्राप्तं सर्वकामार्थान् मृत्युरादाय गच्छति।। शान्ति १७५.२२।।
Weak or strong, full of valour or a coward, a fool or learned, even before his desires are fulfilled, Death takes him away.[38]

इदं कृतमिदं कार्यमिदमन्यत् कृताकृतम्।
एवमीहासुखासक्तं कृतान्तः कुरुते वशे।। शान्ति १७५.२०।।
Man thinks 'I have completed this work; that work remains unfinished; and I have to do that work next.' In the midst of all this planning and agenda, Death gathers him under her control.[39]

In the voice of Medhāvī, the *Mahābhārata* states what is undeniable, but also a paradox.

जातमेवान्तकोऽन्ताय जरा चान्वेति देहिनम्।
अनुषक्ता द्वयेनैते भावाः स्थावरजङ्गमाः।। शान्ति १७५.२४।।
Death is connected with life from the moment one is born.[40]

That is to say, paradoxically, the processes of living are, at the same time, also the processes of dying. It is for this reason, the *Mahābhārata* says to us, that we should first free ourselves of the fear of death; or else it would become the fear of life as well.

Yudhishṭhira's question, 'What causes death?', was not a medical question, seeking to know the biological factors that bring a life to its end. He was seeking the knowledge of those causes that are located *within* a person and bring to his self, or to her self, the *other* death, the psychological death in the first place. It is the *other* dying, the daily death, as much in the collective life of a society as in the life of a family, the death of the mind and of feelings that, the *Mahābhārata* says, we should be concerned with. The *Mahābhārata*'s concern throughout is with life and not with death. Every living being dies a biological death. But, the *Mahābhārata* teaches, biological death alone is not death. Greed is death. Hatred is death. Violence to the *other*, in speech or in thought or in act, is death. Untruth is death. Nor is death some ultimate event. There is a death that takes place every moment, every day. We die to what we had once valued so highly but wrongly. But also we are dead to what we must be intensely alive. There is, every day, a dying and inflicting death—the consequences of one's wrong relationship with one's self and with the *other*. And it is *that* death that Medhāvī resolves to conquer.

सोऽहंह्यहिंस्त्रः सत्यार्थी कामक्रोधबहिष्कृतः ।
समदुःखसुखः क्षेमी मृत्युं हास्याम्यमर्त्यवत् ।। शान्ति १७५.३१ ।।
Doing no violence to another, I will seek truth. Removing from my mind and from my heart desire and anger, and perceiving pleasure and pain to be quite the same, I will thereby free myself from death.[41]

The *Mahābhārata* concludes, in the voice of Medhāvī:

अमृतं चैव मृत्युश्च द्वयं देहे प्रतिष्ठतम् ।
मृत्युमापद्यते मोहात् सत्येनापद्यतेऽमृतम् ।। शान्ति १७५.३० ।।
Both death *and the* deathless *reside together in the human body. From the confusion of perceptions comes death, and from truth, that which death can never touch.*[42]

तस्मात् सत्यव्रताचारः सत्ययोगपरायणः ।
सत्यागमः सदा दान्तः सत्येनैवान्तकं जयेत् ।। शान्ति १७५.२९ ।।
It is only through truth that one conquers death.[43]

The essence of truth is not in *knowing* alone but in *living* as well.[44] The essence of truth is in living in the right relationship with one's self and with the *other*.

The tears of Mrityu, Death, are her tears for us who would not, when we could, conquer greed, untruth, and hatred. If we did, we would conquer Death, as Death herself promised we would. The tears of Death are the tears of sorrow for us who keep creating death all around, when we could as easily create for one's self and for the *other* that which sustains, enhances, enriches, in the worth of life. In a perplexed voice, Death is asking us: '*Why don't you learn to live?*'

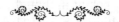

CHAPTER SEVEN

The Question of Truth

- The problem of relativism
- Truth is relational

In answer to a question put to Yudhishṭhira, 'What is the most astonishing thing in the world?', he had said: 'Seeing that everyday people are dying, that those who remain still think that death would not come to *them*. What can be more astonishing than this?'[1] There *is*. Even a more astonishing thing about us human beings is that we all are together and alike when we lie; the moment we begin talking about *truth*, we fly at each other's throat. What can be more astonishing than *this*? There has hardly been anything in human history that has produced greater violence and killing than the conflicting perceptions of what *truth* is. Even before the question '*What is truth?*' could be formulated, there is already present the question '*Whose truth?*' There has been in human relationships no other question at once more intimate and more agonising than this, in one form or another. Not only between one person and another, but also between one religion and another even more.

To begin with, the *Mahābhārata* offers the definition of 'truth' as being:

यथा श्रुतं यथा दृष्टमात्मना यद् यथा कृतम् ।
तथा तस्याविकारेण वचनं सत्यलक्षणम् ।। अनुशासन २३२.१७ ।।

The way it was heard, the way it was seen, and the way it was done, to represent it through speech without distortion is truth.[2]

All schools of Indian philosophy, excepting the Materialists taken as a general group, were united in regarding truth as a great deal more than correspondence with facts. That did not imply disregard to correspondence with facts as an essential aspect of truth. But to say that it is truth that sustains and enhances human worth is not to say that correspondence with facts is all that there is to *truth*. Jainism and Buddhism, like Yoga and the other philosophical schools, subjected 'correspondence with facts' to a much deeper view of truth, *satya*.

Motives and feelings that lead to acts pertain to 'truth' as much as the acts themselves do. To conceal them, or to withhold them, will be untruth. Acts are manifest and verifiable, although there is serious uncertainty even about *that*. Motives and feelings, in being inner states of the mind, are not visible, nor verifiable, in the ordinary meanings of these words. They can only be inferred; and about the inferences drawn as to the motives, there can be legitimate differences of opinion. It is perfectly conceivable that I 'truthfully' state external facts which, on verification, will be found to be true; and yet, in concealing the inner states of my mind inseparably connected with my external acts, I turn them into a lie. What is factually true, if separated from the motives that led to it, may yet be a lie. Anything knowingly stated incompletely will be untruth. Therefore, in the voice of Shiva, the *Mahābhārata* adds:

यच्छलेनाभिसंयुक्तं सत्यरूपं मृषैव तत्। अनुशासन २३२.१८ ।।

What is externally true, but contains clever distortion, is in fact a lie.[3]

Thus, correspondence with facts that are external cannot be by itself a sufficient criterion of truth. For that reason, the *Mahābhārata* is far more concerned with the states of the mind and of feelings than with *acts*.

On the question of truth the *Mahābhārata* engages us simultaneously at three different levels. They are, however, interrelated in a deep coherence suggested by life itself and are not artificial products of some *theory* of truth. *One*, it shows the manifest relativity of truth. *Two*, it shows that the undoubtedly disturbing implications of truth being relative are resolved in perceiving truth to be at the same time relational as well. That is to say, the attributes of truth are to be seen in the quality of one's relationship with one's self and with the *other*. And, *three*, it shows that truth is not *knowing* alone, but *living* quite as much. There have been in the history of philosophy, and of modern science too, quarrels about the ways of *knowing*, and even about what *knowing* is. And there have been even greater quarrels about ways of *living*, which in their substance have been quarrels about the sources of sanction for them. Above all, knowing and living came to be looked upon as two entirely separate domains, epistemology separated from ethics, cognition from character. In the *Mahābhārata*, these three perspectives are brought into a unity.

Truth and the problem of relativism

The *Mahābhārata* takes up in relation to truth the manifest problem of relativity, as it did in relation to *dharma*. Truth and untruth are regarded as relative to *desha* and *kāla*.[4] On first sight, this would seem to be inconsistent with the absolute value placed upon truth.

तपांसि यानि चीर्णानि चरिष्यन्ति च यत् तपः ।
शतैः शतसहस्रैश्च तैः सत्यान्न विशिष्यते ।। शान्ति १९९.६३ ।।

Were all the austerities done in the past, and would be done in the future, multiplied by tens of thousands, truth would outweigh them still.[5]

सत्यमेकाक्षरं ब्रह्म सत्यमेकाक्षरं तपः ।
सत्यमेकाक्षरो यज्ञः सत्यमेकाक्षरं श्रुतम् ।। शान्ति १९९.६४ ।।

Truth alone is the abiding reality, truth alone is the abiding austerity, truth alone is the abiding sacrifice, and truth alone is the abiding knowledge.[6]

सत्यं वेदेषु जागर्ति फलं सत्ये परं स्मृतम् ।
सत्याद् धर्मो दमश्चैव सर्वं सत्ये प्रतिष्ठितम् ।। शान्ति १९९.६५ ।।

It is truth that is manifest in knowledge, and truth is the highest reward. Social order and self-discipline are aspects of truth. Indeed everything is founded upon truth.[7]

प्राणिनां जननं सत्यं सत्यं संततिरेव च ।
सत्येन वायुरभ्येति सत्येन तपते रविः ।। शान्ति १९९.६७ ।।

Truth is the creator: truth is the creation. The wind flows by the power of truth, and it is by the power of truth that the sun has its fire.[8]

सत्येन चाग्निर्दहति स्वर्गः सत्ये प्रतिष्ठितः ।
सत्यं यज्ञस्तपो वेदाः स्तोभा मन्त्राः सरस्वती ।। शान्ति १९९.६८ ।।

It is from truth that fire burns; it is upon truth that the heavens are based. Yajña, *austerity, knowledge, mystical words, and the Goddess of Learning—all these are as many forms of truth.*[9]

तुलामारोपिता धर्मः सत्यं चैवेति नः श्रुतम् ।
समकक्षां तुलयतो यतः सत्यं ततोऽधिकम् ।। शान्ति १९९.६९ ।।

I hear that dharma *and truth were once placed on a weighing scale, to determine their relative weights. Truth was found to be of greater weight.*[10]

यतो धर्मस्ततः सत्यं सर्वं सत्येन वर्धते ।
किमर्थमनृतं कर्म कर्तुं राजंस्त्वमिच्छसि ।। शान्ति १९९.७० ।।

Where there is dharma, *there is truth; and it is through truth, all are enhanced. To what purpose do you then wish to act untruthfully?*[11]

सत्यं ब्रह्म तपः सत्यं सत्यं विसृजते प्रजाः।
सत्येन धार्यते लोकः स्वर्गं सत्येन गच्छति।। शान्ति १९०.१।।
Truth is the reality pervading the universe. Truth is true austerity. It is truth that sustains the world. It is through truth that one gains all that is heaven.[12]

अनृतं तमसो रूपं तमसा नीयते ह्यधः।
तमोग्रस्ता न पश्यन्ति प्रकाशं तमसाऽऽवृताः।। शान्ति १९०.२।।
Untruth is darkness, and darkness takes people down. In the confusion of perceptions, people are unable to see the light.[13]

तत्र यत् सत्यं स धर्मो यो धर्मः स प्रकाशो यः प्रकाशस्तत् सुखमिति।
तत्र यदनृतं सोऽधर्मो योऽधर्मस्तत् तमोयत् तमस्तद् दुःखमिति।। १९०.५।।
What is truth is also what sustains and enhances life. What sustains and enhances is also light. What debases and degrades is darkness; and what is darkness, is pain and suffering.[14]

नास्ति सत्यात् परो धर्मो नानृतात् पातकं परम्।।
स्थितिर्हि सत्यं धर्मस्य तस्मात् सत्यं न लोपयेत्।। शान्ति १६२.२४।।
There is no greater dharma *than truth, nor worse demerit than untruth. In truth alone is* dharma *preserved. Let not truth be therefore obscured.*[15]

सत्यं स्वर्गस्य सोपानं पारावारस्य नौरिव।
नास्ति सत्यात् परं दान नास्ति सत्यात् परं तपः।। अनुशासन ५९८८.३।।
Just as the boat takes us across the sea, truth is the means to all that is heaven. There is no greater sharing, no greater gift, than truth. Neither is there a greater self-discipline than truth.[16]

सत्यस्य वचनं साधु न सत्याद् विद्यते परम्।
सत्येन विधृतं सर्वं सर्वं सत्ये प्रतिष्ठितम्।। शान्ति २५९.१०।।
It is good to speak the truth; for greater than truth there is nothing. Truth sustains everything; and it is in truth that everything has its foundation.[17]

सत्यं सत्सु सदा धर्मः सत्यं धर्मः सनातनः।
सत्यमेव नमस्येत सत्यं हि परमा गतिः।। शान्ति १६२.४।।

Goodness has truth as its essence, and truth is the eternal foundation. Offer your salutations, bow your head, to truth; for truth is the highest state of being.[18]

Tirukkuraḷ, the ancient Tamil classic, says:

Not all lamps are lamps; the lamp of truth is the lamp of the wise.[19]

Then how could truth be *conditional*, relative to 'place' and 'time'? Whatever is conditional is a function of something else. If truth were a function of place and time, then, like them, it must be forever shifting. In that case, *history*, and not *truth*, ought to be life's apotheosis. But here, as elsewhere, the *Mahābhārata* holds that:

नात्यन्तं गुणवत् किंचिन्न चाप्यत्यन्तनिर्गुणम् ।
उभयं सर्वकार्येषु दृश्यते साध्वसाधु वा ।। शान्ति १५.५० ।।
There is nothing that has qualities alone, nor is there anything that is devoid of all qualities; in every act, both good and bad are to be seen together.[20]

As to the questions brought up by Yudhishṭhira:

सत्यं चैवानृतं चोभे लोकानावृत्य तिष्ठत: ।
तयो: किमाचरेद् राजन् पुरुषो धर्मनिश्चत: ।। शान्ति १०९.२ ।।
Everything in the world is a mixture of truth and untruth. Then how does one act in order to act according to dharma*?*[21]

किंस्वित् सत्यं किमनृतं किंस्विद् धर्म्यं सनातनम् ।
कस्मिन् काले वदेत् सत्यं कस्मिन् कालेऽनृतं वदेत् ।। शान्ति १०९.३ ।।
What is truth and what is untruth? At what time must one speak the truth? At what time must one speak the untruth?[22]

The answer was that, 'It is indeed difficult to determine this.'[23] Bhīshma, however, suggests that:

सत्यस्य वचनं साधु न सत्याद् विद्यते परम् ।
यत्तु लोकेषु दुर्ज्ञानं तत् प्रवक्ष्यामि भारत ।। शान्ति १०९.४ ।।

भवेत् सत्यं न वक्तव्यं वक्तव्यमनृतं भवेत् ।
यत्रानृतं भवेत् सत्यं सत्यं वाप्यनृतं भवेत् ।। शान्ति १०९.५ ।।

Undoubtedly, it is good to speak the truth; for greater than truth there is nothing. Yet, I shall speak to you of that which is exceedingly difficult to judge. Where truth turns into untruth, it is better not to speak the truth; for there untruth acts as truth.[24]

तादृशो वध्यते बालो यत्र सत्यमनिष्ठितम् ।
सत्यानृते विनिश्चत्य ततो भवति धर्मवित् ।। शान्ति १०९.६ ।।
One who can discriminate between the relative value of truth and untruth, he alone understands dharma; *the one who doesn't is harmed greatly.*[25]

These views were ambiguous; for it was not explained *what* it was that turned truth into untruth. What was still required to be indicated was a principle of the highest order, to which *truth* must be subordinate, and of which 'place' and 'time' themselves were aspects. That principle was contained in the following propositions, put forth both by Bhīshma and Krishna, in almost identical words, at two separate places. Both of them acknowledge:[26]

सत्यस्य वचनं साधु न सत्याद् विद्यते परम् ।
यत्तु लोकेषु दर्शानं तत् प्रवश्यामि भारत ।। शान्ति १०९.४ ।।
It is best to speak the truth, for there is nothing greater than the truth; yet it is also exceedingly difficult to grasp its substance.[27]

तत्र ते लक्ष्णोद्देश: कश्चिदेवं भविष्यति ।। कर्ण ६९.५४ ।।
दुष्करं परम ज्ञानं तर्केणानुव्यवस्यति ।
श्रुतेर्धर्म इति ह्येके वदन्ति बहवो जना: ।। कर्ण ६९.५५ ।।
तत् ते न प्रत्यसूयामि न च सर्वं विधीयते ।
प्रभवार्थाय भूतानां धर्मप्रवचनं कृतम् ।। कर्ण ६९.५६ ।।
There are those who try to understand the very complex nature of dharma *by means of logic and argument. There are many who say that it is from the Veda that one learns* dharma. *There are others who dispute this. I do not criticise any one of these views, but it is true that the Veda do not provide for everything.*[28]

If some indication was still required to decide between *dharma* and *adharma*, that is, to decide when it is that truth becomes *adharma*, and untruth *dharma*, the principle is:

यत् स्यादहिंसासंयुक्तं स धर्म इति निश्चयः।
अहिंसार्थाय भूतानां धर्मप्रवचनं कृतम्।। कर्ण ६९.५७।।

Whatever does not do violence, that certainly is dharma*; for all the sayings on* dharma *are meant primarily to prevent violence to living beings.*[29]

धारणाद् धर्ममित्याहुर्धर्मो धारयते प्रजाः।
यत् स्याद् धारणसंयुक्तं स धर्म इति निश्चयः।। कर्ण ६९.५८।।

Dharma *is propounded with the aim of securing the good of all living beings; hence whatever fufils that aim is* dharma*—this is certain.*[30]

सर्वं प्रियाभ्युपगतं धर्ममाहुर्मनीषिणः।
पश्यैतं लक्षणौद्देशं धर्माधर्मे युधिष्ठिर।। शान्ति २५९.२५।।

What comes from love for all beings is dharma*; this is the criterion to judge* dharma *from* adharma.[31]

लोकयात्रार्थमेवेह धर्मस्य नियमः कृतः।। शान्ति २५९.४।।
लोकसंग्रहसंयुक्तं विधात्रा विहितं पुरा।। शान्ति २५९.२६।।

Dharma *was created for the orderly progress and the welfare of the people.*[32]

The relativistic character of *dharma* and truth was inherent, however, in the foregoing propositions as well. For what sustains people, and what secures their good, keeps changing with time and place; and also there are many different perceptions of them. It follows that whoever always *speaks* the truth without regard to them, might injure others thereby, and so is liable to reproach. Truth is not confined to 'truth speaking'.

भवेत् सत्यमवक्तव्यं न वक्तव्यमनुष्ठितम्।
सत्यानृते विनिश्चत्य ततो भवति धर्मवित्।। कर्ण ६९.३५।।

What is truth only formally in speech is not necessarily truth; one should discriminate between truth and untruth with regard to their effect.[33]

प्राणिनामवधस्तात सर्वज्यायान् मतो मम।
अनृतां वा वदेद वाचं न तु हिंस्यात् कथंचन।। कर्ण ६९.२३।।

To save others from being killed is a most exalted dharma. *If by speaking a lie, a life is protected, then speak the lie, and protect that life.*[34]

सर्वस्वस्यापहारे तु वक्तव्यमनृतं भवेत्।
तत्रानृतं भवेत् सत्यं चाप्यनृतं भवेत्।। कर्ण ६९.३४।।
तादृशं पश्यते बालो यस्य सत्यमनुष्ठितम्।

Where everything of a person is being threatened, one may speak a lie so as to protect him; for there the lie has the effect of truth, and there the truth speaking will have the effect of being the untruth. Only a fool will think that formal truth is a requisite in all circumstances.[35]

भवेत् सत्यमवक्तव्यं वक्तव्यमनृतं भवेत्।
यत्रानृतं भवेत् सत्यं सत्यं चाप्यनृतं भवेत्।। कर्ण ६९.३२।।

Where the result of speaking a lie is good, akin to speaking the truth, and where speaking the truth will bring great harm, akin to speaking a lie, there one must not speak the truth. There one had better speak a lie.[36]

Moreover:

प्राणात्यये विवाहे वा सर्वज्ञातिवधात्यये।
नर्मण्यभिप्रवृत्ते वा न च प्रोक्तं मृषा भवेत्।। कर्ण ६९.६२।।
अधर्मं नात्र पश्यन्ति धर्मतत्त्वार्थदर्शिनः।

There are occasions when a lie is not a lie: when there is danger to one's life; when one's relatives are threatened with death; at the time of contracting a marriage;[37] *and in fun or good humour.*[38]

To the list of occasions when a lie spoken will not be a lie, the *Bhāgvata-purāṇa* charmingly adds one more: *if one lies to please a woman.*[39]

यः स्तेनैः सह सम्बन्धान्मुच्यते शपथैरपि।। कर्ण ६९.६३।।
श्रेयस्तत्रानृतं वक्तुं तत् सत्यमविचारितम्।

If by speaking untruth one may save oneself, say, from robbers, then one should do so unhesitatingly, and regard that piece of untruth as truth.[40]

This is illustrated with the parable of Kaushika, a *brahmana* ascetic, well read but not too wisely, reputed for his vow that he shall always speak the truth. One day a gang of robbers, asking him whether he had seen a rich young couple whom they were following come that way, and holding him to his vow, he tells them truthfully which way he had seen them go. The robbers found them, robbed them of their belongings, and also killed them. For this '*misuse of speech*', Kaushika the ascetic incurred great demerit and fall.[41]

The *Tirukkuraḷ* says: *'Even falsehood has the nature of truth, if it confers a benefit that is free from fault.'*[42]

However, the *truth* is *relative* argument may easily degenerate into opportunism, and what is palpably wrong and untruthful sought to be justified on one ground or another, in bad faith. It is for this reason that the *Mahābhārata* places the *conditionality* of ethical norms and social functions in the larger context where *dharma* is defined as the force which sustains the people and secures the good of all living beings. However, the suggestion that:

> तस्माद् धर्मार्थमनृतमुक्त्वा नानृतभाग् भवेत् ।। कर्ण ६९.६५ ।।
> एष ते लक्षणोद्देशो मयोद्दिष्टो यथाविधि ।
> *If for the sake of* dharma *one must take recourse to untruth, one does not incur any blame thereby.*[43]

is not to be interpreted, mistranslating *dharma* as 'religion', as saying that one may take recourse to untruth and to lies in advancing one's 'religious' or sectarian cause. That is not the meaning at all. That is not at all the meaning.

Neither does the *Mahābhārata* lessen in any way the importance of 'truth speaking', speaking truthfully, *satya-vāc* or *satya-vachana*.[44] In saying that truth, *satya*, is manifestly very much more than 'truth speaking', it is not being suggested that one may, therefore, speak untruthfully to serve one's purpose, and cleverly justify it with the metaphysics of relativity. '*Speaking truthfully*' as the plain meaning of truth is never abandoned. The plain meaning of the two words *satyam vada*, 'speak truthfully', of the *Taittirīya Upanishad*,[45] was never lost in a truthful discussion of truth that followed in the *Mahābhārata*.

Indeed, how an ignoble but very clever distortion of truth led to the killing of Droṇāchārya or Droṇa on the battlefield, in the war between the Pāṇḍava-s and the Kaurava-s, is narrated in the *Mahābhārata*[46]—and condemned. Droṇāchārya, who had taught archery to both, and was their teacher, but was fighting on the side of the Kaurava-s, had a son, his only son, Ashvatthāmā by name, whom he loved most dearly. When Droṇa proved to be invincible in the battle, a strategy was crafted by Krishna,[47] and under his supervision carried out flawlessly, that would make Droṇa numb with grief and thus unable to fight any more. In the fierce battle of the day, Bhīma announced to Droṇa, in a way that Droṇa could not miss hearing, '*Ashvatthāmā is killed*'.[48] He was, so far as those three words were concerned, indeed speaking truthfully, for meanwhile, according to the plan drawn up by Krishna, Bhīma had killed a magnificent war elephant of his own army, also called Ashvatthāmā.[49] On hearing Bhīma say, '*Ashvatthāmā is killed*', Droṇa was stunned, but he did not believe it, knowing the invincible strength of his son.[50] Wanting to make certain whether his son Ashvatthāmā was or was not killed, he asked Yudhishṭhira.[51] For he always had faith in the man that even if he could, by telling a lie, secure the lordship of all the worlds, he would not lie.[52] Having that faith in Yudhishṭhira being a truthful person and known for his truth speaking, it was from *him* that Droṇa sought the confirmation or the denial of the news that Bhīma had announced. On the urging of Krishna, Yudhishṭhira is made to say, '*Ashvatthāmā is killed*', in a loud voice, but the other part, '*It was Ashvatthāmā the elephant*', in almost a whisper that Droṇa could not hear.[53] Believing that it was his son Ashvatthāmā who was killed, Droṇa abandons the fight, sits in his chariot, his eyes closed, and his head bent low with immeasurable grief, wanting to live no more. At that opportune moment, when Droṇa was not even looking around, Dhrishṭadyumna, the brother of Draupadī, rushed at him, seized him by his hair, and cut off his head with one blow of his sword.[54] Seeing that Droṇa had laid aside his arms, and was completely vulnerable, many soldiers began to shout, 'Don't kill him, don't kill him.' Arjuna, always Droṇa's most favoured pupil, rushed to save his guru from being killed in this manner, even though he, too, was a part of the plan. But by that time the deed was done. That foul strategy soon became widely known, and created in all hearts a deep revulsion, in the heart of Yudhishṭhira the truthful no less. Outwardly his answer to Droṇa was truthful, but Yudhishṭhira had lied, if cleverly, and he knew that he was lying.

In a conversation that takes place soon after the killing of Droṇa, Arjuna calls Yudhishṭhira 'a mean despicable liar', 'in the garb of a truth-speaking person, a hypocrite', and 'a killer of his guru'.[55] He equally bitterly reproaches himself.[56] What is witnessed is an exchange of hurtful and wounding words, flying like arrows, between Bhīma and Arjuna,[57] between Arjuna and Dhrishṭadyumna,[58] and between Sātyaki and Dhrishṭadyumna who justifies his act.[59]

The *Mahābhārata* describes, in a language of symbols, the punishment to Yudhishṭhira in the very next moment of his lying. Until then, because of the force of his truthfulness in speech, his chariot would remain a little above the earth; now it touched the ground.[60] Much later, he would be conducted through a dreadful tour of Hell, and when he asked *why*?, he was told that *that was because he had lied.* But his punishment would not stop there. At the end of the war, won by the Pāṇḍava-s, and Ashvatthāmā still alive, burning with the fire of anger and revenge for the manner of his father's killing, would kill all the sons of the Pāṇḍava-s from Draupadī, when they all were asleep. Before that, he would kill Dhrishṭadyumna, the killer of his father, in a most cruel way, and then rejoice.[61]

It is repeatedly stated in the *Mahābhārata* that the nature of *dharma*, and of truth likewise, is exceedingly subtle and difficult to grasp. It is another way of the *Mahābhārata* saying that human relationships, of one's self with the self and with the *other*, are full of complexities and ambiguities, and are subject to the changing *desha* and *kāla*, besides. Once that is understood, then its consistent advocacy, in the voice of Bhīshma, of the relativistic nature of truth would not seem at variance with his own last words:

सत्येषु यतितव्यं वः सत्यं हि परमं बलम् ।। अनुशासन १६७.४९ ।।
Exert in truth, for truth is the greatest force.[62]

Truth is relational

The problem with theory, with *theory* as such, is that it begins with a conclusion, which appears to be a hypothesis but is in fact a certainty. And since there have always been many theories about the same thing, one conflicting with the other, it means that there are as many conflicting certainties. Human history shows that, by some mysterious transformation, they turn into a luxurious ground for violence of every variety, the 'certainties' about *truth* most of all.

Besides the conception of truth as correspondence with facts as one knows them, there is in the whole of the *Mahābhārata* a deeper view of truth which, in relation with human life and its potentiality, consists in self-discipline as its chief feature. In other words, truth is viewed not merely as correspondence with facts but as the actual *living* of an ethical and rational life. Morality and reason, taken together, have as their aim the individual person in relation with others. For that relation to be ethical, one has first to conquer oneself.

आनृशंस्यं परो धर्मः क्षमा च परमं बलम् ।
आत्मज्ञानं परं ज्ञानं न सत्याद् विद्यते परम् ।। शान्ति ३२९.१२ ।।

> *Not to be cruel is a great* dharma*: forgiveness, the greatest strength: self-knowledge is the highest knowledge: and there is nothing greater than truth.*[63]

> सत्यस्य वचनं श्रेय: सत्यादपि हितं वदेत्।
> यद् भूतहितमत्यन्तमेतत् सत्यं मतं मम।। शान्ति ३२९.१३।।
> *It is good to speak the truth; but the truth must be spoken for the good of others. What is conducive to the greatest good of all beings, I believe that to be the truth.*[64]

In answer to the question: *What is truth and what are its predicates?*,[65] the *Mahābhārata* mentions *thirteen attributes of truth.*[66]

> सत्यं च समता चैव दमश्चैव न संशय:।
> अमात्सर्यं क्षमा चैव ह्रीस्तितिक्षानसूयता।। शान्ति १६२.८।।

> त्यागो ध्यानमथार्यत्वं धृतिश्च सततं स्थिरा।
> अहिंसा चैव राजेन्द्र सत्याकारास्त्रयोदश।। शान्ति १६२.९।।
> *Including itself as a predicate, they are: equality (*samatā*), self-control (*dama*), absence of envy (*amātsarya*), forgiveness (*kṣhmā*), modesty (*hri*), endurance (*titikṣhā*), not to find fault with others (*anasūyā*), renunciation (*tyāga*), concentration (*dhyāna*), nobility of conduct (*āryata*), forbearance (*dhṛti*), and not-violence (*ahiṃsā*).*[67]

Each of them is then defined as follows:

> सत्यं नामाव्ययं नित्यमविकारि तथैव च।
> सर्वधर्माविरुद्धेन योगेनैतदवाप्यते।। शान्ति १६२.१०।।
> *'Truth' is that which is undifferentiated, eternal, and without any defect; it is obtained through the discipline of not doing anything against any* dharma.[68]

> आत्मनीष्टे तथानिष्टे रिपौ च समता तथा।
> इच्छाद्वेषक्षयं प्राप्य कामक्रोधक्षयं तथा।। शान्ति १६२.११।।
> *'Equality' lies in displaying the same attitude towards friend and foe; it is achieved by destroying the feelings of attachment, antipathy, desire, and anger.*[69]

दमो नान्यस्पृहा नित्यं गाम्भीर्यं धैर्यमेव च।
अभयं रोगशमनं ज्ञानेनैतदवाप्यते।। शान्ति १६२.१२।।

'Self-control' consists in not desiring things that belong to others; in the seriousness and steadfastness of purpose; in the absence of deviousness; and in the conquest of anger; it is obtained by knowledge.[70]

अमात्सर्यं बुधाः प्राहुर्दाने धर्मे च संयमः।
अवस्थितेन नित्यं च सत्येनामत्सरी भवेत्।। शान्ति १६२.१३।।

'Absence of envy' consists in mental restraint while giving gifts and in doing one's appointed duty; it is achieved through truthfulness.[71]

अक्षमायाः क्षमायाश्च प्रियाणीहाप्रियाणि च।
क्षमते सम्मतः साधुः साध्वाप्नोति च सत्यवाक्।। शान्ति १६२.१४।।

'Forgiveness' consists in being able to bear a conduct that is unbearable and a speech that is unpleasant; it is achieved through truthfulness.[72]

कल्याणं कुरुते बाढं धीमान् न ग्लायते क्वचित्।
प्रशान्तवाङ्मना नित्यं ह्रीस्तु धर्मादवाप्यते।। शान्ति १६२.१५।।

'Modesty' consists in securing for others, without regret and always at peace within, what is good; it is achieved by following dharma.[73]

धर्मार्थहेतोः क्षमते तितिक्षा क्षान्तिरुच्यते।
लोकसंग्रहणार्थं वै सा तु धैर्येण लभ्यते।। शान्ति १६२.१६।।

'Endurance' is the capacity to bear difficulties in pursuing dharma *and one's desired object; it is obtained through patience.*[74]

'Not to find fault with others' consists in seriousness; it is achieved by generosity.[75]

त्यागः स्नेहस्य यत् त्यागो विषयाणां तथैव च।
रागद्वेषप्रहीणस्य त्यागो भवति नान्यथा।। शान्ति १६२.१७।।

'Renunciation' consists in giving up partiality to things as well as sense gratification; it is achieved by rising above attraction and revulsion.[76]

'Concentration' is achieved through silence.[77]

आर्यता नाम भूतानां यः करोति प्रयत्नतः।
शुभं कर्म निराकारो वीतरागस्तथैव च।। शान्ति १६२.१८।।

'Nobility of conduct' consists in working constantly for the good of others; it is achieved through giving up attachment to things for oneself.[78]

धृतिर्नाम सुखे दु:खे यथा नाप्नोति विक्रियाम्।
तां भजेत सदा प्राज्ञो य इच्छेद् भूतिमात्मन:।। शान्ति १६२.१९।।
सर्वथा क्षमिणा भाव्यं तथा सत्यपरेण च।
वीतहर्षभयक्रोधो धृतिमाप्नोति पण्डित:।। शान्ति १६२.२०।।

'Forbearance' consists in rising above happiness and suffering; it is achieved by constant forgiveness, by sticking to the truth, and by conquering fear and anger.[79]

अद्रोह: सर्वभूतेषु कर्मणा मनसा गिरा।
अनुग्रहश्च दानं च सतां धर्म: सनातन:।। शान्ति १६२.२१।।

'Not-violence' consists in malice towards none, in act or in thought or in speech, and in showing kindness and generosity to others.[80]

एते त्रयोदशाकारा: पृथक् सत्यैकलक्षणा:
भजन्ते सत्यमेवेह बृंहयन्ते च भारत।। शान्ति १६२.२२।।

These thirteen distinct attributes of truth together point to truth, strengthen it and enhance it.[81]

The above thirteen attributes of truth, although each mentioned as distinct, are regarded as aspects of one indivisible whole. That is the reason why each one of them is connected with the rest, and each is described as the 'highest *dharma*'. Each invariably includes the rest.[82] Truth is indivisible. There are no 'parts' to *truth*. Above all, as its attributes, *laksana*, indicate, truth is a state of being in the right relationship with one's self and with the *other*. That is the main concern of the *Mahābhārata*, as it is the main concern of being human.

At the same time, after saying what each of the thirteen attributes of truth in itself is, in the voice of Bhīshma the *Mahābhārata* adds that नान्ता: शक्यो गुणानां च वक्तुं सतस्य पार्थिव. '*The limits of truth's attributes cannot be stated.*'[83] In other words, no one *definition* of truth, nor any one *theory* of truth, can ever state what truth really is. Neither can it be confined within any fixed number of attributes.

However, if one still looks for one word that will indicate clearly the centrality of truth in human life, it will be the word *samāhita*, which means '*held together*', '*connected*', '*united*'. It also means '*held together, united, for the good of the self and for the good of the other, for their good together'*. The relativity of truth is always subject to *this*. The *Mahābhārata* is saying: 'T*ruth is samāhita in every movement of life that sustains, and* *holds together, and enhances the worth of life; and whatever enhances, holds together, and sustains, is samāhita in truth.*

Through various stories of human situations, the *Mahābhārata* is saying that 'knowledge', or *jñāna*; 'intellect', or *buddhi*, and learning, or *vidyā*, are *samāhita* in truth likewise, and truth in them. Cognition is not to be separated from character. When it is, then one sees:

सुमहान्त्यपि शास्त्राणि धरयन्ति बहुश्रुताः ।
छेत्तारः संशयानां च क्लिश्यन्तीहाल्पबुद्धयः ।। शान्ति १५८.१६ ।।
Highly well-read scholars just memorise the shāstra-s. They are even adepts at solving all doubts. Yet, possessed by greed, their intellect gets clouded, and they suffer as a result.[84]

द्वेषक्रोधप्रसक्ताश्च शिष्टाचारबहिष्कृताः ।। शान्ति १५८.१७ ।।
अन्तःक्रूरा वाङ्मधुराः कूपाश्छन्नास्तृणैरिव ।
धर्मवैतंसिकाः क्षुद्रा मुष्णन्ति ध्वजिनो जगत् ।। शान्ति १५८.१८ ।।
As a consequence, occupied with aggression and anger they abandon good manners and cultured conduct. Cruel at heart but sweet of tongue, they are like a well that is covered with misleading grass. Waving the flag of dharma, *they only deceive others.*[85]

The *Mahābhārata* is showing in clear, straightforward, and reasoned language that truth is the very breath of life, without which nothing can survive. Truth is *samāhita* in seeking material prosperity and earning wealth. Truth is *samāhita* in sexual happiness and joy. Truth is *samāhita* in law and governance, however diverse their forms. Truth is *samāhita* in being human and in transcending the human condition: in the pleasures and the pains of the one, and in the tranquillity of the other. Truth is *samāhita* in speech, as it is *samāhita* in silence. When each of them is discussed separately in the *Mahābhārata*, with care and deep concern, never in the abstract, but always in relation to concrete human situations, truth invariably forms a central part of that relation. They all are brought together in the unity of life, and life is brought together in unity with truth. And since the word *samāhita* at the same time means '*the good together*', truth secures that good for all.

यद् भूतहितमत्यन्तं तत् सत्यमिति धारणा ।
विपर्ययकृतोऽधर्मः पश्य धर्मस्य सूक्ष्मताम् ।। वनपर्व २०९.४ ।।
What secures the greatest good of all living beings is truth.[86]

सत्यस्य वचनं श्रेयः सत्यं ज्ञानं हितं भवेत्।
यद् भूतहितमत्यन्तं तद् वै सत्यं परं मतम्।। वनपर्व २१३.३१।।

To speak the truth is the good. True knowledge leads to the good. What secures the greatest good of all beings is believed to be the truth.[87]

वेदस्योपनिषत् सत्यं सत्यस्योपनिषद् दमः।
दमस्योपनिषद् दानं दानस्योपनिषत् तपः।। शान्ति २५१.११।।
तपसोपनिषत् त्यागस्त्यागस्योपनिषत् सुखम्।
सुखस्योपनिषत् स्वर्गः स्वर्गस्योपनिषच्छमः।। शान्ति २५१.१२।।
दमस्योपनिषत् त्यागः शिष्टाचारेषु नित्यदा।। वनपर्व २०७.६७।।

Truth is the essence of knowledge; self-discipline, the essence of truth; to sacrifice for others is the essence of self-discipline. Happiness is the essence of sacrifice; heaven, the essence of happiness. And the essence of heaven is peace. And that is the mystical meaning of cultured conduct always.[88]

वेदस्योपनिषत् सत्यं सत्यस्योपनिषद् दमः।
दमस्योपनिषन्मोक्ष एतत् सर्वानुशासनम्।। शान्ति २९९.१३।।

Truth is the essence of knowledge; self-control, the essence of truth; freedom, the essence of self-control. And that is the mystical meaning of all disciplines.[89]

न मृत्युसेनामायान्तीं जातु कश्चित् प्रबाधते।
ऋते सत्यमसत् त्याज्यं सत्ये ह्यमृतमाश्रितम्।। शान्ति १७५.२८।।

No one can, without truth, face the mighty assault of death. Therefore, give up untruth, for what is beyond death, is dependent upon truth.[90]

अमृतं चैव मृत्युश्च द्वयं देहे प्रतिष्ठितम्।
मृत्युमापद्यते मोहात् सत्येनापद्यतेऽमृतम्।। शान्ति १७५.३०।।

Both death and the deathless are established in the human body. From the confusion of perceptions comes death; and from truth, that which death can never touch.[91]

सोऽहं ह्यहिंस्त्रः सत्यार्थी कामक्रोधबहिष्कृतः।
समदुःखसुखः क्षेमी मृत्युं हास्याम्यमर्त्यवत्।। शान्ति १७५.३१।।

Henceforth, keeping away from violence, I will search for truth. Removing desire and anger from my heart, and tranquil in happiness and suffering alike, I will thus conquer death.[92]

CHAPTER EIGHT

Human Attributes—neither Neglect, nor Idolatry

- *Svārtha* and *niti*: self-interest and prudence

The *Mahābhārata* shows, in great detail, that disrespect to any human attribute, such as self-interest, or sexuality, or desire for material prosperity, or to the more fundamental desire for pleasure, must invite violence. But it shows at the same time how their *idolatry* must invite even greater violence. In one case, the violence is to the individual and to his, or her, relationships: in the other case, because it enters political and economic thought, and becomes an ideology, the idolatry of wealth, power and pleasure, the violence is collective and extensive. The question is one of their proper valuation, of knowing the true place of everything; which, everything in the *Mahābhārata* shows, is quite as fundamental as the desire for pleasure itself, and is inseparably linked with it. It shows that the origins of disorder, *adharma*, lie not in the concern with self-interest, or in the desire for pleasure, but in the *false valuation* we place upon them. We estimate them *either* so low as to look upon them as coarse, ignoble, or even evil; *or* we estimate them so high as to look upon them as the only good. Both are false. And both are self-destructive.

Svārtha, 'self-interest', and *sukha*, 'pleasure', and their intricate workings in human relationships, occupy a large space in the *Mahābhārata*, because they occupy a large space in human living.

येन येन हि यस्यार्थ: कारणेनेह कर्मणि।
तत्तदालम्बते सर्व: स्वे स्वे स्वार्थपरिग्रहे।। शान्ति ३२०.४३।।
Whatever means are required to serve one's self-interest, everybody in every matter adopts them.[1]

It often speaks of *svārtha*, with such stark realism that it may sound even cynical. But that is in the context of an agonising inquiry Yudhishṭhira had raised as regards a familiar situation in human life.

Yudhishṭhira (*to Bhīshma*)

You spoke of the intelligence that foresees a danger and avoids it. You spoke of the intelligence that quickly finds a way out of the danger suddenly materialised. Now I want to hear from you about that intelligence that keeps a king, knowledgeable in matters of *dharma* and economic realities but assailed by enemies, from being overwhelmed?[2]

When assailed at the same time by several enemies, what should a king do? On seeing him in a difficult situation, when the enemies that were put down earlier combine, and try to destroy him by the roots; and they are more powerful than he, and he is helpless and alone besides, what kind of intelligence must he have recourse to in order to survive that crisis?[3]

When someone who had earlier shown all signs of being a friend turns into an enemy, then how should a king behave towards him, and what should he do to remain happy still?[4]

With whom should one struggle? With whom should one seek alliance?[5]

Only you can guide me through these agonising questions. After examining them with care, kindly instruct me.[6]

Bhīshma (*to Yudhishṭhira*)

Your questions are legitimate and right. And I will say something on the difficult subject you have brought up. Listen, son!

अमित्रो मित्रतां याति मित्रं चापि प्रदुष्यति।
सामर्थ्ययोगात् कार्याणामनित्या वै सदा गतिः।। शान्ति १३८.१३।।

Circumstances often combine in such a way that an enemy turns into a friend, and a friend begins harbouring feelings of enmity. Friendship and enmity do not remain the same all the time.[7]

यो ह्यमित्रैर्नरो नित्यं न संदध्यादपण्डितः।
न सोऽर्थं प्राप्नुयात् किंचित् फलान्यपि च भारत।। शान्ति १३८.१६।।

The fool who does not in any circumstance seek peace with the enemy, achieves nothing, gains nothing.[8]

यस्त्वमित्रेण संदध्यान्मित्रेण च विरुद्ध्यते।
अर्थयुक्तिं समालोक्य सुमहद् विन्दते फलम्।। शान्ति १३८.१७।।

It is foolish to think that there is no alliance with the enemy, and no falling out between friends. In his self-interest, the prudent man approaches the enemy with alliance and friendship, and gives up a friend, doing himself much good thereby.[9]

Bhīshma then narrates the story of a wild cat and a mouse trapped together in a hunter's net.[10] Two natural enemies, because one the natural food of the other, desperately needing each other's help when faced with a stronger common danger; and after that danger had passed, one professing undying love and friendship for the other, and the other smelling in that declaration only a threat to oneself. Through that story the *Mahābhārata* conveys many lessons in the power and wisdom of self-interest. They are conveyed in the gentle voice of the mouse who the wild cat invites to his bosom as an abiding friend; and the mouse tells him that he knows he would before long find a permanent place in the cat's stomach, and not in his bosom. He delivers a long discourse,[11] the substance of which is as follows:

नास्ति जातु रिपुर्नाम मित्रं नाम न विद्यते।
सामर्थ्ययोगाज्जायन्ते मित्राणि रिपवस्तथा।। शान्ति १३८.१३९।।

There exists neither enemy nor friend: it is necessity that creates them, friends and enemies alike.[12]

नास्ति मैत्री स्थिरा नाम न च ध्रुवमसौहृदम्।
अर्थयुक्त्यानुजायन्ते मित्राणि रिपवस्तथा।। शान्ति १३८.१४१।।

Neither is friendship permanent, nor is enmity permanent: it is due to self-interest that somebody is now a friend and then an enemy.[13]

मित्रं च शत्रुतामेति कस्मिंश्चित् कालपर्यये।
शत्रुश्च मित्रतामेति स्वार्थो हि बलवत्तरः।। शान्ति १३८.१४२।।

With circumstances changed, sometimes friend turns into enemy, and enemy into friend. Indeed, self-interest alone is the great force.[14]

यो यस्मिन् जीवति स्वार्थं पश्येत् पीडां न जीवति।
स तस्य मित्रं तावत् स्याद् यावन्न स्याद् विपर्ययः।। शान्ति १३८.१४०।।

So long as the other serves one's self-interest, and on his death there is the feeling of loss, only that long is one a friend to the other.[15]

अर्थयुक्ता हि जायन्ते पिता माता सुतस्तथा।। शान्ति १३८.१४५।।
मातुला भागिनेयाश्च तथा सम्बन्धिबान्धवाः।

It is self-interest alone that binds one to father and mother, to son, to uncle, and nephew, indeed to all relatives and friends.[16]

अर्थार्थी जीवलोकोऽयं न कश्चित् कस्यचित् प्रियः।
सख्यं सोदर्ययोर्भ्रात्रोर्दम्पत्योर्वा परस्परम्।। शान्ति १३८.१५२।।
कस्यचिन्नाभिजानामि प्रीतिं निष्कारणामिह।

This material world is shot through with self-interest, and no one is beloved of anyone. The affection between brother and brother, as between man and wife, is based solely on self-interest. I know of no love or affection that is without some purpose.[17]

उत्पन्ना कारणे प्रीतिरासीन्नौ कारणान्तरे।। शान्ति १३८.१५५।।
प्रध्वस्ते कारणस्थाने सा प्रीतिर्विनिवर्तते।

The love that is born out of some purpose, exists only so long as that purpose lasts: that purpose gone, love vāṇīshes, too.[18]

कालो हेतुं विकुरुते स्वार्थस्तमनुवर्तते।। शान्ति १३८.१५७।।
स्वार्थं प्राज्ञोऽभिजानाति प्राज्ञं लोकोऽनुवर्तते।। शान्ति १३८.१५८।।

Reasons are altered by time; and self-interest is altered likewise: the wise know self-interest only too well; and in this, the common folk follow the wise.[19]

अकाले हि समर्थस्य स्नेहतुरयं तव।
तस्मान्नाहं चले स्वार्थात् सुस्थिरः संधिविग्रहे।। शान्ति १३८.१५९।।

You are powerful, and yet you are displaying affection for me. Your self-interest can be the only reason for this, and I know my self-interest too; and with that, I know the nature of alliance and enmity.[20]

अभ्राणामिव रूपाणि विकुर्वन्ति क्षणे क्षणे।
अद्यैव हि रिपुर्भूत्वा पुनरद्यैव मे सुहृत्।। शान्ति १३८.१६०।।
पुनश्च रिपुरद्यैव युक्तीनां पश्य चापलम्।

Friendship and enmity keep changing every moment, as the formations in the clouds do. Today my enemy, you can today turn my friend; and again today become my enemy. See, how unstable the two are, because based on changing self-interest.[21]

Furthermore:

अहमन्नं भवान् भोक्ता दुर्बलोऽहं भवान् बली।। शान्ति १३८.१६६।।
नावयोर्विद्यते संधिर्वियुक्ते विषमे बले।

I am your food, and I am weak. You are strong. There is between us no equality, only great difference in strength. There can be no alliance between us therefore.[22]

In brief, लोको रक्षति चात्मानं पश्य स्वार्थस्य सारताम् । '*Everyone wishes to protect oneself: see, self-interest is the essence of the world.*'[23]

This is honestly acknowledged by Bhīshma, the most venerable figure in the story of the *Mahābhārata*, about his own conduct, too. Just when the war was about to begin, and the two armies poised to rush at each other, Yudhishṭhira got down from his chariot, unarmed, and began to walk towards Bhīshma. That startled everybody, his brothers most of all. 'Where are you going? Why are you doing this?' He does not answer them; keeps walking; and the brothers follow him. A comment is heard from the other side: 'Coward! What a disgrace to his family! He is walking towards Bhīshma, to ask that his life be spared.' He salutes Bhīshma, and says:

'I could not have begun the battle without seeking your permission to fight you, and your blessings, too. That is what I have come for. Permit me to fight you, and bless me.'[24]

Greatly pleased by that extraordinary expression of respect, Bhīshma says about himself something that he had never acknowledged before, maybe not even to himself.

अर्थस्य पुरुषो दासो दासस्त्वर्थो न कस्यचित् ।
इति सत्यं महाराज बद्धोऽस्म्यर्थेन कौरवैः ।। भीष्म ४३.४१ ।।
Man is the slave of self-interest. Self-interest is no one's slave. This is the truth. I am tied to the Kaurava-s with the bond of self-interest.[25]

अतस्त्वां क्लीबवद् वाक्यं ब्रवीमि कुरुनन्दन ।
भृतोऽस्म्यर्थेन कौरव्य युद्धादन्यत् किमिच्छसि ।। भीष्म ४३.४२ ।।
Therefore today I speak to you like an impotent man. The Kaurava-s have supported me with the means of subsistence. Short of switching sides, do tell me what you want from me.[26]

That was a stunningly honest confession, made in plain words, without apology. Yudhishṭhira then approaches Droṇāchārya, Kripāchārya, and Shalya, who were, like Bhīshma, venerable figures of the realm, but are now to be fought. Each one of them, although pleased, says about himself, and in the same words, what Bhīshma had said, and without apology likewise,[27] '*Man is the slave of self-interest.*'

The *Mahābhārata* does not disperse the question of self-interest by raising the metaphysical question, 'What *is* this *sva*, self, whose interest is the spring of one's action?' Here, the 'self' is understood as it is experienced, the psychophysical self, one's distinct individuality, in all its natural attributes of being human. And 'self-interest' has its plain meaning.

Self-interest acknowledged as a human attribute and the moving force behind most actions, the *Mahābhārata* proceeds to show that, in actual fact, though, most of us do not act even out of self-interest, or self-love. For if we *did* take self-interest seriously, it would take us in two interrelated directions. In the first place, it would, by the very logic of self-interest, return us to our self. For in that logic

आत्मैव ह्यात्मनो बन्धुरात्मैव रिपुरात्मनः ।
आत्मैव ह्यात्मनः साक्षी कृतस्यापकृतस्य च ।। स्त्री २.३५ ।।

One's self alone is one's friend, and also one's enemy: one's self alone is the witness to what one does or does not do.[28]

आत्मनाऽऽत्मानमन्विच्छेन्मनोबुद्धीन्द्रियैर्यतैः ।
आत्मा ह्येवात्मनो बन्धुरात्मैव रिपुरात्मनः ।। उद्योग ३४.६४ ।।

बन्धुरात्माऽऽत्मनस्तस्य येनैवात्माऽऽत्मना जितः ।
स एव नियतो बन्धुः स एवानियतो रिपुः ।। उद्योग ३४.६५ ।।

Let one understand one's self through one's body and the mind. One's self is one's friend, and one's self one's enemy. Whoever has conquered his self, has his self as his friend. Conquered, the self is a friend; left uncontrolled, an enemy.[29]

and

न विक्रमो न चाप्यर्थो न मित्रं न सुहृज्जनः ।
तथोन्मोचयते दुःखाद् यथाऽऽत्मा स्थिरसंयमः ।। स्त्री ७.२२ ।।

It is neither bravery, nor wealth, nor friends, nor relatives, that can free one from suffering, but only one's self, stable and self-controlled.[30]

In a long conversation between a husband and wife, referred to only as 'Brāhmaṇa' and 'Brāhmaṇī', about 'the field of acts', or the *kṣhetra*, and about the human person, the doer, or the *kshetrajña*, he says to her:

एक: शास्ता न द्वितीयोऽस्ति शास्ता
यो हृच्छयस्तमहमनुब्रवीमि।। आश्वमेधिक २६.१।।

There is only one ruler, and not another, who, I say to you, resides in one's heart.[31]

एको गुरुर्नास्ति ततो द्वितीयो
यो हृच्छयस्तमहमनुब्रवीमि।। आश्वमेधिक २६.२।।

There is only one teacher, and not another, who, I say to you, resides in one's heart.[32]

एको बन्धुर्नास्ति ततो द्वितीयो
यो हृच्छयस्तमहमनुब्रवीमि।। आश्वमेधिक २६.३।।

There is only one friend, and not another, who, I say to you, resides in one's heart.[33]

एक: श्रोता नास्ति ततो द्वितीयो
यो हृच्छयस्तमहमनुब्रवीमि।। आश्वमेधिक २६.४।।

There is only one listener, and not another, who, I say to you, resides in one's heart.[34]

एको द्वेष्टा नास्ति ततो द्वितीयो
यो हृच्छयस्तमहमनुब्रवीमि।। आश्वमेधिक २६.५।।

There is only one enemy, and not another, who, I say to you, resides in one's heart.[35]

गुरुर्बोद्धा च श्रोता च द्वेष्टा च ह्रादि नि:सृत:।। आश्वमेधिक २६.१३।।

The teacher, the seeker, the listener, the enemy, manifest themselves in one's heart.[36]

The logic of self-interest, if understood properly, would simultaneously return us to the *other*. For even a moment's reflection will show, apparently a paradox, that it is only by serving the interest of the *other* that one serves one's self-interest best. That is to say, the happiness of the *other* is an essential condition of one's own happiness. The two are inseparably bound. Likewise, the pain and sorrow of the *other* is also one's own.

न दु:खं परदु:खे वै केचिदाहुरबुद्धय:।
यो दु:खं नाभिजानाति स जल्पति महाजने।। शान्ति १३९.६५।।

यस्तु शोचति दुःखार्तः स कथं वक्तुमुत्सहेत् ।
रसज्ञः सर्वदुःखस्य यथाऽऽत्मनि तथा परे ।। शान्ति १३९.६६ ।।

There are some fools who think that one does not feel pain at the pain of the other. Only he who does not know the meaning of pain can ever say that. Who feels his pain, and knows the essence of his and the other's pain as well, will never say that.[37]

In every situation, at every turn, this is what the *Mahābhārata* is showing as one of its abiding themes; for it is an abiding theme of human relationships. *Sva-artha*, self-interest, is then to be seen in the brighter light of what is *sva-hita,* for one's good. And one's good consists in securing *para-hita*, the good of the *other*. The two are inseparable. The *Mahābhārata* narrates the following story to illustrate this.[38] And like the other stories the *Mahābhārata* narrates as the stories of the human condition, this one, too, says many things simultaneously.

In order to protect themselves from the increasing harassment by their first cousins, the Kaurava-s, and from any future attempts on their lives, the five Pāṇḍava brothers and their mother, Kuntī, are advised to live for a while in a safer place, incognito. Vyāsa arranges for them to live with the family of a brāhmaṇa, without his ever knowing their true identity.[39] Disguised as brāhmaṇa-s, they maintain themselves by seeking from the people their daily food as the customary *bhikṣhā*, or 'offering', to a brāhmaṇa. The people of the village provide them happily, wondering, though, who they could be; for they looked like of a royal stock, and had by their conduct endeared themselves to the people.[40] One day, while the other brothers had gone seeking their daily *bhikṣhā*, but Bhīma had stayed back, Kuntī heard loud laments emanating from a room of their host. The laments were so very distressful that she herself felt deeply distressed, and said to Bhīma:

Kuntī

Son! We have been living in this brāhmaṇa's home; and we have received from him so much affection and respect that we have, indeed, forgotten our own troubles. I keep thinking in what way can I do some good to him? To a person who has done good, one should repay by doing good to him in a greater measure still.

It seems that some great misfortune has befallen this brāhmaṇa. If I can be of some help to him, I could repay my debt of gratitude thereby.[41]

Bhīma (*to his mother*)

But first find out what is troubling him, and its cause. On knowing that, I will do my best to relieve him of his suffering, even if it be exceedingly difficult to do so.[42]

Kuntī entered the brāhmaṇa's room, where she saw him with his wife, son and daughter. She stood there, unnoticed by them, hearing what they were saying to each other in deep distress.

The Brāhmaṇa (*to his wife*)

Damned be this human life! It has no meaning; it has no purpose; it is the root of pain and suffering; the cause of dependence upon others, and of the exceedingly unpleasant. There is in life only great suffering; and anxiety while one lives. Whoever lives this human life is forever subject to pain and suffering.[43]

Many times in the past I had suggested to you that we go and live in a happier place, but you would not listen to me. Each time you would say, 'I was born here, I grew up here, my father lived here.' Good Lord! Your father, and your mother, departed long ago for heaven! Then why this foolish attachment to this place? But you would not listen to me. And now we are faced with this greatest danger, which for me is a cause of deepest sorrow and anxiety. I know it is I who will have to die; for, while I live, I will let no one else be sacrificed.[44]

सहधर्मचरीं दान्तां नित्यं मातृसमां मम।
सखायं विहितां देवैर्नित्यं परमिकां गतिम्।। आदि १५६.३१।।

You have been my wife, my companion, my friend, you have taken care of me as a mother would. You always did what was for my good. In order to protect my life, I will not sacrifice you. I will consider myself low if I did.[45]

Neither would I sacrifice this little son of ours, still a child, not yet an adolescent. Nor would I sacrifice our daughter. A daughter, it is said, is given to a man as a trust by the gods of the universe. Giving her life, how can I now push her into the jaws of death?

मन्यन्ते केचिदधिकं स्नेहं पुत्रे पितुर्नराः।
कन्यायां केचिदपरे मम तुल्यावुभौ स्मृतौ।। आदि १५६.३७।।

Some people think that a father loves his son more. Some others think that a father loves his daughter more. For me both are equal in my love.[46]

यस्यां लोका: प्रसूतिश्च स्थिता नित्यमथो सुखम् ।
अपापां तामहं बालां कथमुत्स्त्रष्टुमुत्सहे ।। आदि १५६.३८ ।।

Upon whom depend this world, and the continuation of a family line, and all human happiness—how can I sacrifice that innocent daughter?[47]

But sacrificing myself, I would still be greatly troubled after my death; for our children wouldn't be able to survive without me. And I do not have the capacity to take us across this calamity.[48]

The Brāhmaṇī (*to her husband*)

You are learned, and you are wise. You must not, like an ordinary man, be distressed when faced with this calamity. Death will one day or another certainly come to every mortal. That being definite, it is no good lamenting over it. Wife, son, daughter, all are sought for one's own sake. You should live. *I* will go there. To a wife, the great abiding thing is to do what is for the good of her husband, even by sacrificing her life.[49]

The things one seeks a wife for, you have obtained them all through me. You have a son, and you have a daughter. And you have the means to bring them up and protect them; which I wouldn't have, should you die. What would become of them if you were to die?[50]

Furthermore, just as the birds of prey fasten on a piece of meat lying on the ground, so do men on a woman without a husband. When men will approach me again and again, I wouldn't be able to keep myself on the straight path of virtue.[51]

Undeserving, arrogant men would seek this innocent daughter of yours, who is endowed with the best of human qualities. If they were rejected, they would take her away forcibly. How would I then guide her, the only daughter in your family, on the path of cherished goodness?[52] How would I, without you, guide this little son of ours on the path of goodness and nobility? Failing to do both, I would surely end my life. What would become of them then? Without you and me, their father and mother, they would be destroyed.[53]

As for me, I have enjoyed all the pleasures of life. In having you as my husband, and these two as my children, I feel fulfilled. I will have no regret whatsoever if I now die, to protect you all from this calamity. I say to you truly, I wouldn't be able to live without you. Therefore, you should let *me* go to that human-eating *rākṣhasa*.[54]

In the course of deciding what is *dharma* and what is *adharma*, it was established, too, that women are never to be killed. And even *rākṣhasa*-s have a sense of *dharma*. It is likely that if a *woman* goes to him, he would not eat her; whereas if a man does, he would no doubt eat him. Taking into consideration all that I've said to you, protect yourself and these two children, and sacrifice me instead.[55]

Hearing his wife speak thus, the Brāhmaṇa felt exceedingly sad. He took her in his arms, and both began to cry softly.[56] Seeing her parents in such distress, and crying, the daughter is overcome with sorrow and addresses her father thus.[57]

The Daughter (*to her father*)

Why do you cry like one who has nobody to take care of him? You listen to me, and then do what you can.[58]

It is certain that, in accordance with *dharma*, you will have to give me away one day or another, to perpetuate a family line. If, as a girl, I am *tyājyā*, one 'to be given away', then give me away today; and thus protect this whole family.[59]

If you die, neither I nor this little brother of mine will be able to survive. Without you, I will be seen as one who has no protector, is helpless; and, unprotected, I will be forced to go with others, and there would be for me no greater suffering. I would rather prefer death. But if I could protect you all from a calamity, and die thus, I would feel blessed, indeed. No, not you, it is I who will go to that human-eating *rākṣhasa*.[60]

The Son

'Don't cry, father! Don't cry, mother! Send me there. *I* will destroy that demon.' 'See,' he picked up a straw, 'with *this*!' On hearing the boy say that, although troubled and distressed, their hearts filled with very great delight.[61]

At this point Kuntī made her appearance.

Kuntī (*to the Brāhmaṇa*)

What is causing you this great sorrow? I wish to know. And if it can be removed, I shall try to remove it.[62]

The Brāhmaṇa (*to Kuntī*)

What you said, a noble person would say. But I don't think that the cause of my distress can be removed by a human being.

Two leagues away from here, on the banks of the river Yamunā, lives a violent, man-eating *rākṣhasa*. His name is Baka. Fed on human flesh, he is extremely strong and fierce. He is the lord of this town and of this area. He oppresses the people exceedingly, and they have been suffering. But also with his brute force he protects this area from outside invasions and from other troubles. In turn, by way of a tax, we have to supply him every day considerable quantities of food that is taken to him by a man whom he, being a cannibal, then eats. Every household has to supply, by rotation, one man for his consumption. Although a family's turn comes after many years, when it does, it causes greatest distress. This time it is *my* turn.[63]

The king of this area is actually someone else; but he is so weak, irresolute, uncaring, that he does nothing to free the people of this menace. Perhaps we deserve such a ruler. We have settled here permanently, in the kingdom of a wicked king.[64]

राजानं प्रथमं विन्देत् ततो भार्यां ततो धनम् ।
त्रयस्य संचयेनास्य ज्ञातीन् पुत्रांश्च तारयेत् ।। आदि १५९.१२ ।।

One should first choose a good king; then take a wife; and earn money thereafter. These three obtained, one should then bring up one's family well.[65]

I did all these three things wrong. As a result, we are now in deep trouble. I see no way of freedom from that *rākṣhasa*. And I'm drowned in this indescribable sorrow.[66]

Kuntī (*to the Brāhmaṇa*)

Don't feel distressed. You have a small little son, and a daughter full of goodness and virtue. I can't imagine that either of them, or your wife, or you, should go there. I have thought of a way of your being freed from this trouble. I have five sons. I'll send one of them instead.[67]

The Brāhmaṇa (*to Kuntī*)

No, I will not let that happen just to save my life. A brāhmaṇa, and also a guest in my home—to send him to his certain death, and serve my self-interest? No, that is impossible. Such a low act is not to be seen even among those who in other ways negate *dharma.* Rather, to protect one given to knowledge and learning and teaching, one should sacrifice one's self and even one's own son.[68]

अभिसंधिकृते तस्मिन् ब्राह्मणस्य वधे मया ।
निष्कृतिं न प्रपश्यामि नृशंसं क्षुद्रमेव च ।। आदि १६०.९ ।।

आगतस्य गृहं त्यागस्तथैव शरणार्थिनः ।
याचमानस्य च वधो नृशंसो गर्हितो बुधैः ।। आदि १६०.१० ।।

Giving consent to what will cause the death of a brāhmaṇa, will be a cruel, low and despicable act. To abandon the one who has come to one's home; to give up one seeking protection; and to have a seeker killed to save one's own life—these are cruel and despicable acts.[69]

कुर्यान्न निन्दितं कर्म न नृशंसं कथंचन ।
इति पूर्वे महात्मान आपद्धर्मविदो विदुः ।। आदि १६०.११ ।।
श्रेयांस्तु सहदारस्य विनाशोऽद्य मम स्वयम् ।
ब्राह्मणस्य वधं नाहमनुमंस्ये कदाचन ।। आदि १६०.१२ ।।

Even in times of the greatest calamity, one must not do what is cruel and despicable, those knowing the law of such times say. It is better that today, I, with my wife, die; but never will I consent to the killing of a brāhmaṇa.[70]

Kuntī (*to the Brāhmaṇa*)

It is not that I love any of my sons less, even if I had a hundred sons. But I know that man-eating *rākṣhasa* will be unable to destroy my son; for my son is strong and has the knowledge of a *mantra.* This I know, my son will take that *rākṣhasa*'s food to him, and free you from your distress. I have seen before many a *rākṣhasa*; and whoever of them contended with my son was himself destroyed. But there is one condition: you shall not speak about this to anyone; for many will then come to my son, wanting to know that *mantra*, and trouble him evermore.[71]

On being told what he had to do to relieve their host of his distress, Bhīma said: 'I promise I will do it.' Just then the other brothers returned from their errand, and Yudhishṭhira saw that Bhīma wanted to tell him something. Kuntī told him what it was. 'On my asking, Bhīma would do a great deed to free our host and this whole town from a calamity.'[72] Yudhishṭhira reproaches his mother. 'You have been very rash in this, committing Bhīma to a great danger. You know he is our strength, and we depend upon him. To save the life of another man's son, you are prepared to sacrifice your own? Yourself, suffering much, you seem to have lost your head.'[73]

Kuntī (*to her son Yudhishṭhira*)

न चायं बुद्धिदौर्बल्याद्व्यवसायः कृतो मया।। आदि १६१.१२।।
नेदं लोभान्न चाज्ञानान्न च मोहाद् विनिश्चितम्।
बुद्धिपूर्वं तु धर्मस्य व्यवसायः कृतो मया।। आदि १६१.२०।।
No, I did not do this from any weakness of the mind, no.
What I've done, I've done not from any selfish motive, nor out of ignorance, nor from confusion. My decision is based on careful reflection and on the dictates of dharma.[74]

> We have been living in this brāhmaṇa's home happily. In this home we have received so much respect that, indeed, we have forgotten our own past troubles and suffering, even our anger. This seemed to me to be the only way of repaying a debt of gratitude.[75] And remember:

एतावानेव पुरुषः कृतं यस्मिन् न नश्यति।। आदि १६१.१४।।
यावच्च कुर्यादन्योऽस्य कुर्याद् बहुगुणं ततः।। आदि १६१.१५।।
Only he is human who does not let an act of kindness go in vain.
The good that the other did to one should be repaid by doing good to the other in even a greater measure.[76]

Furthermore:

यो ब्राह्मणस्य साहाय्यं कुर्यादर्थेषु कर्हिचित्।
क्षत्रियः स शुभाँल्लोकानाप्नुयादिति मे मतिः।। आदि १६१.२२।।

The kṣhattriya who helps the one devoted to learning and knowledge obtains the highest blessings. This I believe.[77]

क्षत्रियस्यैव कुर्वाणः क्षत्रियो वधमोक्षणम् ।
विपुलां कीर्तिमाप्नोति लोकेऽस्मिंश्च परत्र च ।। आदि १६१.२३ ।।

If a kṣhattriya saves the life of another kṣhattriya he obtains much acclaim in this world and the next.[78]

वैश्यस्यार्थे च साहाय्यं कुर्वाणः क्षत्रियो भुवि ।
स सर्वेष्वपि लोकेषु प्रजा रञ्जयते ध्रुवम् ।। आदि १६१.२४ ।।

The kṣhattriya who helps those devoted to creating the material conditions of human living certainly creates happiness among the people.[79]

शूद्रं तु मोचयेद् राजा शरणार्थिनमागतम् ।
प्राप्नोतीह कुले जन्म सद्द्रव्ये राजपूजिते ।। आदि १६१.२५ ।।

The king who protects in every way the one devoted to the services is honoured among the kings and in this life endowed with great prosperity, is born again as a king in the next.[80]

एवं मां भगवान् व्यासः पुरा पौरवनन्दन ।
प्रोवाचासुकरप्रज्ञस्तस्मादेवं चिकीर्षितम् ।। आदि १६१.२६ ।।

This is what the venerable Vyāsa had said to me once; and I acted accordingly.[81]

> Neither should you be anxious about Bhīma. He has the strength of a mountain.[82]

Kuntī went inside and once again reassured their host and his family. Next morning, while it was still dark, taking the immense quantity of his stipulated food Bhīma went to Baka the *rākshasa*, who was inside his cave. Bhīma began calling him and, meanwhile, merrily began eating the food meant for Baka. On emerging from the cave Baka saw that scene: the man meant to be eaten by him, himself eating the other food he had brought as offering. Enraged, he rushed at Bhīma, abusing him, and an awesome physical fight began between the two. Baka uprooted a tree, and, with it, rushed at Bhīma, who did likewise. Many trees were thus destroyed in that fight between a human and a demon. At one point, Bhīma lifted Baka, rotated him in the air, and flung him on the ground with great force. But that was not yet his end. Now locking each other in a deadly embrace, the physical intimacy of two bodies fighting for conquest, Baka and Bhīma shook the earth. Getting a deadly hold of the demon, the human twisted his body so fiercely that the demon screamed loudly, and died.[83] On hearing his screams, Baka's attendants came out, and were struck with great terror at what they saw. Bhīma reassured them, but made them take a vow.

न हिंसया मानुषा भूयो युष्माभिरिति कर्हिचित् ।
हिंसतां हि बधः शीघ्रमेवमेव भवेदिति ।। आदि १६३.४ ।।

Henceforth do no violence to the humans. Those who will do violence, will by violence die.[84]

And to this they all gave their pledge. Bhīma flung Baka's bloodied body at the gate of the town, and returned home, unseen by the people. When the day broke, and people came out of their homes, they saw the huge, ugly carcass of Baka, who had terrorised them for long, and all were astonished. Reckoning which family's turn it was to supply a man to the man-eating ruler, they came to the brāhmaṇa, and asked him how all that was possible. The brāhmaṇa, keeping Bhīma's identity a secret, said to them, 'It was a brāhmaṇa, having the power of a *mantra*, who has delivered us from our pain and misery. We shall never have to fear again.'[85] And there was great celebration.

The *Mahābhārata* initiates us into that *mantra* and its power. *In the good of the others lies one's own good.*

For that reason, in the voice of Bhīshma the *Mahābhārata* suggests:

यदन्यैविर्हितं नेच्छैदात्मनः कर्म पूरुषः ।
न तत् परेषु कुर्वीत नानन्नप्रियमात्मनः ।। शान्ति २५९.२० ।।

What one would not have the other do to one, that one should not do to the other: what is unpleasant to oneself cannot be pleasant to the other.[86]

In other words, '*Whatever one desires for oneself, let one desire that also for the other.*' For instance, 'He who desires himself to live, how can he kill the other?' And everything in the *Mahābhārata* is saying that life is not in its physicality alone, nor is killing the killing only of the body. One keeps killing the *other* in so many different ways. What one does not see is that in killing the *other* one is killing one's self as well.

The *Mahābhārata* shows the undeniable need, then, *in one's own interest*, of the *self*-related three disciplines: of *dama*, or self-control; *dāna*, or sharing, and *ahiṃsā*, or not-violence. And it shows the equally undeniable need of the *other*-related three disciplines: of endearing *vāṇī*, or speech; *ārjavam*, or simplicity of attitude and lack of deviousness; and of subjugating one's ego to the greater good of others. They are the essence of *dharma*, the foundation of fulfilling relationships. And the attributes of *dharma*, inseparable one from another, are evenly divided between the *self* and the *other*.

In relation to one's self: *satya*, truth; *dama*, self-control; *shaucha*, purity: *ārjava*, lack of deviousness; *hri*, endurance; *achapalam*, resoluteness of character; *dāna*, giving and sharing; and *tapas* and *brahmacharya*, which are not, as generally translated, 'austerity' and 'sexual continence', but, as we shall see later in this book,[87] the other names of truth and self-control. In relation to the *other*: *ahiṃsā*, not to violate the other's being; *samatā*, the attitude of equality; *shāntih*, peace or tranquillity; *anraśansyam*, lack of aggression and cruelty; and *amātsara*, absence of envy. Both flow into each other. *Dharma*, like truth, is a state of being in right relation with oneself and with the *other*.

Svārtha and nīti : self-interest and prudence

Whatever serves self-interest is prudence. Lessons in prudence are conveyed in a great many stories in the *Mahābhārata*, which are the stories of human situations everywhere. The larger number of *prudence*-maxims, *nīti*, are related to certain personal qualities which everybody, but more especially the king and the merchant, must develop if they hoped to be successful in their respective callings. All these maxims centre on *the need for self-control*, of which the control on one's tongue is the most essential. 'All functions of the world are tied to speech, *vāṇī*.'[88] 'He who can see the subtlety of *dharma* and wishes to cultivate proper speech should speak such that what he says is true as well as free from violence and denunciation of others.'[89] Hence one finds throughout the *Mahābhārata* warnings against harshness of speech, not in its form alone but in its spirit as well. It describes the effects that hurtful and dry words produce on others.

> *They burn the bones and the heart and the life of their victim: the prudent man should therefore give up forever speech that is hurtful.*[90]
> *The wound caused by an arrow is healed, and so is the wound caused by a sword; but the wound of hurtful speech is never healed.*[91]

What is spoken without regard to place and time is bitter in result; is unpleasant; displays one's meanness; and is spoken without cause—that is not speech but poison.[92]
He whose speech is dry and whose heart hard; who by his speech hurts and causes pain to others; should among men be regarded as the poorest of all, carrying in his mouth poverty and death.[93]
Harsh words make instant enemy of friends, even those of long standing and the ones who are honoured; for the sting of sharp words cannot be removed from the mind.[94]
Neither the splendour of ornaments, nor kingdom, nor bravery, nor learning, nor wealth, is comparable to courtesy and gentleness.[95]

Hence the teaching, repeated everywhere in the *nīti*-literature, that one speak gently and pleasantly.

वात्सल्यात्सर्वभूतेभ्यो वाच्याः श्रोत्रसुखा गिरः।
परितापोपघातश्च पारुष्यं चात्र गर्हितम्।। शान्ति १९१.१४।।
One's speech should be marked with affection and tenderness towards all human beings, and with pleasantness to the ears. To cause anguish to others by hurting and wounding words are low acts.[96]

अभ्यावहति कल्याणं विविधं वाक् सुभाषिता।
सैव दुर्भाषिता राजन्ननर्थायोपपद्यते।। उद्योग ३४.७७।।
Spoken pleasantly, speech brings happiness in many ways; spoken harshly, it causes disaster.[97]

There is the corresponding injunction against speaking ill of others, which pollutes one's own mind and does injury to others.[98]

The *Mahābhārata* finds no conflict between strength and gentleness,[99] or between pleasant speech and truth. The central point of Dharmic prudence has been: speak the truth, speak pleasantly, but do not speak the truth if it is unpleasant.[100] The definition of 'truth', in the *Mahābhārata*, as indeed in the whole of prudence-literature is thoroughly secular.[101] Bhīshma says:

सत्यस्य वचनं श्रेयः सत्यादपि हितं वदेत्।
यद् भूतहितमत्यन्तमेतत् सत्यं मतं मम।। शान्ति ३२९.१३।।
It is best to speak the truth: and speak the truth for the good. I call only that truth that serves universal good.[102]

That includes, of course, one's own good, *sva-hita*, and self-interest, *svārtha*, cannot be by its very definition anything but what is to one's good, *sva-hita*. This, too, is clearly stated, and the harmony between the two is made the very source of all achievement.[103]

हितं यत् सर्वभूतानामात्मनश्च सुखावहम् ।
तत् कुर्यादीश्वरे ह्येतन्मूलं सर्वार्थसिद्धये ।। उद्योग ३७.४० ।।

However, there are times and circumstances that are abnormal. A different kind of prudence is required then. The *Mahābhārata* does not avoid the requirements of such times—the requirements of expediency. To do so would be dishonest with those human situations over which one has little control. In the stories of abnormal times, the maxims of prudence are naturally different. However, if one reads them without the context in which they are being suggested, they would appear to be maxims of dreadful cynicism and not of rational prudence. The following are a few examples.

न विश्वसेदविश्वस्ते विश्वस्ते नातिविश्वसेत् ।। शान्ति १३८.१४४ ।।
विश्वासाद् भयमुत्पन्नमपि मूलानि कृन्तति ।
न विश्वसेदविश्वस्ते विश्वस्ते नातिविश्वसेत् ।
नित्यं विश्वासयेदन्यान् परेषां तु न विश्वसेत् ।। शान्ति १३८.१९४ ।।

न विश्वसेदविश्वस्ते विश्वस्ते नातिविश्वसेत् ।
विश्वासाद् भयमभ्येति नापरीक्ष्य च विश्वसेद् ।। शान्ति १४०.४३ ।।

संक्षेपो नीतिशास्त्राणामविश्वासः परो मतः ।
नृषु तस्मादविश्वासः पुष्कलं हितमात्मनः ।। शान्ति १३८.१९६ ।।

One should not trust anybody untrustworthy, but let one not trust too much even somebody who is trustworthy; the fear born out of trust destroys everything. The substance of the philosophy of prudence is that it is best not to trust anybody. In not trusting anybody lies one's good the more especially.[104]

अमित्रो मित्रतां याति मित्रं चापि प्रदुष्यति ।
सामर्थ्ययोगात् कार्याणामनित्या वै सदा गतिः ।। शान्ति १३८.१३ ।।

यस्त्वमित्रेण संदध्यान्मित्रेण च विरुद्ध्यते ।
अर्थयुक्तिं समालोक्य सुमहद् विन्दते फलम् ।। शान्ति १३८.१७ ।।

कालेन रिपुणा संधिः काले मित्रेण विग्रहः ।। शान्ति १३८.२०७ ।।
कार्य इत्येव संधिज्ञाः प्राहुर्नित्यं नराधिप ।

It is foolish to think that there is no alliance with the enemy, and no falling out between friends. In his self-interest, the prudent man approaches even the enemy with an offer of friendship, and gives up a friend, doing much good to himself thereby.[105]

अञ्जलिं शपथं सान्त्वं प्रणम्य शिरसा वदेत्।
अश्रुप्रमार्जनं चैव कर्तव्यं भूतिमिच्छता।। शान्ति १४०.१७।।

वहेदमित्रं स्कन्धेन यावत्कालस्य पर्ययः।
प्राप्तकालं तु विज्ञाय भिन्द्याद् घटमिवाश्मनि।। शान्ति १४०.१८।।

Let one greet one's enemy with folded hands; make promises; reassure him; touch his feet with one's head; even wipe his tears; indeed, take him on one's shoulders—as long as the time remains unfavourable. No sooner is the time on one's side than let one smash the enemy like a pot against the stone.[106]

ऋणशेषमाग्निशेषं शत्रुशेषं तथैव च।
पुनः पुनः प्रवर्धन्ते तस्माच्छेषं न धारयेत्।। शान्ति १४०.५८।।

वर्धमानमृणं तिष्ठेत् परिभूताश्च शत्रवः।
जनयन्ति भयं तीव्रं व्याधयश्चाप्युपेक्षिताः।। शान्ति १४०.५९।।

A debt, a fire and an enemy, if left alone, grows again and again; therefore nothing of these should be left unfinished.
A debt remaining unpaid; a humiliated, defeated enemy; and a serious illness; all these create great fear.[107]

आत्मार्थे संततिस्त्याजया राज्यं रत्नं धनानि च।। शान्ति १३८.१७८।।
अपि सर्वस्वमुत्सृज्य रक्षेदात्मानमात्मना।

ऐश्वर्यधनरत्नानां प्रत्यमित्रे निवर्तताम्।। शान्ति १३८.१७९।।
दृष्टा हि पुनरावृत्तिर्जीवतामिति नः श्रुतम्।

न त्वात्मनः सम्प्रदानं धनरत्नवदिष्यते।। शान्ति १३८.१८०।।
आत्मा हि सर्वदा रक्ष्यो दारैरपि धनैरपि।

One's first duty is to keep alive; towards that end, if one has to sacrifice one's kingdom, one's wealth, and even one's family, one should do so.[108]
If one is alive, one may still retrieve what one has lost.[109] *Better than surrendering oneself to the enemy, one should surrender rather one's wealth and woman.*[110]

These maxims were to be a guide, though, in an environment in which there was neither goodness nor justice, and were simply crucial in *āpad-kāla*, times of misfortune.

It is rationally prudent that, for example:

> तस्माद् वैरं न कुर्वीत दुर्बलो बलवत्तरैः ।
> शोचेद्धि वैरं कुर्वाणो यथा वै शाल्मलिस्तथा ।। शान्ति १५७.९ ।।
> *Therefore one should not begin enmity with anybody stronger and more powerful than oneself; in doing so, one only invites distress for oneself.*[111]

> आत्मरक्षणतन्त्राणां सुपरीक्षितकारिणाम् ।। शान्ति १३८.१८१ ।।
> आपदो नोपपद्यन्ते पुरुषाणां स्वदोषजाः ।
> *Those who protect themselves, and act after assessing everything carefully, are protected from the results of their own faults.*[112]
> *Anyone who takes too long to assess a situation invites disaster; the one who can quickly think in the face of danger gets away from it; and the one who provides for his safety beforehand is of course the wisest.*[113]

The prudence-literature displays at the same time the awareness that, understanding neither self-interest nor the importance of *desha* and *kāla*, most of us might as easily misinterpret the maxims of prudence. *In order to prevent prudence from turning into a lack of principles, and the talk of 'time' and 'place' into lack of scruple, every prudence-maxim is balanced by the qualification attached to it.* But self-interest, in the sense of self-good, is still kept as the basis of that balance.

For example, the advice against speaking unpleasant truth, if taken too literally, or pressed too far, may turn against one's own best interest; for there *are* occasions when unpleasant truth must be spoken. Vidura says:

> *Men who always speak pleasantly are easily met; rare are the people who speak and listen to words that are unpleasant but to one's good.*[114]

> *Based on* dharma, *and regardless of pleasant or unpleasant, he who speaks for the good of the other, even if what is spoken be unpleasant, is a true friend to the king.*[115]
> *One should not speak unpleasant truth; but one should not speak pleasant falsehood either.*[116]

It is no doubt prudent not to trust others indiscriminately; but from this it does not follow that one should not trust others at all.

For what kind of world will it be where nobody trusted anybody? It will be lifeless, dead. Therefore, in the voice of king Brahmadatta, who was being read the lesson about the wisdom of not trusting even the one who is trustworthy, the *Mahābhārata* says:

नाविश्वासाद् विन्दतेऽर्थानीहते चापि किंचन।
भयात् त्वेकतरान्नित्यं मृतकल्पा भवन्ति च।। शान्ति १३९.७५ ।।

Without trust no purpose can ever be gained, nor can any effort be made. Always fearing the other will be like being dead.[117]

यस्मिन्नाश्वासते कश्चिद् यश्च नाश्वसिति क्वचित्।
न तौ धीराः प्रशंसन्ति नित्यमुद्विग्नमानसौ।। शान्ति १३८.५९ ।।

He whom nobody trusts, and who himself trusts nobody, is not regarded much, for such a person is full of agitation always.[118]

न श्रद्दधाति कल्याणं परेभ्योऽप्यात्मशङ्कितः।
निराकरोति मित्राणि यो वै सोऽधमपूरुषः।। उद्योग ३६.१९ ।।

Distrustful of himself, who never expects any good to come from others, and does not make friends, is verily a low man.[119]

न तन्मित्रं यस्य कोपाद् बिभेति
यद् वा मित्रं शङ्कितेनोपचर्यम्।
यस्मिन् मित्रे पितरीवाश्वसीत
तद् वै मित्रं सङ्गतानीतराणि।। उद्योग ३६.७ ।।

He whose anger one must fear, and in whose company one must remain distrustful, is not a friend: a friend is one who can be trusted like a father, others are mere companions.[120]

As for the maxim that an enemy should not be left unfinished, there are also the following injunctions, both to be read together. The latter of the two was *dharma*:

श्रान्तं भीतं भ्रष्टशस्त्रं रुदन्तं
पराङ्मुखं पारिवर्हैश्च हीनम्।
अनुद्यन्तं रोगिणं याचमानं
न वै हिंस्याद् बालवृद्धौ च राजन्।। शान्ति २९७.४ ।।

The enemy who is exhausted; who is fearful; who has laid down his arms; who is crying; who is running away; who has no weapons left to fight with; who has given up the fight; who is sick; who is pleading for his life; who is young or who is old; must never be killed.[121]

भग्नशस्त्रो विपन्नश्च कृत्तज्यो हतवाहनः ।
चिकित्स्यः स्यात् स्वविषये प्राप्यो वा स्वगृहे भवेत् ।।

Whoever is in such a state, and has fallen in one's hand, must indeed be protected. His wounds must be tended; and he should be escorted to his home.[122]

There has been no greater gift in the past, nor will there be in the future, than the gift of life, for doubtless there is nothing dearer than one's self.[123]

For that reason one should be kind to all beings.[124]

Avoidance of *ati*, excess, is the final principle of prudence. And it is in the light of this that self-interest is seen as connected even more with the interest of others. Let one pursue what one would: excitement of sexual pleasure, exultation of great wealth, or the power of political supremacy; but all these are eventually destructive if carried to an excess. One's destruction in that case will be brought about not by God, or by some supernatural agency, but by the very logic of excess. The *Shukranīti* says:

अतिदानेन दारिद्र्यं तिरस्कारोऽतिलोभतः ।। शुक्र ३.२२० ।।
अत्याग्रहान्नरस्यैव मौर्ख्यं संजायते खलु ।

Poverty comes through excessive charity; insult through excessive greed; and foolishness is born of excessive zeal.[125]

The *Mahābhārata* dwells upon the excesses of virtue, of learning, of wealth, and of royal power, and shows how each has an inglorious end. It dwells, in a far more realistic manner than the works on ethics do, on the supreme need for control over one's senses, especially over one's speech, and over one's mind.[126]

The *Mahābhārata* does not pretend that a simple recognition of how essential the *self*-related and the *other*-related disciplines are to happiness, individual and collective, will itself be sufficient to achieve happiness. Nor will any discourse on virtues be ever sufficient to create a virtuous world. There is, first of all, this puzzling human phenomenon that, professing self-interest and pleasure as two basic motives of life, we negate both in actual practice. The way in which we mostly relate to each other, far from bringing pleasure and happiness, produces pain and suffering instead. That this is also a part of the human condition is fully acknowledged in the *Mahābhārata* as the very first step towards self-understanding. It will not do to explain it away by saying that it is humanly not always possible to put into practice an ideal. Those who have advanced the principle of self-interest have done so not as an *ideal*, because they deny ethical ideal apart from self-interest, but as the very first motive force of human life. In that case, they must explain, which they don't, why most human beings then act and live in a way manifestly self-destructive. The *Mahābhārata* confronts us with this question in every context.

The *Mahābhārata* shows how all disorders, psychological, economic, and political arise when I begin to think, wrongly, that my self-interest is secured, and thus my happiness, by using others to my purpose. I turn the *other* into an object, to be controlled and manipulated. Eventually that creates a world where, self-interest wrongly perceived, everyone tries to use everyone else, in ways from very crude to very subtle. Such a world is a world where there can be neither truth nor happiness. And that is the very reverse of what we claim: that what we do we do in the quest for happiness.

Self-control is thus related with self-interest; as self-interest is related with one's good. The ultimate source of this rationality exists in man himself: *conquered, one's self is the best friend one has; uncontrolled, one's only enemy.*[127]

CHAPTER NINE

Human Attributes—*Sukha* and *Duḥkha*, Pleasure and Pain

- 'Pleasure' and 'pain': experienced facts
- The reasons why there is more pain than pleasure
- 'Perhaps *that is why* you look pale and weak?'
  The psychosomatic link
- From the same facts three different paths to happiness
  - *Indriya-nigraha*, self-discipline
  - *Vairāgya*, renouncing the world
  - *Moksha*: towards freedom from the human condition
- A radical shift in the '*because–therefore*' reasoning
- The *Mahābhārata*'s teachings of happiness

A central concern of Indian thought, including of course the materialist but also the upanishadic, were the two related questions: how do *sukha* and *duḥkha*, pleasure and pain, affect man? And what is their nature? Just as on other subjects relating to human life, Indian thinkers saw with many eyes and spoke with many tongues, so did they on the subject of pleasure and pain. That was because human life is so immensely varied, and human capacities so diverse, that pleasure and pain, though they come equally to all human beings, do not govern them equally.

All systems of philosophy in India frankly acknowledged the evident fact that man has desires, primarily *sukha-prāpti* and *duḥkha-nivritti*, those of seeking pleasure and avoiding pain. The self-interest underlying these was likewise acknowledged as a naturally given human fact. The analysis of desire, and how pleasure and pain affect man, is connected with everything else in their philosophies. The *Brhadāraṇyaka Upanishad* speaks of three main motives behind human acts: *putraishaṇa*, the desire for progeny, and *vittaishaṇa,* the desire for wealth; and *lokaishaṇa*, the desire for recognition and wanting to be respected in the world.

In Ayurveda, the three motives spoken of are: *prāṇaishana*, the desire for self-preservation; *dhanaishaṇa,* the desire for material prosperity and the comforts that come from it; and *paralokaishaṇa*, the desire for happiness in the life hereafter.

The Vaisheshika assumes attraction to pleasure and aversion to pain as the two chief motives in all human actions. The Nyāya mentions (a) *rāga*, attachment to the objects of pleasure; (b) *dvesha*, antipathy to what is disagreeable; and (c) *moha*, confusion, as the three sources that prompt human actions.

In Buddhism and Jainism, desire and arising from it 'thirst', or *trishṇā*, are seen as the two primary causes of human suffering.

There was in all schools of Indian philosophy a detailed discussion on the manner in which pleasure and pain affect human life. But each school analysed *sukha* and *duḥkha*, in the particular framework of its own metaphysics, which influenced the perceptions each had about the ways of living.

Let us again have a brief look at the one most general characteristic of Dharmic thought, especially in the *Mahābhārata*. Dharmic thought was firmly rooted in empirical realities, which it set out to examine and understand. As a consequence, hardly any one of the main concepts of philosophy in India was of the *a priori* kind, and there were really no presuppositions, although *a priori* thinking was not entirely absent. The systems of philosophy were thus not rationalistic in the philosophic sense of that word. All of them began their inquiry with empirical phenomena. When, however, in their investigations they went beyond the evidence of physical senses, or even of the instruments of the mind, that still did not negate the fact that all their conclusions, no matter how derived, had to have a reference to empirical realities, and from them have their validation. But neither did this mean that the method followed by Indian thinkers was exclusively one of empiricism as opposed to that of rationalism. They simply did not turn either of the two into an *ism*. They proceeded on the basis that there is no essential conflict between the empirical and the rational, and that the thinking about man and the world is a process that involves both. Dharmic thought moved from empirical facts to generalisations, rather than the other way about. The generalisations themselves were arrived at in a hierarchy, from less general to more general. The absence of presuppositions had the singular beneficial result of empirical facts not being forced *somehow* into any particular preconceived mould.

Furthermore, in the *Mahābhārata*, the discussions on pleasure and pain take place for the most part in concrete personal situations as being experienced by concrete human persons. Pleasure and pain are sensations and feelings, not abstract concepts.

'*Pleasure*' and '*pain*': experienced facts

While the problem of pleasure and pain became increasingly technical in the systems of philosophy, all the basic propositions concerning the two are contained in the *Mahābhārata*. They form a coherent and self-consistent picture, which has the merit, moreover, of scientific simplicity.[1] Pleasure and pain are defined in simple terms:

यद् यत्प्रियं यस्य सुखं तदाहु-
स्तदेव दुःखं प्रवदन्त्यनिष्टम् ।। शान्ति २०१.१० ।।

Whatever is agreeable to one is 'pleasure', whatever is disagreeable is 'pain'.[2]

The following universally observable empirical facts are then set out.

दुःखादुद्विजते सर्वः सर्वस्य सुखमीप्सितम् ।। शान्ति १३९.६२ ।।
Everyone wishes to have pleasure, and everybody is distressed by pain.[3]

तत् खलु द्विविधं सुखमुच्यते शारीरं मानसं च। इह खल्वमुष्मिश्च लोके वस्तुप्रवृत्तयः सुखार्थमभिधीयन्ते। न ह्यतः परं त्रिवर्गफलं विशिष्टतरमस्ति स एव काम्यो गुणविशेषो धर्मार्थगुणारम्भस्तद्धेतुरस्योत्पत्तिः सुखप्रयोजनार्थ आरम्भः ।। शान्ति १९०.९ ।।
Pleasure is of two kinds: physical and mental. All human tendencies are towards pleasure. Indeed, dharma, artha, *and* kāma, *the three ends of life, have no other aim but pleasure: it is for obtaining pleasure that every act is begun.*[4]

नैव त्यागी न संतुष्टो नाशोको न निरामयः ।
न निर्विधित्सो नावृत्तो नापवृत्तोऽस्ति कश्चन ।। शान्ति २६९.४६ ।।
There is in this world nobody who has renounced everything; nor is there anybody who is wholly contented; nor anybody without suffering, nor anybody who is completely healthy. There is no one who is completely free from desire, or who is completely without attachment, or who has no object whatsoever towards which he works.[5]

एवं चतुर्णां वर्णानामाश्रमाणां प्रवृत्तिषु ।
एकमालम्बमानानां निर्णये किं निरामयम् ।। शान्ति २६९.४८ ।।
Everybody, of whatever calling, or varna, at whatever stage of life, is dependent on pleasure, and has pleasure as his goal.[6]

शरीरमेवायतनं सुखस्य
दुःखस्य चाप्यायतनं शरीरम् ।
यद्यच्छरीरेण करोति कर्म
तेनैव देही समुपाश्नुते तत् ।। शान्ति १७४.२१ ।।
The body is the basis of pleasure as well as pain. Whatever is done through the physical body, pleasures and pains follow it.[7]

जीवितं च शरीरेण जात्यैव सह जायते ।
उभे सह विवर्तेते उभे सह विनश्यतः ।। शान्ति १७४.२२ ।।
Life and body are born together, grow together, and end together.[8]

द्विविधो जायते व्याधि: शारीरो मानसस्तथा।
परस्परं तयोर्जन्म निर्द्वन्द्वं नोपलभ्यते।। शान्ति १६.८।।
Pains are of two kinds: physical and mental; they arise from each other: without the one, the other cannot exist.[9]

शारीराज्जायते व्याधिर्मानसो नात्र संशय:।
मानसाज्जायते वापि शारीर इति निश्यच:।। शान्ति १६.९।।
There is no doubt that mental illness arises from physical illness. And it is certain that when the mind is sick, the body will be sick too.[10]

मानसेन हि दु:खेन शरीरमुपतप्यते।
अय:पिण्डेन तप्तेन कुम्भसंस्थमिवोदकम्।। वन २.२५।।
When there is pain in the mind, the body burns too; just as the cold water turns hot when a burning hot iron is put into it.[11]

व्याधेरनिष्टसंस्पर्शाच्छ्रमादिष्टविवर्जनात्।
दु:खं चतुर्भि: शारीरं कारणै: सम्प्रवर्तते।। वन २.२२।।
Physical pain has four causes: disease, accidents, hard labour, and the loss of persons who are dear to one.[12]

दु:खं जरा ब्रह्मदत्त दु:खमर्थविपर्यय:।
दु:खं चानिष्टसंवासो दु:खमिष्टवियोजनम्।। शान्ति १३९.६३।।

वधबन्धकृतं दु:ख स्त्रीकृतं सहजं तथा।
दु:खं सुतेन सततं जनान् विपरिवर्तते।। शान्ति १३९.६४।।
Mental pain is caused by old age, loss of wealth, to have to live with those who one does not like and to lose those who one does, bondage, woman and on account of one's son. All beings suffer pain.[13]

रुजन्ति हि शरीराणि रोगा: शारीरमानसा:।
सायका इव तीक्ष्णाग्रा: प्रयुक्ता दृढधन्विभि:।। शान्ति ३३१.३।।
Physical and mental illnesses are like sharp arrows shot by a resolute archer and cause pain to one's body.[14]

सुखस्यानन्तरं दु:खं दु:खस्यानन्तरं सुखम्।
सुखदु:खे मनुष्याणां चक्रवत् परिवर्तत:।। शान्ति १७४.१९।।
Pain follows pleasure, and pleasure follows pain: both move in a cycle.[15]

Pleasure, like pain, is also of two kinds: physical and mental. Suffering is the absence of happiness and happiness is the absence of suffering; but, paradoxically, suffering arises from pleasure, and pleasure can arise from suffering.[16]

एवमेव किलैतानि प्रियाण्येवाप्रियाणि च।
जीवेषु परिवर्तन्ते दुःखानि च सुखानि च।। शान्ति १७४.४८।।

Thus, the agreeable and the disagreeable, pleasure and pain, come in succession to all beings.[17]

सुखस्यानन्तरं दुखं दुःखस्यानन्तरं सुखम्।
न नित्यं लभते दुःखं न नित्यं लभते सुखम्।। शान्ति २५.२३।।

There is pain after pleasure, and pleasure after pain. No one experiences always pain; nor does anyone experience always pleasure.[18]

सुखात् त्वं दुःखमापन्नः पुनरापत्स्यसे सुखम्।
न नित्यं लभते दुःखं न नित्यं लभते सुखम्।। शान्ति १७४.२०।।

There is no one who experiences always suffering, nor anyone who experiences always happiness.[19]

But:

सुखाद् बहुतरं दुःखं जीविते नात्र संशयः।
स्निग्धत्वं चेन्द्रियार्थेषु मोहान्मरणमप्रियम्।। शान्ति ३३०.१६।।

There is no doubt that there is in life more pain than pleasure.[20]

पश्य भूतानि दुःखेन व्यतिषिक्तानि सर्वशः।
उत्तमाधममध्यानि तेषु तेष्विह कर्मसु।। शान्ति १७४.१३।।

You can see that the great, the middling, and the lowly, all human beings, everywhere, acting their respective acts, are suffering with pain.[21]

मनोदेहसमुत्थाभ्यां दुःखाभ्यामर्दितं जगत्।। वन २.२१।।

The whole world is in the grip of physical and mental pain.[22]

शोकस्थानसहस्त्राणि भयस्थानशतानि च।
दिवसे दिवसे मूढमाविशन्ति न पण्डितम्।। शान्ति १७४.४०।।

There are a thousand places for sorrow and a hundred places for fear.[23]

The reasons why there is more pain than pleasure

The reasons, all of them universally verifiable, why there is in the world more pain than pleasure, more suffering than happiness, when the most abiding human wish is for the very opposite, are set out in the *Mahābhārata* as follows:

अनित्यं यौवनं रूपं जीवितं रत्नसंचयः ।
ऐश्वर्यं प्रियसंवासो गृध्येत् तत्र न पण्डितः ।। वन २.४७ ।।

All objects of pleasure are transitory—beauty, youth, wealth, good health, and the company of dear ones.[24]

सर्वे क्षयान्ता निचयाः पतनान्ताः समुच्छ्रयाः ।
संयोगा विप्रयोगान्ता मरणान्तं हि जीवितम् ।। शान्ति ३३०.२० ।।

Accumulation ends in destruction, rise ends in fall, the coming together ends in parting, and life ends in death.[25]

अस्थिरत्वं च संचिन्त्य पुरुषार्थस्य नित्यदा ।
तस्योदये व्यये चापि न चिन्तयितुमर्हसि ।। वन ७९.१२ ।।

All things gained by human effort are unstable and perishable.[26]

निमेषमात्रमपि हि वयो गच्छन्न तिष्ठति ।
स्वशरीरेष्वनित्येषु नित्यं किमनुचिन्तयेत् ।। शान्ति ३३०.२२ ।।

One's life is passing, does not stop even for a moment. When one's own life is transitory, then what thing of life can be considered abiding?[27]

स्त्रवन्ति न निवर्तन्ते स्त्रोतांसि सरितामिव ।
आयुरादाय मर्त्यानां रात्र्यहानि पुनः पुनः ।। शान्ति ३३१.५ ।।

Life constantly moves, does not stop even for a moment.[28] *Like the flow of the rivers that does not ever turn back, the days and the nights keep flowing onwards, robbing a man of his life.*[29]

सुखदुःखानि भूतानामजरो जरयत्यसौ ।
आदित्यो ह्यस्तमभ्येति पुनः पुनरुदेति च ।। शान्ति ३३१.७ ।।

Itself eternal, the sun rises and sets, again and again, making human pleasures and pains subject to decay and death.[30]

अदृष्टपूर्वानादाय भावानपरिशङ्कितान् ।
इष्टानिष्टान् मनुष्याणामस्तं गच्छन्ति रात्रयः ।। शान्ति ३३१.८ ।।

Bringing to man the desired and the disastrous, the unseen and the fantastic, the nights come and pass.[31]

क्षणं बालो भूत्वा क्षणमपि युवा कामरसिकः
क्षणं वित्तैर्हीनः क्षणमपि च संपूर्णाविभवः ।
जराजीर्णैङ्गैर्नट इव वलीमण्डिततनु-
र्नरः संसारन्ते विशति यमधानीयवनिकाम् ।। वैराग्य ५० ।।

For a moment, man is a boy; for a moment, a lovesick youth; for a moment, bereft of wealth; for a moment, at the height of prosperity; then, at life's end, with limbs worn out by old age, and wrinkles adorning his face, like an actor he retires behind the curtain of death.[32]

The sources of pleasure being transitory, the pleasure that is derived from them is naturally momentary. The moments of pleasure are, therefore, the moments of fear and anxiety as well.

संचये च विनाशान्ते मरणान्ते च जीविते ।
संयोगे च वियोगान्ते को नु विप्रणयेन्मनः ।। शान्ति १०४.४४ ।।

When the end of all accumulation is in its destruction, and the end of life is in death, all unions ending in parting, then who will put his mind into them?[33]

* * *

Even if one's life and the sources of pleasure were never ending, there would still be more unhappiness than happiness, more pain than pleasure. The reason for this lies in *desire* itself. Its nature is such that it remains forever unquenched. For desire invariably turns into unending 'thirst', *trishṇā*.

अनाद्यन्ता तु सा तृष्णा अन्तर्देहगता नृणाम् ।
विनाशयति भूतानि अयोनिज इवानलः ।। वन २.३७ ।।

Existing within the human body, 'thirst', trishṇā, *has neither beginning nor end; it keeps destroying people even as the fire does.*[34]

न जातु कामः कामानामुपभोगेन शाम्यति ।
हविषा कृष्णवर्त्मेव भूय एवाभिवर्धते ।। आदि ७५.५० ।।

Not by appeasing it, is desire satisfied; with that it only grows, like fire when more fuel is added to it.[35]

कामस्यान्तं च क्षुत्तृड्भ्यां क्रोधस्यैतत्फलोदयात्।
जनो याति न लोभस्य जित्वा भुक्त्वा दिशो भुवः।। भागवत १८०.२६।।

Desire for food ends with hunger appeased, and anger subsides with its purpose achieved; but should one conquer and enjoy even the whole universe, there would still be no end to one's greed.[36]

मनुष्या ह्याढ्यतां प्राप्य राज्यमिच्छन्त्यनन्तरम्।
राज्याद् देवत्वमिच्छन्ति देवत्वादिन्द्रतामापि।। शान्ति १८०.२४।।

भवेस्त्वं यद्यपि त्वाढ्यो न राजा न च दैवतम्।
देवत्वं प्राप्य चेन्द्रत्वं नैव तुष्येस्तथा सति।। शान्ति १८०.२५।।

On acquiring wealth, men want to acquire a kingdom; having acquired a kingdom, they want to become gods; and then, among gods they want to become Indra.[37]

Even if one becomes wealthy, one may not become a king or a god; if one does become a god, and among gods Indra, one would remain dissatisfied still.[38]

न तृप्तिः प्रियलाभेऽस्ति तृष्णा नाद्भिः प्रशाम्यति।
सम्प्रज्वलति सा भूयः समिद्भरिव पावकः।। शान्ति १८०.२६।।

Contentment does not come even if one should obtain all that one finds pleasurable.[39]

The same is true of sexual pleasure, as Yayāti discovered after a thousand years of his resolute dedication to it. He found that his desire for it had in no way diminished. Thereupon he concluded:

यत् पृथिव्यां व्रीहियवं हिरण्यं पशवः स्त्रियः।
एकस्यापि न पर्याप्तं तस्मात् तृष्णां परित्यजेत्।। आदि ८५.१३।।

Not all the grain in the world, not all the gold, nor all the women, are sufficient even for one man: man grows old, but not desire.[40]

आशा हि परमं दुःखं नैराश्यं परमं सुख।। शान्ति १७४.६३।।

And desire is the greatest pain; not-desire, the greatest happiness.[41]

यद् यत् यजति कामानां तत् सुखस्याभिपूर्यते।
कामानुसारी पुरुषः कामाननुविनश्यति।। शान्ति १७४.४५।।

Whichever desire is given up, that brings happiness in that measure. The one who pursues desire, is by desire destroyed.[42]

* * *

Even if life and the sources of pleasure were not transitory, and there were also ways of containing desire within reasonable bounds, the pleasures would still turn into pains. The reason for this consists *in* those very things that bring man pleasure.

यद्यत्प्रीतिकरं पुंसां वस्तु मैत्रेय जायते ।
तदेव दुःखवृक्षस्य बीजत्वमुपगच्छति ।। विष्णु ६-५.५५ ।।
कलत्रपुत्रमित्रार्थगृहक्षेत्रधनादिकैः ।
क्रियते न तथा भूरि सुखं पुंसां यथाऽसुखम् ।। विष्णु ६-५.५६ ।।
Whatever things are desired by men, those things become the seed from which grows the tree of pain.[43]
Wife, son, friend, wealth, house, property and money—from all these, the pleasure men get is not so much as the opposite of it.[44]

परिग्रहो हि दुःखाय यद् यत्प्रियतमं नृणाम् ।। भागवत ११-९.१ ।।
The grasping of the things most desired by man is the cause of pain.[45]

Therefore, stated again,

यद् यत् त्यजति कामानां तत् सुखस्याभिपूर्यते ।
कामस्य वशगो नित्यं दुःखमेव प्रपद्यते ।। शान्ति १७७.४८ ।।
Whichever desire is given up, that brings happiness in that measure. Being under the control of desire, brings always pain.[46]

Let us take, for example, wealth as a universally desired object, feverishly desired and equally feverishly pursued. However, the problem with this is:

त्यज्यनते दुःखमर्थहि पालने न च ते सुखाः ।
दुःखेन चाधिगम्यन्ते नाशमेषां न चिन्तयेत् ।। शान्ति ३३०.१८ ।।
अन्यामन्यां धनावस्थां प्राप्य वैशेषिकीं नराः ।
It is difficult to earn wealth, painful to part with it, nor is there any pleasure in guarding it, and of course human beings are never satisfied with any amount of it, wanting more and more.[47]

राजतः सलिलादग्नेश्चोरतः स्वजनादपि।
भयमर्थवतां नित्यं मृत्योः प्राणभृतामिव।। वन २.३९।।

Just as all human beings are in constant fear of death, the rich are in constant fear of the king, water, fire, thief, and relatives.[48]

यथा ह्यामिषमाकाशे पक्षिभिः श्वापदैर्भुवि।
भक्ष्यते सलिले मत्स्यैस्तथा सर्वत्र वित्तवान्।। वन २.४०।।

Just as a piece of meat is eaten by vultures in the sky, and by carnivorous animals on the earth, and by the fish in the sea, so is a rich man nibbled everywhere.[49]

* * *

Then there are the physical senses and faculties with their natural tendencies.

विज्ञानार्थं मनुष्याणां मनः पूर्वं प्रवर्तते।
तत् प्राप्य कामं भजते क्रोधं च द्विजसत्तम।। वन २१०.२।।

ततस्तदर्थं यतते कर्म चारभते महत्।
इष्टानां रूपगन्धानामभ्यासं च निषेवते।। वन २१०.३।।

ततो रागः प्रभवति द्वेषश्च तदनन्तरम्।
ततो लोभः प्रभवति मोहश्च तदनन्तरम्।। वन २१०.४।।

ततो लोभाभिभूतस्य रागद्वेषहतस्य च।
न धर्मे जायते बुद्धिर्व्याजाद् धर्मं करोति च।। वन २१०.५।।

First comes the awareness of objects; then springs the desire for them; then the resolution to obtain them; then the acts, followed by their results.[50] *Whatever a man finds agreeable, he develops a tendency towards it: whatever he finds disagreeable, that he looks upon with aversion. He endeavours to obtain what is agreeable and wants to experience it again. From that arises attachment,* rāga, *and afterwards aversion,* dvesha: *then comes greed,* lobha, *followed by confusion,* moha. *Overpowered by all these, he moves away from* Dharma.[51]

रागाभिभूतः पुरुषः कामेन परिकृष्यते।
इच्छा संजायते तस्य ततस्तृष्णा विवर्धते।। वन २.३४।।

या दुस्त्यजा दुर्मतिभिर्या न जीर्यति जीर्यतः।
योऽसौप्राणान्तिको रोगस्तां तृष्णां त्यजतः सुखम्।। वन २.३६।।

The one overcome by attraction towards sensory objects is troubled and tormented by the desire, which turns into trishṇā, *'thirst'. And to 'thirst', there is no end: neither does it weaken. To renounce this fatal disease called* trishṇā *is happiness.*[52]

न संत्यजन्त्यात्मकर्म यो न जीर्यति जीर्यतः।
यो न पूरयितुंशकयो लोभः प्राप्त्या कुरूद्वह।। शान्ति १५८.१२।।

नित्यं गम्भीरतोयाभिरापगाभिरिवोदधिः।
न प्रहृष्यति यो लाभैः कामैर्यश्च न तृप्यति।। शान्ति १५८.१३।।

Since there is in this world no substance that can fill a man's greed, which is like an ocean that never gets filled by all the rivers that flow into it,[53] *greed leads man to endless striving and confusion, from which arise untruth, fear and aggression, indeed every conceivable human disorder.*[54]

In the voice of Bhīshma and some other thinkers, the *Mahābhārata* traces the causal chain of *lobha*, greed, *leading to every kind of unhappiness and pain to one's self and to the other*. Bhīshma says:

अज्ञानान्निरयं याति तथाज्ञानेन दुर्गतिम्।
अज्ञानात् क्लेशमाप्नोति तथापत्सु निमज्जति।। शान्ति १५९.३।।

It is ignorance that takes a person into darkness. It is ignorance that causes his sorry state. It is ignorance that brings him suffering and pain, in which he is then drowned.[55]

Yudhishṭhira seeks to know from him:

अज्ञानस्य प्रवृत्तिं च स्थानं वृद्धिक्षयोदयौ।
मूलं योगं गतिं कालं कारणं हेतुमेव च।। शान्ति १५९.४।।

श्रोतुमिच्छामि तत्त्वेन यथावदिह पार्थिव।
अज्ञानप्रसवं हीदं यद् दुःखमुपलभ्यते।। शान्ति १५९.५।।

What is the origin, the place, the increase and the decrease, the root, the connections, the time, the cause, and the support, of ignorance?
I wish to know systematically the truth of it; for ignorance is the cause of pain and suffering.[56]

Bhīshma replies:

रागो द्वेषस्तथा मोहो हर्ष: शोकोऽभिमानिता।
काम: क्रोधश्च दर्पश्च तन्द्री चालस्यमेव च।। शान्ति १५९.६ ।।

इच्छा द्वेषस्तथा ताप: परवृद्ध्युपतापिता।
अज्ञानमेतन्निर्दिष्टं पापानां चैव या: क्रिया:।। शान्ति १५९.७ ।।

Attraction, aversion, confusion of perceptions, joy and sorrow, pride, covetousness and anger, arrogance, malice, envy on seeing the prosperity of others, and conduct that is offensive—all these are as many forms of ignorance.[57]

उभावेतौ समफलौ समदोषौ च भारत।
अज्ञानं चातिलोभश्चाप्येकं जानीहि पार्थिव।। शान्ति १५९.९ ।।

लोभप्रभवमज्ञानं वृद्धं भूय: प्रवर्धते।
स्थाने स्थानंक्षये क्षैण्यमुपैति विविधां गतिम्।। शान्ति १५९.१० ।।

Because their results and disorders are alike, consider ignorance and excessive greed to be the same.
Ignorance arises from greed, and increases in the same proportion as greed does. And with the decrease in greed, decreases ignorance: they have the same place, creating different conditions of existence.[58]

मूलं लोभस्य मोहो वै कालात्मगतिरेव च।
छिन्ने भिन्ने तथा लोभे कारणं काल एव च।। शान्ति १५९.११ ।।

Confusion of perceptions is the root of greed, conditioned by time; and with time as its cause, greed is then dispersed.[59]

तस्याज्ञानाद्धि लोभो हि लोभादज्ञानमेव च।
सर्वदोषास्तथा लोभात् तस्माल्लोभं विवर्जयेत्।। शान्ति १५९.१२ ।।

Thus, from ignorance, greed, and from greed, ignorance. It is from greed that all disorders arise. Therefore, one must give up greed.[60]

लोभात् क्रोध: प्रभवति लोभात् काम: प्रवर्तते।
लोभान्मोहश्च माया च मान: स्तम्भ: परासुता।। शान्ति १५८.४ ।।

अक्षमा ह्रीपरित्याग: श्रीनाशो धर्मसंक्षय:।
अभिध्याप्रख्यता चैव सर्वं लोभात् प्रवर्तते।। शान्ति १५८.५ ।।

It is from greed that aggression and anger arise; and from greed covetousness. From greed arise confusion, delusion, pride, arrogance, and servitude of others.[61]

अत्यागश्चातितर्षश्च विकर्मसु च या: क्रिया: ।
कुलविद्यामदश्चैव रूपैश्वर्यमदस्तथा ।। शान्ति १५८.६ ।।

सर्वभूतेष्वभिद्रोह: सर्वभूतेष्वसत्कृति: ।
सर्वभूतेष्वविश्वास: सर्वभूतेष्वनार्जवम् ।। शान्ति १५८.७ ।।

Intolerance; shamelessness; the end of well-being and prosperity; weakening of the foundations of relationships; longing for renown—all these arise from greed.

Grasping and excessive longing; drunken pride in one's lineage and learning; drunken pride in one's beauty and affluence: ill will towards all beings; and towards all beings, disrespect; distrust of all beings, and towards all beings, deviousness too. All these arise from greed.[62]

Furthermore, greed produces

हरणं परवित्तानां परदाराभिमर्शनम् ।
वाग्वेगो मनसो वेगो निन्दावेगस्तथैव च ।। शान्ति १५८.८ ।।
उपस्थोदरयोर्वेगो मृत्युवेगश्च दारुण: ।
ईर्ष्यावेगश्च बलवान् मिथ्यावेगश्च दुर्जय: ।। शान्ति १५८.९ ।।

रसवेगश्च दुर्वार्य: श्रोत्रवेगश्च दु:सह: ।
कुत्सा विकत्था मात्सर्यं पापं दुष्करकारिता ।। शान्ति १५८.१० ।।
साहसानां च सर्वेषामकार्याणां क्रियास्तथा ।

The mad rush of speech; the mad rush of the mind; and the mad rush of denigrating others. It produces the mad rush of envy and jealousy; the fearful rush of untruth; the rush of tastes and sounds. To take away forcibly others' money, and force oneself upon the wives of others, are the workings of greed. To revile and abuse others; indeed, every kind of offensive conduct in whatever one does. Inviting the dreadful rush of death.[63]

What the *Mahābhārata* is showing is that greed, *lobha*, puts one in a completely wrong relationship with one's self, and as a consequence in a wrong relationship with the *other*. That can bring only pain and suffering. Therefore,

स लोभ: सह मोहेन विजैतव्यो जितात्मना ।। शान्ति १५८.१५ ।।

Who has conquered greed and its deluding confusion has conquered his self.[64]

'Perhaps *that is why* you look pale and weak?' The psychosomatic link

However, when a human being is unhappy, in whatever measure, he, or she, does not ordinarily link it with any of the four root causes of pain and suffering recounted above. Rather, there are always more immediate causes as experienced by ordinary people in their ordinary lives. It is certainly true that, on a deeper reflection, all of these can be seen as the varied products of those four fundamental causes inherent in the human condition. But it is also true that, when a person is unhappy, and that mental state of being unhappy and troubled affects his, or her, physical health, to hear only a discourse on those four root causes of pain and suffering does little to remove one's unhappiness. The *Mahābhārata* is one universal work concerning the human condition that is perfectly aware of it. Therefore, in its countless stories of human happenings, it narrates first of all the universally experienced ordinary causes of one's unhappiness and pain, created by one's own self, or by the *other*, or by both together. It does that even before tracing them to deeper causes; and then, always, without dispersing the immediate, the personal, into abstractions of one kind or another.

Even Lord Krishna is portrayed as having his immediate troubles, of which he speaks to the sage Nārada, as one would to a friend.[65]

Krishna (*to Nārada*)

स ते सौहृदमास्थाय किञ्चिद् वक्ष्यामि नारद।
कृत्स्नं बुद्धिबलं प्रेक्ष्य सम्पृच्छेस्त्रिदिवंगम।। शान्ति ८१.४।।

Trusting your friendship, I want to say something to you. It is only on seeing the strength of intelligence and wisdom of another that one seeks counsel from him.[66]

दास्यमैश्वर्यवादेन ज्ञानीतां न करोम्यहम्।
अर्धं भोक्तास्मि भोगानां वाग्दुरुक्तानि च क्षमे।। शान्ति ८१.५।।

आरणीमग्निकामो वा मथाति हृदयं मम।
वाचा दुरुक्तं देवर्षे तन्मे दहति नित्यदा।। शान्ति ८१.६।।

I don't wish to lord over my relatives and treat them as slaves. What I get, a half of it I distribute among them, and the other half I keep for myself and for my family. Still I hear from my relatives only wounding words; and I forgive them.

But their bitter words hurt me deeply and keep burning my heart.[67]

बलं संकर्षणे नित्यं सौकुमार्यं पुनर्गदे।
रूपेण मत्तः प्रद्युम्नः सोऽसहायोऽस्मि नारद।। शान्ति ८१.७।।

My elder brother, Balarāma, is wholly taken up by his immense physical strength. And my younger brother is far too tender and gentle and lazy. And my son, Pradyumna, is drunk with his own beauty. And I feel so utterly helpless.[68]

My two chief advisers, Bāhuka and Akrūra, are busy in their mutual hostility. What greater unhappiness can there be when one has friends like Bāhuka and Akrūra fighting with each other all the time? Yet, what greater unhappiness can there be for one to be without friends like them? I do not play favourite one against the other, and I try to see their respective viewpoints.[69]

ममैवं क्लिश्यमानस्य नारदोभयतः सदा।
वक्तुमर्हसि चरूछ्रेयो ज्ञातीनामात्मनस्तथा।। शान्ति ८१.१२।।

Always wishing the good of the other side, Nārada, as a consequence I am deeply unhappy on account of both. Tell me, what do I do to secure my own good and the good of the others?[70]

Through another story the *Mahābhārata* lists many more familiar reasons why a person could be unhappy and troubled, and therefore weak and ill.[71] These must have been familiar stories then; as they are familiar stories now. There is not much in contemporary human experience that could be added to them substantially. Therefore, let us have a look at all of them. For, at the same time as the following lines from the *Mahābhārata* are being translated here, many human beings are perhaps expressing their unhappiness in the same words.

A *brāhmaṇa* was passing through a forest where a *rākṣhasa* caught hold of him and threatened to make a meal out of him. Intelligent and of quick wit, the *brāhmaṇa* felt neither frightened nor lost. He spoke to the *rākṣhasa* very peacefully instead. Praising his peaceful speech, the *rākṣhasa* said that he would let him go only if he could answer his question, the question being: '*Why have I become so weak and pale?*' The *brāhmaṇa* thought for a moment, and began answering the *rākṣhasa*'s question thus:

विदेशस्थो विलोकस्थो विना नूनं सुहृज्जनैः।
विषयानतुलान् भुङ्क्षे तेनासि हरिणः कृशः।। अनुशासन १२४.९।।

Although enjoying wonderful pleasures, you live in a foreign land, far away from your dear ones, and that is the reason why you have become weak and pale.[72]

नूनं मित्राणि ते रक्षः साधूपचरितान्यपि।
स्वदोषादपरज्यन्ते तेनासि हरिणः कृशः।। अनुशासन १२४.१०।।

Due to the disorders of their own character, your friends have abandoned you when you have been so good to them. That is the reason why you have become weak and pale.[73]

धनैश्वर्याधिकाः स्तब्धास्त्वद्गुणैः परमावराः।
अवजानन्ति नूनं त्वां तेनासि हरिणः कृशः।। अनुशासन १२४.११।।

Of much lower qualities than you are, but because they are very rich and glowing, some people ignore you and hardly recognise you. That is the reason why you have become weak and pale.[74]

गुणवान् विगुणानन्यान् नूनं पश्यसि सत्कृतान्।
प्राज्ञोऽप्राज्ञान् विनीतात्मा तेनासि हरिणः कृशः।। अनुशासन १२४.१२।।

A man of qualities, and learned, yet humble, you get no recognition; whereas those of no qualities, and having no mind either, you see them being respected. That is the reason why you look weak and pale.[75]

अवृत्त्या क्लिश्यमानोऽपि वृत्त्युपायान् विगर्हयन्।
माहात्म्याद् व्यथसे नूनं तेनासि हरिणः कृशः।। अनुशासन १२४.१३।।

Maybe you have no means of livelihood, only anxiety; but you are too proud to ask, indeed consider asking as undignified. Perhaps that could be a reason why you have become weak and pale.[76]

सम्पीड्यात्मानमार्यत्वात् त्वयाकश्चि दुपस्वृतः।
जितं त्वां मन्यते साधो तेनासि हरिणः कृशः।। अनुशासन १२४.१४।।

From your goodness, when you do some good to another, he thinks it is from your weakness, and that he has reduced you. Maybe that is one reason why you have grown weak and pale.[77]

प्रज्ञासम्भावितो नूनमप्रज्ञैरुपसंहितः।
हीयमानोऽसि दुर्वृत्तैस्तेनासि हरिणः कृशः।। अनुशासन १२४.१६।।

Although of a noble mind, you are deserving of respect, but those who have no claims to knowledge make little of you, and those who are wicked insult you. Maybe that is why you have become weak and pale.[78]

नूनं मित्रमुखः शत्रुः कश्चिदार्यवदाचरन् ।
वञ्चयित्वा गतस्त्वां वै तेनासि हरिणः कृशः ।। अनुशासन १२४.१७ ।।

An enemy pretending to be a friend came; behaved as a cultured person would; but deceived and cheated you and then left. Maybe that is why you have become weak and pale.[79]

प्रकाशार्थगतिर्नूनं रहस्यकुशलः कृती ।
तज्ज्ञैर्न पूज्यसे नूनं तेनासि हरिणः कृशः ।। अनुशासन १२४.१८ ।।

Your attitudes towards the material things of life are in the open, and you are good at explaining things that are complex; but the learned regard you little. Maybe that is why you have become weak and pale.[80]

असत्स्वपि निविष्टेषु ब्रुवतो मुक्तसंशयम् ।
गुणास्ते न विराजन्ते तेनासि हरिणः कृशः ।। अनुशासन १२४.१९ ।।

In the midst of those who are simply argumentative, you speak authoritatively. But your qualities remain unrecognised. Maybe that is why you have become weak and pale.[81]

धनबुद्धिश्रुतैर्हीनः केवलं तेजसान्वितः ।
महत् प्रार्थयसे नूनं तेनासि हरिणः कृशः ।। अनुशासन १२४.२० ।।

Devoid of money and intelligence, you still aspire for higher things on the strength of your force alone, and have failed. Maybe that is why you have become weak and pale.[82]

तपः प्रणिहितात्मानं मन्ये त्वारण्यकाङ्क्षिणम् ।
बान्धवा नाभिनन्दन्ति तेनासि हरिणः कृशः ।। अनुशासन १२४.२१ ।।

Or, maybe, you have set your heart on austerities and want to live in the forest, but your relatives do not approve of it. And that is why you have become weak and pale.[83]

सुदुर्विनीतः पुत्रो वा जामाता वा प्रमार्जकः ।
दारा वा प्रतिकूलास्ते तेनासि हरिणः कृशः ।। अनुशासन १२४.२१अ ।।

Your son is of rude behaviour; your son-in-law has his eyes on your property; and your wife is out of harmony with you. That is why you have become weak and pale.[84]

भ्रातरोऽतीव विषमाः पिता वा क्षुत्क्षतो मृतः ।
माता ज्येष्ठो गुरुर्वापि तेनासि हरिणः कृशः ।। अनुशासन १२४.२१ब ।।

Or your brothers have differences with you. Or maybe your father and your mother, or some other relative, perhaps your teacher, died of starvation. And that is why you have become weak and pale.[85]

ब्राह्मणो वा हतो गौर्वा ब्रह्मस्वं वा हृतं पुरा।
देवस्वं बाधिकं काले तेनासि हरिणः कृशः।। अनुशासन १२४.२१स।।

In the past, you had killed a person devoted to knowledge and learning, or had stolen his money, or you had killed a cow. That is why you have become weak and pale.[86]

हृतदारोऽथ वृद्धो वा लोके द्विष्टोऽथ वा नरैः।
अविज्ञानेन वा वृद्धस्तेनासि हरिणः कृशः।। अनुशासन १२४.२१ड।।

Someone has taken away your wife; or you are growing old; or people are antagonistic towards you; and you keep worrying about them. And that is why you have become weak and pale.[87]

वार्धक्यार्थं धनं दृष्ट्वा स्वा श्रीर्वापि परैर्हृता।
वृत्तिर्वा दुर्जनापेक्षा तेनासि हरिणः कृशः।। अनुशासन १२४.२१इ।।

Or, maybe, the money that you had set aside for your old age, others have taken it by force; or, deprived of your money, you now have to depend for your subsistence upon the wicked and the ignoble. And that is why you have become weak and pale.[88]

इष्टभार्यस्य ते नूनं प्रातिवेश्यो महाधनः।
युवा सुललितः कामी तेनासि हरिणः कृशः।। अनुशासन १२४.२२।।

Maybe you love your wife dearly, and you have as a neighbour someone who is very rich, and young, and charming, and pleasure loving. And, out of that anxiety, you have become weak and pale.[89]

नूनमर्थवतां मध्ये तव वाक्यमनुत्तमम्।
न भाति कालेऽभिहितं तेनासि हरिणः कृशः।। अनुशासन १२४.२३।।

In the midst of the rich you say things high and noble, and they do not like it. Maybe that is why you have become weak and pale.[90]

दृढपूर्वं श्रुतं मूर्खं कुपितं हृदयप्रियम्।
अनुनेतुं न शक्नोषि तेनासि हरिणः कृशः।। अनुशासन १२४.२४।।

Maybe someone once very dear to you is, out of his foolishness, now angry with you, and you are not able to pacify him. And that is why you have become weak and pale.[91]

नूनमासंजयित्वा त्वां कृत्ये कस्मिंश्चिदीप्सिते।
कश्चिदर्थयते नित्यं तेनासि हरिणः कृशः।। अनुशासन १२४.२५।।

Or, maybe, someone has appointed you for some desired work, but is only using you to serve his own purpose. That is why you have become weak and pale.[92]

नूनं त्वां सुगुणैर्युक्तं पूजयानं सुहृद्ध्रुवम्।
ममार्थ इति जानीते तेनासि हरिणः कृशः।। अनुशासन १२४.२६।।

Maybe you are greatly respected for your own noble qualities; but some friend of yours thinks that you are flourishing due to his influence. And that is why you have become weak and pale.[93]

अन्तर्गतमभिप्रायं नूनं नेच्छसि लज्जया।
विवेक्तुं प्राप्तिशैथिल्यात् तेनासि हरिणः कृशः।। अनुशासन १२४.२७।।

Or, maybe, out of your modesty, you do not wish to disclose what you intend doing, for you are doubtful of your success. And that is why you have become weak and pale.[94]

नानाबुद्धिरुचो लोके मनुष्यान् नूनमिच्छसि।
ग्रहीतुं स्वगुणैः सर्वास्तेनासि हरिणः कृशः।। अनुशासन १२४.२८।।

There are in this world human beings of different perceptions and of different inclinations, but you want to please them all by your own qualities. And maybe that is why you have become weak and pale.[95]

अविद्वान् भीरुरल्पार्थे विद्याविक्रमदानजम्।
यशः प्रार्थयसे नूनं तेनासि हरिणः कृशः।। अनुशासन १२४.२९।।

With no learning, you wish to have the acclaim of being learned; a coward, you wish to be known as brave; having little to give, you want the acclaim of being a great giver. And maybe that is why you have become weak and pale.[96]

नूनमात्मकृतं दोषमपश्यन् किंचिदात्मनः।
अकारणेऽभिशप्तोऽसि तेनासि हरिणः कृशः।। अनुशासन १२४.३१।।

You see no fault within yourself; but others, for no reason whatsoever, keep cursing you. That is maybe why you have become weak and pale.[97]

चिराभिलषितं किंचित्फलमप्राप्तमेव ते ।
कृतमन्यैरपहृतं तेनासि हरिणः कृशः ।। अनुशासन १२४.३० ।।

Or maybe you did not get the fruits for long desired from your work, and others stole it. That is why you have become weak and pale.[98]

धर्म्यमर्थ्यं च काम्यं च काले चाभिहितं वचः ।
न प्रतीयन्ति ते नूनं तेनासि हरिणः कृशः ।। अनुशासन १२४.३४ ।।

What you say is in accordance with dharma, artha, *and* kāma, *and appropriate to the time as well, but people do not believe in you. Maybe that is why you have become weak and pale.*[99]

सुहृदां दुःखमार्तानां न प्रमोक्ष्यसि चार्तिजम् ।
अलमर्थगुणैर्हीनं तेनासि हरिणः कृशः ।। अनुशासन १२४.३३ ।।

Or maybe your near ones suffer great pain, and there is little that you can do to free them from their suffering, and you are yourself deprived of the gains of material prosperity. That is why you have become weak and pale.[100]

In the voice of that *brāhmaṇa*, the *Mahābhārata* speaks also of several impersonal reasons why a person could be unhappy and troubled, even a *rākṣhasa*.

क्लिश्यमानन् विमार्गेषु कामक्रोधावृतात्मनः ।
मन्ये त्वं ध्यायसि जनांस्तेनासि हरिणः कृशः ।। अनुशासन १२४.१५ ।।

Or maybe you feel concerned for those who are assailed by desire and anger and have taken to a wrong path. That is why you have become weak and pale.[101]

साधून् गृहस्थान् दृष्ट्वा च तथा साधून् वनेचरान् ।
मुक्तांश्चावसथे सक्तांस्तेनासि हरिणः कृशः ।। अनुशासन १२४.३२ ।।

You see hermits becoming householders; those who are wicked pretending to be hermits by living in the forest; and the renouncers getting involved in property. Maybe that is why you have become weak and pale.[102]

पापान् प्रवर्धतोदृष्ट्वा कल्याणानावसीदत: ।
ध्रुवं गर्हयसे नित्यं तेनासि हरिण: कृश: ।। अनुशासन १२४.३६ ।।

You see the wicked flourishing, and the truly good suffering, and you always lament that this is so. And that is why you have become weak and pale.[103]

श्रीत्रियांश्च विकर्मस्थान् प्राज्ञांश्चाप्यजितेन्द्रियान् ।
मन्येऽनुध्यायसि जनांस्तेनासि हरिण: कृश: ।। अनुशासन १२४.३८ ।।

You see the brāhmaṇa-s learned in the vedic lore taking to the ways of adharma, *and the scholars devoted to learning and knowledge indulge in the pleasures of the senses, and you feel troubled. That is why you have become weak and pale.*[104]

The brāhmaṇa showed respect to the rākshasa who, in turn, honoured the brāhmaṇa; made him his friend; gave him money; and let him go.[105]

From the same facts: three different paths to happiness

There were three main directions in which, with a common stock of the indisputable facts concerning pleasure and pain narrated above, the Dharmic effort to avoid pain and seek happiness, branched off, each on its own separate journey.

1. The disciplining of the sense organs and their corresponding faculties: *indriya-nigraha*.
2. A complete withdrawal from the workings of the body and the mind and renouncing the world altogether: *vairāgya*.
3. The journey towards *mokṣha*, a state of being in which *all* opposites, including *sukha-duḥkha*, or pleasure-pain, are transcended in one's consciousness.

Mokṣha was more radical than just renunciation; renunciation more radical than just self-control. The real struggle remained, however, between the philosophies of '1.' and '2.'. Between living one's life in the world fully, of sense-experience, desires and feelings and emotions, but self-controlled for one's own good as well as for the good of others, *and* renouncing the world altogether, in act and in spirit, to achieve what was perceived as the greatest good for oneself. But however radically different their practical aims, and however radically different the psychology each created, each of the three disciplines carried within itself a common stock of the facts regarding pleasure-pain that the *Mahābhārata* has set out most vividly. Indeed, each derived its separate world view from those very facts in common. Their reasoning is set out with equal clarity in the *Mahābhārata*: the rationality of *indriya-nigraha*; the rationality of *vairāgya*; and the rationality of *moksha*. The reasoning in each of these three moves from *because it is evidently so* to *therefore it follows that*.

Indeed, each with such clarity and persuasive force, that if any of those parts was read alone, it would lead to a wrong understanding of what the *Mahābhārata* is teaching on a subject most intimate to human living: *sukha* and *duḥkha*. But so as to avoid any *one* of the three being taken as representing the whole truth, each is to be read in its specific context. And to each, the word *neti* must immediately be added, and repeated twice—'*it is not this alone*', 'it is not this *alone*'. This is what the *Mahābhārata* consistently does, as an intellectual and ethical attitude.

According to the *Mahābhārata*:

ये च मूढतमा लोके ये च बुद्धेः परं गताः।
ते नराः सुखमेधन्ते क्लिश्यत्यन्तरितो जनः।। शान्ति १७४.३३।।

ये च मूढतमा लोके ये च बुद्धेः परं गताः।
त एव सुखमेधन्ते मध्यमः क्लिश्यते जनः।। शान्ति २५.२८।।

Only two types of human beings are indeed happy: the fools, and those who have transcended understanding itself: the unhappy ones are those who fall in the middle.[106]

अन्त्येषु रेमिरे धीरा न ते मध्येषु रेमिरे।
अन्त्यप्राप्तिं सुखामाहुर्दुःखमन्तरमन्तययोः।। शान्ति १७४.३४।।

Covered with the blanket of profound ignorance, the fools rest in pleasure, unmindful of the recompense of their acts;[107] *even like the gods they are forever happy, for their consciousness is smeared with sense-pleasure.*[108]

ये च बुद्धिसुखं प्राप्ता द्वन्द्वातीता विमत्सराः।
तान् नैवार्था न चानर्था व्यथयन्ति कदाचन।। शान्ति १७४.३५।।

अथ ये बुद्धिमप्राप्ता व्यतिक्रान्ताश्च मूढताम्।
तेऽतिवेलं प्रहृष्यन्ति संतापमुपयान्ति च।। शान्ति १७४.३६।।

And those who have obtained the happiness of true understanding, they are affected neither by the joy of prosperity nor by the anguish of disaster.[109]

Those who have overcome foolishness, but have not obtained true understanding yet, it is they who are either overjoyed or deeply distressed.[110]

The fools and the knowing are, at either extreme, beyond self-interest. In a real sense one communicates with neither: with the one it is futile, with the other it is not necessary. It is to the vast middle class of humankind, therefore, that the thinkers in the *Mahābhārata* addressed themselves. For it is among that class that self-interest most operates at various levels. And their thinking on pleasure-pain throughout assumed the sturdy fact of self-interest, *svārtha*; and to that, in all their formulations, they constantly appealed. At the same time, they made the point that it is only too easy for us human beings to have a wrong perception of self-interest itself.

a. *Indriya-nigraha*, disciplining the body–mind

Self-interest dictates that since the sense-organs naturally rush towards the objects that are agreeable, and withdraw from those that are disagreeable, the variety of human experience arising from the ground that lies between *rāga* and *dvesha*, *inclination* and *aversion*, the sense-organs and faculties must be kept under control.[111] They, and under their influence the will, tend to run riot if they are not disciplined, and can only produce pain. The *Mahābhārata*'s favourite metaphor in this regard is of the chariot drawn by five horses.

रथ: शरीरं पुरुषस्य राज-
न्नात्मा नियन्तेन्द्रियाण्यस्य चाश्वा: ।
तैरप्रमत्त: कुशली सदश्वै-
र्दान्तै: सुखं याति रथीव धीर: ।। उद्योग ३४.५९ ।।

The body is the chariot, the five sense-organs its horses, and the mind the charioteer. The man who holds firmly the reins of the five horses is a happy charioteer.[112]

इन्द्रियाण्येव तत् सर्वं यत् स्वर्गनरकावुभौ ।
निगृहीतविसृष्टानि स्वर्गाय परकाय च ।। वन २११.१९ ।।

And there is no heaven and there is no hell apart from what the sense-organs, controlled or left wild, create for oneself.[113]

एष योगविधि: कृत्सन्नो यावदिन्द्रियधारणम् ।
एतन्मूलं हि तपस: कृत्स्नस्य नरकस्य च ।। वन २११.२० ।।

Thus, disciplining the body and the mind is the discipline of yoga, and also the root of all austerity, tapas. If not, the hell of all disorder.[114]

इन्द्रियाणां प्रसङ्गेन दोषमार्च्छन्त्यसंशयम् ।
संनियम्य तु तान्येव तत: सिद्धिं समाप्नुयात् ।। वन २११.२१ ।।

Indulgence in the sense-organs leads to all disorder, of this there is no doubt. Disciplined, they bring all fulfilment.[115]

एतान्यनिगृहीतानि व्यापादयितुमप्यलम् ।
अविधेया इवादान्ता हया: पथि कुसारथिम् ।। उद्योग ३४.६० ।।

Just as the untrained and uncontrolled horses can hurt a bad charioteer, so do the physical organs of a man if they are not disciplined.[116]

This was the foundation for the theory of *indriya-nigraha*, which occupies a common ground in dharmic thought. Acts being also of the mind and of speech, these are to be controlled as well. The general proposition is:

इन्द्रियेभ्य: परे ह्यर्था अर्थेभ्य: परमं मन: ।
मनसस्तु परा बुद्धिर्बुद्धेरात्मा महान् पर: ।। शान्ति २४६.३ ।।

Stronger than the sense-organs are their objects; stronger than the sense-objects is the will; stronger than the will is the discriminating mind; and stronger than that is the soul.[117]

It was from this proposition that the various steps to self-discipline, of the body as well as of the mind, are then worked out in clearest details.

The aim of self-discipline is not a withdrawal from the pleasures as such, for that would be unnatural and therefore harmful; but to avoid obsessive attachment to them. In reality that means a detachment from oneself, not from things.

In the voice of Vidura, the *Mahābhārata* says to us:

चक्षु: श्रोत्रे नासिकात्वक् च जिह्वा
ज्ञानस्यैतान्यायतनानि जन्तो: ।
तानि प्रीतान्येव तृष्णाक्षयान्ते
तान्यव्यथो दु:खहीन: प्रणुद्यात् ।। उद्योग ३२.२५ ।।

The eyes, the ears, the nose, the skin, and the tongue, are the instruments through which all living beings sense the world. On the excessive greed, the obsessive 'thirst' for objects, coming to an end, these sense-organs create happiness and joy. Therefore, so as to be free of pain, one should discipline them.[118]

In the voice of Bhīshma, the *Mahābhārata* provides the indisputable reasoning for *dama*, self-discipline, as the way to happiness.[119] That is in answer to the question asked by Yudhishṭhira:

बहुधा दर्शने लोके श्रेयो यदिह मन्यसे।
अस्मिँल्लोके परे चैव तन्मे ब्रूहि पितामह।। शान्ति १६०.२।।
In this world, there are many philosophies of the Good. Among them, which, in your view, is the best, and the most practical?[120]

Bhīshma
धर्मस्य विधयो नैके ये वै प्रोक्ता महर्षिभिः।
स्वं स्वं विज्ञानमाश्रित्य दमस्तेषां परायणम्।। शान्ति १६०.६।।
दमं निःश्रेयसं प्राहुर्वृद्धा निश्चितदर्शिनः।
The great sages have propounded, each according to his understanding, not one but several ways to dharma*. But they all have self-discipline,* dama*, as their common foundation.*[121]
The elders who know with certainty consider self-discipline to be the way to the highest good and beatitude.[122]

दमस्तेजो वर्धयति पवित्रं च दमः परम्।
विपाप्मा तेजसा युक्तः पुरुषो विन्दते महत्।। शान्ति १६०.९।।
Self-discipline increases one's strength, and is the highest purity. Removing the disorders of conduct, the one who has achieved self-discipline has gained the universe.[123]

सुखं दान्तः प्रस्वपिति सुखं च प्रतिबुध्यते।
सुखं पर्येति लोकांश्च मनश्चास्य प्रसीदति।। शान्ति १६०.१२।।
Who has disciplined himself sleeps peacefully, and happily awakes, relates with the world with happiness, and is joyful at heart.[124]

अदान्तः पुरुषः क्लेशमभीक्ष्णं प्रतिपद्यते।
अनर्थांश्च बहूनन्यान् प्रसृजत्यात्मदोषजान्।। शान्ति १६०.१३।।

The one without self-discipline invites great suffering; and, from the lack of self-discipline, keeps creating numerous other disorders too.[125]

Bhīshma then lists 'the signs' that constitute the meaning of *dama*, self-control.[126] In this too, as on every other subject concerning life, there is in the *Mahābhārata* an extraordinary inner coherence. Those 'signs' relate to one's relationship with one's self and one's relationship with the *other*.

क्षमा धृतिरहिंसा च समता सत्यमार्जवम् ।
इन्द्रियाभिजयो दाक्ष्यं मार्दवं ह्रीरचापलम् ।। शान्ति १६०.१५ ।।

अकार्पण्यमसंरम्भः संतोषः प्रियवादिता ।
अविहिंसानसूया चाप्येषां समुदयो दमः ।। शान्ति १६०.१६ ।।

Forgiveness and reconciliation; steadfastness; not-violence; attitude of equality; truthfulness; simplicity of character; conquest of one's sense-organs and faculties; skillfulness; gentleness; generosity; self-containment; endearing speech; not to hurt anyone; and not to find fault in others—these are the signs of self-discipline.[127]

And in so far as they constitute one's happy relationship with one's self and with the *other*, they bring freedom from pain and suffering. In answer to the most pressing question of all men:

क्लिश्यमानेषु भूतेषु तैस्तैर्भावैस्ततस्ततः ।
दुर्गाण्यतितरेद् येन तन्मे ब्रूहि पितामह ।। शान्ति ११०.१ ।।

All living beings are in the grip of pain and suffering, in different ways, in different circumstances. Tell me, Pitamaha, by what means can they cross over suffering?[128]

The *Mahābhārata* in the voice of Bhīshma, suggests the right relationship with one's self, and simultaneously with the *other* as the way to living a happy and meaningful life.[129]

The need for physical and mental discipline over one's self, to be exercised in one's self-interest, was enforced by another reasoning; which, like the previous ones, was self-evident. Since everybody can see that there is no end to desire, and each desire on its fulfilment creates a new one, leading to a perpetual sense of want, which is pain, what is clearly then required is inner contentment *santosha*. And in the same measure as one achieves inner contentment, is the sense of want, with its accompanying feeling of pain, reduced.

असंतोषोऽसुखायेति लोभादिन्द्रियसम्भ्रमः।
ततोऽस्य नश्यति प्रज्ञा विद्येवाभ्यासवर्जिता।। शान्ति २९५.२५।।

Discontent is lack of happiness. From greed comes the agitation of the sense-organs, and because of that, understanding is destroyed in the same way as learning is destroyed without application.[130]

अन्तो नास्ति पिपासायास्तुष्टिस्तु परमं सुखम्।
तस्मात् संतोषमेवेह धनं पश्यन्ति पण्डिताः।। शान्ति ३३०.२१।।

To 'thirst' there is no end; and contentment is great happiness: therefore the wise perceive contentment alone to be the most superior.[131]

यावन्तो विषयाः प्रेष्ठास्त्रिलोक्यामजितेन्द्रियम्।
न शक्नुवन्ति ते सर्वे प्रतिपूरयितुं नृप।। भागवत ८-१९.२१।।

Not even all the objects of pleasure in the world are capable of satisfying one man's desires if he has not mastered his faculties.[132]

दुःखेन चाधिगम्यन्ते तस्मान्नाशं न चिन्तयेत्।
असंतोषपरां मूढाः संतोषं यान्ति पण्डिताः।। वन २.४५।।

यदृच्छयोपपन्नेन संतुष्टो वर्तते सुखम्।
नासं तुष्टस्त्रिभिर्लोकैरजितात्मोपसादितैः।। भागवत ८-१९.२४।।

The ignorant are always discontented, the wise always contented.[133] *The wise know contentment to be the most superior wealth.*[134] *He who is contented with whatever he gets through providence is alone happy; but he who burns in the fire of discontent would be unhappy should he gain even the three worlds.*[135]

After demonstrating that *parigraha*, grasping, can produce neither pleasure nor happiness, all schools of Indian philosophy, including some groups of materialists like the Ājīvika-s, pointed to *a-parigraha*, not-grasping, as the one single most important element in genuine happiness. The general principle in this regard was:

विस्तराः क्लेशसंयुक्ताः संक्षेपास्तु सुखावहाः।
परार्थं विस्तराः सर्वे त्यागमात्महितं विदु।। शान्ति २९८.२०।।

To expand is connected with trouble and suffering; to limit is conducive of happiness.[136]

Therefore, in the voice of Vidura, the *Mahābhārata* says to us:

अर्थानामीश्वरो यः स्यादिन्द्रियाणामनीश्वरः ।
इन्द्रियाणामनैश्वर्यादैश्वर्याद् भ्रश्यते हि सः ।। उद्योग ३४.६३ ।।
In being the lord even of immense wealth, if a person is not in possession of his self; then his sense-organs possessing him, he is dispossessed of all that is good and glorious.[137]

It follows that:

आत्मनाऽऽत्मानमन्विच्छेन्मनोबुद्धीन्द्रियैर्यतैः ।
आत्मा ह्येवात्मनो बन्धुरात्मैव रिपुरात्मनः ।। उद्योग ३४.६४ ।।
Disciplining one's body, mind and intellect, let one conquer one's self with one's self; for one's self alone is one's friend, and one's self also one's enemy.[138]

The *Mahābhārata* entertains, however, no illusion that not to be feverishly attached to persons and things would be easy for most human beings to achieve, however observably true it might be that it is from that sort of attachment that all pain does arise. For if it were easy, the incredible repetitiveness of the warning against it would not have been necessary.

Whether one is free to create one's happiness and suffering, or whether they are predetermined, is another important concern of the *Mahābhārata*'s inquiry into the human condition. It covers as large a ground as *sukha* and *duḥkha*. But free or not, the necessity of physical and mental discipline remains unaltered. That discipline, at its most primary level, consists in not letting oneself be overwhelmed either by the joy of prosperity or by the pain of disaster. Of this, the *Mahābhārata* speaks again and again, and forever again; not as an ethical imperative, however, but as an evident psychological necessity in self-preservation. And in doing that, it assumes freedom over our thoughts, if not altogether over our outward circumstances.

b. *Vairāgya,* renunciation of the world

The argument regarding *pleasure* and *pain* had taken another turn—the path of total withdrawal from the world—which, if in its own logic consistent and based on the same undeniable facts as regards pain and pleasure and their workings as the disciplining of the body-mind was, was nevertheless psychologically fraught with danger. To the individual who moved in that direction, it was a denial of life. The *Mahābhārata* states the *vairāgya* argument as well, with its full force. In that view, *indriya-nigraha*, self-control, alone is not sufficient, though it is evidently necessary. Withdrawal from the *things* of the world is even a greater requisite. For, it is argued, *any* contact with the objects of sense-pleasure is capable of involving in them even a man most self-controlled. Numerous parables were created, all of them no doubt based on human experience, so as to demonstrate how that might happen only too easily. What is further required, if one really wished to obtain true happiness, and freedom from pain, is a complete withdrawal from *the objects* of pleasure themselves. For not only what seems on first sight wholly pleasurable turns out to be conducive to pain, but also the recurrent thirst for pleasure from things that are themselves unstable and transient must produce confusion and pain when they pass; for one tends to behave as if they would endure.

यथा यथा च पर्येति लोकतन्त्रमसारवत् ।
तथा तथा विरागोऽत्र जायते नात्र संशयः ।। शान्ति १७४.४ ।।
In the same measure as a man perceives the things of the world as without substance, he feels repulsed by them. In this there is no doubt.[139]

Carrying the logic of renunciation, *tyāga* or *vairāgya*, to its extreme point, it ended in denying the body and the mind their natural nourishment: the path of extreme asceticism It ended, most of all, in withdrawing from all human ties of relationships. It consisted in the following reasoning. It ended, most of all, in withdrawing from all human ties of relationships.[140]

तृष्णार्तिप्रभवं दुःखं दुःखार्तिप्रभवं सुखम् ।
सुखात् संजायते दुःखं दुःखमेवं पुनः पुनः ।। शान्ति १७४.१८ ।।
The 'thirst' of Desire is pain, and pleasure arises when that pain is assuaged; pleasure leads to the pain of further desire, and thus there is pain again and again.[141]

स्नेहपाशैर्बहुविधैराविष्टविषया जनाः ।
अकृतार्थाश्च सीदन्ते जलैः सैकतसेतवः ।। शान्ति १७४.२३ ।।

Human beings are bound to the numerous objects of this world with the cord of attachment; but because those objects decay and perish, there is anguish as a result. It is like building a bridge on a pile of sand.[142]

संचिन्वानकमेवैनं कामानामवितृप्तकम् ।
व्याघ्रः पशुमिवादाय मृत्युरादाय गच्छति ।। शान्ति १७५.१९ ।।

Till such time as a man is satiated with the objects of pleasure, he keeps accumulating them.[143] *Then one day, one's desires still unfulfilled, death carries one away.*[144]

रात्र्यां रात्र्यां व्यतीतायामायुरल्पतरं यदा ।
गाधोदके मत्स्य इव सुखं विन्देत कस्तदा ।। शान्ति १७५.११ ।।

With each succeeding night one's life ebbing away, who can, like a fish in shallow waters, be happy?[145]

दुर्बलं बलवन्तं च शूरं भीरुं जडं कविम् ।
अप्राप्तं सर्वकामार्थान् मृत्युरादाय गच्छति ।। शान्ति १७५.२२ ।।

Whether a man is weak or powerful, courageous or a coward, a fool or learned, even before his longings are fulfilled death takes him away.[146]

त्वया हि मे प्रणुन्नस्य गतिरन्या न विद्यते ।
तृष्णाशोकश्रमाणां हि त्वं काम प्रभवः सदा ।। शान्ति १७७.३३ ।।

कामानुबन्धं नुदते यत् किंचित् पुरुषो रजः ।
कामक्रोधोद्भवं दुःखमह्रीररतिरेव च ।। शान्ति १७७.४९ ।।

As long as one lives, desire, kāma, *is the origin of the thirst for more, of grief, and of strenuous labour.*[147] *From desire arises aggression, and from them arise pain, shamelessness, discontent.*[148]

यद् यत् त्यजति कामानां तत् सुखस्याभिपूर्यते ।
कामस्य वशगो नित्यं दुःखमेव प्रपद्यते ।। शान्ति १७७.४८ ।।

Whichever desire one renounces, with that one becomes the happier; under the power of desire one remains forever unhappy.[149]

Furthermore, relationships were seen as only full of pain. There is for a short while pleasure and happiness in them; but when they come to an end, there is unbearable pain. To avoid that, one has to withdraw from all relationships. For, eventually, there is only the alone-ness of the individual.

यथा काष्ठं च काष्ठं च समयातां महोदधौ।
समेत्य च व्यपेयातां तद्वद् भूतसमागमः।। शान्ति २८.३६।।

Just as two pieces of wood floating in the ocean touch each other for a while, and then separate, so do the human beings.[150]

नैवास्य कश्चिद् भविता नायं भवति कस्यचित्।
पथि सङ्गतमेवेदं दारबन्धुसुहृज्जनैः।। शान्ति २८.३९।।

No one belongs to me, and I belong to no one. Just as the travellers on a road become companions for a while, so do the wife, brother, and good-hearted friends.[151]

अनित्ये प्रियसंवासे संसारे चक्रवद्नतौ।
पथि सङ्गतमेवैतद् भ्राता माता पिता सखा।। शान्ति २८.४१।।

This world is a moving wheel. Being with the loved ones is transitory, passing. Brother, father, mother, friend are like companions on the road.[152]

क्वासे क्व च गमिष्यामि को न्वहं किमिहास्थितः।
कस्मात् किमनुशोचेयमित्येवं स्थापयेन्मनः।। शान्ति २८.४०।।

कुतोऽहमागतः कोऽस्मि क्व गमिष्यामि कस्य वा।
कस्मिन् स्थितः क्व भविता कस्मात्किमनुशोचसि।। शान्ति ३१९.१४।।

In one's mind one should rather ask, 'Where am I? Where will I go? Who am I? Why am I here? For whom should I grieve?'[153]

एकः प्रसूयते राजन्नेक एव विनश्यति।
एकस्तरति दुर्गाणि गच्छत्येकस्तु दुर्गतिम्।। अनुशासन १११.११।।

असहायः पिता माता तथा भ्राता सुतो गुरुः।
ज्ञातिसम्बन्धिवर्गश्च मित्रवर्गस्तथैव च।। अनुशासन १११.१२।।

मृतं शरीरमुत्सृज्य काष्ठलोष्टसमं जनाः।
मुहूर्तमिव रोदित्वा ततो यान्ति पराङ्मुखाः।। अनुशासन १११.१३।।

One is alone in birth; one is alone in death. One is alone in one's pain; and one is alone in crossing over.[154]

Father, mother, brother, son, guru, relatives and friends are of no help.[155]

They weep over his body for a while when he dies, and then turn their face away.[156]

अहमेको न मे कश्चिन्नाहमन्यस्य कस्यचित् ।
न तं पश्यामि यस्याहं तन्न पश्यामि यो मम ।। शान्ति ३२१.८६ ।।

I am in my being alone. There is no one who belongs to me; and I belong to no one. I see no one to whom I belong; nor do I see anyone who is mine.[157]

Therefore:

Indifferent to all desires, to all emotional ties, let one travel beyond them:

नास्ति विद्यासमं चक्षुर्नास्ति सत्यसमं तपः ।
नास्ति रागसमं दुःखं नास्ति त्यागसमं सुखम् ।। शान्ति १७५.३५ ।।

There are no eyes like knowledge, no austerity like truth, no pain like attachment, and no happiness like renunciation.[158]

The foregoing reasoning was undoubtedly based on experience, not on assumptions. All the things that a man normally desires—wealth, sexual pleasure, a house of one's own, properties, a happy family, children who one would be proud of, success in one's calling, fame in the world—were assessed as to their intrinsic value, and to each felicity was seen a pain attached.

आक्रोन्तं मरणेन जन्म जरया चात्युज्ज्वलं यौवनं
संतोषो धनलिप्सया शमसुखं प्रौढाङ्गनाविभ्रमैः ।
लोकैर्मत्सरिभिर्गुणा वनभुवो व्यालैर्नृपा दुर्जनै-
रस्थैर्येण विभूतयोप्युपहता ग्रस्तं न किं केन वा ।। वैराग्य ३२ ।।

'By death is life assailed; by old age the delight of youth departs, by greed contentment, the calm of inner joy through the coquetries of forward ladies; envy attacks our virtues, snakes trees, villains kings; all power is transient. What is there that another doth not overwhelm it?'[159]

भोगे रोगभयं कुले च्युतिभयं वित्ते नृपालाद्भयं
माने दैन्यभयं बले रिपुभयं रूपे जराया भयम् ।
शास्त्रे वादभयं गुणे खलभयं काये कृतान्ताद्भयं
सर्वं वस्तु भयान्वितं भुवि नृणां वैराग्यमेवाभयम् ।। वैराग्य ३२ ।।

In the enjoyment of the pleasures, the fear of disease; in the high lineage, the fear of fall; in wealth, the fear of the king; in acclaim, the fear of humbling; in power, the fear of the enemy; in beauty, the fear of old age; in learning, the fear of challenge and dispute; in being good, the fear of others' malice; in one's body, the fear of its weakening. All things of the world are shot through with fear. The withdrawal from the world has in it no fear.[160]

Up to this point there was no defect in the statement of facts. But the *vairāgya* literature went very much farther than that. Apart from pointing out that there is no real pleasure in things that are uncertain, unstable and transient, it also concentrated, in the most extravagant language, on the less flattering aspects of the human body. Since the body is the physical instrument of experiencing the pleasures, the offending aspects of the body itself were now enumerated in detail. From this arose the ascetic condemnation, bordering very nearly on hatred, of the human body. That was undoubtedly an excess—and, like all excesses, it was profoundly destructive. Hence the struggle against it was not at the level of philosophic thought alone, but in the realm of the social order as well. Philosophically, it was the very reverse of the Dharmic attitude to the human body, one of immense respect and wonder. It was repeatedly pointed out that to punish one's body, under the impression that one would secure true happiness thereby, was senseless. *For the ascetic denial of the body must eventually lead to a hatred of all that is human.*

Mokṣha: Towards freedom from the human condition

The *Mahābhārata*'s view of *mokṣha* as human freedom will be discussed in a later chapter.[161] However, since every discussion on *moksha* necessarily contains an analysis of *sukha* and *duḥkha*, and the other way around too, its basic logic may briefly be stated here as well.

Earlier in the *Kathopanisad* a distinction was made between *preya*, 'the pleasurable', and *shreya*, 'the Good'. The logic of the one is distinct from the logic of the other. This had been clearly stated:

अन्यच्छ्रेयोऽन्यदुतैव प्रेयस्ते उभे नानार्थे पुरुषं सिनीत: ।
तयो: श्रेय आददानस्य साधु भवति हीयतेऽर्थाद्य उ प्रेयो वृणीते । ।

The Good is different from the Pleasurable: both attract man towards themselves. Of the two, he who seeks the Good is truly blessed; whereas he who seeks the Pleasurable is deprived of the true gain.[162]

श्रेयश्च प्रेयश्च मनुष्यमेतस्तौ सम्परीत्य विविनक्ति धीर: ।
श्रेयो हि धीरोऽभि प्रेयसो वृणीते प्रेयो मन्दो योगक्षेमाद् वृणीते । ।

> *Both the Good and the Pleasurable encounter man. Who is discriminating, he perceives them as different from each other. The discriminating man seeks only the Good rather than the Pleasurable; whereas the less discriminating, desiring the earthly well-being, seeks the Pleasurable.*[163]

The reason why the pleasurable cannot be the abiding *Good*, nor can there be a true seeking in the objects of pleasure, is that they all are limited and transitory.[164] But nowhere did this *Upanishad* say that, *for that reason*, pleasure is to be despised on principle. Nor did it say that *preya*, the pleasurable, is wholly excluded from *shreya*, the Good. The *vairāgya* denial of the natural human attributes forms no part whatever of the philosophy of the *Upanishad*-s.

Given the separate workings of *the Pleasure* and *the Good*, which, excepting the materialists, all other schools of philosophy in India had posited, the consequences of that distinction formed a common ground of Dharmic thinking as a whole. The most general conclusion was that: since pleasure and pain are invariably linked together, what is to be aimed at is not some form of pleasure that is devoid of pain, which would be impossible to find, but a state in which *pleasure* and *pain* as a set of opposites ceased to have effect on a person's consciousness. It was admitted that neither of them could be eliminated as a physical and psychological fact; but through an understanding of their workings, and with a certain discipline of the body and the mind, it is indeed possible to achieve genuine distance to them. And that state of being is called, *mokṣha*, the supreme Good, where all opposites within which human life is ordinarily lived cease to operate upon a man's consciousness, freeing him thereby from the incessant cycle of birth and death, because all his acts would then become *no-acts*.

Mokṣha in that sense is, however, so overwhelmingly difficult to achieve that, despite the harassing repetition of its clear rationality, it was hardly ever a subject of general practical concern, at any rate not in its classical form. Rather, of greater consequence are those parts of the *Mahābhārata* that assume *pleasure* and *pain* to remain two immensely vital factors in the general course of human life. And then they proceed to demonstrate how, in the interest of self-preservation alone, if nothing else, we must so order our lives as not to be destroyed by the pain that invariably comes from feverish attachment, *asakti*, to persons and things. Self-preservation being at different levels, from the preservation of one's physical life to the seeking of the highest good, ordering of life and relationships naturally contains a hierarchy of levels. As a result, the argument concerning pleasure and pain took different directions, each with its specific logic, but eminently practical forms. All of them remained, however, as interrelated parts of a unified perception of life, where each part, by itself perfectly coherent, invariably pointed to the level above it, and remained incomplete without that.

The compelling desire for pleasure, and the simultaneous ideal of *mokṣha*, created a deep tension between the two, and, when that tension remained unresolved, violence. There has not been in human history another society more resolutely dedicated to pleasure than the Dharmic society; nor was there in the world another system of thinking than Dharmic ethics that had worked out more thoroughly the inexorable logic of pleasure from which must arise also pain. That had several results. One result was that the Dharmic man could do nothing wholeheartedly: he could neither pursue pleasure, untroubled by reflection on its melancholy; nor could he give up completely the desire for it. He was meditating on how what is pleasure is also pain, and disaster often takes the form of prosperity. At the same time, he was also mastering the techniques of obtaining the most pleasure from sex, from food, from drinks, from elegance of clothes and perfumes and jewellery, from music, and dance, and poetry, and from numerous intricate combinations of these. There is not the slightest doubt that Indian society has been a very hedonistic society; though one hears of it only rarely. But it has been also a society overcome by a profound melancholy arising from the knowledge that every pleasure, should it last even for a thousand years, carried within itself the shadow of pain. With extreme hedonism in India there existed extreme asceticism, with the awareness besides, that the one is impossible and the other senseless.

A radical shift in the '*because–therefore*' reasoning

Each of the three paths to happiness and to freedom from suffering has its reasoning, in the form '*because–therefore*', as described above. And that reasoning is stated with its fullest force. It is preached in the same words today as well to every 'religious' or 'spiritual' gathering. One hears, though, more of *vairāgya* and *mokṣha* and less of *indriya-nigraha*, self-discipline. And very little is known, or hardly anything, about the *Mahābhārata*'s radical shift in that '*because–therefore*' reasoning attached to each of the three. That radical break concerning *mokṣha*, interpreted mostly as release from the endless cycle of birth and rebirth, and that alone, will be taken up later in this book, and in that context, the reasoning for *vairāgya*.[165] That radical break from the path of *vairāgya*, in the form in which it was being perceived, and is perceived today too, a feeling of repulsion and therefore renunciation of the world, is manifest throughout the *Mahābhārata*. It is manifest in its discussion on the interrelation between the material and the spiritual; the material conditions of life; human sexuality; the foundations of the life-in-family; social arrangements; and the foundations of law and governance. As we will see, from the same stock of undeniable human facts, the *Mahābhārata* draws different conclusions, *which are a joyful affirmation of life and not its violent negation*. The plain reasoning it puts forth has the form '*because* it is true that—*it does not follow* that *therefore*'.

It is true that all things of the world are transitory.[166] But it does not follow that, for that reason, they are worthless. Human life itself is transitory, but it does not follow that, therefore, it is worthless. The *Mahābhārata* teaches that the worth of a thing is derived not from its *duration* but from the quality of what it *creates*.

It is true that, in one's innermost, one is alone, अहम् एको, *aham eko*.[167] But it does not follow that all human relationships are, therefore, in the nature of 'two pieces of wood floating in the sea touching each other for a while and then drifting away'.[168] That was said when a sage was trying to console a king, Senajit, who had lost his son.[169] But the *Mahābhārata* does not turn it into a theory of relationships and a reason for turning away from all human bonds of love and affection and friendship, as *vairāgya* does.

It is true that the sense organs and their respective faculties tend to run riot if not disciplined. But it does not follow that *therefore* one must declare war against them. *Indriya-nigraha*, is not a denial of pleasure; rather, self-discipline is the very first condition of pleasure. Self-discipline is not a morose, joyless, dark discipline; rather, it is the very first condition of coming into the light and joy of being fully human. Self-discipline is not an oppressive negation of one's self; rather, self-discipline is the very first condition of finding one's self and reaching the *other*.

In this context, the *Mahābhārata* narrates the story of the war the king Alarka had declared on his physical sense organs and faculties.[170] He had expanded his kingdom greatly, by bringing under his control new domains. But he was also a deeply reflective person, who now wanted to conquer the inner domain of his self, which he thought he could achieve by means of the same weapons with which he had conquered much else. He said to himself:

मनसो मे बलं जातं मनो जित्वा ध्रुवो जय: ।
अन्यत्र बाणान् धास्यामि शत्रुभि: परिवारित: ।। आश्व ३०.५ ।।
यदिदं चापलात् कर्म सर्वान् मर्त्यांश्चिकीर्षति ।
मन: प्रति सुतीक्ष्णाग्रानहं मोक्ष्यामि सायकान् ।। आश्व ३०.६ ।।
It is with the power of the mind that I have conquered what I have. If I can conquer this mind, I would have a conquest that is abiding. Not shooting my arrows at the enemies outside, I would shoot my arrows at the enemies that are within instead. It is this restless and fickle mind which prompts all human actions: and it is this mind that I will now attack with my deadly arrows, and gain freedom.[171]

The Mind laughed mockingly, and said to Alarka:

नेमे बाणास्तरिष्यन्ति मामलर्क कथंचन ।
तवैव मर्म भेत्स्यन्ति भिन्नमर्मा मरिष्यसि ।। आश्व ३०.७ ।।
अन्यान् बाणान् समीक्षस्व यैस्त्वं मां सूदयिष्यसि ।
These arrows of yours cannot touch me, Alarka. They will only destroy an intimate part of your own self, and it is you who will die. Think of some other weapon with which you can conquer me.[172]

Alarka reflected for a while; and, in quick succession, then threatened his physical sense organs: his nose, his tongue, his skin, his ears, and his eyes. For, he reckoned,

आघ्राय सुबहून् गन्धांस्तानेव प्रतिगृध्यति । आश्व ३०.९ ।।
It is my nose which, enjoying many fragrances, longs for more.

इयं स्वादून् रसान् भुक्त्वा तानेव प्रतिगृध्यति । आश्व ३०.१२ ।।
It is my tongue which, enjoying many tastes, longs for more.

स्पृष्ट्वा त्वग्विविधान् स्पर्शोस्तानेव प्रतिगृध्यति । आश्व ३०.१५ ।।
It is my skin which, enjoying a great many touches, longs for more.

श्रुत्वा तु विविधाञ्शब्दांस्तानेव प्रतिगृध्यति । आश्व ३०.१८ ।।
It is my ears which, enjoying many sounds, long for more.

दृष्ट्वा रूपाणि बहुशस्तामेव प्रतिगृध्यति। आश्व ३०.२१।।

It is my eyes which, enjoying many sights, long for more.[173]

'Therefore I will aim my sharp arrows at my nose, my tongue, my skin, my ears, and at my eyes.' And each one of them, in turn, said to him, in identical words, what the Mind had said:

नेमे बाणास्तरिष्यन्ति मामलर्क कथंचन।
तवैव मर्म भेत्स्यन्ति भिन्नमर्मा मरिष्यसि।। आश्व ३०.१०।।
अन्यान् बाणान् समीक्षस्व यैस्त्वं मां सूदयिष्यसि।

These arrows of yours cannot touch me, Alarka. They will only destroy an intimate part of your self, and it is you who will die. Think of some other weapon with which you can conquer me.

Finally, Alarka threatens his Intellect; for, he reckoned, that it is Intellect, with its power, which makes all kinds of misleading resolutions. If he could destroy his Intellect by his arrows, he would have a great conquest. And he receives from his Intellect the same reply that he had received from his Mind and his physical sense organs.[174]

After meditating for a long while, he concluded that it is the reflective *yoga* with which he will conquer his Mind, his body, and the Intellect, by bringing them into a unity. The word *yoga* means 'that which unites, which joins'. Alarka discovered that he had mistakenly declared war on himself, which was not the way of achieving freedom of the self.[175]

The *Mahābhārata* shows that *to be at war with one's self is to be at war with everyone else.*

The *Mahābhārata*'s teachings of happiness

The *Mahābhārata* teaches at every turn, in every context, that pleasure and happiness, *sukha*, and pain and suffering, *duḥkha*, individual and collective, are *created*; they do not descend just like that. They are created by certain conditions, some of them external, some within. Some of them are *sva-krita*, self-created; some *para-krita*, created by the *other*, both individually and collectively. This is the very first thing that the sage Nārada said to Krishna on hearing about the latter's unhappiness.

आपदो द्विविधाः कृष्ण बाह्याश्चाभ्यन्तराश्च ह।
प्रादुर्भवन्ति वार्ष्णेय स्वकृता यदि वान्यतः।। शान्ति ८१.१३।।
Troubles are of two kinds, Krishna: external and those within. Both are self-created and created by others.[176]

And those conditions are interrelated; any one of them creating the rest. The *Mahābhārata*'s teachings of *sukha-duḥkha*, happiness and suffering, are, therefore, inherent in its analysis of *dharma* and *adharma*; of truth and untruth; of *hiṃsā*, violence, and *ahiṃsā*, not-violence; of the attitudes towards *having* and *not-having*; of sexuality; of the life-in-family and life-alone; of self-knowledge and self-discipline or the absence of them; and in its explorations in the question of causality and human freedom, *mokṣha*. Those teachings are contained in the *Mahābhārata*'s discussions on the foundations of law and governance. And they are contained in its analysis of the logic and psychology of *karma*.[177] However, some of them may again be stated here as well. The *Mahābhārata* teaches the one least condition of keeping one's inner balance in pain and pleasure, in suffering and happiness, alike.

एवमेतानि पुरुषा दुःखानि च सुखानि च।
आप्नुवन्ति महाबुद्धे नोत्कण्ठां कर्तुमर्हसि।। वन २१६.१०।।
Human beings thus keep having suffering and happiness both. Do not let them paralyse you with anxiety.[178]

सुखस्यानन्तरं दुःखं दुःखस्यानन्तरं सुखम्।
न नित्यं लभते दुःखं न नित्यं लभते सुखम्।। शान्ति २५.२३।।
There is pain after pleasure, and pleasure after pain. No one experiences always pain; nor does anyone experience always pleasure.[179]

सुखदुःखे मनुष्याणां चक्रवत् परिवर्ततः।। शान्ति १७४.१९।।
Suffering and happiness move in a cycle.[180]

This being the simple truth, then pride and exultation in success and glory *and* anxiety and grief in adversity and trial are futile alike. The reasoning in this regard is equally simple and manifestly true.

प्रीत्याशोकः प्रभवति वियोगात् तस्य देहिनः।
यदा निरर्थकं वेत्ति तदा सद्यः प्रणश्यति।। शान्ति १६३.१३।।

On the loss of the person one loves, one grieves; but no sooner does one see that grief is futile than the grief is quietened.[181]

प्राक्सम्प्रयोगाद् भूतानां नास्ति दुःखं परायणम् ।
विप्रयोगात् तु सर्वस्य न शोचेत् प्रकृतिस्थितः ।।

There is no pain of parting before the coming together. And there is a parting after coming together and its pain. Seeing this, one should remain centred in one's self and not grieve for what has separated.[182]

And it is well known that parting need not necessarily be physical; an emotional parting is even more of a parting.

Therefore:

भैषज्यमेतद् दुःखस्य यदेतन्नानुचिन्तयेत् ।
चिन्त्यमानं हि चाभ्येति भूयश्चापि प्रवर्तते ।। शान्ति २०५.२ ।।

The most effective remedy for suffering is not to think too much about it; for the more one thinks about suffering, the more it increases.[183]

प्रज्ञया मानसं दुःखं हन्याच्छारीरमौषधैः ।
एतद् विज्ञानसामर्थ्यं न बालैः समतामियात् ।। शान्ति २०५.३ ।।

The suffering of the mind is to be removed through understanding, and that of the body through medicine, that is within the competence of science.[184]

दुःखोपघाते शारीरे मानसे चाप्युपस्थिते ।
यस्मिन् न शक्यते कर्तुं यत्नस्तं नानुचिन्तयेत् ।। शान्ति २०५.१ ।।

But should there be some physical or mental suffering about which nothing could be done, or what was done was ineffective, then let one not worry about it.[185]

सुखं वा यदि वा दुःखं प्रियं वा यदि वाप्रियम् ।
प्राप्तं प्राप्तमुपासीत हृदयेनापराजितः ।। शान्ति १७४.३९ ।।

Pleasure or pain, the agreeable or the disagreeable, whichever one gets, that let one accept, and accept with respect, and not feel ever defeated in one's heart.[186]

शोकस्थानसहस्त्राणि भयस्थानशतानि च।
दिवसे दिवसे मूढमाविशन्ति न पण्डितम्।। शान्ति १७४.४०।।
There are a thousand places for sorrow and a hundred places for fear: they affect only the ignorant, not the wise.[187]

अथाप्युपायं पश्येत दुःखस्य परिमोक्षणे।
अशोचन्नारभेतैवं मुक्तश्चाव्यसनी भवेत्।। वन २१६.२७।।
Leaving anxiety and worry, one should rather see how one can free oneself from pain and suffering, and act, and one does become free.[188]

शोचतो न भवेत् किंचित् केवलं परितप्यते।
परित्यजन्ति ये दुःखं सुखं वाप्युभयं नराः।। वन २१६.२१।।
Anxiety and worry do not help; they only increase one's pain. Only those who transcend the duality of 'pain' and 'pleasure', or 'suffering' and 'happiness', are truly happy.[189]

असंतोषस्य नास्त्यन्तस्तुष्टिस्तु परमं सुखम्।
न शोचन्ति गताध्वानः पश्यन्तः परमां गतिम्।। वन २१६.२३।।
To wanting and to its unrest, there is no end: therefore contentment is the greatest happiness.[190]

त एव सुखमेधन्ते ज्ञानतृप्ता मनीषिणः।
असंतोषपरा मूढाः संतोषं यान्ति पण्डिताः।। वन २१६.२२।।
Happy are those who have the inner contentment of knowledge and wisdom; the unhappy fools are always discontented.[191]

संतापाद् भ्रश्यते रूपं संतापाद् भ्रश्यते बलम्।
संतापाद् भ्रश्यते ज्ञानं संतापाद् व्याधिमृच्छति।। उद्योग ३६.४४।।
Sorrow destroys one's form; sorrow destroys one's strength. Sorrow destroys knowledge and awareness; and sorrow leads to illness.[192]

न विषादे मनः कार्यं विषादो विषमुत्तमम्।
मारयत्यकृतप्रज्ञं बालं क्रुद्ध इवोरगः।। वन २१६.२४।।
Let not one's mind be drowned in anguish and sorrow; for inner anguish is like a deadly poison. In being like a fierce snake does it kill the one devoid of that higher sense of balance and discrimination.[193]

Say again that:

शोकस्थानसहस्त्राणि भयस्थानशतानि च।
दिवसे दिवसे मूढमाविशन्ति न पण्डितम्।। शान्ति १७४.४०।।

There are a thousand places for sorrow and a hundred places for fear: they effect only the ignorant, not the wise.[194]

संयोगानां क्षयं दृष्टा युगानां च विशेषतः।
क्षयं च दृष्ट्वा शैलानां क्षयं च सरितां तथा।। शान्ति ३०१.४९।।
वर्णानां च क्षयं दृष्ट्वा क्षयान्तं च पुनः पुनः।
जरामृत्युं तथा जन्म दृष्ट्वा दुःखानि चैव ह।। शान्ति ३०१.५०।।

Have a look at the end of all unions; (the more especially at the end each cycle of time has.) Look at how the hills crumble, and the rivers go dry. Look at the end of social divisions again and again. Look at the pain of decaying and dying, and the pain of being born again. Look also at the end of the end itself.[195]

आत्मदोषांश्च विज्ञाय सर्वानात्मनि संश्रितान्।
स्वदेहादुत्थितान् गन्धांस्तथा विज्ञाय चाशुभान्।। शान्ति ३०१.५२।।

Becoming aware of the disorders of one's self, and of the smell of pain and suffering that arises from them, one should try to gain knowledge of those disorders.[196]

नार्थो न धर्मो न यशो योऽतीतमनुशोचति।
अप्यभावेन युज्येत तच्चास्य न निवर्तते।। शान्ति ३३०.७।।

Who grieves for what is past, gains neither prosperity, nor dharma, *nor renown. Sorrowing for an absence does not fill the absence, only increases the pain of it.*[197]

गुणैर्भूतानि युज्यन्ते वियुज्यन्ते तथैव च।
सर्वाणि नैतदेकस्य शोकस्थानं हि विद्यते।। शान्ति ३३०.८।।

Everybody gains and loses good things of life. It is not that the occasion for pain comes only to one person.[198]

मृतं वा यदि वा नष्टं योऽतीतमनुशोचति।
दुःखेन लभते दुःखं द्वावनर्थौ प्रपद्यते।। शान्ति ३३०.९।।

The one who grieves for the dead, for what has perished, for what is past, suffers in that yet another pain, thus suffering twice over.[199]

शारीरं मानसं दु:खं योऽतीतमनुशोचति।
दु:खेन लभते दु:खं द्वावनर्थौ च विन्दति।। शान्ति १६.१०।।
Who keeps grieving for a past suffering, physical and mental, suffers a second time, one suffering arising from another.[200]

अहान्यस्तमयान्तानि उदयान्ता च शर्वरी।
सुखस्यान्तं सदा दु:खं दु:खस्यान्तं सदा सुखम्।। आश्वमेधिक ४४.१८।।
The day ends in the setting of the sun; and there is a new dawn at the end of the night. Pleasure ends in pain; and the end of pain is always happiness.[201]

सर्वं कृतं विनाशान्तं जातस्य मरणं ध्रुवम्।
अशाश्वतं हि लोकेऽस्मिन् सदा स्थावरजङ्गमम्।। आश्वमेधिक ४४.२०।।
Whatever is created, must perish too. Whatever is born, would certainly die too. Nothing of this world is permanent.[202]

यो विद्वान् सहवासं च विवासं चैव पश्यति।
तथैवैकत्वनानात्वे स दु:खात् प्रतिमुच्यते।। आश्वमेधिक ४७.७।।
The wise who sees in a coming together already a parting, and sees likewise unity in diversity, is forever from pain and suffering.[203]

नास्त्यनन्तं महाराज सर्वं संख्यानगोचर:।
पुनर्भावोऽपिविख्यातो नास्ति किंचिदिहाचलम्।। शान्ति २७९.६।।
Suffering is not endless. Everything in the world is within the limit of numbers; nothing is countless, nothing is fixed and permanent. What again comes into existence is known for its passing too.[204]

All these are in relation to one's self. But the *Mahābhārata*'s teachings on happiness do not stop there. One's happiness and good are inseparably linked with the happiness and the good of the *other.*

Therefore:

अहिंसा सत्यवचनं सर्वभूतेषु चार्जवम्।
क्षमा चैवाप्रमादश्च यस्यैते स सुखी भवेत्।। शान्ति २१५.६।।
Not to do violence to the other; to adhere to truth; simplicity in conduct towards all being, and not deviousness; forgiveness and reconciliation; and vigilance—whoever has these qualities becomes a happy person.[205]

यश्चैनं परमं धर्मं सर्वभूतसुखावहम्।
दुःखान्निःसरणं वेद सर्वज्ञः स सुखी भवेत्।। शान्ति २१५.७।।

Whoever knows these to be the foundations of life and relationships, and knows them to be conducive of the happiness of all beings, becomes happy too.[206]

Above all, to remain within the conflicting duality of 'pleasure' and 'pain', 'sorrow' and 'joy', one quickly changing into the other, is to remain a dangling man, or a dangling woman, dangling between the two. Therefore:

ये च बुद्धिसुखं प्राप्ता द्वन्द्वातीता विमत्सराः।
तान् नैवार्था न चानर्था व्यथयन्ति कदाचन।। शान्ति १७४.३५।।

Those who have the happiness of the mind, and have gone beyond the play of the opposites, and are free of envy, are affected neither by gain and prosperity nor by loss and adversity.[207]

उभे सत्यानृते त्यक्त्वा शोकानन्दो भयाभये।
प्रियाप्रिये परित्यज्य प्रशान्तात्मा भविष्यति।। शान्ति १७४.५३।।

On transcending the conflicting opposites of 'truth' and 'untruth', 'sorrow' and 'joy', 'fear' and 'not-fear', 'agreeable' and 'disagreeable', one becomes peaceful and tranquil in one's innermost.[208]

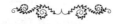

CHAPTER TEN

Material Prosperity and Wealth, *Artha*

- Importance of wealth in the *Mahābhārata*
- The other truth concerning wealth

The place of wealth in human living; the *attitudes* which its possession or the lack of it generate; the kind of life, personal and social, they produce; the manner in which they determine the quality of relationships; and whether, as their result, there is freedom and justice or bondage and oppression—these are the subjects of inquiry in the *Mahābhārata*. They are taken up in other works too, but nowhere as systematically as in the *Mahābhārata*.

Their substance may be stated here first. The *Mahābhārata* says:

आकिंचन्ये न मोक्षोऽस्ति किंचन्ये नास्ति बन्धनम् ।
किंचन्ये चेतरे चैव जन्तुर्ज्ञानेन मुच्यते ।। शान्ति ३२०.५० ।।

Neither is bondage in wealth, nor is freedom in mokṣha. *Whether it is the one or the other will depend upon one's attitude towards having and not-having.*[1]

This conclusion is reached after the view that 'all good things of life flow from money' was stated as strongly as was the opposite view that 'acquisition of money is the main source eventually of all disorder and violence, personal and collective'. Praise of wealth, and the awareness of its hold upon human affairs, were notable parts of dharmic culture in all ages and times. Equally notable in all ages was the dharmic disdain of wealth and its apparent power. The dharmic man produced immense wealth, and worshipped it with singular devotion. But by curtailing his needs step by step, he also repudiated wealth and its power.

There were two general attitudes to *artha*, wealth, radically opposed to each other, and both having deep roots in dharmic life in all periods of its very long history. On the one hand, wealth was regarded as the first condition not only of a happy and dignified family life but also of a stable social order. In this view, even *dharma* and *mokṣha* are dependent on *artha*. On the other hand, wealth, when accumulated in private hands, was believed to give rise to a further desire for it, and therefore to lack of happiness and peace; when accumulated in the hands of the State, to aggression and hatred as well. In this view, wealth at all times is profoundly destructive of spiritual life, in so far as the aim of all spiritual effort is the extinction of desire, because desire leads to bondage. Beyond these attitudes to wealth, to be sought, preserved and augmented according to the one, and to be abjured altogether according to the other, there is in the *Mahābhārata* the journey towards balance.

Importance of wealth in the *Mahābhārata*

First, with utmost realism and candour, the *Mahābhārata* attaches great importance to wealth and material prosperity as long as one lives in society. After the Great War, with its enormous destruction and bloodshed, Yudhishṭhira, the embodiment of *dharma*, is overcome with remorse. He feels repelled by the kingdom that he and his brothers have gained after a stupendous loss of life, though the kingdom was always rightfully theirs. He decides to renounce everything and live the life of a mendicant. That is the road he wants to take for *himself*. Eventually he is dissuaded from taking that step by his brothers, by their wife Draupadī, by Krishna, and by others, each of them putting forward a seemingly weighty argument against his inclination to give up the hard-won kingdom.

One line of argument, propounded by his brother Arjuna, dwells upon the pre-eminence of wealth.[2] Arjuna had planted his feet firmly on material prosperity and wealth, *artha*, as the basis of all that is good and desirable in human life.

अश्वस्तनमृषीणां हि विद्यते वेद तद् भवान् ।
यं त्विमं धर्ममित्याहुर्धनादेष प्रवर्तते ।। शान्ति ८.१२ ।।

अकिंचन्यं मुनीनां च इति वै नहुषोऽब्रवीत् ।
कृत्वा नृशंसं ह्यधने धिगस्त्वधनतामिह ।। शान्ति ८.११ ।।

You know very well that the life of a mendicant is not the dharma *of one born in a royal family, and wealth is essential to fulfilling the duties of a king.*[3]

King Nahusha had said: 'While poor I did many cruel deeds. Poverty is a curse.'[4]

अभिशस्तं प्रपश्यन्ति दरिद्रं पार्श्वतः स्थितम् ।
दरिद्रं पातकं लोके न तच्छंसितुमर्हति ।। शान्ति ८.१४ ।।

People look at a man with no means as if he were also a sinner, proving poverty to be a sin in this world. Don't praise poverty to me.[5]

पतितः शोच्यते राजन् निर्धनश्चापि शोच्यते।
विशेषं नाधिगच्छामि पतितस्याधनस्य च।। शान्ति ८.१५।।

Just as a sinner is a regrettable figure, so is the man who is poor; there is no difference between a fallen man and a man without money.[6]

यस्यार्थास्तस्य मित्राणि यस्यार्थास्तस्य बान्धवाः।
यस्यार्थाः स पुमाँल्लोके यस्यार्थाः स च पण्डितः।। शान्ति ८.१९।।

Whoever is wealthy has friends as well; whoever is wealthy has his family and clan with him; only he who has wealth is known as a man; and then only he is considered to be learned.[7]

अर्थेन हि विहीनस्य पुरुषस्याल्पमेधसः।
विच्छिद्यन्ते क्रियाः सर्वाग्रीष्मे कुसरितो यथा।। शान्ति ८.१८।।

Just as small streams dry up in summer, the efforts of a man without wealth come to nothing.[8]

अर्थभ्यो हि विवृद्धेभ्यः सम्भृतेभ्यस्ततस्ततः।
क्रियाः सर्वाः प्रवर्तन्ते पर्वतेभ्य इवापगाः।। शान्ति ८.१६।।

From increased wealth flow all the good works, as do the rivers from the mountains.[9]

धनात् कुलं प्रभवति धनाद् धर्मः प्रवर्धते।
नाधनस्यास्त्ययं लोको न परः पुरुषोत्तम।। शान्ति ८.२२।।

On wealth depends the rise of a family, and on wealth depends the rise of dharma; *for him who has no wealth, there is happiness neither in this world nor in the next.*[10]

नाधनो धर्मकृत्यानि यथावदनुतिष्ठति।
धनाद्धि धर्मः स्त्रवति शैलादभि नदी यथा।। शान्ति ८.२३।।

A man who is poor cannot fulfil his obligations properly: as the mountain is the source of a river, wealth is the source of dharma.[11]

यः कृशार्थः कृशगवः कृशभृत्यः कृशातिथिः।
स वै राजन् कृशो नाम न शरीरकृशः कृशः।। शान्ति ८.२४।।

He who has little wealth, has few cattle and few servants, and fewer are the guests who come to him: only such a man is truly weak, not the one who is of weak body.[12]

अर्थाद् धर्मश्च कामश्च स्वर्गश्चैव नराधिप।
प्राणयात्रापि लोकस्य विना ह्यर्थं न सिद्ध्यति।। शान्ति ८.१७।।
Through wealth alone can one gain dharma *and* kāma *and the heavens too; without wealth, human beings cannot even live.*[13]

अर्थस्यावयवावेतौ धर्मकामाविति श्रुतिः।
अर्थसिद्ध्य विनिर्वृत्तावुभावेतौ भविष्यतः।। शान्ति १६७.१४।।
Dharma *and* kāma *are the two limbs only of* artha*: it is by gaining wealth that they are obtained too.*[14]

आस्तिका नास्तिकाश्चैव नियताः संयमे परे।
अप्रज्ञानं तमोभूतं प्रज्ञानं तु प्रकाशिता।। शान्ति १६७.१९।।
Not to know the importance of wealth is to remain in darkness; to have the knowledge of the primacy of wealth is to have the light of understanding.[15]

तद्गतार्थं हि पुरुषं विशिष्टतरयोनयः।
ब्रह्माणमिव भूतानि सततं पर्युपासते।। शान्ति १६७.१५।।
Indeed, just as everybody worships the god Brahmā, even the best of men worship a man with wealth.[16]

His brother Bhīma likewise draws Yudhishṭhira's attention to the prime importance of money in human living. He says:

धर्ममूलं जगद् राजन् नान्यद् धर्माद् विशिष्यते।
धर्मश्चार्थेन महता शक्यो राजन् निषेवितुम्।। वन ३३.४८।।
Dharma *is the foundation of this world; and there is nothing of greater value than* dharma. *But undoubtedly* dharma *requires money. Always,* dharma *is a factor in wealth; but wealth is to be grasped for securing the ends of* dharma.[17]

न चार्थो भैक्ष्यचर्येण नापि क्लैब्येन कर्हिचित्।
वेत्तुं शक्यः सदा राजन् केवलं धर्मबुद्धिना।। वन ३३.४९।।
And money cannot be had by begging, or by cowardice, much less by concentrating on dharma *alone.*[18]

न हि केवलधर्मात्मा पृथिवीं जातु कश्चन।
पार्थिवोव्यजयद् राजन् न भूतिं न पुनः श्रियम्।। वन ३३.५८।।
No king has ever gained glory or wealth by thinking only of dharma.[19]

प्रतिषिद्धा हि ते याञ्च्या यथा सिद्ध्यति वै द्विजः।
तेजसैवार्थालिप्सायां यतस्व पुरुषर्षभ।। वन ३३.५०।।

भैक्ष्यचर्या न विहिता न च विट् शूद्रजीविका।
क्षत्रियस्य विशेषेण धर्मस्तु बलमौरसम्।। वन ३३.५१।।

And your calling, your station in life, is that of a king, not that of a brāhmaṇa, or that of a merchant, or of the one who provides services. And you need wealth to fulfil your obligations as a ruler.

सत्त्वं हि मूलमर्थस्य वितथं यदतोऽन्यथा।
न तु प्रसक्तं भवति वृक्षच्छायेव हैमनी।। वन ३३.६४।।

Inner strength alone is the source of all wealth, all else is vain talk. Just as the shadow of trees is no protection in autumn days, similarly, weakness of self is no good.[20]

But, unlike Arjuna, his other brother, Bhīma was not advocating *idolatry of wealth*. Rather, he was trying to correct Yudhishthira's fragmented emphasis on the ethical foundations of relationships, of self with the self, and of the self with the *other*. It is this one-sided, fragmented importance attached to any one of the human attributes that, the *Mahābhārata* shows, is the source of all violence, to one's self in the first place, and then to the *other*. Hence Bhīma's advocacy of the equal importance of ethical foundations, *dharma*; of material prosperity, *artha*; and of the desire for pleasures, *kāma*. Here the reader should turn to the next chapter of this book, where Bhīma's remaining argument in that regard is stated.[21] In the main, he says to Yudhishṭhira:

मोक्षो वा परमं श्रेय एष राजन् सुखार्थिनाम्।
प्राप्तिर्वा बुद्धिमास्थाय सोपायां कुरुनन्दन।। वन ३३.४३।।

तद् वाऽऽशु क्रियतां राजन् प्राप्तिर्वाप्यधिगम्यताम्।
जीवितं ह्यातुरस्येव दुःखमन्तरवर्तिनः।। वन ३३.४४।।

For the one who wishes liberation from the human condition, mokṣha is the greatest good. Through your mental faculties, try to achieve that.
But so long as one lives in this world, and desires happiness, he should pay equal attention to the foundations, dharma; *to securing material prosperity,* artha; *and the pleasures,* kāma.
It is the one who, undecided, dangles between the two who earns only misery.[22]

The dying Bhīshma, immensely wise but less coarse than Arjuna, reinforces the utmost necessity of great wealth for one who would be king. But he does it with certain important qualifications. His propositions are clear and straightforward.

राज्ञः कोशबलं मूलं कोशमूलं पुनर्बलम्।
तन्मूलं सर्वधर्माणां धर्ममूलाः पुनः प्रजाः।। शान्ति १३०.३५।।

The strength of a king is based on treasury and army; army is based on treasury; the social order is based on army; and the people are based on dharma.[23]

अबलस्य कुतः कोशो ह्यकोशस्य कुतो बलम्।
अबलस्य कुतो राज्यमराज्ञः श्रीर्भवेत् कुतः।। शान्ति १३३.४।।

Where is the treasury when the king is weak: and army, where there is no treasury? If there is no army, how can there be kingdom, and majesty if there is no kingdom?[24]

हीनकोशं हि राजानमवजानन्ति मानवाः।
न चास्याल्पेन तुष्यन्ति कार्यमप्युत्सहन्ति च।। शान्ति १३३.६।।

The king whose treasury is empty is treated with indifference even by common men; nobody is satisfied with the little that he gives, and none is eager to work for him.[25]

श्रियो हि कारणाद् राजा सत्क्रियां लभते पराम्।
सास्य गूहति पापानि वासो गुह्यमिव स्त्रियाः।। शान्ति १३३.७।।

Only due to his wealth is a king successful in whatever he does; and just as clothes cover the private parts of women, wealth covers the defects of kings.[26]

स्वराष्ट्रात् परराष्ट्राच्च कोशं संजनयेन्नृपः।
कोशाद्धि धर्मः कौन्तेय राज्यमूलं च वर्धते।। शान्ति १३३.१।।

तस्मात् संजनयेत् कोशं सत्कृत्य परिपालयेत्।
परिपाल्यानुतनुयादेष धर्मः सनातनः।। शान्ति १३३.२।।

Therefore, let the king fill the treasury: having filled it, protect it: protecting it, increase it: for in all ages that is the dharma *of the king.*[27]

न कोशः शुद्धशौचेन न नृशंसेन जातुचित्।
मध्यमं पदमास्थाय कोशसंग्रहणं चरेत्।। शान्ति १३३.३।।

Great wealth can be earned neither by those who are too pure nor by those who are too cruel; follow the middle path, and thus collect great wealth.[28]

कामक्रोधौ पुरस्कृत्य योऽर्थं राजानुतिष्ठति।
न स धर्मं न चाप्यर्थं प्रतिगृह्णाति बालिशः।। शान्ति ७१.७।।

Through wealth alone can one gain dharma *and* kāma *and the next world as well; but wealth should be earned through* dharma, *never through* adharma.[29]

देवताश्च विकर्मस्थ पातयन्ति नराधमम्।
व्याजेन विन्दन् वित्तं हि धर्मात् स परिहीयते।। शान्ति १३२.१८।।

The wealth earned through deceit is destroyed by dharma.[30]

अर्थमूलोऽपि हिंसां च कुरुते स्वयमात्मनः।
करैशास्त्रदृष्टैर्हि मोहात् सम्पीडयन् प्रजाः।। शान्ति ७१.१५।।

Moved by nothing but desire for more wealth, the king who taxes his subjects against the dictates of dharma, *and harasses them thus, surely does violence to himself.*[31]

Respect for wealth and its careful husbandry were taught through popular literature as well. Subject to the principle that too much greed brings ruin, and too little of it brings nothing,[32] the *Pañchatantra*, like the *Mahābhārata*, puts great store by wealth, and warns against the misery and disrespect which its lack must invite.[33] Hence the following words of wisdom in that ancient book of fables.

न हि तद्विद्यते किञ्चद्यदर्थेन न सिद्ध्यति।
यत्नेन मतिमांस्तस्मादर्थमेकं प्रसाधयेत्।। पञ्चतन्त्र १.२।।

There is nothing in the world that cannot be obtained through wealth; let a prudent man therefore earn wealth by his effort.[34]

वरं वनं व्याघ्रगजादिसेवितं जनेन हीनं बहुकण्टकावृतम्।
तृणानि शय्या परिधानवल्कलं न बन्धुमध्ये धनहीनजीवितम्।। ५.२३।।

A forest infested with lions and elephants, devoid of human beings, and full of thorns, is preferable, and a bed of straw and a garment made from the hide of a tree welcome, but not a life without wealth in the midst of friends.[35]

स्वामी द्वेष्टि सुसेवितोऽपि सहसा प्रोज्झन्ति सद्बान्धवा:
राजन्ते न गुणासत्यजन्ति तनुजा: स्फारीभवन्त्यापद: ।
भार्य्या साधु सुवंशजापि भजते नो यान्ति मित्राणि च
न्यायारोपितविक्रमाण्यपि नृणां येषां न हि स्याद्धनम् ।। ५.२४ ।।

The services of those without wealth are repaid with contempt: their friends and relatives abandon them: their qualities never get known: their sons leave them: they harvest trouble in plenty: a wife, even of good lineage, does not look after them: nor do friends gained through unselfish conduct come near them anymore.[36]

शूर: सुरूप: सुभगश्च वाग्मी शस्त्राणि शास्त्राणि विदांकरोति ।
अर्थं बिना नैव यशश्च मानं प्राप्नोति मर्त्योऽत्र मनुष्यलोके ।। ५.२५ ।।

Maybe he is brave, handsome, of a sound body, clever in talk, and well versed in the use of weapons and the shāstra; *but if a man is without wealth, he gets in this world neither fame nor respect.*[37]

तानीन्द्रियाण्यविकलानि तदेव नाम
सा बुद्धिरप्रतिहता वचनं तदेव ।
अर्थोष्मणा विरहित: पुरुष: स एव
बाह्य: क्षणेन भवतीति विचित्रमेतत् ।। ५.२६ ।।

Everything remains the same for him, his faculties, his name, his intelligence, and his speech, but no sooner does a man lack the warmth of wealth than he becomes an outcast.[38]

गतवयसामपि पुसां येषामर्था भवन्ति ते तरुणा: ।
अर्थेन तु ये हीना बृद्धास्ते यौवनेऽपि स्यु: ।। पञ्चतन्त्र १.१० ।।

Old men with wealth appear young; whereas those who have no wealth turn old even in their youth.[39]

पूज्यते यदपूज्योऽपि यदगम्योऽपि गम्यते ।
वन्द्यते यदवन्द्योऽपि स प्रभावो धनस्य च ।। १.७ ।।

He who is disreputable becomes venerable; unworthy of approach, he becomes worthy of access; undistinguished, he becomes an object of praise—such is the influence of wealth.[40]

The other truth concerning wealth

In respect of wealth and its place in life, the opposite view is stated quite as strongly, in the vcice of Yudhishthira mainly, but in other voices as well. His answer to the argument for wealth as thc chief source of everything desirable in life is as follows.

यदेतन्मन्यसे पार्थ न ज्यायोऽस्ति धनादिति ।
न स्वर्गो न सुखं नार्थो निर्धनस्येति तन्मृषा ।। शान्ति २६.२ ।।

The opinion that nothing is greater than wealth and material prosperity, and that the poor have neither happiness nor heavens, is wholly wrong.[41]

स्वाध्याययज्ञसंसिद्धा दृश्यन्ते बहवो जनाः ।
तपोरताश्च मनुयो येषां लोकाः सनातनाः ।। शान्ति २६.३ ।।

Men devoted to learning and yajña *are known to have achieved great powers; and there were ascetics who gained access to the eternal worlds.*[42] *There were men given to studying the Veda and the* shāstra, *or to acquiring true understanding of all things, or to pursuing things not of this world, who are known to have achieved a state beyond which there is nothing.*[43]

तत्रोत्तरां गतिं पार्थ प्रशंसन्ति पुराविदः ।
संतोषो वै स्वर्गतमः संतोषः परमं सुखम् ।। शान्ति २६.११ ।।

तुष्टेर्न किञ्चत् परमं सा सम्यक् प्रतितिष्ठति ।
विनीतक्रोधहर्षस्य सततं सिद्धिरुत्तमा ।। शान्ति २६.१२ ।।

Hence there is no heaven higher than contentment and no happiness that is greater.
Nothing is greater than contentment. He who has gained mastery over anger and delight alike gains inner harmony, and gains thereby all that is truly good.[44]

धर्ममन्ये वृत्तमन्ये धनमीहन्ति चापरे ।।
धनहेतोर्य ईहेत तस्यानीहा गरीयसी ।
भूयान् दोषो हि वित्तस्य यश्च धर्मस्तदाश्रयः ।। शान्ति २६.१७-८ ।।

Some men pursue dharma, *others virtue, and some others wealth. He who works towards wealth, it is better for him not to do anything at all, because in wealth and in the things dependent upon it, one can see only demerit.*[45]

ये वित्तमभिपद्यन्ते सम्यक्त्वं तेषु दुर्लभम् ।
द्रुह्यतः प्रैति तत् प्राहुः प्रतिकूलं यथातथम् ।। शान्ति २६.२० ।।

Those who are only after wealth have little goodness in them; for wealth comes mostly to those who are aggressive against others; but such wealth turns out to be not agreeable in the long run.[46]

Furthermore,

दुष्यन्त्याददतो भृत्या नित्यं दस्युभयादिव ।
दुर्लभं च धनं प्राप्य भृशं दत्त्वानुतप्यते ।। शान्ति २६.२२ ।।

Servants, paid regularly, still harbour resentment; and should a wealthy man, on getting still greater wealth, give to his servants more, he would then burn as much from this as he would from fear of robbers.[47]

अधनः कस्य किं वाच्यो विमुक्तः सर्वशः सुखी ।
देवस्वमुपगृह्यैव धनेन न सुखी भवेत् ।। शान्ति २६.२३ ।।

Who can say anything to one who is poor, for in being free from fear he is also forever happy: no one is happy even after obtaining the wealth of gods.[48]

Those who are wise know of course that wealth does not stay forever with any one.[49]

There were other facts to prove that wealth must produce greed; and from greed would arise a host of other inclinations, all destructive of happiness and public peace.[50] Leaving aside spirituality, at least this much is certain: that like the desire for sexual pleasure, there is no end to the desire for wealth.

मनुष्या ह्याढ्यतां प्राप्य राज्यमिच्छन्त्यनन्तरम् ।
राज्याद् देवत्वमिच्छन्ति देवत्वादिन्द्रतामापि ।। शान्ति १८०.२४ ।।

On acquiring wealth, men want to acquire a kingdom; having acquired a kingdom, they want to become gods; and then among gods they want to become Indra.[51]

भवेस्त्वं यद्यपि त्वाढ्यो न राजा न च दैवतम् ।
देवत्वं प्राप्य चेन्द्रत्वं नैव तुष्येस्तथा सति ।। शान्ति १८०.२५ ।।

Even if one becomes wealthy, one may not become a king or god; if one does become a god, and among gods Indra, one would remain dissatisfied still.[52]

The paradox that *the more one has*, the greater is the discontent, was brought up everywhere in dharmic literature in one context or another. The *Bhāgvata-purāṇa* observes:

> कामस्यान्तं च क्षुत्तृड्भ्यां क्रोधस्यैतत्फलोदयात् ।
> जनो याति न लोभस्य जित्वा भुक्त्वा दिशो भुवः ।। ८-१९.२० ।।
> *Desire for food ends with hunger appeased, and anger subsides with its purpose achieved; but should one conquer and enjoy even the whole universe, there would still be no end to one's greed.*[53]

But why is it that one is not satisfied even with obtaining all that one desires? The answer is that the nature of *desire* itself is such that it must remain forever unquenched, just as fire can only grow with more fuel added to it.[54] It is vain to think that the way to quench desire is to appease it.[55]

If read properly, the *Mahābhārata* is not rejecting wealth and material prosperity as of any value, or as a natural human attribute. On the contrary, it is showing its great importance in human affairs. Money and property are material objects, which bring with them, however, a host of *attitudes*; which a lack of them does, too. It is with those attitudes, the inner states of the mind, which *having* and *not-having* produce, with which the *Mahābhārata* is even more concerned; for they have consequences both for the individual person and for the society. *The paradox of desire and its logic* come into focus in *that* context.

Yudhishṭhira asks Bhīshma:

> ईहमानः समारम्भान् यदि नासादयेद् धनम् ।
> धनतृष्णाभिभूतश्च किं कुर्वन् सुखमाप्नुयात् ।। शान्ति १७७.१ ।।
> *If a person driven by the thirst for money still doesn't get it, what should he do that he might still be happy?*[56]

It is clear that Yudhishṭhira was not asking from a man of the world advice as to the most efficient means of making money. He was asking what state of the mind should one strive for, if all one's efforts to make money bear no fruits. In answer to *that*, in the voice of Bhīshma the *Mahābhārata* suggests two things straightaway.

> सर्वसाम्यमनायासं सत्यवाक्यं च भारत ।
> निर्वेदश्चाविधित्सा च यस्य स्यात् स सुखी नरः ।। शान्ति १७७.२ ।।

An attitude of equality towards all; truthfulness; distance from the world and its workings; avoiding fruitless labour; and excessive involvement—whoever has these five is indeed a happy person.[57]

एतान्येव पदान्याहुः पञ्च वृद्धाः प्रशान्तये ।
एष स्वर्गश्च धर्मश्च सुखं चानुत्तम मतम् ।। शान्ति १७७.३ ।।
Those mature in knowledge regard these five steps as the source of peace. They are believed to be heaven, dharma, *and the highest happiness.*[58]

It is legitimate for us to ask whether the five steps enumerated above as steps to peace and happiness are only high-minded consolation for one's failure in making money *or* will they hold good even when one has been immeasurably successful in becoming immeasurably rich? Only then will they have an abiding universal meaning. And even in that case, they will, at least in first impressions, sound the more convincing if they came from the one who was successful and not from the one who was a failure. So far as this is concerned, it would on a second look prove to be incorrect reasoning. For the question is about the essential truth of a thing. In any case, the demonstration of the ills and the demerit of striving for wealth and owning it came from a man, Yudhishṭhira, who would now be emperor. But it came also from a sage, Mańki by name,[59] who had tried hard to earn some money but had failed.[60]

Sage Mańki addresses simultaneously his heart *and* desire, *kāma*. About money and wealth, he had reached, after deep reflection, the following definite conclusions.

ईहा धनस्य न सुखा लब्ध्वा चिन्ता च भूयसी ।
लब्धनाशे यथा मृत्युर्लब्धं भवति वा न वा ।। शान्ति १७७.२६ ।।
Striving for money is certainly not conducive to happiness. When obtained, one is overcome with the anxiety to protect it. If lost, after gaining it, it is quite as painful as death. Neither is it certain if, after making all the efforts to get it, one will get it or not.[61]

धननाशेऽधिकं दुःखं मन्ये सर्वमहत्तरम् ।
ज्ञातयो ह्यवमन्यन्ते मित्राणि च धनाच्च्युतम् ।। शान्ति १७७.३४ ।।
The suffering arising from the loss of money and wealth, I think that to be the most painful; for he who is deprived of money, even his relatives and friends show him scant respect.[62]

अवज्ञानसहस्त्रैस्तु दोषाः कष्टतराऽधने।
धने सुखकला या तु सापि दुःखैर्विधीयते।। शान्ति १७७.३५ ।।
He who is poor, for him are reserved a thousand expressions of indifference. Poverty has in it many a great demerit; but also the happiness of having money and wealth is laced mostly with pain.[63]

नान्तं सर्वविधित्सानां गतपूर्वोऽस्ति कश्चन।
शरीरे जीविते चैव तृष्णा मन्दस्य वर्धते।। शान्ति १७७.१७ ।।
No one has hitherto fully understood all the workings of money and wealth. The thirst for this body and life only keeps increasing.[64]

Addressing Desire, *Kāma*, Mańki therefore says:

अनुतर्षुल एवार्थः स्वादु गाङ्गमिवोदकम्।
मद्विलापनमेतत्तु प्रतिबुद्धोऽस्मि संत्यज।। शान्ति १७७.२८ ।।
Kāma! *Like the sweet waters of the Ganga, money only increases the unending thirst for it. I've now clearly seen that this thirst is also my drunkenness. Leave me alone!*[65]

अर्थलोलुपता दुःखमिति बुद्धं चिरान्मया।
यद् यदालम्बसे काम तत्तदेवानुरुध्यसे।। शान्ति १७७.३७ ।।
Greed for money is suffering, this I've understood after a long time. Kāma! *whoever hosts you, you possess him!*[66]

अतत्त्वज्ञोऽसि बालश्च दुस्तोषोऽपूरणोऽनलः।
नैव त्वं वेत्थ सुलभं नैव त्वं वेत्थ दुर्लभम्।। शान्ति १७७.३८ ।।
Kāma! *Not understanding the truth of things, you are a fool. It is difficult to fill your appetite, as it is difficult to fill the appetite of fire. You understand neither the possible nor the impossible.*[67]

पाताल इव दुष्पूरो मां दुःखैर्योक्तुमिच्छसि।
नाहमद्य समावेष्टुं शक्यः काम पुनस्त्वया।। शान्ति १७७.३९ ।।
Kāma! *It is as difficult to make you complete as it is difficult to fill the space under the earth. You wish to involve me in pain and suffering: but you can live within me no longer.*[68]

आत्मना सप्तमं कामं हत्वा शत्रुमिवोत्तमम्।
प्राप्यावध्यं ब्रह्मपुरं राजेव स्यामहं सुखी।। शान्ति १७७.५२ ।।

Desire, Anger, Greed, Confusion of perceptions, Arrogance, Sloth, and Attachments, are the seven enemies of man, of whom Desire is the strongest. Conquering them, and with them conquering Desire, I will be happy like a king.[69]

परित्यजामि काम त्वां हित्वा सर्वमनोगतीः ।
न त्वं मया पुनः काम वत्स्यसे न च रंस्यसे ।। शान्ति १७७.४२ ।।
Adieu, Desire, adieu! I leave you, Kāma, *adieu! No longer will you possess me. Nor will you enjoy me anymore.*[70]

Furthermore, in other voices, the *Mahābhārata* says what is manifestly true:

तस्मादर्थागमाः सर्वे मनोमोहविवर्धनाः ।
कार्पण्यं दर्पमानौ च भयमुद्वेग एव च ।। वन २.४२ ।।

अर्थजानि विदुः प्राज्ञा दुःखान्येतानि देहिनाम् ।
अर्थस्योत्पादने चैव पालने च तथा क्षये ।। वन २.४३ ।।

सहन्ति च महद् दुःखं घ्नन्ति चैवार्थकारणात् ।
अर्था दुःखं परित्यक्तुं पालिताश्चैव शत्रवः ।। वन २.४४ ।।
The ways of making money are the ways also that produce mental obsession, miserliness, arrogance, pride, fear and anxiety. For human beings, these are money-created pain and suffering.
It is difficult to earn wealth, painful to part with it; nor is there pleasure in guarding it; and of course human beings are never satisfied with any amount of it: seeing this, the wise look upon wealth as productive only of pain, and neither aspire for it, nor do they grieve at the loss of it.[71]

यथा ह्यामिषमाकाशे पक्षिभिः श्वापदैर्भुवि ।
भक्ष्यते सलिले मत्स्यैस्तथा सर्वत्र वित्तवान् ।। वन २.४० ।।
Just as a piece of meat is eaten by the vultures in the sky, by the carnivorous animals on the earth, and by the fish in the sea, so is a rich man nibbled everywhere.[72]

राजतः सलिलादग्नेश्चोरतः स्वजनादपि ।
भयमर्थवतां नित्यं मृत्योः प्राणभृतामिव ।। वन २.३९ ।।
The rich are in constant fear of the king, water, fire, thief, and relatives, just as all human beings are in constant fear of death.[73]

अनित्यं यौवनं रूपं जीवितं रत्नसंचयः।
ऐश्वर्यं प्रियसंवासो गृध्येत् तत्र न पण्डितः।। वन २.४७।।
Accumulated wealth, like beauty, youth, health, and the company of dear ones, is transitory.[74]

सर्वे क्षयान्ता निचयाः पतनान्ताः समुच्छ्रयाः।
संयोगा विप्रयोगान्ता मरणान्तं हि जीवितम्।। शान्ति ३३०.२०।।
Accumulation ends in destruction, rise ends in fall, the coming together ends in parting, and life ends in death.[75]

आन्तो नास्ति पिपासायास्तुष्टिस्तु परमं सुखम्।
तस्मात् संतोषमेवेह धनं पश्यन्ति पण्डिताः।। शान्ति ३३०.२१।।
The wise, therefore, regard contentment to be the greatest wealth.[76]

The picture of the ills that come from striving for wealth, which often includes taking what belongs to another, is drawn in the *Mahābhārata*, in the first place to correct the extreme view that material wealth is everything. Or that, in the words of Bhartrihari, सर्वे गुणाः काञ्चनमांश्रयन्ते, '*All good qualities are dependent upon money.*'[77]

For, 'There are many who, driven by their greed for money, often lose even their lives. Such people perceive nothing but money as the sole purpose of life.'[78]

The *Mahābhārata* corrects this view at two levels of argument, both self-evident and indisputably rational. *First*, stated briefly, in the voice of Yudhishṭhira:

कुले जातस्य वृद्धस्य परवित्तेषु गृद्ध्यतः।
लोभः प्रज्ञानमाहन्ति प्रज्ञा हन्ति हता ह्रियम्।। उद्योग ७२.१८।।
Born in a good family, and mature in age, should a person still take what belongs to another, then his greed destroys first his faculty of thought. Faculty of thought destroyed, the sense of shame is destroyed.

ह्रीर्हता बाधते धर्मं धर्मो हन्ति हतः श्रियम्।
श्रीर्हता पुरुषं हन्ति पुरुषस्याधनं वधः।। उद्योग ७२.१९।।
Shame destroyed, dharma *is destroyed. When* dharma *is destroyed, all that is benevolent and good is destroyed. With that, man's prosperity is destroyed. And the destruction of a man's prosperity is akin to his death.*

अधनाद्धि निवर्तन्ते ज्ञातयः सुहृदो द्विजाः।
अपुष्पादफलाद् वृक्षात् तथा कृष्ण पतत्रिणः।। उद्योग ७२.२०।।
When bereft of money and wealth, his relatives and friends vanish in the same way as the birds fly away from a tree that bears neither flower nor fruit any more.[79]

Second, it is undeniable, as a sage says to a king who had lost his kingdom and all his wealth but had not lost his longing for them, that:

संचये च विनाशान्ते मरणान्ते च जीविते।
संयोगे च वियोगान्ते को नु विप्रणयेन्मनः।। शान्ति १०४.४४।।
Accumulation ends in its destruction; life ends in death; coming together ends in separation. Then who will put too great a value upon them?[80]

धनं वा पूरुषो राजन् पुरुषं वा पुनर्धनम्।
अवश्यं प्रजहात्येव तद् विद्वान् कोऽनुसंज्वरेत्।। शान्ति १०४.४५।।
Whether a person abandons wealth, or wealth abandons him, that this will happen one day is certain. Then which man will still put his mind to so shifting a commodity as wealth?[81]

सुखमर्थाश्रयं येषामनुशोचामि तानहम्।
मम ह्यर्थाः सुबहवो नष्टाः स्वप्न इवागताः।। शान्ति १०४.८।।
I grieve for those who regard money as everything.[82]

But correcting the perception of the primacy of money and wealth in human affairs is no advocacy of poverty either. Therefore the *Mahābhārata* draws at the same time a picture of the ills that come from unsought poverty.

नातः पापीयसीं काञ्चिदवस्थां शम्बरोऽब्रवीत्।
यत्र नैवाद्य न प्रातर्भोजनं प्रतिदृश्यते।। उद्योग ७२.२२।।
When food for today and tomorrow is not to be seen, there is no situation more painful than that, as Sambara the wise had said.[83]

धनमाहुः परं धर्मं धने सर्वं प्रतिष्ठितम्।
जीवन्ति धनिनो लोके मृता ये त्वधना नराः।। उद्योग ७२.२३।।
It is through money that dharma *exists, and everything is dependent upon money. In this world, the rich alone seem to live. The poor are as good as dead.*[84]

एतामवस्थां प्राप्यैके मरणं वव्रिरे जनाः।
ग्रामायैके वनायैके नाशायैके प्रवव्रजुः।। उद्योग ७२.२५।।
Falling into poverty, many chose to kill themselves; many left one place to go and live in another, some even in a forest; and some left their homes, if only to kill themselves.[85]

उन्मादमेके पुष्यन्ति यान्त्यन्ये द्विषतां वशम्।
दास्यमेके च गच्छन्ति परेषामर्थहेतुना।। उद्योग ७२.२६।।
Many persons go mad; many get into the clutches of men of ill will. In need of money, some accept the servitude of others.[86]

तं तदा मन्युरेवैति स भूयः सम्प्रमुह्यति।
स मोहवशमापन्नः क्रूरं कर्म निषेवते।। उद्योग ७२.३२।।
In the state of poverty, a man is full of anger, which makes him lose his faculty of judging between right and wrong, and then he takes to cruel deeds.[87]

आपदेवास्य मरणात् पुरुषस्य गरीयसी।
श्रियो विनाशस्तद्ध्यस्य निमित्तं धर्मकामयोः।। उद्योग ७२.२७।।
The loss of money and property is for a man a great misfortune, greater than even death; for they, money and wealth, are also the means to his fulfilling his desires and dharma *as well.*[88]

धनेन जयते लोकावुभौ परमिमं तथा।
सत्यं च धर्मवचनं यथा नास्त्यधनस्तथा।। शान्ति १३०.४३।।
Given money, a person masters this world as well as the next, and gains access to truth and dharma. *With no money, his life is no life at all.*[89]

अधनं दुर्बलं प्राहुर्धनेन बलवान् भवेत्।
सर्वं धनवता प्राप्यं सर्वे तरति कोशवान्।। शान्ति १३०.४९।।
Having no money, he is looked upon as weak: it is with money that he becomes strong. By the one who is rich, everything can be had; and the one who has reserves of cash sails through.[90]

The Dharmic balance, far from being mechanical, or one of finding a middle position between two absolutely opposite points of view, consisted in the acknowledgement that human beings are diverse in their capacities, and have numerous perceptions, not all of equal value, but all deserving recognition. Hence there are contexts in which it is legitimate to regard wealth as a primary factor; and there are contexts in which it is foolish to do so. Both contexts have their respective rationality. The former related to the social world. But given its economic functions, and in them the importance of wealth, there would remain still the need for social control over the means of acquisition of wealth and its proper use. For, '*artha*, the wealth, not put to good use, becomes a source of *anartha*, disaster'.[91] The proper distribution of wealth is to be the principle.

कथं न भिद्येत न च स्त्रवेत
 न च प्रसिच्येदिति रक्षितव्यम् ।
अरक्ष्यमाणं शतधा प्रकीर्येद्
 ध्रुवं न नाशोऽस्ति कृतस्य लोके ।। वन २३६.२७ ।।

If wealth is not distributed, it will be wasted as the water stored in an unfired clay pot is wasted. It is therefore one's duty to preserve it. Wealth not properly distributed is wasted in a hundred different ways.[92]

More than social control, there would remain, in one's own interest, the necessity of self-control. Towards that end, the first step is to understand *the logic of having*, and what it leads to, unless disciplined. Taking up the social order, *loka-saṁgraha*, as one of the main concerns of human living, in unity with the ordering of one's individual life, the aim in the *Mahābhārata* is to prevent the necessity of wealth from turning into greed, and greed into lawlessness.

The qualification that Bhīshma had attached to his statements on the importance of wealth is as crucial as those statements are important. While it is undeniable that material prosperity and sexual pleasure are central among human attributes, wealth should be earned through *dharma*, never through *adharma*. What that means, in the very first place, is that desire for wealth and its fruits as a natural human attribute must, however, never be wrenched from the other attributes and turned into the only goal of life. When that happens, that goal turns upon itself and becomes self-destructive, but not without destroying so much else besides. That is true of sexual desire as well. The *Mahābhārata* tells us, as does the collective experience of life, that their *fulfilment is possible only within the wholeness of human attributes—in neither their neglect, nor in their idolatry*.

It is, in a sense, true:

क: कस्य चोपकुरुते कश्च कस्मै प्रयच्छति ।
प्राणी करोत्ययं कर्म सर्वमात्मार्थमात्मना ।। शान्ति २९२.१ ।।
Who does a good turn to the other? Who gives to the others? Whatever one does, one does only for one's self.[93]

But it is also true that:

येऽर्था धर्मेण ते सत्या येऽधर्मेण धिगस्तु तान् ।
धर्मं वे शाश्वतं लोके न जह्याद् धनकाङ्क्षया ।। शान्ति २९२.१९ ।।
Only that wealth is truly wealth that has been earned in the ways of dharma. *What has been collected through* adharma *to others is a wealth damned. One should not, in one's greed for money, abandon what is universally right and good.*[94]

न धर्मार्थी नृशंसेन कर्मणा धनमर्जयेत् ।
शक्तित: सर्वकार्याणि कुर्यान्नर्द्धिमनुस्मरेत् ।। शान्ति २९२.५ ।।
One should not gather wealth by doing cruel deeds. The best thing is to make efforts to one's best capacities, and not be anxious how to make the most money.[95]

न्यायागतं धनं चैव न्यायेनैव विवर्धितम् ।
संरक्ष्यं यत्नमास्थाय धर्मार्थमिति निश्चय: ।। शान्ति २९२.४ ।।
The wealth that has been lawfully earned, and lawfully increased, is also to be preserved with care—in order to secure the good of others. This is certain.[96]

The influence of wealth is, therefore, subordinated to the nobility of conduct, *sadāchāra*. Vidura says:

प्राप्नोति वै वित्तमसद्बलेन
नित्योत्थानात् प्रज्ञया पौरुषेण ।
न त्वेव सम्यग् लभते प्रशंसां
न वृत्तमाप्नोति महाकुलानाम् ।। उद्योग ३६.२१ ।।
A man may obtain wealth through force, constant effort, intelligence, and through one's prowess; but that does not still give him the excellence of conduct of one born in a good family.[97]

Vidura provides also the definition of 'nobility of conduct', which is this:

न तत् परस्य संदध्यात् प्रतिकूलं यदात्मनः।
संग्रहेणैष धर्मः स्यात् कामादन्यः प्रवर्तते।। उद्योग ३९.७१।।
Do not do unto others what one would not do unto oneself: this in brief is dharma. *All else is selfishness.*[98]

अक्रोधेन जयेत् क्रोधमसाधुं साधुना जयेत्।
जयेत् कदर्यं दानेन जयेत् सत्येन चानृतम्।। उद्योग ३९.७२।।
Let one conquer anger with not-anger, wickedness with goodness, meanness with generosity in giving, and untruth with truth.[99]

Avoidance of *ati*, excess, was the final principle of prudence. It is this principle that is to form the basis of professional and social ethics. And it is in the light of this that self-interest is seen as connected with the interests of others. Let one pursue what one would: excitement of sexual pleasure, exultation of great wealth, or the power of political supremacy; but all these were eventually destructive if carried to an excess. One's destruction in that case will be brought about not by God, or by some supernatural agency, but by the very logic of excess. The *Shukranīti* says:

मार्दवान्नैव गणयेदपमानोऽतिबादतः।
अतिदानेन दारिद्र्यं तिरस्कारोऽतिलोभतः।। शुक्र ३.२२०।।
Poverty comes through excessive charity, insult through excessive greed, and foolishness is born of excessive zeal.[100]

The *Mahābhārata* dwells upon the excesses of virtue, of learning, of wealth, and of royal power, and shows how each has an inglorious end, for each generates pride and arrogance. It dwells, in a far more realistic manner than the other works on ethics do, on the supreme need for control over one's senses, especially over one's speech, and over one's mind.[101] *Self-control is thus identified with self-interest*. The ultimate source of this rationality exists in man himself:

आत्मनाऽऽत्मानमन्विच्छेन्मनोबुद्धीन्द्रियैर्यतैः।
आत्मा ह्यवात्मनो बन्धुरात्मैव रिपुरात्मनः।। उद्योग ३४.६४।।
बन्धुरात्माऽऽत्मनस्तस्य येनैवात्माऽऽत्मनाजितः।
स एव नियतो बन्धुः स एवानियतो रिपुः।। उद्योग ३४.६५।।

Conquered, one's self is the best friend one has; uncontrolled, one's only enemy.[102]

None of this means, though, that Indian history has been one of self-control by everyone, everywhere and always. The teaching, repeated throughout in the prudence literature, *that one should not seek material prosperity at the expense of others*, was not always followed in practice; nor is it now. The teaching is:

तस्मादहं ब्रवीमि त्वां राजन् संचिन्त्य शास्त्रत: ।
संसिद्धाधिगमं कुर्यात् कर्म हिंसात्मकं त्यजेत् ।। शान्ति २९४.२४ ।।

न संकरेण द्रविणं प्रचिन्वीयाद् विचक्षण: ।
धर्मार्थं न्यायमुत्सृज्य न तत् कल्याणमुच्यते ।। शान्ति २९४.२५ ।।

By all means endeavour towards prosperity, but give up aggression towards others.[103]

It was recognised quite early in Indian thought that that maxim would be seldom remembered. The very long list of fines mentioned in Kauṭilya's *Arthashāstra*[104] indicates the prevalence of deception and cheating in various ways: adulteration; false weights and measures; enhancing the value of articles and lowering their quality; deception in the manufacture of articles and in their sale; charging unauthorised rates of interest; claiming more than the amount loaned; misappropriation of deposits and wages; manufacturing counterfeit notes; fabricating accounts and king's orders; extortion and bribery; cheating by goldsmiths; dishonest judgements by judges, and unjust punishments. Kauṭilya was evidently familiar with all the tricks of the trade.

The *Mahābhārata* likewise had no illusion that everybody would accumulate wealth lawfully. It was painfully familiar with the unscrupulous pursuit of wealth and pleasure against one's self-interest as well as against the interest of others. Cheating and fraudulent practices must have had already a long history by the time the *Mahābhārata* came to be written. Hence the anguished and puzzled cry of Vyāsa:

ऊर्ध्वबाहुर्विरौम्यष न च कश्चिच्छृणोति मे ।
धर्मादर्थश्च कामश्च स किमर्थं न सेव्यते ।। स्वर्गारोहण ५.६२ ।।

With my arms raised I am shouting, but nobody listens to me: when both wealth and pleasure can be had from dharma, *why do people not follow it?*[105]

The *Mahābhārata* leaves with us a last suggestion on material prosperity and wealth:

> धनस्य यस्य राजतो भयं न चास्ति चोरतः।
> मृतं च यन्न मुञ्चति समर्जयस्व तद् धनम्।। शान्ति ३२१.४६।।
> *Earn that wealth which is free of the fear of the state, of the fear of being stolen, and free of the fear that it will all end with one's death.*[106]

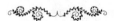

CHAPTER ELEVEN

Sexual Energy and Relationship, *Kāma* and *Saha-dharma*

- Conflicting attitudes towards woman
- Comparative pleasure of man and woman
- The question regarding the primacy of sexuality
- Sexuality and relationship
- Possession of the mind
- *Kāma* subject to *dharma*

The *Mahābhārata* had set out to understand human life in all its expressions. The nature of desire and its workings was one of its fundamental inquiries. The quest for pleasure and happiness was from the very beginning acknowledged to be the spring of all human actions. *Sukha*, or 'pleasure and happiness', which included sexual pleasure, was a subject of inquiry in the major *Upanishad*-s. At least forty long chapters are devoted to it in the *Mahābhārata*. And it is there most of all, long before Vātsyāyana compiled his *Kāmasūtra*, that the human sexual impulse is investigated systematically. But there was in all this, a certain method of understanding. It is not until that method is understood that human life and relationships could be understood, the relations between man and woman above all.

Of the many attributes of that method of understanding life, we need to concentrate here mainly on two. *First*, it is plain that every person wants to understand experience, and not just go through it without making sense, in whatever measure, of what one is experiencing. Understanding is, therefore, experiential; it is not merely intellectual. The problem, however, is that: *one*, we generally see experience as something happening *to* us, as something from outside, and hardly ever see that every person is also an active creator of his, or her, experience. Thus, self-understanding is the very first step towards meaning. And, *two*, we tend to fragment one experience from another, and then seek to understand it; which, of course, is impossible, for the attributes of a human being are interrelated in a way that one flows into the other, and can be understood only in their *togetherness*. That is to say, self-understanding, as the first step towards pleasure and happiness, is to experience oneself in one's inner togetherness, and not as a fragmented being.

Second, therefore, the method is to show the natural inner unity of human attributes. The physical body is not separated from the mind; nor are they as a unity separated from emotions and feelings. In their integral togetherness, they constitute *prāṇa*, or the *life force*. Neither is man separated from nature; for the five elements of nature, that is, the earth, the fire, the water, the air, and the space, are already within man as the generative parts of his physical and mental being. Thus, the material and the spiritual are not two separate domains. The physical and the material, as forms of energy, are also the spiritual, and equally worthy of reverence. The human body with all its natural attributes is as sacred as the spirit. This is the clearly stated position of the *Upanishad*-s, the first human striving towards understanding the self and the world in their innermost relation. And so it is in the *Mahābhārata*.

Like everything else in Indian culture, sex was perceived at many different levels. And, like everything else, it has been discussed hitherto in isolation from other areas of Indian thought and life, which are as universal as they are particular. The problem is that sexual life in Indian society was for the most part centred in the undeniable functionality of human living, but also moved away from it in different directions, exploring the limits of sex, often taking a course that was socially reckless. Hence *the two languages of sexuality: one of functionality, the other of ecstasy.* What is more, having investigated with scientific thoroughness the nature of sexual energy, as well as different sexual practices, Indian culture concluded sex to be *anirvachanīya*, meaning that about which nothing definite can be said. That means that almost anything can be said about sexual energy.

However, through Bhīma, one of the five Pāṇḍava brothers, the *Mahābhārata* provides us with the definition of *kāma*.

> इन्द्रियाणां च पञ्चानां मनसो हृदयस्य च।
> विषये वर्तमानानां या प्रीतिरुपजायते।। वन ३३.३७।।
> स काम इति मे बुद्धिः कर्मणां फलमुत्तमम्।
> *The pleasure, the joy, that arises at the time of the physical senses and the mind and the heart enjoying their natural objects, is, in my opinion,* kāma, *and is the best product of all acts.*[1]

Kāmadeva is the god of erotic desire, *kāma*. The various names given to him illustrate the view that dharmic culture generally had of sex and sensuousness. He is called Abhi-rūpa, the beautiful; Darpaka, the inflamer; Gridhu, the lustful or sharp, Kamana and Kharu, the desirous; Kāntu, the happy; Kalakeli, the merry or the wanton; Māra, the destroyer; Māyī, the deluder, Muhira, the bewilderer; Rāga-vṛnta, the stalk of passion, Rupāstra, the weapon of beauty; Raṭa-nārīcha, the voluptuary, Samantaka, the destroyer of peace, Saṅsāra-guru, the teacher of the world; and Shringāra-yoni, the origin of desire.[2] Rati is his wife. Together they are the deities of the erotic and the desirable.

Sex is the primeval force that moves every living being, and from which the gods are not exempt either. Like all forces of nature, sexual force was raised to the status of a deity, in whose presence the virtuous and the wise alike are humbled. Even the great god Shiva, the fierce destroyer of everything in his aspect of Mahā-kāla, and so the god also of renewal and reproduction, found himself being distracted, while in deep meditation, by a sudden rush of desire for Pārvāti, his wife. Seeing with clarity the source of his disturbance, he opens his 'third eye' and reduces Kāmadeva, hiding behind a bush, to ashes. On the pathetic pleading of Rati, Kāmadeva's wife, Shiva restores him to life but on the condition that the god of erotic desire would forever remain disembodied and invisible. Thus, Anańga is one of the names of Kāmadeva. Thus also, besides the divine nature of sexual force, the hidden forms of its working. In this view, the force of sex must be acknowledged with humility, cultivated with knowledge and sensitivity, but at all times bound within limits. This is the view of the *dharmashāstra*.

In another view, sex is compared to a mighty tree.[3]

हृदि कामद्रुमश्चित्रो मोहसंचयसम्भवः ।
क्रोधमानमहास्कन्धो विधित्सापरिषेचनः ।। शान्ति २५४.१ ।।

तस्य चाज्ञानमाधारः प्रमादः परिषेचनम् ।
सोऽभ्यसूयापलाशो हि पुरा दुष्कृतसारवान् ।। शान्ति २५४.२ ।।

सम्मोहचिन्ताविटपः शोकशाखो भयाङ्कुरः ।
मोहनीभिः पिपासाभिर्लताभिरनुवेष्टितः ।। शान्ति २५४.३ ।।

Growing in the heart of man from the seed of confusion, kāma *is a many-coloured, brilliant, strange tree. Anger and ego are its two main trunks. Ignorance is its root. Ambition is the water by which it is watered; carelessness is the water. Finding fault with others, its leaves; the demerit of one's previous life, its sap.*

Sorrow, its branches; anxiety, its twigs; and fear, its buds. Longing is the climber that covers it from all sides. The roots of this mighty kāma*-tree are very widespread.*[4]

उपासते महावृक्षं सुलुब्धास्तत्फलेप्सवः ।
आयसैः संयुताः पाशैः फलदं परिवेष्ट्यतम् ।। शान्ति २५४.४ ।।

यस्तान् पाशान् वशे कृत्वा तं वृक्षमपकर्षति ।
गतः स दुःखयोरन्तं जरामरणयोर्द्वयोः ।। शान्ति २५४.५ ।।

संरोहत्यकृतप्रज्ञः सदा येन हि पादपम् ।
स तमेव ततो हन्ति विषग्रन्थिरिवातुरम् ।। शान्ति २५४.६ ।।

People with greed, chained to their desires, sit all around this mighty tree—in the hope of enjoying its fruits.

Whoever by the sword of knowledge, having first mastered his desires, cuts at the very roots of this tree, becomes free from the sorrows of old age and death.[5]

But the fool who climbs the kāma*-tree to gather its fruits is sure to be destroyed by it.*

In other words, while *kāma*, sexual desire, is a human attribute, confusion, anger, ego, ignorance, sorrow, anxiety, and fear are the attributes of *kāma*. This is the view of rational asceticism, fully represented in the *Mahābhārata*, in the context where the ascetic denial and its logic are being recounted.

In yet another view, the force of sex can be transmuted into the highest spiritual energy. But that can be achieved neither by confining sex within arbitrary social norms, nor by renouncing it, but by the utmost submission to it in the first place. The cosmic energy stored in sex, though its acts are mostly blind and wasteful, can be released into human consciousness by means primarily of those very acts. But not before sex has been perceived, and worshipped, as *shakti*, the primal force. The human body is the storehouse of that force, which lies dormant and can be awakened. It is a psychic force that exists in a hierarchy of energy levels, the highest of which is the *kuṇḍalini*, sleeping like a coiled snake, unmindful of its awesome power. It is ethically neutral. It is indifferent whether, awakened at the end of a long and intricate system of discipline, where sex plays the chief role, it is directed towards gaining miraculous powers; or, since that will still be a low level of attainment, it is directed towards the spiritual awareness of the true nature of all things. This path of adoration of sexual force in the person of the female, and of submission to its numerous forms, so that the human limits may flow into the limitlessness of the divine, is not meant for weak constitutions but only for the strong. For the path is not only tortuous and exceedingly difficult but also shot through with mystery. This is the view of *tantra*, of which there are nearly as many branches as there are philosophic sects.

The tāntric view of the transforming power of sex is historically older than the sastric view of sex regulated and enjoyed. It is almost certain that tāntric practices in one form or another had existed even before the vedic times. As a result of the later sastric battle against them, mainly on the question of their social implications, they were contained. But the battle was at no time fully resolved. The history of the battle between the two has not yet been written beyond saying that a prominent cause of the decline of Buddhism in India was the revulsion felt at the excesses of Buddhist tāntric cults. But there were other tāntric cults as well. Not only was the battle against them never altogether won, but in the great measure that it was, it was not before some of the main ideas of the latter had been incorporated into dharmic language.

In a large part of the ancient Tamil literature the predominant sentiment is sex. The main body of that literature consists of the *Tolkāppiyam*, the earliest extant Tamil grammar, the ten idylls, and the eight anthologies. A considerable part of the *Tolkāppiyam* is devoted to erotic emotion, designated by the word *aham*, which is also the word for the entirety of one's self. *Aham* is an experience that cannot be expressed; it has to be spoken as something wholly impersonal; hence the injunction that on no occasion must the identity of the hero and the heroine be revealed even by indirect reference to them. Furthermore, sex, like the rest of human life, is seen as related to nature. The *Tolkāppiyam* gives the grammar of sex by providing a complex network of erotic behaviour. It charts the progress of erotic love as a relationship between land and life, season and sentiment. Here is the fullest approval of sexual relations before marriage; that state called *kaḍavu* or stealing. Outside marriage, sexual relations were permitted to men, though confined to courtesans, who are mostly spoken of in terms of respect, because seen as fulfilling a social function, but also as greedy and wily, often bringing great misfortune. Sex for married women was to be kept strictly within the framework of marriage where it had its full play. In the post-Pallavan period, the erotic sensibility of the Tamils is influenced almost entirely by the sanskritic.[6] From the seventh century onwards almost the whole of Tamil literature was devotional and religious. The earlier concern with sexual love did not flower into secular literature.

The tāntric texts, the *Ṛg-veda* and the *Atharva-veda*, the *Upanishad*-s, and the *Mahābhārata* speak of sexuality as a human attribute in terms of respect, free from conventional moral judgement, and realistic to a high degree besides. The sastric ordering of sexual impulse, allowing it free expression within marriage, was tempered, however, with the realistic thought that men and women being human, subject to time, place and opportunity, there would always be transgressions. Underlying the tolerant and rational attitudes towards them, there were two principles of a general kind. *First*: if sexual appetite cannot always be contained within the bounds of marriage, it must remain within the bounds of social conduct. *Second*: of greater consequence than sexual weakness is the waywardness of the mind. These principles inform the laws of the *dharmashāstra* as regards sexual relations outside marriage and the children born thereby.[7]

Acknowledging that there are excesses of virtue and of knowledge, and warning against both, the dharmic sexual ideal was eminently one of balance. Hence the functional view of sex. Its aim was to secure at all times social stability, and to treat individual transgressions with charity. But this high-minded functionalism was threatened from three sides: *(a)* tāntric *cults, (b) ecstasy cults,* and *(c) asceticism.* Incompatible with each other, these were also at variance with the sastric attitude towards sex. But in all likelihood that was one expression of a more fundamental difference: the attitude to caste. The question whether they arose primarily as a reaction against the social rigidity of *varṇa* and *jātī*, or whether that reaction was only an incidental product, remains unresolved. Assuming, what is a commonly held view, that these cults were in their intention a departure from the *varṇa-āshrama* scheme of life, they not only did not go far enough in that direction, but they were also contained by the sastric law. Their temper was anti-intellectual, adding to the non-intellectual temper of *varṇa-āshrama-dharma*. The guru was the moving force in the numerous sects within the three groups mentioned above, strengthening thereby the role of authority in dharmic society. Above all, they fortified a tradition of perceptions, and of language, in which one moved simultaneously at vastly different levels. As a result, it became very nearly impossible to make a definitive statement about any fact, neither leaving out any one of its several aspects, nor letting it remain unconnected with the rest of the universe, for in the *connectedness* lay its meaning. With this qualification we may next have a brief look at some of the aspects of the three movements.

In the first place, an absolute distinction has been drawn between an idea and its abuse. The sexual connection of tāntric cults, Buddhist or non-Buddhist, in many cases ending in corruption and debauchery, had proved to be socially disruptive. But whereas the social consequences of those cults were not immediately discernible, their presuppositions, considered in their own terms, carried with them a high degree of plausibility. That is because of the most general underlying principle of dharmic culture, namely, *the limits of the possible cannot be decided arbitrarily.* Combined with the habit of experimenting with an idea to its very last limits, when the tāntric belief that sexual force, if concentrated on one point, can awaken hidden powers, produced also licence and degeneracy, there was disapproval of the excesses but the idea itself never lost support. Often the disapproval remained mute, and the original idea was reasserted and propounded with skill and vigour.[8] Despite the socially dangerous aspects of the tāntric sexual practices, a fascination for them remained, and is evident even today.

Gopinath Kaviraj argues: 'Due to various reasons, the tāntric practice was polluted, but that was not due to any inherent defect of the practice itself. Rather, it was due to its abuse by the inept'.[9] 'When, inevitably, incompetent people took to the tāntric path,' he further says, 'not everybody could keep the purity of the high ideals of Nāgārjuna and Asaṅga. Hence in Buddhism, too, as in other schools, there was progressive increase in laxity and social transgression. There is no doubt that, of all the factors in the decline of Buddhism, this was the main; for the society is founded upon social discipline. But when faced with individual and collective falling-off from the ideal, the significance of the original ideal is not to be forgotten.'[10] These observations, although true, seem to suggest, however, that an idea and its excess are two separate things. In actual fact, their distinction cannot be maintained beyond a point. The perversion of an idea must in some sense follow from the nature of the idea itself, particularly when the idea, such as that lying beneath the tāntric practices, mysterious and complicated, is of the kind that its purity must be rare and its abuse natural and common.

The luxuriant growth of *tantra*, and later of *bhakti*, had some of their roots in the reaction against the functional view of sex, though it would be wrong to say that they had no other foundation. In domesticated sex there was little place for ecstasy, and ecstasy was the one thing that the dharmic man prized the most. *Ānanda*, or 'ecstasy', was the goal of the *bhakti* cults, and *mahā-sukha*, or 'great delight', that of the tāntric. These were not primarily sexual in their deepest experience; but to release sexual energy from its narrow confines was the primary means of reaching them. The tāntric goal and techniques being wrapped in *rahasya*, mystery, they were in the reach only of rare masters, but the worship of the naked female, followed by sexual intercourse, was within the grasp of the majority. Their lure was heightened by the functionality of domestic sex and, therefore, the absence in it of ecstasy.

The sensual language and rituals of the *bhakti* sects were the other facts. Their significance lies not in turning a sacred emotion into something profane, but chiefly in the fact that those cults, with individuality of emotion as their main characteristic, were seemingly a new development in a society where individual-ness of experience was regarded as of little value. Emotional abandon into the awareness of a personal relationship with God stood in such bold relief against the dry functionality of the *dharmashāstra*, that its appeal was irresistible. The one inevitable route it took, as in the Krishna–Rādhā cults, was erotic. Its visible forms were, however, more sensuous than sexual. The emotional lyrics, sung in a chorus, with drums and cymbals, garlands of jasmine worn around the neck and the arms and the waist, the yellow and ochre garments made of pure silk, swaying in a trance-like dance, beyond *varṇa*, beyond *āshrama*, into a region of pure emotion. The *bhakti* emotion being dependent neither upon birth nor upon learning, naturally the largest following of the ecstasy cults, like those of the tāntric cults, came from the so-called lower castes. The interrelation among these three—reaction against the functional view of sex, the assertion of one's individuality and therefore of personal relationships, and denial of caste as any barrier to them—constitutes another area that deserves to be understood a great deal more than it has been so far. For those connections were neither invariable nor always coherent.

Asceticism was another factor that the sastric sexual ideal had to contend with. In all probability, the history of asceticism is older than even the Veda. Indian asceticism has several faces, to be distinguished one from the other. Their common outward feature was their view of sensuousness, and therefore of sex, as a cosmic snare into which, in a thousand different ways, man is forever drawn, only to squander his psychic energy. It was a denial of the body and its pleasures, of personal ties and their comfort, of social relations and their security. In its extreme form it starved the body and the mind of their nourishment. Struck by the sight of disease, decay, and death, the Buddha also at first had taken to the path of harsh penance, only to discover that that was the wrong path. Then, breaking his long fast that had very nearly killed him, it was from a woman that he accepted some sweet food, and she watched over him for several days—from a respectful distance. He discovered later, in one sweep of a magnificent vision, that salvation was not in punishing the body, but in knowing the causal chain of suffering and decay, and in destroying that chain with singular determination. Before the Buddha, there had been in the *Upanishad*-s a similar turning away from senseless asceticism. And yet, however varied their goals, the *munī*, the *yati*, the *yogin*, the *sādhū*, the *sannyāsī*, the *bairāgi*, or by whatever other names the ascetic was known, remained at all times a visible presence.

To the shrewd legislator, that presence was a potential danger to the social order, because the figure of the ascetic was one of immense attraction—to women. And that was so for reasons that were paradoxical. The very act of denial is also an act of obsession, both generating a kind of power, and all power is a mysterious invitation to women. The ascetic denial was mostly the sexual denial, and hence the denial of woman, in the logic of which she became the eternal seducer. To have created that role for woman was one of the paradoxical results of Indian asceticism. Seduction of the ascetic remained an abiding theme of Indian mythology and literature.

Conflicting attitudes towards woman

At this point, let us consider the greatly conflicting perceptions that were prevalent at all times as regards the nature of woman. They are connected mostly with sexuality. There is the view of woman as divine fullness from which man draws sustenance.[11]

Side by side exists also the view of her as wily, mendacious, a seeker of sexual pleasure regardless of time, place, and person. Alongside the woman as *shakti*, divine energy, stood the woman as *māyā*, the deluder,[12] a source at once of fascination and fear. Fear, because she was believed to carry within her an insatiable sexual hunger, inviting confusion and ruin. We do not know exactly at what point in Indian history this view of woman arose. But it is certain that it had found its harshest expression in the *Pañchatantra*,[13] among the earliest books of fables. The stories of the unbounded sexual appetite of women were drawn in a work of great artistry and wisdom with such unrelieved harshness that one might suspect them to be the ravings of one deeply hurt by women.

But neither at the time that the work was written, around 300 B.C., nor at any subsequent period of Indian history, was the author of the *Pañchatantra* alone in his views, some of them given below,[14] on the alleged faithless and treacherous nature of woman. In fact, many of them were taken almost word for word from the *Anushāsana-parva* of the *Mahābhārata*.[15] There a nymph, Pañchachuḍā, on being questioned half-seriously half-laughingly by the sage Nārada about the nature of woman is persuaded to reveal the secret of womankind. She is depicted as being initially hesitant to do so: 'I am a woman and I cannot denigrate women.'[16]

जल्पंति सार्द्धमन्येन पश्यन्त्यन्यं सविभ्रमा: ।
हृद्गतं चिन्तयन्त्यन्यं प्रिय: को नाम योषिताम् ।। पञ्चतन्त्र १.१४६ ।।
एकेन स्मितपाटलाधररुचो जल्पन्त्यनल्पाक्षरं
वीक्षन्तेऽन्यमित: स्फुटत्कुमुदिनीफुल्लोल्लसल्लोचना: ।
दूरोदारचरित्रचित्रविभवं ध्यायन्ति चान्यं धिया
केनेत्थं परमार्थतोऽर्थवदिव प्रेमास्ति वामभ्रुवाम् ।। पञ्चतन्त्र १.१४७ ।।

While talking with one, and looking at another with lust, they think of another in their heart. Who can really be their beloved?[17]

नाग्निस्तृप्यति काष्ठानां नापगानां महोदधि: ।
नान्तक: सर्वभूतानां न पुंसां वामलोचना ।। पञ्चतन्त्र १.१४८ ।।

Fire is not satisfied with all the wood, nor the ocean with all the rivers, nor death by claiming all that lives, nor a woman with all men.[18]

रहो नास्ति क्षणो नास्ति नास्ति प्रार्थयिता नर: ।
तेन नारद नारीणां सतीत्वमुपजायते ।। पञ्चतन्त्र १.१४९ ।।

There is no privacy, there is no time, there is not the man who asks—it is for these reasons, O Nārada, that women are sometimes faithful.[19]

अनर्थित्वान्मनुष्याणां भयात्परिजनस्य च ।
मर्य्यादायाममर्य्यादा: स्त्रियस्तिष्ठन्ति सर्वदा ।। पञ्चतन्त्र १.१५३ ।।

Only because they are not wanted, and because they fear people not their own, do reckless women remain within bounds.[20]

नासां कश्चिदगम्योऽस्ति नासाञ्च वयसि स्थिति: ।
विरूपं रूपवन्तं वा पुमानित्येव भुज्यते ।। पञ्चतन्त्र १.१५४ ।।

To women, none is inaccessible; nor do they discriminate between the young and the old, the ugly and the handsome. Every man is the object of their pleasure.[21]

दुर्दिवसे घनतिमिरे दु:सञ्चारासु घनवीथीषु ।
पत्युर्विदेशगमने परमसुखं जघनचपलाया: ।। पञ्चतन्त्र १.१८४ ।।

A day that is cloudy, the darkness that is deep, the lanes with little movement, and the departure of husband for abroad, these greatly delight women who are faithless.[22]

अनृतं साहसं माया मूर्खत्वमतिलोभता।
अशौचं निर्दयत्वञ्च स्त्रीणां दोषा: स्वभावजा:।। पञ्चतन्त्र १.२०७।।
Untruth, daring, deception, foolishness, extreme greed, uncleanliness and cruelty are the defects natural to women.[23]

यदि स्यात्पावक: शीत: प्रोष्णो वा शशलाञ्छन:।
स्त्रीणां तदा सतीत्वं स्याद्यदि स्याद्दुर्जनो हित:।। २०३।।
Only if fire should become cold, and the moon become hot, and the wicked turn good, that the faithfulness of women could be trusted.[24]

यदन्तस्तन्न जिह्वायां यज्जिह्वयां न तद्बहि:।
यद्धितं तन्न कुर्वन्ति विचित्रचरिता: स्त्रिय:।। पञ्चतन्त्र ४.५६।।
What is in their heart, is not what is on their tongue; what is on their tongue, is not what comes out. What is good, that they do not desire. The ways of women are indeed strange.[25]

उशना वेद यच्छास्त्रं यच्च वेद बृहस्पति:।
स्त्रीबुद्ध्या न विशिष्येत तास्तु रक्ष्या: कथं नरै:।। अनुशासन ३९.८।।
The knowledge Shukrāchārya has, and the knowledge Brihaspati has, is not greater than the cunning intelligence of women. Who can then protect women?[26]

Although such views were in the nature of mindless generalisations, and were nasty as well, the *Mahābhārata*, consistent with its method of recounting different perceptions of human life, was stating *also* what must certainly have been among the prevalent perceptions of woman. And given the belief in woman's lust,[27] mostly hidden but seeking opportunities, came about the view of sex itself as the gateway to ruin. Sex came to be looked upon as a delirious waste of physical energy as well as a threat to one's peace of mind. This was the very opposite both of the *dharmashāstra* and the tāntric views of sex, though between even them there was a great conflict. Several factors contributed to that development: asceticism, superstition, sexual fear, folk wisdom, and in some ways the *dharmashāstra* as well. To trace their tangled influence upon one another is exceedingly difficult. It is even doubtful whether the unflattering opinion about the prodigious sexual appetite of women can be attributed primarily to ascetic traditions. The cynical language of the aphorisms about women is not the language of asceticism but apparently of 'worldly knowledge'. The *Pañchatantra*, where the depressing portrait of the unrestrained sexuality of women is sketched relentlessly, is a book of worldly prudence, not of asceticism. In any event, those aphorisms do *not* constitute the final dharmic assessment of the nature of woman, and it will be wrong to quote them without the qualifying statements with which they are surrounded always in the *Mahābhārata*.

The use of the phrase 'qualifying statements' is itself, however, misleading. For it would seem to imply that the aphorisms in question formed the main body of the *Mahābhārata*'s opinion about women but that they were—very graciously—qualified. That is not the case at all. It is true that alongside woman as the sustaining energy, *shakti*, there stood also the woman as *māyā*. But it will be wrong to muddle the perception of woman as *māyā*, which had the grandeur at least of a principle, with the perception of woman as a sexually lawless being, which leaves her neither sense nor dignity. It was this latter view that the *Mahābhārata* sought to repudiate no sooner than it was expressed.

First. To correct the stupid impression that sexual need was a primary need of women only, the *Mahābhārata* states the obvious:

इमे वै मानवा लोके स्त्रीषु सज्जन्त्यभीक्ष्णशः ।
मोहेन परमाविष्टा देवसृष्टेन पार्थिव ।। अनुशासन ३९.१ ।।

स्त्रियश्च पुरुषेष्वेव प्रत्यक्षं लोकसाक्षिकम् ।। अनुशासन ३९.२ ।।

All men of this world desire women: likewise women desire men. This is evident and everybody in the world is a witness to it.[28]

सज्जन्ति पुरुषे नार्यः पुंसां सोऽर्थश्च पुष्कलः ।। अनुशासन ४३.१५ ।।

Just as women desire men, so also men have the same feeling towards women.[29]

भार्यापत्योर्हि सम्बन्धः स्त्रीपुंसोः स्वल्प एव तु ।
रतिः साधारणो धर्म इति चाह स पार्थिवः ।। अनुशासन ४५.९ ।।

The relationship between wife and husband, as between woman and man, is very intimate and subtle, with sexual intimacy as its common characteristic.[30]

Second. Bhīshma unreservedly shares the depressing perception of woman as sexually lawless, and primarily *that*.[31] But, assuming that women by their very nature were inclined to sexual anarchy, he emphasises that they should be protected for that very reason.[32] Bhīshma states:

स्त्रियः साध्व्यो महाभागाः सम्मता लोकमातरः ।
धारयन्ति महीं साजन्निमां सवनकाननाम् ।। अनुशासन ४३.२० ।।

The women who are virtuous and noble are honoured in the world as mother, and they sustain the world by their own strength; but the women who are inclined to waywardness, and may easily destroy the family, need to be protected from themselves.[33]

एवमेतासु रक्षा वै शक्या कर्तुं महात्मभिः ।। अनुशासन ४३.२२ ।।

नासां स्नेहो नरैः कार्यस्तथैवेर्ष्या जनेश्वर ।। अनुशासन ४३.२५ ।।

But it is only a man who is noble and strong himself who can protect women;[34] *that is, if he is neither taken up too much by them, nor is he jealous of them.*[35]

Correspondingly, Bhīshma reserves the strongest condemnation for those men who deceive and take advantage of women left unprotected.

अनाथां प्रमदां बालां बृद्धां भीतां तपस्विनीम् ।
वञ्चयन्ति नरा ये च ते वै निरयगामिनः ।। अनुशासन २३.६४ ।।

Those men who deceive women who have no one to take care of them, women who are old, women who are young, or a girl-child, women who are fearful, and women who have become ascetics, are certainly damned to hell.[36]

He exhorts Yudhishṭhira who would now be king:

तस्माद् ब्रवीमि पार्थ त्वां स्त्रियो रक्ष्याः सदैव च ।
उभयं दृश्यते तासु सततं साध्वसाधु च ।। अनुशासन ४३.१९ ।।

Therefore I say to you that you should protect women always. Both good and bad can be seen in women.[37]

It is in *this* context, and not independent of it, that there comes the famous, or in certain circles rather infamous, pronouncement:

पिता रक्षति कौमारे भर्ता रक्षति यौवने ।
पुत्राश्च स्थाविरे भावे न स्त्री स्वातन्त्र्यमर्हति ।। अनुशासन ४६.१४ ।।

The father protects her in her childhood; the husband protects her in her youth; and sons protect her in her old age: for woman there is no independence.[38]

Since this verse occurs in the *Manu-smṛti* as well, Manu has been depicted as the enemy of women's freedom. The verse has been interpreted as saying that women *ought* not to be independent, and must forever remain under the control of men. If we take the totality of what had been said about women, and about their equal place in the social order, that interpretation would seem absurd.

Third. A plainly logical objection in this regard is raised by Yudhishṭhira, who puts it to Bhīshma.

अनृताः स्त्रिय इत्येवं सूत्रकारो व्यवस्यति।
यदानृताः स्त्रियस्तात सहधर्मः कुतः स्मृतः।। अनुशासन १९.६।।

If it were true that women by nature were given to untruth, anrta, *as maintained by the authors of the* dharmasutra *and even in the Veda, what sense would there be then in describing marriage as 'the state of* saha-dharma, *that is, observing* dharma *together?*[39]

अनृताः स्त्रिय इत्येवं वेदेष्वपि हि पठ्यते।
धर्मोऽयं पूर्विका संज्ञा उपचारः क्रियाविधिः।। अनुशासन १९.७।।

How, should one of the partners be given to untruth by her very nature, would the togetherness in dharma *be possible? For it would then mean that untruth is included in that* saha-dharma; *which can never be the case, for untruth can never be a part of* dharma. *Or can it simply be that what man and woman do together is given the conventional name* saha-dharma?[40]

Bhīshma does not answer this objection; but from what he announces,[41] after all his statements have been made about woman's inborn incapacity to remain sexually within the bounds of marriage, it can plainly be inferred that those statements were quietly given up, that is, if they were ever taken seriously. Besides, *there is in the Mahābhārata not a single woman who answers, even remotely, Pañchachūḍā's description of women and shared, at least in theory, by Bhīshma.* The fifteen verses that form Chapter 46 of the *Anushāsana-parva* may be taken as a final statement of dharmic attitudes towards women. Of them, ten are as follows:

पितृभिर्भ्रातृभिश्चपि श्वशुरैरथ देवरैः।
पूज्या भूषयितव्याश्च बहुकल्याणमीप्सुभिः।। अनुशासन ४६.३।।

Desirous of good of many kinds, let father, brother, father-in-law, and brother-in-law honour her with jewels and clothes.

यदि वै स्त्री न रोचेत पुमांसं न प्रमोदयेत्।
अप्रमोदात् पुनः पुंसः प्रजनो न प्रवर्धते।। अनुशासन ४६.४।।
पूज्या लालयितव्याश्च स्त्रियो नित्यं जनाधिप।

If the woman's wishes are not fulfilled, she cannot please her husband; if he is not pleased, the progeny does not rise. Let women be honoured and pleased always.

स्त्रियो यत्र च पूज्यते रमन्ते तत्र देवताः।। अनुशासन ४६.५।।
अपूजिताश्च यत्रैताः सर्वास्तत्राफलाः क्रियाः।

Where women are honoured, there the gods reside; where they remain not honoured, there nothing can bear fruit.

तदा चैतत् कुलं नास्ति यदा शोचन्ति जामयः।। अनुशासन ४६.६।।
जामीशप्तानि केहानि निकृत्तानीव कृत्यया।
नैव भान्ति न वर्धन्ते श्रिया हीनानि पार्थिव।। अनुशासन ४६.७।।

That family does not survive where the daughters-in-law lament. The homes that are cursed by them are destroyed as if by a malevolent ghost; bereft of fortune, those homes do not prosper.

स्त्रियः पुंसां परिददे मनुर्जिगमिषुर्दिवम्।
अबलाः स्वल्पकौपीनाः सुहृदः सत्यजिष्णवः।। अनुशासन ४६.८।।
ईर्षवो मानकामाश्च चण्डाश्च सुहृदोऽबुधाः।
स्त्रियस्तु मानमर्हन्ति ता मानयत मानवाः।। अनुशासन ४६.९।।
स्त्रीप्रत्ययो हि वै धर्मो रतिभोगाश्च केवलाः।
परिचर्या नमस्कारास्तदायत्ता भवन्तु वः।। अनुशासन ४६.१०।।

On ascending to heaven, Manu entrusted women to the protection of men, saying: 'They are weak; with few clothes; good-hearted; triumphant in truth; jealous; capricious; given to violence; kind-hearted, and foolish. Women deserve to be honoured, and all of you shall honour them. For womankind is the basis of all order. Sexual pleasure, attendance and service, and adoration—all are dependent upon them.

उत्पादनमपत्यस्य जातस्य परिपालनम्।
प्रीत्यर्थं लोकयात्रायाः पश्यत स्त्रीनिबन्धनम्।। अनुशासन ४६.११।।
सम्मान्यमानाश्चैता हि सर्वकार्याण्यवाप्स्यथ।

The birth of progeny, the nourishing of the young, and the happy progress of society, are seen as tied to women. Only if they are respected and honoured will everything succeed.

श्रिय एताः स्त्रियो नाम सत्कार्या भूतिमिच्छता।
पालिता निगृहीता च श्रीः स्त्री भवति भारत।। अनुशासन ४६.१५ ।।
Women are the glory. If happiness and well-being are desired, let them be treated kindly and with honour: when a woman is protected and with loving care, she becomes the splendour and the good fortune.

As for the woman as mother, the *Mahābhārata* holds:

दशाचार्यानुपाध्याय उपाध्यायान् पिता दश।। अनुशासन १०५.१४ ।।
दश चैव पितृन् माता सर्वां वा पृथिवीमपि।
गौरवेणाभिभवति नास्ति मातृसमो गुरुः।। अनुशासन १०५.१५ ।।
In status, greater than ten scholars is the teacher and the preceptor; higher than ten preceptors, is the father; and higher than ten fathers is the mother: she is higher in status than even the entire Earth. There is no guru greater than the mother.[42]

In matters of inheritance, too, the *Mahābhārata* clearly stipulates that there is no distinction between son and daughter. Both are equal.

स्त्रियास्तु यद् भवेद् वित्तं पित्रा दत्तं युधिष्ठिर।
ब्राह्मण्यास्तद्धरेत् कन्या यथा पुत्रस्तथा हि सा।। अनुशासन ४७.२५ ।।
सा हि पुत्रसभा राजन् विहिता कुरुनन्दन।। अनुशासन ४७.२५ ।।
In the money and property of a woman inherited from her father, the daughter has a right as the son has, because as the son so the daughter. Daughter is like son—this is the established principle.[43]

In the light of these, in the light of the status of woman in the *Upanishad*-s, it should be absolutely clear that what the *dharmashāstra*-s and the *shāstri*-s later did, for example, to women who had lost their husbands was a complete negation of *dharma*. That was because side by side with the lure and fear of unattached women, there was the lure and fear of widows. Because they continued to be a part of their dead husband's family, the fear of their sexual involvement, with consequent disruption of the family and the social order, was deep.[44] Therefore, reversing the attitudes of the

Mahābhārata, and quite as much the law of the *Arthashāstra*, the one single object of the sastric legislation as regards widows was to starve their senses, and disfigure them for the rest of their lives. The sastric repression of widows was primarily sexual. They were expected to eat only once a day, and no more than a subsistence diet. They were not to wear colours, or adorn themselves with flowers and perfume. Their heads were shaved; their bodies were bereft of all ornament; they were required to not even brush their teeth. Their place for sleeping was on the floor, and during festivities in an unseen corner. The sāstric aim was to destroy their sexual impulse and to leave them sexually unattractive. Should any sexual thought still enter their heads, they were voluntarily to undergo a series of purificatory rituals. They were brainwashed into fearing that since their widowhood was a consequence of their past *karma*, any laxity in observing 'the *dharma* of a widow', which the *shastri*-s decided what it would be, was sure to invite a similar punishment in the future life. The later *dharmashāstra*-s, which were in actual fact only *adharma-shāstras*, that is, the codes of injustice, inequity and violence, *a-dharma*, governed much of a woman's life. The *Mahābhārata*, which is the greatest friend of women the world has ever known, remained neglected—even today. The *Mahābhārata* portrays women as teachers of life and relationships, many of them in a later book—'The Women of the *Mahābhārata*'. Meanwhile, let us hear these words of the *Mahābhārata*:

य: कश्चिन्नयाय्य आचार: सर्वं शास्त्रमिति श्रुति: ।
यदन्याय्यमशास्त्रं तदित्येषा श्रूयते श्रुति: ।। शान्ति २६९.५८ ।।

Whatever is just and fair is shastra; *whatever is unjust and unfair is* a-shastra.[45]

Comparative pleasure of man and woman

In the *Mahābhārata*, a question is raised as to who enjoys sexual pleasure more, the man or the woman?[46] The answer is suggested through the story of Bhańgāsvana, a king.[47] He had angered Indra, the chief of the gods, by withdrawing from him his customary tribute, and not giving him the first place in a sacrificial rite that he had set up. Indra wreaks his vengeance on Bhańgāsvana by transforming him into a woman when the king was bathing in a lake. Everyone was shocked and dismayed, his wife and children most of all. by his metamorphosis. Bhańgāsvana now began his life as a woman, with all the desires a woman has. Later, he, now she, married a man of her choice, and raised a large family. Meanwhile, reconciled with Indra, the god offered to change him back into his masculine self. But Bhaṅgāsvana declined that offer, saying that he wanted to remain as a woman, for he was happier in that gender. That is because, he said, it was as a woman that he experienced the deeper pleasure of sexual union between man and woman than he did as a man.[48] And that pleasure was indescribable. Bhaṅgāsvana acknowledged, too, that the children she had given birth to, as a woman, were infinitely more dear to her than those whom he had fathered as a man. 'A woman has greater love for her sons than a man has.'[49]

The question regarding the primacy of sexuality

Of the three ends of life, *trivarga*, namely, the right ordering of life and relationships, *dharma*; material prosperity and wealth, *artha*; fulfilment of sexual desire, *kāma*; which one is fundamental, of which the other two are secondary expressions? This question has occupied the human mind at all times everywhere. The *Mahābhārata* reflected upon it likewise.

The five Pāṇḍava brothers are having a long conversation about this very question.[50] Vidura is there, too. The conversation opens with Yudhishṭhira asking:

धर्मे चार्थे च कामे च लोकवृत्तिः समाहिता ।
तेषां गरीयान् कतमो मध्यमः को लघुश्च कः ।। शान्ति १६७.२ ।।

कस्मिंश्चात्मा निधातव्यस्त्रिवर्गविजयाय वै ।
संहृष्टा नैष्ठिकं वाक्यं यथावद् वक्तुमर्हथ ।। शान्ति १६७.३ ।।

People are generally motivated by dharma, *by the desire for material prosperity,* artha, *and the desire for sexual fulfilment,* kāma: *of these three, which one is of the highest value, which is of the middling value, and which is the lowest?*
Examine this question, and say only what you truly believe.[51]

This 'say only what you truly believe' pervades the whole of the *Mahābhārata. Nothing is asked, and nothing answered, from a passing curiosity only.*

Vidura, the detached observer in the *Mahābhārata*, advocates in a few quick steps the primacy of *dharma*.[52]

बाहुश्रुत्यं तपस्त्यागः श्रद्धा यज्ञक्रिया क्षमा।
भावशुद्धिर्दया सत्यं संयमश्चात्मसम्पदः।। शान्ति १६७.५।।
एतदेवाभिपद्यस्व मा तेऽभूच्चलितं मनः।
एतन्मूलौ हि धर्मार्थावेतदेकपदं हि मे।। शान्ति १६७.६।।

It is in dharma *that all beings are established.*
Study and reflection, devotion, sacrifice, forgiveness, compassion, truth and self-control: these constitute the real wealth of the self. They are the roots both of the right ordering of relationships, dharma, *and material prosperity,* artha. *Thus, material prosperity is already assumed in* dharma.

धर्मो राजन् गुणः श्रेष्ठो मध्यमो ह्यर्थ उच्यते।
कामो यवीयानिति च प्रवदन्ति मनीषिणः।। शान्ति १६७.८।।

Those who are wise say that dharma *is the highest; material prosperity and wealth middling; and the fulfilment of sexual desire inferior in comparison to these two.*

तस्माद् धर्मप्रधानेन भवितव्यं यतात्मना।
तथा च सर्वभूतेषु वर्तितव्यं यथात्मनि।। शान्ति १६७.९।।

So, the right ordering of relationships should be one's highest aim, behaving towards all beings in the same way as one would towards oneself.[53]

Arjuna settles, as he had done on an earlier occasion,[54] for the incontestable supremacy of material prosperity and wealth in human affairs.[55] His main argument is:

This world is the field of action, and all things are done here as a means of livelihood. Without economic prosperity and wealth, neither can dharma *be had, nor* kāma. *Indeed, they are the subsidiary attributes of wealth itself, and cannot survive independent of it.*

अप्रज्ञानं तमोभूतं प्रज्ञानं तु प्रकाशिता।। शान्ति १६७.११।।

Not to know the primacy of wealth is the darkness of ignorance; to know the importance of wealth is to have the light of knowledge.[56]

Nakula and Sahadeva, the twins, support Arjuna, but with a significant shift.[57] 'There is no question that wealth is as rare as it is most desired:

there is no doubt whatever, that on obtaining wealth a person can fulfil all his desires, and this is proved by direct experience.'[58] But they point also to the *unity between the two, dharma* and *artha,* and *do not grade one over the other.* They say:

अनर्थस्य न कामोऽस्ति तथार्थोऽधर्मिण: कुत: ।
तस्मादुद्विजते लोको धर्मार्थाद् यो बहिष्कृत: ।। शान्ति १६७.२५ ।।
A person who is poor has not the means of fulfilling his desires; and nor can a person who is bereft of dharma *be prosperous; and he who has not the wealth combined with* dharma, *is treated as an outcast.*[59]

तस्माद् धर्मप्रधानेन साध्योऽर्थ: संयतात्मना ।
विश्वस्तेषु हि भूतेषु कल्पते सर्वमेव हि ।। शान्ति १६७.२६ ।।
Therefore what one should aim at is to earn wealth combined with the right ordering of relationships, and have the right ordering of relationships combined with wealth.

धर्मं समाचरेत् पूर्वं ततोऽर्थं धर्मसंयुतम् ।
तत: कामं चरेत् पश्चात् सिद्धार्थ: स हि तत्परम् ।। शान्ति १६७.२७ ।।
Exercising self-control, and keeping dharma *foremost in the mind, let one earn wealth that is combined with* dharma; *and, maintaining the harmony between the two, fulfil one's erotic impulse.*[60]

Bhīmasena upholds what he says is the demonstrable primacy of *kāma* in life, which means, in the first place, the primacy of *desire* as the motivating force.[61] There can be no arguing about it. It is evident, he says, that: 'Every act begins with a desire for *something*. In the absence of desire, there would neither be any effort at earning wealth, nor any interest in the ordering of relationships; nor would there be even any impulse towards sexual pleasure.'[62] Then he quickly lists very many human activities, from the highest form of spiritual effort to the most ordinary acts of commerce and agriculture, each one of them motivated evidently by the desire for one thing or another.[63]

समुद्रं वा विशन्त्यन्ये नरा: कामेन संयुता: ।
कामो हि विविधाकार: सर्वं कामेन संततम् ।। शान्ति १६७.३३ ।।
And of desire, there are many different forms, and every act is suffused with desire.

नास्ति नासीन्नाभविष्यद् भूतं कामात्मकात् परम्।
एतत् सारं महाराज धर्मार्थावत्र संस्थितौ।। शान्ति १६७.३४।।

There is not one human being, nor there ever was, nor will there be in the future, who is without desire. Therefore, kāma *is the essence of life, and* dharma *and* artha *have only that as their foundation.*[64] *Indeed, they are only the other expressions of* kāma, *which should be regarded as the substance of life.*[65]

He even advises his elder brother Yudhishṭhira, light-heartedly of course,

सुचारुवेषाभिरलंकृताभि-
मदोत्कटाभिः प्रियदर्शनाभिः।
रमस्व योषाभिरुपेत्य कामं
कामो हि राजन् परमो भवेन्नः।। शान्ति १६७.३८।।

Seek the company of women who are beautiful, are dressed elegantly, and are intoxicated with their beauty, and make merry with them. Kāma *alone is the highest.*[66]

But, after saying that he has thought on this question deeply, he concludes that the most important of all is:

धर्मार्थकामाः सममेव सेव्या
यो ह्येकभक्तः स नरो जघन्यः।
तयोस्तु दाक्ष्यं प्रवदन्ति मध्यं
स उत्तमो योऽभिरतस्त्रिवर्गे।। शान्ति १६७.४०।।

One should enjoy all the three, dharma, artha, *and* kāma, *together. He who worships only one of them is the most pitiable; he who is an adept in enjoying two of them is of the middle class; but he who enjoys all the three in a harmonious way is the best.*[67]

The *Mahābhārata* thus starts with a legitimate question, and examines it, recounting different opinions concerning it. The question is about the primacy either of the right ordering of human relationships, *or* of economic prosperity, *or* of sexual impulse, one over the other. But it is finally suggested that this question itself is a misleading question; for, in asking it, it presupposes that one is more fundamental than the other. The evident truth is that all these human attributes are interrelated, and neither the one nor the other has any *primacy*. The main question will then be, not of assessing the relative importance of any one of them, in principle, but of their harmonious working in the man–woman relationship. *To fragment any one of them from the other two will result in its idolatry, and is sure to invite violence to one's own self and to the other.* This is the position of the *Mahābhārata* throughout; and it is in that light that human sexuality is to be seen. It is to be seen in the light of relationships—the relationship of the self with the self and of the self with the *other*.

Sexuality and relationship in the *Mahābhārata*

Dharmic civilisation knew also the incontestable truth that to sexual desire there is no end, even when the body is stricken with infirmity and old age. For sexual pleasure is not entirely of the body. Given the longest duration of it, marred by no external circumstance, it will leave *desire* unsatisfied still. The myth of Yayāti conveys this truth most strikingly.[68] Since it depicts much besides, let us consider it in some detail.

During one of his wanderings in his kingdom, Yayāti finds Devayānī in a well, into which Sharmishṭhā, her younger companion and the daughter of the king of the Asura-s, had pushed her after they had a quarrel resulting from the mixing up of their clothes. Yayāti rescues her from the well, and Devayānī, a dazzling beauty, offers herself as a wife to the king. That offer is refused on the ground that she is the daughter of a brāhmaṇa and he is a kṣhattriya, and that their union would be against the rules of *varṇa*. She vows that she would marry only him and would persuade her father, Shukrāchārya, the great guru of the Asura-s, to consent to it. After a long time, the scores between the two girls, meanwhile settled by Sharmishṭhā being obliged to act as maid to Devayānī, Yayāti chances to meet Devayānī again—this time happily sporting in a grove. He had forgotten the earlier episode, but Devayānī had not. Finally, the king marries her, after the father had waived the scruple about the mixing of the two *varṇa*-s. Sharmishṭhā is offered to the king as part of Devayānī's personal entourage. But the father subjects this to a condition, namely, Yayāti must respect Sharmishṭhā in every way, but should not talk with her in private, or touch her, much less invite her to his bed.

Yayāti breaks that condition, but not of his volition wholly. Herself of a royal stock, a woman of great beauty but cloistered, one day Sharmishṭhā finds the king alone in the palace garden. She approaches him and frankly asks him that he satisfy her desire. Greatly tempted, Yayāti nevertheless reminds her of the condition imposed upon him at the time he married Devayānī. He says he would be lying if he breaks the promise he had given in that regard. And it is wrong for a king to lie.

राजा प्रमाणं भूतानां स नश्येत् मृषा वदन्।
अर्थकृच्छ्रमपि प्राप्य न मिथ्या कर्तुमुत्सहे।। आदि ८२.१८।।

To the people, the king is the authority. He would be destroyed if he were to speak untruthfully. Should I be faced with economic crisis, I would even then not lie.[69]

Sharmishṭhā argues that:

न नर्मयुक्तं वचनं हिनस्ति
  न स्त्रीषु राजन् न विवाहकाले।
प्राणात्यये सर्वधनापहारे
  पञ्चानृतान्याहुरपातकानि।। आदि ८२.१६।।

There are five occasions when a lie is not a lie: in jest; in conversation with one's wife; at the time of contracting a marriage; when one's life is in danger; and if one faces the threat of being ravished against one's will.[70]

पृष्टं तु साक्ष्ये प्रवदन्तमन्यथा
  वदन्ति मिथ्या पतितं नरेन्द्र।
एकार्थतायां तु समाहितायां
  मिथ्या वदन्तं त्वनृतं हिनस्ति।। आदि ८२.१७।।

In order to save an innocent life, on being questioned should one bear false witness, it would be false to hold him fallen. But to tell a lie only to save one's own life when two lives are together threatened, then that lie would doubtless be a fall.[71]

Moreover, she argues, there are three kinds of persons who have no independent right to ownership of property—wife, servant, and son. Their wealth belongs to whoever controls them. Husband has the right over the property of his wife, master over that of his servant, and father over that of his son.[72] She is under the control of Devayānī, being her maid; and Devayānī is under the control of Yayāti, being his wife; so he has under his control the maid as well. He has a lawful right to both the women. Perfect syllogism. Besides, giving to a woman a son, and offering oneself for erotic pleasure, are gifts far greater than the gift of money and jewels. Did he not have it announced in the town that whoever asks him for whatever gift, should be given? Now he must give her the one gift she most desires—himself, or fall into a lie. All these arguments were of course self-serving, but not without a sense of humour. She was laughing within herself, pressing into her service some of those very customs she would have condemned, noticing clearly that Yayāti was greatly willing but, being a man of honour, needed some semblance of justification. She provided him with that. Persuaded thus, Yayāti takes Sharmishṭhā as another wife, in secret. They enjoy each other for a long while, and then return to their respective apartments, happy and glowing.

Sharmishṭhā is now with child. Whereupon, truly concerned about her, Devayānī scolds her with words of shame, and wants to know the name, the family, the clan of the father of the child. Without giving a direct answer, Sharmishṭhā says that far from doing anything shameful, she has begotten the child in a perfectly legitimate manner 'from a noble man learned in the lore of the Veda whom I asked for the gift of love'. Devayānī says no more; the two women laugh; and then they part. Earlier Devayānī had had two sons from Yayāti; in the years to follow, Sharmishṭhā has three sons by him. Devayānī discovers that fact when, the five children playing together, Sharmishṭhā's sons being questioned by Devayānī who their father is, point to Yayāti. In great anger and hurt, Devayānī turns to the king, saying that he had insulted and deceived her, and she would live with him no longer. She prepares to return to her father; Yayāti follows her to the hermitage. On hearing the tearful complaint of his daughter, but before hearing Yayāti's explanation, Shukrāchārya curses the king to fall into old age. In that very moment Yayāti is transformed into a man bent with great age, his strength gone.

He pleads that his relationship with Sharmishṭhā, although against the condition imposed by the guru, was just and right all the same. The king reminds the guru of the law that when a maiden rightly asks from a man the gift of *kāma*, whoever spurns her is guilty of killing a foetus, as it were. To avoid that crime, he gave the woman the gift she most desired; and in doing that, he had done no wrong. Since his longings remained still unsatisfied, the king begs the guru that the curse be annulled.

Moved, but unable to undo the effect of his own curse, once pronounced, Shukrāchārya offers the king a boon instead—should any of his five sons be willing to transfer to him his own youth, the king would become young again. Yayāti asks all his five sons, and all refuse—except the youngest,

Puru, born of Sharmishṭhā. Puru gives up his youth and bestows it upon his father, for a thousand years, taking upon him his father's cursed old age.

Full of youthful vigour again, Yayāti enjoys fully all the pleasures of sexuality, this time in the company of Vishvāchī, the divine nymph.

यथाकामं यथोत्साहं यथाकालं यथासुखम् ।
धर्माविरुद्धं राजेन्द्र यथार्हति स एव हि ।। आदि ८५.२ ।।

As his impulse, the degree of ardour, and the appropriateness of time would dictate, he enjoyed the pleasures and their happiness. Without doing anything, though, that was against dharma.[73]

This is important, that he did nothing against *dharma*. What this means here is that, in the process of enjoying the pleasures of *kāma*, he did nothing that would degrade, debase, hurt, and do violence to any one. Neither did he ignore his kingly duties, his royal obligations to others.

अतिथीनन्नपानैश्च विशश्च परिपालनैः ।
आनृशंस्येन शूद्रांश्च दस्यून् संनिग्रहेण च ।। आदि ८५.४ ।।
धर्मेण च प्रजाः सर्वा यथावदनुरञ्जयन् ।
ययातिः पालयामास साक्षादिन्द्र इवापरः ।। आदि ८५.५ ।।

He would give liberally to those who were poor and had no one to take care of them. He would offer food and water to the guests. He would protect the merchants and traders. He would be kind and generous to those who provided services. He would punish the robbers and thieves. He would, governing in the light of dharma, *keep the people happy and contended, and took care of them thus.*[74]

The teaching through this story would have been ruined if Yayāti were portrayed as turning into a selfish degenerate as a result of his hunger for sexual pleasure, *kāma*. The *Mahābhārata*'s teaching is that there is, rather, something inherent in *kāma* itself that would keep it unsatisfied and, even in its own terms, remain forever unfulfilled. This truth Yayāti began to see.

स सम्प्राप्य शुभान् कामांस्तृप्तः खिन्नश्च पार्थिवः ।
कालं वर्षसहस्रान्तं सस्मार मनुजाधिपः ।। आदि ८५.७ ।।
परिसंख्याय कालज्ञः कलाः काष्ठाश्च वीर्यवान् ।
यौवनं प्राप्य राजर्षिः सहस्रपरिवत्सरान् ।। आदि ८५.८ ।।

In the very moments of his enjoying the pleasures he experienced, too, the melancholy thought that, given even a thousand years, they would all come to an end. Knowing the workings of Time, that certain prospect made him feel sad.[75]

There is sadness at the very heart of the pleasures of *kāma*.

At the end of a thousand years, but his sexual appetite still keen and undiminished, he returns to his son Puru the manhood that he had borrowed. Then he declares:

न जातु कामः कामानुपभोगेन शाम्यति।
हविषा कृष्णवर्त्मेव भूय एवाभिवर्धते।। आदि ८५.१२।।
The hunger for pleasure can never be satisfied by more pleasure, just as the fire can only grow higher when fed with more oil.[76]

यत् पृथिव्यां व्रीहियवं हिरण्यं पशवः स्त्रियः।
एकस्यापि न पर्याप्तं तस्मात् तृष्णां परित्यजेत्।। आदि ८५.१३।।
Not all the grain in the world, not all the gold, not all the women, are sufficient even for one man. Let one therefore renounce the 'thirst' of desire.[77]

या दुस्त्यजा दुर्मतिभिर्या न जीर्यति जीर्यतः।
योऽसो प्राणान्तिको रोगस्तां तृष्णां त्यजतः सुखम्।। आदि ८५.१४।।
Exceedingly difficult to give up, by the ones having wrong perceptions, which does not ever weaken although man does, and is like a fatal disease, only in renouncing that 'thirst' of desire is there true happiness.[78]

पूर्णं वर्षसहस्त्रं मे विषयासक्तचेतसः।
तथाप्यनुदिनं तृष्णा ममैतेष्वभिजायते।। आदि ८५.१५।।
तस्मादेनामहं त्यक्त्वा ब्रह्मण्याधाय मानसम्।
निर्द्वन्द्वो निर्ममो भूत्वा चरिष्यामि मृगैः सह।। आदि ८५.१६।।
In the pleasures of the physical senses I have spent complete one thousand years. Even then my 'thirst' for them rises every day.[79]
Therefore, giving it up, I shall henceforth live, with the deer of the forest, a life of the mind, inquiring into the ultimate reality of the universe.[80]

Saying this, he anoints his youngest son Puru, born of Sharmishṭhā, to be the next king,[81] and retires from the world. But not before giving his son sage counsel on the foundations of good governance and what his conduct as king ought to be.[82]

Among several other things, through the dramatic story of Yayāti, the *Mahābhārata* is teaching us the truth that desire *alone* cannot be the basis of the man–woman relationship. In saying 'Let one renounce the thirst of desire', what is being also suggested is that one should abandon the mistaken notion that satisfaction of desire is all what erotic love is.

(b) The *Mahābhārata* conveys at the same time another truth. Not only can the man–woman relationship not be limited to the satisfaction of desire *alone*, but also that erotic love, in order to be truly erotic, requires a sense of *togetherness, sam-bhoga, which has the meaning of 'enjoying together, experiencing together.'* And togetherness requires a sense of direction, *dishā*, as well. If a person is to live a sane life, then his, and her, perceptions of the man–woman relationship have to be those of *togetherness*, *saha*, *with a direction, dishā*. The story of Ashṭāvakra and Uttara-Dishā[83] conveys this truth.

In the earlier part of the *Anushāsana-parva*, a conversation between Yudhishṭhira and Bhīshma is narrated, which is about the foundation of marriage. It begins with a question, raised by Yudhishṭhira.

'What is this *saha-dharma*, the ordering of life together, which binds man and woman in marriage? To me, it appears doubtful whether there is any such thing.

When one of them dies, does anything of *saha-dharma* remain in the one who lives?

Besides, when men and women have many different natures, different temperaments; are obliged by various circumstances to live at two different places, then how can there be between them this togetherness, this *saha-dharma*?

Some of the lawgivers are of the firm opinion that women are given to untruth. If that is true, then how can one living with a woman live with her in *dharma* together?

Since one reads even in the Veda that women are given to untruth, it follows that their untruth must form part of *saha-dharma*: but untruth can never be a part of *dharma*. It seems to me, therefore, that *saha-dharma* is nothing more than a secondary attribute of marriage; and what husband and wife do together is given the name *dharma* on purely functional grounds.

The more I think about it, the more does this subject appear to me highly complex. Can you throw some light on this subject?[84]

Bhīshma then narrates the story of Ashṭāvakra and Uttara-Dishā. Ashṭāvakra was born deformed, bent in eight joints. That was the result when, his mother still carrying him, he corrected his father, a great scholar, on the pronunciation of a certain word, which his father was pronouncing wrongly. Greatly angered at the gross impertinence of one not even born yet, he cursed the child to be born 'crooked in eight places'. Hence his name *Ashṭa-vakra*. Later he is made whole. Now himself a scholar of great repute, he wants to marry Suprabhā, the daughter of the sage Vadānya. She is incomparable in beauty; is endowed with great character, with charm no less; and she had stolen the heart of Ashṭāvakra. Her father wants to make certain that Ashṭāvakra is truly worthy of his daughter. Vadānya lists the qualities a man must have, so as to be deserving of his daughter. He must have no other woman in his life; must not be living abroad; must be learned, of pleasant speech, highly respected, brave, good mannered, capable of enjoying the pleasures, and in looks handsome.[85] As if all these were not sufficient for a man to claim a woman's hand, Vadānya plans to subject Ashṭāvakra to a further test of character. 'I will certainly give my daughter in marriage to you, but first you make a journey northward where you will meet a person,' Vadānya says to him vaguely.

'But where exactly in the north must I go? Who is it that I should meet?' Ashṭāvakra asks him.

The father then charts the precise, but long and complicated, route that the young man should take. 'To Alkāpurī, the home of Kubera, in the Himalayas. In going beyond it, you will cross the Himalaya, and reach Kailāsha, the home of Shiva. Turning north-east, you will see another mountain, called Mahāparshva, where the four seasons, the day and the night, the Time, the human nature and also what is divine, live in their embodied forms. Go beyond them: and you will enter into a deep blue forest. There, in that land of enchantment, you will meet a woman, who is old and impressive and a teacher. After you have met her, showing her all the marks of respect and adoration, come back; and you will marry my daughter. If this condition is acceptable to you, Ashṭāvakra, start right now.'[86]

Ashṭāvakra had set his heart on Suprabhā so much that he would have accepted any condition, and leaves on the journey prescribed by Vadānya.

Eventually he arrives at his destination, a mansion worthy of the gods, and is welcomed by *seven* glorious young girls, one more beautiful than the other, who usher him inside. There, in a hall, he sees an old woman, seated on a beautifully carved bed, and she welcomes him most warmly. It was already night, and she asks all the girls there to leave, excepting one. And then begins the story. After conversing with her for a while, Ashṭāvakra says to the old woman: 'It is already late in the night, you go to sleep, too.' And he himself goes to another bed, kept near her own.

Not long thereafter, the old woman climbs on to the bed on which the young man was trying to sleep, pretending that she was feeling cold. He is still polite and courteous to her. Her arrival in his bed is followed soon by her embracing him close. Ashṭāvakra remains unresponsive and cold, as if he were only a piece of dried wood. Looking unhappy,

The Woman (*to Ashṭāvakra*)

> In the proximity of a man, a woman desires nothing but erotic union. Driven by sexual impulse, I've come to you. Accept me. The moment I saw you, I felt irresistibly drawn. My riches and all that you see here, whatever I have, are yours, and I, too, am yours. We will enjoy all the pleasures of life. I will satisfy all your desires. Of that, you need have no doubt![87]

Ashṭāvakra

> Of these things I have but little knowledge. I swear, I intend marrying someone I love, the daughter of a sage. Moreover, I shall not touch a woman who is another's and earn a demerit thereby.[88]

The Woman

> In taking me, you would earn no demerit whatever, for I am nobody's woman, I am independent. I truly say to you that I am independent, I am free. And should our sexual union invite demerit, let that come to *me*. And can't you see that I am trembling with sexual desire for you?[89]

What Ashṭāvakra saw, most of all, was that she was old, and terribly ugly and repulsive. And he felt great compassion for her. The night passed, and the day; and he still thought, 'What could have made her so repulsive? The deity of this magnificent palace, and yet so ugly? A curse, maybe? Must I ask her? But no, I must not transgress into her secret.'[90]

While pressing her attention, the woman was pronouncing, too, upon the innate nature of woman, in words that had in them neither shame nor self-reproach, just plain speech.

ब्रह्मन्नकामतोऽन्यास्ति स्त्रीणां पुरुषतो धृतिः ।। अनुशासन १९.८० ।।
To women, nothing is more desirable than the company of a man.[91]

आत्मच्छन्देन वर्तन्ते नार्यो मन्मथचोदिताः ।। अनुशासन १९.८७ ।।
न च दह्यन्ति गच्छन्तयः सुतप्तैरपि पांसुभिः ।
Driven by sexual desire, they do whatever they want to do. They can walk on burning sand, but their feet will not burn thereby.[92]

नानिलोऽग्निर्न वरुणो न चान्ये त्रिदशा द्विज ।। अनुशासन १९.९१ ।।
प्रियाःस्त्रीणां यथा कामो रतिशीला हि योषितः ।

सहस्त्रे किल नारीणां प्राप्येतैका कदाचन ।। अनुशासन १९.९२ ।।
तथा शतसहस्त्रेषु यदि क्वाचित् पतिव्रता ।
Nothing, no other god, is more desired by women than Kāma. By their very nature, women seek sexual pleasure and that alone. There will not be one, among a hundred women, who is not greedy for sexual pleasure; nor one, among a hundred thousand, who is faithful.[93]

नैता जानन्ति पितरं न कुलं न च मातरम् ।। अनुशासन १९.९३ ।।
न भ्रातन् न च भर्तारं न च पुत्रान् न देवरान् ।
लीलार्यन्त्यः कुलं घ्नन्ति कूलानीव सरिद्वराः ।। अनुशासन १९.९४ ।।
Then they know neither father, nor family, nor mother. They regard neither brother, nor husband, nor children. Driven by their desire, they break the limits of family, even as the great rivers overflow their own banks.[94]

स्थविराणामपि स्त्रीणां बाधते मैथुनज्वरः ।। अनुशासन २१.५ ।।
Why, as you have seen, the fever of sexual desire burns even old women.[95]

Hearing this mindless denigration of women, Ashṭāvakra asks her to hold her tongue. But he is still kind to her. The old woman was so terribly ugly, besides, that the more he looked at her, the more repulsed he felt. But he felt also sorry for her.

The next morning, she bathed him, and served him with food that was almost ambrosia, and he felt he could not have enough of it. In the night, she approached him again, saying: 'I am hungry for an erotic union with you. Can't you see how much I want it from you? Accept me.' By now she had transformed herself into a dazzlingly beautiful young woman. Greatly perplexed by these happenings, but keeping control over himself,

Ashṭāvakra (*to the woman*)

Look, I have no inclination towards you. I honestly say that I am in love with the daughter of a sage and I want to marry her. Peace be with you, and leave me alone.

By now he was also certain of being tested by the sage Vadānya. 'Earlier she was an old woman; and now a young girl, in magnificent clothes and jewels! It is a great wonder, how did this transformation take place?' When the day breaks, he says to the woman: 'Who are you? Please tell me the truth.'

The Woman (*to Ashṭāvakra*)

Know me as North Direction, *Uttara-Dishā*. Yes, it is true that the sage Vadānya had sent you to me, for you to learn what is of the greatest importance in the man–woman relationship. Wherever men and women live, their *proximity* itself creates sexual desire. And you saw that *maithuna jvara*, sexual fever, can wreck an old woman no less. But you were self-controlled throughout, and steadfast in your love for the girl you want to marry. May you two be happy in the togetherness of *dharma*. Only he who has disciplined his self is worthy of a woman, and can be happy.[96]

On returning from his journey that was full of insights, Ashṭāvakra marries Suprabhā, and establishes for all time to come the man–woman relationship as a state of *saha-dharma*. *Togetherness, with a sense of direction, dishā*. It is not a function of physical proximity alone. Uttara-Dishā had deliberately mounted her reckless denigration of women with a view to testing whether Ashṭāvakra would permanently be discouraged. His self-control consisted in being neither distracted by physical proximity nor discouraged by stupid notions about women.

The *Mahābhārata* avoids alike the feverish pursuit of sexual pleasure and abjuring it altogether. In the one, there is neither rest nor satisfaction; in the other, only harm. To steer clear of all excess, of physical enjoyment and of ascetic denial alike, sexual pleasure is given a decided place: within the institution of marriage. Having understood sex from all sides, it was assigned its own 'place' and 'time', but no more. Wild and free, like the raging fire in the forest, sexual energy could destroy everything; given bounds, it could be wholesome and creative, like the fire in the hearth. Hence, *kāma* subject to *dharma.*

In a final movement, all the three, *dharma*, *artha* and *kāma*, are then made dependent upon woman as wife.[97] Being the other half of man, the wife is declared to be *the protector* of wealth, of human body, of society, of social order, of heaven, and even of ancestors.[98]

That established, distance is made an essential factor in keeping sexual interest in the *other* alive. Distance, and not crippling intimacy, has been the most noticeable aspect of the dharmic view of the man–woman relationship. The dharmic man had acquired the wisdom that indifference or hatred is the ultimate fruit of unrelieved intimacy.

Possession of the mind

It is through the story of Vipula and Ruchi, the young wife of his guru Devasharmā, that the *Mahābhārata* conveys even a subtler truth—that sexuality is not of the body alone but of the mind even more. Hence the possession of the *other's* mind can be quite as much a 'sexual' act as the possession of the *other's* body.[99] *Kāma* is psychic energy above all.

Ruchi was indescribably beautiful, so resplendent in her youth and beauty that even the gods desired her, *Indra*, most of all. The sage Devasharmā knew it all. He knew the natural inclinations of women, as he knew what Indra was like; therefore, he was even more vigilant about his wife.[100] Obliged to participate in a sacrificial rite at a place far away, he had at the same time his anxiety about the protection of his wife from Indra; he entrusts this task to Vipula, his student, staying with the guru at his hermitage. After cautioning Vipula that Indra was such an accomplished trickster besides that he could at will assume any form in order to deceive others,[101] he left, saying to Vipula: 'Protect my wife from Indra who is like a dog wanting to lick what remains of the offerings at a *yajña.*'[102]

Indra was waiting just for that moment. Soon thereafter he entered the hermitage, looking exceedingly attractive, and burning with desire for Ruchi. Meanwhile, Vipula had reflected deeply on the situation. 'In what way can I protect my guru's wife, for I have heard that, besides being cunning, Indra is very strong, too? Even if one closed all the doors and windows of the house, it may still be impossible to prevent Indra's entry, for he could make himself invisible and enter somehow. I am not strong enough to challenge him physically in any case. I will protect Ruchi by means of my psychic powers instead. I will enter her body and occupy her inner space, and control her responses. There is no other way in which I can protect her from being taken by Indra. In doing so, I myself will do no wrong; for just as a wayfarer occupies for a while a room in an inn, I will occupy her inner space without touching her in any way, myself free of desire.'[103] Resolving to adopt that method, Vipula engages Ruchi in telling her many stories. And after he had made her feel comfortable with him, he looks deeply into her eyes, and uniting the light of his eyes with hers, and her mouth with his mouth, he enters her being, like wind.[104] Thus possessing psychically her inner space, he begins to reside there, Ruchi completely unaware of what had happened.[105]

When Indra entered the hermitage, Ruchi was astonished by the appearance of a resplendently handsome man, and wanted to welcome him, not knowing who he was. But she could not move, for Vipula, sensing her own desire to respond to the visitor, had her completely motionless. In a most endearing speech, Indra said to her: 'I am Indra, the lord of gods, and I have come here for *you*. My desire for you is so very great that it is almost a pain. Come to me, waste no more time.'[106] But held by the psychic force of Vipula inside her, she could neither say what she wanted to, that she was open to his urging, nor could she move towards him. Instead, Vipula changed her intended words of warm welcome into the cold words of inquiry as to 'the purpose of his visit there'. At the same time as she felt unhappy in saying those cold words, Indra, too, quickly saw the changed expression in her eyes, as if being prompted by someone else. By his own powers he now saw Vipula inside her, as one would one's reflection in a mirror.[107] And he began to tremble with fear. Leaving Ruchi's inner space, Vipula emerged only to confront Indra and chastise him in the strongest of language.[108] 'If I wish, I could burn you to ashes; but, out of my kindness, I will let you go. Never attempt any such thing again. Not only do you not have any control over your reckless sexual passions, you are a fool as well. For you do not seem to know the fire of an ascetic's anger. Go away from here the way you came.'[109] Without speaking a word, Indra hastened to depart.

When Devasharmā returned, Vipula narrated to him the happenings, and that he was able to protect Ruchi from Indra's sexual advances. In return he received from his guru words of the greatest praise and blessings. *But Vipula kept from him the knowledge of the method that he had adopted in order to protect his wife—of possessing her psychically and controlling thereby her openness to Indra's sexual urgings.*[110]

With the blessings of his guru, Vipula leaves the hermitage and devotes himself to greater austerities and, in the process, acquires even greater psychic powers. That made him full of self-pride and even arrogance, imagining that he had now mastered the universe.[111] In one of his wanderings one day into a deep forest, he saw a man and a woman in a sexual embrace, holding each other by their hands and moving in a rhythmic circle like a potter's wheel. Soon the couple began to quarrel. One was saying to the other 'You are moving too fast'; and the other saying 'No, no, *you* are moving too fast.' Then looking at Vipula, they said to each other: 'Of the two of us, whoever is speaking falsely would meet the same fate as destined for this Vipula in his life hereafter.'[112] On hearing this, Vipula felt exceedingly distressed, saying to himself: 'If some dreadful fate awaits me, then what good have these austerities brought me? What great offence could I have committed?'[113]

Thereafter he saw six men playing the game of dice, the dice made of silver and gold. They, too, looking at him, were saying: 'Whoever among us should try to cheat in this game would meet the same fate that is destined for Vipula in his life hereafter.'[114] Feeling distressed even more, as if he were thrown into a burning fire, he began to reflect upon his whole life, but could find in it nothing that was blameworthy. 'Could it be that the *means* I had adopted in protecting Ruchi were the offence? In filling her with my subtle presence, my physical body united with hers, organ with organ, I had possessed her as well. Could *that* have been the offence? And also I withheld that truth from my guru.'[115] He concluded that *that*, indeed, was the offence; which was also the truth.[116] And Vipula fell into a deep depression.

In that state of mind, visiting Devasharmā soon thereafter, Vipula learns from him that the couple he had encountered in the forest was *Day* and *Night*, who move in a circular movement as in a wheel, and who knew him intimately, even as they knew Ruchi intimately. And the six men playing the game of dice were *the six seasons*; and they, too, were the 'witnesses' of one's innermost being, of the good and the bad alike that one does even when no one else is a witness to them.[117]

न मां कश्चिद् विजानीत इति कृत्वा न विश्वसेत्।
नरो रहसि पापात्मा पापकं कर्म वै द्विज।। अनुशासन ४३.६।।

कुर्वाणं हि नरं कर्म पापं रहसि सर्वदा।
पश्यन्ति ऋतवश्चापि तथा दिननिशेऽप्युत।। अनुशासन ४३.७।।

Doing something wrong unnoticed by others, let no one think that what he is doing is going unnoticed altogether.[118]

The wrongs that one does are being witnessed by day and night and by the six seasons always.[119]

Devasharmā (*to Vipula*)

This is what they were conveying to you directly. For in your pride and self-congratulation you had begun to entertain also the notion that you were wholly free from any blemish; when, in fact, your entering Ruchi's body and concealing that fact from me were both grievously wrong.[120]

At the same time, it was not within your ordinary power to protect a woman intoxicated with herself. You did no wrong intentionally. And I have love and affection for you.[121]

Had I seen impure intent in what you did, I would have cursed you without regret. Women feel drawn towards men, as men do towards women: had there been in your mind any other thought towards her than that of protecting her, you would have incurred my curse no doubt. You protected my wife, and I have love and affection for you, my son. May the blessings of good health and heavens be with you.[122]

This is a very complex story. It is saying many different things at the same time, as all stories of human emotions do, and can thus be read in many different ways. In the first place, Vipula was protecting Ruchi from *herself*. For in certain situations, those of the workings of sexual impulse especially, the greater dangers are from one's self than they are from the *other*, because those dangers are far more subtle. But it is not always so. Quite as often the dangers are from the *other*, and they come in different forms, which at first sight may not seem to be dangers at all. Hence the need of protection, just as from one's own self, so from the *other*. But the act of protecting may as well become a means of exercising power over the one being protected. It often does, but not *always*. Whether, in any given case, it is the one or the other can be judged only in the light of the nature of the relationship itself, which may sometimes be judged wrongly.

The main point of the story is not that of protection, but one of possessing the inner being of the *other* so completely that its *psychic intimacy is infinitely greater than any physical intimacy can ever be.* Its implications are so very dangerous that the story itself, and through it the *Mahābhārata*, declares it clearly to be a great offence. Vipula was exonerated by the husband, whose wife's inner space he had filled by his psychic presence, but only after taking into account the purity of his motives. That makes the point that motives are to be understood in judging acts. But, equally important, it suggests that, independent of motives, acts themselves set up a logic that runs its own course. Therefore, the means are as important as the ends. Above all, to withhold an inner truth, while recounting truthfully the outward facts, may turn the whole thing into a lie.

Kāma subject to *dharma*

Finally, what does the *Mahābhārata* mean in suggesting that *kāma*, like *artha*, be subject to *dharma*?[123] We saw the meaning of *dharma* in its three main attributes. *Prabhava*, which means 'nurturing, cherishing, providing more amply, prospering, increasing, enhancing'. *Dhārana*, which means 'supporting, sustaining, bringing together, upholding'. And *ahiṃsā*, which means 'not to do violence to another's being'. This is what the togetherness in *kāma* should achieve even in erotic terms, which will be *saha-kāma*.

Conversely, whatever has the characteristic of depriving, starving, diminishing, debasing, degrading, separating, uprooting, hurting, and doing violence to the inner space and rhythms of the other, is *adharma*, the negation of *dharma*. The very first thing it destroys is the erotic impulse. However, it is also true that the greater the degradation, and the greater the hurting and the violence, the more thrilling is the sexual experience *for some people*. But there, it is not the sexual experience that is primary, but the thrill of degrading oneself and the *other*, and of doing violence to both. In other words, debasing, degrading, reducing, hurting and doing violence can be for some people an experience akin to sexuality.

Similarly, seduction is where there is no relationship, even of mutual sexual pleasure, but where the aim is to employ sexual power to reduce and degrade the other, and then depart. This truth the *Mahābhārata* conveys through numerous stories of seduction, where the irresistible lure of sexuality is a means to securing some end other than pleasure. And all seductions are depressingly alike.

There is also in sex 'selling' and 'buying', both in their actual and metaphorical meaning, sexuality, not as relationship, but as a transaction, a human being as a commodity. In the voice of Bhīshma, the *Mahābhārata* says:

> यो मनुष्यः स्वकं पुत्रं विक्रीय धनमिच्छति।
> कन्यां वा जीवितार्थाय यः शुल्केन प्रयच्छति।। अनुशासन ४५.१८।।
>
> सप्तावरे महाघोरे निरये कालसाह्वये।
> स्वेदं मूत्रं पुरीषं च तस्मिन् मूढः समश्नुते।। अनुशासन ४५.१८।।
>
> *The man who, by selling his son wishes to obtain money, and, by selling his daughter, earns a living, is destined for the darkest of all hells.*[124]
>
> अन्योऽप्यथ न विक्रेयो मनष्यः किं पुनः प्रजाः।
> अधर्ममूलैर्हि धनैस्तैर्न धर्मोऽथ कश्चन।। अनुशासन ४५.२३।।
>
> *No human being should be sold, what to say of selling one's own children. Where money is had through means of* adharma, *there nothing can be enhancing.*[125]

The force of erotic impulse is to be subject, most of all, to *a-parigraha*, which has the meaning of 'not encircling, not engulfing, not imprisoning'. For the most part, sexual energy comes to be used as a weapon of power over the *other*. Man and woman encircle, engulf, overpower, and imprison each other in the world of sexuality; which must, in the end, produce its own violence and ill-being; whereas *sam-bhoga* implies a deeper experience of *togetherness* between man and woman in a way that without the *other* the self is incomplete. In saying that *kāma* be subject to *dharma*, the *Mahābhārata* is teaching that the sense of the sacredness of the *other* shall always remain the emotional foundation of sexual pleasure and happiness.[126]

In brief,

> अर्थश्चात्यर्थलुब्धस्य कामश्चातिप्रसङ्गिणः।। शल्य ६०.२१।।
> धर्मार्थौ धर्मकामौ च कामार्थौ चाप्यपीडयन्।
>
> धर्मार्थमानान् योऽभ्येति सोऽत्यन्तं सुखमश्नुते।। शल्य ६०.२२।।
>
> *The* artha *of the excessively greedy, and the* kāma *of the one obsessed with it—both these do injury to* dharma.

The one who does no injury to dharma *and material well-being by obsessive sexuality; or to sexuality and* dharma *by the obsessive greed for wealth; or to material well-being and sexual impulse by* dharma *misconceived; but enjoys them together, in their inner harmony, gains the greatest happiness of all.*[127]

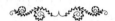

CHAPTER TWELVE

Grihastha and *Grihiṇī*, the Householder; *Grihastha-āshrama*, Life-in-family

- Family as a stage in life
- The highest place for the householder and the family
- Obligations and duties, and 'the three debts'
- Not obligations and duties alone, also *feelings*
- The place of the wife in the life-in-family
- The place of the mother in the life-in-family
- Conversations between husband and wife as part of family life
- Life-in-family in the larger context of life

There has been the *anthropology* of family; the *sociology* of family; and the *political ideology* of family. Their outcome is the enormous amount of modern literature on the structure of the family and family relationships in different societies. The most painstaking studies by anthropologists and sociologists have contributed to modern knowledge concerning the family. What it has brought into focus at the same time is the question of the *methodology* employed by them in studying the family, especially in those societies described as 'primitive' or 'tribal'. Can one understand people other than one's own in the same way that a geologist would determine the age of earth and stone? The question of *methodology* has itself produced, in anthropology and sociology, as in philosophy and the study of history, literature full of argument and contention. It is also, in the first two disciplines, about the seeing of the *other* from the presuppositions, of one kind or the other, that the observer carries as a part of his, or her, own cultural baggage. The writings of the political ideologists of different persuasions have added passion and heat to the debate between those who perceive family from the eye of tradition and those who see it as the playground of gender bias and exploitation. There are considerable differences, though, even among them—the difference being equally in the degree of heat and passion in their writings. But can it honestly be said that they have added anything that is truly universal about the family, in the light of which a human being can *reorder* one's relationship to the family, and the relationship of the family to the society, in a way that enhances human worth?

What is truly universal must also be a matter of foundations. In discussing the life of the householder, the *griha-stha*, 'the one living in family', the *Mahābhārata* is concerned with the foundations of family life everywhere as a human attribute. In that, as in everything else concerning the human being, it clearly breaks away from the world of the earliest of the *dharmasūtra*-s, and from their lust for legislation. There was perhaps no other area of human living than the life of the householder to which the lawgivers, the *shāstri*-s, devoted their attention more. That attention reached a point of legislative insanity. It can be seen in the *details* of the prescribed rituals that filled the daily life of a householder, from the time he awoke to the time he went to sleep, and filled his entire life, from the moment he was born till the moment of his death. Although even a brief look at those details is necessary for an adequate understanding of the shāstric mind, I propose not to describe them here; for they will occupy almost this entire volume. They are to be found in Pandurang Vaman Kane's authoritative *History of Dharmasastra (Ancient and Mediaeval Religious and Civil Law)*.[1]

Those details tell us what the lawgivers would have the householder do; and exactly *how*; and precisely *when*; and strictly *where*. And if he did what was forbidden, and did not do what was enjoined, or did not do it in the manner prescribed, or did it even one time less than the number of times prescribed, then what he must do in expiation thereof. And then followed the legislation on the *how*, and the *when*, and the *where* of the acts of expiation as well—in the minutest detail.

After we have travelled through the shāstric legislation on the householder and family, and have breathed in the air it had created, we can clearly draw the following picture in the main, and contrast it straightaway with the picture that emerges in the *Mahābhārata*.

1. In the shāstric schemes for human life, everything, *everything*, was classified and divided into numerous groups, which were of course created artificially. Not only did the *dharmashāstra*-s divide people into different castes, which themselves arose from a most intricate caste calculus, but also families in each *varṇa* on one basis or another. For example, the brāhmaṇa-s were classified into four groups, depending upon the different ways in which they earned their livelihood. And not human beings alone were classified. The rituals prescribed for them were similarly classified, those that were to be observed by them daily and were to be conducted at different times of their lives. If they were done in *this* way, they were called *that*; if done in *that* way, *this*. On the difference between *this* and *that*, or whether there should be any difference at all, there were different opinions among the lawgivers, which gave rise to intricate discussions, occupying the *shāstri*-s quite as much as the rituals occupied the householder.

   The *Mahābhārata* is concerned that every person overcomes *divisions*—divisions within the self, and the divisions between the self and the *other*, created by wrong perceptions of the self and of the *other* and of the relation between the two. Not rituals but overcoming self-division; not prescriptions but self-knowledge; not the artificial complexities but the simplicity of life; are the *Mahābhārata*'s concerns for the individual, for 'the one living in family', *griha-stha*, above all.

2. One main concern of the lawgivers everywhere has been to protect and perpetuate a given social structure. That was the case with the *dharmashāstra*-s as well. Towards that end, life-in-family was to be regulated and controlled; here by means of ritualistic legislation first. The daily rituals, if they were followed to their last prescribed detail, must have so exhausted the householder that little mental energy was left to look at one's social contexts critically. The energy of self-knowledge, when the self is not separated from the social, can be quite subversive. For it is the energy of asking questions in the first place.

   The philosophic inquiry into the human condition, as in the *Upanishad*-s, and so in the *Mahābhārata*, had released the immense mental and spiritual energy inherent in every human individual. In the *Mahābhārata*, that energy is directed, for example, towards examining the foundations of law and governance equally with the inquiry into the nature of the Self. And in that inquiry, the *grihastha*-s, the householders, men and women alike, occupy a prominent place. The seers of the *Upanishad*-s, most of them at any rate, were householders. What is described is the outcome of their daily mental and spiritual life. What rituals they followed are not mentioned, for in the life of the spirit, in one's inner journey, ritual acts are of no importance at all. It was decidedly on that point, among many others, that the *Upanishad*-s were a radical turning away. The air one breathes in the *Upanishad*-s and in the *Mahābhārata* is not the air of prescribed rituals but the liberating air of self-awareness.

3. Life in the family everywhere is lived through *feelings*—of love, caring, and gratitude mostly, but, because feelings are also problematic, disregard, hurt, envy, aggression, and hatred as well. And feelings are not rituals. No amount of washing one's hands can either create love or wash off hatred. Nor can they be commanded by legislation. The chief concern of the *dharmashāstra*-s was with the outward ritualistic *acts* prescribed for the householder, and not with *feelings* that nourish life in the family. The range of the former touches the fantastic; the stock of the latter is poor, or very nearly absent.

The *Mahābhārata* concentrates on *relationships* and not on ritualistic *acts*.[2] It is a systematic inquiry into the foundations of relationships, personal *and* social, which support, sustain, and enhance life: their *dharma*. It is therefore at the same time an inquiry also into what uproots, degrades, and does violence to life: the *adharma* of relationships, their 'disorder'.

4. Underlying most rituals and rites was the notion of 'impurity' or 'pollution'. Taking possession of the shāstric mind to an almost pathological degree, the idea of pollution pervaded at once the *dharmashāstra*-s and the householder in every single act. Certain kinds of human beings were polluting. Certain occasions were polluting. And certain places were polluting. There were intricate discussions as to the degree of pollution attached to each. The touch of a *shudra* was polluting, although, according to some *dharmashāstra*-s, not always. The touch of a woman in her menstruating period, *rajasvalā*, mother or wife or sister or daughter, was polluting. The touch of a widow, even her very presence on happy occasions, was polluting. Birth, the act of eating, and death were the three main occasions in a family when the obsession with the idea of pollution found its fullest force. The prescribed rituals and rites for the whole family at the time of a birth or a death in the family cover a large part of every *dharmashāstra*. Impurities were to be removed by purificatory baths and other rites spread over many days. Concerning them there were many intricate and learned discussions. Instead of four baths, will three not do?

The *Upanishad*-s, and especially the *Mahābhārata*, draw our attention to the real and not imaginary impurities of life: the impurities of the mind and the heart. They teach us that no human being is impure; nor is any occasion impure; nor is any place impure. Greed, anger, deviousness, arrogance, and untruth are the sources of all pollution, which reside in man's heart. And those can be removed, not by taking ritual baths, or by ritual rites, but only by self-knowledge and self-discipline. This does not mean that the *Mahābhārata* is against keeping one's body thoroughly clean, which is undoubtedly a good habit. It only means that one may be thoroughly clean in one's body and yet may be thoroughly unclean in one's relationship with one's self and with the *other*. Neither does it mean that the *dharmashāstra*-s were wholly unmindful of keeping one's mind and heart also clean in a relational sense.

The issue was the rituality of *acts* turning into a belief that ritual acts and rites themselves, if done exactly as legislated, were sufficient foundations of a happy life; and that belief turning *meaning* itself into something purely ritualistic.

Therefore, the *Mahābhārata* gives to the idea of *shaucha*, 'cleanness', 'purity', as to everything else in life, a deeply relational meaning, away from its rituality. 'Of all the places of pilgrimage, *tīrtha*, one's heart is the highest; of all the purities, *shuchi*, the purity of the heart the greatest.'[3]

तीर्थानां हृदयं तीर्थं शुचीनां हृदयं शुचिः ।। शान्ति १९३.१८ ।।

Family as a stage in life

Man's life was divided into the familiar 'four stages', or *āshrama*. *Brahmacharya*, a period of study; *grihastha*, a time for raising a family; *vānaprastha*, a time for freedom from the cares of the family, and for reflection on the higher concerns of life; which literally means 'moving towards the forest'; and, finally, *sannyāsa*, the time for total withdrawal from the world. If people were taught to honour those in the stage of *vānaprastha*, and the stage of *sannyāsa* was in certain circles considered the apotheosis of life, it was 'the life in family', *grihastha-āshrama*, that was without question the most important.[4] Family was considered to be the support of the other three. Both Gautama and Baudhayāna, the authors of the earliest of the *dharmasūtra*-s, were greatly in favour of the householder. There is, they said, only one *āshrama*, that of the householder; to them, none other was more important.[5] If there were some, like Bādarāyaṇa, who would that a person went through his life in an orderly progression of the four *āshrama*-s;[6] there were others, like Manu, Vasishṭha, Vishnu and Daksha, who looked upon the family as the nucleus of social order.[7] Kane concludes: 'On the whole the tendency of most of the *Dharmasastra* works is to glorify the status of a householder and push into the background the two *āshramas* of vānaprastha and sannyāsa.'[8]

On this subject there was, however, a great deal of conflict. Asceticism and the figure of an ascetic have always had to the Indian mind an irresistible attraction. The lawgivers were concerned with the potentially disruptive effect of asceticism on social progress, *loka-yātrā*, and hence, so far as they were concerned, legislation for the life of an ascetic as well, to keep it within bounds. And that legislation was as thoroughgoing in its range, of rituals and rites, as was the legislation for the life of the householder. The concerns of the *Mahābhārata* are very different. Consistent with its *method* in reflecting upon the human condition, which I have described elsewhere, the *Mahābhārata* first narrates, at its strongest, a prevalent view; and then shows how very limited it is, or how very mistaken. Both are done, not in the abstract, but in the light of the concrete situations of human living. Thus, it narrates the two hardy notions of *tyāga*, or 'giving up', 'renouncing', 'leaving', and *tapas*, 'austerity', underlying the argument for renouncing the family in the service of a supposed higher spiritual goal; and then gives them a radically inner meaning. Before moving on to the *Mahābhārata*'s advocacy of life-in-family as the most important state for the individual and for society alike, let us have a quick look at what it says *tyāga* truly is, and what it is not.

The context is the crisis in the family of the Pāṇḍavas created by the decision of the eldest brother, Yudhishṭhira, to renounce everything and walk, alone, on the path of total withdrawal from the world. That is because, he says, he is so appalled by the enormous destruction of human lives in the War that they have just won against their first cousins, and have reclaimed the kingdom that was justly always theirs, that he sees no meaning in what was gained at such cost.[9] He advances the familiar rationale of renunciation.

कुशलाकुशलान्येके कृत्वा कर्माणि मानवाः ।
कार्यकारणसंश्लिष्टं स्वजनं नाम विभ्रति ।। शान्ति ९.३० ।।
आयुषोऽन्ते प्रहायेदं क्षीणप्राणं कलेवरम् ।
प्रतिगृह्याति तत् पापं कर्तुः कर्मफलं हि तत् ।। शान्ति ९.३१ ।।
Tied with their relatives due to the workings of cause and effect, human beings take care of them well or not so well. In either case, at the time of one's death one reaps the consequences of one's own acts, good or bad.[10]

एवं संसारचक्रेऽस्मिन् व्याविद्धे रथचक्रवत् ।
समेति भूतग्रामोऽयं भूतग्रामेण कार्यवान् ।। शान्ति ९.३२ ।।
The world moving like a wheel, human beings in it meet each other for definite reasons.[11]

जन्ममृत्युजराव्याधिवेदनाभिरभिद्रुतम् ।
अपारमिव चास्वस्थं संसारं त्यजतः सुखम् ।। शान्ति ९.३३ ।।
In this world, one is constantly assailed by birth, death, old age, diseases,

and by pain. Only he is happy who renounces this seemingly endless world.[12]

दिव: पतत्सु देवेषु स्थानेभ्यश्च महर्षिषु ।
को हि नाम भवेनार्थी भवेत् कारणतत्त्ववित् ।। शान्ति ९.३४ ।।

The gods fall from their heavens; the sages fall from their high stature. Then why would anyone, knowing the workings of cause and effect, want to have anything to do with this world?[13]

Yudhishṭhira, who would now be emperor, extols the many philosophic virtues of the life of a mendicant instead, and announces his resolve to live that way hereafter. It is in the conversations between him and his four brothers, and between him and his wife, that follow his announcement,[14] that the *Mahābhārata* lifts 'renunciation' and 'austerity', *tyāga* and *tapas*, from their meaning as only outward ritualistic *acts*, to their ethical relational meaning.

Angered firstly by what he regards as the complete irrationality of his elder brother's resolve to renounce, and not just because of his mistaken notions of 'renunciation', Bhīma speaks to him thus, clearly with contempt.

Bhīma

You don't seem to understand the true meaning of anything, just as the intelligence of a vedic scholar who keeps only chanting the *mantra*-s is dimmed and destroyed thereby. If you wanted to live the lazy life of a mendicant, then why did you engage yourself and *us* in this dreadful war? After our victory, you talk of *renunciation*. It is like a person travelling long with a certain aim and desire, turning back just when he has reached his destination. Or it will be like a person killing himself as well, after killing his enemies. Or it will be like a hungry person not eating when he gets the food. Or like a person burning with sexual desire, not touching the woman he had desired when he gets her. Had we known earlier that you wanted to renounce the world, we would not have engaged in this cruel war. Like you, we also would have till our last days lived as beggars and mendicants. The truth is that here we ourselves are to be blamed—for following you, because you are our eldest brother, but a man with little intelligence.[15]

Bhīma continues:

शक्यं पुनररण्येषु सुखमेकेन जीवितुम् ।
अबिभ्रता पुत्रपौत्रान् देवर्षीनतिथीन् पितॄन् ।। शान्ति १०.२२ ।।

Only he who is incapable of providing for his children and grandchildren, and cannot offer hospitality to the guests who come, can live by himself happily in a forest.[16]

शक्यं तु मौनमास्थाय बिभ्रताऽऽत्मानमात्मना ।
धर्मच्छद्मं समास्थाय च्यवितुं न तु जीवितुम् ।। शान्ति १०.२१ ।।

But, under the guise of dharma, *observing silence and filling only one's own stomach, without having to take care of others, is only to fall from one's duties, not to live a worthy life.*[17]

नेमे मृगा: स्वर्गजितो न वराहा न पक्षिण: ।
अथान्येन प्रकारेण पुण्यमाहुर्न तं जना: ।। शान्ति १०.२३ ।।

Living in forests, neither the antelopes, nor the pigs, nor the birds, have ascended to Heaven. Merit is gained by other means, not by living in the forest alone.

यदि संन्यासत: सिद्धिं राजा कश्चिदवाप्नुयात् ।
पर्वताश्च द्रुमाश्चैव क्षिप्रं सिद्धिमवाप्नुयु: ।। शान्ति १०.२४ ।।

If a king were to achieve life's highest by taking to sannyāsa *and living in a forest, then the hills and the trees there would, too, quickly.*[18]

On the question 'what is true renunciation?', the *Mahābhārata* suggests, in the voice of Nakula, the other brother of Yudhishṭhira:

वित्तानि धर्मलब्धानि क्रतुमुख्येष्ववासृजन् ।। शान्ति १२.७ ।।
कृतात्मा स महाराज स वै त्यागी स्मृतो नर: ।। शान्ति १२.८ ।।

Only he who spends his lawfully earned money on the works of higher purposes, and has self-discipline, is known as the true renouncer.[19]

क्रोधहर्षावनादृत्य पैशुन्यं च विशेषत: ।
विप्रो वेदानधीते य: स त्यागी पार्थ उच्यते ।। शान्ति १२.११ ।।

इति य: कुरुते भावं स त्यागी भरतर्षभ ।
न य: परित्यज्य गृहान् वनमेति विमूढवत् ।। शान्ति १२.१४ ।।

He who has conquered anger and excessive joy alike, especially the habit

of talking ill behind one's back, and is devoted to pursuing knowledge, is called the true renouncer.
He who leaves his home for a forest is no renouncer, only a fool.[20]

अनवेक्ष्य सुखादानं तथैवोर्ध्वं प्रतिष्ठितः।
आत्मत्यागी महाराज स त्यागी तामसो मतः।। शान्ति १२.९।।

Who has never known and understood the joys of the life-in-family, and has moved on to the next stage of life, he is only a renouncer confused in his perceptions.[21]

अन्तर्बहिश्च यत् किंचिन्मनोव्यासंगकारकम्।
परित्यज्य भवेत् त्यागी न हित्वा प्रतितिष्ठति।। शान्ति १२.३५।।

Only by giving up what, within one's self or outside, entangles the mind, does one truly renounce, not by leaving one's home.[22]

आश्रमांस्तुलया सर्वान् धृतानाहुर्मनीषिणः।
एकतश्च त्रयो राजन् गृहस्थाश्रम एकतः।। शान्ति १२.१२।।

समीक्ष्य तुलया पार्थ कामं स्वर्गं च भारत।
अयं पन्था महर्षीणामियं लोकविदां गतिः।। शान्ति १२.१३।।

Once the life-in-family was weighed in a scale along with the three other stages of life. Kept in the weighing scale of analysis, it was found to be of greater weight; for there is in it both the fulfilment of desire and heaven. It has been ever since considered the way of the sages and of the worldly alike.[23]

Sahadeva, Nakula's twin, adds:

न बाह्यं द्रव्यमुत्सृज्य सिद्धिर्भवति भारत।
शारीरं द्रव्यमुत्सृज्य सिद्धिर्भवति वा न वा।। शान्ति १३.१।।

By renouncing only outer things, one does not achieve the highest. Whether one gains that, or doesn't, by giving up material things related to one's body: even that is doubtful.[24]

द्व्यक्षरस्तु भवेन्मृत्युस्त्र्यक्षरं ब्रह्म शाश्वतम्।
ममेति च भवेन्मृत्युर्न ममेति च शाश्वतम्।। शान्ति १३.४।।

ब्रह्ममृत्यू ततो राजन्नात्मन्येव समाश्रितौ।
अदृश्यमानौ भूतानि योधयेतामसंशयम्।। शान्ति १३.५।।

True renunciation consists in giving up the notion 'this is mine' and the entanglements that come from that notion. The notion of the ownership of things is the place of death; freedom from it, the place of what death can never touch. And both death and the freedom from it exist in one's self, leading imperceptibly people to fight each other. Of this there is no doubt.[25]

अथवा वसतो राजन् वने वन्येन जीवत: ।
द्रव्येषु यस्य ममता मृत्योरास्ये स वर्तते ।। शान्ति १३.१० ।।

बाह्यान्तरं भूतानां स्वभावं पश्य भारत ।
ये तु पश्यन्ति तद् भूतं मुच्यन्ते ते महाभयात् ।। शान्ति १३.११ ।।

Living in a forest, if one's mind still thinks of the things of the world, and one's ownership of them, then surely one is living in death. Do give a thought to the fact that people are one thing outwardly and quite another within. Those who perceive this, free themselves from great fear.[26]

The very considerable *vairāgya*-literature in India, which is forcefully represented in the *Mahābhārata*, is full with the sound of renunciation: 'renounce *this*, renounce *that*'; 'leave *this*, leave *that*', leading to a completely wrong understanding of what *mokṣha*, or human freedom, truly is. External renunciation is no path to *mokṣha*. Neither is a withdrawal from family and its bonds, on principle, any part of human freedom, if *mokṣha* is properly understood. The *Mahābhārata* is full with the sound of the freedom of the mind. For it is in the *mind*, and not in the external *things* of the world, that both bondage and freedom lie.[27] The *Mahābhārata* says to us:

आकिंचन्ये न मोक्षोऽस्ति किंचन्ये नास्ति बन्धनम् ।
किंचन्ये चेतरे चैव जन्तुर्ज्ञानेन मुच्यते ।। शान्ति ३२०.५० ।।

Neither is mokṣha *in lack of possessions; nor is bondage in possessions. Whether it is the one or the other, having or not-having, it is knowledge that sets one free.*[28]

In that, it is a woman, Kausalyā, the wife of King Janaka, who is our teacher, as she was a teacher to her husband, who suddenly decided to leave everything and take to *sannyāsa* in search of *mokṣha*. She said to him: 'To wear ochre robes; to shave one's head; to carry a trident and a begging bowl—these are mere signs of *tyāga*, renunciation: in themselves they do not lead to *mokṣha*. Since discriminating awareness is the only means to *mokṣha*, all external signs are irrelevant.'[29] She further says:

त्यागान्न भिक्षुकं विद्यान्न मौढ्यान्न च याचनात् ।
ऋजुस्तु योऽर्थं त्यजति नसुखं विद्धि भिक्षुकम् ।। शान्ति १८.३० ।।

असक्तः सक्तवद् गच्छन् निःसंगोमुक्तबन्धनः ।
समः शत्रौ च मित्रे च स वै मुक्तो महीपते ।। शान्ति १८.३१ ।।

परिव्रजन्ति दानार्थं मुण्डाः काषायवाससः ।
सिता बहुविधैः पाशैः संचिन्वन्तो वृथामिषम् ।। शान्ति १८.३२ ।।

If passions, kasaya, *are not removed from one's heart, then wearing the ochre robe should be regarded as nothing more than a means to selfish ends. In my opinion, it is another profession adopted by those shaven-heads waving the flag of* dharma *but insincerely.*

No one is a monk merely because he has renounced and he begs. He alone is a genuine monk who has naturally risen above one's petty self-interests and is not attached to pleasures.[30]

A wife advancing such an argument may appear to be self-serving, for she and her family would be affected the most by her husband's decision to take to the ochre robe and to the life-alone. At another place, therefore, the *Mahābhārata* states the same reasoning, this time in the voice of the sage Mārkaṇḍeya, in conversation with Yudhishṭhira, on the subject of what true renunciation is. Mārkaṇḍeya says:

त्रिदण्डधारणं मौनं जटाभारोऽथ मुण्डनम् ।
वल्कलाजिनसंवेष्टं ब्रतचर्याभिषेचनम् ।। वन २००.९६ ।।

अग्निहोत्रं वने वासः शरीरपरिशोषणम् ।
सर्वाण्येतानि मिथ्या स्युर्यदि भावो न निर्मलः ।। वन २००.९७ ।।

To carry a trident; to vow silence; to carry the weight of long hair; or to have a shaven head; to wrap one's body with the hide of a tree or of an animal; to observe vows, ritual bathing, and the ritual stoking of the ritual fire; to live in a forest; and to starve one's body—all these have no meaning if one's feelings are not pure and clean.[31]

Equally importantly, in the context of the discussion on the family and the householder, King Janaka's wife asks her husband to keep in mind (what was true then, and what is true now) that:

अन्नाद् गृहस्था लोकेऽस्मिन् भिक्षवस्तत एव च।
अन्नात् प्राण: प्रभवति अन्नद: प्राणदो भवेत्।। शान्ति १८.२८।।

गृहस्थेभ्योऽपि निर्मुक्ता गृहस्थानेव संश्रिता:।
प्रभवं च प्रतिष्ठां च दान्ता विन्दन्त आसते।। शान्ति १८.२९।।

In this world, the household is sustained by food; and the renouncers are sustained by the households. Life depends on food; the giver of food is the giver of life as well.

Free from family, the renouncers depend for their sustenance upon families nevertheless. They arise from there; and it is from there that they receive respect and acknowledgement.[32]

The highest place for the householder and the family

The conflict between *grihastha-āshrama*, life-in-family, and *sannyāsa*, life-alone, for being ranked one over the other, must have been so great that the *Mahābhārata* thought it necessary to dwell upon it throughout. It states the arguments for life-alone at their strongest. Yet, human life being a complex system of relationships and of interdependence from birth to death, it is the life-in-family that the *Mahābhārata* sets out to study, and to show how very demanding and exacting its living is. And so demanding is its discipline that it is described, in one word, as *dushkara*, that is 'exceedingly difficult', 'arduous'.

Therefore, during the same conversation between Yudhishṭhira and his brothers, and between him and his wife Draupadī, the *Mahābhārata* holds in the clearest of words:

आश्रमांस्तुलया सर्वान् धृतानाहुर्मनीषिण:।
एकतश्च त्रयो राजन् गृहस्थाश्रम एकत:।। शान्ति १२.१२।।

समीक्ष्य तुलया पार्थ कामं स्वर्गं च भारत।
अयं पन्था महर्षीणामियं लोकविदां गति:।। शान्ति १२.१३।।

इति य: कुरुते भावं स त्यागी भरतर्षभ।
न य: परित्यज्य गृहान् वनमेति विमूढवत्।। शान्ति १२.१४।।

Once the wise weighed in a scale the relative weight of the four stages of life, and kept life-in-family on one side and the other three on the other. Weighing them on the scale of close analysis, life-in-family was found to be of greater weight; for it is in it that the fulfilment of desires and the higher purposes of life, the earthly and the heavenly, get combined.[33]

At another place, in a conversation between sage Kapila and another sage, Syūmarashmi, the same view is put forth quite as strongly; assigning to the *grihastha-āshrama*, and not to the *sannyāsa*, the highest place in human life.[34] Bhīshma recalls that conversation when Yudhishṭhira asks him: 'The life-in-family and the *yoga-dharma* are not far from each other. Yet, of the two which is more conducive to the highest Good?'[35] Here *yoga-dharma* has the meaning of the life of a *sannyāsī*. Bhīshma begins by saying: 'Both are conducive to the highest Good. Both are exceedingly difficult. Both have been practised by people who were great.' And then he narrates the dialogue between Kapila and Syūmarashmi on that very question.

Kapila

> We have heard it said that the *sannyāsī* obtains the highest state of existence; and so does the one who is in the stage of *vānaprastha*, now free from the cares of life-in-family; and so does the householder; and the young student likewise. All these four stages are regarded as the four different paths to the same goal—highest consciousness. Of them, that this is 'higher' and that is 'lower', this 'stronger' and that 'weaker', is only a manner of speaking with reference to their results.[36]
> However, soon after saying this, he extols the inner transformation of a *sannyāsī* to the highest degree, and concludes: 'His having gained the highest state of consciousness, of what use will then the life-in-family be for him?'[37]

Syūmarashmi

> If what you describe as the highest state of consciousness be also the greatest result of human effort, then the relative importance of the life-in-family becomes manifest even more. For it is evident that without the support of the household no other *āshrama* can survive.[38]

यथा मातरमाश्रित्य सर्वे जीवन्ति जन्तवः ।
एवं गार्हस्थ्यमाश्रित्य वर्तन्त इतराश्रमाः ।। शान्ति २६९.६ ।।

Just as all living beings are able to survive owing to the loving care of their mothers, likewise all other stages of life are possible because of the support that the households provide.

गृहस्थ एव यजते गृहस्थस्तप्यते तपः ।
गार्हस्थ्यमस्य धर्मस्य मूलं यत्किंचिदेजते ।। शान्ति २६९.७ ।।

It is the householder who performs the yajña; *and it is he who engages in* tapas: *it is life-in-family that is the foundation of all good that is done.*

प्रजनाद्यभिनिर्वृत्ताः सर्वे प्राणभृतो जनाः ।
प्रजनं चाप्युतान्यत्र न कथंचन विद्यते ।। शान्ति २६९.८ ।।

All living beings find pleasure in the acts of procreation; but it is only in life-in-family, and nowhere else, where creation takes place.[39]

However, it is to be noted that Syūmarashmi assigns a pre-eminent place to the life-in-family on the same ground on which he dismisses the life-alone, *sannyāsa*, as worthless—that is, the performance of vedic rituals and rites, the *acts*, by the householder; and the freedom from them that a *sannyāsī* gives himself, or herself, in the belief that it is knowledge and not *acts* that bring enlightenment. He thought that, in advocating *sannyāsa* as the path primarily of knowledge and inner transformation of the self, Kapila was also repudiating the Veda, which had emphasised the *acts*. Syūmarashmi had some harsh words to describe those who believed that there could be no *moksha* in living a life-in-family but in renouncing the *acts* as well. He called them faithless, devoid of subtle thinking, unstable, lazy, tired, ignorant, fools.[40] The debate between the two was in actual fact about another issue altogether, a perennial issue in Indian philosophical thought. Between the path of *knowledge* and the path of *acts*, which is more conducive to the greatest good of the Self? The arguments for life-in-family by Syūmarashmi, and for life-alone by Kapila, were incidental. Through this device, as a part of its *method*, the *Mahābhārata* is showing that neither is a sound rational ground. Both remained as respective arguments for one or the other, but wrong in their exclusiveness.

If rituals and rites form a central part of life, then of course the life-in-family becomes central, too, for it is the householder, and not the one who lives a life-alone, who performs those rites. That was one perception. After stating it, the *Mahābhārata* proceeds to show the pre-eminence of the life-in-family *because* the family is the very first natural context in which life begins and where human beings grow as persons. At the same time it shows, not at any one place but throughout, that marriage and the family are not in themselves any hindrance to the seeking of spiritual freedom, which both come, the freedom and hindrance to it, from within one's own self.

In the voice of Shiva, in conversation with his wife Umā, the *Mahābhārata* says again:

शीलवृत्तविनीतस्य निगृहीतेन्द्रियस्थ च । ।
आर्जवे वर्तमानस्य सर्वभूतहितैषिण: ।
प्रियातिथेश्च क्षान्तस्य धर्माजितधनस्थ च । ।
गृहाश्रयमपदस्थस्य किमन्यै: कृत्यमाश्रमै: ।

Who has the nobility of conduct and humility of spirit; has disciplined his physical senses and mental faculties; is simple and straightforward; has in his heart the good of all beings; offers affectionate hospitality to his guests; is forgiving; and who has earned his money in accordance with dharma—*what need has such a householder of any other* āshrama?[41]

यथा मातरमाश्रित्य सर्वे जीवन्ति जन्तव: । ।
तथा गृहाश्रमं प्राप्य सर्वे जीवन्ति चाश्रमा: ।

Just as all living beings live with the protection of the mother, so do all other stages of life live with the householder as their support.[42]

Obligations and duties, and 'the three debts'

The *Mahābhārata* is full of descriptions of the family ideal and duties, not only of one member towards the rest, but also of the family as a whole towards society. The foundation of family relationships is not the individual will and its changing content, but obligation and its unchanging form. Members of a family remained united by means of duties that were held to be sacred and not merely civil. Those duties were to be met irrespective of character and circumstance. For example, no matter what the character or the circumstances of a father or a mother might be, their children owed to them certain duties. Similarly, the parents owed to their children certain duties. Providing protection, loving care, a disciplined upbringing, and honest advice were the duties of parents towards children; obedience, holding them in honour, and looking after them in their old age were the duties of children towards parents.

Besides the specific obligations and duties of one member of the family towards another; the obligation of the family as a unit towards others, consisting of kindness, charity, and hospitality, are equally emphasised in the *Mahābhārata*. One is trained to deem it a great honour if a guest comes, and a greater honour if he, or she, is pleased. One earns *puṇya*, great merit, thereby. Nothing is more reprehensible than to ignore or insult a guest; in doing so, one invites severe demerit. Furthermore, the family duties extended to animals as well, particularly to those that did not belong to any one person; they had to be protected and fed and looked after. The householder of the *Mahābhārata* is obliged not only to the living, but to the dead as well—and to the gods of the universe, too. Just as he eats only after the others in the family have eaten, he does not eat without first making a symbolic offering to the ancestors and to the gods who are the elements of Nature: the earth, the space, the sun, the wind, and the fire. These are not to be, in the *Mahābhārata* at any rate, simply ritualistic acts, but are meant to invoke a feeling of oneness with so much else in which a family is sustained.

Those obligations and duties, the *Mahābhārata* shows, are neither arbitrary nor capricious. Their foundations are in the concept of 'three debts', *ṛṇa*, that every person owes, and that must be discharged: a debt to one's ancestors; a debt to one's teachers; and a debt to society.[43] The debt to one's ancestors is to be repaid by raising a family; the debt to one's teachers, by contributing further to the advancement of knowledge; and the debt to society, by living a self-regulated and self-disciplined life. To these three debts, two more are added. A debt to guests, for a person has been himself, or herself, a guest in another household, and has been received with feelings of respect and affection. But *one owes a debt to one's self, too.*[44]

How is the debt one owes to one's self to be repaid?

Not obligations and duties alone, also feelings

In the *Mahābhārata*, the foundations of family relationships are discussed not in the terms of *rules* but in the language of *feelings*—through the stories of human situations everywhere.

It is true that a sense of obligation, or a sense of duty, is often a weighty criterion that determines how one behaves in one way rather than in another. And that criterion is often invoked in the stories of family happenings that the *Mahābhārata* narrates. What it narrates also as the problematic, however, are the moral dilemmas that often arise when there is a direct conflict between one duty and another, both inviolable. The most famous example of this was the deep moral dilemma that confronted Arjuna. At the very beginning of the war between the Kaurava-s and the

Pāṇḍava-s, first cousins to each other, he surveys the two armies poised to rush at each other. He sees on the other side not only his close relatives but many of those, too, whom he shall, as his duty, honour and cherish and protect from harm. It was equally his duty to fight, if it had come to that, to regain the kingdom that was his and of his brothers, the five Pāṇḍava-s, of which they were unjustly deprived, to the accompaniment of many cruel deeds done to the family moreover. To fight for justice, that was one duty; not to wage war against one's relatives and the elders of the realm, that was another duty. Which of the two must he choose when there was a serious conflict between them? There were other weighty considerations as well: the social consequences of what would certainly be a most terrible and bloody war. And neither could *they* be ignored. What was his duty: to fight or not to fight? His responsibility for either of the two conflicting decisions would have been too much for him to bear. Śrī Krishna, acting as Arjuna's charioteer, resolves his paralysing dilemma by means of a long discourse to him on the battlefield, famous as the *Bhagvad-Gītā*.[45]

It is a different story that Arjuna forgot that lesson not long after the war was over and won. One evening he said to Śrī Krishna: 'I vaguely remember your giving me a long lecture on the battlefield. What was it that you had said? I have forgotten it. Will you kindly tell me again?'[46] Naturally, the teacher felt disappointed and irritated.[47] He said to Arjuna: 'You are indeed a man of little faith, and of intelligence even less. To repeat what I had said then is beyond my capacity now.'[48] Nevertheless, 'in order to please his friend,' Śrī Krishna gives another discourse, known as *Anu-Gītā*,[49] 'secondary *Gītā*'. *By design*, it has neither the grandeur nor the philosophic depth of the original. *By design again*, it is so rambling besides that it is most unlikely that Arjuna would have retained much of what was being said this time either. Through this episode, the *Mahābhārata* is pointing out that even the profoundest of philosophy is the product of feelings and emotions felt strongly at a particular point in time.

What is done as a duty is done independent of feelings. And what is done without feelings is done but incompletely. Feelings are said to be 'subjective'; and what is subjective is believed to change, sometimes from one day to another. Obligation and duty are 'objective' and, therefore, 'fixed'. As yet another characteristic of its method, the *Mahābhārata* shows the presumed dichotomy between the subjective and the objective to be false. Life is a system of relationships; and relationships are lived through feelings. The quality of a life will be determined by the quality of relationships, and they, by the quality of the feelings that run through them. Feelings arise from perceptions, in which the mind and its instruments play a central part. But feelings can also cloud perceptions. In order to change feelings, perceptions have to change. Thus, in the *Mahābhārata*, knowledge is brought in relation to feelings, philosophy in relation to the life-in-family enacted everyday everywhere.

However, the *Mahābhārata* is not a catalogue of human feelings and their play. The feelings through which life-in-family is lived are to be suffused with *dharma*. And here we must again focus on the meaning of *dharma*.

प्रभवार्थाय भूतानां धर्मप्रवचनं कृतम्।
यः स्यात् प्रभवसंयुक्तः स धर्म इति निश्चयः।। शान्ति १०९.१०।।

All the sayings of dharma *are with a view to nurturing, cherishing, providing more amply, enriching, prospering, enhancing all living beings, securing their* prabhava. *Therefore, whatever has the characteristic of doing that, is* dharma. *This is certain.*

धारणाद् धर्ममित्याहुर्धर्मेण विधृताः प्रजाः।
यः स्याद् धारणसंयुक्तः स धर्म इति निश्चयः।। शान्ति १०९.११।।

All the sayings of dharma *are with a view to supporting, sustaining, bringing together, and in their togetherness upholding, all living beings, securing their* dharma. *Therefore, whatever has the characteristic of doing that is* dharma. *This is certain.*

अहिंसार्थाय भूतानां धर्मप्रवचनं कृतम्।
यः स्यादहिंसासम्पृक्तः स धर्म इति निश्चयः।। शान्ति १०९.१२।।

All the sayings of dharma *are with a view to securing for all living beings freedom from violence. Therefore, whatever has the characteristic of not doing violence is* dharma. *This is certain.*[50]

Conversely, *whatever* has the characteristic of depriving, starving, diminishing, separating, uprooting, hurting, doing violence, debasing and degrading, is the negation of *dharma*. Whatever brings that about is, in one word, *adharma*.

The place of the wife in life-in-family

What was the status of the wife in the Indian household from the earliest times of Indian history? A great deal has been written on this subject; and it is needless to repeat what is already familiar. The question of the *actuality* of the status of woman in the Indian life-in-family, in contrast with the *ideal*, became a matter of intense controversy in the latter half of the nineteenth century, and has again come to the fore. The ideal itself may be restated here briefly, because concerning even that there are several misconceptions. The wife in the Indian household has been the subject of much discussion—in the tone both of 'woman the exploited' and 'woman the goddess'. If the disorders, the *adharma*, of actual behaviour, individual and collective, are to be set right, then there have to be unquestionable foundations, in the light of which a reordering of relationships is to take place. The *Mahābhārata* provides us with those universal foundations upon which the *attitudes* and *feelings* in the man–woman relationship are to be based.

Whereas for the *shāstri*-s, the learned lawgivers, the place of the wife is primarily functional, in the *Mahābhārata*, it is primarily relational. In the *dharmashāstra*-s, the presence of the wife is required by the side of her husband to enable him to perform the prescribed rituals and rites; in the *Mahābhārata*, it is only by the presence of the wife that a house is called a home. This is not to say that the one is necessarily a negation of the other. What is relational may in some ways also be functional. The main point is about the meaning of the word *saha-dharminī*, 'the one who is together in observing *dharma*', as the wife is called in most of the *dharmashāstra*-s, where the word *dharma* has itself a narrow and ritualistic meaning.

As we saw above, the *Mahābhārata* gives to the word *dharma* a radically different meaning, and in that light sees the wife with altogether different eyes. In all the conversations between a husband and a wife that the *Mahābhārata* narrates, he does not, as far as I know, ever call her '*saha-dharminī*'. He always addresses her in words of love and endearment—'*priye*', or 'my loved one'; '*shubhe*', or 'you so good', 'you so splendid'; '*shubhanāne*', or 'you so beautiful', and the like. And love and endearment, in the *Mahābhārata*, are not functional things of use, and neither is the wife ever so, in relation to her husband.

न गृहं गृहमित्याहुर्गृहिणी गृहमुच्यते।
गृहं तु गृहिणीहीनमरण्यसदृशं मतम्।। शान्ति १४४.६।।

A house is not a home: only through the wife is a house called the home. Where there is no wife, that dwelling is like wilderness.[51]

पुत्रपौत्रवधूभृत्यैराकीर्णमपि सर्वतः।
भार्याहीनं गृहस्थस्य शून्यमेव गृहं भवेत्।। शान्ति १४४.७।।

Even when his home is full with his son, daughter-in-law, and grandchildren, and other dependents too, a man's home is still empty without his wife.[52]

वृक्षमूलेऽपि दयिता यस्य तिष्ठति तद् गृहम्।
प्रासादोऽपितया हीनः कान्तार इति निश्चितम्।। शान्ति १४४.१२।।

With one's wife, even a place under a tree is home; without her, even a palace is empty. This is certain.[53]

भार्या हि परमो ह्यर्थः पुरुषस्येह पठ्यते।
असहायस्य लोकेऽस्मिल्लोकयात्रासहायिनी।। शान्ति १४४.१४।।

The greatest wealth of a man is his wife. For him who is lost and helpless in the journey of life, his wife is his support.[54]

तथा रोगाभिभूतस्य नित्यं कृच्छ्रगतस्य च।
नास्ति भार्यासमं किंचन्नरस्यार्तस्य भेषजम्।। शान्ति १४४.१५।।

For him who is afflicted with illness, and troubled for long and deeply, there is no better cure than his wife.

नास्ति भार्यासमोबन्धुर्नास्ति भार्या समागतिः।
नास्ति भार्यासमो लोके सहायो धर्मसंग्रहे।। शान्ति १४४.१६।।

There is no friend like the wife, no support like the wife, nor anyone in the world like the wife, who helps one live a meaningful life.[55]

The status of the wife is derived from the fundamental supposition that 'the wife is a man's other half'.[56] Therefore, in the voice of Shakuntalā,[57] the *Mahābhārata* says:

अर्धे भार्या मनुष्यस्य भार्या श्रेष्ठतमः सखा।
भार्या मूलं त्रिवर्गस्य भार्या मूलं तरिष्यतः।।आदि ७४.४१।।

The wife is a man's other half; the wife is his best friend. The wife is the root of all order, of material prosperity, of the fulfilment of desires.[58]

भार्यावन्तः क्रियावन्तः सभार्या गृहमेधिनः ।
भार्यावन्तः प्रमोदन्ते भार्यावन्तः श्रियान्विताः ।।आदि ७४.४२।।

Only they who have a wife are full of endeavour, and only they are truly householders. Those having a wife are happy and cheerful, and they are the ones endowed with all that is good in life.[59]

सखायः प्रविविक्तेषु भवन्त्येताः प्रियंवदाः ।
पितरो धर्मकार्येषु भवन्त्यार्तस्य मातरः ।।आदि ७४.४३।।

In the moments of deepest intimacy, of loving speech; in the ordering of life, like a father; and in the moments of crisis, the wife acts like a mother.[60]

सुसंरब्धोऽपि रामाणां न कुर्यादप्रियं नरः ।
रतिं प्रीतिं च धर्मं च तास्वायत्तमवेक्ष्य हि ।।आदि ७४.५१।।

Sexual satisfaction, love, and the ordering of life, depend upon the wife. Let no man, therefore, even if angry, do ill to his wife.[61]
But surely not every wife is all these. Therefore, the Mahābhārata adds:

यस्य भार्या गृहे नास्ति साध्वी च प्रियवादिनी ।
अरण्यं तेन गन्तव्यं यथारण्यं तथा गृहम् ।। शान्ति १४४.१७ ।।

The home where the wife has in her no goodness, nor is of pleasant speech, that man might as well go into the wilderness; for there is no difference between such a dwelling and the wilderness.[62]

However, as far as I know, there is in the *Mahābhārata* not a single woman who turns a home into a wilderness. There has been this general impression that the shāstric law concerning a man's relationship with his wife gave liberty to the man to behave with her as he liked, while imposing on the woman all kinds of restrictions in that respect. This is not true, in the *foundations* at any rate. This ground will have to be covered in detail by taking as examples the shāstric law both of divorce and of no-divorce. And a study of Kauṭilya's *Arthashāstra* in this context is essential. But this is not the place for undertaking such an exercise. It will suffice here to say that in that regard the husband had no greater privileges than the wife had. A husband's duties towards his wife are, in the foundations of *grihastha āshrama*, no less demanding than are the duties of a wife towards her husband. And in the complexities of the man–woman relationship, both are equally placed.

There has been, too, the impression that the word *rakṣhā*, 'protection', that occurs in many verses pertaining to woman, in the *Mahābhārata* as well,[63] was a device to keep her under man's control. There are some women in India, and elsewhere too, who bristle at the very mention of the word 'protection' in the context of the husband–wife relationship, for they presume that 'protection' is a word in the vocabulary of power relationship, and that the life-in-family is a field where the man exercises power over the woman the most. Submission is the price of protection. Even on a superficial reading of the *Mahābhārata*, one will hear again and again, and yet again, that self-control, and not power over the *other*, is the very first natural foundation of relationships. *All* relationships, personal and collective, should be lived in *dharma*, so that they support, enhance, bring together, and protect from fear of violence, and do not debase, degrade, separate, and do violence. Thus, for example, in its most systematic philosophy of governance and law, *rāja-dharma*, the *Mahābhārata*'s main justification for the existence of the state is to protect the people from fear of every kind, including their fear of the state itself.[64] The foundation of family relationships, the *Mahābhārata* is saying to us, often in an anguished tone, can never be one's power over the other but love and caring, which require power over one's own self in the first place. In any case, in the many stories of family happenings, it is the woman, the wife, or the mother, who is demonstrably doing the *protecting*. And protection is not physical alone. In the *Mahābhārata*, the wife is often seen as protecting the husband from his wholly mistaken notions of one thing or another concerning life.

The *Mahābhārata* is mainly talking about the conditions within the family whereby a woman is made happy. They are not some acts of charity towards her; they are plainly demanded even by one's self-interest. In the same breath, it talks about the paradox of self-interest: one's self-interest is best served by serving the interest of the *other*. That is to say, *the happiness of the other is an essential condition of one's own happiness*. In the realm of sexual relations between husband and wife, this is so even more. Hence *saha-kāma*, the feeling of *togetherness* as the foundation of sexual happiness, without which sexuality is nothing; it is dead.[65]

The following verses contain the substance of what the *Mahābhārata* says should be the position of the woman in the life-in-family, and not of the wife alone:[66]

स्त्रियो यत्र च पूज्यन्ते रमन्ते तत्र देवता: ।
अपूजिताश्च यत्रैता: सर्वास्तत्राफला: क्रिया: ।। अनुशासन ४६.५ ।।

Where women are honoured, there the gods reside; where they remain unhonoured, there nothing can bear fruit.[67]

तदा चैतत् कुलं नास्ति यदा शोचन्ति जामय: ।। अनुशासन ४६.६ ।।
जामीशप्तानि गेहानि निकृत्तानीव कृत्यया ।
नैव भान्ति न वर्धन्ते श्रिया हीनानि पार्थिव ।। अनुशासन ४६.७ ।।

That family does not hold where the daughters-in-law lament. The homes that are cursed by them are destroyed as if by a malevolent ghost. Bereft of fortune, those homes do not prosper.[68]

ईर्षवो मानकामाश्च चण्डाश्च सुहृदोऽबुधा: ।
स्त्रियस्तु मानमर्हन्ति ता मानयत मानवा: ।। अनुशासन ४६.९ ।।
स्त्रीप्रत्ययो हि वै धर्मो रतिभोगाश्च केवला: ।
परिचर्या नमस्कारास्तदायत्ता भवन्तु व: ।। अनुशासन ४६.१० ।।

Womankind is the foundation of all order. Sexual pleasure; attendance and service; and adoration—all these are dependent upon women.[69]

यदि वै स्त्री न रोचेत पुमांसं न प्रमोदयेत् ।
अप्रमोदात् पुन: पुंस: प्रजनो न प्रवर्धते ।। अनुशासन ४६.४ ।।
पूज्या लालयितव्याश्च स्त्रियो नित्यं जनाधिप ।

If the woman's wishes are not respected, she cannot please her husband; and if he is not pleased, progeny cannot be. Let women be honoured and pleased always.[70]

उत्पादनमपत्यस्य जातस्य परिपालनम् ।
प्रीत्यर्थं लोकयात्राया: पश्यत स्त्रीनिबन्धनम् ।। अनुशासन ४६.११ ।।
सम्मान्यमानाश्चैता हि सर्वकार्याण्यवाप्स्यथ ।

The birth of progeny, the nourishing of the young, and the happy progress of society, are seen as tied to women. Only if they are respected and honoured can everything succeed.[71]

श्रिय एता: स्त्रियो नाम सत्कार्या भूतिमिच्छता ।
पालिता निगृहीता च श्री: स्त्री भवति भारत ।। अनुशासन ४६.१५ ।।

Women are the glory. If well-being is desired, they should be treated with kindness and respect. When the woman is protected, and with loving care, she becomes the splendour and the good fortune.[72]

साध्वी कुलं वर्धयति साध्वी पुष्टिर्गृहे परा।
साध्वी लक्ष्मी: रति:साक्षात् प्रतिष्ठा संततिस्तथा।। अनुशासन पृ ५५४६।।

A good woman enhances the family. A good woman nourishes the family. A good woman is the goddess of good fortune, the source of sexual happiness, the embodiment of what the family is founded upon, and of creation.[73]

A daughter is to be cherished greatly; for in a tone full of tenderness and love, the *Mahābhārata* says:

नित्यं निवसते लक्ष्मी: कन्यकासु प्रतिष्ठिता।
शोभना शुभयोग्या च पूज्या मगंलकर्मसु।। अनुशासन पृ ५५४६।।

In a daughter the goddess of prosperity lives always. She is established in her always. A daughter is glorious, endowed with all that is good, to be honoured at the beginning of every good work.[74]

आकरस्थं यथा रत्नं सर्वकामफलोपगम्।
तथा कन्या महालक्ष्मी: सर्वलोकस्य मगंलम्।। अनुशासन पृ ५५४६।।

Just as a precious jewel makes everything worthy, a daughter is like the great goddess of good fortune, for everything good in this world.[75]

Here it is important to note that the above propositions are neither in the nature of moral *ought* nor prescribed rules. However, this can be seen only after studying the *Mahābhārata* with attention both to what it is saying and to its *method* of saying it. These are clearly, first, the natural foundations of the family. They require to be stated; but after they have been stated, there was no self-consciousness about them; they appeared as natural as breathing. It is true that there had to be, besides, laws concerning, for instance, inheritance of property by a widow or by a daughter. The *dharmashāstra*-s were concerned with that and not quite so much with the *quality* of personal relationships, say, as between husband and wife. It is undeniable that inheritance and property are important, too. That area will have to be studied in order to see whether in the scheme of things as perceived in any given society a woman was at a disadvantage, on principle, because she was a woman. Whether any disadvantage attached to her in the foundations themselves, or whether it was a crude disorder, is to be distinguished sharply, as it always is in the *Mahābhārata*. What is important here is that the *anthropology*, the *sociology*, the *political ideology*, the *phenomenology*, of the family are all brought together in the *Mahābhārata*'s view of the family. *(a)* Indisputably, the first natural context where human life begins; and *(b)* for a human life to grow with a sense of joy and worth, the life within the family has naturally to be suffused with *dharma*, with that which protects, enhances, and brings freedom from fear. Everything else flows from that, in whichever direction it may be. Everything else is to have its validation in that. Almost as a first foundation, in the context of law and politics surrounding the family above all, the *Mahābhārata* states this at every turn.

In the story of Ashṭāvakra, who had set his heart on Suprabha and wanted to marry her, but was put to the test by another woman, the main conclusion is that, in order to be worthy of a woman, the man has to have control over himself first.[76] Correspondingly, the *Mahābhārata* reserves its strongest condemnation for those men who deceive and take advantage of women left unprotected.[77] Above all, it is saying again and again, and yet again, in the light of concrete human situations, that marriage is a state of emotional togetherness, *saha-dharma* and *saha-kāma*, and not a theatre of struggle for power between man and woman.

The place of the mother in the life-in-family

To the *Mahābhārata*, the mother has the most exalted status in the life-in-family.

दशाचार्यानुपाध्याय उपाध्यायान् पिता दश। अनुशासन १०५.१४ ।।
दश चैव पितॄन् सर्वां वा पृथिवीमपि।
गौरवेणाभिभवति नास्ति मातृसमो गुरुः ।। अनुशासन १०५.१५ ।।

Greater than ten teachers is the preceptor: greater than ten preceptors is the father: and greater than ten fathers is the mother. The mother is greater than even the earth. There is no guru greater than the mother.[78]

At another place, in another context of a family happening, it is said:

मातादेहारणिः पुंसां सर्वस्यार्तस्य निर्वृतिः।
मातृलाभे सनाथत्वमनाथत्वं विपर्यये।। शान्ति २६६.२६ ।।

It is only the mother who gives comfort and heals those in distress. Only that long does a person feel protected as long as the mother is alive; without her, he feels he is unprotected wholly.[79]

न च शोचति नाप्येनं स्थाविर्यमपकर्षति।
श्रिया हीनोऽपि यो गेहमम्बेति प्रतिपद्यते।। शान्ति २६६.२७।।
So long as the mother is there, he feels he has no worry; neither does age wither him. Maybe poor, he is still rich on entering his home, calling out to his mother.[80]

पुत्रपौत्रोपपन्नोऽपि जननीं यः समाश्रितः।
अपि वर्षशतस्यान्ते स द्विहायनवच्चरेत्।। शान्ति २६६.२८।।
Himself now a father, and a grandfather too, and of age one hundred, he behaves with his mother as if two years old.[81]

कुक्षिसंधारणाद् धात्री जननाज्जननी स्मृता।
अगंनां बर्धनादम्बा वीरसूत्वेन वीरसूः।। शान्ति २६६.३२।।

शिशोः शुश्रूणाच्छुश्रूर्माता देहमनन्तरम्।। शान्ति २६६.३३।।
Because she bears, she is called dhātrī: *for giving birth, she is called* jananī: ambā, *because she nourishes the limbs: and* vīrasu *because she carried child with courage. In rearing with love and care, she is* śhushru: *the mother is one's own intimate body.*[82]

नास्ति मातृसमा छाया नास्ति मातृसमा गतिः।
नास्ति मातृसमं त्राणं नास्ति मातृसमा प्रिया।। शान्ति २६६.३१।।
There is no better cover than the mother; no greater support than she; neither a greater protector; and there is none dearer than she.[83]

Therefore, in the *Mahābhārata*, and in the *dharmashāstra*-s too, there is nothing more reprehensible than to disregard one's mother.[84] The father may be repudiated but never the mother.

Yet, in one of its central stories of human tragedy, the *Mahābhārata* narrates the story of a mother, Kuntī, who had cast away her firstborn, for he was born while she was still not married and was a girl almost.[85] For fear of the shame and disgrace that she would bring upon her family, she floated the child in a basket on the waves of a river. She took great care, though, to seal the basket so perfectly that water would not get into it, but air would to keep the child alive. Down the stream, a childless couple, Adhiratha and his wife Rādhā, would notice the basket and the child in it. And a child born a prince would be brought up in the humble circumstances of the woman who was to be his true mother. Karṇa is perhaps the most tragic, and also the most noble, figure in the *Mahābhārata*, whose tragedy began with his birth. He would learn the truth many years later. Just before the war was to begin, Kuntī went to see him—but only to ask for a favour.[86] She addresses Karṇa as *Kaunteya*, 'the son of Kuntī'. Still polite and courteous to her, he says: 'I am *not Kaunteya*. I am *Rādheya*, the son of Rādhā. Tell me, Princess, if there is something that I can still do for you.'[87] On her saying that he was in actual fact her eldest son, and she his mother, Karṇa says to her: 'What *you* did to me, what worse could an enemy have done to another?' 'Never before did you think of my good, though my mother. Today you come to me, but only to serve your own purpose.' 'Even so, your visit will not be in vain.'[88]

Through that happening, enacted everywhere in the world today as well, in different forms, the *Mahābhārata* is saying that a biological mother may not answer any of the descriptions of the mother cited above, but another woman may, *all of them*, and quite often does. Motherhood, undoubtedly a biological fact, is not biological alone. Thus, what is said about the mother remains unaltered, disorders apart.

Then there is the opposite, equally extreme, story of Chirakārī, who was commanded to kill his mother, and that by his father, the sage Gautama, when Gautama found that his wife had been seduced by the god Indra.[89] Chirakārī was given that name due to *his habit of reflecting on a thing long, and taking even longer to act upon it.* As it turned out to be in this particular case, it is not a bad habit at all. In fact, after giving the command and going away, the father now desperately hoped that his son would be true to his name Chirakārī. The son reflects on that family situation very carefully and for long. To obey his father was undoubtedly a duty enjoined upon a son, but to protect his mother from any harm was equally a son's duty towards the mother. Of these two equally inviolable duties, which one must he choose? And he began to reflect upon this grave moral dilemma. Meanwhile, his father began to feel horrified at what he had done. He came to the conclusion, as his son already had, that:

एवं स्त्री नापराध्नोति नर एवापराध्यति ।
व्युच्चंरश्च महादोषं नर एवापराध्यति ।। शान्ति २६६.३८ ।।

In situations such as these, the fault is not of the woman but only of the man.[90]

Moreover, Gautama was honest with himself and acknowledged:

ईर्ष्याजं व्यसनं प्राहुस्तेन चैवोर्ध्वरेतसः ।
ईर्ष्यया त्वहमाक्षिप्तो मग्नो दुष्कृतसागरे ।। शान्ति २६६.५१ ।।
It was out of a sense of jealousy that I behaved in the dreadful way that I did. Jealousy is the root of all that is painful.[91]

He rushes back home, happily to find that Chirakārī, true to his name, was still reflecting upon what he should do. The father expresses his deepest gratitude to his son for having saved him from the darkest misdeed of having his wife killed when she was deserving of receiving from her husband respect, loving care, and protection from harm.

Respect and loving care for one's mother and father are greatly emphasised in the *Mahābhārata*. They were not just *duties* towards the parents, to be performed somehow. *Feelings* of respect and loving care are equally emphasised. In the story of the humbling of an arrogant brāhmaṇa first by an ordinary woman, a housewife, and then by a meatseller,[92] the latter takes him home and introduces him to his old parents.[93] Kaushika the brāhmaṇa notices the simple elegance of a modest home vibrating with happiness. After the old couple had welcomed the visitor, Dharmavyādha the meatseller, his eyes shining with love for his mother and father, says to Kaushika:

पिता माता च भगवन्नेतौ मद्दैवतं परम् ।
यद् दैवतेभ्यः कर्तव्यं तदेताभ्यां करोम्यहम् ।। वन २१४.१८ ।।
My mother and father are the gods I worship. What I am expected to do for the gods of the universe, I do for them.[94]

एतदर्थं मम प्राणा भार्या पुत्रः सुहृज्जनः ।
सपुत्रदारः शुश्रूषां नित्यमेव करोम्यहम् ।। वन २१४.२३ ।।
My own life, my wife, my children, and my other loved ones, all of us are devoted to caring for them.[95]

अनुकूलं तथा वच्मि विप्रियं परिवर्जये ।
अधर्मेणापि संयुक्तं प्रियमाभ्यां करोम्यहम् ।। वन २१४.२५ ।।

I say only what is pleasing to them, and not what may hurt them, and nor do I do what is adharma *and they will not approve.*[96]

धर्ममेव गुरुं ज्ञात्वा करोमि द्विजसत्तम।
अतन्द्रितः सदा विप्र शुश्रूषां वै करोम्यहम्।। वन २१४.२६।।

Believing that the caring of one's father and mother is dharma *of great substance, I serve them diligently.*[97]

पञ्चैव गुरवो ब्रह्मन् पुरुषस्य बुभूषतः।
पिता माताग्निरात्मा च गुरुश्च द्विजसत्तम।। वन २१४.२७।।

For the one desirous of his welfare, there are five guru-s: father, mother, the fire, the Self, and the preceptor.[98]

एतेषु यस्तु वर्तेत सम्यगेव द्विजोत्तम।
भवेयुरग्नयस्तस्य परिचीर्णास्तु नित्यशः।
गार्हस्थ्ये वर्तमानस्य एष धर्मः सनातनः।। वन २१४.२८।।

Whoever acts towards them well, will serve the life-in-family well. This is the abiding dharma *of all times.*[99]

The meatseller then delivers his final words to Kaushika:

त्वया विनिकृता माता पिता च द्विजसत्तम।
अनिसृष्टेऽसि निष्क्रान्तो गृहात् ताभ्यामनिन्दित।। वन २१५.७।।

वेदोच्चारणकार्यार्थमयुक्तं तत् त्वया कृतम्।
तव शोकेन वृद्धो तावन्धीभूतौ तपस्विनौ।। वन २१५.८।।

Learned Brāhmaṇa! You have neglected your mother and father. You set out in search of knowledge, leaving your home without even their knowing, much less with their consent. That was wrong on your part. Pained thereby, your elderly parents, sorrowing for you, have become blind.[100]

तौ प्रसादयितुं गच्छ मा त्वां धर्मोऽत्यगादयम्।
तपस्वी त्वं महात्मा च धर्मे च निरतः सदा।। वन २१५.९।।

सर्वमेतदपार्थं ते क्षिपं तौ सम्प्रसादय।
श्रद्दधस्व मम ब्रह्मन् नान्यथा कर्तुमर्हसि।
गम्यतामद्य विप्रर्षे श्रेयस्ते कथयाम्यहम्।। वन २१५.१०।।

मातापित्रोः सकाशं हि गत्वा त्वं द्विजसत्तम।

अतन्द्रित: कुरु क्षिप्रं मातापित्रार्हि पूजनम् ।
अत: परमं धर्मं नान्यं पश्यामि कंचन ।। वन २१५.१३ ।।

In not keeping your parents happy, your devotion to knowledge is a waste. Go back to them. Have faith in what I say to you; for what I say to you is for your utmost good. Go and serve your parents. I see no dharma *greater than that.*[101]

Conversations between husband and wife as part of family life

A question is asked in the *Mahābhārata*: 'What kind of life do two brilliant persons, husband and wife, lead as householders?' The answer is: 'Well, they live the ordinary life of the life-in-family, *grihastha*; raise a family—and have brilliant conversations with each other.' The whole of the *Mahābhārata* resounds with those brilliant, and profound, conversations between husband and wife. It is as much through *them* as through the conversations between a king and a thinker, or between one thinker and another, that the *Mahābhārata* explores the universal questions of human experience, the universal foundations of human life. The conversations are often between a mother and her son. And quite often they are between a woman, as wife or mother, or neither, and a person who is not a member of the family.

Indeed, much of the Mahābhārata can be rearranged, absolutely faithfully to the text, in terms of those conversations in which women have demonstrably a central place as teachers.

Those conversations between a husband and wife take place in as many different tones as are known to human beings. For example, a wife says to the man: 'Frankly, with *you* as my husband, I am quite worried as to my future. You *do* nothing, only keep thinking on the great questions of life, unaware that I am dependent upon you.'[102] The husband replies: 'My dear wife, I am not offended by what you say, for I know that what you say comes from the goodness of your heart. But may we discuss what it is *to act*, and *who* acts, and what is *the field of action*?' The wife must have rolled her eyes, 'There he goes again! May we *discuss*?' A long conversation takes place between them, during which she puts to him many searching questions, the substance of which is: *It is not by outward acts but by transforming one's mind and heart that one experiences the true blessedness of life.*[103]

Spread over many days, another conversation takes place between a husband and wife, Siva and Umā, in the tone of a detached inquiry, touching many philosophical questions concerning the human condition, which include the foundations of good governance.[104] Being a highly intelligent woman, along with being a great beauty, Umā, also called Pārvatī, knew how contentious, and therefore how unpleasant, philosophical discussions can be. Therefore, she begins every discussion by paying her husband handsome compliments. He returns her compliments even more handsomely. The conversation between them is one of the profoundest parts of the *Mahābhārata*.

The conversations between Yudhishṭhira and his wife Draupadī, spread over many years, in different places, have a different tone altogether. Haunted by the memory of her dreadful humiliation, when she expresses to her husband her feelings of deep hurt that would not leave her, he gives her a lecture on the virtues and the rationality of forgiveness. She knows very well all those arguments. She was talking like a woman deeply hurt; her husband Yudhishṭhira would talk like a professor of philosophy, insensitive to her feelings. She would correct his wholly mistaken notion that forgiveness can be independent of 'the time', 'the occasion', and 'the person concerned'. She would teach him, and us, that neither is forgiveness *always* a virtue, nor is force *always* the best means.

In contrast, Draupadī's second eldest husband, Bhīma, would respect her every whim, and not give her a lecture. One day, when they were still in exile, a breeze brings to her lap some exquisitely fragrant flowers, and she says to Bhīma: 'Look, look, I want lots and lots of them. They are so beautiful and fragrant.'[105] And Bhīma sets out to trace their origin, and bring to his wife lots of them. In the process he trespasses on another's estate that was out of bound; a fight follows; and he very nearly loses his life[106]—but brings those flowers to her all the same. On another occasion, when the Pāṇḍava-s had to spend the thirteenth year of their exile incognito, and Draupadī, herself a princess, worked as a maid to the queen of Virāṭa, and Bhīma as a cook in the royal kitchen, she was the object of indecent attention from the queen's brother. Deeply troubled, she goes in the middle of the night to where Bhīma is sleeping, and wakes him up. Seeing how distressed his wife is, he takes her hands in his, and says, 'Once so very beautiful, how rough they have become by the work that you have to do.' Saying this, Bhīma presses his wife's hands on his face—and begins to cry.[107]

In a later part of this work, 'The Women of the *Mahābhārata*', we will hear other conversations between husband and wife.

Life-in-family in the larger context of life

The life-in-family is the natural context in which most of human life is lived. Most human beings will feel lost without that context. In a large measure it gives to their individual life its meaning, however exacting, in different measures, its living may be. The living of the life-in-family is determined by the very nature of that context, and every context has its own logic. But no context can in itself be either self-sufficient or self-fulfilling. The context of the family is evidently located in the larger context of life itself. A *grihastha* and a *grihinī* are concerned no less, as human beings, with all those questions that touch human life intimately, some of them constantly, some others at different points of one's life. Therefore, constantly, the *Mahābhārata* suggests that the personal concerns of an individual living the life-in-family are not uniquely personal, and that they are best understood by understanding what exists beyond the personal, understood in a way, however, that what exists beyond the personal neither devalues nor negates the distinctly personal. For, it is only through oneself that one can sense, experience, and live. It is through the happenings in a family, through the experiences of a man or a woman or of a child, that the *Mahābhārata* reflects upon the fundamental questions as regards the human condition that those experiences invariably give rise to. Those happenings and experiences are the common stock of human living. *In that sense*, all families are alike. They all speak a common language. Yet, it is also true that growing in vastly different historical and cultural conditions, families in different places have different perceptions of life, of family itself.

But whatever the diversities, the *foundation of family* is, everywhere, and at all times, *saha*, 'togetherness'. And, in its very essence, there is in the *saha* no exercise of power of the one over the other. Neither is this *togetherness* a swallowing of one by the other, as of a lamb by a lion, and the lion declaring cheerfully, 'We two are *now* together.' Nor is *togetherness* an abolition of individuality and its distinct colours. Togetherness, by definition, requires the existence of the self and of the *other*.

In the ceremony of marriage by vedic rites, the man and the woman together take seven steps around the fire before which the ceremony takes place, fire being a witness, along with other elements of nature present. On taking the seventh step, they turn towards each other, and say:

सखा सप्तपदा भव
सख्यं ते गमेयं सख्यात्ते मायोषं
सख्यान्मे मा योष्ठास्मयाव
सङ्कल्पावहै संप्रियौ रोचिष्णू सुमनस्यमानौ।
इषमूर्जमभिसंवसानौ सन्नौ मनांसि
संव्रता समु चित्तान्याकरम्।।
With these seven steps, become my friend.
I seek your friendship. May you never deviate from this friendship.
May we walk together.
May we resolve together.
May we love each other and enhance each other.
May our vows be congruent and our desires shared.[108]

Marriage as friendship, not as theatre of a power struggle. Nor is *saha* limited to the family. It is the foundation of *all* relationships. There has been, for example, this famous resolve, of teacher and student together, and its sound heard through countless centuries:

ॐ सह नाववतु। सह नौ भुनक्तु। सह वीर्यं करवावहै।
तेजस्वि नावधीतमस्तु। मा विद्विषावहै।
May we together protect each other. And together nourish each other. May we gain strength together. What we have together learnt and studied, may it in splendour and force grow. May we never have for each other repugnance and dislike.[109]

Then follows the two-word invocation to peace that *togetherness* brings, and is repeated three times.

ॐ शान्तिः शान्तिः शान्तिः

CHAPTER THIRTEEN

Varṇa-dharma, Social Arrangements; *Loka-saṁgraha*, towards Social Wealth

- The origin of *varṇa*
- *Varṇa*—a function, not a person
- By conduct, not by birth
- By birth, not by conduct alone
- The humbling of arrogance
- Antagonism among social functions: its psychology
- Harmony among social functions: the way to social wealth

Equally with the highest human aspiration of *mokṣha*, spiritual freedom, the *Mahābhārata* is concerned with the social conditions that make human freedom possible. That takes us into the famous fourfold division of labour, or callings, or *varṇa*, which was firmly in place already in the vedic times, much before the *Mahābhārata* came to be written. But, also, it had degenerated into the *assumed* theocratic superiority of one division over the other; and, because they were believed to have had a theocratic origin, it had become oppressively divisive in social relations above all. As the Buddha would do centuries later, the *Mahābhārata* showed the *adharma* of a natural and perfectly rational division of callings turning into a social system of *castes* determined by one's birth, and they into 'superior' and 'inferior', 'upper' and 'lower. Producing arrogance in the 'upper caste', and resentment in the 'lower caste', it became a negation of what it was meant to be, turning *varṇa-dharma* into the *adharma* of *varṇa*. And whereas, in its foundations, the division of callings, *varṇa-dharma* is demonstrably universal, the wholly mistaken notion of *jātī-dharma* became something characteristically Indian, dominating Indian life and social relationships ever since, right up to our own times. Much of the modern research on Indian society, in anthropology and sociology and history, is obsessed with the caste system, even as all the reform movements in Indian history have had the caste as their focus of social struggle. However, what is of concern here is not Indian social *history* but the *foundations* of *loka-yātrā*, social living, and *loka-saṁgraha*, social wealth, the concerns of civil society everywhere, to which the *Mahābhārata* devoted anxious attention. That history is to be read and judged in the light of those foundations.

In the classical theory of *varṇa*, there was ideally a division of social functions.[1] Of the four *varṇa*, and the numerous *jātī* that arose connected with them, the economic functions of animal husbandry, agriculture, and trade were assigned to the *vaishya*. Manual labour and services for economic operations were provided by the *shūdra*. The *vaishya* and the *shūdra*, often clubbed together, with numerous artisan groups coming under that combination, were the producers of commodities and wealth.

The chief function of the *kṣhattriya* was not to participate in the production of wealth, but to govern and create harmonious social conditions by regulating the social behaviour of one group towards another group, where every *varṇa* and *jātī* could pursue its appointed function. The people on their part owed the king their allegiance, which was, however, not an allegiance to a person but to *dharma* as the foundation of governance, to which the governing class was itself to be subject in every way.

Likewise, the *brāhmaṇa*, as a calling, was to have nothing to do with the production of wealth. His function was to study the various branches of knowledge, the Veda; teach those competent to learn; perform sacred rituals and preserve their sanctity; and to act as counsel to the king and as teacher to all *varṇa*. In return for these services, expected to be of high quality, he was to receive for his maintenance, and for the maintenance of his family, gifts and grants from those to whom he attended.

The purely economic functions, assigned to the *vaishya* and the *shūdra*, were set apart from the governing and the intellectual functions, undoubtedly interrelated but each distinct nonetheless. Next was created, in successive stages, an intricate system of social control over wealth, its overriding principle being that wealth be produced and owned according to the dictates of *dharma*. That is to say, the relationships involved in the economic functions of a society are to be regulated by *dharma*. And here again the reader should return to the fundamental meaning of *dharma*. Hence the detailed laws and arrangements as regards the social uses to which a part of wealth ought to be put. Their foundations were laid in the *Mahābhārata*.

The Dharmic aims were: *one*, to confine the production of wealth to specified sections of society. *Two*, to control, distribute, and employ wealth for social purposes. And, *three*, in a world view where concern with the social order went hand in hand with the ultimate aspiration for *mokṣha*, to ensure that one did not conflict with the other. Any one of these aims would have been difficult enough to achieve wholly in any society with luxuriant diversity. To have made them together the ultimate social ideal was nothing less than inspired madness. Yet, it is hardly possible to say that they were altogether a failure. That they were not entirely a success either, and that occupation with wealth did not remain limited to the castes with economic functions, and extended even to monks, is indisputable. This made the Dharmic scene still more complex.

The four-*varṇa* social order has five aspects: (a) its origin; (b) the status of one *varṇa* in relation to another; (c) the scale of their legal accountability;

(d) reflecting the previous three, their social relations; and (e) their relative disciplines. They may be considered here, *in their essence*, so far as the *Mahābhārata* perceives them.

The origin of *varṇa*

As regards this, there were three distinct theories, which, like most things, got mixed up. The first is the divine-origin theory. The division of society into four *varṇa*s is attributed, in the *Ṛg-veda* itself, in its famous *Puruṣa-sūkta* hymn,[2] to the cosmogenic Male, who created the *brāhmaṇa* from His mouth; the *kṣhattriya* from His arms; the *vaishya* from His thighs; and the *shūdra* from His feet. An identical view of the divinely created *varṇa* is to be found in the *Vājneya-saṁhita* of the *Yajur-veda*;[3] in the *Taittirīya-saṁhita* of the Sama-veda;[4] in the *Atharva-veda*; and in the *Bṛhadāraṇ-yaka Upanishad*.[5] The God of the *Bhagvad-Gītā* tells us that the four *varṇ a* were created by Him, dividing them according to distinct aptitudes and functions.[6] Elsewhere in the *Mahābhārata*, generally it is to Brahmā that the origin of the four *varṇa* is attributed;[7] often enough it is to Krishna;[8] at least at one place, it is to Shiva.[9] However, this discrepancy is not material. That the *varṇa* order had its origin in the divine will, and is therefore inviolable, is something that has been believed for many centuries.

The other two theories are secular, are of equally ancient origin, and have had in diverse ways much influence. Of them, one is racial, and the other economic. Then there are variants of both. The racial theory is that *varṇa*, literally meaning 'colour', came to denote the two different peoples, the fair-skinned, or the *shukla-varṇa*, Aryan and the dark-skinned, or the *krishna-varṇa*, indigenous Dasyu and/or Dasa, struggling to achieve supremacy one over the other.[10] Because it was a prevalent view, therefore it is represented in the *Mahābhārata*. On account of their dark colour, *krishna-varṇa*, the latter were treated as racially distinct, and as inferior. To begin with, those were the only two *varṇa*: when subjugated, the dark-skinned people were soon given a position in the social hierarchy, but a lower one, and were called *shūdra*.[11] Their dark colour associated with the meanest of human attributes, as recorded in the *Mahābhārata*,[12] the prejudice against dark skin was laid deep in the Indian mind, and yet, not without being redeemed. For Krishna, one of the ancient gods of the Hindu pantheon, is portrayed as a dark-skinned god, as his very name suggests. One of the main characters of the *Mahābhārata*, Draupadī, who dominates the story from the beginning to the end, is known also as Krishnā, because of her dark colour. And she is portrayed also as an indescribably great beauty.

There is evidence of internal struggle among the Aryans themselves.[13] That probably put them into separate groups, each in turn called *varṇa*, namely, *brāhmaṇa*, *kṣhattriya*, and *vaishya*. The membership of each was determined purely by birth, and each was recognised, according to the theory, by a separate colour of the skin—the *brāhmaṇa* by the white, the *kṣhattriya* by the red, the *vaishya* by the yellow, and the *shūdra* by the black.[14]

No sooner was recounted, in the voice of the sage Bhrigu, what must have been the prevalent colour theory of the origin of the *varṇa* social structure than the *Mahābhārata* dismissed it straightaway, in the voice of the sage Bharadvāj.

Bhrigu *(describing the creation of the world)*

ब्राह्मणा: क्षत्रिया वैश्या: शूद्राश्च द्विजसत्तम।
ये चान्ये भूतसङ्घानां सङ्घास्तांश्चापि निर्ममे।। शान्ति १८८.४।।

Brahmā then created four varṇa-s: brāhmaṇa, kṣhattriya, vaishya *and* shūdra, *and other groups among humans.*[14a]

ब्राह्मणानां सितो वर्ण: क्षत्रियाणां तु लोहित:।
वैश्यानां पीतको वर्ण: शूद्राणामसितस्तथा।। शान्ति १८८.५।।

The colour of brāhmaṇa *was white, of* kṣhattriya *red, of* vaishya *yellow, and of* shūdra *black.*[14b]

Bharadvāj

स्वेदमूत्रपुरीषाणि श्लेष्मा पित्तं सशोणितम्।
तनु: क्षरति सर्वेषां कस्माद् वर्णो विभज्यते।। शान्ति १८८.८।।

But every human body bleeds, defecates, sweats, and has phlegm and life, alike. How can the human beings then be divided into varṇa *of different colours?*[15]

काम: क्रोधो भयं लोभ: शोकश्चिन्ता क्षुधा श्रम:।
सर्वेषां न: प्रभवति कस्माद् वर्णो विभिद्यते।। शान्ति १८८.७।।

Desire, anger, fear, greed, sorrow, anxiety, and hunger affect all human beings alike. How can there be then this difference of varṇa *at all?*[16]

The *Mahābhārata* is throughout concerned not with the colour of one's skin, but with the colours of one's thoughts, feelings, and acts. It is concerned with the human colours of desire, anger, fear, greed, sorrow, and hunger.

The economic theory, always brought up along with the divine-origin and the racial-origin theories, emphasises division of labour, and of social functions, as mentioned earlier. As the society grew increasingly complex, resulting in the emergence of numerous professions, the latter hardened into different *jātī*, caste properly called. Kane mentions the evidence that there were (with some doubts) at least sixty-three castes existing at the close of the vedic period itself,[17] which is generally reckoned to be about 1000 B.C..

A further division took place and newer castes came into being. The increasing division of *varṇa* into *jātī*, or caste, reflected then the need to acknowledge another human fact: free sexual union between men and women of different *varṇa*. This, called *varṇa-sankara*, or 'the mixing up of the *varṇa*-s', was forbidden in theory so very strongly that it must have been a common occurrence, indeed. If a higher *varṇa* man took a woman of a lower *varṇa*, as frequently happened, the union, with or without marriage, was called *anuloma*, 'in the natural order'. If, on the other hand, a higher *varṇa* woman took a man from a lower *varṇa*, as also must have frequently happened, the union was called *pratiloma*, 'against the natural order'. The progeny outside wedlock were similarly classified as *anuloma* and *pratiloma*, and each was given a specific name, and assigned a specific profession. The *shāstris*, or the lawgivers, all *brāhmaṇa*-s, were by now obsessed with the caste-game. For they proceeded to divide people further into sub-castes. That was done by classifying the following progeny. First, born of an *anuloma*, or a *pratiloma*, caste with any one of the main four *varṇa*-s, the belief obviously being that some in that *varna* were left still uncorrupted and of 'pure stock'. Second, born of inter-*anuloma*. Third, of inter-*pratiloma*. And then by classifying those born of *anuloma* with *pratiloma*, or the other way around. The result was a highly intricate calculus of the ensuing castes and sub-castes, with specific names and assigned particular professions.[18]

All this reached a point of total insanity. The *Mahābhārata* rejected it all, in different ways, in different contexts. While the so-called '*dharmashāstra*-s' of the *shāstris* were busy separating people in a fashion thoroughly artificial, an attribute of *adharma*, the *Mahābhārata* was showing what brings people together in their innate human unity, *dharma*.

Varṇa—a function, not a person

The single most important contribution of the *Mahābhārata* in regard to *varṇa* has been to insist that *varṇa* is a social *function* and not a *person*. Hence to each of the four *varna* a corresponding discipline was attached, an expectation from each, which was functional in the first place. The respective disciplines, naturally interrelated, were to be, together, the foundation of social progress and social wealth, *loka-yātrā* and *loka-saṁgraha*. In that sense, it was a collective discipline of *dharma*. What is functional has to be at the same time also ethical. Hence the common ethical discipline, or *sāmānya-dharma*, common to all social functions; and the specific discipline, or *vishesha-dharma*, specific to each calling. In the event of a conflict between the two, that is, between the ethical and the functional, which one should be decisive? This question, too, was taken up by the *Mahābhārata*.

By conduct, not by birth

Excepting the abnormal times, during which the functional duties of the four *varṇa* could be transposed, there is a strong and persistent element in the *Mahābhārata* which emphasised the relativity of *varṇa* itself. It was repeatedly held that the positions of *brāhmaṇa* and *shūdra*, for example, were relative to their conduct. Those were not to be regarded as positions fixed unalterably by virtue of birth.[19] Some of the propositions that the *Mahābhārata* put forth in that regard are as follows.

जातिरत्र महासर्प मनुष्यत्वे महामते ।
संकरात् सर्ववर्णानां दुष्परीक्ष्येति मे मति: ।। वन १८०.३१ ।।
It is difficult to determine the jātī *of a person because all the* varṇa *have become hopelessly mixed.*[20]

सर्वे सर्वास्वपत्यानि जनयन्ति सदा नरा: ।
वाङ्मैथुनमथो जन्म मरणं च समं नृणाम् ।। वन १८०.३२ ।।
All men everywhere are producing children with women of all castes: speech, sexual intercourse, birth and death are common to all human beings:[21]

इदमार्षं प्रमाणं च ये यजामह इत्यपि ।
तस्माच्छीलं प्रधानेष्टं विदुर्ये तत्त्वदर्शिन: ।। वन १८०.३३ ।।

Those who understand things and are wise regard cultured behaviour, therefore, to be more important.[22]

सत्यं दानं क्षमा शीलमानृशंस्यं तपो घृणा ।
दृश्यन्ते यत्र नागेन्द्र स ब्राह्मण इति स्मृतः ।। वन १८०.२१ ।।

Brāhmaṇa is one in whom can be seen truth, generosity, forgiveness, humility, absence of cruelty, austerity and kindness.[23]

चातुर्वर्ण्यं प्रमाणं च सत्यं च ब्रह्म चैव हि ।
शूद्रेष्वपि च सत्यं च दानमक्रोध एव च ।
आनृशंस्यमहिंसा च घृणा चैव युधिष्ठिर ।। वन १८०.२३ ।।

But these qualities are found in a shūdra *as well.*[24]

शूद्रे तु यद् भवेल्लक्ष्म द्विजे तच्च न विद्यते ।
न वै शूद्रो भवेच्छूद्रो ब्राह्मणो न च ब्राह्मणः ।। वन १८०.२५ ।।

यत्रैतल्लक्ष्यते सर्प वृतं स ब्राह्मणः स्मृतः ।
यत्रैतन्न भवेत् सर्प तं शूद्रमिति निर्दिशेत् ।। वन १८०.२६ ।।

If they are present in a shūdra, *and are absent in a* brāhmaṇa, *then that* shūdra *is not a* shūdra, *and that* brāhmaṇa *is not a* brāhmaṇa:[25] *only that person who has those qualities is to be regarded as* brāhmaṇa, *and the one who does not have them is to be regarded as a* shūdra.[26]

ब्रह्म च ब्राह्मणत्वं च येन त्वाहमचूचुदम् ।
सत्यं दमस्तपो दानमहिंसा धर्मनित्यता ।।
साधकानि सदा पुंसां न जातिर्न कुलं नृप । वन १८१.४२-३ ।।

It is neither family nor caste, but truth, and self-control, and penance, and discipline of the body and mind, and non-violence, and constant pursuit of knowledge, which help a man succeed in his aims.[27]

In the voice of Yakṣha, the *Mahābhārata* again clearly asks:

राजन् कुलेन वृत्तेन स्वाध्यायेन श्रुतेन वा ।
ब्राह्मण्यं केन भवति प्रब्रूह्येतत् सुनिश्चतम् ।। वन ३१३.१०७ ।।

Finally, profession, studies in scriptures, and philosophy of these, which determines brāhmaṇahood? *Tell me definitely.*[27a]

And equally clearly, in the voice of Yudhishṭhira, it answers this question by saying in a firm tone:

श‍ृणु यक्ष कुलं तात न स्वाध्यायो न च श्रुतम् ।
कारणं हि द्विजत्वे च वृत्तमेव न संशयः ।। वन ३१३.१०८ ।।

Brāhmaṇa*hood is determined by conduct, and not by family, nor by studies, nor by listening to scriptures—of this there is no doubt.*[28]

Again:

न योनिर्नापि संस्कारो न श्रुतं यत्र शूद्रेऽपि तिष्ठति ।
विशिष्टः स द्विजातेर्वै विज्ञेत इति मे मतिः ।। अनुशासन १४३.५० ।।

सर्वे वर्णा ब्राह्मणा ब्रह्मजाश्च
सर्वे नित्यं व्याहरन्ते च ब्रह्म ।
तत्त्वं शास्त्रं ब्रह्मबुद्ध्या ब्रवीमि
सर्वं विश्वं ब्रह्म चैतत् समस्तम् ।। शान्ति ३१८.८९ ।।

Born from Brahmā, all varṇa *are* brāhmaṇa.[29]

प्राप्य ज्ञानं ब्राह्मणात् क्षत्रियाद् वा
वैश्याच्छूद्रादपि नीचादभीक्ष्णम् ।
श्रद्धातव्यं श्रद्दधानेन नित्यं
न श्रद्धिनं जन्ममृत्यू विशेताम् ।। शान्ति ३१८.८८ ।।

A man of faith should obtain knowledge from whomsoever it is available, from the brāhmaṇa, *the* kṣhattriya, *the* vaishya, *or the* shūdra, *even from a man born in a low* varṇa.[30]

मनश्शौचं कर्मशौचं कुलशौचं च भारत ।
शरीरशौचं वाक्छौचं शौचं पञ्चविधं स्मृतम् ।। आश्व. ९२.पृ ६३७७ ।।

पञ्चस्वेतेषु शौचेषु हृदि शौचं विशिष्यते ।
हृदयस्य च शौचेन स्वर्गं गच्छन्ति मानवाः ।। आश्व. ९२.पृ ६३७७ ।।

There are five kinds of purity: the purity of the heart, the purity of acts, the purity of family, the purity of the body, and the purity of speech.[31] *Of these five, the purity of the heart is the most superior. It is only through the purity of the heart that human beings go to heaven.*[32]

Some centuries later, the voice of the Buddha would only add force to the *Mahābhārata*'s voice raised against distinctions based on castes, and against the assumed purity of the *brāhmaṇa*-s by virtue of birth alone. On the question of the relative purity of the castes, the Buddha declared: 'I do not say that there is any difference in freedom as against freedom.'[33] To him there was no distinction in striving after 'faith, health, honesty, output of energy, wisdom' except in the degree of success in it.[34]

In all likelihood, the immense popular appeal of the Buddha and his teachings was more due to the freedom they offered from the yoke of *varṇa* and *jātī*. The relativist propositions regarding *varṇa* were meant, most probably, to reverse the absolutist trends of the caste system that had already become unacceptable in the time of the *Mahābhārata*, and by the time of the Buddha, oppressive. But his teachings on social questions were a restatement of the original principles underlying the *varṇa* order. Their spirit was embodied in the proposition: *varṇa is a function and not the status of a person*. This is clearly stated in the theory of *varṇa*, whatever be the reversals and complexities of that theory in its historical development.

The *Shukranītī* states the position without any ambiguity.[35] It says:

न जात्या ब्राह्मणश्चात्र क्षत्रियो वैश्य एव च।
न शूद्रो न च वै म्लेच्छो भेदिता गुणकर्मभिः।। शुक्र I. १.३८।।

Not by birth is one brāhmaṇa, *or* kṣhattriya, *or* vaishya, *or* shūdra, *or* mleccha, *but by virtue of one's function and conduct.*[36]

ज्ञानकर्मोपासनाभिर्देवताराधने रतः।
शांतो दांतो दयालुश्च ब्राह्मणस्तु गुणैः कृतः।। शुक्र I. १.४०।।

The brāhmaṇa *is so called because he is given to knowledge, to the worship of the gods, to prayers, and is peaceful, restrained and kind.*[37]

लोकसंरक्षणे दक्षश्शूरो दांतः पराक्रमी।
दुष्टनिग्रहशीलो यस्स वै क्षत्रिय उच्यते।। शुक्र I. १.४१।।

He who protects the people; is dexterous, and is brave; is restrained and powerful; and punishes the wicked; is called kṣhattriya.[38]

क्रयविक्रयकुशला ये नित्यं पण्यजीविनः।
पशुरक्षाकृषिकरास्ते वैश्याः कीर्तिता भुवि।। शुक्र I. १.४२।।

Those who are experts in sale and purchase, who live by commerce, who tend to cattle and take to agriculture, are called vaishyas *in the world.*[39]

द्विजसेवार्चनरताश्शूराश्शांता जितेन्द्रियाः।
सीरकाष्ठतृणवहास्ते नीचाश्शूद्रसंज्ञिकाः।। शुक्र I. १.४३।।

Those, of the lower order, who provide services; who are brave, peaceful and have mastered their senses; who are drivers of the plough and cutters of the wood, are called shūdra-*s.*[40]

ब्रह्मणस्तु समुत्पन्नास्सर्वे ते किं नु ब्राह्मणाः ।
न वर्णतो न जनकाद्ब्राह्मचं तेजः प्रपद्यते ।। शुक्र I. १.३९ ।।
Born from Brahmā, all varṇa *are* brāhmaṇa.

त्यक्तस्वधर्माचरणा निर्घृणाः परपीडकाः ।
चण्डाला हिंसका नित्यं म्लेच्छास्ते ह्यविवेकिनः ।। शुक्र I. १.४४ ।।
Those who have abandoned their functional duties, who are cruel and cause pain to others, and who are always agitated, are mleccha-*s.*[41]

In order to emphasise, once again, that *shūdra* is a social function and not a person, Shiva, after indicating the social functions of the *brāhmaṇa*, the *kṣhattriya,* and the *vaishya*, declares:

तथैव शूद्रा विहिताः सर्वधर्मप्रसाधकाः ।
शूद्राश्च यदि ते न स्युः कर्मकर्ता न विद्यते ।। अनुशासन पृ. ५९२१ ।।
Similarly, shūdra *is the basis of all* dharmas: *if there were no* shūdra, *there would be no services:*[42] *the other three* varṇa-*s are founded on* shūdra. ’[43]

त्रयः पूर्वे शूद्रमूलाः सर्वे कर्मकराः स्मृताः । अनुशासन पृ. ५९२१ ।।
All social functions are shūdramūlaka.

By birth, not by conduct alone

But the contention that *brāhmana*, *kshattriya*, *vaishya*, and *shūdra* were functional terms, and therefore who is what one is must depend on one’s character, linked respectively with the four broad groups of social functions, could hardly amount to much in practical terms. For not only was it impossible to assign to a person a *varna* after observing his, or her, character and conduct, but also these were neither always self-consistent nor always coherent in themselves. Nor was it inconceivable that a person could exhibit, at the same time, or at different times, the diverse characteristics that each *varṇa* was supposed to embody as something distinctive to it. It was quite conceivable that a person be simultaneously intellectual, energetic, and shrewd in matters concerning money and trade, the traits chiefly associated in the *varṇa* theory with *brāhmaṇa*-s, *kṣhattriya*-s, and *vaishya*-s respectively. Thus it was practically impossible to assign *varṇa* simply on the basis of conduct and propensity. These were by nature uncertain, ambiguous, and changing, and no social structure could be based solely on them, even if undoubtedly they were important factors in social relations. For this reason, quietly ignoring the view that one's place in the structure of *varṇa* must be relative to conduct and character, birth remained the sole basis to one's *varṇa*. That was the chief premise of the *dharmashāstra*, and is represented fully in the *Mahābhārata* as well.

The concept of *sva-dharma* as something absolute was emphasised again with full vigour. The functional duties of different *varṇa* were reiterated at every opportunity,[44] and so was the principle: 'Let no one discard the duties that are attached to him with birth into a *varṇa*, no matter if those duties be without superior qualities.'[45] The next step was to maintain that even if a person was devoid of ethical qualities required of his particular *varṇa*, it did not deprive him of the status of that *varṇa*.

To take the *brāhmaṇa* as an illustration of this, we find it stated without any ambiguity:

> दुर्वृत्ता वा सुवृत्ता वा प्राकृता वा सुसंस्कृताः।
> ब्राह्मणा नावमन्तव्या भस्मच्छन्ना इवाग्नयः।। आश्वमेधिक पृ. ६३१७।।
> *Whether the* brāhmaṇa*s are of evil or of good character, whether they are crude or cultured, they should never be insulted, because they are like the fire concealed under the ash.*'[46]

Then followed a fulsome eulogy of the *brāhmaṇa*.[47] How weighty that eulogy was meant to be is evident from the fact that it was spoken by Krishna, presented already in the *Mahābhārata* as an incarnation of Vishnu. He pronounces:

> नास्ति विप्रसमं दैवं नास्ति विप्रसमो गुरुः।
> नास्ति विप्रात् परो बन्धुर्नास्ति विप्रात् परो निधिः।। आश्वमेधिक पृ. ६३१८।।
> *There is no god greater than the* brāhmaṇa, *and greater than him there is no guru. There is no friend greater than the* brāhmaṇa, *and greater than him there is no treasure.*

> नास्ति विप्रात् परं तीर्थं न पुण्यं ब्राह्मणात् परम्।
> न पवित्रं परं विप्रान्न द्विजात् पावनं परम्।
> नास्ति विप्रात् परो धर्मो नास्ति विप्रात् परा गतिः।। आश्वमेधिक पृ. ६३१८।।

There is no place more sacred than the brāhmaṇa, *and no merit greater than him. There is nothing purer than the* brāhmaṇa, *nor is there anything more purifying than him. There is no* dharma *greater than the* brāhmaṇa, *and greater than him there is no state of existence.*[48]

उत्पत्तिरेव विप्रस्य मूर्तिर्धर्मस्य शाश्वती।। आश्वमेधिक पृ. ६३१७।।
By his very birth he is the abiding symbol of eternal dharma.[49]

ये केचित् सागरान्तायां पृथिव्यां द्विजसत्तमाः।
मम रूपं हि तेष्वेवमचिंतेष्वर्चितोऽस्म्यहम्।। आश्वमेधिक पृ. ६३२१।।

ब्राह्मणे पूजिते नित्यं पूजितोऽस्मि न संशयः।
आक्रुष्टे चाहमाक्रुष्टो भवामि भरतर्षभ।। आश्वमेधिक पृ. ६३२०।।
तर्जयन्ति च ये विप्रान् क्रोशयन्ति च भारत।
आक्रुष्टस्तजितश्चाहं तैर्भवामि न संशयः।। आश्वमेधिक पृ. ६३२१।।
Therefore the brāhmaṇa *is to be worshipped; wherever he is worshipped, I am worshipped too—in this there is no doubt, and the rude words directed at the* brāhmaṇa *are in fact directed at me.*[50]

बहवस्तु व जानन्ति नरा ज्ञानबहिष्कृताः।
यदहं द्विजरूपेण वसामि वसुधातले।। आश्वमेधिक पृ. ६३२१।।
For many ignorant people do not know, it is I who reside on the earth in the form of the brāhmaṇa.[51]

In the voice of Bhīshma, the *Mahābhārata* states an altogether different perception of the *brāhmaṇa*-s, who were of many different kinds.

सन्त्येषां सिंहसत्त्वाश्च व्याघ्रसत्त्वास्तथापरे।
वराहमृगसत्त्वाश्च जलसत्त्वास्तथापरे।। अनुशासन ३५.१४।।
Some have the strength of a lion, some of a tiger. The strength of some is that of a wild boar, of some others, that of a deer. And some are as slippery as the fish.[52]

सर्पस्पर्शसमाः केचित् तथान्ये मकरस्पृशः।
विभाष्यधातिनः केचित् तथा चक्षुर्हणोऽपरे।। अनुशासन ३५.१५।।
The touch of some is like the touch of a snake; of others, like the touch of a crocodile. Some can kill by cursing; some others, only by their look of anger.[53]

सन्ति चाशीविषसमा: सन्ति मन्दास्तथापरे ।
विविधानीह वृत्तानि ब्राह्मणानां युधिष्ठिर ।। अनुशासन ३५.१६ ।।
Some are dangerous like a poisonous snake; but some others are of a gentle nature. In this world the temperament and conduct of brāhmaṇas *are of many kinds.*[54]

Furthermore, a *brāhmaṇa*, should he even be a sage, was not averse to singing the glory, in the most extravagant terms, of a king, with a view to receiving from him as reward, riches. The *Mahābhārata* records this honestly. The *brāhmaṇa* as a definite social function was expected to devote himself to knowledge, to learning and teaching, and not seek material affluence, for these two generally do not go together. But, on the urging of his wife, the sage Atri frees himself from that discipline.[55] He proposes to his wife that they and the family go and live in the forest, 'for life in a forest is much better than life in a village'.[56] The wife suggests that before he and she do that, he should make their children financially secure, and that he should for that purpose approach King Prithu, who was at that time having a *yajña* conducted, during which gifts are given to *brāhmaṇa*-s.[57] 'The only obstruction to that,' Atri says to his wife, 'is that the *brāhmaṇa*-s who would have assembled there are hostile to me. Whatever I will say on the subjects of *dharma*, material prosperity, and fulfilment of sexual impulse, they will say the very contrary of it. Even so, I will go there, for your suggestion is a good one, and King Prithu will give me much money.'[58]

Arriving there, sage Atri says to the king: 'You are on this earth the greatest king, blessed are you. All the sages sing glory to you. For, other than you, there is no king on this earth who is rooted in *dharma*.'[59] On hearing this lavish praise of the king, the sage Gautama got angry—violating the discipline that a *brāhmaṇa*, most of all, master anger—and said to Atri: 'Never say that again. In the form of god Indra, Prajāpati himself is present here. You are not in your senses. You know nothing of *dharma*. You do not even know what the purpose of *dharma* is. You are a fool. I know you have come here to serve your selfish end, to secure money from the king.'[60] Atri retorted: 'Gautama, it is *your* intelligence that is clouded. King Prithu is truly 'the dispenser of destinies', the *vidhātā*, and it is he who is also the Prajāpāti.'[61]

The assembled *brāhmaṇas* there asked, 'Who are these two, quarrelling, and so loudly? Who allowed them to come here?'[62] They were informed that the dispute was about the sage Atri maintaining that King Prithu was the dispenser of destinies and the sage Gautama challenging it.[63] Since a firm decision was required on that point of dispute, they all rushed to the sage Sanatkumāra for resolving it. He decided in favour of Atri describing the king as the dispenser of destinies.[64] Very pleased, Atri's view of the king upheld, King Prithu said to him: 'You have called me the greatest among men, and equal to the gods. Therefore I shall give you gold coins one hundred million; ten full measures of gold; diamonds and rubies and other jewels; beautiful clothes, and also a hundred young women to be in your service. I give all these to you, right now. In my opinion, you are the wisest of all.'[65] Loaded with those riches, the sage Atri returns home, distributes that wealth among his children, and goes with his wife to live in the forest.[66]

In order to reject Krishna's declaration that 'by birth is *brāhmaṇa* a great god', irrespective of his actual character, the *Mahābhārata* narrates the story of a *brāhmaṇa*, Gautama, who was cruel and greedy, an ungrateful wretch, killing his friend and benefactor without a scruple, without a thought. On the orders of the king, he is seized, and cut into pieces. But when that meat was fed to animals, even they, who lived on all kinds of meat, found the meat of a human who was an ungrateful wretch and the betrayer and killer of his loving friend unacceptable.[67]

मित्रद्रोही नृशंसश्च कृतघ्नश्च नराधमः।
क्रव्यादैः कृमिभिश्चैव न भुज्यन्ते हि तादृशाः।। शान्ति १७२.२६।।

The one who is a betrayer of a friend; is cruel; is ungrateful; is the lowliest among humans; even the carnivorous animals, not even the insects, would eat the flesh of such a being.

To Krishna, irrespective of moral excellence the *shūdra* was forever *shūdra*. This position was reached in a complete reversal of the view that should a *shūdra* distinguish himself ethically and spiritually, he be regarded as *brāhmaṇa*. For there was no reason why a *shūdra* could not excel himself thus. Now it was held that he was not fit for a superior life other than what his birth as *shūdra* had destined him to lead. He was kept from learning the Veda and reciting them. Krishna declares:

न भयं देवदैत्येभ्यो रक्षोभ्यश्चैव मे नृप।
शूद्रवक्त्राच्च्युतं ब्रह्म भयं तु मम सर्वदा।। आश्वमेधिक. पृ. ६३७९।।

I fear neither gods nor demons; but I always fear when the Veda are recited by the shūdra.[68]

त्रैलोक्येऽस्मिन् निरुद्विग्नो न बिभेमि कुतश्चन।
न दिवा यदि वा रात्रावुद्वेग: शूद्रलङ्घनात्।।. आश्वमेधिक पृ. ६३७९।।
It is the transgression of limits by the shūdra *that agitates me.*[69]

यान्युक्तानि मया सम्यग् विद्यास्थानानि भारत।
उत्पन्नाति प्रवित्राणि भुवनार्थं तथैव च।।
तस्मात् तानि न शूद्रस्य स्पृष्टव्यानि युधिष्ठिर।
सर्वं च शूद्रसंस्पृष्टमपवित्रं न संशय:।।. आश्वमेधिक पृ. ६३७७।।
There are fourteen areas of knowledge. The four Veda, their six accessories, the mīmāṁsā, the nyāya, *the* dharmashāstra *and the* purāna*: these were created for the good of the three worlds: the* shūdra *must not touch them; for all things that come in contact with the* shūdra *are polluted—in this there is no doubt.*[70]

लोके त्रीण्यपवित्राणि पञ्चामेध्यानि भारत।
श्वा च शूद्र:श्वापाकश्च अपवित्राणि पाण्डव।। आश्वमेधिक पृ. ६३७७।।
The dog, the shūdra, *and the* chandala *are impure.*[71]

> *For this reason the brāhmaṇa was forbidden to eat the food offered or touched by the shūdra*[72]*—except in times of distress. Neither was the shūdra to be instructed by the brāhmana in higher learning, or in the details of shastric ritual, even if he had by his austere efforts risen to the status of the ascetic.*[73] *This was in complete reversal of the position taken in one of the major Upanishad-s, namely, whoever is truthful, he is worthy of being initiated into vedic studies, even if he has no known father and therefore no known lineage.*[74]

The *Mahābhārata* was honestly recording that reversal.

And after recording that reversal, it took a strong position against it, in different contexts, in different voices. The voice of the sage Parāshara, the father of the author of the *Mahābhārata*, was one of them. In a long discourse to King Janaka, which is described as the *Parāshara-Gītā*,[75] he maintains, in complete contrast to what Krishna had said about the *shūdra*:

न चापि शूद्र: पततीति निश्चयो
  न चापि संस्कारमिहार्हतीति वा।
श्रुतिप्रवृत्तं न च धर्ममाप्नुते
  न चास्य धर्मे प्रतिषेधनं कृतम्।। शान्ति २९६.२७।।
It is certain that the shūdra *is not a lowly being.*[76]

वैदेह कं शूद्रमुदाहरन्ति
 द्विजा महाराज श्रुतोपपन्ना: ।
अहं हि पश्यामि नरेन्द्र देवं
 विश्वस्य विष्णुं जगत: प्रधानम् ।। शान्ति २९६.२८ ।।

Those who are truly learned in the Veda and the shastra *regard the* shūdra *verily as the Prajāpati, the creator and the protector of life. But, dear King, I see the* shūdra *as Vishṇu, the main protector of the world and the source of its nourishing.*[77]

In an invocation to Shiva, it is said:

ब्राह्मणा: क्षत्रिया वैश्या: शूद्रा वर्णावराश्च ये ।
त्वमेव मेघसंघाश्च विद्युत्स्तनितगर्जित: ।। शान्ति २८४.१२२ ।।

Brāhmaṇa, kṣhattriya, vaishya, shūdra, *and those beyond, are all your forms.*[78]

In the voice of Parāshara, the *Mahābhārata* is reiterating that social arrangements have a common goal, one of creating social wealth, of creating conditions in which each person can fulfil his or her human worth. Parāshara restates the familiar origin of *varṇa* in a natural division of labour and describes the *specific functions* of each.[79] And to each specific social function, a specific discipline is attached, without which that social function can never be fulfilled. Then follows a quick statement of the requirements of ethical conduct common to them all.[80]

आनृशंस्यमहिंसा चाप्रमाद: संविभागिता ।
श्राद्धकर्मातिथेयं च सत्यमक्रोध एव च ।। शान्ति २९६.२३ ।।
स्वेषु दारेषु संतोष: शौचं नित्यानसूयता ।
आत्मज्ञानं तितिक्षा च धर्मा: साधारणा नृप ।। शान्ति २९६.२४ ।।

Absence of cruelty; not-violence; vigilance; a feeling of gratitude towards one's ancestors; warm hospitality to guests; truthfulness; freedom from anger; contentment with one's own wife; cleanliness; not finding faults in others; self-knowledge; and forbearance—these are the dharma-*s common to all.*

In the context of *varṇa-dharma*, 'the specific social callings', into which, to begin with, one is born, and quite aware that some of those callings were being looked upon as 'inferior' and 'impure', King Janaka asks Parāshara:

किं कर्म दूषयत्येनमथो जातिर्महामुने।
संदेहो मे समुत्पन्नस्तन्मे व्याख्यातुमर्हसि।। शान्ति २९६.३१।।
A doubt has arisen in my mind: is it by one's birth, or is it by one's conduct, that one invites impurity into one's life? Will you examine this for me?[81]

Parāshara's answer is:

असंशयं महाराज उभयं दोषकारकम्।
कर्म चैव हि जातिश्च विशेषं तु निशामय।। शान्ति २९६.३२।।
By both does one attract impurity to one's station in life—of this, there is no doubt. However, there is a distinctive aspect to this question, which I will mention.[82]

जात्या च कर्मणा चैव दुष्टं कर्म न सेवते।
जात्या दुष्टश्च यः पापं न करोति स पूरुषः।। शान्ति २९६.३३।।
Only that person who, regardless of where he is born, behaves in a way not blameworthy, is worthy of being called a human person.[83]

जात्या प्रधानं पुरुषं कुर्वाणं कर्म धिक्कृतम्।
कर्म तद् दूषयत्येनं तस्मात् कर्म न शोभनम्।। शान्ति २९६.३४।।
Born in a superior station in life, if he still behaves in a way that is shameful, that person falls low. Therefore, one should not act in ways that do no good.[84]

The humbling of arrogance

Were the *brāhmaṇa* a person, independent of the social functions allotted to the *varṇa* called '*brāhmaṇa*', and irrespective also of the intellectual and moral qualities required to fulfil that function, then, to take one example, the imparting of knowledge should have been the privilege only of those born in the families called '*brāhmaṇa*'. That this was never the case, and that any such implication was on the contrary refuted, can be seen in several of those parables in the *Mahābhārata* in which an arrogant *brāhmaṇa* is humbled and made to receive instruction at the hands now of a *kṣhattriya*, then of a *vaishya*, and equally often at the hands of a *shūdra*.

Jājali, a *brāhmaṇa* ascetic, who had persuaded himself that he knew everything about *dharma*, for the sole reason that he had practised severe austerities, was cured of his arrogance by being made to visit Tulādhāra, a *vaishya*, a grocer, who then instructs him in the real meaning of *dharma*.[85]

Then there is the long parable of Kaushika, the *brāhmaṇa* scholar and also an ascetic. Kaushika had mastered the Veda, had mastered all knowledge, but not anger.[86] One day, as he was studying, sitting under a tree, a bird soiled him and his books with her droppings. He looks up in great anger, and so great is the force in his eyes that the offending bird drops dead. Somewhat remorseful at what he had done, he sets out to beg for his daily food. Reaching the doorsteps of a house, he gives the call of a *brāhmaṇa* with a begging bowl. From inside the house a woman answers: 'Please wait.' The woman was then attending to her husband, who had only a little while earlier returned from a long journey and was tired and hungry. After she finished her duties to him, she comes out with food for the *brāhmaṇa*, who in the meantime is most wrathful, because he was made to wait, and felt insulted thereby. Full of anger, he addresses her with words of reproach. She explains what had held her. But Kaushika continues to address her in a menacing language. Once again, most respectfully, the woman explains what had delayed her giving him the offering of food. Kaushika is still angry, and abusive. At this point, the woman says to him: 'Do forgive me, sir, I did not mean to insult you;[87] *but I am not that little bird either, whom you could kill with your angry look.*'[88] Kaushika is astonished by her pre-knowledge of that event. Noticing his astonishment, but ignoring it, she gently continues her brief address to him, saying: '*There is one enemy of men that resides in their bodies, its name is anger.*'[89] 'It is because of the anger of *brāhmaṇas* that the water of the sea turned salty.'[90] Then, in five clear and crisp verses, she tells him what kind of man do the gods acknowledge as *brāhmaṇa*.

यः क्रोधमोहौ त्यजति तं देवा ब्राह्मणं विदुः ।
यो वदेदिह सत्यानि गुरुं संतोषयेत च।। वन २०६.३३ ।।
हिंसितश्च न हिंसेत तं देवा ब्राह्मणं विदुः ।

He who gives up anger and confusion; speaks the truth; keeps his teacher contented; does not return violence with violence; do the gods acknowledge as a brāhmaṇa.[91]

जितेन्द्रियो धर्मपरः स्वाध्यायनिरतः शुचिः ।। वन २०६.३४ ।।
कामक्रोधौ वशौ यस्य तं देवा ब्राह्मणं विदुः ।

He who has mastered his sense organs, and has thereby mastered anger and lust; is given to study, and is clean; do the gods acknowledge as a brāhmaṇa.[92]

यस्य चात्मसमो लोको धर्मज्ञस्य मनस्विनः ।। वन २०६.३५ ।।
सर्वधर्मेषु च रतस्तं देवा ब्राह्मणं विदुः ।
He who feels himself to be one with the world; and treats all dharmas *alike; do the gods acknowledge as a* brāhmaṇa.[93]

योऽध्यापयेदधीयीत यजेद् वा याजयीत वा ।। वन २०६.३६ ।।
दद्याद् वापि यथाशक्ति तं देवा ब्राह्मणं विदुः ।
He who studies and teaches; gives whatever lies in his capacity to give; do the gods acknowledge as a brāhmaṇa.[94]

ब्रह्मचारी वदान्यो योऽधीयीत द्विजपुङ्गवः ।। वन २०६.३७ ।।
स्वाध्यायवानमत्तो वै तं देवा ब्राह्मणं विदुः ।
He who is restrained in his natural impulses; is noble-minded; and is mindful in his studies; do the gods acknowledge as brāhmaṇa.[95]

In other words, she tells Kaushika that he is *not* a *brāhmaṇa* by conduct, not yet at any rate. Not only that, she tells him in plain language that.

न तु तत्त्वेन भगवन् धर्मं वेत्सीति मे मतिः ।। वन २०६.४३ ।।
Venerable sir, you do not, in my opinion, know the substance of dharma.[96]

The woman then suggests to the young ascetic that he go to the city of Mithilā and meet Dharmavyādha, a meatseller, from whom he would learn a great deal more about *dharma*. At the same time, very charmingly, she delivers her final words to him:

अत्युक्तमपि मे सर्वं क्षन्तुमर्हस्यानिन्दित ।
स्त्रियो ह्यवध्याः सर्वेषां ये च धर्मविदो जनाः ।। वन २०६.४६ ।।
Should I have said something which I should not have, then I seek your forgiveness. In the eyes of those who know dharma, *women are above punishment!*[97]

Far from saying anything she should not have said, she had said what a sage, Syūmarashmi, would say to another sage, Kapila, at another time.[98]

Sufficiently humbled, Kaushika says to the woman: 'On the contrary, your words of reproach have done me great good. You are a good woman.'[99] After expressing his gratitude for what she had said to him, he leaves. It is significant that the woman's *varṇa* is not mentioned, nor even her name. It was sufficient that she was a woman, and that she was a good woman. She must have undoubtedly heard the prudent advice

> त्रीन् कृशान् नावजानीयाद् दीर्घमायुर्जिजीविषुः ।
> ब्राह्मणं क्षत्रियं सर्पं सर्वे ह्याशीविषास्त्रयः ।। अनुशासन १०४.७७ ।।
> *Whoever wishes to live long, must not trifle with, even if they were weak, a* brāhmaṇa, *a* kṣhattriya, *and a snake; for they all are very poisonous.*[100]

Refusing to be overawed, she had decided to cure the arrogance of a *brāhmaṇa* scholar and ascetic, and advised him that he should further learn—from a *meatseller*.

Kaushika takes her advice and travels to Mithilā. On making inquiries about Dharmavyādha, he is directed to a shop where a man is selling the meat of goat and buffalo. *After* he had attended to his customers, he turns, as the woman had done *after* she had attended to her tired and hungry husband who had come home from a long journey, to Kaushika and tells him that he knows who he is and the purpose of his visit. 'This is the *second* astonishment!' Kaushika mutters to himself. 'But this is not the place for a man like you,' the meatseller says to him, 'Come, let us go home, and we shall talk there.' On reaching home, he attends to his old parents first. Then follows a long discourse, slow, measured, and profound,[101] from the meatseller to the *brāhmaṇa*. It contains the very substance of *dharma*.[102]

It is noteworthy that the instruction on the ethical and spiritual core of *dharma*, came to a *brāhmaṇa* from a meatseller, ranked amongst the lowest in the scale of *varṇa* and *jātī*. It is equally noteworthy that neither the housewife nor the meatseller mentions *sva-dharma*, that is, '*one's allotted calling*', directly. When it is mentioned indirectly, it is done only to make the point that should a *brāhmaṇa* fail to develop the ethical qualities necessarily required of his functional status, then he was not to be regarded as a *brāhmaṇa*.

Kaushika takes leave of Dharmavyādha after expressing his deep gratitude to him.

इहाहमागतो दिष्ट्या दिष्ट्या मे सङ्गतं त्वया।
ईदृशा दुर्लभा लोके नरा धर्मप्रदर्शकाः।। वन २१५.१४।।

It was my great good fortune that I came here and had your company. It is rare to find in the world a man like you who shows the path to dharma.[103]

एको नरसहस्त्रेषु धर्मविद् विद्यते न वा।
प्रीतोस्मि तव सत्येन भद्रं ते पुरुषर्षभ।। वन २१५.१५।।

Maybe there is, or maybe there is not, one man in a thousand who knows the essence of dharma. *I am happy in the truth you've shown me.*[104]

पतमानोऽद्य नरके भवतास्मि समुद्धृतः।
भवितव्यमथैवं च यद् दृष्टोऽसि मयानघ।। वन २१५.१६।।

I was descending into a hell; but you have liberated me. In the future, too; now that I have seen you.[105]

The *Mahābhārata* equally dwells on the arrogance of power and its humbling. It narrates numerous stories of the humbling of a king, in different ways; and, as every human story does, each one of them says many things simultaneously about human conduct. The story of sage Shamīka and King Parīkṣhita is narrated in the very first few chapters of the *Mahābhārata*, in the *Ādi-parva*.[106]

Parīkṣhita was the grandson of Arjuna, and was in many respects a good king. One day he went hunting, and was chasing a deer that he had already injured by his arrow. The deer eluded him, and the king in the meantime felt exceedingly tired, thirsty, and hungry as well. In that state, he chanced to enter the hermitage of sage Shamīka, and saw him sitting under a tree. He approached him and asked him whether he had seen a deer with an arrow embedded in its body running that way. Shamīka does not answer. That was because that day was his day of silence. The king repeats his question; the sage remains silent. Exasperated at this, Parīkṣhita picks up with one end of his bow a dead snake that he sees lying there, and places it around the neck of the silent sage, who does not react even to this, and keeps his silence.[107] Grievously insulted by the king, sage Shamīka does not insult him in turn.[108] He does not speak one word. And the king leaves.

The sage had a young son, Shringī by name. He was known for his learning, for leading an austere life, and for his force of character. But he was known even more for his quick hot temper, and he was difficult to please. While returning home, he encountered his friend Krisha, son of another sage, who narrated to him the earlier events.[109] On being asked more closely, Krisha said: 'Your father had done nothing to the king that was improper. If he did not answer the king, that was because he was, at that time, observing his discipline of silence. To see the king put that dead snake around your father's neck, I was as grieved as I would have been had my own father been insulted like that.'[110] 'The king has gone away; but your father is sitting there, with a dead snake around his neck.' On hearing this, by now his eyes red with the fire of anger, Shringī pronounces a curse upon King Parīkṣhita thus: 'For placing a dead snake around my old father's neck, and insulting him, seven nights after today Takṣhaka, the king cobra, impelled by the power of my words, will bite that arrogant king and make him die a horrible death.'[111]

On reaching the hermitage, and greatly distressed by what was done to his father, he tells him about the curse that he had earlier pronounced upon Parīkṣhita[112] Thereupon sage Shamīka speaks to his angry son thus:

न मे प्रियं कृतं तात नैव धर्मस्तपस्विनाम्।
वयं तस्य नरेन्द्रस्य विषेये निवसामहे।। आदि ४१.२०।।

न्यायतो रक्षितास्तेन तस्य शापं न रोचये।
सर्वथा वर्तमानस्य राज्ञो ह्यस्मद्विधैः सदा।। आदि ४१.२१।।

क्षन्तव्यं पुत्र धर्मो हि हतो हन्ति न संशयः।
यदि राजा न संरक्षेत् पीडा नः परमा भवेत्।। आदि ४१.२२।।

Dear son! By acting in that manner, which is not the dharma *of us ascetics, you have done me no good. We live in the realm of King Parīkṣhita, who protects us in every lawful way. Therefore he deserves to be forgiven in every way. Your cursing him has not pleased me at all. When* dharma *is transgressed, that transgression itself destroys us. If the king does not protect, there is great disorder.*[113]

न शक्नुयाम चरितुं धर्मं पुत्र यथा सुखम्।
रक्ष्यमाणा वयं तात राजभिर्धर्मदृष्टिभिः।। आदि ४१.२३।।

चरामो विपुलं धर्मं तेषां भागोऽस्ति धर्मतः।
सर्वथा वर्तमानस्य राज्ञः क्षन्तव्यमेव हि।। आदि ४१.२४।।

Protected by a king who acts in the light of dharma*, we are ourselves able to live in accordance with* dharma*, which will not be possible without the* *protection of governance. Hence, in the merit that we earn, the king has a share, too. The present king is to be forgiven.*[114]

तेनेह क्षुधितेनाद्य श्रान्तेन च तपस्विना।
अजानता कृतं मन्ये व्रतमेतदिदं मम।। आदि ४१.२६।।

Today he chanced to come here, tired, thirsty and hungry. He didn't know about my day of silence. It seems to me that that is the reason why, angry when I did not speak to him, he behaved in the way that he did.[115]

कस्मादिदं त्वया बाल्यात् सहसा दुष्कृतं कृतम्।
न ह्यर्हति नृपः शापमस्मत्तः पुत्र सर्वथा।। आदि ४१.३३।।

But without considering the circumstances, you acted in a way that was impulsive and wrong. The king does not deserve our curse.[116]

Shringī said to his father: 'Whether that was impulsive; whether what I did was wrong; whether you like it or you don't, my curse will not go in vain. I've never spoken a lie—not even in jest. My curse will come true.'[117]

Shamīka said to his son: 'By nature you are hard. I know that the curse you have pronounced will not come untrue. Even so, a father should instruct even his grown-up son, so that he might live a life of virtue. You are still a child; even those who have distinguished themselves and are great souls are sometimes overcome with anger. Therefore, on seeing that your childishness is taking you away from *dharma*, I consider it necessary that I instruct you.'[118]

क्रोधो हि धर्मं हरति यतीनां दुःखसंचितम्।
ततो धर्मविहीनानां गतिरिष्टा न विद्यते।। आदि ४२.८।।

Anger destroys what the seekers would have with great difficulty achieved in dharma. *Bereft of* dharma, *they become bereft of a higher state of life.*[119]

शम एव यतीनां हि क्षमिणां सिद्धिकारकः।
क्षमावतामयं लोकः परश्चैव क्षमावताम्।। आदि ४२.९।।

Self-restraint and forgiveness is the path of all true seekers. Those who are forgiving, for them this world and the next are good.[120]

तस्माच्चरेथाः सततं क्षमाशीलो जितेन्द्रियः।
क्षमया प्राप्स्यसे लोकान् ब्रह्मणः समनन्तरान्।। आदि ४२.१०।।

Keeping your faculties under control, learn to be forgiving. It is through forgiveness that you will achieve the highest.[121]

'As far as I am concerned,' Shamīka says to his son, 'with peace in my heart I will do what can still be done. I will send a message to the king: 'On coming to know your insulting behaviour towards me, my son, impulsive and of little intelligence, has pronounced a curse upon you.' And he sends his pupil, Gauramukha, to the royal palace with that message, which was delivered.[122] The messenger said to the king: 'Sage Shamīka has forgiven you, but not his son, who has cast a curse upon you. On the seventh night from today, Takṣhaka, the king cobra, will be the cause of your death. Do all you can to protect yourself.'[123]

When all this became widely known, a physician of the greatest skill, Kāshyapa by name, set off for the royal palace on the seventh day. 'When Takṣhaka causes the king's death, I will bring him back to life by the power of my *mantra*-s, and I will earn both money and merit thereby.' Takṣhaka interrupts the physician's journey, saying to him: 'I will give you twice as much money as you expect from the king after you have revived him. Besides, it is possible that you may not be able to; in which case, your reputation as a great physician will be ruined. So, go back.' But the king cobra first wanted to make sure that Kāshyapa did indeed possess the medical power to bring back to life a person who had died from the poison of a snake. He asks the physician to revive a tree into which he will inject his deadly poison, which the physician does. Convinced, Takṣhaka gives him the promised money. And the physician, the money secured, cheerfully abandons the merit part of reviving a dead king, and goes back.[124]

On receiving sage Shamīka's message, the king's ministers had set up the most elaborate arrangements in order to protect the king from being bitten by a snake. But on the fateful day, Takṣhaka does reach, through cleverly devised means, Parīkṣhita's body, injects into it its deadly poison, and that very instant the king drops dead.[125] The curse comes true.

Parīkṣhita was born still—when Ashvatthāmā, in revenge of his father Droṇāchārya's death on the battlefield by manifestly devious means adopted by the Pāṇḍavas, had fired on the womb of Uttarā, carrying Parīkṣhita, a weapon of the greatest power. But Krishna had brought the dead child back to life then. This time, there was no one to enact another miracle.

Antagonism among social functions: its psychology

With increasing diversity of economic and administrative functions, the concept of *sva-dharma*, 'one's allotted calling', had lost its functional meaning long before the Christian era began. It is now settled that the *kṣhattriya*-s had contributed much to the new thought in the *Upanishad*-s, even if it did not originate entirely in their circle.[126] Some of them had influenced the break from that part of the vedic world view that was magical, animistic, and ritualistic. They had participated in that great adventure of the human spirit, which concluded with the view that there is one eternal reality, not to be known entirely through reasoning, but on knowing which everything else is known. The one *atman*, the *Upanishad*-s declared, is that eternal reality which is the essence not of man alone, but of all living beings.

The subsequent break even from that teaching was a product decidedly of the *kṣhattriya*-s. The Buddha and the Mahavira, both *kṣhattriya*-s, founded two systems of thought that were pluralistic and atheistic in their metaphysics, empirical in their method, and immeasurably more systematic in their ethical outlook, than were the *Upanishad*-s. They were among the greatest teachers of all times. Not all those who later developed Indian logic and epistemology were *brāhmana*-s. And there were some *brāhmaṇa*-s who were kings. From the fifth and the sixth centuries A.D., on account of land grants and other privileges accorded to them in perpetuity, many *brāhmaṇa*-s became feudal landlords.[127] Some *brāhmaṇa*-s took to trade. Many *brāhmaṇa*-s remained priests, conducting various rituals and ceremonies, but known neither for their learning nor for their exemplary character always. The *shūdra*-s, far from remaining in the service of the upper three *varṇa*-s, shared with the *vaishya* the production of commodities and wealth. Some of the *shūdra*-s became kings and founded their own dynasties. The *kṣhattriya varṇa* never existed in the South, there being only two main divisions that were acknowledged, *brāhmaṇa* and the rest. The history of 'the rest' in terms of caste is very complicated, the word '*shūdra*' being applied to them often, but with a connotation that was very different from what it had in other parts of India. The fact is that the scheme of the original four *varṇa* hardly ever applied to South India. The celebrated eighty-four *siddha*-s, 'masters' or 'adepts', of the tantric traditions were *shūdra*-s. Not a few of the leading lights of the *bhakti* movement were *vaishya*-s or *shūdra*-s.

The least that these facts illustrate is that social positions, in real terms, were determined mostly by time, place, circumstance, and the character of the person concerned, and that this was a stated part of the theory. But that relativity was reversed, in theory and in practice, more especially after Buddhism had ceased to be the force that it once was. The enormous complexity of the adjustments that continued to be made in consequence forms yet another door in the labyrinth of *varṇa* and *jātī*.

There were several very definite reasons behind the reversal of the relativistic direction of dharmic thought and life. Those reasons belonged to different areas; and in each area, to different levels of perception. But all of them had one common source—the need for certainty.

It is difficult to say at what point of Indian history caste tended to become absolutist. The use of the word 'reversal' implies a sequence, but it is not easy to say anything definite about its historical beginning, particularly when the relativistic outlook on caste was juxtaposed with that view of it which was absolutist, and when both so continued throughout Indian history. What we do know is that the concept of *varṇa*, and with it the concept of *sva-dharma*, became increasingly formal; and that it was *jātī*, caste properly called, that became the social unit, its membership being by birth and not by temperament or conduct. *Jātī* had to be something fixed and not shifting, if the laws relating to it were to be tangible and firm. This, however, gives us only a partial picture. That is because *varṇa*, however formal it might have become, remained always linked with *jātī*, though that relation was far from certain. For instance, while it is true that one's social identity was derived from the caste or the sub-caste into which one was born, each caste felt nevertheless obliged to link itself generally with one or the other *varṇa*. When particular claims were made in that regard, there were serious disputes. Whatever else the relation between *varṇa* and *jātī* meant, it meant lack of certainty first of all. The absolutist trends that had emerged, taken at their purest, were in response to a need for principles that were clear and certain and not subject to place and time. While that need was seemingly in harmony with the philosophic quest for the permanent behind the ever-changing phenomena, it also became a source of all the complexities of Indian social life. For that relation between what was believed to be changeless and the changing phenomena, clear in its formulation but ambiguous in its practice, was hardly amenable to a unified social theory.

When *varṇa* and *jātī* were presented in the later *dharmashāstra*-s as a self-consistent and absolute social theory, they were at complete variance with the pluralistic facts of Indian life. They were at complete variance, too, with the ethical *foundations* of social relationships, without which nothing that is sane and moral can ever survive anywhere. The *Mahābhārata* is concerned with the foundations, with the *dharma*, of all social arrangements everywhere. But it was the *dharmashāstra* and their literal exponents, the shastri, and not the *Mahābhārata*, that came to dominate the social structure in India. They laid the foundations of a social system that could produce only social conflict and human degradation. The *Mahābhārata* is saying in a voice impassioned, often even anguished, that should any social arrangement degrade and debase human worth, it would be *adharma*, and will produce only violence.

At the same time the *Mahābhārata* recognised the antagonism seemingly inherent in the division of callings, the more especially when its origin was attributed to the divine source. It is concerned, therefore, with the psychology of antagonism that exists among the various social callings, side by side with their interdependence. That antagonism, expressed in different ways, must have been so sharp then, as they are now, everywhere, that the *Mahābhārata* honestly records it all. For, if a division of callings is natural to social existence, the antagonisms that this division produces seem to be quite as natural.

The problem clearly arose from too *literal* an understanding of *brāhmaṇa* being created from the head of the Primeval Being, Brahmā; *kṣhattriya* from His arms; *vaishya* from His thighs; and *shūdra* from His feet. *Although a very picturesque way of describing the organic unity of the four main social callings, it was quickly misinterpreted to mean that what pertains to 'head' is 'higher', and that which pertains to 'feet' is 'lower', in human worth, and thus in social status*. It was forgotten that human beings stand on their *feet* and not on their *head*. Therefore, in the voice of Shiva, the *Mahābhārata* wants it to be remembered that all social existence is *shūdramūlaka*, rooted in *shūdra*, that is to say, in services. Neither are the functions of 'the thighs' inferior to the functions of 'the arms'. That this had to be stated at all, and even emphasised, was owing to the fact that the notions of 'the higher' and 'the lower', 'the superior' and 'the inferior', in respect of different social functions, had already taken a strong hold.

A related attitude that had simultaneously taken hold was that *services*, as a function of *shūdra*, were functions mean and lowly, whereas pursuit of knowledge and governance, as functions respectively of *brāhmaṇa* and *kṣhattriya*, were elevated and powerful; and trade and commerce that generated wealth, as functions of *vaishya*, equally worthy of respect. It was said earlier in this chapter that the single most important contribution of the *Mahābhārata*, in the context of social arrangements, has been that *varṇa* pertains not to a person but to a social function, and to each social function a corresponding ethical discipline is invariably attached. Therefore, when it was said that *shūdra* is to provide the other three *varṇa* with services, it clearly meant that without *services* there can be no society. It was so then; it is so now. But the provider of services was not a personal slave of the other social functionaries. Neither was he a lowly being by virtue of his calling alone. In the *Mahābhārata*, *shūdra* is never depicted as such—except in the places where a wrong perception, a wrong attitude, in that regard is narrated as *adharma*.

However, antagonisms there were. And the antagonism most commonly narrated in the *Mahābhārata* was between *brāhmaṇa* and *kṣhattriya*. *It was an antagonism that has existed throughout human history, as it exists today, between the thinker and the intellectual and those invested with the governing power of the state. The intellectual asks questions; the functionaries of the state resist any questioning*. The thinker points to a greater reality from which the power of the state must derive its justification; the functionaries of the state believe power to be its own and the only justification. The *Mahābhārata* depicts that antagonism through the metaphor of '*the right of way*'. Between the thinker and the king, who has the right of way? In the following story,[128] *to be read throughout metaphorically, as it was meant to be*, the quarrel was '*who* should give way, even physically: the *brāhmaṇa* to the king, or the king to the *brāhmaṇa*?'

Once upon a time there was a king, Kalmāshpāda by name, and he was a very powerful king. Going on a hunt one day, he wandered around strenuously for game, and hunted down many animals. On his way back, thirsty and hungry, he happened to come to a pathway so narrow that only one person could pass through it.[129] On that path, he saw a sage, Shakti by name, the eldest son of the sage Vasishṭha, coming from the opposite side. The king said to him: 'Move out of my way.' Very gently, Shakti said to the king: 'The established *dharma* is that it is the king who should give way to a *brāhmaṇa*. It is *you* who should move out of my way.'[130] A quarrel broke between them on the right of way. And neither of them gave way to the other. Thereupon, seeing that as an insult to his majesty as king,

Kalmāshpāda started whipping Shakti brutally.[131] Blinded with hurt and anger, Shakti used the only weapon a helpless *brāhmaṇa* always had—the power of a curse. He pronounced a curse upon the king: 'You so low among kings, like a demon you are hitting an ascetic. Be a demon from now on, a man-eating demon, and wander around hungry for humans for the rest of your life. Now, go from here.'[132] And the curse comes true: a demon takes possession of the king. Thus possessed, Kalmāshpāda lost awareness of everything except his demonic power.[133]

But a sage had a weapon of even greater force than the weapon of pronouncing a curse—*kṣhmā*, forgiveness. Shakti's father, the sage Vasishṭha, the most venerable among the sages, showed, in the face of the gravest provocation, his limitless power of forgiveness.[134] But Vasishṭha was made of a different mettle than his son. A most demanding test for him materialised one day when King Vishvāmitra chanced to arrive at his hermitage.[135] The king was received with all the marks of respect due to a guest. Soon his eyes fell upon that very special cow of the hermitage, a *kāmadhenu*, 'fulfiller of all wishes', and a beautiful animal, whose name was Nandinī.[136] King Vishvāmitra looked at Nandinī admiringly, so very admiringly, indeed, that he offered a hundred million cows, and even his kingdom, in exchange for Nandinī.[137] 'Nandinī lives here,' Vasishṭha said, '*She will not be given away, in exchange not even for a kingdom*.'[138] King Vishvāmitra announced, in grossest disregard of the hospitality shown to him, that he was anyway going to take her away. 'I am a kṣhattriya and a king,' he said to Vasishṭha. 'You are a *brāhmaṇa* given to studies, and have little strength. If I want this cow, you cannot refuse. I have a right to use the force of my arms. I am a kṣhattriya and not a *brāhmaṇa*. I will take away this cow by force.'[139] Vasishṭha replied: 'You are with your army, you are a king, and you believe in the force of your arms. Do as you wish.'[140]

The king's men seized Nandinī, forced her to move, and when she would not move, began whipping her, so as to make her move. In great distress, she began to cry, looking at Vasishṭha, who said to her:

शृणोमि ते रवं भद्रे विनदन्त्याः पुनः पुनः ।। आदि १७४.२४ ।।
ह्रियसे त्वं बलाद् भद्रे विश्वामित्रेण नन्दिनि ।
किं कर्तव्यं मया तत्र क्षमावान् ब्राह्मणो ह्यहम् ।। आदि १७४.२५ ।।

I can see that Vishvāmitra is taking you away by force. Nandinī! I hear your distressed crying. But I feel helpless. I am a forgiving brāhmaṇa.[141]

Himself much distressed, Vasishṭha nevertheless remained steady in his mind, saying: क्षत्रियाणां बलं तेजो ब्राह्मणानां क्षमा बलम्। 'The strength of a kṣhattriya is in his force; the strength of a *brāhmaṇa* is in his power of forgiveness.'[142]

Nandinī asked him: 'Have *you* abandoned me? If you have not, then nobody can take me away by force.' 'No, I have *not* abandoned you,' Vasishṭha said to her. 'Remain here, if you *can*.' Hearing that loving answer *remain here*, Nandinī raised her head in the air—and turned into an awesome fury.[143]

Her eyes red with anger, on being forced and assaulted and hurt, Nandinī charged with incredible force the soldiers of Vishvāmitra—and then followed one miracle after another. From her angry eyes, and from her tail, and from the froth of her mouth, and from her sweat, and from her urine, emerged a large number of warriors of frightening physical strength and armed with weapons of every description. They all charged the king's soldiers, who soon began to run away, scattered, but were chased for a long distance, thoroughly punished, but not one of them killed. And the king, now left alone, watched all this with utter disbelief. He began to shoot his arrows at Vasishṭha, who waved them all away with a twig of a tree in his hand. For that simple twig of a tree was invested with the moral force of the one who had been treated unjustly but was still forgiving. The *Mahābhārata* suggests that a simple twig of a tree in the hands of a forgiving sage has infinitely greater power than all the weapons of a king. Now totally reduced, King Vishvāmitra declared:

धिग् बलं क्षत्रियबलं ब्रह्मतेजोबलं बलम्।। आदि १७४.४५।।

'The force of a kṣhattriya *be damned. The true force is the force that comes from a life lived in knowledge, truth and peace.'*[144]

Making that declaration, Vishvāmitra, the *kṣhattriya*, devotes himself earnestly to *becoming brāhmaṇa*. But feelings of peace towards Vasishṭha he never could have. He retained feelings of unceasing rivalry and envy towards him. *In that sense*, because still full of envy and antagonism towards another, manifestations of *krodha*, 'anger', he never did become *brāhmaṇa*. For a true *brāhmaṇa* is the one who conquers those first. When it is said that he did indeed become *brāhmaṇa*, it is at the same time said that he did so through his many acts of kindness to those in difficult situations.[145] But his acts of violence are mentioned, too.[146]

The extreme, and the most dramatic, expression of the antagonism between the *brāhmaṇa*-s and the *kṣhattriya*-s was Parashurāma[147] emptying the earth of *kṣhattriya*-s twenty-one times,[148] in a continuing bloody massacre. His hostility began when the arrogant sons of an equally arrogant king burnt down the hermitage of sage Jamadagni, Parashurāma's father, and killed him. This story, like many others, is to be read metaphorically and not literally.

The antagonism between the *brāhmaṇa*-s and the *kṣhattriya*-s often revolved around money. Of that, as one of the extreme examples, the *Mahābhārata* narrates the following story, the story of Aurva.[149] And again, like every other story of human relationships, this one also says many things simultaneously. The sage Vasishṭha recounted it to his grandson Parāshara.

Once upon a time there was a king called Kritavīrya. He gave plenty of money to the priests who had conducted for him an elaborate rite. They belonged to the lineage of the sage Bhrigu, and were known as Bhārgava-s. After the king had died, his successors fell for some reasons in great need of money. They knew that the Bhrigu *brāhmaṇa*-s had still with them the very considerable amount of money the King Kritavīrya had gifted them. They went to them with a request that that money be given back to them. Some of those *brāhmaṇa*-s hid their immense amount of money in vaults they dug in the earth.[150] Some quickly distributed what they had among other *brāhmaṇa*-s; but some, assessing the situation, and thinking it to be prudent to do so, gave to the princes the money they had.[151]

Some royals, not satisfied, began to look for the money that might have been hidden, and chanced upon a huge amount of it concealed in the earth. And all the princes assembled began to have a look at the find. Feeling tricked, they began to insult the *brāhmaṇa*-s, and killed many of them right there. In their anger, that the Bhārgava-s should have estimated them so low in intelligence as to trick them, the kṣhattriya-s began to kill them wherever they could be found. With a view to wiping out the last sign of the line of Bhrigu, they began to kill the Bhārgava women who were pregnant. Many of them, struck with fear, hid themselves in the remote caves of the snowy mountains.[152]

One of the pregnant Brāhma*ṇī*-s performed upon herself a surgical miracle. She cut open her stomach; took out from her womb her unborn child; made a deep cavity in one of her thighs, and placed the child there, so that she would not appear to be pregnant, and her child would be safe.

But another brāhma*ṇī*, who came to know about it, informed the princes, who came there to kill the woman and her unborn child.[153]

On arriving there with that purpose they saw the woman glow in her own strength. Another miracle then took place. Just at that time, the child emerged from the thigh of his mother, having on his face the brightness of the midday sun. He looked at them, and in that very instant, they lost their eyesight.[154] The infant, given the name Aurva, because he was born from his mother's *uru*, thigh,[155] blinded them all. *They were already blind, with nothing but the darkness of greed in their eyes, and cruelty in their hearts.* Now they were even physically blind, and in that state, with sharp burning pain in their eyes, they began to wander around on that mountain. They soon found their way back to the woman, and sought her forgiveness and pardon.[156]

'It is not *I* who took away your sight. I am not even angry with you,' the Brāhma*ṇī* said to the blinded descendants of King Kritavīrya.

'It is my son, a descendant of the sage Bhrigu, who is angry with you. There is no doubt that, remembering how you had killed his many relatives and friends, it is he who has deprived you of your eyesight. Children! When you began to kill even the women who were pregnant, I protected my own child by keeping him hidden in my thigh for a hundred years. True to his lineage of a seeker of knowledge, it was during the time that I was carrying him, and protecting him, that he gained the knowledge he has. But recalling how his father was killed, he is resolved to kill you all. And therefore he has first blinded you. Seek the pardon of my son Aurva. Should he be pleased with your abject humbling of yourselves, he would restore the light of your eyes.'[157]

The princes do precisely that, and Aurva restores the vision in their eyes.[158] But he is even more resolved to bring *all* kṣhattriya-s to their knees, indeed, to destroy that very world where the drunkenness of power could so easily destroy men and women and many an unborn child.[159] He is full of anger at a cruel and unjust world, and resolves that such a world shall not exist.

There is more to this story, which we will see in the context of the following question.

Why does the *Mahābhārata* portray *brāhmaṇa* as perpetually an 'angry man'? Exceptions apart, like the sage Vasishṭha. Particularly when it keeps emphasing, a recurring theme, that *krodha*, anger, is one of the three main doors to self-ruin, the other two being unrestrained lust and greed?

If we keep in mind the *Mahābhārata*'s chief premise that, like the other *varṇa, brāhmaṇa is not a person but a calling to fulfil certain social functions*, then the question will become: *is there not something in that calling itself that produces anger*? Since, moreover, to each calling a corresponding ethical discipline was attached, the question would also be: *is not the ethical discipline required of brāhmaṇa of such impossibly high order that, when subject to it, that discipline itself would create a grinding feeling of resentment—and anger?*

In the first place, *brāhmaṇa*, as a calling, was to devote himself to learning and knowledge; to study and teach; to think, to question, to seek light; to open doors for one's self and for others. He could not then also seek pleasures. For the two don't go together. In the voice of Vidura, the *Mahābhārata* is stating what has always been true, as it is true today:

> सुखार्थिन: कुतो विद्या नास्ति विद्यार्थिन: सुखम् ।
> सुखार्थी वा त्यजेद् विद्यां विद्यार्थी वा त्यजेत् सुखम् ।। उद्योग ४०.६ ।।
> *Where is learning for those who want pleasures? For the one who seeks learning, there are no pleasures. If you want pleasures, give up learning: if you want learning, give up pleasures.*[160]

But to seek pleasure, in all its meanings, is a natural attribute of being human. All human acts have *sukha*, as their aim. This is acknowledged by the *Upanishad*-s, and is a main premise in the *Mahābhārata*'s analysis of *sukha* and *duḥkha*.[161] It is undeniable that most of us have a very limited perception of 'pleasure', though. It is true that 'pleasure' is so related to the other attributes of being human that if we wholly separate it from them, and make it the sole aim of life, it is always self-defeating. The path of *vidya*, knowledge, is a difficult path; for the mind plays such tricks at every turn that what seemed to be unassailably true turned out to be demonstrably false. But it is entirely a different thing to say that it is a joyless path. Moreover, to say that pleasures are not for him who seeks knowledge is one thing, but it is altogether a different thing to conclude that he *shall not* seek joy. Somehow that became one of the prescriptions for brāhmaṇa, an expectation from him. It made him a joyless character. And where there is no joy, the ground is fertile for anger.

Furthermore, he who belonged to the calling called *brāhmaṇa* saw around him the power and the glory of the ruling class, *kṣhattriya*, and the great affluence of the trader and the merchant, *vaishya*, but he was excluded from both—on principle. A *brāhmaṇa* was to have neither power nor affluence. Yet, for his and his family's subsistence, he was dependent on those who had both, when there was no reason why, given the intelligence he devoted to the service of learning and knowledge, he could not use the same intelligence in making himself quite as affluent. Desire for money, and for the pleasures that come from it, is another natural attribute of being human. But he was required to have nothing to do with money and pleasures. He was thus cut off from the fulfilment of a natural attribute. His calling as *brāhmaṇa* was different, for which he and the members of his family were to receive the highest respect from the other three *varṇa*—and occasional gifts and endowments. That is all that he had. Therefore, at the slightest sign of what he interpreted as disrespect towards him, he flew into anger and rage—ready to pronounce a curse upon the offender. In fact, with no joy in his heart and a stern eye, *he looked for* any sign of disrespect, which might not have been that at all. With a simmering resentment at being on principle excluded from what he could have had, he acquired a temperament that was 'difficult to please', except with the most lavish signs of respect and welcome. The *Mahābhārata* throughout describes, in extravagant language, but with a hidden sense of laughter, those signs of respect with which a visiting brāhmaṇa was received either in a royal court or in a humble household, adding invariably that the great personage was *pleased* thereby. *To please a brāhmaṇa, and keep away from his ready anger, became gradually not only a duty but also an art.* The *Mahābhārata* describes that, too, but again with a hidden sense of laughter.

The sound of that laughter can be heard in the story of the sage Agastya and his wife Lopāmudrā.[162] She was the daughter of the king of Vidharba. When Agastya asked the king for his daughter Lopāmudrā's hand in marriage, the father was most reluctant to give his daughter in marriage to a poor sage, but was at the same time full of fear of Agastya's anger, if he did not. For the sage could destroy them with *kopa-agni*, 'the fire of his anger', on being refused.[163] On seeing her parents fearful and worried, Lopāmudrā announced that she was ready to marry Agastya, and they could save themselves thereby.[164] Lopāmudrā was given in marriage to Agastya.

The very first thing Agastya said to his wife, on their arrival at his hermitage, is: 'The clothes and the ornaments you are wearing are expensive beyond description. Throw them away.'[165] That she did, and in their place put on clothes, rough and coarse, appropriate for the wife of a poor sage given to learning and knowledge.[166] She devoted herself to her husband, even in the circumstances that had changed her life dramatically, and he loved her, too. One day he desired her and invited her to sexual union. Thereupon, bashful and shy, she said to him: 'I know that you married me with the sole purpose of carrying on your line, but I think you have for me love as well. It is my wish that before we make love I adorn myself, and you do likewise, with resplendent clothes, and with jewels resplendent even more. Besides, I wish to make love on the kind of bed I had in the palace. I do not wish to sully your sacred calling by having physical union with you in these sacred clothes of the wife of a sage.'[167]

Agastya said to his wife: 'But, my dearest Lopāmudrā, the kind of riches and affluence there were in your father's home, neither you nor I have them. How are your wishes then to be met? How is the money to be had without lowering myself?'[168] And she replied: 'I have stated my wishes. But neither do I want you to lower yourself in fulfilling them. Do what you consider to be the best, but don't delay.'[169] Agastya said: 'Very well, if that is what you have decided, I will go in search of money. Meanwhile, take care of yourself.'[170]

The sage Agastya first approached King Śhrutarva, whom he thought to be the richest among kings. On learning that the sage was on his way to meet him, the king, with all his ministers in attendance, received him at the border of his kingdom; showed him all the signs of respect due to a sage; escorted him to his palace; and standing with folded hands, asked the sage what might be the purpose of his visit.[171] 'I have come here to ask you for some money,' Agastya said. 'Without doing any violence to anybody, give me whatever you can.'[172] King Śhrutarva places before him a full statement of the financial accounts of the kingdom: 'Take from it whatever you wish.'[173] On having a look at the account, *receipts and expenditure*, Agastya saw that they were evenly balanced. 'I can take nothing from this without causing hurt to others.'[174]

Thereafter he approached King Bṛadhanaśva; and then King Trasadasyu, and the same scene was re-enacted by those two kings as well. *The receipts and expenditure accounts of the kingdoms were evenly balanced, and Agastya could take nothing from them without causing hurt to others.*[175] Each preceding king would follow the sage on his visit to the next king. By the time that highly distinguished company reached the King of Demons, *daitya-rāja*, there was in it one sage and three kings. The sage was seeking money with which to buy for his wife some resplendent clothes, some ornaments resplendent even more, and a bed suitable for a woman who had been a princess before she had married him for fear of his anger if he was refused. The kings were seeking money as a reserve for their royal treasuries, for their revenues and expenditure were so precariously balanced that nothing was left for any emergency.

Ilvala, the King of Demons, seemed vastly amused by their visit, receiving them, though, with all the outward signs of honour and respect. He reserved for his distinguished guests even a more special honour. He transformed his brother Vātāpi into a fat lamb and served them his meat.[176] Sensing something was wrong, the three kings looked at Agastya, who said to them: 'Don't touch it. I will eat the whole portion', which was then served to him.[177] On his finishing it, Ilvala laughingly gave a call: 'Vātāpi! Vātāpi! Come out. Come out.' What came out instead, in a loud report, was a huge big fart from Agastya.[178] '*I have digested your demonic power.* There is no Vātāpi any more,' Agastya said to Ilvala.[179]

With all his ministers in full attendance, Ilvala now asked the sage the purpose of their visit there: 'In what way can I be of service to you?' Agastya laughingly replied: 'We consider you a powerful and immeasurably rich king. These kings are not particularly rich, and I need some money. Without hurting others, give us what you can.'[180] Ilvala did not put before the sage, as the other three kings had, a revenue–expenditure account of his treasury. Instead, he said: 'Yes, I will, *provided* you can tell me what in my mind I am thinking of giving.' 'You are thinking of giving to each of these kings ten thousand cows and as many gold coins. To me, you are thinking of giving two times more, and also a chariot covered with gold and equipped with two horses that can run at the speed of wind.'[181] Ilvala gives him very much more, and the sage Agastya returns, at the speed of wind, to his wife Lopāmudrā, and fulfils her wishes.[182] The meaning of this story has many different levels, which are plain and clear, and do not have to be laboured upon.

Let us next briefly consider the question *whether the ethical discipline required of brāhmaṇa, that is, the intellectual, the thinker, the teacher, was not of such an impossibly high order that, when subject to it, that discipline itself would create a grinding feeling of resentment—and anger. From what follows,*[183] *it can be seen that joy in living was no part of the high expectations from him.*

वर्तेत तेषु गृहवानक्रुद्ध्यन्नसूयकः ।
पञ्चभिः सततं यज्ञैर्विघसाशी यजेत च ।। शान्ति २३५.२५ ।।

सतां धर्मेण वर्तेत क्रियां शिष्टवदाचरेत् ।
असंरोधेन लोकस्य वृतिं लिप्सेदगर्हिताम् ।। शान्ति २३५.२६ ।।
The brāhmaṇa *living-in-family, avoiding both anger and the habit of finding fault in others, should perform the prescribed five* yajña-s; *act according to* dharma *and be civilised in his conduct; and adopt that means of livelihood which does not conflict with those of others and is above reproach.*[184]

श्रुतिविज्ञानतत्त्वज्ञः शिष्टाचारो विचक्षणः ।
स्वधर्मेण क्रियावांश्च कर्मणा सोऽप्यसंकरः ।। शान्ति २३५.२७ ।।
He should be learned in the Veda; have knowledge of substance; be polite and courteous but also clever; and remain steadfast in his own calling and not mix it with that of another.[185]

क्रियावाञ्श्रद्दधानो हि दान्तः प्राज्ञोऽनसूयकः ।
धर्माधर्मविशेषज्ञः सर्वं तरति दुस्तरम् ।। शान्ति २३५.२८ ।।

धृतिमानप्रमत्तश्च दान्तो धर्मविदात्मवान् ।
वीतहर्षमदक्रोधो ब्राह्मणो नावसीदति ।। शान्ति २३५.२९ ।।
A brāhmaṇa *who has forbearance, is not careless, is self-controlled; is centred in* dharma, *is an expert in knowing* dharma *from* adharma, *has a sense of reverence and faith, and has risen above the feelings of delight and anger and arrogance, becomes also free from regret and sorrow.*[186]

एषा पुरातनी वृत्तिर्ब्राह्मणस्य विधीयते ।
ज्ञानवत्त्वेन कर्माणि कुर्वन् सर्वत्र सिध्यति ।। शान्ति २३५.३० ।।
This is an ancient calling of Brāhmaṇa. *Living accordingly and acting in the light of knowledge, he achieves all that is worth achieving.*[187]

To these, Vyāsa had added some more. In relation to his own self:

गन्धान् रसान् नानुरुन्ध्यात् सुखं वा
  नालंकाराश्चाप्नुयात् तस्य तस्य ।
मानं च कीर्तिं च यशश्च नेच्छेत्
  स वै प्रचारः पश्यतो ब्राह्मणस्य ।। शान्ति २५१.१ ।।
Only he is to be considered a brāhmaṇa, *who does not take to the pleasures arising from smell and taste, and wishes neither for honours nor for acclaim nor for fame.*[188]

In relation to the *other*, a *brāhmaṇa*

> ज्ञातिवत् सर्वभूतानां सर्ववित् सर्ववेदवित् ।
> नाकामो म्रियते जातु न तेन न च वै द्विजः ।। शान्ति २५१.३ ।।
>
> *Looks upon others as his own; knows what is to be known; has risen above desires; and therefore above death. He fears no one, and no one fears him. He has risen above inclination and aversion alike.*[189]

To these, however, Vyāsa's one-line postscript must immediately be added. The point is not that anyone else, also exhibiting these qualities, is not a *brāhmaṇa*. Rather, the point is that only *he is* a true *brāhmaṇa* who does.[190] The *Mahābhārata* puts the greatest emphasis on this throughout, as we saw earlier in this chapter.[191] But the discussion becomes very confusing when Vyāsa begins clearly to talk not about *brāhmaṇa* as a distinct social function, to which a distinct discipline is attached, but about *brāhmaṇa-ttva*. And then he talks about the state of *mokṣha*, freedom from the human condition, and the attributes of the one who has achieved it.[192] That applies to all human beings.

The mocking irony that can be heard throughout the *Mahābhārata* was that this long list of expectations of every conceivable virtue produced in a *brāhmaṇa* the two things that he was required to conquer in the first place—anger and hurtful speech. The *Mahābhārata* reports, just as a matter of fact, that 'the *brāhmaṇa*-s are by temperament angry men', quick to take offence and even quicker to pronounce a curse upon the offender.[193] That was a natural outcome of the high expectations that *brāhmaṇa* should be more than human.

The pressure that a person belonging to a specific social calling should be more than human often results for that very reason in his turning into less than human.

Brāhmaṇa was not to have anything to do with the production of wealth, or with money. He and his family were to live a life devoid of life's natural pleasures, in its description almost stern. They lived on what was given to him by others, which was often liberal, especially if the giver was a king or a rich merchant. That was in exchange for his services as a priest, conducting *yajña* and other ritual ceremonies. He *expected* liberal gifts. Even if he was not a priest, but a philosopher and sage, or not even that, he expected to be supported by those who had power and by those who had riches. He was turned thereby into a perpetual *yāchaka*, *the one who seeks from others, who asks for*. Hencc the great importance attached to *dāna*, 'giving gifts', to a *brāhmaṇa*. And even a greater importance attached to feeding a *brāhmaṇa*, as a sure means of earning 'merit', *punya.*[194]

It is undeniable, as it was then and so it is now, that to seek something from others, to ask for, is always to lower oneself inwardly. Driven by necessity, one still does, because one is dependent upon others, but one does it at a cost. That must, and always does, produce anger. *One of the expressions of that anger is resentment against the one who gives and from whom one receives. And the other way round, too. The Mahābhārata* is perfectly aware of this strange human psychology—*of being resentful of those upon whom one has to depend—and looks at the psychologically difficult relationship between the giver and the receiver.*

A *brāhmaṇa* arrives at the court of King Yayāti. He says to the king:

इदमन्यच्छ्रूयतां ययातिर्नाहुषो राजा राज्यस्थ: पौरजनावृत आसांचक्रे गुर्वर्थी
ब्राह्मण उपेत्याब्रवीद् भे राजन् गुर्वर्थं भिक्षेयं समयादिति।। वन १९५.१।।

I have come here to seek something from you, but *on one condition.*

Yayāti

ब्रवीतु भगवान् समयमिति।। वन १९५.२।।

Venerable sir, state your condition.

The Brāhmaṇa

विद्वेषणं परमं जीवलोकें
कुर्यान्नर: पार्थिव याच्यमान:।
तं त्वां पृच्छामि कथं तु राजन्
दद्याद् भवान् दयितं च मेऽद्य।। वन १९५.३।।

It is generally seen in this world that, on being asked to give something, the one who gives begins to have feelings of resentment and hatred for him who seeks. King! Tell me, how will you give what I want to be given?[195]

King Yayāti

न चानुकीर्तयेदद्य दत्त्वा
अयाच्यमर्थं न च संभृणोमि।
प्राप्यमर्थं च संश्रुत्य
तं चापि दत्त्वा सुसुखी भवामि।। वन १९५.४।।
ददामि ते रोहिणीनां सहस्त्रं
प्रियो हि मे ब्राह्मणो याचमान:।

न मे मनः कुप्यति याचमाने
दत्तं न शोचामि कदाचिदर्थम् ।। वन १९५.५ ।।

After giving a gift I do not talk about it again and again. Neither do I have anger against the one who asks nor regret after giving. And what I give, I give happily. There is nothing you may want and I do not have. I give you a thousand cows of red colour. The brāhmaṇa *who comes asking is dear to me.*[196]

But *coming and asking* creates also a mentality of *yāchaka*, who then makes a request for only outwardly but actually *demands*; and if his demand is not fulfilled, he is ready to express his displeasure. *The Mahābhārata talks about the attitude with which one should give, and should receive, if there is to be neither resentment and regret after giving nor a feeling of being lowered on receiving. And there is to be no consequent anger both with one's self for having asked and with the other for appearing superior in giving.*[197]

On being questioned what situations in life bring happiness, and what bring pain, Baka the ascetic says:

अष्टमे द्वादशे वापि शाकं यः पचते गृहे ।। वन १९३.२७ ।।
कुमित्राण्यनपाश्रित्य किं वै सुखतरं ततः ।
यत्राहानि न गण्यन्ते नैनमाहुर्महाशनम् ।। वन १९३.२८ ।।

Where days are not counted, and there is no daily anxiety about securing food: where one cooks in one's own home a modest meal of vegetables and doesn't have to depend on those who are no friends: that man is to be counted as happy.[198]

अपि शाकं पचानस्य सुखं वै मघवन् गृहे ।
अर्जितं स्वेन वीर्येण नाप्यपाश्रित्य कंचन ।। वन १९३.२९ ।।

Only he is happy who, earning on his own, cooks in his own home, even if it be a meal of vegetables, and doesn't have to seek from others.[199]

फलशाकमपि श्रेयो भोक्तुं ह्यकृपणं गृहे ।
परस्य तु गृहे भोक्तुः परिभूतस्य नित्यशः ।। वन १९३.३० ।।
सुमृष्टमपि न श्रेयो विकल्पोऽयमतः सताम् ।
श्ववत् कीलालपो यस्तु परान्नं भोक्तुमिच्छति ।। वन १९३.३१ ।।
धिगस्तु तस्य तद् भुक्तं कृपणस्य दुरात्मनः ।

For it is infinitely more desirable to live on fruit and vegetables in one's own home, but without self-pity, than to be dependent upon others, and enjoy in other homes superb food given with ill-grace though.[200]

In the voice of Aurva, whose father was killed by some money-hungry princes, and we heard his story earlier in this chapter, the *Mahābhārata* at the same time gives expression to the other argument that there are occasions in life, when faced with injustice and cruelty one can only be angry and ought to be so. But that is a different inquiry: whether, even in those circumstances, anger will still be self-destructive and, however justified, can correct neither injustice nor cruelty. That is best discussed in the larger context of violence, *hiṃsā*, and not-violence, *ahiṃsā*.[201]

Harmony among social callings: The way to social wealth

There is in the social history of India not much evidence of genuine harmony among the different social callings. There was mostly antagonism and conflict, which came increasingly to the surface, especially from the nineteenth century onwards. But they were always there. They were there while the *Mahābhārata* was being composed. They were there in the times of the Buddha. And they were there while the legal codes, the *dharmasūtra*-s and the *dharmashāstra*-s, governing the domestic and the social life of the people called the Hindu-s, were being compiled. The antagonism and the conflicts arose not from the division of *varṇa-dharma*, social callings, but undoubtedly when they began being graded one over the other, into 'higher' and 'lower', 'superior' and 'inferior', opening the way of power of one over the other. It has always been a very complex and complicated social history, as it is today. But here we are not concerned with *social history* but with the *foundations*. For the *Mahābhārata* suggests that it is only in the light of the universal human foundations of human relationships that the past can be judged and the present made happier.

Those foundations of harmonious social arrangements were, in the clearest of words, laid down in the *Mahābhārata*. Bhīshma stated them briefly.

विशेषेण च वक्ष्यामि चातुर्वर्ण्यस्य लिङ्गतः ।
पञ्चभूतशरीराणां सर्वेषां सदृशात्मनाम् ।। अनुशासन १६४.११ ।।

लोकधर्मे च धर्मे च विशेषकरणं कृतम् ।
यथैकत्वं पुनर्यान्ति प्राणिनस्तत्र विस्तरः ।। अनुशासन १६४.१२ ।।

Now I will speak of the substance of the four different social functions: brāhmaṇa, kṣhattriya, vaishya *and* shūdra. *All persons belonging to them are created alike by the five elements of Nature. They all have in them a similar Self. Even so, each has a different worldly function to fulfil. Fulfilling different social functions, they come again into a unity.*[202]

सर्वेषां तुल्यदेहानां सर्वेषां सदृशात्मनाम् ।
कालो धर्मेण संयुक्तः शेष एव स्वयं गुरुः ।। अनुशासन १६४.१४ ।।
All human beings are alike in their physicality. They are alike, too, in having the same soul. What remains is dharma *shot through with Time: and* dharma *on its own is the guru.*[203]

एवं सति न दोषोऽस्ति भूतानां धर्मसेवने ।। अनुशासन १६४.१५ ।।
In that case, there is in the division of social callings no harm.[204]

Then, knowing how the human mind can be conditioned wrongly but cleverly, very cleverly indeed, Bhīshma adds this as the final lines:

शूद्रोऽहं नाधिकारो मे चातुराश्रम्यसेवने ।
इति विज्ञानमपरे नात्मन्युपदधत्युत ।। अनुशासन १६४.१० ।।
A shūdra *may think to himself, 'I have no rights in the superior ways of living.' But those who are good never take recourse to cunning falsehood.*[205]

In the same way as the *Mahābhārata* depicts antagonism and conflict among social callings as being mostly between *kṣhattriya* and *brāhmaṇa*, it talks about the need for harmony, towards the social good, chiefly among these two. *In actual reality, their antagonism was between the power of the state and its instruments of governance, if that is what kṣhattriya be, and the thinker and the philosopher and the sage, if that is what brāhmaṇa be.* The struggle between them was, metaphorically, about 'the right of way'.[206] And that was considered greatly harmful to the social good.

मिथोभेदाद् ब्राह्मणक्षत्रियाणां
प्रजा दुःखं दुःसहं चाविशन्ति ।
एवं ज्ञात्वा कार्य एवेह नित्यं
पुरोहितो नैकविद्यो नृपेण ।। शान्ति ७३.२८ ।।

> *Because of the conflict between* kṣhattriya *and* brāhmaṇa, *the people suffer intolerable suffering.*[207]

But so did the king—in ways that were quickly manifested. Hence the exhortation to him, again and again, to appoint a good *purohita*, in the interest not of his reign alone but also in the interest of the good of the people.

It is of the utmost importance here to have a correct understanding of *purohita*. He was not a family priest. A *purohita* was to be, to the one who governs, his philosopher, guide, and mentor. Apart from the clearest description of what *purohita* was meant to be in relation to the king, the word itself makes its meaning abundantly clear. It is composed of two words: *pura* and *hita*. The word *pura* means 'stronghold', 'fortress' and 'one who goes before, one who leads'. And the word *hita* means 'beneficial, good, welfare, good advice, friendly, affectionate, kind'. Two of its many derivatives are *hita-vādin*, 'a friendly counsellor or advisor', and *hita-mitra*, 'a benevolent friend'. That is what a *purohita* is meant to be. And that is what *brāhmaṇa* as a social calling is meant to be, the *Mahābhārata* throughout maintains. That means that whoever, himself unselfish, is a benevolent friend, is truly a *brāhmaṇa*, or even that such a person alone is *brāhmaṇa*. This also the *Mahābhārata* maintains throughout.

Thus, when it is said:

> ब्रह्म वर्धयति क्षत्रं क्षत्रतो ब्रह्म वर्धते ।
> एवं राज्ञा विशेषेण पूज्या वै ब्राह्मणाः सदा ।। शान्ति ७३.३२ ।।
> Brāhmaṇa *enhances* kṣhattriya, *and* kṣhattriya *enhances* brāhmaṇa*: therefore, the state, and those entrusted with governance, must particularly respect* brāhmaṇa.[208]

It will be a completely wrong understanding to hear this as saying that the persons born in the families called '*brāhmaṇa*-s' have, for that reason alone, a special claim to being respected. What it means is that, just as sovereignty belongs to *dharma* and not to the king,[209] the king should specially respect a philosopher and sage, यः सत्करोति ज्ञानानि,[210] and seek his counsel in matters pertaining to the foundations of governance being in *dharma* and truth. This he should do in his self-interest, and in the interest of the people above all. The *Mahābhārata* is saying this in the clearest of words—again, and again, and yet again.

In saying that न ब्राह्मणविरोधेन शक्या शास्तुं वसुन्धरा,[211] 'the world cannot be governed in opposition to *brāhmaṇa*', what is being said is that good governance cannot be in opposition to truth and knowledge. Governance shall seek the light of *dharma*, which keeps power from turning into its own justification and end.

That light cannot come from within governance itself. Hence, in order to create conditions for *loka-yātrā*, the happy progress of life, and *loka-saṁ graha*, social wealth, the abiding need for having the unity of *kṣhattriya* and *brāhmaṇa* as two distinct social functions. Hence the abiding need for a king to have a good *purohita*, who would be to him a philosopher and a guide and a mentor. Together they symbolised the unity of power and philosophy.

योगक्षेमो हि राष्ट्रस्य राजन्यायत्त उच्यते ।
योगक्षेमो हि राज्ञो हि समायत्तः पुरोहिते ।। शान्ति ७४.१ ।।

The welfare of a nation is dependent upon the state, and the welfare of the state is dependent upon the direction that a philosopher as advisor provides.[212]

There remained nevertheless a huge confusion concerning *varṇa* as a social function and the individual person belonging to it. Thus arose the confusion between *brāhmaṇa* as a social function, to which a corresponding ethical discipline was attached, and 'a *brāhmaṇa*' as a particular individual. One of its results was that the very high importance given to knowledge and philosophy, to learning and teaching, as a distinct social calling given the name brāhmaṇa, was quickly transferred to them and misinterpreted as the eulogy of individuals called '*brāhmaṇa*-s' independent of their character. This confusion had first to be stated, which the *Mahābhārata* did. Thereafter it proceeded to remove that wrong notion, which had turned a natural and also a perfectly rational social arrangement upside down.

In the story of the humbling of an arrogant *brāhmaṇa* by an ordinary housewife[213] the *Mahābhārata* is correcting a thoroughly mistaken notion. She tells him why a person may be a *brāhmaṇa* and yet not be *brāhmaṇa*. She makes this distinction perfectly clear to him. In that continuing story the *Mahābhārata* is saying, besides, that a thinker and a philosopher and a teacher doesn't have to be a *brāhmaṇa*.

He may be a meatseller by profession, or a grocer. Thus, Kaushika the arrogant brāhmaṇa is made to receive lessons in the true meaning of *dharma*, and much else, from Dharmavyādha, a meatseller and another arrogant brāhmaṇa, Jājali, from a grocer, Tulādhāra.

Likewise, *purohita* is not an individual, much less a *brāhmaṇa* necessarily. In his person, as a *purohita* to a king, he is a symbol of detached, disinterested, unselfish, friendly, and wise counsel as to how the power of the state is to be exercised and towards what end. He is a symbol of *dharma*; in being that, he is a symbol of truth and justice. Only in the measure that he is all these is he a *purohita*. Thus, 'what leads', 'what goes before', as a part of the meaning of the word '*purohita*', is that of which he is a symbol. All the marks of great respect to *purohita* are the marks of the acknowledgement that it is *dharma* and truth and justice that should lead and go before and not the power of the state. They show the awareness of the necessity of friendship between philosophy and power—for *loka-hita*, the good of the people.

> ब्रह्मक्षत्रमिदं सृष्टमेकयोनि स्वयम्भुवा।
> पृथग्बलविधानं तन्न लोकं परिपालयेत्।। शान्ति ७४.१३।।
> *Both* brāhmaṇa *and* kṣhattriya *have a common origin, in Brahmā. If their force and purpose become separate, then neither can nourish the world.*[214]

> तपो मन्त्रबलं नित्यं ब्राह्मणेषु प्रतिष्ठितम्।
> अस्त्रबाहुबलं नित्यं क्षत्रियेषु प्रतिष्ठितम्।। शान्ति ७४.१४।।
> ताभ्यां सम्भूय कर्तव्यं प्रजानां परिपालनम्।
> *In* brāhmaṇa *it is the force of the life lived in austerity and concentration: in* kṣhattriya *it is the force of arms that is manifest. Therefore, fulfilling their respective functions, they should together serve and nourish the people.*[215]

In that sense, Vidura in the *Mahābhārata* is the greatest *purohita* the world has ever known. His counsel, mostly addressed to his half-brother, King Dhritirashtra, is addressed to all human beings. His sayings are clearly divided between what concerns a person's relationships with his, and her, self and with the other. Clear and straightforward, they constitute an important part of the *Mahābhārata* as leading to self-knowledge and sane living.[216] Vidura was neither a *brāhmaṇa* nor a *kṣhattriya*. He was born of a *shūdra* woman; and he described himself as a *shūdra*.[217] In the person of Vidura, as in the persons of Dharmavyādha and Tulādhāra and the unnamed housewife, the *Mahābhārata* is saying: *on the path of truth and knowledge there are no distinctions between one person and another except what he makes of himself, or she makes of herself.*

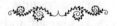

CHAPTER FOURTEEN

Dharma—The Foundation of *Rāja-dharma,* Law and Governance

- The purpose of governance: *danda*
- The main attribute of governance
- The discipline of *dharma* is the discipline of the king
- Self-discipline of the king
- Impartiality, truth, and trust in governance
- Trust as the foundation of republics
- Public wealth under the control of *dharma*
- Fear as the basis of the social order?
- Reconciliation *or* force?
- The law of abnormal times: *āpad-dharma*
- An argument against capital punishment
- The king creates historical conditions, not they him

Much of Indian thought, particularly political thought, has been surrounded by very many wrong understandings, and misunderstandings, western or Indian. They have a long history. However, although it is necessary to remove them, that exercise eventually becomes very tiresome, and in the end it is not very productive either. Who misunderstood what, or wrongly understood it, quickly involves one in what may justly be called misunderstanding of misunderstandings. It is best to state, therefore, what is demonstrably true about the foundations of Indian thought beyond its diversities; state what is clear and verifiable, and is not subject to any one person's interpretation of it. Then coming to those foundations, order our social life and relationships in the same way as we should order our individual lives and relationships. It may be, as some philosophers have argued, that human life in its daily transactions is anyway only a series of *interpretations* of truth, some of them right, some of them wrong, the mind playing its familiar tricks at every turn. The result is, in their view, that we human beings can only live from one misunderstanding to another, some of them beautiful, some of them ugly, and move from ignorance to ignorance. That distinct possibility was fully taken into account in the *Mahābhārata*, and later in the *Yoga-Vāsishṭha*, which then demonstrate, step by step, how the conquest *of* the mind, *by* the mind, is the very first foundation of sane living.

Earlier in this book we saw that one of the characteristics of the *Mahābhārata* has been that, in the place of *definitions* of things, it asks for their attributes, or *Lakṣaṇas*. All definitions are arbitrary, whereas the *Lakṣaṇas*, or the attributes, are what *show* a thing, through which a thing becomes manifest. Thus, not the 'definition' of truth, or of love, but the attributes of truth and love, by which they are known. The question *what is dharma*? is answered likewise in terms of its *Lakṣaṇas*, attributes, which are clear, straightforward, and genuinely universal. And yet, there is perhaps no other word that has been misunderstood more than *dharma*. It has always been translated, wrongly, as 'religion'. The result is that, since our perceptions are governed by that incorrect translation, the statement that *dharma* is the foundation of law and governance, is quickly interpreted to mean that that foundation is 'religious' in character, which it is not. Here we must recall what was said in the earlier chapter on the meaning of *dharma*.

The *Mahābhārata* says,[1] *one*:

> प्रभवार्थाय भूतानां धर्मप्रवचनं कृतम् ।
> यः स्यात्प्रभवसंयुक्तः स धर्म इति निश्चयः ।।
> *All the sayings of* dharma *are with a view to nurturing, cherishing, providing more amply, endowing more richly, prospering, increasing, enhancing, all living beings: securing their* prabhava. *Therefore, whatever has the characteristic of bringing that about is* dharma. *This is certain.*

Two,

> धारणाद् धर्ममित्याहुर्धर्मेण विधृताः प्रजाः ।
> यः स्याद् धारणसंयुक्तः स धर्म इति निश्चयः ।।
> *All the sayings of* dharma *are with a view to supporting, sustaining, bringing together, upholding, all living beings—in one word, their* dhārana. *Therefore, whatever has the characteristic of doing that is* dharma. *This is certain.*

And *three*,

> अहिंसार्थाय भूतानां धर्मप्रवचनं कृतम् ।
> यः स्यादहिंसासम्पृक्तः स धर्म इति निश्चयः ।।
> *All the sayings of* dharma *are with a view to securing for all living beings freedom from violence. Therefore, whatever has the characteristic of not doing violence is* dharma. *This is certain.*

Conversely, whatever has the characteristic of depriving, starving, diminishing, debasing, degrading, separating, uprooting, hurting, doing violence, is the *negation of dharma*. Whatever brings these about, is, in one word, *adharma*. This is the case both in our individual relationships and in our social relationships. In whatever way you define 'justice', 'law', and 'good governance', they must have everywhere as their basic attributes *prabhava*, *dhārana*, and *ahimsā*. *Dharma* is their natural foundation. 'Injustice', 'tyranny', and 'anarchy' are likewise known by their attributes, which are the attributes of *adharma*, all of them destructive of the self and of the *other*.

What are the elements of political theory, of which law and governance are essential parts? To begin with, there is the individual, as the concrete unit of life, placed in a system of social relations. Who decides how these relations are to be regulated? In the event of conflict between the interests of the individual and those of society, what principle can settle the issue between these two? These questions are answered variously depending upon what precisely is the concept of *law*. A further question arises whether law is given unto man as divine commands, and is therefore immutable, and the Church is the interpreter of those commands. Or is law an outcome of the material conditions of a society, and must keep changing even as those conditions do? Since the idea of law is intimately connected with the idea of *power*, the legitimate sources of power, the manner of its use, the limits on its exercise, and the moral rightness of revolt against it when it turns tyrannical, are other questions that follow immediately. Next, through what institutions is the power of law exercised? The concepts of sacred and temporal powers arise in answer to that question. Their mutual relationship, the relation between the state and the church, as well as the range of authority which either may claim over the individual, are the other elements of political thought. So is the question of *ends* towards which the individual person, a group, or a whole society moves, and the *means* through which those ends are secured. Are *ends* their own justification, and the question of means only a functional one? Or are *means* ethically as important as *ends* are, and do both require justification of a higher order which neither of them can by itself provide? Then there are questions concerning *freedom* and *justice*. Always connected with each other, all of the foregoing questions are related, above all, with the idea of *history*. History is the crucible in which political ideas mature and human decisions arise. *Desha* and *kāla*, 'time' and 'place', are evidently the two coordinates of history; they are in a flux, and so are ideas and human decisions. In that case, can there ever be such a thing as 'foundation', which is not subject to the changing *desha* and *kāla*?

Many of the questions listed above, including the one mentioned the last, form part of the *Mahābhārata*'s inquiry into the foundations of law and governance. We must here make a clear distinction, though. There are certain questions that are universal, while some questions belong only to a particular history. For example, the question concerning the legitimate sources of power, the manner of its exercise, and the limits to which it must be subject, is a question that is universal. But the question as regards the relation between the state and the church in their competing claims over the allegiance of the individual person is a product only of western history. It formed no part of dharmic reflections on man and society. The issue between the sacred and the temporal power posed no challenge of the kind that it did for many centuries in the history of western societies, for *dharma* perceived no polarity between the two. Similarly, the question as to whether law is given as divine commands and is therefore immutable, or is a product of the material conditions of a society and must keep changing with them, posed no theoretical problem in dharmic political thought. The idea of *dharma* cuts across this issue by showing that:

a. in its attributes of *prabhava* and *dhāraṇa* and *ahiṃsā*, *dharma* as the ordering reality of life is always and everywhere necessarily the basic condition of human living, and, in that sense, is not subject to the particularities of *desha* and *kāla*.
b. But insofar as a particular time, a particular place, and a particular society are the determining factors of legislated law, no one set of laws can be called either universal or unchanging. And
c. The particularities of *desha* and *kāla*, undoubtedly important in their own place, cannot be invoked as always decisive in going against the foundations of human living.

That is to say, no law, no custom, however old, will have any authority if it tends to debase and degrade human worth, if it creates separations, or if it does violence to human dignity. Even the changing laws, made in response to the changing times, must at all times be subject to the unchanging *dharma* as foundation. What the *Mahābhārata* had suggested in saying this is clearly the position also of the modern philosophy of law.

The chief concern of dharmic political thought was power or *bala*: its sources; the purpose for which it is exercised; the limits to it; and the legitimacy of revolt against it when it becomes *adharma*, that is, when it creates conditions of oppression and violence. The *Mahābhārata* enquires into all these in systematic detail.

The question of power is naturally connected with the purpose for which a king, or, in the modern idiom, the state, exists. In all that follows, substitute the word 'state' for the word 'king'.

The purpose of governance, *daṇḍa*

The greatest part of the political thought in the *Mahābhārata* unfolds in the form of a long conversation between Yudhishṭhira and the dying Bhīshma, who often recalls some other conversations that had taken place earlier on the subject of governance. Yudhishṭhira asks Bhīshma:

को दण्डः कीदृशो दण्डः किंरूपः किंपरायणः ।
किमात्मकः कथंभूतः कथंमूर्तिः कथं प्रभो ।। शान्ति १२१.५ ।।
जागर्ति च कथं दण्डः प्रजास्ववहितात्मकः ।
कश्च पूर्वापरमिदं जागर्ति प्रतिपालयन् ।। शान्ति १२१.६ ।।

What is governance? What is it like? What are its forms? What is it based on? What is its purpose? What is its origin? What is its structure?[2] *How does governance keep vigilant in the service of the people? Who keeps awake while ruling the world?*[3]

As regards the purpose of the state and governance, *daṇḍa*, the *Mahābhārata* invokes memories of a time when:

न वै राज्यं न राजाऽऽसीन्न च दण्डो न दाण्डिकः ।
धर्मेणैव प्रजाः सर्वा रक्षन्ति स्म परस्परम् ।। शान्ति ५९.१४ ।।

There was neither kingdom nor king; neither governance nor governor. The people protected each other by means of dharma. *It was in* dharma *that they grew together and were sustained.*[4]

But that happy state did not last long. There arose much confusion among people in their duties of mutual protection. They lost their sense of obligation to each other. Then arose greed, to possess what they did not own. Unrestrained in their appetites, and driven only by their greed, people did violence to each other, in the wrong notion that one might flourish at the cost of the *other*, and there was anarchy. They could no longer discriminate between what is right and what is wrong. Since people could no longer govern themselves in self-governance, there arose the need for an external governing force, so that people might not destroy each other by their self-created anarchy,[5] and destroy human flourishing above all. The king was invested, therefore, with the authority of *daṇḍa*, or governance. For

राजा चेन्न भवेल्लोके पृथिव्यां दण्डधारकः ।
जले मत्स्यानिवाभक्ष्यन् दुर्बलं बलवत्तराः ।। शान्ति ६७.१६ ।।

If there were in the world no daṇḍa, *people would have destroyed each other: it is out of the fear of punishment that people do not engage in mutual killing.*[6]

दण्डश्चेन्न भवेल्लोके विनश्येयुरिमाः प्रजाः ।
जले मत्स्यानिवाभक्षयन् दुर्बलान् बलवत्तराः ।। शान्ति १५.३० ।।

If there were no daṇḍa *in the world, the world would not survive; for just as the big fish swallow the small fish, those who are strong would feed on the weak.*[7]

राजमूलो महाप्राज्ञ धर्मो लोकस्य लक्ष्यते ।
प्रजा राजभयादेव न खादन्ति परस्परम् ।। शान्ति ६८.८ ।।

The order that exists in the world has governance as its foundation. It is out of the fear of punishment that people do not engage in mutual killing.[8]

असम्मोहाय मर्त्यानामर्थसरंक्षणाय च ।
मर्यादा स्थापिता लोके दण्डसज्ञा विशाम्पते ।। शान्ति १५.१० ।।

Governance is the name of the limits set to keep people from the confusion of anarchy and to protect the material conditions of life.[9]

It is governance which establishes this world upon truth; truth secures dharma; *and* dharma *is established in those who have true knowledge of things.*

There is no other justification for the king to exist than to protect in every way the people. For protection is the first foundation of all social order. It is from the fear of governance that people do not consume each other: it is upon governance that all order is based.[10]

Hence, given the fundamental importance of governance against anarchy, also *the fundamental place of the philosophy of governance*, the *rāja-dharma*, and *Mahābhārata* says:

सर्वे धर्मा राजधर्मप्रधानाः सर्वे वर्णाः पाल्यमाना भवन्ति ।
सर्वस्त्यागो राजधर्मेषु राजंस्त्यागंधर्मेचाहुरग्रयंपुराणम् ।। शान्ति ६३.२७ ।।
सर्वे त्यागा राजधर्मेषु दृष्टाः सर्वा दीक्षा राजधर्मेषु चोक्ताः ।
सर्वा विद्या राजधर्मेषु युक्ताः सर्वे लोका राजधर्मे प्रविष्टाः ।। शान्ति ६३.२९ ।।

अल्पाश्रयानल्पफलान् वदन्ति धर्मानन्यान् धर्मविदोमनुष्या: ।
महाश्रयं बहुकल्याणरूपं क्षात्रं धर्मं नेतरं प्राहुरार्या: ।। शान्ति ६३.२६ ।।

Of all the foundations, the foundation of governance is central; for it is through it that all the human callings are cared for. Every human limit is inherent in the foundation of governance; and to observe limits is the deepest foundation of all.[11]

All limits can be seen in the foundation of governance, and in the foundation of governance, every initiation. All aspects of knowledge are united in that foundation, and into it enter all the worlds.[12]

Little is the support, and even less the fruits, of other foundations, according to those who know what foundations are. But the foundation of governance brings good of many kinds as none other does, the tradition announces.[13]

Given the protection of the people as the purpose of creating the king, his practical goal is bound by that purpose: his discipline arises from the goal set for him: and that discipline is the discipline of *dharma*, to which he is at all times absolutely subject himself. In other words, although the king is invested with the authority and power of governance, the true sovereignty belongs to *dharma*, not to him. The *Mahābhārata* states this again and again, and in many ways.[14]

And, again and again, at every turn, in every situation, the *Mahābhārata* states that, in all the acts of governance, the goal of the king, or of the state, is the protection of the people, derived from the evident truth that,[15] 'protection supports the world'. 'Protected, people prosper: prospering, they endow the king in turn.'

Briefly stated,

एष एव परो धर्मो यद् राजा रक्षति प्रजा: ।
भूतानां हि यथा धर्मो रक्षणं परमा दया ।। शान्ति ७१.२६ ।।

तस्मादेवं परं धर्मं मन्यन्ते धर्मकोविदा: ।
यो राजा रक्षणे युक्तो भूतेषु कुरुते दयाम् ।। शान्ति ७१.२७ ।।

The protection of the people, this is the highest dharma *of the king. Indeed, the protecting of all living beings with kindness towards them is the highest* dharma.[16]

Therefore, the king who has the character of protecting with kindness, those who know what dharma *truly is regard as his highest* dharma.[17]

Governance is to ensure for the people protection from fear, for there is nothing more degrading to human worth than living in fear. The *Mahābhārata* enjoins, therefore:

> *Let the king protect his subjects from their fear of him; from their fear of others; from their fear of each other; and from their fear of things that are not human.*[18]

This fundamental principle of governance is then applied by the *Mahābhārata* to all areas of public policy, always keeping freedom from fear, from the fear of violence, as the main purpose of the state. In other words, its purpose lies in 'protecting the small fish from the big fish'.[19] In that process, however, the *Mahābhārata* warns, the state must not turn itself into the biggest fish of all. When that happens, as indeed it did at different times in human history, including our own times, there is oppression and terror, the *adharma* by the state. In contrast,

> पुत्रा इव पितुर्गेहे विषये यस्य मानवा: ।
> निर्भया विचरिष्यन्ति स राजा राजसत्तम: ।। शान्ति ५७.३३ ।।
> *That king is the best in whose realm the people live without fear, just as the sons live without any fear in the house of their father.*[20]

The *Mahābhārata* says that the one class that requires the greatest protection of all is composed of those who are weak, are poor, are exploited, are helpless, and are trampled upon. Indeed, it is to protect them from the strong that the king was created. That large class of the weak is able to exist because of the power of the king.[21]

> दुर्बलार्थे बलं सृष्टं धात्रा मान्धातरुच्यते ।
> अबलं तु महद्भूतं यस्मिन् सर्वे प्रतिष्ठितम् ।। शान्ति ९१.१२ ।।

In the strongest advice to the king, in a language that is impassioned too, the *Mahābhārata* addresses the king thus:

> दुर्बलांस्तात बुध्येथा नित्यमेवाविमानितान् ।
> मा त्वां दुर्बलचक्षूंषि प्रदहेयु: सबान्धवम् ।। शान्ति ९१.१५ ।।
> *Do not ever think that the weak and the helpless are always to be despised. Take care that the eyes of the weak do not burn you and your relatives to death.*[22]

न हि दुर्बलदग्धस्य कुले किंचित् प्ररोहति।
आमूलं निर्दहन्त्येव मा स्म दुर्बलमासदः।। शान्ति ९१.१६।।

Nothing remains in the family of the one destroyed by the anger of the weak, not one sprout of life ever germinates there, not a blade of grass. Therefore, never oppress the weak and the poor.[23]

अबलं वै बलाच्छ्रेयो यच्चातिबलद्बम्।
बलस्याबलदग्धस्य न किंचिदवशिष्यते।। शान्ति ९१.१७।।

The weak are, in actual fact, much stronger than the strong. They have in them decidedly greater strength; for nothing is left of the strong that have been burnt by the weak.[24]

विमानितो हतः क्रुष्टस्त्रातारं चेन्न विन्दति।
अमानुषकृतस्तत्र दण्डो हन्ति नराधिपम्।। शान्ति ९१.१८।।

Where the insulted, the hurt, and the rejected with a heap of abuses, do not find in the king their protector, there the law of the danda *will surely destroy the king.*[25]

यानि मिथ्याभिशस्तानां पतन्त्यश्रूणि रोदताम्।
तानि पुत्रान् पशून् घ्नन्ति तेषां मिथ्याभिशंसनात्।। शान्ति ९१.२०।।

The tears that fall from the eyes of those who are accused falsely, and are helpless, can destroy an entire kingdom.[26]

यत्राबलो वध्यमानस्त्रातारं नाधिगच्छति।
महान् दैवकृतस्तत्र दण्डः पतति दारुणः।। शान्ति ९१.२२।।

Harassed and oppressed, when a person is left defenceless and unprotected, there the oppressor is punished severely by some higher power.[27]

Therefore,

कृपणानाथवृद्धानां यदाश्रु परिमार्जति।
हर्षं संजनयन् नृणां स राज्ञो धर्म उच्यते।। शान्ति ९१.३८।।

When the king wipes the tears of the poor, the dispossessed, and the old, and creates happiness among the people thereby, such conduct on his part is called the king's dharma.[28]

The word '*rakṣhā*', or 'protection', has a somewhat negative meaning, in the sense that protection is always *from* something, or somebody, of which, of whom, one is for good reasons afraid. Or protection is *against* something not desirable. Since there is in human life so much of which one is rightly fearful, especially when it is an organised entity, the function of the state is to protect the individual from that fear. Law and governance are the instruments of that protection. But that is only one of the functions of the state, although a fundamental one. *Rakṣhā*, or 'protection', has also a meaning beyond that. In describing that wider meaning, the *Mahābhārata* enjoins upon the king to create social conditions not only of freedom from fear but, more positively, of human flourishing, where the individual is enabled to come into the fullness of his, or her, being. That is the meaning of *prabhava* as an attribute of *dharma*. There is no denying that there can be no human flourishing where there is violence. *Prabhava*, or enhancing the human worth, is possible only through *ahiṃsā*, or conditions of not-violence, another attribute of *dharma*. But it is also true that not-violence by itself is not sufficient to create conditions of happiness. I may not do any violence to you, but I may not give you my friendship and love either. Where there is love, there must also be not-violence, *ahiṃsā*, but *ahiṃsā* cannot by itself create love. Trust, friendship, and caring are the elements of human bonding, individual and social. *They* lead to not-violence, and not the other way around. Hence 'protection' has, in the *Mahābhārata*, the wider meaning of creating conditions of personal and social bonding. That is the function of the king, or of the state. 'To give protection to people is the highest function of the king; protecting all beings with the utmost kindness to them is his greatest *dharma*.'[29]

The *Arthashāstra* of Kauṭilya, assigned 321 B.C. in the reign of Chandragupta Maurya, speaks of that one supreme maxim to which the king is subject, and to which all his actions shall be subordinate. 'In the happiness of his subjects lies his happiness; in their welfare, his welfare; whatever pleases himself he shall not consider as good, but whatever pleases his subjects he shall consider as good.'[30] The purpose always was to create social conditions where every individual could follow his, or her, *svadharma*, that is, his, or her, inner calling, and also achieve the orderly progress and welfare of the society as a whole, *lokayātrā* or *lokasaṃgraha*.

The main attribute of governance

In answering the questions of Yudhishṭhira, Bhīshma recalls a conversation that took place many years earlier between two kings, Vasuhoma and Mandhātā, on the subject of *daṇḍa*, governance.[31] During that conversation, Vasuhoma describes 'vigilance', *jāgrati,* as the main attribute of *daṇḍa*. In the long chain of inheritance, the power of governance passing from one to another, *daṇḍa* remained *vigilant* throughout.[32] In brief,

प्रजा जागर्ति लोकेऽस्मिन् दण्डो जागर्ति तासुच।
सर्वे संक्षिपते दण्ड: पितामहसमप्रभ: ।। शान्ति १२२.५१ ।।

जागर्ति काल: पूर्वे व मध्ये चान्ते च भारत
ईश्वर: सर्वलोकस्य महादेव: प्रज्ञापति: ।। शान्ति १२२.५२ ।।

इत्येष दण्डो विख्यात आदौ मध्ये तथावरे।
भूमिपालो यथान्यायं वर्ततानेन धर्मवित् ।। शान्ति १२२.५४ ।।

In this world, the people are vigilant; and in the people, it is daṇḍa *that is vigilant, keeping everybody within limits.*[33]
Protecting all the peoples, daṇḍa *is ever vigilant, in the beginning, the middle, and the end of creation.*[34]
Thus, daṇḍa *is known as 'the beginning', 'the middle', and 'the end'. The king, rooted in* dharma, *shall act through it justly.*[35]

The discipline of *dharma* is the discipline of the king

The discipline of the king is to be derived from the purpose for which he was invested with the power of governance. And to that the *Mahābhārata* devotes the utmost attention. The following are the principles to which the exercise of political power shall be subject at all times.

1. आत्मानमेव प्रथमं विनयैरुपपादयेत्।
अनुभृत्यान् प्रजा: पञ्चादित्येष विनयक्रम: ।। अनुशासन २१२.१२ ।।
Let the king first discipline himself. Only then must he discipline his subordinates and his subjects; for that is the proper order of discipline.[36]

2. स्वस्मात् पूर्वतरं राजा विनयत्वेन वै प्रजा: ।
अपहास्यो भवेत्तादृक् स्वदोषस्यानवेक्षणात् ।। अनुशासन २१२.१३ ।।

The king who tries to discipline his subjects without first disciplining himself becomes an object of ridicule in not being able to see his own defects.[37]

3. सर्वेभ्य एष स्थानेभ्यो रक्षेदात्मानमात्मवान्।
प्रजानां रक्षणार्थाय प्रजाहितकरो भवेत्।। अनुशासन २१२.२५।।

In order to protect his subjects, let the king protect himself at all places, and devote himself to doing good to his subjects.[38]

4. प्रजाकार्यं तु तत्कार्यं प्रजासौख्यं तु तत्सुखम्।
प्रजाप्रियं प्रियं तस्य स्वहितं तु प्रजाहितम्।
प्रजार्थं तस्य सर्वस्वमात्मार्थं न विधीयते।। अनुशासन २१२.२६।।

The interest of his subjects alone is his interest, their well-being his well-being; what is pleasing to them is pleasing to him, and in their good lies his own good. Everything he has is for their sake; for his own sake, he has nothing.[39]

5. स्वतश्च परतश्चैव परस्परभयादपि।
अमानुषभयेभ्यश्च स्वाः प्रजाः पालयेन्नृपः।। अनुशासन २१२.४०।।

Let the king protect his subjects from their fear of him, from their fear of others, from their fear of each other, and of things that are not human.[40]

There is no doubt that the *Mahābhārata* speaks of power, *bala*, as that upon which ultimately everything depends for its existence, even *dharma*.[41]

अतिधर्माद् बलं मन्ये बलाद् धर्मः प्रवर्तते।
बले प्रतिष्ठितो धर्मो धरण्यामिव जङ्गमम्।।शान्ति १३४.६।।

I consider power superior to even dharma*; for it is through power that* dharma *progresses.*[42]

धूमो वायोरिव वशे बलं धर्मोऽनुवर्तते।
अनीश्वरो बले धर्मो द्रुमेबल्लीव संश्रिता।।शान्ति १३४.७।।

Just as smoke takes the direction the wind would, so does dharma *follow power. Just as a creeper needs the support of a tree to spread, so does* dharma *require power to remain firm and stable.*[43]

But power is never considered its own justification. On the contrary, *power without dharma* is as much the way to tyranny as *dharma left unprotected* is the way to anarchy. In brief, the power of the state has to exercise discipline upon itself most of all, the discipline of *dharma*. For the state is not an end in itself.

विभज्य दण्ड: कर्तव्यो धर्मेण न यदृच्छया।
दुष्टानां निग्रहोदण्डो हिरण्यं बाह्यत: क्रिया।।शान्ति १२२.४०।।
The power of governance is to be exercised in accordance with dharma, *and not arbitrarily. For its main purpose is to control the lawless, not to accumulate wealth, which is anyway secondary.*[44]

It is by exercising the power of governance in accordance with *dharma* that the people are made secure and free from fear. उभौ सत्याधिकारस्थौ त्रायेते भयात्[45] The *Mahābhārata* exhorts the king again and again, and yet again, in words that are clear and straightforward: 'Subject yourself to the discipline of *dharma*, for it is in the discipline of *dharma* that the discipline of your calling as the king lies.'

मरणान्तमिदं सर्वं नेह किञ्चिदनामयम्।
तस्माद् धर्मे स्थितो राजा प्रजा धर्मेण पालयेत्।। शान्ति ९३.२३।।
Everything in this world perishes in the end; nor is there anything which is not transitory or free from disease. Therefore, remaining steadfast in dharma, *the king should take care of the people in the light of* dharma.[46]

Self-discipline of the king

Bhīshma propounds thirty-six *self-disciplines* that the king should cultivate diligently.[47] The principle underlying them all is—balance.

अयं गुणानां षट्त्रिंशत्षट्त्रिंशद्गुणसंयुत:
यान् गुणांस्तु गुणोपेत: कुर्वन् गुणमवाप्नुयात्।। शान्ति ७०.२।।

1. The king should preserve *dharma* without harshness.
2. Be a believer, but not abandon affection for others.
3. Secure wealth without cruelty.
4. Enjoy the physical senses without excess.
5. Speak pleasingly without being pitiable.
6. Be brave without bragging.
7. Give, but not to the undeserving.
8. Be fearless without being heartless.

9. Have no alliance with the wicked.

10. Have no quarrels with friends.

11. Employ spies, but not those who are not loyal to the state.

12. Accomplish one's work without hurting others.

13. Avoid confiding in those who are wicked.

14. Do not indulge in self-praise.

15. Do not deprive of their money those who are distinguished.

16. Do not be dependent on those who are of low character.

17. Do not punish anyone without carefully examining the facts of the alleged offence.

18. Do not share the secret advice given to him.

19. Do not offer money to those who are greedy.

20. Neither trust those who had done an ill deed to him.

21. Protect his wife, but without jealousy.

22. Remain pure, but not hate others.

23. Enjoy the company of women, but without excess.

24. Enjoy eating food, but not that which is harmful.

25. Give up arrogance, and be hospitable and respectful to those deserving of respect.

26. Serve the elders, but without guile.

27. Worship gods, but without pride.

28. Seek material prosperity, but not by questionable means.

29. Love, without being stubborn.

30. Be competent and skilful, but not without knowing the proper occasion.

31. Never give false assurance.

32. Be kind, but without being sarcastic.

33. He must not attack anyone without warning;

34. Do not be angry without cause;

35. nor regret after destroying the enemy.

36. Be gentle, but not to those whose conduct had been harmful.

> *It is best that the king does not abandon truth: is not devious and cunning in his conduct towards others: remains steadfast in self-control, in* dharma, *in civilised behaviour, in his royal obligations, and in the good of the people.*[48]

He should never hesitate in answering straightforwardly when a question is put to him; but neither should he say anything without thinking; never be hasty in his actions, and never speak ill of others.[49]

The idea of balance is carried in the later works as well. For example, discussing the whole range of polity in his *Arthashāstra*, Kauṭilya says:

Whoever imposes severe punishment becomes repulsive to the people, while he who awards mild punishment becomes contemptible. But whoever imposes punishment as deserved becomes respectable. For punishment, when awarded with due consideration, makes the people devoted to righteousness and to the works productive of wealth and enjoyment; whereas punishment, when ill-awarded, under the influence of greed and anger owing to ignorance, excites fury even among hermits and ascetics dwelling in forests, not to speak of householders.[50]

Nor can daṇḍa *be kept in abeyance; for then, it gives rise to such disorder as is implied in the proverb of the fishes (a great fish swallowing a small one); for, in the absence of a magistrate, the strong will swallow the weak, but under his protection the weak will resist the strong.*[51]

The *Mahābhārata* exhorts the king to keep himself free from the arrogance, *darpa*, of power and authority above all. For

यत्राधर्मं प्रणयते दुर्बले बलवत्तरः ।
तां वृत्तिमुपजीवन्ति ये भवन्ति तदन्वयाः ।। शान्ति ९३.९ ।।
By abusing his great power, where the king begins to oppress the weak, and takes to adharma, *there his officials make that kind of behaviour their means of livelihood as well.*[52]

राजानमनुवर्तन्ते तं पापाभिप्रवर्तकम् ।
अविनीतमनुष्यं तत् क्षिप्रं राष्ट्रं विनश्यति ।। शान्ति ९३.२ ।।
In that they follow the behaviour of the king. Full of such arrogant people, that kingdom is soon destroyed.[53]

दर्पो नाम श्रियः पुत्रो जज्ञेऽधर्मादिति श्रुतिः ।
तेन देवासुरा राजन् नीताः सुबहवो व्ययम् ।। शान्ति ९०.२७ ।।

राजर्षयश्चय बहवस्तथा बुध्यस्व पार्थिव।
राजा भवति तं जित्वा दासस्तेन पराजित:।। शान्ति ९०.२८।।

From a part of adharma, *arrogance is the son of plenitude: he has destroyed gods and kings and scholars alike. Reflect on this. He who conquers arrogance is truly a king; he who is conquered by it is merely a slave.*[54]

राजैव कर्ता भूतानां राजैव च विनाशक:।
धर्मात्मा य: स कर्ता स्यादधर्मात्मा विनाशक:।। शान्ति ९१.९।।

The king is at once both the protector of people and their destroyer. He who conducts himself according to dharma *is a protector; he who takes to* adharma *turns into a destroyer.*[55]

That is to say, the king has to have first a right relationship with his own self before he can fulfil his responsibility to the *other*.

आत्मा जेय: सदा राज्ञा ततो जेयाश्च शत्रव:।
आजितात्मा नरपतिर्विजयेत कथं रिपून्।। शान्ति ६९.४।।

When the king has conquered his own self, he has conquered his enemies too. The king who remains defeated by his own self, how can he be victorious against an enemy?[56]

The very first element in his right relationship with his self is his own freedom from deviousness and cunning.[57] Every other discipline comes from that freedom.

उभे प्रज्ञे वेदितव्ये ऋज्वी वक्रा च भारत।
जानन् वक्रां न सेवेत प्रतिबाधेत चागताम्।। शान्ति १००.५।।

Intelligence is of two kinds: one which is devious and crooked, the other which is simple and straightforward. The king should know one from the other. He should knowingly not take recourse to the first. Should deviousness come to him naturally, he should try to remove it.[58]

Not only must the king be not devious in his conduct towards those he is supposed to protect, the people, but also in his conduct towards an enemy. The *Mahābhārata*, in the strongest statement on this subject, holds that

सर्वं जिह्मं मृत्युपदमार्जवं ब्रह्मण: पदम् ।
एतावाञ्ज्ञानविषय: किं प्रलाप: करिष्यति ।। शान्ति ७९.२१ ।।
All deviousness is the place of death: simplicity and straightforwardness, the place of highest reality. This alone is the subject of knowledge; all the rest are empty words.[59]

Simplicity and straightforwardness are attitudes of the mind; courteous and sincere speech is their expression. When asked what advice he gave to his son Puru while anointing him his successor, King Yayāti says[60] that among the many disciplines that he advised him to cultivate with vigilance, the very first was: 'A truly strong person forgives always, and one who is of weak character shows anger always.'[61] 'The man who is not full of anger is superior to the one who is; and better than the man who is intolerant is the man who can bear much.'[62] The power of governance must at all times be exercised without anger and intolerance. That means also exercising self-control over one's speech.

नारुन्तुद: स्यान्न नृशंसवादी न हीनत: परमभ्याददीत ।
ययास्य वाचा पर उद्विजेत न तां वदेदुषतीं पापलोक्याम् ।। आदि ८७.८ ।।

अरुन्तुदं परुषं तीक्ष्णवाचं वाक्कण्टकैर्वितुदन्तं मनुष्यान् ।
विद्यादलक्ष्मीकतमं जनानां मुखे निबद्धां निर्ऋतिं वहन्तम् ।। आदि ८७.९ ।।
Out of anger, don't speak in a way that is hurtful and creates in the other only agitation.
The man who is given to hurtful speech, consider him *to be truly poor; for, in the form of cruel speech, he is carrying within him a demon.*[63]

The language of governance, of *daṇḍa*, need never be a language that offends the dignity of others, and turns friends into enemies. Rather, Yayāti suggested to his son:

न हीदृशं सवननं त्रिषु लोकेषु विद्यते ।
दया मैत्री न भूतेषु दानं च मधुरा च वाक् ।। आदि ८७.१२ ।।

तस्मात् सान्त्वं सदा वाच्यं न वाच्यं परुषं क्वचित् ।
पूज्यान् सम्पूजयेद् दद्यान्न च याचेत् कदाचन ।। आदि ८७.१३ ।।
Kindness and friendship to all beings, sharing, and speech that is endearing—there is in the world nothing that can win people than these three. Speak in a way that is reassuring, never in a way that is hurtful.

Respect those worthy of respect. Give to others, but never ask anything for yourself.[64]

Impartiality, truth, and trust in governance

But, the *Mahābhārata* says, protection of the people is possible only when governance is impartial, and the law is not 'held in abeyance'. The fundamental principle of dharmic law is: 'The king shall not punish one for the offence committed by another.' That, in turn, is possible only when:

तद्दण्डविन्नृप: प्राज्ञ: शूर: शक्नोति रक्षितुम् ।
न हि शक्यमदण्डेन क्लीबेनाबुद्धिनापि वा ।। शान्ति ९१.४९ ।।

न जात्वदक्षो नृपति: प्रजा: शक्नोति रक्षितुम् ।
भारो हि सुमहांस्तात राज्यं नाम सुदुष्करम् । शान्ति ९१.४८ ।।

संग्रह: सर्वभूतानां दानं च मधुरं वच: ।
पौरजानपदाश्चैव गोप्तव्यास्ते यथासुखम् ।। शान्ति ९१.४७ ।।

The king, besides being intelligent, also knows the principles of punishment. He who is afraid of dispensing just punishments is impotent as king and is devoid of intelligence and can never protect the people.[65] *Because governance is a complex affair, and a burden too, the ruler who is not skilful in the art of governing can never protect the people.*[66]

Therefore, the king is advised: 'By uniting yourself with the people, through giving and by endearing speech, you shall protect them in a way that brings them happiness.[67]

The elements of professional skill and competence are laid in the *Mahābhārata* with great care and thought. But what is required at the very foundation of the state is its *moral competence*. For it is from *that*, that the authority of the state flows. The very first element of law and governance is the attitude of impartiality, or *saṁyag-daṇḍa*.

सम्यग्दंण्डधरो नित्यं राजा धर्ममवाप्नुयात् ।
नृपस्य सततं दण्ड: सम्यग् धर्म: प्रशस्यते ।। शान्ति ६९.३० ।।

The king who governs always with equality and impartiality obtains dharma. *And the king who has the* dharma *of equality and impartiality is applauded and praised.*[68]

No one shall be exempt from the law, for no one is above the law, *adaṇḍanīya*.

पापमाचरतो चत्र कर्मणा व्याहृतेन वा।
प्रियस्यापि न मृष्येत स राज्ञो धर्म उच्यते।। शान्ति ९१.३५।।
Should somebody even dear to the king commit an offence by act or speech, the king shall punish him, too. That behaviour is called the king's dharma.[69]

गुरोरप्यवलिप्तस्य कार्याकार्यमजानतः।
उत्पथप्रतिपन्नस्य दण्डो भवति शाश्वतः।। शान्ति ५७.७।।
If, from arrogance, losing the sense of what is right and what is wrong, a person adopts a wrong course, he should be punished, even if he were the king's guru.[70]

माता पिता च भ्राता च भार्याचैव पुरोहितः।
नादण्ड्यो विद्यते राज्ञो यः स्वधर्मे न तिष्ठति।। शान्ति १२१.६०।।
Neither mother, nor father, nor brother, nor wife, nor the priest, no one is above the law; and should any of them transgress dharma, *the king shall punish him, or her, too. To the king, no one is beyond the law of punishment.*[71]

यथा पुत्रास्तथा पौत्रा द्रष्टव्यास्ते न संशयः।
भक्तिश्चैषां न कर्तव्या व्यवहारे प्रदर्शिते।। शान्ति ६९.२७।।
श्रोतुं चैव न्यसेद् राजा प्राज्ञान् सर्वार्थदर्शिनः।
व्यवहारेषु सततं तत्र राज्यं प्रतिष्ठितम्।।शन्ति ६९.२८।।
Undoubtedly, the king should look upon his subjects as his sons and grandsons. But in dispensing justice he shall display no partiality arising from any feeling of affection. While dispensing justice, the king should, in hearing both sides to a case, have men of knowledge and understanding to assist him. For it is upon justice that the state is based.[72]

प्रकृतीनां हि रक्षार्थे रागद्वेषौ व्युदस्य च।
उभयोः पक्षयोर्वादं श्रुत्वा चैव यथातथम्।।
तमर्थं विमृशेद् बुद्ध्या स्वयमातत्त्वदर्शनात्।। अनुशासन २१२.२७।।

तत्त्वविद्भाश्च बहुभिः सहासीनो नरोत्तमैः।
कर्तारमपराधं च देशकालौ नयानयौ।।
ज्ञात्वा सम्यग्यथाशास्त्रं ततो दण्डं नयेन्नृषु।। अनुशासन २१२.२८।।

एवं कुर्वेल्लभेद् धर्मं पक्षपातविवर्जनात्।
प्रत्यक्षाप्तोपदेशाभ्यामनुमानेन वा पुनः।।
बोद्धव्यं सततं राज्ञा देशवृत्तं शुभाशुभम्।। अनुशासन २१२.२९।।

It is only after he has heard without prejudice both sides in a case; has reflected long enough to come to the right conclusion; has consulted those who know the principles of good governance; has carefully examined the nature of the alleged offence and the character of the accused; has taken into consideration the context and the circumstances; and has understood what is justice and what is injustice; that the king should punish a person.[73]

यमो यच्छति भूतानि सर्वाण्येवाविशेषतः।
तथा राज्ञानुकर्तव्यं यन्तव्या विधिवत् प्रजाः।। शान्ति ९१.४४।।

The king who dispenses justice thus, without any partiality, gains the merit of dharma.[74]

लोकरञ्जनमेवात्र राज्ञां धर्मः सनातनः।
सत्यस्य रक्षणं चैव व्यवहारस्य चार्जवम्।। शान्ति ५७.११।।

Just as the Lord of Death, Yama, rules equally over all living beings, so should the king govern the people without discriminating among them.[75]

Impartiality in the acts of the state is then related to truth.[76]

न हि सत्यादृते किंचिद् राज्ञां वै सिद्धिकारकम्।
सत्ये हि राजा निरतः प्रेत्य चेह च नन्दति।। शान्ति ५६.१७।।

For the kings, no means are more effective than truth, no wealth greater than truth. For it is upon the trust of the people that the state is founded; when that trust is destroyed, because of the untruthfulness of the king, the state is destroyed, too.

Of that there is no doubt, the *Mahābhārata* suggests.

ऋषीणामपि राजेन्द्र सत्यमेव परं धनम्।
तथा राज्ञां परं सत्यान्नान्यद् विश्वासकारणम्।। शान्ति ५६.१८।।

Just as for the sages truth is their greatest wealth, similarly for the kings there is no other means of creating trust among the people than truth.[77]

In brief,

प्रियाप्रिये परित्यज्य समः सर्वेषु जन्तुषु।
कामं क्रोधं च लोभं च मानं चोत्सृज्य दूरतः।। शान्ति ५९.१०४।।
Freeing your self from likes and dislikes, and keeping preferences, anger, greed and vanity far away, treat all beings with a sense of equality.[78]

What that means in actual practice is that:

भयार्तानां भयात् त्राता दीनानुग्रहकारणात्।
कार्याकार्यविशेषज्ञो नित्यं राष्ट्रहिते रतः।।
सत्यः संधस्थितो राज्ये प्रजापालनतत्परः।
अलुब्धो न्यायवादी च षड्भागमुपजीवति।।
कार्याकार्यविशेषज्ञः सर्वे धर्मेण पश्यति।
स्वराष्ट्रेषु दयां कुर्यादकार्ये न प्रवर्तते।। अनुशासन।।
The king should free the fearful from fear: be kind to the helpless and the poor: understand what is proper and what is improper: keeping his governance rooted in truth, enhance and sustain the people: without greed, say only that which is just: discriminate between right and wrong: look upon everybody with the eyes of truth and justice: and never take a course of action which is unbecoming of him.[79]

What is also essential is a feeling of trust among the people towards the assembly, *sabhā*, that legislates, directs, and controls the public acts of the state. Regarding the royal assembly, the *Mahābhārata* prescribes:

न सा सभा यत्र न सन्ति वृद्धा
न ते वृद्धा ये न वदन्ति धर्मम्।
नासौ धर्मो यत्र न सत्यमस्ति
न तत् सत्यं यच्छलेनाभ्युपेतम्।। उद्योग ३५.५८।।
That assembly is no assembly that does not have in it elders. Those are no elders who do not speak according to dharma. *That* dharma *which is not rooted in truth is no* dharma. *And that truth is no truth which is full of deviousness and cunning.*[80]

To summarise, the *Mahābhārata* describes the foundations of good governance as follows:

त्रायते हि यदा सर्वं वाचा कायेन कर्मणा।
पुत्रस्यापि न मृष्येच्च स राज्ञो धर्म उच्यते।। शान्ति ९१.३२।।

When the king, with his heart and speech and body, protects the people, and does not pardon a wrongdoing even by his own son, that is called the 'Dharma *of Governance.*[81]

संविभज्य यदा भुङ्क्ते नृपतिर्दुर्बलान् नरान्।
तदा भवन्ति बलिन: स राज्ञो धर्म उच्चते।। शान्ति ९१.३३।।

When the king tends to the weak and the helpless first, and only then to himself, the weak and the helpless gaining strength thereby, that is called the 'Dharma *of Governance'.*[82]

यदा रक्षति राष्ट्राणि यदा दस्यूनपोहति।
यदा जयति संग्रामे स राज्ञो धर्म उच्यते।। शान्ति ९१.३४।।

When the king protects the nation, subdues the robbers and thieves, and is victorious in battle, that is called the 'Dharma *of Governance'.*[83]

पापमाचरतो यत्र कर्मणा व्याहृतेन वा।
प्रियस्यापि न मृष्येत स राज्ञो धर्म उच्यते।। शान्ति ९१.३५।।

When the king punishes a wrongdoing even by one dear to him, that is called the 'Dharma *of Governance'.*[84]

यदा शारणिकान् राजा पुत्रवत् परिरक्षति।
भिन्नत्ति च न मर्यादां स राज्ञो धर्म उच्यते।। शान्ति ९१.३६।।

When the king protects the merchants as he would his own children, and does not transgress his limits, that is called the 'Dharma *of Governance'.*[85]

यदाऽऽप्तदक्षिणैर्यज्ञैर्यजते श्रद्धयान्वित:।
कामद्वेषावनादृत्य स राज्ञो धर्म उच्यते।। शान्ति ९१.३७।।

When the king, without greed or aversion, donates liberally, and with faith, to the rites of invocation to the gods of the universe, that is called the 'Dharma *of Governance'.*[86]

कृपणानाथवृद्धानां यदाश्रु परिमार्जति।
हर्षं संजनयन् नृणां स राज्ञो धर्म उच्यते।। शान्ति ९१.३८।।

When the king wipes the tears of the poor, the abandoned, and the old, and thereby creates happiness among the people, that is called the 'Dharma *of Governance'.*[87]

विवर्धयति मित्राणि तथारींश्चापि कर्षति।
सम्पूजयति साधूंश्च स राज्ञो धर्म उच्चते।। शान्ति ९१.३९।।

When the king increases his friends, and limits his enemies, and honours those who are good, that is called the 'Dharma *of Governance'.*[88]

सत्यं पालयति प्रीत्या नित्यं भूमिं प्रयच्छति।
पूजयेदतिथीन् भृत्यान् स राज्ञो धर्म उच्यते।। शान्ति ९१.४०।।

When the king perseveres in truth with sincerity; gifts lands; and is hospitable to those who deserve to be taken care of; that is called the 'Dharma *of Governance'.*[89]

Trust as the foundation of republics

Most of all, if the people were not to destroy each other, they have to have a feeling of trust for each other. Where trust is absent, nothing can survive. In describing *gaṇa-rājya*, the constitution of republics, the *Shānti-parva* speaks also of the causes of their decline.[90] 'The republics have been destroyed mostly because of dissension between one people and another.'[91] Bhīshma says: 'In the republics, in the families, and between one state and another, the two factors that ignite the fire of enmity are greed and arrogance.'[92] A republic is normally a happy place. 'Those with wisdom praise the citizens of a republic. Bound with a sense of unity, they do not cheat each other. Rather, serving each other, they create for themselves happiness.'[93] For that reason, he further says, in order that the state may protect the people, it has to protect them first from their fear of each other, which must arise when there is distrust among them. For that, he has to be sensitive to what causes the feeling of distrust. If not, 'the internal fears uproot the roots of a republic'.[94] Bhīshma concludes by saying:

अकस्मात् क्रोधमोहाभ्यां लोभाद् वापि स्वभावजात्।
अन्योन्यं नाभिभाषन्ते तत्पराभवलक्षणम्।। शान्ति १०७.२९।।

Out of anger, or confusion, or because of greed, when the various peoples of a republic can no longer communicate with each other, then it is a sure sign of their defeat already.[95]

Public wealth under the control of *dharma*

One of the concerns of the *Mahābhārata* is to show that *lobha*, greed, is profoundly destructive of all relationships—of the self with the self, and of the self with the other. After showing the decided importance of *artha*, wealth, in human living, it concentrates on the equally important condition that the need for money in order to live does not turn into greed, and greed into lawlessness. Hence wealth, especially public wealth, should be under the control of *dharma*. And we must keep returning to the meaning of *dharma* as the foundation of relationships, personal and social. Let us next look at the principles to which the state earnings are to be subject.

a. The king must confine himself to his lawful sources of income.[96] What those sources were, as prescribed in the *Dharmasūtra*, in the *Mahābhārata*, and in Kauṭilya's *Arthashāstra*, have been described in detail by others.[97] Briefly they were: one-sixth of the produce from individual lands; an irrigation cess on them; tax on the products of artisans; tolls and duties on all kinds of merchandise; a protection tax on the caravans of traders; fees on the use of waterways; and monies collected as fines for wrongdoing. There was provision also for a special tax on wealthy merchants,[98] for wealthy men were considered to be the main limb of the nation.[99] Above all, it was lawful for the king to call upon the people, during an emergency arising from external attack, to meet the defence expenses,[100] which were to be treated, however, as a loan to the State.

b. Should the king, out of greed, attempt to collect wealth by taxing the people far too much, he would neither keep the wealth thus accumulated, nor preserve the social order,[101] indeed might destroy the very means on which the livelihood of the people depends.[102] No nation can progress where the people are squeezed unlawfully.[103]

c. Taxes must be high or low according to the capacity of the people;[104] on no account must they be oppressive. Out of greed, should the king impose on the people oppressive taxes, not only would the traders and merchants as well as the artisans leave his realm,[105] but he would invite also hatred,[106] destroying himself thereby.[107]

d. The capacity to pay must be carefully investigated before settling the amount to be collected as royal revenue. While assessing the capacity, regard must be paid to production expenses, loans incurred, and losses that might take place; and tax must be linked with the relative grades of a product.[108]

e. The royal revenues, to be collected diligently but without harshness,[109] must be spent, with equal diligence but with prudence, in protecting the people and in their welfare in every possible way—the two paramount duties of a king, his *dharma*.

f. The treasury is a source of power,[110] and on power depends the kinghood;[111] but in the last count, the power of the king depends on whether, by spending his wealth, he has ensured the welfare of his people. The royal wealth must be spent on public works, like highways, waterways, sources of drinking water, wells, and ponds and lakes, temples and public gardens, and also on maintenance of certain kinds of individuals. Those whose maintenance from royal funds is the responsibility of the king includes destitutes, widows, orphans, the sick, and the aged.[112] Where they are not looked after, that kingdom is doomed.

g. One should be free from *lobha*, greed, because from greed arise all evils;[113] and one should give, *dāna*, because that increases wealth as well as merit.

h. Where there is cheating, there is resentment and loss of trust, both sufficient to destroy the social and economic fabric. The king's officials, appointed to keep a watch on every department of economic activity, must ensure the quality of products, the reasonableness of their price, and the conditions in which they are sold and bought.[114]

i. Wealth that is hoarded, like the honey in a beehive, invites only its plunder.[115] Hence the surplus must be employed in charity and in public works. Where these conditions are not fulfilled, the king is entitled to take from traders and merchants their surplus wealth and put it to public use.

j. Only the wealth earned through *dharma* is legitimate wealth; that which comes through *adharma* is improper. Let no one earn wealth through cruel deeds.[116]

ऊधश्छिन्द्यात तु यो धेन्वा: क्षीरार्थी न लभेत् पय: ।
एवं राष्ट्रमयोगेन पीडितं न विवर्धते ।। शान्ति ७१.१६ ।।
यो हि दोग्ध्रीमुपास्ते च स नित्यं विन्दते पय: ।
एवं राष्ट्रमुपायेन भुञ्जानो लभते फलम् ।। शान्ति ७१.१७ ।।

अथ राष्ट्रमुपायेन भुज्यमानं सुरक्षितम्।
जनयत्यतुलां नित्यं कोशवृद्धिं युधिष्ठिर।। शान्ति ७१.१८।।

मालाकारोपमो राजन् भव माऽऽङ्गारिकोपमः।
तथायुक्तश्चिरं राज्यं भोक्तुं शक्ष्यसि पालयन्।। शान्ति ७१.२०।।

Just as the one who wishes to obtain milk cannot get it by cutting off the udders of a milk-giving cow, similarly a nation cannot progress where the people are exploited greatly.

Only he who tends to the milk-giving cow every day gets milk in plenty; so the king who tends to his people by all proper means receives the benefits of caring.

The royal treasury is increased when the people are protected in every way that is just.

The king should act rather like a gardener, and not like a coal miner.[117]

Therefore:

मा स्म लुब्धांश्च मूर्खांश्च कामार्थे च प्रयूयुजः।
अलुब्धान् बुद्धिसम्पन्नान् सर्वकर्मसु योजयेत्।। शान्ति ७१.८।।

मूर्खो ह्यधिकृतोऽर्थेषु कार्याणामविशारदः।
प्रजाः क्लिश्नात्ययोगेन कामक्रोधसमन्वितः।। शान्ति ७१.९।।

कामक्रोधौ पुरस्कृत्य योऽर्थे राजानुतिष्ठति।
न स धर्मं न चाप्यर्थे प्रतिगृह्णाति बालिशः।। शान्ति ७१.७।।

मा स्माधर्मेण लोभेन लिप्सेथास्त्वं धनागमम्।
धर्मार्थावध्रुवौ तस्य यो न शास्त्रपरो भवेत्।। शान्ति ७१.१३।।

अपशास्त्रपरो राजा धर्मार्थान्नाधिगच्छति।
अस्थाने चास्य तद् वित्तं सर्वमेव विनश्यति।। शान्ति ७१.१४।।

अर्थमूलोऽपि हिंसां च कुरुते स्वयमात्मनः।
करैरशास्त्रदृष्टैर्हि मोहात् सम्पीडयन् प्रजाः।। शान्ति ७१.१५।।

Don't ever put financial matters into the hands of those who are greedy and foolish. Employ only those who are intelligent and free from greed.[118]

If a person who is aggressive and is driven by his desire for pleasure, and is not efficient and knowledgeable either, is entrusted with the work of raising finances, he will only oppress the people.[119]

Never try to accumulate wealth by means of adharma *and greed. For whatever is against the just principles of governance is unstable. The*

> *king who oppresses the people by taxing them against all the dictates of the* shastra, *does violence to himself by his own hands. Such a king gains neither material prosperity nor* dharma, *and is verily a fool. Should he obtain much wealth, he would squander it away on improper deeds.*[120]

The first thing to be observed about these principles is their secular character. They invoke nothing theological but only what is just and right in creating the social good. The repeated saying that *daṇḍa*, governance, must in all circumstances be subject to *dharma* upheld the sovereignty of law and not anything religious. And the law whose sovereignty it upheld is not merely law as legislated but is the law, *dharma*, which is the foundation of all relationships, and supports, sustains, and enhances human worth. The nearly obsessive dharmic fear of greed had its basis in the logic of desire, which is such that unless desire is kept within limits, it must end in destroying everything that is of human worth. In other words, control is self-control, which may come naturally if that logic is understood, not cerebrally alone but with one's whole being.

Fear as the basis of the social order

At this point, let us recall, if only one of its characteristics, which is also the one most important, the *method* employed in the *Mahābhārata* in its enquiry into the human condition.

It is evident that human relationships are marked by numerous complexities. Those constitute a substantial part of human reality. If they are not fully acknowledged, and taken into account, then any discussion as regards the foundations will in practical terms remain empty, however noble and grand it may be. But it is also true that without a clear understanding of the foundations, the practical details of social arrangements would remain equally empty, the for then they would have no direction, no principles by which social conflicts can be settled. The *Mahābhārata* suggests that both these dangers be avoided, if the reflections on law and governance are to be realistic and meaningful.

Therefore, the method of the *Mahābhārata* is to confront one reality with another reality, one truth with another truth, when the two are in evident conflict in the same context. Let us take one example of how this method is then applied to the processes of law and governance—to the question of freedom from fear.

Earlier we saw that a justification of the existence of the state is that it shall create social conditions of freedom from fear, where freedom from the fear of the state, fear of organised tyranny, is the very first freedom. This is one inviolable truth.

Arjuna, the great hero in the *Mahābhārata*, brings up the opposite truth. His argument is as follows.[121]

दण्डे स्थिता: प्रजा: सर्वा भयंदण्डे विदुर्बुधा: ।
दण्डे स्वर्गो मनुष्याणां लोकोऽयं सुप्रतिष्ठित: ।। शान्ति १५.४३ ।।

विष्वग्लोप: प्रवर्तेत भिद्येरन् सर्वसेतव: ।
ममत्वं न प्रजानीयुर्यदि दण्डो न पालयेत् ।। शान्ति १५.३८ ।।

Daṇḍa, *or governance, is the basis of social order, and the fear of punishment is the basis of governance. Both this life and the next are based upon governance.*[122]
It is the fear of daṇḍa, *in the sense both of rule and punishment, which secures the world from anarchy. Were there not, in the minds of the people, this fear, all limits would be breached, and no one would even care which thing is his and which is not.*[123]

If there were no fear of rule, there would be only the rule of fear. Arjuna further says:

दण्डश्चेन्न भवेल्लोके विनश्येयुरिमा: प्रजा: ।
जले मत्स्यानिवाभक्ष्यन् दुर्बलान् बलवत्तरा: ।। शान्ति १५.३० ।।
It is without doubt the fear of rule that alone keeps the people on the path of proper conduct towards each other. In its absence, just as in the waters the big fish swallow the small fish, those who are powerful would feed on those who are weak.[124]

राजदण्डभयादेके पापा: पापं न कुर्वते ।
यमदण्डभयादेके परकोभयादपि ।। १५.५ ।।

परस्परभयादेके पापा: पापं न कुर्वते ।
एवं सांसिद्धके लोके सर्वंदण्डे प्रतिष्ठितम् ।। शान्ति १५.६ ।।
It is in the nature of the world that many men restrain themselves from wrongdoing for fear of punishment by law. Some restrain themselves from the fear of Death: some, from the fear of what might happen to them

in the life hereafter: and some others restrain themselves simply from the fear of each other. Everything is based on the fear of rule.[125]

दण्डस्यैव भयादेके न खादन्ति परस्परम् ।
अन्धे तमसि मज्जेयुर्यदि दण्डो न पालयेत् ।। शान्ति १५.७ ।।
It is only out of fear that people do not swallow each other.[126]

सर्वो दण्डजितो लोको दुर्लभो हि शुचिर्जनः ।
दण्डस्य हि भयाद् भीतो भोगायैव प्रवर्तते ।। शान्ति १५.३४ ।।
Only rarely is a person found who is good and clean by nature; only out of fear, and not out of goodness, do most people keep within bounds.[127]

Social order is possible only when there is among the people the fear of law and its rule.

In his long and very systematic exposition of the foundations of law and governance, Bhīshma maintains that fear must then be, on principle, an essential part of social regulation. Regulation sets limits—limits on one man's conduct towards another. And limits will be observed only when there is the fear of punishment when they are transgressed. It is for this reason that, paradoxically, fear is the basis of governance, and the purpose of governance is to secure for the people freedom from fear.

How was this paradox resolved? How were these two conflicting realities reconciled?

There was no way in which that troublesome paradox *could* be resolved. And there was no attempt to resolve it *somehow* either. It remains—to be faced honestly. But it does not cripple the purpose of governance. It is only that the fear that both Arjuna and Bhīshma were talking about, as the basis of social order, was the fear of *adharma*, not of the ruler. Therefore, with perfect consistency, Bhīshma places the king himself, who wields the *daṇḍa* more than anyone else, under the fear of *daṇḍa*. He is told that he should fear one thing most of all—the tears of the poor, the weak and the oppressed, for their tears have the power of destroying an entire kingdom. Deriving his authority, political and moral, from *dharma* as justice, and from justice as truth, he must fear, more than even death, his own acts of injustice and untruth, acts of *adharma*.

After pointing out the role of fear as the restraining factor in human relationships, the *Mahābhārata* then returns to freedom from fear as the very first condition of social peace and of human dignity. For:

शब्दे स्पर्शे रसे रूपे गन्धे च रमते मनः।
तेषु भोगेषु सर्वेषु न भीतो लभते सुखम्।। शान्ति ७२.२३।।

अभयस्य हि यो दाता तस्यैव सुमहत् फलम्।
न हि प्राणसमं दानं त्रिषु लोकेषु विद्यते।। शान्ति ७२.२४।।

Human beings take delight in sounds, touch, tastes, beauty, and in fragrance. But the one who is full of fear can derive from them no happiness whatever.

Therefore whoever can give the gift of freedom from fear himself obtains great good. For there is no greater gift in all the worlds than the gift of life.[128]

Hence the suggestion Vidura makes to Dhritarāshṭra, the king:

चक्षुषा मनसा वाचा कर्मणा च चतुर्विधम्।
प्रसादयति यो लोकं तं लोकोऽनुप्रसीदति।। उद्योग ३४.२५।।

यस्मात् त्रस्यन्ति भूतानि मृगव्याधान्मृगा इव।
सागररन्तामपि मही लब्ध्वा स परिहीयते।। उद्योग ३४.२६।।

पितृपैतामहं राज्यं प्राप्तवान् स्वेन कर्मणा।
वायुरभ्रमिवासाद्य भ्रंशयतयनये स्थितः।। उद्योग ३४.२७।।

The looks, the heart, the speech, and the deeds—when, with these four, the king makes the people happy, it is with him that the people are happy.[129]

Where the living beings have a feeling of terror, as the deer do towards the hunter, there the king, should he gain the whole earth stretching up to the sea, is discarded by them.[130]

By his acts of injustice, he destroys the kingdom he inherited from his father and forefathers, in the same manner as the wind disperses the clouds.[131]

Freedom from fear is the very first foundation of good governance.

स्वतश्च परतश्चैव परस्परभयादपि।
अमानुषभयेभ्यश्च स्वाः प्रजाः पालयेन्नृपः।। अनुशासन ।।

Let the king protect his subjects from their fear of him; from their fear of others; from their fear of each other; and from their fear of things that are not human.[132]

Reconciliation or force?

Let us next consider the other two conflicting truths, both essential to every kind of human relationship, personal as well as social: the evident necessity of *kṣhmā*, reconciliation, as freedom from the insanity of hatred and revenge, and the equally evident necessity of using *bala*, force, for self-protection. Both have their own indisputable rationality. The question is: 'Of forgiveness and force, which is the superior?'[133]

Advocated by Yudhishṭhira, in his conversation with his wife, Draupadī, who had been some years earlier grievously insulted and humiliated in the open assembly of the Kuru kingdom, and who had been burning for thirteen years with the desire for revenge, the rationality of *kṣhmā*, or reconciliation, is as follows:

> *The opposite of forgiveness is anger and intolerance. And anger, uncontrolled, destroys men.*[134]

क्रोधमूलो विनाशो हि प्रजानामिह दृश्यते।। वन २९.३।।
क्रुद्धः पापं नरः कुर्यात् क्रुद्धो हन्याद् गुरूनपि।
क्रुद्धः परुषया वाचा श्रेयसोऽप्यवमन्यते।। वन २९.४।।

वाच्यावाच्ये हि कुपितो न प्रजानाति कर्हिचित्।
नाकार्यमस्ति क्रुद्धस्य नावाच्यं विद्यते तथा।। वन २९.५।।

हिंस्यात् क्रोधादवध्यांस्तु वध्यान् सम्पूजयीत च।
आत्मानमपि च क्रुद्धः प्रेषयेद् यमसादनम्।। वन २९.६।।

That anger destroys human beings, this can be observed.[135] *It brings destruction all around because a man in anger does not know what should be said and what should not be said; to him, there is then nothing that must not be done, nor anything that must not be said.*[136]

Driven by anger, a man can commit any offence: can kill the respected elders: by his offensive speech insult men who are noble: or can kill even himself.[137]

That is because he is not able to see a thing in its proper light and is unable to see the limits.[138]

Answering a probable question, *Why* forgiveness? *Why* reconciliation? Why *not* revenge?', Yudhishṭhira says:

आक्रुष्टः पुरुषः सर्वं प्रत्याक्रोशेदनन्तरम्।
प्रतिहन्याद्धतश्चैव तथा हिंस्याच्च हिंसितः।। वन २९.२७।।

If there were not men willing to forgive, and to subdue their anger, there would be no peace among men, for anger is the origin of all discord.[139]

हन्युर्हि पितरः पुत्रान् पुत्राश्चापि तथा पितॄन्।
हन्युश्च पतयो भार्याः पतीन् भार्यास्तथैव च।। वन २९.२८।।

In that case, people will return aggression with aggression, hurt with hurt, violence with violence.[140]

एवं संकुपिते लोके शमः कृष्णे न विद्यते।
प्रजानां संधिमूलं हि शमं विद्धि शुभानने।। वन २९.२९।।

Fathers will kill sons, and sons will kill fathers. Husbands will kill wives, and wives will kill husbands.

क्षन्तव्यं पुरुषेणेह सर्वापत्सु सुशोभने।
क्षमावतो हि भूतानां जन्म चैव प्रकीर्तितम्।। वन २९.३२।।

In this way there will be no peace anywhere, and peace is based on reconciliation.[141]
Therefore, a prudent man, a man who is wise, controls his anger at all times and is ready to forgive the transgressions of others.[142]
In this world, reconciliation is the best.[143]

This is the rationality of *kshmā*.

Through Yudhishthira, the *Mahābhārata* places, therefore, the utmost emphasis upon forgiveness and reconciliation in the following words,[144] which are as lyrical as they are profound:

क्षमा धर्मः क्षमा यज्ञः वेदाः क्षमा श्रुतम्।
य एतदेवं जानाति स सर्वं क्षन्तुमर्हति।। वन २९.३६।।

क्षमा ब्रह्म क्षमा सत्यं क्षमा भूतं च भावि च।
क्षमा तपः क्षमा शौचं क्षमयेदं धृतं जगत्।। वन २९.३७।।

क्षमा तेजस्विनां तेजः क्षमा ब्रह्म तपस्विनाम्।
क्षमा सत्यं सत्यवतां क्षमा यज्ञः क्षमा शमः।। वन २९.४०।।

Forgiveness is dharma*: forgiveness is sacrifice: forgiveness is Veda: forgiveness is* sruti*: he who knows this can forgive everything.*

> *Forgiveness is Brahma, forgiveness is truth, forgiveness is the past and the future, forgiveness is austerity, forgiveness is purity: it is in reconciliation alone that the world is sustained.*
> *Forgiveness is the force of the forceful, the Brahma of the ascetics, the truth of the truthful, the control of the mind.*[145]

It is reconciliation that keeps the world together,[146] क्षमयैव धृतं जगत् ।

> आत्मानं च परांश्चैव त्रायते महतो भयात् ।
> क्रुध्यन्तमप्रतिक्रुध्यन् द्वयोरेष चिकित्सकः ।। वन २९.९ ।।
> *He who does not return anger with anger saves himself and the other from great fear. He becomes a healer both to himself and to the other.*[147]

Without disputing that forgiveness, *kṣhmā*, is a good quality, and reconciliation may be the best, Draupadī argued, on the other hand, that it would be a great mistake to think that they are so *always*.[148] Neither force nor reconciliation is good always: न श्रेयः सततं तेजो न नित्यं श्रेयसी क्षमाः ।[149]

He who is always forgiving invites several defects. His relatives, his subordinates, his enemies, and even those who are neutral to him, treat him with disrespect, nor does anybody ever show him courtesy, because forgiveness is seen as weakness, and weakness invites disrespect. Therefore, to forgive always is unwise even for the wise.[150] The capacity to hurt and to harm makes people afraid, and what one is afraid of, one does not take lightly. The king who can do neither good nor harm is of little worth.

Draupadī narrates a conversation between King Bali and his grandfather, Emperor Prahlāda, on the question: 'Of forgiveness and force, which is the superior?' Prahlāda maintained that neither is good always. To be forgiving *always* is unwise even for the wise. But the man who uses force *always*, and never forgives, also invites many wrong things.[151] Without regard to place and occasion, full of anger and force, he keeps punishing people; he alienates friends and becomes an object of hatred on the part of his own people; because he insults others, he suffers losses, and in turn is treated with reproach and disrespect; all around he generates anguish, hostility and agitation, and in the process loses everything, often his life.[152]

Draupadī admonishes her husband, Yudhishṭhira, that, for these reasons, one should neither be always gentle nor be always forceful; rather, according to different contexts and times, *desha* and *kāla*, one should be now gentle and then forceful.[153]

काले मृदुर्यो भवति काले भवति दारुणः।
स वै सुखमवाप्नोति लोकेऽमुष्मिन्निहैव च।। वन २८.२४।।

क्षमाकालांस्तु वक्ष्यामि शृणु मे विस्तरेण तान्।
ये ते नित्यमसंत्याज्या यथा प्राहुर्मनीषिणः।। वन २८.२५।।

There is a time for forgiveness, and there is a time for force.[154] *If a person has done in the past a good turn to one, then, remembering that, even a serious offence on his part is to be forgiven.*[155] *Likewise, he who has offended out of ignorance must be forgiven, for it is not possible for anybody to be wise everywhere.*[156] *Just one offence is to be forgiven to everybody; the second offence, or if having knowingly committed an offence a person pretends innocence, however small the offence, then it must be punished.*[157] *If it were found, after careful examination, that the offence was a result of ignorance, then it is to be forgiven surely.*[158]

The principle to be relied upon in these matters is this, she says:

मृदुना दारुणं हन्ति मृदुना हन्त्यदारुणम्।
नासाध्यं मृदुना किंचित् तस्मात् तीव्रतरं मृदु।। वन २८.३१।।

देशकालौ तु सम्प्रेक्ष्य बलाबलमथात्मनः।
नादेशकाले किंचित् स्याद् देशकालौ प्रतीक्षताम्।
तथा लोकभयाच्चैव क्षन्तव्यमपराधिनः।। वन २८.३२।।

Whereas truly nothing is difficult with gentleness, and gentleness can conquer harshness, whether force should be applied or reconciliation must depend on a rational grasp of desha and kāla, 'time' and 'place'; of one's own relative strength and weakness; and of the nature of the given situation and its cause.[159] *Gentleness achieves nothing if practised in a wrong place and at a wrong time and in relation to a wrong person.*

In brief,

मृदुर्भवत्यवज्ञातस्तीक्ष्णादुद्विजते जनः।
काले प्राप्ते द्वयं चैतद् यो वेद स महीपतिः।। वन २८.३६।।

मृदुरित्यवजानन्ति तीक्ष्ण इत्युद्विजन्ति च।
तीक्ष्णकाले भवेत् तीक्ष्णो मृदुकाले मृदुर्भवेत्।। शान्ति १४०.६५।।

If he is always gentle, the people ignore him; if he uses force always, they become agitated. He should be gentle when it is time for gentleness, and be forceful when it is time for force.[160]

Bhīshma expresses the same view through a metaphor:

तस्मान्नैव मृदुर्नित्यं तीक्ष्णो नैव भवेन्नृपः ।
वासन्ताक्र इव श्रीमान् न शीतो न च धर्मदः ।। शान्ति ५६.४० ।।

न च क्षान्तेन ते नित्यं भव्यं पुत्र समन्ततः ।
अधर्मो हि मृदू राजा क्षमावानिव कुञ्जरः ।। शान्ति ५६.३७ ।।

मृदुर्हि राजा सततं लङ्घ्यो भवति सर्वशः ।।
तीक्ष्णाच्चोद्विजते लोकस्तस्मादुभयमाश्रय ।। शान्ति ५६.२१ ।।

In the same way as the autumn sun gives neither too great heat nor too great cold, the king should be neither too gentle nor too forceful.[161]
You should not be forgiving always and everywhere. For, in being like a gentle elephant, such a king creates conditions only of adharma.[162]
A gentle and forgiving king is ignored; the one who is severe and harsh always, hurts and agitates people. Therefore, according to the circumstances, take recourse to gentleness and firmness.[163]

In these lies the skill of governance. 'One's own self; one's grasp of *desha* and *kāla*; adequacy of means; clarity of purpose; reliable assistants; and honest but competent advice: these are the six elements of good governance.'

राज्यं हि सुमहत् तन्त्रं धार्यते नाकृतात्मभिः ।
न शक्यं मृदुना वोढुमायासस्थानमुत्तमम् ।। शान्ति ५८.२१ ।।

The state is a great instrument. The kings who have not conquered their minds and are cruel, and those who are of gentle disposition, cannot alike hold the weight of that instrument.[164]

Vidura acknowledged that:

एकः क्षमावतां दोषो द्वितीयो नोपपद्यते ।
यदेनं क्षमया युक्तमशक्तं मन्यते जनः ।। उद्योग ३३.४८ ।।

In those who are forgiving, there seems to be only one defect, none other: which is this, that people consider a forgiving person to be a weak person.[165]

But

सोऽस्य दोषो न मन्तव्यः क्षमा हि परमं बलम्।
क्षमा गुणो ह्यशक्तानां भूषणं क्षमा।। उद्योग ३३.४९।।

That should not be considered a defect; rather, forgiveness is the greatest strength. Forgiveness is a good quality in those who are helpless; in those who are powerful, their adornment as well.[166]

एको धर्मः परं श्रेयः क्षमैका शान्तिरुत्तमा।
विद्यैका परमा तृप्तिरहिंसैका सुखावहा।। उद्योग ३३.५२।।

Dharma *alone is the greatest good; forgiveness and reconciliation the best way to peace; knowledge alone brings the deepest satisfaction; and not-violence, happiness.*[167]

The law of abnormal times: *āpad-dharma*

Yudhishṭhira asks another important question: 'How should one order one's conduct towards one's self and towards the *other* in times that are abnormal?' In the context of governance more than even personal relationships, the *Mahābhārata* develops a whole rationality of abnormal times, or *āpad-dharma.*[168] When social and economic conditions change so dramatically as to produce anarchy, and life itself is threatened, one must order, the *Mahābhārata* says, one's life and relationships with solely one aim—to preserve oneself. That is the law of abnormal times, *āpad-dharma*, during which, *but only then*, the requirements of normal ethical social behaviour are waived. In such circumstances whatever helps preserve oneself is *dharma*. Here the underlying principle is: 'It is better to be alive than dead; alive, a person can order his life again.'[169]

Here the issue was not between ethical standards and royal power. Rather, the question was whether, faced with treachery and corruption among his officials, invasion and war from his enemies, and threat to the social order from among his own subjects, should the king in dealing with them be guided still by scruple, truth, fairness, and kindness? It was this inescapable question, of a very practical kind, that engages the *Mahābhārata*. A king in distress, with many enemies and few friends, his treasury and army weakened, with a wicked minister to advise him, and threatened with the loss of his kingdom, was permitted to raise financial resources from among his people somehow, by force if necessary, against the principles of *dharma*. That sanction was based on three grounds, as mentioned by Bhīshma:

a. The *dharma* of a man in distress being different from that of a man who is strong, and only if the king lives can he preserve *dharma*, to preserve himself is then, in such circumstances, a duty greater than any *dharma*.[170]
b. His strength depends on the treasury and the army, the army depends on the treasury, social order is protected by the army, and the people are protected by social order.[171]
c. And without hurting others in one way or another, one cannot, in *abnormal times*, collect material resources; and without money in the treasury there can be no army.[172] It was therefore held that no blame would attach to the king if, in times that are abnormal, he should be forced to collect material resources even by hurting his people.[173] 'What door is barred to a man in distress?'[174]

But no sooner is all this said, in honest acknowledgement of the requirements of abnormal times, than, at the same place, the *Mahābhārata* says also this. The king must always remember, however, that whatever be the compulsions of distressful times, there is no denying that anything that goes against *dharma* must eventually produce resentment and violence. Thus, wealth collected by hurting the people can never last; nor can it ever produce any good. Therefore, as soon as social conditions become normal, the king must return to the people what he had taken from them to save himself. At no time must he press the rule of expediency in his own favour and against the interests of the people. Distressful times must not become an alibi for doing things that are wrong anyway. Rather,

> परस्परं हि संरक्षा राज्ञा राष्ट्रेण चापदि।
> नित्यमेव हि कर्तव्या एष धर्मः सनातनः।। शान्ति १३०.३०।।
> *The king and the people should, in times of distress, protect each other: this is the abiding* dharma *of all times.*[175]

Where the king is unable to do so, there even a *brāhmaṇa* should bear arms so as to protect the people, and in doing so he incurred no blame,[176] though in normal times it was no part of a *brāhmaṇa*'s functions to take to arms. Neither was it any part of the functions of the *vaishya* and the *shūdra* to bear arms and assume the duty of protecting the people, which belonged solely to the *kṣhattriya*. However, in conditions of anarchy, persons of all *varṇa* might take to arms with a view to preserving social order.[177] Consistent with its rational and pragmatic attitudes to questions concerning society, the *Mahābhārata* takes the following unambiguous position. Whoever, be he a *shūdra*, helps the people at a time of calamity, and acts like a boat to the drowning, is worthy of respect in all manner.[178] Himself fearless, whoever is able to relieve people of their suffering, is worthy of respect given to a king.[179] Indeed, whoever is able to protect social order and put an end to disorder, he alone should be king.[180] Just as an elephant made of wood, a deer made of leather, a barren land, and a cloud that does not bear rain, are useless, so is the *brāhmaṇa* who is illiterate and the king who does not protect.[181]

In any event, distressful times don't arise just like that. They are the products of the logic of *adharma*. They arise when, separated from the good of the people, the exercise of power becomes its own end. They arise from greed and its dismal workings. They arise when governance is thoughtless and has no direction. They arise when government begins to govern in the place of law. They arise when wealth and power are pursued cynically. They arise when there is carelessness and lack of vigilance. And they arise when people would not respect each other's spiritual space, and in that sense, too, do violence to each other. The *Mahābhārata* holds, therefore, that such times are created by *swakrit* and *parakrit*, the cumulative logic of one's own self or by the other, or the two together. To repeat in this context as well: there are two kinds of intelligence, one that is *kuṭila*, devious; and the other which is simple and *sarala*, straightforward. The king, particularly the king, because he is invested with the power of governance, should, even in his own self-interest, cultivate the second of the two, the simple and straightforward intelligence. Should devious intelligence come to him naturally, he should try to remove it.[182] Deviousness may seem to help one survive a crisis, but it always leaves its own logic behind, the logic of distrust, of self-destruction, nowhere manifest more than in the acts of governance.

An argument against capital punishment

Perhaps for the first time anywhere, it is in the *Mahābhārata* that an argument against capital punishment was advanced. It develops in answering the question of Yudhishṭhira, put to Bhīshma: 'How should the king protect the people in a way that he does not also have to cause violence to anybody?'[183]

Bhīshma narrates a conversation that had taken place between Satyavān and his father, Dhyumatsena, a king.[184]

On seeing many convicts being led to be put to death, on the orders of his father, the king, Satyavān approached him, and said to him 'what had not been said before'. 'It is true that sometimes what looks like *dharma* in actual fact is only *adharma*; and what may appear to be *adharma* turns out to be *dharma*. But to put someone to death can never be an act of *dharma*.'[185] The king replied: 'Not to put a criminal to death ever, if that is *dharma*, then, prey, what can *adharma* be? If thieves and robbers are not put to death, then there would surely arise confusion of functions and lawlessness.'[186] 'In the Kali-yuga, some people may by force take what belongs to another, saying "this is *mine*, not his", making the orderly progress of society impossible. If you have a solution to that, tell me what it is.'[187]

Satyavān puts forth his argument against capital punishment as any part of a civilised penal code, as follows:

तत्त्वाभेदेन यच्छास्त्रं तत् कार्यं नान्यथाविधम् ।
असमीक्ष्यैव कर्माणि नीतिशास्त्रं यथाविधि ।। शान्ति २६७.९ ।।

One should use only that system of punishment that does not dismember the body. Neither should anybody be punished without first carefully examining the alleged offence of a person and applying to it the established principles of law.

दस्यून् निहन्ति वै राजा भूयसो वाप्यनागसः ।
भार्या माता पिता पुत्रो हन्यन्ते पुरुषेण ते ।
परेणापकृतो राजा तस्मात् सम्यक् प्रधारयेत् ।। शान्ति २६७.१० ।।

On putting a robber to death, the king renders his wife and children, his father and mother, without any means of sustenance, which is like putting them to death as well. Therefore, the king must think carefully.

असाधुश्चैव पुरुषो लभते शीलमेकदा ।
साधोश्चापि ह्यसाधुभ्यः शोभना जायते प्रजा ।। शान्ति २६७.११ ।।

Besides, a wicked person often turns over a new leaf and acquires goodness, and the children of the wicked often grow into good human beings.

न मूलघातः कर्तव्यो नैष धर्मः सनातनः ।
अपि स्वल्पवधेनैव प्रायश्चित्तं विधीयते ।। शान्ति २६७.१२ ।।

Therefore, by sentencing a person to death, one should not destroy his very roots. Rather, some other form of ordinary punishment may quite be the opportunity for him to repent and reform himself.

अद्वेजनेन बन्धेन विरूपकरणेन च ।
वधदण्डेन ते क्लिश्या न पुरोहितसंसदि ।। शान्ति २६७.१३ ।।

यदा पुरोहितं वा ते पर्येयु: शरणैषिण: ।
करिष्याम: पुनर्ब्रह्मन् न पामिति वादिन: ।। शान्ति २६७.१४ ।।
तदा विसर्गमर्हा: स्युरितीदं धातृशासनम्
बिभ्रद् दण्डाजिनं मुण्डो ब्राह्मणोऽर्हतिशासनम् ।। शान्ति २६७.१५ ।।

गरीयांसो गरीयांसमपराधे पुन: पुन: ।
तदा विसर्गमर्हन्ति न यथा प्रथमे तथा ।। शान्ति २६७.१६ ।।

Should he go to a preceptor, and promise that he would not do wrong again, he should be pardoned. But if a person does wrong again and again, then he should receive a punishment greater than what he would have for his first offence. For he would have then forfeited his pardon as in the earlier case.[188]

King Dhyumatsena lists instead the following reasons for imposing increasingly harsher punishments to protect the people from wrongdoers.[189] Whatever is required to keep the people within the bounds of *dharma*, to do that is all *dharma*—until those bounds are breached. In times long ago, it was easy to govern people, for they were gentle, given to truth, and there was in them very little enmity and aggression. In those times, to put a wrongdoer to shame was itself a great punishment. When wrongdoing increased, it was still sufficient to give him *vāgdaṇḍa*, that is, chastise him in harsh words, and then let him go. Then followed the practice of imposing fines and other financial punishments. And now has arisen the necessity to impose the death penalty; even then, it seems impossible to keep the wicked within bounds. To a robber, there is none dear to him. Why, he would rob even a corpse in the cremation ground, and is not averse to robbing a deity either. Whoever trusts a robber must indeed be a fool.

What Satyavān was arguing against was not the need for *any* punishment, but *against punishment by death, because it is final and closes forever any other possibility for the condemned.*

तान् न शक्नोषि चेत् साधून् परित्रातुमहिंसया ।
कस्यचिद् भूतभव्यस्य लाभेनान्तं तथा कुरु ।। शान्ति २६७.२३ ।।
If you can find no way to protecting good people except by sentencing the robbers to death, or cannot reform the wicked without doing violence to them, then, keeping their past and their future in mind, do what is for their good.

वित्रास्यमानाः सुकृतो न कामाद् घ्नन्ति दुष्कृतीन् ।
सुकृतेनैव राजानो भूयिष्ठं शासते प्रजाः ।। शान्ति २६७.२५ ।।
The purpose of governance is not to kill the wicked, but to create conditions in which the people can be good.[190]

Satyavān moves to another ground.[191] He argues that, in order to create social conditions where people can be good, the king himself has to live and govern in a way that he sets an example of true goodness, which includes upholding the impartiality of law.

आत्मैवादौ नियन्तव्यो दुष्कृतं संनियच्छता ।
दण्डयेज्च महादण्डेरपि बन्धूननन्तरान् ।। शान्ति २६७.२९ ।।
Wishing to control the wicked, the king must exercise control over himself first. Should his relatives do wrong, he should impose upon them severe punishments, too.

श्रेयसः श्रेयसोऽप्येवं वृत्तं लोकोऽनुवर्तते ।
सदैव हि गुरोर्वृत्तमनुवर्तन्ति मानवाः ।। शान्ति २६७.२६ ।।
The people follow the good conduct of a good and noble king. It is in the nature of things that people follow what men of substance do.[192]

आत्मानमसमाधाय समाधित्सति यः परान् ।
विषयेष्विन्द्रियवशं मानवाः प्रहसन्ति तम् ।। शान्ति २६७.२७ ।।
Should the king, himself a slave of his appetites, with little discipline over himself, give a lecture on good conduct to others, he would invite from the people only mocking ridicule.[193]

The king creates historical conditions, not they him

The *Mahābhārata* takes up another question: 'Do historical conditions create the character of the state, or does the character of the state create historical conditions?'[194] Given his considered view that *kāla*, Time, is not the force that governs human affairs, but that it is the human mind that decides the quality of human relationships, Bhīshma says to Yudhishṭhira: 'Entertain no doubt whether it is Time that creates the king *or* the king who creates the times. It is the king who creates the times.'[195]

कालो वा कारणं राज्ञो राजा वा कालकारणम्।
इति ते सशंयो मा भूद् राजा कालस्य कारणम्।। शान्ति ६९.७९ ।।

Far from propounding any theory of historical human *progress* in a collective sense, the whole of Indian thought speaks rather of collective human *decline*. However, progress or decline, it is not some inner mysterious teleology that is at work, but the consequences of the collective *karma*. For just as the logic of a person's *karma* determines his, or her, individual times, which can be changed, for the better or for the worse, so will the collective *karma* of a society determine its collective times, which can be changed likewise. In other words, it is not some inherent *telos* of history that determines the course of events but the *logic of acts*.

There is in the *Mahābhārata* the familiar division of 'times', or the *yuga*-s, in the *krita*, *tretā*, *dvāpara*, and the *kali-yuga*. On the two ends, there is the *krita-yuga*, often called *satya-yuga*, which was the 'golden age' of mankind, and the *kali-yuga*, or the times when there is a collective collapse of all that sustains life and its worth in all its forms. In between are the other two, *tretā* and *dvāpara*, *tretā* much less in the quality of life than *krita*, and *dvāpara* even less. The *kali* is the worst of all times, the times in which man has lived for many centuries, which are also the times, only the worse, in which he lives *now*. At different places, the *Mahābhārata* enumerates, in detail, the relative characteristics of each of these four *yuga*-s, 'the times'.[196] Those details need not distract us here from the following two truths that they point towards.

a. Of progress or of decline, the main characteristics of the four *yuga*-s, 'the times', revolve around the quality of one's relationship with one's self and one's relationship with the *other*. Human beings create the times, and not the other way around. And this is what the *Mahābhārata* is saying to us, in very many different stories, which are the stories of human relationships everywhere.

b. It is the quality of governance that determines, visibly, the quality of the social conditions in which we human beings enact the stories of our lives. The two are inseparable. And, again, the social conditions revolve around one's relationship with one's self and with the *other* and their quality. Therefore, the *Mahābhārata* says, in the voice of Bhīshma:

दण्डनीत्यां यदा राजा सम्यक् कार्त्स्न्येन वर्तते।
तदा कृतयुगं नाम कालसृष्टं प्रवर्तते।। शान्ति ६९.८०।।

When the king uses with honour, truth, and care the instrument of governance, he creates the times called krita-yuga.[197]

दण्डनीतिं परित्यज्य यदा कार्त्स्न्येन भूमिपः।
प्रजाः क्लिश्नात्ययोगेन प्रवर्तेत तदा कलिः।। शान्ति ६९.९१।।

When the king abandons honour, truth, and care in the acts of governance and, by indefensible means, oppresses the people, then arise the times called kali.[198]

राजा कृतयुगस्रष्टा त्रेताया द्वापरस्य च।
युगस्य च चतुर्थस्य राजा भवति कारणम्।। शान्ति ६९.९८।।

It is the king who creates the social conditions that are distinctive to each of the four times.[199]

रसाः सर्वे क्षयं यान्ति यदा नेच्छति भूमिपः।
प्रजाः संरक्षितुं सम्यग् दण्डनीतिसमाहितः।। शान्ति ६९.९७।।

When the king, equipped with governance, does not wish to protect the people, then the world loses all its flavours.[200]

लोकस्य सीमन्तकरी मर्यादा लोकभाविनी।
सम्यङ्नीता दण्डनीतिर्यथा माता यथा पिता।। शान्ति ६९.१०३।।

When the instruments of governance are used in ways that are just, truthful, and caring, then governance becomes like father and mother, and keeps the world within its proper limits.[201]

यस्यां भवन्ति भूतानि तद् विद्धि मनुजर्षभ।
एष एव परो धर्मो यद् राजा दण्डनीतिमान्।। शान्ति ६९.१०४।।

You should know that all living beings exist by means of governance alone. The greatest dharma *of the king is for him to be just and caring in governing.*[202]

तस्मात् कौरव्य धर्मेण प्रजा: पालय नीतिमान्।
एवंवृत्त: प्रजा रक्षन् स्वर्गं जेतासि दुर्जयम्।। शान्ति ६९.१०५।।
Therefore, if you will, rooted in dharma *and justice, tend to the people, you can conquer even the heavens most difficult to conquer.*[203]

In different words,

यदह्न कुरुते पापमरक्षन् भयत: प्रजा:।
राजा वर्षसहस्त्रेण तस्यान्तमधिगच्छति।। शान्ति ७१.२८।।
यदह्न कुरुते धर्मे प्रजा धर्मेण पालयन्।
दशवर्षसहस्त्राणि तस्य भुक्ते फलं दिवि।। शान्ति ७१.२९।।
The demerit that a king invites by not protecting the people from fear lasts for one thousand years; whereas the merit that he earns by governing in accordance with dharma, *that lasts for ten thousand years.*[204]

What it clearly means is that the consequences of the conditions of fear, injustice, untruth, and abuse of power last a long time collectively. In brief,

धर्मेण राज्यं विन्देत धर्मेण परिपालयेत्।
धर्ममूलां श्रियं प्राप्य न जहाति न हीयते।। उद्योग पर्व ३४.३१।।
Obtain the royal power through dharma, *and through* dharma *nourish and enhance it; the prosperity that comes from* dharma *neither decreases nor dies.*[205]

धर्मे तिष्ठन्ति भूतानि धर्मो राजनि तिष्ठति।
तं राजा साधु य: शास्ति स राजा पृथिवीपति:।। शान्ति ९०.५।।
All living beings have dharma *as the foundation of their existence, and* dharma *exists over and above the king. Only he remains the king, who lives and governs in accordance with* dharma.[206]

धर्मे वर्धति वर्धन्ति सर्वभूतानि सर्वदा।
तस्मिन् ह्रसति हीयन्ते तस्माद् धर्मं न लोपयेत्।। शान्ति ९०.१७।।
When dharma *prospers, all living beings prosper always; with the decline of* dharma, *they decline as well.*

प्रभवार्थं हि भूतानां धर्म: सृष्ट: स्वयम्भुवा।
तस्मात् प्रवर्तयेद् धर्मं प्रजानुग्रहकारणात्।। शान्ति ९०.१९।।

It is with a view to enhancing, ennobling, providing more richly, and taking upwards, all living beings, securing their prabhava, *that* dharma *was created; it is imperative for the king, so as to do good to the people, that he preserve* dharma.[207]

तस्माद्धि राजशार्दूल धर्म: श्रेष्ठतर: स्मृत: ।
स राजा य: प्रजा: शास्ति साधुकृत् पुरुषर्षभ ।। शान्ति ९०.२० ।।

कामक्रोधावनादृत्य धर्ममेवानुपालय ।
धर्म: श्रेयस्करतमो राज्ञां भरतसत्तम ।। शान्ति ९०.२१ ।।

For dharma *is the highest; and he alone is king who governs with justice and truth. Rising above desire and aggression, persevere in* dharma, *for* dharma *is the greatest good for the king.*[208]

And all these necessarily involve caring for the individual, that is, creating social conditions where no individual is degraded or debased and has to live in constant fear of one kind or another, especially those who are weak and poor. Hence the *Mahābhārata*'s repeated injunctions to the king, the state:

वृद्धबालधनं रक्ष्यमन्धस्य कृपणस्य च ।
न खातपूर्वं कुर्वीत न रुदन्ती धनं हरेत् ।। अनुशासन ६१.२५ ।।

The king shall protect the material means of the old, of the young, of the blind, and of the poor. And never shall he deprive a woman in distress of her material means.[209]

हृतं कृपणवित्तं हि राष्ट्रं हन्ति नृपश्रियम् ।
दद्याच्च महतो भोगान् क्षुद्भयं प्रणुदेत् सताम् ।। अनुशासन ६१.२६ ।।

When the material means of the already poor are snatched, it destroys the entire kingdom and the king's prosperity, too. Therefore, the king shall provide them with ample means of living, and ensure that people do not suffer hunger.[210]

धिक् तस्य जीवितं राज्ञो राष्ट्रे यस्यावसीदति ।
द्विजोऽन्यो वा मनुष्योऽपि शिबिराह वचो यथा ।। अनुशासन ६१.२९ ।।

King Shibi had said: 'Damned be the life of that king in whose domains those devoted to knowledge and learning, or any other human being, suffer hunger.'[211]

क्रोशन्त्यो यस्य वै राष्ट्राद्ध्रियन्ते तरसा स्त्रियः।
क्रोशतां पतिपुत्राणां मृतोऽसौ न च जीवति।। अनुशासन ६१.३१।।
In whose domains women are taken away forcibly and cry helplessly, and whose husband and children cry helplessly, too, such a king is like dead, not living.[212]

अरक्षितारं हर्तारं विलोप्तारमनायकम्।
तं वै राजकलिं हन्युः प्रजाः सन्नह्य निर्घृणम्।। अनुशासन ६१.३२।।
The king who does not protect the people, only keeps exploiting them, and does not have an able and good minister to lead, such a king is not king, but the very embodiment of Kali, the dark times. The people should destroy such a king.[213]

Moreover, after narrating a dreadful war and its human suffering on both sides, the *Mahābhārata* shows that nothing that is of enduring worth was ever achieved by war. This is an evident truth of history.

Therefore:

अयुद्धेनैव विजयं वर्धयेद् वसुधाधिपः।
जघन्यमाहुर्विजयं युद्धेन च नराधिप।। शान्ति ९४.१।।
Let the king increase what he has obtained, without recourse to war, for the victory that is obtained through war is of a very low quality indeed.[214]

नाधर्मेण महीं जेतुं लिप्सत जगतीपतिः।
अधर्मविजयं लब्ध्वा को नु मन्येत भूमिपः।। शान्ति ९६.१।।
Let no king ever desire to obtain victory through adharma. *Who can ever gain in respect in obtaining victory through* adharma?[215]

अधर्मयुक्तो विजयो ह्यध्रुवोऽस्वर्ग्य एव च।
सादयत्येष राजानं महीं च भरतर्षभ।। शान्ति ९६.२।।
The victory gained by adharma *is both ignoble and insecure. Such a victory takes both the king and his kingdom only to ruin.*[216]

सर्वविद्यातिरेकेण जयमिच्छेन्महीपतिः।
न मायया न दम्भेन य इच्छेद् भूतिमात्मनः।। शान्ति ९६.२४।।
A king who wishes to be victorious should achieve his victory by enhancing all areas of knowledge, and not by cunning and arrogance.[217]

धर्ममेवानुवर्तस्व न धर्माद् विद्यते परम्।
धर्मेस्थिता हि राजानो जयन्ति पृथिवीमिमाम्।। शान्ति १२.६।।

Follow dharma, *for greater than* dharma *there is nothing. The kings established in* dharma *conquer the whole world.*[218]

Furthermore,

य: सत्करोति ज्ञानानि ज्ञेये परहिते रत:।
सतां वर्त्मानुगस्त्यागी स राजा राज्यमर्हति।। शान्ति ५७.३८।।

Only that king is considered worthy of being king who honours knowledge and those devoted to it; is himself given to reflection and to the welfare of others; has no selfish ends; and follows the path shown by those who have in them goodness.[219]

न यस्य कूटं कपटं न माया न च मत्सर:।
विषये भूमिपालस्य तस्य धर्म: सनातन:।। शान्ति ५७.३७।।

In whose domain there is neither insincerity nor deviousness, neither intrigues nor envy, only there do the foundations hold.[220]

In the voice of the sage Mārkaṇḍeya, on describing the lives of the kings who were truly great, the *Mahābhārata* says to those who govern:

नेशे बलस्येति चरेदधर्मम्।

Because you have power, do not do what is unjust, oppressive, full of violence, adharma.[221]

At the end, let us hear the voice of Bhartrihari, which resonates with what the *Mahābhārata* has been saying, again and again, and yet again, on the foundations of law and governance being in justice, truth, and in the concern for the welfare of the people:

निन्दन्तु नीतिनिपुणा यदि वा स्तुवन्तु
लक्ष्मी: समाविशतु गच्छतु वा यथेष्टम्।
अद्यैव वा मरणमस्तु युगान्तरे वा
न्याय्यात्पथ: प्रविचलन्ति पदं न धीरा:।।

Let those learned in statecraft praise or blame: let the goddess of wealth come or go as she pleases: let death come today or ages later: persons who are steadfast do not ever swerve from the path of justice.[222]

CHAPTER FIFTEEN

Sage Nārada's Questions to King Yudhishṭhira

- Questions concerning Yudhishṭhira's self
- Questions concerning the principles of sound statecraft
- Questions concerning the principles of sound administration
- Questions concerning the security of the realm
- Questions concerning the foundations of good governance

The sage Nārada visits King Yudhishṭhira, and is received with all the marks of great respect and welcome. Nārada inquires about the well-being of Yudhishṭhira, as any friend would. But his concern is very much more than ordinary courtesy. And it is expressed in the form of many questions that he asks Yudhishṭhira, and they are asked in the spirit of *I hope that you are doing this* or *I hope that you are taking care not to do that. Not sermons, but just asking; not interrogating, but expressing a hope. But asking with sincere concern, not interrogating as a magistrate would.* The questions, which are very many, are heard with the utmost attention—and without any interruption, excepting once. Here the *Mahābhārata* develops a method of instructing in the form of asking questions, gentle and friendly. Some of them are about Yudhishṭhira's relationship with his own self; some are concerning the principles of sound statecraft; some are about the principles of good administration; and the rest about his relationship as a king with the people. They are simple and straightforward, instructions as gentle questions, and questions as hopes—about one's sound relationship with one's self, and about the foundations of good governance, which are inseparable.[1]

Concerning Yudhishṭhira's relation with his self

कच्चिदर्थाश्च कल्पन्ते धर्मे च रमते मनः।
सुखानि चानुभूयन्ते मनश्च न विहन्यते।। सभा ५.१७।।

Is the money you have sufficient for your upkeep? Do you observe dharma *with your heart? Do you have means of comfort and pleasure as you would wish? I hope that you are in your heart not distressed.*[2]

कच्चिदर्थेन वा धर्मं धर्मेणार्थमथापि वा।
उभौ वा प्रीतिसारेण न कामेन प्रबाधसे।। सभा ५.१९।।

कच्चिदर्थे च धर्मे च कामं च जयतां वर।
विभज्य काले कालज्ञः सदा वरद सेवसे।। सभा ५.२०।।

In greed for wealth, I hope that you do not harm dharma*; or, obsessed only with* dharma*, do not neglect material concerns; or, taken up too* *much with sensual pleasures, neglect both material concerns and* dharma. *I hope that you divide your time evenly among them, knowing that there is a proper time for everything.*[3]

कच्चिदात्मानमेवाग्रे विजित्य विजितेन्द्रियः ।
परान् जिगीषसे पार्थ प्रमत्तानजितेन्द्रियान् ।। सभा ५.६१ ।।

I hope that it is only after you have conquered your own self that you expect to conquer others.[4]

षडनर्था महाराज कच्चित् ते पृष्ठतः कृताः ।
निद्राऽऽलस्यं भयं क्रोधोऽमार्दवं दीर्घसूत्रता ।। सभा ५.१२६ ।।

Have you put aside the six disorders: too much sleep; and sloth; fear; anger; hardness of feelings; and taking too long to take a decision?[5]

नास्तिक्यमनृतं क्रोधं प्रमादं दीर्घसूत्रताम् ।
अदर्शनं ज्ञानवतामालस्यं पञ्चवृत्तताम् ।
एकचिन्तनमर्थानामनर्थज्ञैश्च चिन्तनम् ।। सभा ५.१०८ ।।
निश्चितानामनारम्भं मन्त्रस्यापरिरक्षणम् ।
मगंलाद्यप्रयोगं च प्रत्युथानं च सर्वतः ।। सभा ५.१०९ ।।
कच्चित्त्वं वर्जयस्येतान् राजदोषांश्चतुर्दश ।
प्रायशो यैर्विनश्यन्ति कृतमूलापि पार्थिवाः ।। सभा ५.११० ।।

I hope that you have overcome the fourteen defects in matters concerning governance—lack of faith; untruth and lies; anger; carelessness; the habit of putting off and delaying; not keeping company with men of understanding and knowledge; laziness; far too great an attachment to the pleasures of the five senses; taking decisions wholly on your own; in matters of finances, consulting those who have little knowledge of them; once a decision has been taken to do something, then putting it off; not keeping confidential advice confidential; ignoring celebrations that are auspicious; and waging war against all the enemies at the same time. Even the kingdoms established securely are destroyed by these fourteen defects.[6]

कच्चिच्छारीरमावाधमौषधैर्नियमेन वा ।
मानसं वृद्धसेवाभिः सदा पार्थापकर्षसि ।। सभा ५.९० ।।

Do you, taking wholesome and healthy food, and proper medicines, take care of your physical health, and by serving the elderly keep your mind at peace?[7]

कच्चिच्छृणोषि वृद्धानां धर्मार्थसहिता गिर:।
नित्यमर्थविदां तात यथाधर्मार्थदर्शिनाम्।। सभा ५.११७।।
Are you always attentive to what those elderly people, who are learned in dharma *and in matters concerning the material conditions of life, show?*[8]

कच्चित् ते सफला वेदा: कच्चित् ते सफलं धनम्।
कच्चित् ते सफला दारा: कच्चित् ते सफलं श्रुतम्।। सभा ५.१११।।
Is your knowledge fruitful? Is your wealth fruitful? Is your wife fruitful? Is your learning fruitful?[9]

In the only interruption by him, when Yudhishṭhira asks: 'How do the Veda become fruitful? How does wealth become fruitful? How does a wife become fruitful? How does learning become fruitful?',[10] Nārada says:

अग्निहोत्रफला वेदा दत्तभुक्तफलं धनम्।
रतिपुत्रफला दारा: शीलवृत्तफलं श्रुतम्।। सभा ५.११३।।
It is by the purifying fire that knowledge becomes fruitful. By sharing, and by enjoying it, does wealth become fruitful. In sexual happiness, and in raising a family, does a wife become fruitful. And learning becomes fruitful in sila *and in good conduct.*[11]

Concerning the principles of sound statecraft

मित्रोदासीनशत्रूणां कच्चिद् वेत्सि चिकीर्शितम्।
कच्चित् संधिं यथाकालं विग्रहं चोपसेवसे।। सभा ५.२५।।
Do you have the knowledge of what the friends, the indifferent, and the foes plan to do and when? I hope that it is only after considering the time that you decide whether it is time for unity or time for aggression.[12]

कच्चिद् वृत्तिमुदासीने मध्यमे चानुमन्यसे।
कच्चिदात्मसमा वृद्धा: शुद्धा: सम्बोधनक्षमा:।। सभा ५.२६।।

कुलीनाश्चानुरक्ताश्च कृतास्ते वीर मन्त्रिण:।
विजयो मन्त्रमूलो हि राज्ञो भवति भारत ।। सभा ५.२७।।
Do you know what your conduct should be towards those who are indifferent, and towards those who are middling? I hope that you have as advisers and ministers only those who are trustworthy, elderly, uncorrupted, and who can address a problem with understanding, are

well-born, and who have feelings of affection for you. The roots of a state's flourishing are in sound advice.[13]

कच्चित् संवृतमन्त्रैस्तैरमात्यैः शास्त्रकोविदैः।
राष्ट्रं सुरक्षितं तात शत्रुभिर्न विलुप्यते ।। सभा ५.२८।।

Is your nation's security safe in the hands of your ministers who keep their counsel secret? And is not being destroyed by the enemies?[14]

कच्चिन्न कृतकैर्दूतैर्ये चाप्यपरिशङ्किताः।
त्वत्तो वा तव चामात्यैर्भिद्यते मन्त्रितं तथा ।। सभा ५.२४ ।।

I hope that those who you do not suspect, pretending to be friends, do not obtain from your ministers your secrets and make them known.[15]

कच्चिन्मन्त्रयसे नैकः कच्चिन्न बहुभिः सह।
कच्चित् ते मन्त्रितो मन्त्रो न राष्ट्रं परिधावति ।। सभा ५.३० ।।

I hope that you do not decide on a matter of consequence all on your own, but neither do you discuss it with far too many people so that your secrets travel to hostile nations.[16]

कच्चिन्नैको बहूनर्थान् सर्वशः साम्परायिकान्।
अनुशास्ति यथाकामं कामात्मा शासनातिगः ।। सभा ५.५२ ।।

Could there be among your staff someone who does what he wishes and uses all the means as he pleases, transgressing your discipline?[17]

कच्चिन्मुख्या महत्स्वेव मध्यमेषु च मध्यमाः।
जघन्याश्च जघन्येषु भृत्याः कर्मसु योजिताः ।। सभा ५.४३ ।।

कच्चिद् विदित्वा पुरुषानुत्तमाधममध्यमान्।
त्वं कर्मस्वनुरूपेषु नियोजयसि भारत ।। सभा ५.७५ ।।

Have you assigned the most important work to those who are most competent, to those who are of middling competence works that are of middling importance, and small ordinary tasks to those who are ordinary—to each according to the level of his competence?[18]

अमात्यानुपधातीतान् पितृपैतामहाञ्छुचीन्।
श्रेष्ठाञ्छ्रेष्ठेषु कच्चित् त्वं नियोजयसि कर्मसु ।। सभा ५.४४ ।।

Do you assign to the ministers who are above reproach, behave as their forefathers did, and are distinguished, the works of the realm that are of the greatest import?[19]

एकोऽप्यमात्यो मेधावी शूरो दान्तो विचक्षणः ।
राजानं राजपुत्रं वा प्रापयेन्महतीं श्रियम् ।। सभा ५.३७ ।।

Even one minister, if he is of great intellect, is brave and courageous, is self-restrained and skilful, is sufficient to help the king, or the prince, to obtain the greatest good.[20]

कच्चिन्न लुब्धाश्चौरा वा वैरिणो वा विशाम्पते ।
अप्राप्तव्यवहारा वा तव कर्मस्वनुष्ठिताः ।। सभा ५.७६ ।।

I hope that you have not employed in your service people who are greedy, are thieves, bear ill will, and are devoid of practical experience.[21]

कच्चित् कारणिकाधर्मे सर्वशास्त्रेषु कोविदाः ।
कारयान्ति कुमारांश्च योधमुख्यांश्च सर्वशः ।। सभा ५.३४ ।।

Do those whom you have employed to educate the princes and the chief defence officials, do so only first themselves knowing the meaning of dharma *and other subjects?*[22]

कच्चित् सहस्रैर्मूर्खाणामेकं क्रीणासि पण्डितम् ।
पण्डितो ह्यर्थकृच्छ्रेषु कुर्यान्निःश्रेयसं परम् ।। सभा ५.३५ ।।

Instead of employing a thousand fools, I hope you honour one wise man, for in times of crisis, it is only a man of wisdom who is of the greatest help.[23]

Concerning the principles of sound administration

a. *Questions about the likely misuse and abuse of state authority either by the king himself or by his officials*

कच्चिदर्थेषु सम्प्रौढान् हितकामाननुप्रियान् ।
नापकर्षसि कर्मभ्यः पूर्वमप्राप्य किल्विषम् ।। सभा ५.७४ ।।

I hope that you don't dismiss, without first examining their alleged offence, officials who are mature, of good will, and lovable?[24]

कच्चिन्न लोभान्मोहाद् वा मानाद् वापिविशाम्पते ।
आर्थिप्रत्यर्थिनः प्राप्तान् न पश्यसि कथंचन ।। सभा ५.९२ ।।

Does it happen that, from greed, confusion, or arrogance, you do not even look at those who have come to you with a petition, or at those wrongly treated and have come to seek relief from you?[25]

कच्चिन्न लोभान्मोहाद् वा विश्रम्भात् प्रणयेन वा।
आश्रितानां मनुष्याणां वृत्तिंत्वं संरुणत्सि वै।। सभा ५.९३।।

Does it happen that, from greed, confusion, or arrogance, you terminate the livelihood of those who are dependent on you?[26]

कच्चिदार्यो विशुद्धात्मा क्षारितश्चौरकर्मणि।
अदृष्टशास्त्रकुशलैर्न लोभाद् वध्यते शुचिः।। सभा ५.१०५।।

Does it happen that your officials, out of greed, falsely accuse of theft a good person, take his money, and even kill him?[27]

दुष्टो गृहीतस्तत्कारी तज्ज्ञैर्दृष्टः सकारणः।
कच्चिन्न मुच्यते स्तेनो द्रव्यलोभान्नरर्षभ।। सभा ५.१०६।।

Does it happen that a man caught stealing, and caught with the stolen goods as well, is then let off in return for money received?[28]

उत्पन्नान् कच्चिदाढ्यस्य दरिद्रस्य च भारत।
अर्थान् न मिथ्या पश्यन्ति तवामात्या हृता जनैः।। सभा ५.१०७।।

I hope that your ministers do not think that a poor person coming suddenly into much money would have got it necessarily by wrong means, and take it away from him.[29]

कच्चिदभ्यागता दूराद् वाणिजो लाभकारणात्।
यथोक्तमवहार्यन्ते शुल्कं शुल्कोपजीविभिः।। सभा ५.११५।।

Do your officials collect only admissible taxes from those merchants who come from faraway places in the hope of earning good money?[30]

कच्चित् ते पुरुषा राजन् पुरे राष्ट्रे च मानिताः।
उपानयन्ति पण्यानि उपधाभिरवञ्चिताः।। सभा ५.११६।।

Do merchants, feeling welcome and respected, bring for sale into your realm things that are of use? I hope your men do not cheat them by devious means.[31]

b. *Questions whether those who have worked diligently and sincerely for the good of the state are honoured and rewarded*

कच्चिद् बलस्य ते मुख्याः सर्वयुद्धविशारदाः।
धृष्टावदाता विक्रान्तास्त्वया सत्कृत्य मानिताः।। सभा ५.४८।।

Are the chief commanders of your army experts in all kinds of warfar, and are they fearless and brave? I hope that you honour them and reward them.[32]

कच्चित् पुरुषकारेण पुरुषः कर्म शोभयन् ।
लभते मानमधिकं भूयो वा भक्तवेतनम् ।। सभा ५.५३ ।।

Whoever, by his endeavour, does some good work, does he get from you much appreciation and higher salary?[33]

कच्चिद् विद्याविनीतांश्च नराञ्ज्ञानविशारदान् ।
यथार्हं गुणतश्चैव दानेनाभ्युपपद्यसे ।। सभा ५.५४ ।।

By rewarding them with money, do you honour and respect the scholars who have learning in many areas of knowledge, and have the humility that knowledge brings?[34]

कच्चिद् दारान्मनुष्याणां तवार्थे मृत्युभीयुषाम् ।
व्यसनं चाभ्युपेतानां बिभर्षि भरतर्षभ ।। सभा ५.५५ ।।

Do you take care of the family of those who willingly die for the sake of the State, or put themselves in great danger?[35]

कच्चित् कृतं विजानीषे कर्तारं च प्रशंससि ।
सतां मध्ये महाराज सत्करोषि च पूजयन् ।। सभा ५.१२० ।।

Dear King! Do you ever get to know a good turn done to you by someone? Do you praise such a person, and in the assembly full of good people do you express your gratitude to him and show him your respect?[36]

c. *The question whether salaries are paid on time*

कच्चिद् बलस्य भक्तं च वेतनं च यथोचितम् ।
सम्प्राप्तकाले दातव्यं ददासि न विकर्षसि ।। सभा ५.४९ ।।
कालातिक्रमणादेते भक्तवेतनयोर्भृताः ।
भर्तुः कुप्यन्ति यद्भृत्याःसोऽनर्थ सुमहान् स्मृतः ।। सभा ५.५० ।।

Do you give to your army provisions and their salary at the appointed time? I hope that you neither reduce nor delay what is their due. When provisions and salaries are delayed for too long, servants get angry, and their anger is said to be a cause of great disaster.[37]

d. *Questions about the welfare of farmers and workers*

कच्चिद् राष्ट्रे तडागानि पूर्णानि च बृहन्ति च।
भागशो विनिविष्टानि न कृषिर्देवमातृका।। सभा ५.७८।।

Have you had big water ponds constructed everywhere in your realm? Agriculture cannot be done only on the hope of good rains.[38]

कच्चिन्न भक्तं बीजं च कर्षकस्यावसीदति।
प्रत्येकं च शतं वृद्ध्या ददास्यृणमनुग्रहम्।। सभा ५.७९।।

I hope that the crops and the seeds of farmers in your realm are not wasted. Do you do good to each farmer by giving him loans on one per cent interest for agriculture?[39]

कच्चित् स्वनुष्ठिता तात वार्ता ते साधुभिर्जनैः।
वार्तायां संश्रितस्तात लोकोऽयं सुखमेधते।। सभा ५.८०।।

Are agriculture and trade in your realm done by people who are competent and good, for it is only those who live by these professions who live happily?[40]

कच्चिन्न सर्वे कर्मान्ताः परोक्षास्ते विशङ्किताः।
सर्वे वा पुनरुत्सृष्टाः संसृष्टं चात्र कारणम्।। सभा ५.३२।।

I hope that the farmers and the workers of your realm are not unknown to you. Are you aware of what they do? Are they happy with you? Their happiness is one single cause of social prosperity.[41]

कच्चिज्ज्ञातीन् गुरून् वृद्धान् वणिजः शिल्पिनः श्रितान्।
अभीक्ष्णमनुगृह्णासि धनधान्येन दुर्गतान्।। सभा ५.७२।।

By providing them with the means they need, do you look after the members of your family; the elderly; the merchants and the artisans; and those who are poor and unhappy?[42]

द्रव्योपकरणं किंचित् सर्वदा सर्वशिल्पिनाम्।
चातुर्मास्यावरं सम्यङ् नियतं सम्प्रयच्छसि।। सभा ५.११९।।

Do you provide regularly the artisans of your realm with the materials of production in a measure that will suffice for their work for four months at the least?[43]

Questions concerning the security of the realm

The *Mahābhārata* suggests that the best security for a nation is to be had in the happy conditions that exist within, which were indicated by the foregoing questions as instructions, and by the questions that followed. Security is not merely a military question. *That nation is most secure where the people feel secure and happy by the kind of governance with which they are governed.* That is the main direction in which Nārada's questions lead King Yudhishṭhira. But undoubtedly there are other factors as well, including the valour and vigilance of the army, about which he asks many questions, and, in asking them, instructs the king.[44] However, those factors, too, lie within.

कच्चिन्नगरगुप्त्यर्थे ग्रामा नगरवत् कृताः ।
ग्रामवच्च कृताः प्रान्तास्ते च सर्वे त्वदर्पणाः ।। सभा ५.८२ ।।
In order that the towns be secure, have the villages been made equally secure? And, like those villages, have the villages in the border regions been provided with similar security? Do all the regions, towns, and villages of your realm offer tribute as taxes?[45]

कच्चित् पौरा न सहिता ये च ते राष्ट्रवासिनः ।
त्वया सह विरुध्यन्ते परैः क्रीताः कथंचन ।। सभा ५.९४ ।।
I hope that the people in the towns and in your nation, coming together, do not oppose you. Nor that they have been bribed and bought by your enemies.[46]

Equally important is the *Mahābhārata*'s view that the vigilance and security of the realm does not at the same time mean also uncivilised conduct or brutality towards 'the enemy'. Rather, the very opposite of it. Therefore, Nārada asks Yudhishṭhira:

कच्चिद् भयादुपगतं क्षीणं वा रिपुमागतम् ।
युद्धे वा विजितं पार्थ पुत्रवत् परिरक्षसि ।। सभा ५.५६ ।।
Do you guard and protect, as you would your son, he who has, fearful, or having lost all that he had, come to you seeking protection, or the enemy whom you have vanquished in a war?[47]

Above all, questions concerning the foundations of good governance

कच्चिच्छूरा: कृतप्रज्ञा: पञ्च पञ्च स्वनुष्ठिता: ।
क्षेमं कुर्वन्ति संहत्य राजञ्जनपदे तव ।। सभा ५.८१ ।।

Dear King! In all the villages of your provinces, does the Assembly of the Five, or Pancha, consisting of those who are wise and competent, keep working for the good of the people?[48]

कच्चिदाचरितं पूर्वैर्नरदेव पितामहै ।
वर्तसे वृत्तिमक्षुद्रां धर्मार्थसहितां त्रिषु ।। सभा ५.१८ ।।

*I hope your conduct towards the various social callings—*brāhmaṇa-*s,* vaishya-*s, and* shūdra-*s—is as liberal, and in accordance with* dharma, *as was the conduct of your forbears towards them.*[49]

कच्चिन्नोग्रेण दण्डेन भृशमुद्विजसे प्रजा: ।
राष्ट्र तवानुशासन्ति मन्त्रिणो भरतर्षभ ।। सभा ५.४५ ।।

Dear King! I hope you do not create distress among the people by inflicting upon them harsh punishments. Do your ministers sustain and preserve your realm by their own lawful and just conduct?[50]

कच्चिन्न चौरेर्लुब्धैर्वा कुमारै: स्त्रीबलेन वा ।
त्वया वा पीड्यते राष्ट्रे कच्चित् तुष्टा: कृषीवला: ।। सभा ५.७७ ।।

I hope your nation does not feel oppressed due to thieves, and the greedy, and the conduct of your princes or princesses, or due to your own conduct. Are the farmers in your realm contented and happy?[51]

कच्चिद् दण्ड्येषु यमवत्पूज्येषु च विशाम्पते ।
परीक्ष्य वर्तसे सम्यगप्रियेषु प्रियेषु च ।। सभा ५.८९ ।।

I hope you are like Yamarāja towards the guilty deserving punishment, and like Dharmaraja towards those who are to be respected. Do you distinguish between the lovable and the nasty only after careful thought?[52]

कच्चिच्छोको न मन्युर्वा त्वया प्रोत्पाद्यतेऽनघ ।
अपि मङ्गलहस्तश्च जन: पार्श्वे नु तिष्ठति ।। सभा ५.१०२ ।।

I hope you do not create in anybody's heart anger and sorrow.[53]

कच्चिदग्निभयाच्चैव सर्वे व्यालभयात् तथा ।
रोगरक्षोभयाच्चैव राष्ट्रं स्वं परिरक्षसि ।। सभा ५.१२४ ।।

Do you protect your nation from fear—of fire, poisonous snakes, diseases, and from the fear of the wicked?[54]

कच्चित् त्वमेव सर्वस्या: पृथिव्या: पृथिवीपते ।
समश्चानभिशङ्क्यश्च यथा पिता ।। सभा ५.५७ ।।

Do the people of your nation trust you as one would one's father and mother?[55]

Conquest first of one's self; sound statecraft; good administration; security of the realm; and good governance—all these, the *Mahābhārata* teaches us, are interrelated. And all of them, together, have one aim—the welfare of the people.

CHAPTER SIXTEEN

Fate *or* Human Endeavour? The Question of Causality

- *Daiva*, fate
- *Purushārtha,* human endeavour,
- Endeavour and providence together
- *Kāla,* time
- *Svabhāva:* Innate disposition
- The question of accountability in what happens
- The question of causality unresolved
- Beyond 'causality'

The theory of *karma* had held the individual so completely responsible for what he made of himself that the burden of it seemed far too much for him to bear alone. In the domain of *karma* there is neither grace nor reprieve. These are granted by the Other, and there is no Other. One is entirely alone with one's acts and their inevitable fruition.[1] This, the freedom to choose but the subjection to the results thereof, is something which the individual, weak and irresolute, cannot live with. Hence his emotional need for something beyond himself, greater and more powerful than he, a cosmic force, to which he could transfer the accountability that belonged to him. That need was answered by three major shifts in the theory of *karma*, each one of them growing into a controversy as to the factors that govern a man's circumstances. In the first place, there arose the belief in *daiva*, providence, as a force over and above *purushārtha*, human endeavour. But although the belief in providence was more comforting than the awareness of one's own accountability, *daiva* seemed a little too mysterious and inaccessible. Therefore, secondly, providence was identified with 'Time', *kāla*, and then with God. It was most comforting to believe that, in the last count, one's situation is willed by God, to whom one can pray, and whom one may even occasionally curse, for he is accessible, not remote, nor deaf. The dharmic man, putting aside the *mokṣha* ideal for all practical purposes, longed not for freedom but for grace. Freedom implied strength of mind and of character: grace, their weakness. Finally, in order to negate choice and history, as well as their awesome burden, *karma* came to mean no more than ritual acts. In ritual acts there is no choice, no decision, no personal accountability. This, on the face of it, was the very opposite of the theory of *karma*.

The discussion in the *Mahābhārata* on providence *vs.* human endeavour, *daiva vs. purushārtha*,[2] starts with the empirical fact that not always does effort bring the desired result, whereas some people often get what they want without making any effort for it. The *Mahābhārata* mentions different explanations to account for this.[3]

Success or failure is attributed *(a)* solely to providence, *daiva*, or *adṛṣṭā*, the unseen; *(b)* to human endeavour alone, *purushārtha*; *(c)* to the combination of endeavour and providence and to neither of them wholly; *(d)* to the turning of Time, *kāla*; and *(e)* entirely to the innate disposition of things, *svabhāva*. There is, above all, the view that no definite statement could be made as to why things happen the way they happen or do not happen when there is every reason to expect that they would. The *Pañchatantra* is divided equally between human effort and fate.[4] The *Shukranīti* is almost wholly for human effort.[5] The vigorous advocacy for human effort is contained in the *Yoga-Vāsishṭha*, surprisingly, for this work is also philosophically one of uncompromising idealism, that the material world, in being a product of the mind, is an illusion.

Daiva, fate

Providence or fate, or *daiva* was sought to be established on the empirical ground that:

> उपर्युपरि लोकस्य सर्वो गन्तुं समीहते।
> यतते च यथाशक्ति न च तद् वर्तते तथा।। शान्ति ३३१.३८।।
> *Although all people aspire to move higher and higher, and exert themselves to their utmost capacity to reach their goal, not all succeed.*[6]

The least that this proves is that there are factors involved in success and failure other than human effort.

> योऽयमिच्छेद् यथाकामं कामानां तदवाप्नुयात्।
> यदि स्यान्न पराधीनं पुरुषस्य क्रियाफलम्।। शान्ति ३३१.९।।
> *Were the fruits of one's acts not dependent upon another,* parādhīna, *then one might obtain what one wished.*[7]

> न म्रियेरन् न जीर्येरन् सर्वे स्युः सर्वकामिनः।
> नाप्रियं प्रति पश्येयुरुत्थानस्य फले सति।। शान्ति ३३१.३७।।
> *And if the results of man's endeavour were entirely in his own hands, he would neither grow old nor die, and all his wishes would be fulfilled, without his ever having to experience the disagreeable.*[8]

Were endeavour the only factor in success, then what might explain the facts, to be seen everywhere, such as these?[9]

संयताश्च हि दक्षाश्च मतिमन्तश्च मानवा: ।
दृश्यन्ते निष्फला: संत: प्रहीणा: सर्वकर्मभि: ।। शान्ति ३३१.१० ।।

Those who are self-disciplined, intelligent, and competent are often failures, despite their constant endeavour.[10]

अपरे बालिशा: सन्तो निर्गुणा: पुरुषाधमा: ।
आशीर्भिरप्यसंयुक्ता दृश्यन्ते सर्वकामिन: ।। शान्ति ३३१.११ ।।

And there are men who are foolish, are devoid of all qualities, and are low, are seen to be having all that they wish, without the blessings of anyone.[11]

भूतानामपर: कश्चिद्धिंसायां सततोत्थित: ।
वञ्चनायां च लोकस्य स सुखेष्वेव जीर्यते ।। शान्ति ३३१.१२ ।।

There are men who injure and deprive others, but themselves grow old surrounded with pleasure and happiness;[12] *and those who are virtuous and wise who suffer terrible privations.*

अचेष्टमानमासीनं श्री: कञ्चिदुपतिष्ठते ।
कश्चित् कर्मानुसृत्यान्यो न प्राप्यमधिगच्छति ।। शान्ति ३३१.१३ ।।

Wealth and prosperity come to those who make not the slightest effort; and there are those who do not achieve what they desire though they endeavoured for it.[13]

तस्य योनौ प्रयुक्तस्य गर्भो भवति वा न वा ।
आम्रपुष्पोपमा यस्य निवृत्तिरुपलभ्यते ।। शान्ति ३३१.१५ ।।

Sometimes conception takes place, at other times it does not. When it does, there is miscarriage, like the mango flower falling before coming to fruit.[14]

केषाञ्चित् पुत्रकामानामनुसंतानमिच्छताम् ।
सिद्धौ प्रयतमानानां न चाण्डमुपजायते ।। शान्ति ३३१.१६ ।।

देवानिष्टा तपस्तप्त्वा कृपणै: पुत्रगृद्धिभि: ।
दश मासान् परिधृता जायन्ते कुलपांसना: ।। शान्ति ३३१.१८ ।।

People pray and make other efforts that they might get a son, but nothing happens, not an egg fructifies. When they do get a son, after fervent prayers to the gods, he turns out to be a disgrace to the family.[15]

व्याधिभिर्मथ्यमानानां त्यजतां विपुलं धनम्।
वेदनां नापकर्षन्ति यतंमानाश्चिकित्सका:।। शान्ति ३३१.३०।।

People afflicted with many a disease go to physicians to get cured, and pay them a lot of money; the physicians try their best, but fail to relieve their patients of their pain.[16]

ते चातिनिपुणा वैद्याः कुशलाः सम्भृतौषधाः।
व्याधिभिः परिकृष्यन्ते मृगा व्याधैरिवार्दिताः।। शान्ति ३३१.३१।।

The best of physicians are often unable to cure, even with the best medicines at their disposal, and, like an afflicted deer, fall prey to disease themselves.[17]

ऐश्वर्यमदमत्तांश्च मत्तान् मद्यमदेन च।
अप्रमत्ताः शठाञ्छूरा विक्रान्ताः पर्युपासते।। शान्ति ३३१.३९।।

The brave and the distinguished find themselves serving the arrogant, the drunkards, and the wicked.[18]

क्लेशाः परिनिवर्तन्ते केषाञ्चिदसमीक्षिताः।
स्वं स्वं च पुनरन्येषां न किंचिदधिगम्यते।। शान्ति ३३१.४०।।

Some have their problems solved without any care, others get nothing from their own wealth. What is more, acts of the same kind are seen as leading to vastly different results.[19]

These facts, some of them very ironical, puzzle every human being, and every human being seeks an explanation for them. That cannot lie in the theory that happiness and sufferings of this life are the results of good or bad acts done in a previous life, for that raises quite as many questions. Neither is the problem of uneven human situations resolved by tracing them to the good and bad acts of a previous life. For it is hardly plausible that persons of intellectual and moral distinction did something so heinous in a previous life as to pay for it now; and men who are visibly wicked and cruel had done things so remarkably meritorious as to reap their extravagant reward in this life. This, according to the *daiva* theory, points, then, to the existence of unseen fate. Whether a man is prosperous or poor, happy or miserable, must depend upon *that*. For that reason it is best neither to feel elated nor feel depressed.[20]

यथा यथास्य प्राप्तव्यं प्राप्नोत्येव तथा तथा।
भवितव्यं यथा यच्च भवत्येव तथा तथा।। शान्ति २२६.१०।।

A man gets what he is destined to get; and what is destined to happen must happen.[21]

न मन्त्रबलवीर्येण प्रज्ञया पौरुषेण च।
न शीलेन न वृत्तेन तथा नैवार्थसम्पदा।
अलभ्यं लभते मर्त्यस्तत्र का परिदेवना।। शान्ति २२६.२०।।
What he is not destined to get, that even his strength, intelligence, endeavour, humility, blameless conduct, and wealth, are powerless to secure for him.[22]

Namuchi, who was once a king but fell in adverse circumstances, advocates 'fate' as the ruler of all beings,[23] and 'just as water naturally flows towards ground that is lower, every person acts and moves as the fate would have it'.[24] On being asked by Indra, the lord of gods, how he feels on being divested of all his glory as king,[25] Namuchi says:

अनवार्येण शोकेन शरीरं चोपतप्यते।
अमित्राश्च प्रहृष्यन्ति शोके नास्ति सहायता।। शान्ति २२६.४।।
तस्माच्छक्र न शोचामि सर्वं ह्येवेदमन्तवत्।
संतापाद् भ्रश्यते रूपं संतापाद् भ्रश्यते श्रियः।। शान्ति २२६.५।।
Sorrow for the past certainly weakens the body, which will only delight those not one's friends, and will be of no help to one's self either. Therefore, I don't grieve; for all glory comes to an end anyway. Grief for the things of the past can only destroy one's well-being, longevity, and one's inner balance.[26]

एतद् विदित्वा कात्सर्न्येन यो न मुह्यति मानवः।
कुशली सर्वदुःखेषु स वै सर्वधनो नरः।। शान्ति २२६.२३।।
Whoever, on seeing this, is not confused, he alone keeps well in adversity, and he alone is rich in every way.[27]

लब्धव्यान्येव लभते गन्तव्यान्येव गच्छति।
प्राप्तव्यान्येव चाप्नोति दुःखानि च सुखानि च।। शान्ति २२६.२२।।
Whatever one is destined to get, that one gets; wherever one is destined to go, there one goes. Suffering or happiness, what one is meant to have, that one will have.[28]

न मन्त्रबलवीर्येण प्रज्ञया पौरुषेण च।
न शीलेन न वृत्तेन तथा नैवार्थसम्पदा।
अलभ्यं लभते मर्त्यस्तत्र का परिदेवना।। शान्ति २२६.२०।।

What one is not destined to have, that neither any mantra, *nor one's strength, nor intelligence, nor good conduct, nor one's wealth, can ever secure. Having understood this, I think it is futile to grieve.*[29]

न तत्सदः सत्परिषत् सभा च सा
प्राप्य यां न कुरुते सदा भयम्।
धर्मतत्त्वमवगाह्य बुद्धिमान्
योऽभ्युपैति स धुरंधरः पुमान्।। शान्ति २२६.१८।।

For there is no gathering, nor is there any assembly of the good and the wise, nor any group of people, through whom one is never fearful. Who centres oneself in the true meaning of what is, is alone truly learned and wise.[30]

Purushārtha: human endeavour

Faith in human endeavour as the source of every success, and the lack of it as the reason for failure, is based on the equally empirical ground that:

स्वं चेत् कर्मफलं न स्यात् सर्वमेवाफलं भवेत्।
लोको दैवं समालक्ष्य उदासीनो भवेन्ननु।। अनुशासन ६.१९।।

To act would be meaningless if one's efforts did not have recompense, in which case people would look only to the mysterious providence and give up effort altogether.[31]

उत्सीदेरन् प्रजाः सर्वा न कुर्युः कर्म चेद् भुवि।
तथा ह्येता न वर्धेरन् कर्म चेदफलं भवेत्।। वन ३२.११।।

In that event, if people did not make effort, there would be no progress and everything would perish.[32]

Yudhishṭhira seeks to know from Bhīshma: 'Of providence and human effort, which has the greater force?'[33] In answer to this question, Bhīshma narrates what Brahmā, the Primeval Being, had said to Sage *Vāsishṭha* when this very question was put to him.[34] Brahmā gave an irrefutable reasoning for *purushārtha*, having greater force. Its substance is as follows:

नाबीजं जायते किंचिन्न बीजेन बिना फलम्।
बीजाद् बीजं प्रभवति बीजादेव फलं स्मृतम्।। अनुशासन ६.५।।

It is evident that without a seed, nothing can germinate, nor fruits either. Seed grows from seed, and fruit comes from seed.[35]

यथा बीजं विना क्षेत्रमुप्तं भवति निष्फलम्।
तथा पुरुषकारेण विना दैवं न सिध्यति।। अनुशासन ६.७।।

A seed has to be sown in the field before it can germinate, and fructify. Likewise, providence is not effective in the absence of effort.[36]

तपसा रूपसौभाग्यं रत्नानि विविधानि च।
प्राप्यते कर्मणा सर्वं न दैवादकृतात्मना।। अनुशासन ६.१२।।

By his strenuous effort, man gains beauty, good fortune, and other riches. Through endeavour man can achieve everything; by depending on providence, nothing.[37]

कृतः पुरुषकारस्तु दैवमेवानुवर्तते।
न दैवमकृते किंचित् कस्यचिद् दातुमर्हति।। अनुशासन ६.२२।।

Human effort follows providence; but where there is no effort, providence can provide nothing.[38]

यथाग्निः पवनोद्धतः सुसूक्ष्मोऽपि महान् भवेत्।
तथा कर्मसमायुक्तं दैवं साधु विवर्धते।। अनुशासन ६.४३।।
यथा तैलक्षयाद् दीपः प्रहासमुपगच्छति।
तथा कर्मक्षयाद् दैवं प्रहासमुपगच्छति।। अनुशासन ६.४४।।

In the same way as even a small fire stoked with high wind can grow big, providence gains in strength with human effort as support.[39] *And just as the lamp is extinguished when the oil is finished, providence must vanish, too, when effort comes to an end.*[40]

न च फलति विकर्मा जीवलोके न दैवं
व्यपनयति विमार्गं नास्ति दैवे प्रभुत्वम्।
गुरुमिव कृतमग्र्यं कर्म संयाति दैवं
नयति पुरुषकारः संचितस्तत्र तत्र।। अनुशासन ६.४७।।

No one in this world is seen to flourish without making effort. Providence does not have the power to alter the path one has chosen. Just as a disciple walks behind his preceptor, so does providence behind human effort. The accumulated effort can summon providence where it would.[41]

कृती सर्वत्र लभते प्रतिष्ठां भाग्यसंयुताम् ।
अकृती लभते भ्रष्टः क्षते क्षारावसेचनम् ।। अनुशासन ६.११ ।।

अर्थो वा मित्रवर्गो वा ऐश्वर्यं वा कुलान्वितम् ।
श्रीश्चापि दुर्लभा भोक्तुं तथैवाकृतकर्मभिः ।। अनुशासन ६.१५ ।।

तथा स्वर्गश्च भोगश्च निष्ठा या च मनीषिता ।
सर्वं पुरुषकारेण कृतेनेहोपलभ्यते ।। अनुशासन ६.१३ ।।

Effort can secure for a man everything that is desirable. But he who does nothing, relying on providence alone, can enjoy not even what he has been endowed with.[42] *Such a man destroys himself.*[43]

दैवं पुरुषकारश्च स्थितावन्योन्यसंश्रयात् ।
उदाराणां तु सत्कर्म दैवं क्लीबा उपासते ।। शान्ति १३९.८२ ।।

Even if providence and effort were linked with each other, the noble-minded always exert, only the cowards talk of providence.[44]

कर्म चात्महितं कार्यं तीक्ष्णं वा यदि वा मृदु ।
ग्रस्यतेऽकर्मशीलस्तु सदानर्थैरकिञ्चनः ।। शान्ति १३९.८३ ।।

Whatever is for one's good, hard or gentle, that one must do; he who abandons effort, invites poverty and misfortune.[45]

तस्मात् सर्वं व्यपोह्यार्थं कार्य एव पराक्रमः ।
सर्वस्वमपि संत्यज्य कार्यमात्महितं नरैः ।। शान्ति १३९.८४ ।।

Therefore, let one not think of providence; staking all, one must make strenuous effort for one's good.[46]

विद्या शौर्यं च दाक्ष्यं च बलं धैर्यं च पञ्चमम् ।
मित्राणि सहजान्याहुर्वर्तयन्तीह तैर्बुधाः ।। शान्ति १३९.८५ ।।

Learning, courage, dexterity, strength, and patience are the five natural friends of a man; with their help are done all the acts of the wise.[47]

The Pañchatantra

प्रारभ्यते न खलु विघ्नभयेन नीचैः
प्रारभ्य विघ्नविहता रिमन्ति मध्याः ।

विघ्नैः सहस्रगुणितैरपि हन्यमानाः
प्रारब्धमुत्तमगुणा न परित्यजन्ति।। पंचतंत्र III.२५४।।

Those who are inferior begin nothing for fear of obstructions; the middling abandon a thing no sooner than there are obstructions; but the superior men do not leave what they began even if they be hurt by a thousand obstacles.[48]

सस्नेहवर्तिदीपस्य रक्षा वातात् प्रयत्नतः।। शुक्रनीति I.५३।।

With effort it is possible to protect the lamp against the wind.[49]

In a conversation between Yudhishṭhira and his wife Draupadī, during their long years of exile, the years of adversity and trial, Draupadī mounts, in sixty verses, a powerful argument, clear and consistent, for human effort as the means of gaining everything of worth.[50] She engages in an issue that is as central to the *Mahābhārata* as is the question of the ordering of relationships: Is a person free to be what he, or she, is? Or is man determined by some other: Time, or Fate, or God, or History? The substance of what she said is: 'At this moment we are in great adversity. Without arguing endlessly the question of human freedom, or whether you will or will not achieve success, if you devote yourself to effort, and have no doubts as to its efficacy, we can regain what you have lost.' She concludes by saying:

देशकालावुपायांश्च मगंलं स्वस्तिवृद्धये।
युनक्ति मेधया धीरो यथाशक्ति यथाबलम्।। वन ३२.५३।।

Taking into consideration time and place and by judging through intelligence one's capacities and strength, let a man, with untroubled mind, make effort and increase in blessings.

The *Yoga-Vāsishṭha*[51] dismisses *daiva*, fate, as a figment of imagination, just a word, invoked by fools, for there exists no such thing as fate or destiny.[52] If these words are nevertheless used, it is to explain, in a manner of speaking, the accumulation of one's own endeavour: there is no destiny other than one's past efforts coming to fruition *now* as good or bad.[53] In fact, *daiva* refers to nothing substantial that aids or obstructs one's endeavour. And endeavour is concrete, visible action, whereas *daiva* can neither be seen nor inferred. Man, a self-determined being, determines his destiny; as he endeavours so he achieves.[54] One gets only what one has striven for; nothing is ever achieved by sitting idly.[55] Only a fool will depend on *daiva*, and only a fool will ruin himself by refusing to make effort.[56] Indeed, those who depend entirely on their own efforts have the power of overcoming the effects even of acts done in a previous life, although it is true that the latter are responsible for one's circumstances in this life. Even *those* can be changed by effort, but not through the absurd belief in fate. This optimism of the author of the *Yoga-Vāsishṭha* is based on the argument that just as the wrong acts of yesterday can be rectified today, so the efforts of this life can annul the effects of those of the previous one.[57] Of the past and present efforts, it is the stronger that subdues the weaker; in either case, it is one's own effort that succeeds.[58] For that reason one should, through recourse to determined effort, overcome the past, but first one must dispel from one's mind the notion that the past fully determines our present state and the future.[59] There is no question that misfortunes, even if a legacy of the past, can be destroyed through manly effort in the present.[60] There is none among the brave, the successful, the learned and the wise, who waits for destiny.[61]

Endeavour and providence together

The two explanations, 'human endeavour', or *purushārtha*, and 'providence', or *daiva*, were exclusive; and to each there were objections on empirical grounds. Neither of them could wholly account for the vast differences in human situation. Given the ancient tradition of reconciling extreme views, the third position on the subject was propounded briefly by Krishna. That was in the context of his visit to the court of the Kaurava-s as the personal envoy of the Pāṇḍava-s, with the mission to avert a war between them, and to secure for the latter their legitimate share of the kingdom. While departing, Krishna says:

तत्र वै पौरुषं ब्रूयुरासेकं यत्र कारितम् ।
तत्र चापि ध्रुवं पश्येच्छोषणं दैवकारितम् ।। उद्योग ७९.३ ।।

तदिदं निश्चितं बुद्ध्या पूवैरपि महात्मभिः ।
दैवे च मानुषे चैव संयुक्तं लोककारणम् ।। उद्योग ७९.४ ।।

I shall try to achieve what is good for both sides. But however clean and moist the field may be made by human effort, it cannot yield without rains at the proper time; in ploughing and irrigating the field there is human effort, but then there is drought owing to providence. The ancient sages had therefore concluded that the social good is a combined product of providence and human effort.

अहं हि तत् करिष्यामि परं पुरुषकारतः।
दैवं तु न मया शक्यं कर्म कर्तुं कथंचन।। उद्योग ७९.५ ।।

I shall do everything that lies in my power, but it is not in my power to alter providence.[62]

At another place, the same view is attributed to Shiva.[63] In a long dialogue with Umā, his wife, who raises several questions concerning human life, human effort *vs* providence among them. Umā asks:

भगवन् सर्वभूतेश लोके कर्मक्रियापथे।
दैवात् प्रवर्तते सर्वामिति केचिद् व्यवस्थिताः।। अनुशासन पृ ५९७८ ।।

अपरे चेष्टया चेति दृष्ट्वा प्रत्यक्षतः क्रियाम्।
पक्षभेदे द्विधा चास्मिन् संशयस्थं मनो मम।।
तत्त्वं वद महादेव श्रोतुं कौतूहलं हि मे।। अनुशासन पृ. ५९७८ ।।

Some people believe that it is providence in which human acts originate.[64] *Some others, arguing from what is evident, believe that it is in human endeavour, and not in providence, that acts originate. These are the two opposing views. My mind is full of doubt, and I am curious to know. Mahadeva, will you enlighten me what the truth of it is?*[65]

Shiva says:

केवलं फलनिष्पत्तिरेकेन तु न शक्यते।
पौरुषेणैव दैवेन युगपद् ग्रथितं प्रिये।। अनुशासन पृ. ५९७९ ।।

Neither of them is effective by itself, dear one; every act is tied to effort and providence together.[66]

तयोः समाहितं कर्म शीतोष्णं युगपत् तथा।
पौरुषं तु तयोः पूर्वमारब्धव्यं विजानता।।
आत्मना तु न शक्यंहि तथा कीर्तिमवाप्नुयात्।। अनुशासन पृ. ५९७९ ।।

It is by their combination that effort succeeds. Just as heat and cold exist together, providence and human effort work together. It is of course plain that one should begin with making effort; for what cannot materialise by itself, that one should do first.[67]

रोपणं चैव लवनं यच्चान्यत् पौरुषं स्मृतम्।।
काले वृष्टिः सुवापं च प्ररोहः पंक्तिरेव च।
एवमादि तु यच्चान्यत् तद् दैवतमिति स्मृतम्।। अनुशासन पृ. ५९७९ ।।

To sow the seed is the work of man; for the seed to germinate, for the rains to come at the proper time, and for the harvest to be good, is the work of providence. They happen when providence is favourable.[68]

अबुद्धिगम्यं यन्मर्त्यैर्हेतुभिर्वा न विद्यते।।
तादृशं कारणं दैवं शुभं वा यदि वेतरत्।
यादृशं चात्मना शक्यं तत् पौरुषमिति स्मृतम्।। अनुशासन पृ. ५९७९।।
What lies in the capacity of man is called purushārtha*; what cannot be grasped by his intelligence, or by reasoning, is called* daiva*, whether it is beneficial or not.*[69]

नरस्याकुर्वतः कर्म दैवसम्पन्न लभ्यते।
तस्मात् सर्वसमारम्भो दैवमानुषनिर्मितः।। अनुशासन पृ. ५९७९।।
The man who does not make effort, providence does not help him either. Therefore all acts are dependent upon human effort and providence together.[70]

At another place, in a conversation between two persons, Ashvatthāmā and Kripāchārya, planning their next move in a most desperate situation,[71] the same view is put forth in greater detail. Kripā says to Ashvatthāmā:

आबद्धा मानुषाः सर्वे निबद्धाः कर्मणोर्द्वयोः।
दैवे पुरुषकारे च परं ताभ्यां न विद्यते।। सौप्तिक २.२।।
All human beings are bound by two factors alone: providence and effort. Apart from them, there is no other factor.[72]

न हि दैवेन सिद्ध्यन्ति कार्याण्येकेन सत्तम।
न चापि कर्मणैकेन द्वाभ्यां सिद्धस्तु योगतः।। सौप्तिक २.३।।
Goals are achieved neither solely by providence, nor solely by human effort. They are achieved by a combination of those two.[73]

पर्जन्यः पर्वते वर्षन् किन्नु साधयते फलम्।
कृष्टे क्षेत्रे तथा वर्षन् किन्न साधयते फलम्।। सौप्तिक २.५।।
What is achieved if the clouds rain on the hills? And what is it that cannot be achieved if the rains fall on a field that has been ploughed and sown with seeds?[74]

सुवृष्टे च यथा देवे सम्यक् क्षेत्रे च कर्षिते।
बीजं महागुणं भूयात् तथा सिद्धिर्हि मानुषी।। सौप्तिक २.७।।

If there have been good rains, but the field has been prepared well, too, then the seed sown in it will be most fruitful. Likewise, human achievement is dependent both on providence and effort.[75]

उत्थानं चाप्यदैवस्य ह्यनुत्थानं च दैवतम्।
व्यर्थं भवति सर्वत्र पूर्वस्तत्र विनिश्चयः।। सौप्तिक २.६।।

The efforts of a man not favoured by providence will be useless; and so will be the efforts of a man who has providence on his side but has not himself made efforts, and providence is rendered ineffective thereby.[76]

उत्थानं च मनुष्याणां दक्षाणां दैववर्जितम्।
अफलं दृश्यते लोके सम्यगप्युपपादितम्।। सौप्तिक २.११।।

Where the effort made intelligently is bereft, though, of the support of providence, there no effort is seen to be fruitful.[77]

हीनं पुरुषकारेण यदि दैवेन वा पुनः।
कारणाभ्यामथैताभ्यामुत्थानमफलं भवेत्।। सौप्तिक २:१९।।

Providence bereft of effort, and effort bereft of providence—these two alone account for human failures in the world.[78]

प्रायशो हि कृतं कर्म नाफलं दृश्यते भुवि।
अकृत्वा च पुनर्दुःखं कर्म पश्येन्महाफलम्।। सौप्तिक २.१३।।

Generally, effort is hardly ever seen in this world to bear no fruit; and lack of effort is seen mostly producing pain. Therefore, effort should be considered most fruitful.[79]

शक्नोति जीवितुं दक्षो नालसः सुखमेधते।
दृश्यन्ते जीवलोकेऽस्मिन् दक्षाः प्रायोहितैषिणः।। सौप्तिक २.१५।।

Making effort skilfully, a man may still live a happy life: for those who do are generally seen to be achieving what is good for them.[80]

चेष्टामकुर्वल्लँभते यदि किंचिद् यदृच्छया।
यो वा न लभते कृत्वा दुर्दर्शौ तावुभावपि।। सौप्तिक २.१४।।

Without making any effort the man who still gains something due to favourable providence, or after making every effort gains nothing: these two kinds of men are seen only rarely.[81]

यदि दक्षः समारम्भात् कर्मणो नाश्नुते फलम्।
नास्य वाच्यं भवेत् किंचिल्लब्धव्यं वाधिगच्छति।। सौप्तिक २.१६।।

अकृत्वा कर्म यो लोके फलं विन्दति धिष्ठितः।
स तु वक्तव्यतां याति द्वेष्यो भवति भूयशः।। सौप्तिक २.१७।।

After making every effort, should an efficient man achieve nothing, no one would blame him. But the man who achieves everything without doing anything invites low esteem and the hostility of others.[82]

अनारम्भात् तु कार्याणां नार्थः सम्पद्यते क्वचित्।। सौप्तिक २.३४।।
कृते पुरुषकारे तु येषां कार्यं न सिद्ध्यति।
दैवेनोपहतास्ते तु नात्र कार्या विचारणा।। सौप्तिक २.३५।।

Nothing is ever achieved if nothing is ever begun. But whose efforts bear no fruit, they are no doubt defeated already by providence.[83]

Kāla, Time

To the pre-eminently rational dharmic mind, the theory of unseen fate was hardly satisfactory. For not only did it constitute no 'explanation' but it also amounted to abandoning oneself to caprice; and caprice was one thing that the dharmic mind, suffused with the idea of order, had resolutely banished from its scheme of things. So as to bring providence within rational categories of thought, and make it intelligible, it was identified with *kāla*, 'Time', a necessary condition of all life and thought, experienced directly, for one lives and thinks in time. A great many men and women have always drawn their power of survival from, among other things, the deeply-rooted belief, shared by the peasant and the learned alike, in 'Time' as the cause of unceasing creation and events.[84]

It is not man but *kāla*, that determines every human situation. That is the uncompromising view also of Vyāsa, the author of the *Mahābhārata*. He maintained it from the beginning to the end of that work.

कालः सृजति भूतानि कालः संहरते प्रजाः।
संहरन्तं प्रजाः कालं कालः शमयते पुनः।। आदि १.२४८।।

कालो हि कुरुते भावान् सर्वलोके शुभाशुभान्।
कालः संक्षिपते सर्वाः प्रजा विसृजते पुनः।। आदि १.२४९।।

कालः सुप्तेषु जागर्ति कालो हि दुरतिक्रमः।
कालः सर्वेषु भूतेषु चरत्यविधृतः समः।। आदि १.२५०।।

अतीतानागता भावा ये च वर्तन्ति साम्प्रतम् ।
तान् कालनिर्मितान् बुद्ध्वा न संज्ञां हातुमर्हसि ।। आदि १.२५१ ।।

Time creates all beings, and Time destroys what is created. Destroying what is created, Time is then pacified by Time.

Time is the doer of all that happens in the world, of the good and the bad alike. Time contracts and limits what is created; and Time expands and sets free what is limited.

While everything sleeps, Time keeps vigil. None can transgress the movement of Time. Time moves within all beings equally, freely, with nothing to obstruct it. Whatever was in the past, and what will come in the future, and is now, are the creations of Time. Seeing this, do not lose your discriminating awareness.[85]

In brief, **कालमूलमिदं सर्वं भावाभावौ सुखासुखे**. That is, everything is rooted in Time, that which *is* and that which *is-not*, happiness and suffering alike.[85a]

With a view to persuading Yudhishṭhira, distraught with grief and remorse at the end of the Great War, that:

सुखं च दुःखं च भवाभवौ च
लाभालाभौ मरणं जीवितं च ।
पर्यायत: सर्वमवाप्नुवन्ति
तस्माद् धीरोनैव हृष्येन्न शोचेत् ।। शान्ति २५.३१ ।।

Pleasure and pain, creation and destruction, gain and loss, and life and death—these come to everybody in a cycle of time; therefore, who is of a steady mind should not rejoice or grieve for them.[86]

Vyāsa unfolds in the following argument the rationality of his belief that Time determines every event.[87]

न कर्मणा लभ्यते चिन्तया वा
नाप्यस्ति दाता पुरुषस्य कश्चित् ।
पर्याययोगाद् विहितं विधात्रा
कालेन सर्वं लभते मनुष्य: ।। शान्ति २५.५ ।।

What is lost can be regained neither by effort nor by thinking about it. Nor is there anyone who can gift what has been destroyed. Everything is given to man in a cycle of time.[88]

न बुद्धिशास्त्राध्ययनेन शक्यं
  प्राप्तुं विशेषं मनुजैरकाले।
मूर्खोऽपि चाप्नोति कदाचिदर्थान्
  कालो हि कार्यं प्रति निर्विशेषः।। शान्ति २५.६।।

Out of time, one cannot gain even by one's intelligence and learning what is of special value; whereas, when it is time, even a fool gets what he desired. Hence Time is the main factor in everything.[89]

नाभूतिकालेषु फलं ददन्ति
  शिल्पानि मन्त्राश्च तथौषधानि।
तान्येव कालेन समाहितानि
  सिद्ध्यन्ति वर्धन्ति च भूतिकाले।। शान्ति २५.७।।

When it is time for a downward slide, neither skill nor mantra, *nor any medicine, is any good; when it is time for a rise, then all these are effective by the force of Time.*[90]

कालेन शीघ्राः प्रवहन्ति वाताः
  कालेन वृष्टिर्जलदानुपैति।
कालेन पद्मोत्पलवज्जलं च
  कालेन पुष्यन्ति वनेषु वृक्षाः।। शान्ति २५.८।।

The wind blows, the clouds give rain, the lotus in the water blooms, and the trees in the woods grow, in their time.[91]

कालेन कृष्णाश्च सिताश्च रात्र्यः
  कालेन चन्द्रः परिपूर्णबिम्बः।
नाकालतः पुष्पफलं द्रुमाणां
  नाकालवेगाः सरितो वहन्ति।। शान्ति २५.९।।

The nights are bright and dark in their time, and the moon is full only at its given time. Out of time, there are neither flowers nor fruits on the trees, nor do the rivers flow swiftly.[92]

नाकालतो म्रियते जायते वा
  नाकालतो व्याहरते च बालः।
नाकालतो यौवनमभ्युपैति
  नाकालतो रोहति बीजमुप्तम्।। शान्ति २५.११।।

नाकालतो भानुरुपैति योगं
  नाकालतोऽस्तङ्गिरिमभ्युपैति।

नाकालतो वर्धते हीयते च
चन्द्रः समुद्रोऽपि महोर्मिमाली ।। शान्ति २५.१२ ।।

It is not until their time that women conceive, and children are born and begin to speak, or die. Youth does not come before its time, and the seed that was sown does not germinate before its time. The sun rises and the sun sets on its time. The moon does not wax and wane before its cycle; neither do the tides in the sea.[93]

The most forceful expression of that belief is contained in the dialogue that takes place between Shakra, who had just become Indra, the king of gods, and Bali, the man who had ruled the three worlds as the previous Indra but was now vanquished by Shakra.[94]

On looking for Bali everywhere, the new Indra, accompanied by a procession of gods, at last finds him in a cave on the coast of Kerala. Seeing his victor with his glorious retinue, Bali feels neither grief nor nostalgia. Fearless and calm, he stands upright and looks at Shakra. Thereupon the following dialogue takes place between the two.[95]

Shakra as the new Indra

Bali! You are in the hands of your enemies, and have lost your domains. Not long ago the lord of all the worlds, but now in such a mean state. Your wife and your limitless wealth in the hands of others; gone your golden canopy studded with diamonds and rubies and pearls; and gone the celestial singers that amused you day and night; and with them, gone the nymphs attending upon you with their charms. Your generosity boundless, and your gifts without end—and now, nothing of that remains with you.

And yet, there is on your face neither grief for what you have lost, nor pain at your situation.

To what do you owe this impossible equanimity? Is it your courage? Or your services to the old and the infirm? Or some austerities that you undertook? Is it to these that you owe your strength in adversity? How is it that you do not grieve?

Bali

Shakra! Today you have all the power and I have none. I see the glory that you have recently acquired, and I have lost everything, and this must encourage you to address me with words of taunt.

You did not always have the power to speak to me like this. From where do you get it *now*?

The wise say that only the man who treats with dignity a valiant foe, defeated and chained, is truly a superior man. But let that be.

For me it is a time for silence, and forgiveness, not of showing strength. I was what you are today; and what I am today, you will be that tomorrow. For change is in the nature of things, transitory, shifting, one moment here, and gone in the next.

You are not the cause of your glory; nor am I the cause of my misery. There is some other to whom we owe this change. No, not your bravery, nor your effort, it is the changing Time that has made you Indra.

There was a time when I used to thunder, as you do now, and there was none to dispute with me, god or demon, so complete was my sway. Now I am bound and reduced by Time.

Why do I not grieve at my loss?, you ask me. Your question implies that I must; but must I? You always had rather a plain mind, and so it is even today. Or you would be aware that to grieve is futile.

It is futile to grieve, for grief cannot undo what is done, and can only weaken a man further. But there is a reason of greater weight than even this.

There is no other source of movement and change than Time. Creation and destruction, happiness and suffering, victory and defeat, are caused not by human effort, but by Time. Seeing this, I am neither elated in victory, nor assailed by grief in defeat. What the sea is to the rivers, death is to all that lives and moves. Why shall I then grieve?

Neither am I the cause of my defeat, nor are you the cause of your victory. It is Time that keeps changing everything in this world. And everything in all the worlds is in the flow of Time. With Time on a man's side, his actions bring him happiness; the same actions, with Time against him, bring him sorrow. The same acts bring different results at different times—this we all can see.

As we all can see, a man who is born high, and is noble, handsome and strong, lives a life of grief, for such is his destiny; and a man born low, is ignoble, as well as a fool, has a life crowned with happiness, for that is *his* destiny.

Time is no respecter of persons. All are in the grip of Time—to be bent or broken.

Consumed by Time, a thing is later burnt by fire; what is killed by Time, that is then killed by another; what is already destroyed, that alone can be destroyed; and the gain that is destined, that one must have.

The universe is moved by Time. None can stop its flow, nor turn it back, nor influence its ways. Time preserves, and Time destroys; for life and death are in Time. There is no island in the ocean of Time.

With the change of Time you will fall, too—as I did. There have been hundreds of Indras, all of them vanished, crushed by Time. So you will vanish, too. You and I know the names of kings, and of emperors, who seemed invincible, full of glory, and each thought that he owned the universe. Where *are* they now? All gone, nothing left but a name, vanished, borne away on the tide of Time.

When Time turns, everything turns. For what good deeds did *you* do that you became the lords of the gods? And what evil deeds did we do that *we* are today in this sorry state?

There is no reason for you to be arrogant, and none for me to grieve. We are subject to Time, like everything else. And Time is all-powerful. All-powerful is the flow of Time.

Who understands the power of Time does not grieve even when a victim of Time; for grief does not remove one's adversity, only weakens one further. Why should then one grieve?

There is no defying Time, only submission, not the submission of the coward, but of the wise, and wisdom is given to man.

An equally forceful advocacy of Time as the cause of every event is put forth in the *Mahābhārata* in the story also of Arjuna, the great hero, being reduced completely after the Great War was won.[96]

Following the coronation of Yudhishṭhira, Sri Krishna returns to Dwārakā on the eastern coast, carrying with him, though, the curse of Gāndhārī. All her sons being killed in the war, she was disconsolate with grief. In her last conversation with him, she curses Krishna: that just as her whole family was destroyed in that war between the Kaurava-s and the Pāṇḍava-s, which he *could* have prevented but didn't, his own clan would be destroyed in a similar family feud. And that he himself would die, unattended, far away from his home, a mean death. And that is what happens. When the news was brought to the Pāṇḍava-s, in Hastināpura, Arjuna immediately sets off for Dwārakā—alone. Leaving aside his own grief on the death of his beloved friend, his main task now is to escort the wives and the other women of Krishna's household to Hastināpura. There are also the children, the old, and the infirm who had survived to be taken care of. As they begin to leave, the city of Dwārakā itself begins being swallowed by the sea. There were other men, too, some of them even armed, but they were dispirited and wholly confused. The huge caravan, with Arjuna as the only protector of the women and their fabulous wealth, passes through 'the land of the five rivers', where they are attacked by a large number of sturdy Ahir robbers, who wanted the women and their wealth. Arjuna desperately tries to protect them, but in vain.

The arrows he shot from his bow missed their mark and were exhausted. It was only with much effort that he could even string his famous bow. Not much strength was left in his arm. He had lost his skill in archery. Overwhelmed by those strong robbers, he gave up the fight, saying in desperation: 'The knowledge of weapons is not forever.'[97] The robbers forcibly carried away many of the women with their priceless jewels. On reaching Hastināpura, Arjuna settled in different places the remaining women and the others of Krishna's clan.

He now meditates on what he has been reduced to. Not long ago a great warrior, his very name striking terror in his enemies, now he could not protect women from ordinary robbers. In that state of mind he visits Vyāsa and recounts all that had happened, and his distress at his impotence.[98] Vyāsa consoles him, with an admirable philosophic detachment, saying:

एवं बुद्धिश्च तेजश्च प्रतिपत्तिश्च भारत।। मौसल ८.३२।।
भवन्ति भवकालेषु विपद्यन्ते विपर्यये।

When it is time for the rise, one's intelligence, strength, and knowledge, all these rise, too: when it is time for decline, they decline as well.[99]

कालमूलमिदं सर्वं जब्दीजं धनंजय।। मौसल ८.३३।।
काल एव समादत्ते पुनरेव यदृच्छया।

Time is the cause of everything in the world. Time is the seed of creation; and Time then destroys, for no cause.[100]

स एव बलवान् भूत्वा पुनर्भवति दुर्बल: ।। मौसल ८.३४ ।।
स एवेशश्च भूत्वेह परैराज्ञाप्यते पुन: ।

Now forceful, Time then becomes weak; now a ruler, becomes then powerless.[101]

'Don't be disheartened. Don't grieve,' Vyāsa says to Arjuna. 'The work for which you were meant to be has ended. It is now time for you to depart.'[102] What Vyāsa was saying is that it is the historical moment that makes a man a hero; that moment passed, he is nothing.

In consoling Dhritarāshṭra, his half-brother, devastated with grief at the complete destruction of his family in the war, Vidura propounds the same belief: that every event is predetermined by *kāla*, and that what had happened had to happen the way it did.[103]

काल: कर्षति भूतानि सर्वाणि विविधान्युत ।
न कालस्य प्रिय: कश्चिन्न द्वेष्य: कुरुसत्तम ।। स्त्री २.८ ।।

Time gathers into itself all living beings. No one is in special favour of Time; nor is Time hostile to anyone.[104]

न कालस्य प्रिय: कश्चिन्न द्वेष्य: कुरुसत्तम ।
न मध्यस्थ: क्वचित्काल: सर्वं काल: प्रकर्षति ।। स्त्री २.२३ ।।

Time loves no one; nor has any aversion to anyone, nor indifference. Time draws into itself all alike.[105]

यथा वायुस्तृणाग्राणि संवर्तयति सर्वश: ।
तथा कालवशं यान्ति भूतानि भरतर्षभ ।। स्त्री २.९ ।।

Just as the wind keeps blowing hither and thither pieces of straw, all living beings are likewise moved by Time.[106]

एकसार्थप्रयातानां सर्वेषां तत्र गामिनाम् ।
यस्य काल: प्रयात्यग्रे तत्र का परिदेवना ।। स्त्री २.१० ।।

All those who came here at the same time would go away, too. The one whose time comes first, goes earlier. Then why grieve for anyone?[107]

काल: पचति भूतानि काल: संहरते प्रजा: ।
काल: सुप्तेषु जागर्ति कालो हि दुरतिक्रम: ।। स्त्री २.२४ ।।

It is Time that ripens and matures all beings; and it is Time that destroys all that lives. Time is ever vigilant while all sleep; and there is no transgressing Time.[108]

Bhīshma rejects the view that *kāla*, predetermines everything that happens. In his long conversation with Yudhishṭhira, he maintains, on the contrary, that Time is no force. It is only a mental construct to explain sequence. The real force lies in the human heart and in the human mind, and in human acts thereby.[109] Or else man is nothing. If Time determines everything, then a person is not accountable for what he, or she, does. Furthermore, this mysterious entity called 'Time' is at best irrational and capricious in its workings. For it is not at all clear why Time should be on my side today, and turn against me tomorrow. There is no dialogue with Time. But there is a dialogue with my self as to the choices I make and act accordingly. What I am is a result of my acts that sustain and enhance and do no violence to the *other*, the ways of *dharma*, or that uproot, separate, degrade, and violate the *other*, the ways of *adharma*.

> न ह्यधर्मतयाधर्मं दद्यात् कालः कथंचन।
> तस्माद् विशुद्धमात्मानं जानीयाद् धर्मचारिणम्।। अनुशासन १६४.६।।
> *In no way can Time,* kāla, *turn* dharma *into* adharma. *Therefore, the one treading the path of* dharma *should be considered master of his self.*[110]

> सप्रष्टुमप्यसमर्थो हि ज्वलन्तमिव पावकम्।
> अधर्मः संततो धर्मं कालेन परिरक्षितम्।। अनुशासन १६४.७।।
> Dharma *has the radiance of fire, protected by Time.* Adharma *cannot touch* dharma *even remotely.*[111]

> कार्यवितौ हि धर्मेण धर्मो हि विजयावहः।
> त्रयाणामपि लोकानामालोकः कारणं भवेत्।। अनुशासन १६४.८।।
> Dharma *is the cause of the acts inherent in its meaning. They bring true conquest; spread light; and preserve and protect the whole creation.*[112]

Rejecting predetermination by some mysterious *kāla*, rejecting also fate as the decisive factor, Bhīshma suggests to Yudhishṭhira, who would now be king, the preeminence of human effort.

> उत्थानेन सदा पुत्र प्रयतेथा युधिष्ठिर।
> न ह्युत्थानमृते दैवं राज्ञामर्थं प्रसादयेत्।। शान्ति ५६.१४।।

> साधारणं द्वयं ह्येतद दैवमुत्थानमेव च।
> पौरुषं हि परं मन्ये दैवं निश्चितमुच्यते।। शान्ति ५६.१५।।

For your manly rise, son, always make effort. Providence alone, without effort, does not serve the royal ends of governance. Ordinarily, in achieving one's ends, both effort and providence are believed to be the determining factors. Even so, I believe effort to be the more important, providence already decided.[113]

विपन्ने च समारम्भे संतापं मा स्म वै कृथाः ।
घटस्वैव सदाऽऽत्मानं राज्ञामेष परो नयः ।। शान्ति ५६.१६ ।।

Should obstructions arise in what you begin, or what you begin is not successful, feel no anguish in your heart. Put yourself to endeavour always, for that is the best principle for kings.[114]

एतावन्मात्रमेतद्धि भूतानां प्राज्ञलक्षणम् ।
कालयुक्तोऽप्युभयविच्छेषं युक्तं समाचरेत् ।। अनुशासन १६४.४ ।।

With providence and time adverse, persevere still in dharma. *That is the mark of intelligence and wisdom.*[115]

A similar objection to Time being the causal ground of every event is mounted at another place, too—in a conversation between a bird, Pūjanī, and a king Brahmadatta, between whom a most distressful event had taken place.[116] Pūjanī was a rare bird, who understood human languages, lived in the royal palace, and had been for many years a companion to the king. She would every morning fly to a distant place, and bring from there two pieces of a rare fruit, one for the king's little son, and the other for hers. Both children grew strong on that magic fruit. One day, while Pūjanī was away, the little prince, playing with the little bird, smashed him on the floor and killed him. On her return, seeing what had happened, Pūjanī, blinded with grief and anger, took out the eyes of the prince by her deadly claws, saying 'What an ungrateful, cruel, untrustworthy wretch this prince turned out to be.' And then she told the king she would live there no longer and was going away. Brahmadatta had in him a strong sense of justice, and concluded that his little boy's cruel karma invited instant punishment, which was just and right. He sought reconciliation with Pūjanī the bird by invoking several arguments, one of which was that since Time, *kāla*, is the prime mover of everything, who could then be held guilty to whom?

कालेन क्रियते कार्यं तथैव विविधाः क्रियाः ।
कालेनैते प्रवर्तन्ते कः कस्येहापराध्यति ।। शान्ति १३९.४९ ।।

Pūjanī! Time alone is the prime mover, and all events are owing to Time. Who is then guilty to whom?[117]

नाहं प्रमाणं नैव त्वमन्योन्यं कारणं शुभे।
कालो नित्यमुपादत्ते सुखं दुःखं च देहिनाम्।। शान्ति १३९.५२।।

In this hurt that we have caused each other, neither are you the cause, nor am I the occasion. It is Time that generates happiness and sorrow for all beings.[118]

एवं वसेह सस्नेहा यथाकाममहिंसिता।
यत् कृतं तत् तु मे क्षान्तं त्वं च वै क्षम पूजनि।। शान्ति १३९.५३।।

Pūjanī! I will not hurt you in any way. Live here as you please, as always, with much affection. I have forgiven what you did, and you now forgive whatever I might have done.[119]

After giving him several reasons from her perspective as to why, after what had happened, she ought not to stay with him any longer,[120] Pūjanī feels sufficiently detached to engage King Brahmadatta as regards his belief in Time as the cause of everything.

यदि कालः प्रमाणं ते न वैरं कस्यचिद् भवेत्।
कस्मात् त्वपचितिं यान्ति बान्धवा बान्धवैर्हतैः।। शान्ति १३९.५४।।

If you consider Time to be the cause of all acts, then there should be no such thing as enmity. And why do then relatives seek revenge when their near ones are killed?[121]

कस्माद् देवासुराः पूर्वमन्योन्यमभिजघ्निरे।
यदि कालेन निर्याणं सुखं दुःखं भवाभवौ।। शान्ति १३९.५५।।

If life and death, pleasure and pain, have Time as their cause, then why did the devas *and the* asuras *in the past kill each other?*[122]

भिषजो भैषजं कर्तुं कस्मादिच्छन्ति रोगिणः।
यदि कालेन पच्यन्ते भेषजैः किं प्रयोजनम्।। शान्ति १३९.५६।।

Why do physicians prescribe medicines for those who are ill? If Time is burning all beings, then what good are the medicines?[123]

प्रलापः सुमहान् कस्मात् क्रियते शोकमूर्च्छितैः।
यदि कालः प्रमाणं ते कस्माद् धर्मोऽस्ति कर्तृषु।। शान्ति १३९.५७।।

If you consider Time to be the prime cause of everything, then why do human beings grieve so exceedingly, and lament so loudly? And also why should there be, in that case, prescriptions and prohibitions in observing dharma*?*[124]

तव पुत्रो ममापत्यं हतवान् स हतो मया।
अनन्तरं त्वयाहं च हन्तव्या हि नराधिप।। शान्ति १३९.५८।।

Your son killed my son, and I clawed the eyes of your son and blinded him. And now, you will kill me.[125]

The conversation between the king and the bird continues. It now focuses on the fearful question whether either of them could hereafter trust the other. Rejecting the *Time* theory as an inadequate explanation for things happening the way they happen, Pūjanī puts forth a strong plea, as Bhīshma had, for human effort and action, *purushārtha*, instead.

दैवं पुरुषकारश्च स्थितावन्योन्यसंश्रयात्।
उदाराणां तु सत्कर्म दैवं क्लीबा उपासते।। शान्ति १३९.८२।।

Fate and human effort depend on each other. However, the liberally endowed persevere in beneficial acts; the impotent, worship fate.[126]

कर्म चात्महितं कार्यं तीक्ष्णं वा यदि वा मृदु।
ग्रस्यतेऽकर्मशीलस्तु सदानर्थैरकिञ्चनः।। शान्ति १३९.८३।।

Hard or gentle, let one do what is to one's good. The one who gives up endeavour invites poverty and disaster.[127]

तस्मात् सर्वं व्यपोह्यार्थं कार्य एव पराक्रमः।
सर्वस्वमपि संत्यज्य कार्यमात्महितं नरैः।। शान्ति १३९.८४।।

Therefore, not depending on Time, or on fate, or on innate disposition of things, one should by all means do what is good for one.[128]

विद्या शौर्यं च दाक्ष्यं च बलं धैर्यं च पञ्चमम्।
मित्राणि सहजान्याहुर्वर्तयन्तीह तैर्बुधाः।। शान्ति १३९.८५।।

Knowledge, bravery, competence, strength—and patience: these are the five natural friends of man. It is through them that the wise do what they do.[129]

Pūjanī the bird ends the long association she had with King Brahmadatta, and leaves, still full of sadness at her son's death. But before she leaves, she offers some fundamental principles of good governance as her parting gift to the king.[130] We will return to them in the following chapter on *dharma* as the foundation of law and governance.

Svabhāva, innate disposition

The theory of *svabhāva*, 'innate disposition', or 'nature of things', or 'property of things', was another way of explaining the diversity of creation and events.[131] Things are what they are on account of their innate disposition; there is no cause outside them; they are self-determined. Events are accounted for by the nature of things. *Svabhāva*, and not human endeavour as such, is the source of all that happens, which is not to say that endeavour is excluded from *svabhāva*. Those who believed in *svabhāva* shared,[132] with *providence* theory and *Time* theory, the argument that if man were the master of his destiny, he would succeed in all that he did. The experience is that so far from achieving what they did desire, men's actions bring them to grief: where is the force, then, in human exertion?[133] It is nothing but ignorance that makes a man regard his actions alone as being responsible for his situation, when all happenings, happy or unhappy, flow from the innate disposition of things.[134] Once this is understood, there is place neither for pride nor for grief.[135]

Svabhāva, as a theory of causation, is the theory of the inner teleology of nature. It had its adherents in various philosophical schools, such as the Sāṃkhya, the Lokāyata, and in the schools of ancient Indian medicine, Āyur-veda. The Sāṃkhya traces the origin of the world to the constant tension among the three forces, *sattva*, *rajas*, and *tamas*, always found together, their totality called *prakṛiti*, Nature. To put it simply, *sattva* is intelligence-energy; *rajas* is action-energy; and *tamas* is confusion. As long as the force of any one of them is equal to the other two, there is no creation, no movement, all three held in a balanced tension. The moment that balance is disturbed, things start happening. Their combination in different proportions, with virtually countless possibilities, then determines the *svabhāva* of a thing, giving it the limits within which it moves and lives. To say that a thing is self-determined is to point to its innate *svabhāva*, over which the human will has no control. Neither is it subject to any arbitrary moral government. But this does not imply chaos in nature. It only means that it has its own teleology that cannot be forced into moral categories. The function of science is to understand the innate disposition of things and individuals.

According to the Sāṃkhya theory of *svabhāva* as propounded in the *Mahābhārata*,[136] the mind invariably carries within itself the three energies, *sattva*, *rajas*, and *tamas*. To each of these are attributed a separate cluster of *feelings*.[137]

सत्त्वं रजस्तमश्चैव प्राणिनां संश्रिताः सदा।
त्रिविधा वेदना चैव सर्वसत्त्वेषु दृश्यते।। शान्ति १९४.२९।।

सात्त्विकी राजसी चैव तामसी चेति भारत।
सुखस्पर्शः सत्त्वगुणो दुःखस्पर्शो रजोगुणः।
तमोगुणेन संयुक्तौ भवतोऽव्यावहारिकौ।। शान्ति १९४.३०।।

तत्र यद् प्रीतिसंयुक्तं काये मनसि वा भवेत्।
वर्तते सात्त्विको भाव इत्याचक्षीत तत् तथा।। शान्ति १९४.३१।।

अथ यद् दुःखसंयुक्तमप्रीतिकरमात्मनः।
प्रवृत्तं रज इत्येव तन्न संरभ्य चिन्तयेत्।। शान्ति १९४.३२।।
अथ यन्मोहसंयुक्तमव्यक्तविषयं भवेत्।
अप्रतर्क्यमविज्ञेयं तमस्तदुपधारयेत्।। शान्ति १९४.३३।।

प्रहर्षः प्रीतिरानन्दः सुखं संशान्तचित्तता।
कथंचिदभिवर्तन्त इत्येते सात्त्विका गुणाः।। शान्ति १९४.३४।।

अतुष्टिः परितापश्च शोको लोभस्तथाक्षमा।
लिगांनि रजसस्तानि दृश्यन्ते हेत्वहेतुभिः।। शान्ति १९४.३५।।
अवमानस्तथा मोहः प्रमादः स्वप्नतन्द्रिता।
कथंचिदभिवर्तन्ते विविधास्तामसा गुणाः।। शान्ति १९४.३६।।

The feelings, with or without cause, of happiness, love, delight, and peace are sattvic, *the feelings of discontent, sorrow, regret, greed and intolerance are* rajasic; *of lack of respect, confusion, sloth and sleepiness,* tamasic.[138]

Sometimes the mind experiences cheerfulness, clarity, and happiness; at other times unhappiness; and sometimes only confusion, neither clearly happiness nor clearly unhappiness.[139]

Happiness is the outcome of sattva. *Discord, strife, unhappiness, arise from* rajas. *And confusion is produced by* tamas. *All conceivable feelings are contained within these three.*[140]

These general types of dispositions are found on their own accord in all beings; and they may then be characterised accordingly.[141]

> *Whenever, without any apparent cause, one has a feeling of happiness or clarity, it may be interpreted as an infusion of* sattva *into the mind. A sudden feeling of vague unhappiness, or depression, is to be attributed to the activity of* rajas*: in the moments where nothing is clear, nor anything seems to have any logic, and nothing makes any sense, it is certain that the force of* tamas *has overpowered one.*[142]

Added to these non-theistic categories comprising the physical world, the concepts of *buddhi*, *ahamkāra*, and *manas*, approximately translated as 'the discriminating faculty', 'the ego', and 'the mind', completed the psychological apparatus with which the Sāṃkhya explained the diversity of created beings. The interaction among human beings and its varying quality could be understood only in terms of different *svabhāva*. The diverse circumstances of human beings could be traced to the natural and constant reaction among them, each individual with its own *svabhāva*, determined by the relative dominance of one or the other of the three forces, *sattva* and *rajas* and *tamas*. That is to say, the human situation could be explained in human and natural terms, without recourse to any cause, *daiva*, or *kāla*, or 'God', outside and beyond man.

The science of ancient Indian medicine treated, therefore, disorders, *doṣa*, of the body and mind, strictly in psychophysical terms, tracing every disease to the three *gunas*, in their relation with the natural environment, active in an individual. According to Surendranath Dasgupta, 'Āyur-veda is closely associated with the Sāṃkhya and the Nyāya-Vaiśeṣika, which alone deal with sort of physics in Indian philosophy.'[143] He refers to the *Vivaraṇa-siddhānta-cintāmaṇi* of Narasiṃha Kavirāja, who maintained that, according to Sāṃkhya, 'it is the *doṣa* transforming itself from a state of equilibrium to a state of unbalanced preponderance of any of them that is to be called a disease.'[144] The analysis of the disorders of the mind is among the most scientific part of Āyur-veda. Dasgupta quotes Śuṣruta as saying that even in the medical school, some attributed creation to 'Time', *kāla*; some to the natural processes of *niyati*, blind destiny, some others to *svabhāva*, the nature of things; some to *yadṛcchā*, mere accident; and some others to *pariṇāma*, evolution by the will of God—each calling these causes *prakṛiti*, nature.[145] Since this would appear to go against the indisputable fact that the theory of *svabhāva* constituted the theoretical framework of Āyur-veda, Dasgupta adds by way of explanation:

> *'The primary use of prakṛiti may have been due to the idea of an enquiry regarding the source and origin of the world. Prakṛiti literally means "source" or "origin". So the term was probably used in reference to other speculations regarding the origin of the world before it was technically applied as a Sāṃkhya term. The ideas of svabhāva, kāla, etc. seem to have been combined to form the technical Sāṃkhya concept of prakṛiti, and the two schools of Sāṃkhya, the Kapila and the Patañjali schools, arose in connection with the dispute as to the starting of the evolution of prakṛ iti accidentally (yadṛcchā) or by the will of God. The idea of prakṛiti was reached by combining all the alternative sources of world-manifestation that were current before, and so they are all conserved in the notion of prakṛiti.*[146]

In two separate conversations, one between the Sāṃkhya philosopher Pañchashikha and King Janaka, and the other between Indra and Prahlāda, the *Mahābhārata* speaks of the innate dispositions, *svabhāva*, as the cause of everything. Indra asks Prahlāda whether it was from self-knowledge or from some other sustaining power that he had that extraordinary steadiness of the mind even in his extreme adversity.[147] Prahlāda says:

स्वभावत् सम्प्रवर्तन्ते निवर्तन्ते तथैव च।
सर्वे भावास्तथाभावा: पुरुषार्थो न विद्यते।। शान्ति २२२.१५।।

What is and what is-not, both originate in the innate disposition, svabhāva, *of things. Human effort plays no real part in them.*[148]

पुरुषार्थस्य चाभावे नास्ति कश्चिच्च कारक:।
स्वमं न कुर्वतस्तस्य जातु मानो भवेदिह।। शान्ति २२२.१६।।

However, even though human effort is not the cause of what happens, man derives the false notion of his being its cause.[149]

यस्तु कर्तारमात्मानं मन्यते साध्वसाधु वा।
तस्य दोषवती प्रज्ञा अतत्त्वज्ञेति मे मति:।। शान्ति २२२.१७।।

In my opinion, anyone who thinks himself to be the cause of the good or of the ill is of defective intelligence and of little understanding.[150]

यदि स्यात् पुरुष: कर्ता शक्रात्मश्रेयसे ध्रुवम्।
आरम्भास्तस्य सिद्ध्येयुर्न तु जातु परा भवेत्।। शान्ति २२२.१८।।

If man were the cause, then he would achieve success in whatever he did for his good; and he would know no failure.[151]

अनिष्टस्य हि निर्वृत्तिरनिर्वृतिः प्रियस्य च।
लक्ष्यते यतमानानां पुरुषार्थस्ततः कुतः।। शान्ति २२२.१९।।
But it can be seen everywhere that far from achieving what is desired, what one gets is the very opposite. Where, then, is human effort?[152]

अनिष्टस्याभिनिर्वृत्तिमिष्टसंवृत्तिमेव च।
अप्रयत्नेन पश्यामः केषाञ्चित् तत्स्वभावतः।। शान्ति २२२.२०।।

स्वभावप्रेरिताः सर्वे निविशन्ते गुणा यदा।
शुभाशुभास्तदा तत्र कस्य किं मानकारणम्।। शान्ति २२२.२२।।
We can see how, without effort, one loses the desired and gets what was not desired. Both happen due to the innate disposition of things. When the good and the ill alike happen due to the given dispositions, then why should man consider himself to be their cause?[153]

स्वभावादेव तत्सर्वमिति मे निश्चिता मतिः।
आत्मप्रतिष्ठा प्रज्ञा वा मम नास्ति ततोऽन्यथा।। शान्ति २२२.२३।।
I am of the considered view that everything originates in svabhāva. *The faculty of understanding within me does not lead me to a different view either.*[154]

स्वभावभाविनो भावान् सर्वानेवेह निश्चयात्।
बुद्ध्यमानस्य दर्पो वा मानो वा किं करिष्यति।। शान्ति २२२.२७।।
It is certain that all things originate in the innate nature of things. Whoever can see this clearly will be affected neither by pride nor by arrogance.[155]

To the mixture of effort and providence, by definition uncertain as to its precise composition, was added the 'innate nature of things' as the third factor. All this meant that human effort, best made after analysing the nature of persons and situations, was still subject to unseen factors. Thus, there could never be absolute predictions about human affairs, and there was in them necessarily a factor of uncertainty. That factor was called *daiva*.

Excepting the theory of *purushārtha*, all the rest, *daiva*, *kāla*, *niyati*, *svabhāva*, in their extreme as well as in their moderate forms, according to

Gopinath Kavirāj,[156] 'were collateral and had a community of origin. They were all non-theistic assumptions, which had arisen in attempting to find out an explanation of the appearance and disappearance of phenomena. All were more or less of a determinist cast.'[157] What is more, they all had in common their rejection of the principle of 'efficient causation'. Unlike *karma* theory, they denied freedom of will; and there was in them no place for God, and *karma* theory was one with them in *this*.

The question of accountability in what happens

The question of one's accountability for what one does is intimately connected with the question of causality. *If* it has been predetermined by Fate, or by Time, or by Providence, or by God's will, by whichever of these forces over and above me, what I shall *be*, and what course my life shall take, then I was never a free agent in doing what I did, nor shall ever be. In that event, nothing can survive of the fundamental assumption in all relationships: that I am accountable *for*, and responsible *to*, the way I choose to relate and act. Since that cannot survive, man can only live as a creature with neither freedom nor dignity, because controlled by the will of some other, *parādhīna*, from the beginning to the end. *Dharma* and truth, both in their relational sense, can have meaning only if the freedom of the will is assumed unquestionably. Where that is in question, *dharma* and truth will be in question, too.

The question of accountability runs through the whole of the *Mahābhārata*. For it is a question that runs through the whole of human life.

It did equally in the story of Gautamī, an old woman, her only son bitten by a snake and falling dead.[158] Arjunaka, a hunter, grieved at the death of the old woman's only son, caught that snake, bound it with a long cord, and brought it to Gautamī. 'This is the snake that caused your son's death. Tell me how shall I kill it? Throw it into a fire? Or cut it into pieces? In killing a boy, this wicked snake doesn't deserve to live anymore.'

Gautamī

> Arjunaka! Leave this snake free! You shall not kill it. What was destined to happen, happened. Knowing this, who will want to carry the burden of the sin in killing it?
> By killing it, my son will not come back to life. And what harm will it cause you if this snake lives? Then why destroy another life?[159]

The Hunter

Wise lady! I know that is how good people will feel. But the lesson that you are preaching is for those who are in a happy state. No, I will kill this snake. Those who seek peace attribute to Time the cause of every happening, and become reconciled thereby. But those who take revenge, come to peace in that way. Once this snake is killed, you also will.[160]

Gautamī

My son was destined to die; therefore I would not kill this snake. The brahmanas are free from anger. How can they, from anger, then cause pain to another? You, too, forgive this snake, and let him free. What is gained by killing an enemy held in captivity? And what purpose is served by not letting free an enemy in one's hands? Why should I not forgive this snake, and why should I not secure its release? It is not that by killing it, my son will be restored to life. And I can see no other gain in killing it.[161]

The Hunter

But neither can you gain any good by keeping this wicked snake alive. Force is to be answered with force. Many other lives can be saved by killing this snake. It is not right to put other lives in danger by protecting one life. Therefore let me kill it.[162]

Gautamī refuses to be persuaded. At this point, the snake, writhing in pain, speaks in human voice. The following argument takes place between him and the hunter, the latter determined to kill him.

The Snake *(to the Hunter)*

Arjunaka! I am not accountable for the death of that boy. Not from any desire of mine, but because I was prompted by Death to do so. I stung the boy, and he died. I am not a free agent, controlled by another. The accountability is not mine; it is that of Death.[163]

The Hunter *(to the Snake)*

Supposing your wrongdoing was owing to the fact that you were under the control of another, it is *you* who actually committed the crime, and are therefore guilty. Just as the potter's wheel and his rotating stick are accessory causes in the production of a pot, so are you a cause in this boy's death, which you admit you are, and deserve to be killed for what you did.[164]

The Snake *(to the Hunter)*

Arjunaka! From undeniable facts you are drawing wrong conclusions. In your own example, the wheel and the stick are not free agents, but under the control of the potter. Likewise, I am under the control of Death. Therefore your indictment of me is not just. If, as you say, even the accessories who act under the will of another are causes nonetheless, it raises a serious doubt as to who is then mainly accountable—the abettor, the prompter, or the completely dependent accessories? Besides, if you still think someone to be guilty, then that guilt has to apply to the whole group of causes, and not just to any one of them. In these circumstances, I alone am neither guilty nor accountable.[165]

The Hunter *(to the Snake)*

If your argument is accepted, that even after committing a crime its doer has no accountability for it, then the robbers and the murderers can never be punished. You are just trying to be clever.[166]

The Snake *(to the Hunter)*

Hunter! Whether, or not, the prompter, the abetter, is also the doer, it is true that without the actual doer no act can take place. Even so, although Death and I are equally causes in this boy's death, because I actually caused it, I still hold Death to be mainly accountable, being the prompter, the abettor. You are mistaken in thinking that I am the cause of the boy's death. If you think carefully, it will be the prompter, the Death, who will be held culpable.[167]

The snake repeatedly exonerating himself, and transferring the culpability for the boy's death to Death; *mrityu,* Death, appears on the scene. She addresses the Snake and says

Death

I was prompted by *Kāla,* Time, to prompt you to sting the boy. Neither am I the cause in this young boy's death nor are you the cause; it is Time who is the cause.

यथा वायुर्जलधरान् विकर्षति ततस्ततः ।
तद्वज्जलदवत् सर्प कालस्याहं वशानुगः ।। अनुशासन १.५१ ।।

Just as the wind drives the clouds hither and thither, I am, like those clouds, under the control of Time.[168]

सात्त्विका राजसाश्चैव तामसा ये च केचन ।
भावाः कालात्मकाः सर्वे प्रवर्तन्ते हि जन्तुषु ।। अनुशासन १.५२ ।।

Whatever human energies there are, of sattva, rajas, *and* tamas, *they are suffused with Time, and come to all beings accordingly.*[169]

जङ्गमाः स्थावराश्चैव दिवि वा यदि वा भुवि ।
सर्वे कालात्मकाः सर्प कालात्मकमिदं जगत् ।। अनुशासन १.५३ ।।

All that moves on this earth and in the next world, is controlled by Time. This world is in the nature of Time.[170]

प्रवृत्तयश्च लोकेऽस्मिंस्तथैव च निवृत्तयः ।
तासां विकृतयो याश्च सर्वं कालात्मकं स्मृतम् ।। अनुशासन १.५४ ।।

All human acts in their diversity, and in their manifold results, are only as many forms of Time.[171]

आदित्यश्चन्द्रमा विष्णुरापो वायुः शतक्रतुः ।
अग्निः खं पृथिवी मित्रः पर्जन्यो वसवोऽदितिः ।। अनुशासन १.५५ ।।
सरितः सागराश्चैव भावाभावौ च पन्नग ।
सर्वे कालेन सृज्यन्ते ह्रियन्ते च पुनः पुनः ।। अनुशासन १.५६ ।।

The sun, the moon, the water, the wind, the fire, the space, the earth, the rivers, the sea, the friends, and the strangers, that which is, and that which is not—*all these are the creations of Time, and by Time destroyed.*[172]

एवं ज्ञात्वा कथं मां त्वं सदोषं सर्प मन्यसे ।
अथ चैवंगते दोषे मयि त्वमपि दोषवान् ।। अनुशासन १.५७ ।।

Snake! Knowing all this, how can you hold me *culpable? If culpability can still attach to me, then you are culpable no less.*[173]

The Snake

Mrityu! I neither say that you are guilty, nor do I say that you are not guilty. All that I am saying is that you prompted me to cause the boy's death by stinging him.

Whether *Time* is culpable, or he too is not guilty, is not for me to examine. Neither do I have the competence to do so.

I have by all means to defend myself from the accusation brought against me. It is not my aim that, in doing that, Death's culpability be established.[174]

Arjunaka! You heard what Death said. You have now no justification to keep me tied like this and cause me pain.[175]

The Hunter

Yes! I have heard what Death said and what you said. But there is nothing in that which exonerates you. In this boy's death I hold both you and Death to be equally culpable. Shame on this cruel-hearted Death who keeps creating pain and suffering all around. And you—were a cause, too. I am going to kill you.[176]

Death repeats her ontological, moral, and even legal, arguments that when a person acts as he does, being wholly under the control of another force, as both she and the Snake did, then that is a good reason for being exonerated of the culpability for a crime he committed.[177] The Hunter then asks: 'In that case, if both you and the Snake are wholly controlled by Time, and can do nothing as a free agent, then *why* do I, a disinterested observer, feel happy when someone does good to another, and angry when he does ill to another? I want to know that.'[178]

Since Death transfers all accountability for her doings on to Time, as the Snake had transferred to Death the accountability that was his, and the issue that is raised is a serious one no doubt, Time appears on the scene. He addresses the Snake, the Hunter, and Death, as follows:

Time

न ह्यहं नाप्ययं मृत्युर्नायं लुब्धक पन्नगः ।
किल्बिषी जन्तुमरणे न वयं हि प्रयोजकाः ।। अनुशासन १.७० ।।

Hunter! Neither am I accountable for the death of this person, nor is Death accountable, nor is the Snake accountable. In no one's death are we prompters, or agents, or causes.[179]

यदनेन कृतं कर्म तेनायं निधनं गतः ।
विनाशहेतुः कर्मास्य सर्वे कर्मवशा वयम् ।। अनुशासन १.७२ ।।

कर्मदायादवाँल्लोकः कर्मसम्बन्धलक्षणः।
कर्माणि चोदयन्तीह यथान्योन्यं तथा वयम्।। अनुशासन १.७३।।
Arjunaka! It is what the boy did, his own karma, *that caused his death; none other was the cause of his death. The living being himself causes his death. In this world, it is one's own* karma *that follows one: and it is* karma *that is an attribute of all relations. We all are under the control of our* karma.[180]

यथा मृत्पिण्डतः कर्ता कुरुते यद् यदिच्छति।
एवमात्मकृतं कर्म मानवः प्रतिपद्यते।। अनुशासन १.७४।।
Just as, from the clay, a potter makes what he wishes, a person makes everything from his own karma.[181]

यथाच्छायातपौ नित्यं सुसम्बद्धौ निरन्तरम्।
तथा कर्म च कर्ता च सम्बद्धावात्मकर्मभिः।। अनुशासन १.७५।।
Just as the sunshine and the shadow are with each other related always, so are the doer and his karma.[182]

Hearing Time say this with authority, to whom has been attributed the awesome power of being the origin of all that *is* and all that *is not*, Gautamī is reconciled, and is free from grief, and says to the Hunter:

नैव कालो न भुजगो न मृत्युरिह कारणम्।
स्वकर्मभिरयं बालः कालेन निधनं गतः।। अनुशासन १.७८।।
मया च तत् कृतं तत् कृतं येनायं मे मृतः सुतः।
यातु कालस्तथा मृत्युर्मुञ्चार्जुनक पन्नगम्।। अनुशासन १.७९।।
'Arjunaka! Let the Snake go. I am convinced that my son died as a consequence of his karma. *And that my son died was my* karma *as well. No one else was the cause in that.' Thereafter, departed Death, departed Time, departed the Snake, as they came.*[183]

The *Mahābhārata* takes up in several other contexts as well the question of the accountability for one's acts. At the end of the war, won by the Pāṇḍava-s but not without devastation of the greatest magnitude, Yudhishṭhira is wracked with grief and holds himself accountable for what had happened.[184] He acknowledges his guilt in the killings of Bhīshma and Droṇāchārya by means that were foul.[185] 'For gaining this kingdom I have had those killed who ought never to have been touched. Those acts of mine are burning me with guilt.'[186] He announces his decision to end his life.[187]

At this point Vyāsa consoles him that he need feel neither accountable for what had happened, nor feel wracked with guilt. In his voice the *Mahābhārata* then says, addressing of ccurse a person deeply distressed, but addressing equally the question of causality and, connected with it, the moral question of accountability: On the question of the accountability for the killings, there can be four different views.

ईश्वरो वा भवेत् कर्ता पुरुषो वापि भरत।
हठो वा वर्तते लोके कर्मजं वा फलं स्मृतम्।। शान्ति ३२.१२।।

One, what happens, happens by the will of God. Or, two, the individual is accountable for his acts. Or, three, the accountability is upon the very nature of the situation. Or, four, it is one's fate in the form of one's accumulated karma, *in which lies the cause of every happening.*[188]

One

ईश्वरेण नियुक्तो हि साध्वसाधु च भारत।
कुरुते पुरुषः कर्म फलमीश्वरगामि तत्।। शान्ति ३२.१३।।

If it is God's will that prompts man to do what he does, good or evil, then the accountability for it belongs to God and not to man.

यथा हि पुरुषश्छिन्द्याद् वृक्षं परशुना वने।
छेत्तुरेव भवेत् पापं परशोर्न कथञ्चन।। शान्ति ३२.१४।।

When a man cuts a green tree in the woods with his axe, the sin attaches to the man wielding the axe and not to the axe.

अथवा तदुपादानात् प्राप्नुयात् कर्मणः फलम्।
दण्डशस्त्रकृतं पापं पुरुषे तन्न विद्यते।। शान्ति ३२.१५।।

It may also be said that the maker of the axe is accountable in the first place, for it is he who had put the axe in the hands of the man who cut that green tree. In that case, it will not be right to hold the cutter of the tree accountable, for had there been no axe, there would have been no cutting.

न चैतदिष्टं कौन्तेय यदन्येन कृतं फलम्।
प्राप्नुयादिति यस्माच्च ईश्वरे तन्निवेशय।। शान्ति ३२.१६।।

It is not right that for someone's act somebody else should face the consequence. For what happens, the good or the evil, place the accountability then upon God, who is the prime cause of everything.[189]

Two

अथापि पुरुषः कर्ता कर्मणोः शुभपापयोः।
न परो विद्यते तस्मादेवमेतच्छुभं कृतम्।। शान्ति ३२.१७।।

न हि कश्चित् क्वचिद् राजन् दिष्ट प्रतिनिवर्तते।
दण्डशस्त्रकृतं पापं पुरुषे तन्न विद्यते।। शान्ति ३२.१८।।

Should you hold that it is the individual who is wholly accountable for his acts, good or ill, and none else, then, too, no one can anywhere transgress what, in the form of their accumulated bad karma, *providence has writ for him.*[190]

Three

यदि वा मन्यसे राजन् हतमेकं प्रतिष्ठितम्।
एवमप्यशुभं कर्म न भूतं न भविष्यति।। शान्ति ३२.१९।।

If you believe that what happens, happens due to the inherent nature of situations, then, in a situation of war, it is natural that either the one or the other of the two warriors will die. It was a result of something beyond you in the past, as it will be beyond you in the future.[191]

Four

अथाभिपत्तिर्लोकस्य कर्तव्या पुण्यपापयोः।
अभिपन्नमिदं लोके राज्ञामुद्यतदण्डनम्।। शान्ति ३२.२०।।

You may say that what a person gets, the happy or the unhappy, is to be traced to its cause in any event, for nothing happens without a cause, and that cause is one's own acts. Then also you'll have to hold that the wrong deeds of those people had accumulated in the form of their fate. And in their destruction you had done, moreover, what your duties of governance required you to do.[192]

None of this meant that the main question of causality had been settled. Vyāsa did not pretend that it had been. For that reason he once again, as his work the *Mahābhārata* does throughout, talks of different views on this subject, one incompatible with another, but each with irrefutable logic. Here he was mainly concerned that Yudhishthira does not kill himself. And he reasons with him.

स्वधर्मे वर्तमानस्य सापवादेऽपि भारत।
एवमात्मपरित्यागस्तव राजन् न शोभनः।। शान्ति ३२.२३।।

Assuming what in your present station you must do, your dharma, *has defects in it, that is no good reason for a man like you to end your life.*[193]

विहितानि हि कौन्तेय प्रायश्चित्तानि कर्मणाम्।
शरीरवांस्तानि कुर्यादशरीरः पराभवेत्।। शान्ति ३२.२४।।

There is a provision for expiating one's wrong deeds, but that one can do only if one keeps one's body alive.[194]

तद् राजन् जीवमानस्त्वं प्रायश्चित्तं करिष्यसि।
प्रायश्चित्तमकृत्वा तु प्रेत्य तप्तासि भारत।। शान्ति ३२.२५।।

If you live, you can seek expiation. If you die without it, you will be a troubled man in the life hereafter.[195]

Like Yudhishṭhira, Dhritarāshṭra, the old blind king, was a troubled man even at the beginning of the war, and even more troubled at the end of it, all his sons having been killed. Sañjaya, his exceptionally gifted reporter, with the miraculous gift of seeing everything from far away, would report to the blind king the daily events on the battlefield. On hearing Sañjaya narrate the killing of young Abhīmanyu, Arjuna's son, Dhritarāshṭra is full of dread of what would certainly follow by way of punishment for the young prince's treacherous killing by the six great warriors on the side of the Kaurava-s. He begins to lament and hold his eldest son Duryodhana wholly accountable for behaving towards his first cousins, the Pāṇḍava-s, in a manner that had made the war inevitable.[196] He recalls his many admonitions to his son to behave differently, all spurned. 'If he had only listened to my advice, if he had only paid heed to what was said to him by those venerable men of the realm, and had made peace with his cousins, all these dreadful happenings would not be happening. He chose to follow his wicked friends instead.' He asks Sañjaya to report the doings of 'that greedy, lustful for the kingdom, unwise, wicked, and demented son of mine'.[197]

Sañjaya (*to Dhritarāshṭra*)

If you will care to listen to what I say, in all this your own injustice is the cause. Your laments now are of no use, just as it is no use building a dam after all the water has flowed away.[198]

You had already taken over the kingdom. And then, what was

further added to it by your elder brother's sons, you usurped even that. Your own greed was limitless. It isn't right that, confronted with a disaster, you now blame your son.[199]

You *could* have disciplined your son Duryodhana by one means or another. You didn't, to further your own selfish ends. You deprived the Pāṇḍava-s of their rightful inheritance. They were then subjected to all kinds of humiliation. You could have prevented that. You didn't. Even at the point when it all came to the war you could have stopped it. You didn't.[200]

I've heard your laments, King. They are like honey laced with poison.[201]

For that devastating war, the accountability continued being transferred from one to another, either in self-reproach or in reproaching the *other*—the familiar human habit that the *Mahābhārata* recounts. It ended with Queen Gāndhārī, the mother of the Kaurava-s, holding Krishna entirely accountable for the war. Describing the heart-wrenching scenes after the last battle was over, and weeping inconsolably,[202] Gāndhārī turns to Krishna, her whole body shaking now with anger, and says to him:

शक्तेन बहुभृत्येन विपुले तिष्ठता बले।
उभयत्र समर्थेन श्रुतवाक्येन चैव ह।। स्त्री २५.४०।।

इच्छतोपेक्षितो नाशः कुरूणां मधुसूदन।
यस्मात् त्वया महाबाहो फलं तस्मादवाप्नुहि।। स्त्री २५.४१।।

You could have prevented all this from happening, but you didn't. You let the destruction of this family take place.[203]

पतिशुश्रूषया यन्मे तपः किंचिदुपार्जितम्।
तेन त्वां दुरवापेन शप्स्ये चक्रगदाधर।। स्त्री २५.४२।।

If I have earned any merit in living the way I have, then with the force of that merit I curse you.[204]

त्वमप्युपस्थिते वर्षे षट्त्रिंशे मधुसूदन।
हतज्ञातिर्हतामात्यो हतपुत्रो वनेचरः।। स्त्री २५.४४।।
अनाथवदविज्ञातो लोकेष्वनभिलक्षितः।
कुत्सितेनाभ्युपायेन निधनं समवाप्स्यसि।। स्त्री २४.४५।।

In the thirty-sixth year from now, your sons and your relatives and your

advisers will likewise die fighting each other.
You will drift in the deep woods, unseen, unknown, alone, helpless. And you will die a mean death.
As the women of the Bhārata clan are weeping now, the women of your family will likewise weep over their dead.[205]

On hearing these severe words of Gāndhārī, Krishna says to her, smiling somewhat: 'You are only pronouncing in advance what I know is going to happen.'[206] But he doesn't stop with this. He turns upon the sorrow-wracked, grieving Gāndhārī, and, in equally hard and bitter words, accuses her of transferring to *him* the accountability that properly belonged to *her* for not restraining her 'wicked-hearted, vain and jealous, cruel and arrogant, disobedient and disregarding, contemptuous son Duryodhana. How can you blame me for what you should blame yourself for? You are wholly accountable for the destruction of the Kuru clan.'[207]

As every happening in human life does, every happening in the *Mahābhārata* is saying many other things at the same time, apart from itself. And it is left to the self-aware reader to make out what they all are. Here, in this event, too. Put aside the knotted question of causality. Put aside the equally knotted question of culpability. Here was the plain requirement of compassion and grace, kindness and gentle speech, to a sorrowing mother, no matter what her sons might have been like. The *Mahābhārata* portrays Krishna having in him none of these towards her. But he had none of these towards the tragic Karna,[208] or towards the dying Duryodhana, either.[209]

Soon after Duryodhana was killed in the last battle between him and Bhīmasena, in a straight battle by mace, but in a way that was on the part of Bhīma in complete violation of a cardinal rule of such contest, Krishna proclaimed his accountability, though not his culpability. Speaking to Yudhishṭhira, he admitted, but without regret for what he declared was a necessity, that the war could never have been won for the Pāṇḍava-s except through means that were deceitful.[210]

नैष शक्योऽतिशीघ्रास्त्रस्ते च सर्वे महारथा: ।
ऋजुयुद्धेन विक्रान्ता हन्तुं युष्माभिराहवे ।। शल्य ६१.६१ ।।

नैष शक्य: कदाचित् तु हन्तुं धर्मेण पार्थिव: ।
ते वा भीष्ममुखा: सर्वे महेष्वासा महारथा: ।। शल्य ६१.६२ ।।

You never could have, by using fair means, killed Duryodhana, Bhīshma, Droṇa, Karṇa, and Bhūrishrava, great warriors all. Not all the protectors of the world could have, together, conquered any of them by fighting in a way that dharma *would demand one ought.*[211]

Therefore,

मयानेकैरुपायैस्तु मायायोगेन चासकृत् ।
हतास्ते सर्व एवाजौ भवतां हितमिच्छता ।। शल्य ६१.६३ ।।

Desiring your good, I repeatedly used deceitful means to have those great warriors overcome and killed.[212]

यदि नैवंविधं जातु कुर्यां जिह्ममहं रणे ।
कुतो वो विजयो भूयः कुतो राज्यं कुतो धनम् ।। शल्य ६१.६४ ।।

If I had not used in the war those thoroughly wrong means, how could you have had the victory, and the kingdom, and its wealth?[213]

Krishna was unashamedly advocating that the ends justify the means.

न च वो हृदि कर्तव्यं यदयं घातितो रिपुः ।
मिथ्यावध्यास्तथोपायैर्बहवः शत्रवोऽधिकाः ।। शल्य ६१.६७ ।।

You should not think too much about the way that the enemy was killed. Many enemies of greater strength have been killed in the past by using means that were full of lies and cunning.[214]

पूर्वैनुगतो मार्गो देवैरसुरघातिभिः ।
सद्भिश्चानुगतः पन्थाः स सर्वैनुगम्यते ।। शल्य ६१.६८ ।।

Why, even the gods[215] *took to that path in overcoming the* asura*-s. And the path followed by the great is the path that the others also take.*[216]

कृतकृत्याश्च सायाह्ने निवासं रोचयामहे ।
साश्वनागरथाः सर्वे विश्रमामो नराधिपाः ।। शल्य ६१.६९ ।।

Our work is accomplished. The dusk is falling, and I want to take rest.[217]

The entire *Mahābhārata* is about not only that the ends do *not* justify the means, but also about the nature of the ends themselves, in relation to one's self and the *other*.

Here, however, the question is that I can be accountable only if I have a free will. The determinist theories, logically viewed, rule out the individual's accountability in what happens. Everybody above had presupposed that if the *other* had behaved differently, the things would have been different. And that had further presupposed that the other *could* have behaved differently, for he, or she, was free to do so as a free human agent. But these were the very two presuppositions honestly in question.

Towards the end of the tragic drama, the *Mahābhārata*, narrating the seemingly endless chain of self-reproach and blaming the *other*, once again puts forth the belief that, in actual reality, no one person is accountable for what happens. It is some force over and above man, by whatever name you call it, 'Providence', 'Time', or 'God's will', that is the determining cause of everything. In this view, putting aside the conventional, there is room neither for self-reproach, nor room for blaming the *other*. For no one could have behaved differently than what he, or she, did. Although it reiterates only one position on the question of causality, and thereby on the question of personal accountability, it is saying at the same time many other things as well.

Dhritarāshṭra and his wife Gāndhārī, the parents of the slain Kaurava-s, are shown the utmost respect, and every consideration, by the victors, their nephews. After some time the sorrowing old couple decide to change the context of their lives, to make the forest their home. Kuntī, the mother of the Pāṇḍava-s, decides to spend the last days of her life with *them*. In a language, and in manners, that were heart-wrenching, they seek everybody's leave—of the people of the realm above all. For Dhritarāshṭra had been their king for many years, and there was between them a bond. They assemble in large numbers, persons of every social calling and of every status. What he seeks from them is their forgiveness first and foremost.

Dhritarāshṭra

I've decided with Gāndhārī to take to the forest.

We are old and weary. The grief of losing our sons is wrecking us, too. Besides, we've become very weak due to fasting.

There has been between you and us a very close bond of affection, such as not to be seen between other kings and their people. Allow me now to retire to the forest.

I've had much happiness in the kingdom of Yudhishṭhira, indeed, much greater happiness than I had in the glory of my son Duryodhana's rule.

> I'm blind by birth. I'm old. All of my sons have been killed. What better life for me can there be than to take to the forest? Allow me to leave.[218]

On hearing their former king say thus, the people are moved to tears.[219]

Dhritarāshṭra spoke again.

> After Pāṇḍu, my brother, I've served you, in ways good or bad. I seek your forgiveness for the errors there might have been.
> When Duryodhana had the sway of the realm, he, too, had caused no offence to you, though he was of a twisted mind.
> It was his arrogance, injustice, and twisted mind that caused the war in which many were killed, and the earth devastated.
> For my own acts at that time, good or ill, I seek with my hands folded, your forgiveness.
> At no time have you expressed your anger against me, and you have been loyal. I stand before you, my hands folded in salutation to you.
> Dear people! My sons were greedy, with no self-discipline, and minds unstable. With Gāndhārī I seek your forgiveness for the wrongs they did.
> I seek your forgiveness for whatever wrongs were done to you by my sons and by those connected with me.
> 'This King Dhritarāshṭra is old. All his sons have been killed, and he is drowned in grief. And he is a descendant of a long line of kings'—thinking thus, forgive his offences.
> Gāndhārī, too, weak and old and grieving for her sons dead, seeks your forgiveness as I do.
> Forgive these two old people, wracked by the grief of having lost all their sons. We seek refuge in you.[220]

There is complete silence; all those assembled there are far too moved for anyone to say anything.[221] And Dhritarāshṭra is still seeking from them both their forgiveness and their consent to what he and Gāndhārī propose to do.

People's forgiveness for the past: and people's consent to what a king proposes to do with his personal life. In being king, a king's life is not his personal life alone. It is connected with the lives of a great number of other people beyond him and his family.

Dhritarāshṭra speaks to them again.

I am an old man. All my sons have been killed. With my wife I am in many different ways in pitiable grief. My father, Krishna-Dvaipāyana Vyāsa, has given his consent for us to live in the forest. And Yudhishṭhira, too, *his*. Again and again, my head bowed, I offer you my salutations. Give me and Gāndhārī *your* consent for us to lead our lives in the forest.[222]

Sāmba is chosen by the assembled people to express, on their behalf, their sentiments. He is known to be learned and wise, his conduct beyond reproach. A man of great understanding, he is fearless in speech besides.[223]

Sāmba *(to Dhritarāshṭra)*

(After saying how happy the people have been in his reign, how very greatly he would be missed, but that that he should take the path his heart dictates.)[224]

यत् तु ज्ञातिविमर्देऽस्मिन्नात्थ दुर्योधनं प्रति।। आश्रमवासिक १०.२६।।
भवन्तमनुनेष्यामि तत्रापि कुरुनन्दन।

न तद् दुर्योधनकृतं न च तद् भवता कृतम्।। आश्रमवासिक १०.२७।।
न कर्णसौबलाभ्यां च कुरवो यत् क्षयं गताः।

न स राज्ञां वधे सू नुः कारणं ते महात्मनाम्।। आश्रमवासिक १०.३४।।
न भवान् न च ते भृत्या न कर्णो न च सौबलः।

You said something about Duryodhana being the cause of that destructive war. The truth is that neither was Duryodhana the cause, nor were you the cause, nor your officials, nor was Karṇa, nor Shakuni, the cause.[225]

दैवं तत् तु विजानीमो यन्न शक्यं प्रबाधितुम्।। आश्रमवासिक १०.२८।।
दैवं पुरुषकारेण न शक्यमपि बाधितुम्।

In my view, what happened, had to happen, being the writ of Providence. No one could have prevented it. Human will cannot undo what Providence has writ.[226]

King! The magnitude of human destruction in that war, its incredible enormity, was such that no human agency could have wrought it, not even the most powerful. It could have happened only by the power of Providence.[227]

सर्वं दैवकृतं विद्धि कोऽत्र किं वक्तुमर्हति ।। आश्रमवासिक १०.३५ ।।

It all was the doing of Providence. What else can one say?[228]

Sāmba then speaks about Duryodhana

> The way Emperor Shāntanu, and King Chitrāṅgada had protected the people, the way your father Vichitravīrya, assisted by Bhīshma, had looked after his subjects, and the way King Pāṇḍu protected the people, in the same way did Prince Duryodhana protect us and take care of us.[229]
>
> Never did your son do even the smallest injustice to us ever. We trusted Prince Duryodhana as we would our own fathers. In his reign we lived happily, which is known to you as well.[230]
>
> You have looked after our well-being like a father or a brother. Prince Duryodhana, too, never ever behaved towards us in any way offensive.[231]
>
> You are the lord of the realm, and we consider you our guru. We give you our consent that you now live in the forest. And as for your son Duryodhana, we will say this: May he, with the blessings of these good people here, obtain heaven and its happiness and peace.[232]

Through Sāmba's address to King Dhritarāshṭra, the *Mahābhārata* is saying two things of particular importance:

a. whichever view one takes of causality, one should transcend self-reproach and blaming the other alike, for both are useless, and do no good. And,
b. there is in life no one who is an unredeemed villain, nor is there any one an absolute hero.

The question of causality unresolved

The philosophical question regarding causality had been, in one form or another, a part of the *Upanishad*-s seeking to know the nature of reality. There were already the same four or five different perceptions of causality as would later be discussed in the *Mahābhārata*. For example, the *Shvetāshvatara Upanishad* opens with the questions:

किं कारणं ब्रह्म कुतः स्म जाता जीवाम केन क्व च सम्प्रतिष्ठाः ।
अधिष्ठिताः केन सुखेतरेषु वर्तामहे ब्रह्मविदो व्यवस्थाम् ।। श्वेताश्वतर I.१ ।।
What is the causal ground of this world? By what are we created? By what do we live? On what are we based? Controlled by what do we live the happiness and suffering that seem to have in them an order? These questions are asked by some of those seeking to know what Reality is.[233]

कालः स्वभावो नियतिर्यदृच्छा भूतानि योनिः पुरुष इति चिन्त्या ।
संयोग एषां न त्वात्मभावादात्माप्यनीशः सुखदुःखहेतोः ।। I.२ ।।
Kāla, *Time?* Svabhāva, *the innate nature of a thing?* Niyati, *a predetermined cause?* Yaddrchha, *merely accidental? Or Man, the created being? Neither each separately, nor they together, can be the cause, for none of them is a* conscious *entity. Nor can Man be the cause, for his happiness and suffering are caused by some other source. This has to be examined.*[234]

Later, again, the same *Upanishad* says:

स्वभावमेके कवयो वदन्ति कालं तथान्ये परिमुह्यमानाः ।
देवस्यैष महिमा तु लोके येनेदं भ्राम्यते ब्रह्मचक्रम् ।। VI.१ ।
Some philosophers consider svabhāva, *the innate disposition of a thing, to be the cause; some others think it is* kāla, *Time; but both are confused. In actual reality, it is the Divine Being, through whose power and grace, all that there is exists and moves.*[235]

येनावृतं नित्यमिदं हि सर्वं ज्ञः कालकालो गुणी सर्वविद्यः ।
तेनेशितं कर्म विवर्तते ह पृथ्व्यप्तेजोऽलखानि चिन्त्यम् ।। VI.२ ।।
It is with that Divine Being that this whole world is suffused; and the earth and water and light and wind and the space are; and all happenings of the world are governed. And that Divine Being is beyond Time.

Encompassing all attributes, it is all knowing. And yet, it is beyond all the attributes that the human mind can think of.[236]

In the *Upanishad*-s the question of causality, although subject to diverse and conflicting perceptions, was, however, not left unresolved, as it would be in the *Mahābhārata*. Besides, whereas in the *Upanishad* it is examined in abstract terms, in the *Mahābhārata* it is always, and naturally, linked with the concrete realities of human living, which are manifestly uneven and diverse, and their unevenness also the puzzle. Furthermore, the *Upanishad-s* finally assume what is already in question.

In a conversation between Vyāsa; the author of the *Mahābhārata*, and his son, Shukadeva, Vyāsa summarises the incompatible views concerning the cause of events,[237] as follows.

केचित् पुरुषकारं तु प्राहुः कर्मसु मानवाः।
दैवमित्यपरे विप्राः स्वभावं भूतचिन्तकाः।। शान्ति २३२.१९।।

Some people believe in human effort as the cause of all happenings; while some others regard fate to be the cause; and some others, the materialists, believe the innate disposition of things to be the cause.[238]

पौरुषं कर्म दैवं च फलवृत्तिः स्वभावतः।
त्रय एतेऽपृथग्भूता न विवेकं तु केचन।। शान्ति २३२.२०।।

Some other people maintain that these three, effort and fate and innate disposition, are together the cause, and each separately cannot be the cause.[239]

एतमेव च नैवं च न चोभे नानुभे न च।
कर्मस्था विषयं ब्रूयुः सत्त्वस्थाः समदर्शिनः।। शान्ति २३२.२१।।

And there are those who do not say that effort is the cause; nor do they say that fate is the cause; nor that the two together are the cause; and neither do they say that together they are not the cause. That means they are unable to come to any definite conclusion on this question.[240]

But Vyāsa's own conclusion was definite.

दधाति प्रभवे स्थानं भूतानां संयमो यमः।
स्वभावेनैव वर्तन्ते द्वन्द्वयुक्तानि भूरिशः।। शान्ति २३२.४२।।

It is Time, kāla, *that determines the place of everything, keeping all beings within bounds. By nature carrying within themselves the conflict of the opposites, all beings suffer much.*[241]

निश्चितं कालनानात्वमनादिनिधनं च यत्।
कीर्तितं यत् पुरस्तान्मे सूते यच्चात्ति च प्रजाः।। शान्ति २३८.१९।।

It is certain that time has neither beginning nor end, and has many expressions, many forms. Time creates all that is living, and Time destroys all that was created.[242]

यच्चेदं प्रभवः स्थानं भूतानां संयमो यमः।
स्वभावेनैव वर्तन्ते द्वन्द्वसृष्टानि भूरिशः।। शान्ति २३८.२०।।
It is Time that creates, matures, controls, and destroys. It is in Time that, given the innate nature of things, countless beings live their lives with the conflict of the opposites.[243]

On this entire subject the feelings naturally ran very high. Agitated over the incompatible theories of human destiny and change, a large assembly of sages gathered on the banks of a river to find a way out of that confusing maze. Unable to do so, they resorted to abusing each other and physical violence, throwing at each other their sticks, begging bowls, and garments.[244] That, incidentally, proved the rarity of self-control on the part of even the best among men, and it explains why the injunction against anger as the gateway to ruin was repeated at every turn in the *Mahābhārata*. Furthermore, how difficult has been the problem of causation, and each explanation of human diversity unsatisfactory, was indicated by the legend that, on appealing to Vāsishṭha, the wisest of them all, the disputing sages received the cryptic answer: 'I have little knowledge of this subject.'[245] The problem of causality created much discord not only among philosophers but also among the shastris. This was because the question of human freedom had always been of intimate relevance to the individual and his social context. But the discord was never resolved.

For instance, there is a conflict between *santosha*, or contentment, upon which a great value was put throughout, and *purushārtha*. For human effort, at least a part of it, has its origin in *asantosha*, discontentment, with the given situations, and in the will to change them for the better. Besides, effort implies exercise of the will and of individuality, but these two were considered also to be the cause of confusion and suffering. What is more, the praise of human effort was in conflict with shastric ritualism, for rituals cannot be called 'endeavour'. If endeavour, properly called, must consist of acts which, done in individual judgement, have change as their aim, then it can have no place in a society where practically every area of human life was legislated by the *dharmashastra*, and the general structure of that legislation considered immutable. These conflicts were never resolved, at any rate not in theory. On the other hand, the meaning of *purushārtha* was quietly incorporated into shastric ritualism. 'Effort' was not to be understood as the historic action of an individual, of which dissatisfaction with the existing state of things is the spring. *Yoga-*

Vāsishṭha, the most forceful protagonist of human freedom, suggests nevertheless that only those efforts succeed that are undertaken in consonance with the *shastra* and with the approval of good men,[246] 'good men' being those who had imbibed the spirit of the *dharmashāstra*. Thus *karma* and *purushārtha* were sucked into the vortex of shāstric formalism.

Beyond 'causality'

In charting the progress of one's right relationship with one's self and with the *other*, the *Mahābhārata* shows that it is not essential that there should first be a definite answer to the question as to why do things happen the way they happen, or do not happen when there are reasonable expectations that they would. All the contending theories of causality had, however, in common one practical conclusion: in adversity, anxiety and grief, and in success, triumph, and exultation; both these are pointless as well as self-destructive. It is with this that all discussions concerning causality end. That the question of causality remained unresolved, as it always would, need not produce moral paralysis of the will. Faith in *daiva* or *kāla* gave rise to heroic resignation; faith in *purushārtha*, to courage and resolve; faith in *svabhāva*, to the cool detachment of a scientist; faith in God, to a cheerful surrender to what was interpreted as His will. All agreed that it was foolish to exult in triumph and grieve in distress. The *Mahābhārata* says to us what is evidently true:

सुखस्यानन्तरं दुःखं दुःखस्यानन्तरं सुखम् ।
सुखदुःखे मनुष्याणां चक्रवत् परिवर्ततः ।। शान्ति १७४.१९ ।।

After happiness, comes suffering; and after suffering, happiness. Human happiness and suffering move like a wheel.[247]

That being in the nature of things, it is therefore suggested:

सुखं वा यदि वा दुःखं प्रियं वा यदि वाप्रियम् ।
प्राप्तं प्राप्तमुपासीत हृदयेनापराजितः ।। शान्ति १७४.३९ ।।

Happiness or suffering, the pleasant or the unpleasant, whatever comes, receive it with respect, and never feel defeated in your heart.[248]

देशकालावुपायांश्च मङ्गलं स्वस्तिवृद्धये ।
युनक्ति मेधया धीरो यथाशक्ति यथाबलम् ।। वन ३२.५३ ।।

Taking into consideration time and place, and by judging through intelligence one's capacities and strength, let a man, with untroubled mind, make effort and increase one's blessings.[249]

न त्वेवात्मावमन्तव्यः पुरुषेण कदाचन।
न ह्यात्मपरिभूतस्य भूतर्भवति शोभना।। वन ३२.५८।।

Let no man show disrespect to his self, for, defeating himself thereby, he never can gain anything good.[250]

To this, the *Yoga-Vāsishha* would add:

जीर्णं भिन्नं श्लथं क्षीणं क्षुब्धं क्षुण्णं क्षयं गतम्।
पश्यामि नववत्सर्वं तेन जीवाम्यनामयः।। योग.वा ६/१-२६-३३।।

What is worn out, broken, loosened, powerless, disturbed, crushed, or destroyed, consider that a new beginning.[251]

CHAPTER SEVENTEEN

From Ritual *Acts* to Relationships

- What is true *shaucha*, 'purity'?
- What is true *tīrtha*, 'pilgrimage'?
- What is true *tyāga*, 'renunciation'?
- What is *sadāchara*, 'good conduct'?
- What is *shishṭāchāra*, 'cultured conduct'?
- Who is truly *paṇḍita*, 'wise'? who is a fool?
- Who is truly a *santa*, 'saint'?

One of the deepest revolutions that took place in Indian thought was that of the *Upanishad*-s: the second was that of the *Mahābhārata*. And they were not far apart in time.

The Upanishadic revolution consisted in lifting the human mind from the outward vedic ritualistic *acts* that had the aim of obtaining, with their assumed magical power if practised as prescribed, the things of the world one desired. The *Upanishad*-s moved the mind *from acts to understanding, from rituals to inquiry.* The Self was the subject of inquiry. Life was the subject of meditation.

The revolution of the *Mahābhārata* consisted in showing, as the *Upanishad*-s had done, the physical, the mental, and the spiritual attributes of the Self as a unity, in their relatedness with each other, in which nothing could be understood if fragmented from the rest. The Self is a being in relation with itself. At the same time the Self is a being in relation with the *other*. The two are inseparable. The revolution of the *Mahābhārata* consisted in uniting self-awareness with the awareness of the *other*, in uniting self-knowledge with the knowledge of the *other*. And, with both these, uniting one's life with the life of the *other*. It was even a deeper revolution than that of the *Upanishad*-s insofar as it rooted itself in the concrete empirical realties of human experience, and therefore in the questions that invariably arose from their complexities.

The *Mahābhārata* gives to the ideas and the practices that remained solitary a deeply relational meaning. To the idea and practice of *tapas* as burning oneself in austerities; to *tīrtha* as some geographical *place* of pilgrimage one goes *to* in order to remove one's sins; to *shaucha* as outward cleansing and baths; to *dāna* as alms giving in order to earn merit: relational and ethical meaning. From the tedium and the weariness of solitary *acts*, it lifts the human person into the excitement and joy of *relationships*.

What is true *shaucha*, 'purity'?

This is one of the questions that Yudhishṭhira asks the sage Mārkaṇḍeya,[1] who replies:

वाक्शौचं कर्मशौचं च यच्चशौचं जलात्मकम् ।
त्रिभिः शौचैरुपेतो यः स स्वर्गी नात्र संशयः ।। वन पर्व २००.८२ ।।

Purity is of three kinds: the purity of speech; the purity of conduct; and keeping one's body clean.[2]

त्रिदण्डधारणं मौनं जटाभारोऽथ मुण्डनम् ।
वल्कलाजिनसंवेष्टं व्रतचर्याभिषेचनम् ।। वन २००.९६ ।।

अग्निहोत्रं वने वासः शरीरपरिशोषणम् ।
सर्वाण्येतानि मिथ्या स्युर्यदि भावो न निर्मलः ।। वन २००.९७ ।।

To carry a trident; keep a vow of silence; have on one's head the weight of long hair; or to shave one's head; wear garments made of a tree or an animal hide; take to vows; have ritual baths, live in a forest, and starve one's body—all these are of no worth if one's feelings are not clean and unsullied.[3]

न दुष्करमनाशित्वं सुकरं ह्याशनं विना ।
विशुद्धिं चक्षुरादीनां षण्णामिन्द्रियगामिनाम् ।। वन २००.९८ ।।
विकारि तेषां राजेन्द्र सुदुष्करकरं मनः ।

It is not difficult to give up the objects of one's physical sense organs, for that can be achieved by practice. What is most difficult to control is one's mind.[4]

ये पापानि न कुर्वन्ति मनोवाक्कर्मबुद्धिभिः ।
ते तपन्ति महात्मानो न शरीरस्य शोषणम् ।। वन २००.९९ ।।

To starve and oppress one's body is no tapas, *or austerity. The ones who do no evil by thought, or by speech, or by acts, or in the mind—they are great souls truly.*[5]

न ज्ञातिभ्यो दया यस्य शुक्लदेहोऽविकल्मषः ।
हिंसा सा तपसस्तस्य नानाशित्वं तपः स्मृतम् ।। वन २००.१०० ।।

To starve one's body is no tapas. *Who has purified his body by fasting and other vows but has for his near ones no feelings of tenderness, and does violence to them, destroys whatever he might have gained by fasting and other vows.*[6]

न हि पापानि कर्माणि शुद्ध्यन्त्यनशनादिभिः ।
सीदत्यनशनादेव मांसशोणितलेपनः ।। वन २००.१०२ ।।

Fasting does not remove the demerit of one's wrong doings, only weakens this body of flesh and blood.[7]

मासार्धमासोपवासाद् यत् तपो मन्यते जनः।
आत्मतन्त्रोपघाती यो न तपस्वी न धर्मवित्।। अनुशासन ९३.४।।
Those who fast for a month or for less and consider that to be austerity, tapas, *are only oppressing their body; they are neither true ascetics nor do they know* dharma.[8]

तिष्ठन् गृहे चैव मुनिर्नित्यं शुचिरलंकृतः।
यावज्जीवं दयावांश्च सर्वपापैः प्रमुच्यते।। वन पर्व २००.१०१।।
By living a life-in-family, who is full of kind feelings for all beings, can be an ascetic truly, and truly pure.[9]

Elsewhere, it is reiterated:

आहारप्रभवाः प्राणा मनो दुर्निग्रहं चलम्।
मनसश्चेन्द्रियाणां चाप्यैकाग्र्यं निश्चितं तपः।। वन पर्व २६०.२५।।
The mind is always restless, very difficult to control. To concentrate together the mind and the physical senses is the true austerity, the true tapas.[10]

तीर्थानां हृदयं तीर्थं शुचीनां हृदयं शुचिः।। शान्ति १९३.१८।।
The purity of the heart is the true purity; of all pilgrimages, the heart is the greatest.[11]

In the voice of Yudhishṭhira, the *Mahābhārata* raises the question:

यद् वरं सर्वतीर्थानां तन्मे ब्रूहि पितामह।
यत्र चैव परं शौचं तन्मे व्याख्यातुमर्हसि।। अनुशासन १०८.१।।
Which pilgrimage is the highest of all, and also the most purifying?[12]

In the voice of Bhīshma, the *Mahābhārata* then answers:

वृत्तशौचं मनःशौचं तीर्थशौचमतः परम्।
ज्ञानोत्पन्नं यच्छौचं तच्छौचं परमं स्मृतम्।। अनुशासन १०८.१२।।
Purity is said to be of four kinds: the purity of conduct; the purity of the mind; the purity that a pilgrimage gives; and the purity born of knowledge. Of these, the purity born of knowledge is the highest.[13]

समारोपितशौचस्तु नित्यं भावसमाहितः ।
केवलं गुणसम्पन्नः शुचिरेव नरः सदा ।। अनुशासन १०८.१४ ।।
The person who is clean; is ever suffused with feelings clean; and is endowed with qualities that are good—such a person is always pure.[14]

नोदकक्लिन्नगात्रस्तु स्नात इत्यभिधीयते ।
स स्नातो यो दमस्नातः स बाह्याभ्यन्तरः शुचिः ।। अनुशासन १०८.९ ।।
Merely bathing one's body with water is no cleansing. The true cleansing is with the waters of the discipline of the self. He alone is considered clean outside and within.[15]

अतीतेष्वनपेक्षा ये प्राप्तेष्वर्थेषु निर्ममाः ।
शौचमेव परं तेषां येषां नोत्पद्यते स्पृहा ।। अनुशासन १०८.१० ।।
Those who do not dwell on the past, nor have a feeling of ownership in what is given in the present, nor are desirous of this and desirous of that—in them alone is purity truly.[16]

प्रज्ञानं शौचमेवेह शरीरस्य विशेषतः ।
तथा निष्किंचनत्वं च मनसश्च प्रसन्नता ।। अनुशासन १०८.११ ।।
Discerning knowledge is a particular means to the cleansing of the body; and likewise are the freedom from having, and cheerfulness of the mind.[17]

Elsewhere, in the voice of Śrī Krishna:

मनश्शौचं कर्मशौचं कुलशौचं च भारत ।
शरीरशौचं वाक्छौचं शौचं पञ्चविधं स्मृतम् ।। आश्वमेधिक पृ ६३७७ ।।
Purity is said to be of five kinds. Purity of the heart; purity of the acts; purity of the lineage; purity of one's body; and purity of speech.

पञ्चस्वेतेषु शौचेषु हृदि शौचं विशिष्यते ।
हृदयस्य च शौचेन स्वर्गं गच्छन्ति मानवाः ।। आश्वमेधिक पृ ६३७७ ।।
Of these, the purity of the heart is the most special. It is from the purity of the heart that human beings obtain heaven.[18]

What is true *tīrtha*, pilgrimage?

तीर्थानां हृदयं तीर्थं शुचीनां हृदयं शुचिः । शान्ति १९३.१८ ।।

Of all places of pilgrimage, the heart; and the purity of the heart, of all that is pure.[19]

पावनं सर्वतीर्थानां सत्यं गायन्ति सामगाः ।
सत्यस्य वचनं तीर्थमहिंसा तीर्थमुच्यते ।। आश्वमेधिक पृ ६३७९ ।।

Truth is what makes all pilgrimage sacred. To speak the truth, and do no violence to any being, are called pilgrimage.[20]

तपस्तीर्थं दया तीर्थं शीलं तीर्थं युधिष्ठिर ।
अल्पसंतोषकं तीर्थं नारी तीर्थं पतिव्रता ।। आश्वमेधिक पृ ६३७९ ।।

Self-discipline is pilgrimage. Compassion is pilgrimage. Śīla *is pilgrimage. To be content with little is pilgrimage. A good woman is pilgrimage.*[21]

संतुष्टो ब्राह्मणस्तीर्थं ज्ञानं वा तीर्थमुच्यते ।। आश्वमेधिक पृ ६३७९ ।।

A contended seeker of learning and knowledge is pilgrimage. Knowledge is pilgrimage.[22]

यतयस्तीर्थमित्येवं विद्वांसस्तीर्थमुच्यते ।
शरण्यपुरुषस्तीर्थमभयं तीर्थमुच्यते ।। आश्वमेधिक पृ ६३७९ ।।

A renouncer is pilgrimage, and so is the one having knowledge. Who gives protection to another is pilgrimage. To offer all living beings freedom from fear is pilgrimage.[23]

In the voice of Śrī Krishna, the *Mahābhārata* says furthermore:

व्रतस्य पारणं तीर्थमाजवं तीर्थमुच्यते ।
देवशुश्रूषणं तीर्थं गुरुशुश्रूषणं तथा ।। आश्वमेधिक पृ ६३७४ ।।

To keep to a vow; simplicity of character; to be devoted to teachers and to the god like—all these are called tīrtha, *pilgrimage.*[24]

पितृशुश्रूषणं तीर्थं मातृशुश्रूषणं तथा ।
दाराणां तोषणं तीर्थं गार्हस्थ्यं तीर्थमुच्यते ।। आश्वमेधिक पृ ६३७४ ।।

To serve one's parents; to keep women happy; and live a fruitful life in the life-in-family, all these are called tīrtha, *pilgrimage.*[25]

आतिथेयः परं तीर्थं ब्रह्मतीर्थं सनातनम्।
ब्रह्मचर्यं परं तीर्थं त्रेताग्निस्तीर्थमुच्यते।। आश्वमेधिक पृ ६३७४।।

To honour a guest is a great pilgrimage. To pursue knowledge is a great pilgrimage. To live a self-disciplined life is a great pilgrimage.[26]

मूलं धर्मं तु विज्ञाय मनस्तत्रावधार्यताम्।
गच्छ तीर्थानि कौन्तेय धर्मो धर्मेण वर्धते।। आश्वमेधिक पृ ६३७४।।

They all are rooted in dharma. *Undertake that pilgrimage. For* dharma *increases by living in the light of* dharma.[27]

द्विविधं तीर्थमित्याहुः स्थावरं जङ्गमं तथा।
स्थावराज्जङ्गमं तीर्थं ततो ज्ञानपरिग्रहः।। आश्वमेधिक पृ ६३७४।।

There are two kinds of pilgrimage: the fixed, the stationary; and the living, of the mind. Of these two, that of the mind is superior, for one gains knowledge thereby.[28]

कर्मणापि विशुद्धस्य पुरुषस्येह भारत।
हृदये सर्वतीर्थानि तीर्थभूतः स उच्यते।। आश्वमेधिक पृ ६३७४।।

All pilgrimages, all tīrtha-*s, reside in the heart of a person whose acts are unsullied; hence such a person is called 'the embodiment of pilgrimage'.*[29]

गुरुतीर्थं परं ज्ञानमतस्तीर्थं न विद्यते।
ज्ञानतीर्थं परं तीर्थं ब्रह्मतीर्थं सनातनम्।। आश्वमेधिक पृ ६३७४।।

The guru as pilgrimage leads to the highest knowledge, and higher than knowledge there is no pilgrimage.[30]

क्षमा तु परमं तीर्थं सर्वतीर्थेषु पाण्डव।
क्षमावतामयं लोकः परश्चैव क्षमावताम्।। आश्वमेधिक पृ ६३७५।।

Of all pilgrimages, forgiveness is the greatest; who undertakes the pilgrimage of forgiveness and reconciliation is happy now and hereafter.[31]

मानितोऽमानितो वापि पूजितोऽपूजितोऽपि वा।
आक्रुष्टस्तर्जितो वापि क्षमावांस्तीर्थमुच्यते।। आश्वमेधिक पृ ६३७५।।

Honoured or insulted, worshipped or disregarded and done violence to—who remains forgiving is called himself a tīrtha, *pilgrimage.*

आत्मा नदी भारत पुण्यतीर्थ-
मात्मा तीर्थं सर्वतीर्थप्रधानम्।
आत्मा यज्ञः सततं मन्यते वै
स्वर्गो मोक्षः सर्वमात्मन्यधीनम्।। आश्वमेधिक पृ ६३७५।।

The Self is a river the most sacred; and of all pilgrimages, the principal. For the ultimate freedom from the human condition, and the heavens, too, depends upon the Self.[32]

आचारनैर्मल्यमुपागतेन
सत्यक्षमानिस्तुलशीतलेन।
ज्ञानाम्बुना स्नाति हि नित्यमेवं
किं तस्य भूयः सलिलेन तीर्थम्।। आश्वमेधिक पृ ६३७५।।

Who has cleansed himself by sage conduct; and, through truth and forgiveness, has gained incomparable peace—bathing in the waters of knowledge thus, what need does he have of pilgrimage to some sacred waters?[33]

Continuing his conversation with Yudhishṭhira on what 'purity' and 'pilgrimage', *shaucha* and *tīrtha*, in their real meaning are, Bhīshma talks about the 'mind as pilgrimage', *manas tīrtha*:

अगाधे विमले शुद्धे सत्यतोये धृतिह्रदे।
स्नातव्यं मानसे तीर्थे सत्त्वमालम्ब्य शाश्वतम्।। अनुशासन १०८.३।।

The deep unsullied pure waters of truth that hold the heart, in that pilgrimage of the mind bathe, with faith in what is abiding.[34]

तीर्थशौचमनर्थित्वमार्जवं सत्यमार्दवम्।
अहिंसा सर्वभूतानामानृशस्यं दमः शमः।। अनुशासन १०८.४।।

Simplicity of character, truth, compassion for others, self-discipline of the body and of the mind, and to do no violence to any being—these are the attributes of the purity that comes from the pilgrimage of the mind.[35]

निर्ममा निरहंकारा निर्द्वन्द्वा निष्परिग्रहाः।
शुचयस्तीर्थभूतास्ते ये भैक्ष्यमुपभुञ्जते।। अनुशासन १०८.५।।

The embodiments of true pilgrimage are those who are free of the notions of mine-ness, of vanity and egotism, of inner conflicts, and are free of the emotions that injure and imprison.[36]

These are not to be taken as a long catalogue of impossible virtues. The *Mahābhārata* teaches that true pilgrimage is *a journey within,* which takes us at the same time on another pilgrimage—*the journey to the other.*

The sage Pulatsya visits Bhīshma, who receives him with the greatest respect. After they exchange words of mutual love, Bhīshma seeks the resolution of a doubt that has arisen in his mind concerning pilgrimage.[37] 'What *does* a person who travels around the world as on a pilgrimage really gain?'[38]

In the voice of Pulatsya, the *Mahābhārata* says:

यस्य हस्तौ च पादौ च मनश्चैव सुसंयतम् ।
विद्या तपश्च कीर्तिश्च स तीर्थफलमश्नुते ।। वन ८२.९ ।।

Who has brought his body and his mind together in self-discipline, he alone reaps the fruits of pilgrimage truly.[39]

प्रतिग्रहादपावृत्तः संतुष्टो येन केनचित् ।
अहंकारनिवृत्तश्च स तीर्थफलमश्नुते ।। वन ८२.१० ।।

He alone reaps the fruits of pilgrimage truly who has set his mind against wanting and its restlessness, is contented with what he has, and is free of all egotism.[40]

अकल्कको निरारम्भे लघ्वाहारो जितेन्द्रियः ।
विमुक्तः सर्वपापेभ्यः स तीर्थफलमश्नुते ।। वन ८२.११ ।।

Who is free from pride and arrogance is free from the stain of dishonesty, conquering his body and mind; he alone reaps the fruits of pilgrimage truly.[41]

अक्रोधनश्च राजेन्द्र सत्यशीलो दृढव्रतः ।
आत्मोपमश्च भूतेषु स तीर्थफलमश्नुते ।। वन ८२.१२ ।।

He alone reaps the fruits of pilgrimage truly who has freed himself from anger, is firm in truthfulness, and has a feeling of unity with other beings.[42]

While teaching that the true pilgrimage, *tīrtha*, is not to a *place* but is a journey within, the *Mahābhārata* then takes us to the sacred places of India, the *tīrtha*-s: in the north,[43] in the south,[44] in the east,[45] and in the west.[46] It takes us on a pilgrim's journey to some mountain or to a hill; to some rivers and, among them, to some rivers sacred especially;[47] or to a confluence of two rivers;[48] to some lakes; to some forests and woods; and to some villages and towns. But each one of them is sacred *because* with each one of them is associated one story or another of the sacredness of life. An act of upholding a principle even at the cost of one's life; of self-sacrifice in one form or another; of redemption; of healing; and quite as often the memory of a great conversation that took place there, exploring a common, ordinary experience and its meaning.[49] Their sacredness is relational, *not* ritualistic.

The five Pāṇḍava brothers and their wife Draupadī, cheated out of their kingdom by their first cousins, have just begun their thirteen years in exile. That was a precondition for the loser in the game of dice that was fraudulently played, the dice being loaded falsely, and Yudhishṭhira putting everything on the stake had lost everything. With the question *why?*, now uppermost in their minds, they are trying to come to terms with their dramatically altered situation. Yudhishṭhira asks the sage Lomasha:

न वै निगुणमात्मानं मन्ये देवर्षिसत्तम।
तथास्मि दुःखसंतप्तो यथा नान्यो महीपतिः।। वन ९४.१।।

I do not see myself as being devoid of good qualities, yet I know of no other king who burns in suffering and pain more.

परांश्च निर्गुणान् मन्ये न च धर्मगतानपि।
ते व लोमश लोकेऽस्मिन्नृध्यन्ते केन हेतुना।। वन ९४.२।।

These others, on the other hand, I see as men without qualities, not given to dharma, *yet they are becoming more and more prosperous. What could be the reason for that? Why?*[50]

With the sage Lomasha as their guide, thus begins the journey of the Pāṇḍava-s and of Draupadī to the numerous sacred places, which is a journey in self-knowledge, towards the greater truths of life in the light of which man makes sense of his changing personal situations. At the time of their leaving on that pilgrimage, the other sages present there say to them the following words of benediction:

मनो ह्यदुष्टं शौचाय पर्याप्तं वै पराधिप।
मैत्रीं बुद्धिं समास्थाय शुद्धास्तीर्थानि द्रक्ष्यथ।। वन ९३.२२।।

If one's heart is not sullied with wicked thoughts, then that is sufficient to gain purity. With the feelings of friendship for all beings, visit the sacred places of pilgrimage.

ते यूयं मानसैः शुद्धा शरीरनियमव्रतैः ।
दैवं व्रतं समास्थाय यथोक्तं फलमाप्स्यथ ।। वन ९३.२३ ।।

Be unsullied in your heart and disciplined in your body, and you will reap the fruits of pilgrimage.[51]

What is true *tyāga*, 'renunciation'?

a. There is in the *Mahābhārata* throughout, as there had been in the *Upanishad*-s, the teaching away from the mistaken notion of *tyāga*, renunciation, being in 'a giving up of *objects*', or in 'a staying away from the natural attributes of being human'. Renunciation properly understood is an outcome not of mechanically giving up objects but of understanding the proper place of everything in life—in relation to one's self and in relation to the *other*. Renunciation, or *tyāga*, has a profoundly ethical meaning, in consonance with life and not away from it.

वित्तानि धर्मलब्धानि क्रतुमुख्येष्ववासृजन् ।
कृतात्मा स महाराज स वै त्यागी स्मृतो नरः ।। शान्ति १२.८ ।।

Who uses well the money earned justly, and who keeps his mind and its workings under control, is considered a true tyāgi.[52]

अन्तर्बहिश्च यत् किंचिन्मनोव्यासगंकारकम् ।
परित्यज्य भवेत् त्यागी न हित्वा प्रतितिष्ठति ।। शान्ति १२.३५ ।।

The true tyāgi *is the one who sees through the distracting workings within oneself and outside, not the one who leaves home and goes away.*[53]

क्रोधहर्षावनादृत्य पैशुन्यं च विशेषतः ।
विप्रो वेदानधीते यः स त्यागी पार्थ उच्यते ।। शान्ति १२.११ ।।

He who has freed himself from the violence of anger, too great a delight in things and situations, and who has freed himself especially from talking ill of others in their absence, is called a true tyāgi.[54]

इति यः कुरुते भावं स त्यागी भरतर्षभ ।
न यः परित्यज्य गृहान् वनमेति विमूढवत् ।। शान्ति १२.१४ ।।

The one having such attitudes is a tyāgi *truly, not the one who, like a fool, leaves home and goes into the forest.*[55]

It is the conquest of the mind and the cleansing of feelings, not the giving up of *things*, which is what renunciation properly understood is, the *Mahābhārata* teaches.

न बाह्यं द्रव्यमुत्सृज्य सिद्धिर्भवति भारत।
शारीरं द्रव्यमुत्सृज्य सिद्धिर्भवति वा न वा।। शान्ति १३.१ ।।
Nothing good is ever achieved by merely giving up physical things.[56]

यदा कामान् समीक्षेत धर्मवैतंसिको नरः।
अथैनं मृत्युपाशेन कण्ठे बध्नाति मृत्युराट्।। शान्ति १२.१५ ।।
Living in the forest but lusting for the things of the world, such a person may wave the flag of dharma *but only invites the death of his self.*[57]

अभिमानकृतं कर्म नैतत् फलवदुच्यते।
त्यागयुक्तं महाराज सर्वमेव महाफलम्।। शान्ति १२.१६ ।।
A task done with pride and arrogance is never any good. The same work done with humility and a feeling of sacrifice brings immense good.[58]

b. I can share only what I *have*, not what I have *given up*. From this came the question:

भगवन् दानधर्माणां तपसो वा महामुने।
किंस्विद् बहुगुणं प्रेत्य किं वा दुष्करमुच्यते।। वन २५९.२७ ।।
Of sharing, dāna, *and burning in austerity,* tapas, *which is the superior? Of these two, which is the more difficult to practise?*[59]

In the voice of Vyāsa, the *Mahābhārata* says:

दानान्न दुष्करं तात पृथिव्यामस्ति किंचन।
अर्थे च महती तृष्णा स च दुःखेन लभ्यते।। वन २५९.२८ ।।
Nothing on this earth is more difficult than giving and sharing. People have a consuming greed for money, and money comes with great difficulty.[60]

परित्यज्य प्रियान् प्राणान् धनार्थंहि महामते।
प्रविशन्ति नरा वीराः समुद्रमटवीं तथा।। वन २५९.२९ ।।

कृषिगोरक्ष्यमित्येके प्रतिपद्यन्ति मानवाः।
पुरुषाः प्रेष्यतामेके निर्गच्छन्ति धनार्थिनः।। वन २५९.३० ।।

Some daring men, not caring for their safety, plunge into the sea in search of pearls. Some explore forests. Some live by agriculture and animal husbandry. Some others travel far in search of lucrative employment.[61]

तस्माद् दुःखार्जितस्यैव परित्यागः सुदुष्करः ।
न दुष्करतरं दानात् तस्माद् दानं मतं मम ।। वन २५९.३१ ।।
Therefore the money earned, after enduring much pain, is not easy to share. Nothing is more difficult than sharing what one has. In my view, sharing is superior.[62]

विशेषस्त्वत्र विज्ञेयो न्यायेनोपार्जितं धनम् ।
पात्रे काले च देशे च साधुभ्यः प्रतिपादयेत् ।। वन २५९.३२ ।।
The particular thing to keep in mind, though, is that, judging properly 'time', 'place', and 'the person concerned', one should share what has been justly earned, and only with those who are worthy.[63]

अन्यायात् समुपात्तेन दानधर्मो धनेन यः ।
क्रियते न स कर्तारं त्रायते महतो भयात् ।। वन २५९.३३ ।।
The money earned unjustly, even if shared, offers no protection from great fear.[64]

Yudhishṭhira asks again about the relative superiority of burning in austerity, *tapas*, and *dāna*, sharing with others what one has. This time, however, with an addition: 'Learning and knowledge, *vidyā*, austerity, *tapas*, and sharing, *dāna*—of these three, which is the more special?'[65] Bhīshma answers this question by narrating a conversation that Vyāsa and the sage Maitreya once had.

On his travels, one day Vyāsa arrives in Vārāṇasī and, drifting around, with no particular place in mind, chances upon a group of ascetics assembled at the hermitage of Maitreya. He is of course quickly recognised, and is received by Maitreya with the greatest respect. He is offered a wholesome meal, at the end of which he is ready to leave. As he is leaving, Maitreya sees on Vyasa's face a look of amusement, a smile that was almost laughter.[66]

Maitreya *(to Vyāsa)*

With my salutations to you, may I know the reason for that look of amusement on your face? Being serious and resolute, you are not given to laughter. Whence this unexpected look of joy and laughter on your face then?[67]

In myself I see a great good fortune coming to me from burning in ascetic practice. In you, it seems to have come effortlessly. You are amused at something, whereas I'm not. What could be the reason?[68]

That was the reason. Maitreya had earned the blessing of being the person he was, from his affectionate impulse of sharing, but he saw its source in his burning in ascetic practice. Vyāsa had smiled because, on the contrary, he saw the source of Maitreya being blessed not in the *tapas* that he was praising so highly, but in *dāna*, in his affectionate generosity. It was an exceedingly delicate situation. Vyāsa wanted to make Maitreya aware of the much greater gift he had within him, but without making him feel that, in putting so great an emphasis on a thing so limited as *tapas*, he had been also a fool.

Vyāsa *(to Maitreya)*

Venerable sir! I was hungry and thirsty. And you gave me food and water.

It was with an affectionate heart that you offered food and water to one hungry and thirsty, your guest. Even the smallest act of sharing brings the greatest of merit, with which you are so visibly blessed.

This act of yours, of giving and sharing, has made your ascetic practice sacred. Your power is from the power of that merit. To see you is to see the embodiment of that merit of giving and sharing. And I'm happy to see you.

The fragrance you have, I think that to be the fragrance of giving and sharing. Sharing with others is even superior to all the bathing in the places of pilgrimage, and superior, too, to keeping the vedic vows.[69]

In placing far greater value upon the relational giving and sharing, *dāna*, in comparison to the solitary burning of oneself in ascetic practice, *tapas*, Vyāsa, wanting to be neither contentious nor quarrelsome, takes care not to be dismissive of what his host believed in, and lived, according to his belief.

Vyāsa *(to Maitreya)*

अहं दानं प्रशंसामि भवानपि तपःश्रुते।
तपः पवित्रं वेदस्य तपः स्वर्गस्य साधनम्।। अनुशासन १२२.५।।

I praise giving and sharing, and you praise austerity and learning the sacred lore. Undoubtedly, austerity and studying the Veda are means to gaining heaven.[70]

तपसा महदाप्नोति विद्यया चेति नः श्रुतम्।
तपसैव चापनुदेद् यच्चान्यदपि दुष्कृतम्।। अनुशासन १२२.६।।

I have heard it said that both tapas *and* vidyā *take one to high states of being, both removing the effects of one's wrong deeds.*[71]

सर्वविद्यस्तु चक्षुष्मानपि यादृशतादृशम्।
तपस्विनं तथैवाहुस्ताभ्यां कार्यं सदा नमः।। अनुशासन १२२.१०।।

सर्वे पूज्याः श्रुतधनास्तथैव च तपस्विनः।
दानप्रदाः सुखं प्रेत्य प्राप्नुवन्तीह च श्रियम्।। अनुशासन १२२.११।।

Who has learning and knowledge has eyes truly, and so has, in the same way, an ascetic. Both should be saluted. For those rich in knowledge and the ascetics are worthy of respect. Likewise, those who give and share are prosperous in this world and happy in the next.[72]

After praising *vidyā* and *tapas*, and Maitreya even more, Vyāsa returns to giving and sharing, to *dāna*, as incomparably higher. Vyāsa's understanding of the Veda is in being relational in the main, not ritualistic.

त्रीण्येव तु पदान्याहुः पुरुषस्योत्तमं व्रतम्।
न द्रह्येच्चैव दद्याच्च सत्यं चैव परं वदेत्।। अनुशासन १२०.१०।।

The Veda speak of three resolutions as of the greatest quality—to have no hatred for anyone; to give and share what one has; and to be truthful to others.[73]

यानीमान्युत्तमानीह वेदोक्तानि प्रशंससि।
तेषां श्रेष्ठतरं दानमिति मे नात्र संशयः।। अनुशासन १२०.१७।।

Of all the vedic acts that you praise, that of giving and sharing, dāna, *is the highest, of this I have no doubt.*[74]

दानकृद्भिः कृतः पन्था येन यान्ति मनीषिणः ।
ते हि प्राणस्य दातारस्तेषु धर्मः प्रतिष्ठितः ।। अनुशासन १२०.१८ ।।
The path travelled by the givers is the path that the wise take. Those who share are known as the givers of life, and it is in them that dharma *is based.*[75]

c. In all acts of giving and sharing, *motives* on the part of the giver are invariably involved. The *Mahābhārata* speaks of five motives behind *dāna*.[76]

धर्मादर्थाद्भयात् कामात् कारुण्यादिति भारत ।
दानं पञ्चविधं ज्ञेयं कारणैर्यैनिबोध तत् ।। अनुशासन १३८.५ ।।
It is from one of the five motives that one gives: dharma*; or one is flattered; or out of fear; or to fulfil some other desire; or out of simple kindness.*[77]

इह कीर्त्तिमवाप्नोति प्रेत्य चानुत्तमं सुखम् ।
इति दानं प्रदातव्यं ब्राह्मणेभ्योनसूयता ।। अनुशासन १३८.६ ।।
He wishes to earn for himself a good name in this life and peace in the next. This is giving from the motive of dharma*. One should, free of envy, always give to those engaged in learning and knowledge.*[78]

ददाति वा दान्यति वा मह्यं दत्तमनेन वा ।
इत्यर्थिभ्यो निशम्यैव सर्वं दातव्यमर्थिने ।। अनुशासन १३८.७ ।।
One gives on hearing, 'He is a giver; he will give; or he has given me earlier'. This is giving because one is flattered. But one should give.[79]

नास्याहं न मदीयोऽयं पापं कुर्याद् विमानितः ।
इति दद्याद् भयादेव दृढं मूढाय पण्डितः ।। अनुशासन १३८.८ ।।
One gives, even a wise man to a fool, fearing 'If I don't give this man who is asking, he would feel humiliated, and could harm me.' This is giving out of fear.[80]

दीनश्च याचते चायमल्पेनापि हि तुष्यति ।
इति दद्याद् दरिद्राय कारुण्यादिति सर्वथा ।। अनुशासन १३८.१० ।।
One gives thinking, 'He is terribly poor, and is asking from me; whatever little I'll give him, he will be satisfied.' This is giving out of kindness and compassion.[81]

प्रियो मेऽयं प्रियोऽस्याहमिति सम्प्रेक्ष्य बुद्धिमान्।
वयस्यायैवमाक्लिष्टं दानं दद्यादतन्द्रितः।। अनुशासन १३८.९।।
One gives thinking, 'He is dear to me, and I'm dear to him.' An intelligent man, thinking thus, should always give happily.[82]

But the *Mahābhārata* does not among them grade one motive over the other as 'better' or 'worse'. As a postscript, it simply adds:

इति पञ्चविधं दानं पुण्यकीर्तिविवर्धनम्।
यथाशक्त्या प्रदातव्यमेवमाह प्रजापतिः।। अनुशासन १३८.११।।
No matter what the motive be, one should always give and share according to one's capacity. For one earns merit and a good name thereby.[83]

d. If 'giving' is difficult, 'asking' is humiliating.

याच्यमाहुरनीशस्य अभिहारं च भारत।
उद्वेजयन्ति याचन्ति सदा भूतानि दस्युवत्।। अनुशासन ६०.४।।
To ask is considered to be humiliating to the one who asks. Those who always keep asking keep agitating people, as if they were robbers.[84]

Therefore the man who does not ask, an *ayāchaka*, is valued higher than the one who does, a *yāchaka*.[85] 'Among the rulers are those superior who are resolute in protecting the people; among those given to learning and knowledge, the resolute in not asking.'[86]

Knowing that to ask, to be a supplicant, is reducing, the *Mahābhārata* simultaneously speaks of the one who gives without the *other* asking, or without his or her having to ask, as a person far superior to the one who gives only on asking. It places an ethical obligation upon those who *have*, especially upon the king, upon the state, to *look for* those who may be in severe circumstances but will not ask.[87]

आनृशंस्यं परो धर्मो याचते यत् प्रदीयते।
अयाचतः सीदमानान् सर्वोपायैर्निमन्त्रयेत्।। अनुशासन ६०.६।।
To him who asks, to give is undoubtedly a good act, done in the spirit of kindness. But one should rather give to those who do not ask even in situations greatly difficult for them.[88]

कृशाय कृतविद्याय वृत्तिक्षीणाय सीदते।
अपहन्यात् क्षुधां यस्तु न तेन पुरुष: सम:।। अनुशासन ५९.११।।
There is none other who does greater good than the one who removes the hunger of those who are learned but are in difficult days, helpless, weak, and disturbed.[89]

क्रियानियमितान् साधून् पुत्रदारैश्च कर्शितान्।
अयाचमानान् कौन्तेय सर्वोपायैर्निमन्त्रयेत्।। अनुशासन ५९.१२।।
You should by all means reach out to those good people who are suffering because they are not able to support their family but do not ask.[90]

Having a deep understanding of the human, the *Mahābhārata* is perfectly aware that a *dāna*, 'giving', can quite easily turn into an instrument of power over the *other*, in putting him, or her, under a sense of perpetual obligation, and then extracting a price in return. The giving that has a price is no giving. It is for this reason that the virtue of *dāna* is never discussed without at the same time talking about the attitude of the mind, and feelings, with which one should give.[91]

e. Furthermore, the *Mahābhārata* teaches that just as 'the giving up', *tyāga*, is not a giving up of material *things* primarily, the 'giving', *dāna*, is not primarily a giving of *things* either. Therefore, side by side the 'giving of food and water', *anna-dāna* and *jala-dāna*,[92] and a sharing of the earth, *bhūmi-dāna*,[93] the *Mahābhārata* is talking about a sharing of love and affection, *prīti-dāna*: sharing knowledge, *vidyā-dāna* and *jñāna-dāna*: and a giving thereby of freedom from fear, *abhaya-dāna*. It is talking about the sharing of light that they bring into life and its daily experience: *dīpa-dāna*. It is talking about lighting a lamp—even against the wind.

ज्योतिस्तेज: प्रकाशं वाप्यूर्ध्वगं चापि वर्ण्यते।
प्रदानं तेजसां तस्मात् तेजो वर्धयते नृणाम्।। अनुशासन ९८.४६।।
A lamp spreads the light upwards and increases human worth. Therefore, dīpa-dāna *is to light the light of human worth.*[94]

यस्मादूर्ध्वगमेतत् तु तमसश्चैव भेषजम्।
तस्मादूर्ध्वगतेर्दाता भवेदत्रेति निश्चय:।। अनुशासन ९८.४८।।

The flame of the lamp is upwards. It is a cure for the illness of darkness. Who lights a lamp enhances his worth undoubtedly, as does the flame of a lamp.[95]

आलोकदानाच्चक्षुष्मान् प्रभायुक्तो भवेन्नरः।
तान् दत्त्वा नोपहिंसेत न हरेन्नोपनाशयेत्।। अनुशासन ९८.५०।।

Spreading light, āloka-dāna, *one gives to one's eyes light and its effulgence. After lighting a lamp, let one not blow it out, or remove, or destroy.*[96]

दीपहर्ता भवेदन्धस्तमोगतिरसुप्रभः।
दीपप्रदः स्वर्गलोके दीपमालेव राजते।। अनुशासन ९८.५१।।

Who steals a lamp, blind and without radiance and grace of life, falls into the hell of darkness; who lights a lamp is himself full of light, in the radiance and grace of heaven.[97]

'Sharing', *dāna*, in its truest sense is a sharing of one's self.

Above all, in the voice of the sage Nārada the *Mahābhārata* brings together in a deep mystic unity knowledge, truth, self-discipline, sharing, self-sacrifice, happiness, and heaven and peace.

वेदस्योपनिषत् सत्यं सत्यस्योपनिषद् दमः।
दमस्योपनिषद् दानं दानस्योपनिषत् तपः।। शान्ति २५१.११।।

Truth is the essence of knowledge; self-discipline, the essence of truth. Giving and sharing are the essence of self-discipline; and self-sacrifice, the essence of giving and sharing.

तपसोपनिषत् त्यागस्त्यागस्योपनिषत् सुखम्।
सुखस्योपनिषत् स्वर्गः स्वर्गस्योपनिषच्छमः।। शान्ति २५१.१२।।

The giving up is the essence of self-sacrifice; happiness, the essence of giving up. Heaven is the essence of happiness; and peace, the essence of heaven.[98]

What is *sadāchāra*, 'good conduct'? What is *shishṭāchāra*, 'cultured conduct'?

It is in the voice of a meatseller, *Dharmavyādha*, portrayed as among the most cultured of men, that the *Mahābhārata* teaches what 'cultured conduct', *shishṭāchāra*, and 'good conduct', *sadāchāra* in their true meanings are. In his long conversation with Kaushika the arrogant brāhmaṇa, the meatseller says:

कामक्रोधौ वशे कृत्वा दम्भं लोभमनार्जवम्।
धर्ममित्येव संतुष्टास्ते शिष्टाः शिष्टसम्मताः।। वन २०७.६३।।

Those who keep under control their impulses, of sexual pleasure, anger, greed, arrogance, and deviousness, and abide by dharma, *are, in the opinion of the cultured, considered cultured.*[99]

न तेषां विद्यतेऽवृत्तं यज्ञस्वाध्यायशीलिनाम्।
आचारपालनं चैव द्वितीयं शिष्टलक्षणम्।। वन २०७.६४।।

Those who are devoted to self-knowledge and self-understanding, and are in their behaviour all that śīla *means,*[100] *is the second attribute of being cultured.*[101]

गुरुशुश्रूषणं सत्यमक्रोधो दानमेव च।
एतच्चतुष्टयं ब्रह्मन् शिष्टाचारेषु नित्यदा।। वन २०७.६५।।

In those who are cultured, the four good qualities: devotion to the teacher, speaking the truth, absence of anger, and sharing with others what one has, are always found.[102]

शिष्टाचारे मनः कृत्वा प्रतिष्ठाप्य च सर्वशः।
यामयं लभते वृत्तिं सा न शक्या ह्यतोऽन्यथा।। वन २०७.६६।।

Acting thus from one's heart, what one can gain can be gained in no other way.[103]

सत्योपनिषत् सत्यं सत्यस्योपनिषद् दमः।
दमस्योपनिषत् त्यागः शिष्टाचारेषु नित्यदा।। वन २०७.६७।।

Truth is the essence of knowledge; the essence of truth, self-control; the essence of self-control, in sharing with others: and all these are manifest in the one truly cultured.[104]

ये तु शिष्टाः सुनियताः श्रुतित्यागपरायणाः।
धर्मपन्थानमारूढाः सत्यधर्मपरायणाः।। वन २०७.६९।।

Those who are cultured live a life within bounds, given to learning and knowledge, share it with others, abide by dharma, *and consider truth to be the ultimate support.*[105]

नियच्छन्ति परां बुद्धिं शिष्टाचारान्विता जनाः ।
उपाच्यायमते युक्ताः स्थित्या धर्मार्थदर्शिनः ।। वन २०७.७० ।।

Those who are cultured keep also their intelligence within bounds; and, remaining within the limits of dharma, *concern themselves with their material prosperity.*[106]

अक्रुद्ध्यन्तोऽनसूयन्तो निरहंकारमत्सराः ।
ऋजवः शमसम्पन्नाः शिष्टाचारा भवन्ति ते ।। वन २०७.७८ ।।

Those who are free of anger, who do not seek fault in others: free of envy and egotism, have simplicity of temperament, and control over their mind, are cultured truly.[107]

सर्वभूतदयावन्तो अहिंसानिरताः सदा ।
परुषं च न भाषन्ते सदा सन्तो द्विजप्रियाः ।। वन २०७.८४ ।।

Those are truly cultured who are kind to all beings; do no violence to any one; and hurt no one by speaking bitter and wounding words.[108]

अनसूया क्षमा शान्तिः संतोषः प्रियवादिता ।
कामक्रोधपरित्यागः शिष्टाचारनिषेवणम् ।।
कर्म च श्रुतसम्पन्नं सतां मार्गमनुत्तमम् ।। वन २०७.९६ ।।

The truly cultured have manifest in them forgiveness and reconciliation, peace and contentment. Free from wanting and anger and the habit of finding fault in others, they are of loving speech, abiding in cultured conduct.[109]

सर्वत्र च दयावन्तः सन्तः करुणवेदिनः ।। २०७.९४ ।।
गच्छन्तीह सुसंतुष्टा धर्मपन्थानमुत्तमम् ।
शिष्टाचारा महात्मानो येषां धर्मः सुनिश्चितः ।। २०७.९५ ।।

Having always in their heart feelings of compassion; at peace with themselves; abiding on the path of dharma*; they are truly cultured, and great souls.*[110]

अहिंसा सत्यवचनं सर्वभूतहितं परम् ।
अहिंसा परमो धर्मः स च सत्ये प्रतिष्ठितः
सत्ये कृत्वा प्रतिष्ठां तु प्रवर्तन्ते प्रवृत्तयः ।। वन २०७.७४ ।।

Ahiṃsā *and speaking truthfully—these are for the greatest good of all beings.* Ahiṃsā *is the greatest* dharma *of all; and it is upon truth that* ahiṃsā *is based. In whatever they do, those who are truly cultured begin with truth.*[111]

सत्यमेव गरीयस्तु शिष्टाचारनिषेवितम् ।
आचारश्च सतां धर्मः सन्तश्चारलक्षणाः ।। वन २०७.७५ ।।
In those who abide in cultured conduct, truth is of the greatest weight. That is their dharma*; and it is from that, that they are known.*[112]

एतत् ते सर्वमाख्यातं यथाप्रज्ञं यथाश्रुतम् ।
शिष्टाचारगुणं ब्रह्मन् पुरस्कृत्य द्विजर्षभ ।। वन २०७.९९ ।।
Dear brāhmaṇa! Whatever I've understood, and have also heard, about cultured conduct, I've told you.[113]

And once again, lest the scholar ascetic Kaushika had wrongly understood the meaning of *dharma* in all these formulations, the meatseller makes it abundantly clear to him—and to us—what, properly understood, *dharma* is.

आरम्भो न्याययुक्तो यः स हि धर्म इति स्मृतः ।
अनाचारस्त्वधर्मेति इतच्छिष्टानुशासनम् ।। वन २०७.७७ ।।
What has its beginnings in what is just, and fair, and reasonable, is dharma. *Whatever is oppressive, unjust, and unfair, is* adharma.[114]

It may for a moment appear that there is a circularity of definition in what has been said above. 'Cultured conduct is the conduct of those who are cultured.' This does not say much. In the formulations above, there is no circularity of definition of this kind. In answer to a forthright question, 'What is cultured conduct?', what is first being answered is the question, 'Who can be called truly cultured?', and the attributes of a person truly cultured, *shishṭa*, he or she, are clearly described. Those attributes relate to a person in relationship with himself or herself and with the other at the same time.

Sadāchāra, or 'good conduct', is the same: *to bring oneself in right relationship with one's self and with the other.* It pertains not to *acts* alone but to *attitudes and feelings* as well. The *Mahābhārata* teaches that without feelings acts are dead.

Yudhishṭhira asks Bhīshma:

आयुष्मान् केन भवति अल्पायुर्वापि मानवः ।
केन वा लभते कीर्ति केन वा लभते श्रियम् ।। अनुशासन १०४.२ ।।
By what means does a person live long, and how is a person's life shortened? How does a person gain a good name, and how his well being?[115]

In this, Yudhishṭhira was not seeking a prescription for physical longevity. A person may live long and yet live a short life or not live at all. In the voice of Bhīshma, the *Mahābhārata* then says:

आचाराल्लभते ह्यायुराचाराल्लभते श्रियम्।
आचारात् कीर्तिमाप्नोति पुरुषः प्रेत्य चेह च।। अनुशासन १०४.६।।

It is from good conduct that a person gains a long life; and it is from good conduct that a person gains prosperity and well-being. From good conduct he gains a good name here and peace hereafter.[116]

तस्मात् कुर्यादिहाचारं यदीच्छेद् भूतिमात्मनः।
अपि पापशरीरस्य आचारो हन्त्यलक्षणम्।। अनुशासन १०४.८।।

Therefore, who seeks his well-being and his own good should behave in a way that is good and that removes the offences and the unhappy attributes of one's body.[117]

आचारलक्षणो धर्मः सन्तश्चारित्रलक्षणाः।
साधूनां च यथावृत्तमेतदाचारलक्षणम्।। अनुशासन १०४.९।।

Good conduct is the attribute of dharma, *and is that by which a good human being is recognised. Conversely, the way those who have goodness in them behave, is how 'good conduct' is recognised.*[118]

अप्यदृष्टं श्रवादेव पुरुषं धर्मचारिणम्।
भूतिकर्माणि कुर्वाणं तं जनाः कुर्वते प्रियम्।। अनुशासन १०४.१०।।

Good in his conduct, who works for the good of others, even if not met or seen, is recognised by them with feelings of love.[119]

अक्रोधनः सत्यवादी भूतानामविहिंसकः।
अनसूयुरजिह्मश्च शतं वर्षाणि जीवति।। अनुशासन १०४.१४।।

Who has freed himself from anger; is truthful; does no violence to any being; does not seek fault in others; and is not devious; lives a hundred years.[120]

सर्वलक्षणहीनोऽपि समुदाचारवान् नरः।
श्रद्दधानोऽनसूयुश्च शतं वर्षाणि जीवति।। अनुशासन १०४.१३।।

And so does a person, even if he is bereft of qualities but is of good conduct, has faith, and does not seek fault in others.[121]

आचारो भूतिजनन आचार: कीर्तिवर्धन: ।
आचाराद् वर्धते ह्यायुराचारो हन्त्यलक्षणम् ।। अनुशासन १०४.१५४ ।।

आगमानां हि सर्वेषामाचार: श्रेष्ठ उच्यते ।
आचारप्रभवो धर्मो धर्मादायुर्विवर्धते ।। अनुशासन १०४.१५५ ।।

Good conduct creates the good of all, increasing good name, too. It is from good conduct that one gains a long life; and good conduct removes the defects and demerits of character.

In all scriptures, good conduct is considered the best. From good conduct arises dharma, *and from* dharma *a long life.*[122]

Sadāchāra understood thus, not as formal rules of conventional behaviour, but as being in right relationship with one's self and with the *other*, is perceived in the *Mahābhārata* as the basis equally of good governance and all social arrangements. Lest the division of social callings was misinterpreted as designating some individuals as being 'higher' and others as 'lower', and a brāhmaṇa among them being ranked the highest irrespective of his character, it is again reiterated that:

न योनिर्नापि संस्कारो न श्रुतं न च संतति: ।
कारणानि द्विजत्वस्य वृत्तमेव तु कारणम् ।। अनुशासन १४३.५० ।।

No one is a brāhmaṇa by birth or family, by upbringing or learning. Good conduct, sadāchāra, *alone is the main determinant in one being a brāhmaṇa.*[123]

सर्वोऽयं ब्राह्मणो लोके वृत्तेन तु विधीयते ।
वृत्ते स्थितस्तु शूद्रोऽपि ब्राह्मणत्वं नियच्छति ।। अनुशासन १४३.५१ ।।

Sadāchāra is everywhere the discipline required of the social calling known as brāhmaṇa. A shūdra *centred in* sadāchāra *is a brāhmaṇa, too.*[124]

Who is truly a *paṇḍita*, 'wise'? Who is a fool?

The *Mahābhārata* asks these questions, and answers them in the voice of Vidura, the wisest of men, the detached observer to the great tragedy unfolding, which nobody seemed to be able to prevent. Vidura is having a long conversation with his half-brother Dhritarāshṭra, the blind king, counselling him to restrain his son Duryodhana from his unjust acts towards the Pāṇḍava-s, who were the rightful inheritors of the kingdom but cheated out of it. Among the many subjects with which he engages Dhritarāshṭra is also the question, 'Who is truly wise, a *paṇḍita*?' Vidura says:

आत्मज्ञानं समारम्भस्तितिक्षा धर्मनित्यता।
यमर्थान्नापकर्षन्ति स वै पण्डित उच्यते।।
निषेवते प्रशस्तानि निन्दितानि न सेवते।
अनास्तिक: श्रद्दधान एतत् पण्डितलक्षणम्।। उद्योग पर्व ३३.१६।।

Self-understanding; application with a steady mind; the capacity of bearing suffering; and abiding in dharma*: having these qualities, who is not swayed from his path, is alone called wise,* paṇḍita.

Doing what is good, and keeping away from what is ill, having faith, he alone is called wise, paṇḍita.[125]

क्रोधो हर्षश्च दर्पश्च ह्री: स्तम्भो मान्यमानिता।
यमर्थान्नापकर्षन्ति स वै पण्डित उच्यते।। उद्योग ३३.१७।।

He alone is called wise, paṇḍita, *who in his resolution is not swayed by anger, or delight, or pride, or arrogance, or by a feeling of self-importance.*[126]

श्रुतं प्रज्ञानुगं यस्य प्रज्ञा चैव श्रुतानुगा।
असम्भिन्नार्यमर्याद: पण्डिताख्यां लभेत स:।। उद्योग ३३.२९।।

He alone is to be called wise, paṇḍita, *whose learning and knowledge are guided by a higher faculty of the mind, and that in turn enriched by learning and knowledge, and who does not transgress limits.*[127]

Much that is included in 'good and cultured conduct', *sadāchāra* and *shishṭāchāra*, is included also in being wise, a *paṇḍita*. And a plain reading of them will show that they are being addressed not to personages living in idealistic clouds but to those who are concerned with living a happy and meaningful life in this world, the only visible world given to them. Being 'wise', *paṇḍita*, is indisputably a prerequisite of success in one's worldly concerns. Vidura mentions the following other mental and ethical self-disciplines of the one wise, required clearly in one's own interest first of all.[128]

यस्य कृत्यं न जानन्ति मन्त्रं वा मन्त्रितं परे।
कृतमेवास्य जानन्ति स वै पण्डित उच्यते।। उद्योग ३३.१८।।

Who keeps his counsel to himself before he acts, he alone is called wise.[129]

यस्य कृतं न विघ्नन्ति शीतमुष्णं भयं रतिः।
समृद्धिरसमृद्धिर्वा स वै पण्डित उच्यते।। उद्योग ३३.१९।।

Who is not obstructed in his resolve by extreme changes of climate, or by fear and love, or by change of fortunes, prosperity or poverty, he alone is called wise.[130]

यस्य संसारिणी प्रज्ञा धर्मार्थावनुवर्तते।
कामादर्थं वृणीते यः स वै पण्डित उच्यते।। उद्योग ३३.२०।।

Whose worldly intelligence occupies itself with material prosperity in the light of the discipline of dharma, *and who chooses effort and endeavour over the pursuit of pleasures, he alone is called wise.*[131]

यथाशक्ति चिकीर्षन्ति यथाशक्ति च कुर्वते।
न किंचिदवमन्यन्ते नराः पण्डितबुद्धयः।। उद्योग ३३.२१।।

Who wishes to make effort, and also does, according to his capacities, and does not dismiss any work as too worthless to do, he alone is called wise.[132]

क्षिप्रं विजानाति चिरं शृणोति
विज्ञाय चार्थं भजते न कामात्।
नासम्पृष्टो व्युपयुङ्क्ते परार्थे
तत् प्रज्ञानं प्रथमं पण्डितस्य।। उद्योग ३३.२२।।

He listens carefully and for long, but grasps the substance of a subject quickly. He begins a work not from selfish desire but from a sense of the worth of what is to be done. Neither does he engage without cause. This is a main characteristic of one wise, a paṇḍita.[133]

नाप्राप्यमभिवाञ्छन्ति नष्टंनेच्छन्ति शोचितुम्।
आपत्सु च न मुह्यन्ति नराः पण्डितबुद्धयः।। उद्योग ३३.२३।।

Those who do not long for things beyond reach; nor lament for what is lost; and do not lose heart in times of trouble, they have the intelligence of the one wise.[134]

निश्चित्य यः प्रक्रमते नान्तर्वसति कर्मणः।
अवन्ध्यकालो वश्यात्मा स वै पण्डित उच्यते।। उद्योग ३३.२४।।

Who begins a work only after making a careful resolution about it; having begun thus, he does not abandon it midway; does not waste his time; and keeps his mind under control, he alone is called wise.[135]

आर्यकर्मणि रज्यन्ते भूतिकर्माणि कुर्वते।
हितं च नाभ्यसूयन्ति पण्डिता भरतर्षभ।। उद्योग ३३.२५।।
The wise feels drawn towards excellence, works for making things better, and does not seek faults in those working for the good of others.[136]

न हृष्यत्यात्मसम्माने नावमानेन तप्यते।
गाङ्गो ह्रद इवाक्षोभ्यो यः स पण्डित उच्चते।। उद्योग ३३.२६।।
Who is neither filled with too great a delight on being honoured, nor with pain when shown disrespect, and, like the deeps of the river Ganga, has a mind tranquil and quiet, he alone is called wise.[137]

तत्त्वज्ञः सर्वभूतानां योगज्ञः सर्वकर्मणाम्।
उपायज्ञो मनुष्याणां नरः पण्डित उच्यते।। उद्योग ३३.२७।।
Who knows the substance of the things physical, the best way of doing things, and the best method as well, he alone is called wise.[138]

अर्थं महान्तमासाद्य विद्यामैश्वर्यमेव वा।
विचरत्यसमुन्नद्धो यः स पण्डित उच्यते।। उद्योग ३३.४०।।
However much he gains in material prosperity, in learning and knowledge, and in the glory of fame and recognition, and who he does not turn arrogant, he alone is called wise.[139]

The *Mahābhārata* quickly draws a portrait also of a fool, a *mūḍha*.[140]

अश्रुतश्च समुन्नद्धो दरिद्रश्च महामनाः।
अथाश्चाकर्मणा प्रेप्सुर्मूढ इत्युच्यते बुधैः।। उद्योग ३३.३०।।
A fool is one who has no learning but is full of pride; has no money, but dreams great dreams; and without making effort, hopes to make great money.[141]

स्वमर्थं यः परित्यज्य परार्थमनुतिष्ठति।
मिथ्या चरति मित्रार्थे यश्च मूढः स उच्चते।। उद्योग ३३.३१।।
Leaving his own concerns, busying himself with the concerns of others, and behaving towards a friend in a way untruthful.[142]

अकामान् कामयति यः कामयानान् परित्यजेत्।
बलवन्तं च यो द्वेष्टि तमाहुर्मूढचेतसम्।। उद्योग ३३.३२।।

Who wants those who do not want him, and leaves those, who do, and starts hostility with those more powerful than he.[143]

अमित्रं कुरुते मित्रं द्वेष्टि हिनस्ति च।
कर्म चारभते दुष्टं तमाहुर्मूढचेतसम्।। उद्योग ३३.३३।।
Who makes a friend of the one not a friend, and causes pain to the one who is, and begins doing things wicked.[144]

संसारयति कृत्यानि सर्वत्र विचिकित्सते।
चिरं करोति क्षिप्रार्थे स मूढो भरतर्षभ।। उद्योग ३३.३४।।
Who expands his concerns with no use, distrusts everybody, and delays doing what should be done at its proper time.[145]

श्राद्धं पितृयो न ददाति दैवतानि न चार्चति।
सुहृन्मित्रं न लभते तमाहुर्मूढचेतसम्।। उद्योग ३३.३५।।
Who does not keep the remembrance of his forefathers, and does not offer his prayers to the gods of the universe, nor does he find a caring friend.[146]

अनाहूतः प्रविशति अपृष्टो बहु भाषते।
अविश्वस्ते विश्वसिति मूढचेता नराधमः।। उद्योग ३३.३६।।
Who comes uninvited, and speaks without being asked, and puts his trust in those unworthy of trust.[147]

परं क्षिपति दोषेण वर्तमानः स्वयं तथा।
यश्च क्रुध्यत्यनीशानः स च मूढतमो नरः।। उद्योग ३३.३७।।
Himself behaving badly, who talks of the bad behaviour of others, lacking strength, flies into anger yet. Such a person is not just a fool, but an irredeemable fool.[148]

Who is truly a *santa*, 'saint'?

It is in the voice of Sāvitrī, whom we will meet later in this book,[149] that the *Mahābhārata* says what a saint, a *santa*, truly is. What she says about the attributes of a saint is to be found throughout the *Mahābhārata*. In a highly intelligent and charming conversation that she is having with Yama, the Lord of Death, who had claimed the life of Satyavān, her husband whom she loved dearly, she says:

सतां सदा शाश्वतधर्मवृत्तिः
 सन्तो न सीदन्ति न च व्यथन्ति।
सतां सद्भिर्नाफलः सगंमोऽस्ति
 सद्भ्यो भयं नानुवर्तन्ति सन्तः।। वन २९७.४७।।

The saints are rooted always in the abiding universal dharma. *They are neither agitated nor in despair; no one has any fear of them; neither is their company ever in vain.*[150]

आत्मन्यपि न विश्वासस्तथा भवति सत्सु यः।
तस्मात् सत्सु विशेषेण सर्वः प्रणयमिच्छति।। वन २९७.४२।।

People do not trust their own self as they trust saints. Hence their love for them.[151]

सौहृदात् सर्वभूतानां विश्वासो नाम जायते।
तस्मात् सत्सु विशेषेण विश्वासं कुरुते जनः।। वन २९७.४३।।

Trust in the other comes from a caring heart. And because saints have a caring heart, people have a special trust in them.[152]

न च प्रसादः सत्पुरुषेषु मोघो
 न चाप्यर्थो नश्यति नापि मानः।
यस्मादेतन्नियतं सत्सु नित्यं
 तस्मात् सन्तो रक्षितारो भवन्ति।। वन २९७.५०।।

The tranquillity and grace of the saints are never in vain. In their company no one feels reduced; nor does anyone's self-interest suffer. Because grace, and no threat to anyone's self-respect and self-interest, are to be found in the saints always, they are truly the protectors of all.[153]

आर्यजुष्टमिदं वृत्तिमिति विज्ञाय शाश्वतम्।
सन्तः परार्थं कुर्वाणा नावेक्षन्ति परस्परम्।। वन २९७.४९।।

The abiding sadāchāra *manifest in them, the saints work for the good of the others; and among themselves do not look at each other with troubled eyes.*[154]

Sāvitrī concludes:

सन्तो हि सत्येन नयन्ति सूर्यं
 सन्तो भूमिं तपसा धारयन्ति।

सन्तो गतिर्भूतभव्यस्य राजन्
सतां मध्ये नावसीदन्ति सन्तः ।। वन २९७.४८ ।।

It is from the power of truth that the saints keep the sun in its place, and bear the earth. In the saints exist the past, the present and the future. Being with them is to be free of agitation and despair.[155]

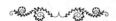

CHAPTER EIGHTEEN

Mokṣha—Liberation from the Human Condition

- The rationality of *mokṣha*
- The radical shift in the *Mahābhārata*
- The attributes of a free person
- *Mokṣha* as freedom *from*
- The paths to *mokṣha*
- *Mokṣha* as freedom *into*

In the ideal of *mokṣha*, as liberation from the human condition, the *Mahābhārata* raised self-interest to its highest level.

कुटुम्बं पुत्रदारांश्च शरीरं संचयाश्च ये ।
पारक्यमध्रुवं सर्वं किं स्वं सुकृतदुष्कृतम् ।। शान्ति ३२९.३२ ।।
The family, the wife and the children, the accumulations, one's body—all these are unstable and impermanent. What remain are one's own order and disorder.

यदा सर्वं परित्यज्य गन्तव्यमवशेन ते ।
अनर्थे किं प्रसक्तस्त्वं स्वमर्थं नानुतिष्ठसि ।। शान्ति ३२९.३३ ।।
When you will have to go too, leaving everything behind, then why are you preoccupied with what is of little concern? Why do you not centre your self in your own self instead?[1]

Simple in its conception, and logical in its formulation, there were reasons, though, to be discussed presently, why the simplicity of *mokṣha* should have vanished into details that are not intrinsic to it, and its universality into limited religiosity. The concept of *mokṣha* in its essentials had nothing to do even with the idea of God, much less with theological doctrines of any kind. It was arrived at entirely through analysis of the nature of *acts* and of their binding consequences in which God has no place.[2] And because it was firmly rooted in that analysis, it has had, like all other concepts in the *Mahābhārata*, a plainly universal meaning. It was not a 'Hindu' concept, nor was it a product of 'Hinduism', although that is how it has been perceived in modern times. Let us trace its outline as given in the *Mahābhārata*. Although in many respects the same as in the rest of the *mokṣha* literature in the systems of philosophy, in the *Mahābhārata* it had taken a radically different perspective, making it a truly universal philosophy of human freedom.[3]

The rationality of *mokṣha*

The *Mahābhārata* begins with the following empirical propositions, to be observed universally.[4] They were set out in an earlier chapter, discussing pleasure and pain, *sukha* and *duḥkha*, as the two human attributes that dominate life. They have to be restated here as well, as they are in the *Mahābhārata* on *mokṣha*.

> *All human beings are in the grip of physical and mental suffering.*[5]
> *There is no doubt that in life there is more suffering than pleasure.*[6]
> *There are a thousand places for sorrow and hundreds for fear.*[7]
> *The body is the basis of pleasure as well as pain. Life and the body are born together and end together.*[8]
> *Sufferings are of two kinds: physical and mental. They arise from each other; without the one, the other cannot exist.*[9]
> *Physical suffering has four causes: disease, accidents, hard labour, and the loss of persons who are dear to one.*[10]
> *Mental suffering is caused by old age, loss of wealth, to have to live with those who one does not like and to lose those who one does, bondage and woman.*[11]
> *The two most general causes of mental suffering are: 'thirst',* trsna, *and 'entanglement',* asakti.[12]
> *Suffering is the absence of happiness, and happiness is the absence of suffering; but, paradoxically, suffering arises from pleasure, and pleasure can arise from suffering.*[13] *Both move in a cycle. There is no one who always experiences suffering, nor is there anyone who always experiences happiness.*[14]
> *It is futile to brood over one's suffering, for not only does pain not become less thereby, but one loses also the capacity to discriminate and act, thus giving rise to suffering twice over.*[15]
> *Awareness of the body is through acts. The acts are of four kinds: seeing, thinking, speaking, and doing; and as one acts, so one becomes.*[16]
> *First there comes the awareness of objects, then springs the desire for them, then the resolution to obtain them, then the acts, followed by the results.*[17]
> *Whatever sensory experience a man finds agreeable, he develops a tendency towards it; whatever he finds disagreeable, that he looks upon with aversion; he endeavours to obtain what is agreeable, and wants to experience it again and again; from that rises attachment,* raga, *and afterwards, aversion,* dvesa; *then comes greed,* lobha, *followed by confusion,* moha; *overpowered by these he moves away from* dharma.[18]

Attraction towards sensory objects creates desire, which turns into trsna, *'thirst'. To desire, there is no end; it neither weakens nor does it ever die, although one's senses do.*[19]

Since there is in the world no substance that can fill a man's desire, which is like an ocean that can never get filled,[20] *desire leads man to endless striving and confusion, from which arise untruth, fear, and aggression.*

From greed arises every conceivable harm to oneself and to others: anger; confusion; egoism; intolerance; shamelessness; loss of prosperity; worry; ill-reputation; miserliness; excessive 'thirst'; arrogance on account of one's family and learning, good looks and plentiful wealth; aggression; disrespect; distrust and deviousness towards all beings; forceful possession of the wealth of others; and rudeness to their women; onslaught of forceful speech and will; the tendency to speak ill of others; envy, lies, hatred; self-praise; dangerous acts; and doing what ought not to be done.[21]

Ignorance is the root cause of greed, and greed feeds ignorance.[22]

Pleasure, like suffering, is also of two kinds: physical and mental. All human tendencies are towards pleasure, for everybody tries to avoid pain and experience pleasure.[23]

Indeed, dharma, artha, *and* kāma, *the three ends of life, have no other aim but pleasure; it is for obtaining pleasure that every act is begun.*[24]

But the pleasures of this world, like suffering, are transitory.[25] *What is more, by their very nature they are shot through with pain; for every act of pleasure has attachment as its mental component, and from attachment invariably comes greed.*

From the foregoing empirical propositions, subject of universal experience, the following two general propositions were abstracted *a posteriori*:

a. pleasure and suffering, *sukha* and *duḥkha*, are the results of one's own acts;
b. from the moment of conception, one suffers the fruits of acts done in one's previous life as well.[26]

These propositions formed the essence of the *karma* theory. They were connected to another proposition, namely, that not all acts come to fruition immediately, and some acts do not fructify in one lifetime. Hence the necessity to posit rebirth, indeed a whole cycle of birth and death. These propositions, if not wholly empirical, still founded the edifice of *karma* theory, not on the idea of God but on the structure of human desire and what followed from it necessarily. As a link to the *mokṣha* theory, but also in their own terms, equally secular were the following propositions, marked as much for the evocative force of their expression as for the simplicity of the underlying idea: *the karma of a man never leaves him.*

सुशीघ्रमपि धावन्तं विधानमनुधावति।
शेते सह शयानेन येन येन यथा कृतम्।। शान्ति १८१.८।।

उपतिष्ठति तिष्ठन्तं गच्छन्तमनुगच्छति।
करोति कुर्वतः कर्मच्छायेवानुविधीयते।। शान्ति १८१.९।।

If he runs fast, it follows him with equal speed; when he sleeps, it sleeps with him, is with him in whatever he does; on getting up, it gets up with him; on walking, it walks with him; his karma *follows him like a shadow.*[27]

स्वकर्मफलनिक्षेपं विधानपरिरक्षितम्।
भूतग्राममिमं कालः समन्तात् परिकर्षति।। शान्ति १८१.११।।

The fruits of one's actions are like a trust, protected by the unseen; on the appointed time, it surely reaches one.[28]

अचोद्यमानानि यथा पुष्पाणि च फलानि च।
स्वं कालं नातिवर्तन्ते तथा कर्म पुरा कृतम्।। शान्ति १८१.१२।।

Just as flowers and fruits appear unasked, so do the acts done earlier; they do not transgress the time of their fruition.[29]

सम्मानश्चावमानश्च लाभालाभौ क्षयोदयौ।
प्रवृत्ता विनिवर्तन्ते विधानान्ते पुनः पुनः।। शान्ति १८१.१३।।

Honour–insult, gain–loss, rise–fall—these are the results of one's acts of the past, and are exhausted once experienced.[30]

आत्मना विहितं दुःखमात्मना विहितं सुखम्।
गर्भशय्यामुपादाय भुज्यते पौर्वदेहिकम्।। शान्ति १८१.१४।।

Pain is a result of one's own acts, and pleasure and happiness likewise. From the time of conception, one has to suffer the consequences of acts done in a previous life.[31]

यथा धेनुसहस्त्रेषु वत्सो विन्दति मातरम्।
तथा पूर्वकृतं कर्म कर्तारमनुगच्छति।। शान्ति १८१.१६।।

Just as a calf reaches its mother among a hundred cows, one's previous karma *reaches its doer.*[32]

Mokṣha has been the ultimate point in the logic of *karma*. Together they constitute a rational system of thought in which all its essential propositions are derived from the main premise that every act, good or ill, if done with a motive, binds its doer. At the same time, they are rooted in empirical experience. That is to say, the rationality of *karma* and *mokṣha* is not of *a priori* kind. None of the propositions concerning them was a pure logical abstraction, which experience could neither confirm, nor deny. Their basis remained always empirical, the sensible world of experience, where there are visible differences of personal capacity and circumstance.

The rationality of *mokṣha* consists in the following argument. *Trishṇā*, or 'thirst', and obsessive entanglement, or *āsakti*, lead to a virtually endless chain of acts. Only those acts that are done with a desired objective bind the doer. Acts that are disinterested do not count as '*acts*' in the logic of *karma*. In other words, it is the mind and not the outward act that is the decisive factor. In order to play out fully their inherent logic, acts require a series of lives. Thus, time is of fundamental importance in acts coming to their fruition, even as a seed comes to fruition in time. To have release from that repetitive series of life and death, one must overcome the 'thirst' of desire, *trishṇā*, and dissolve all entanglements. That is what stops forever the moving wheel of *karma*—for oneself. That this is what *mokṣha* meant, and that it had reference to nothing beyond the logic of *karma*, is clearly stated, and repeatedly, in the *Mahābhārata*.[33] For example:

कर्मणा जायते प्रेत्य मूर्तिमान् षोडशात्मकः।
विद्यया जायते नित्यमव्यक्तं ह्यव्ययात्मकम्।। शान्ति २४१.८।।

From acts arises, after death, another life with the manifest sixteen psychophysical attributes of human personality; from knowledge arises a state where one's self remains, in the unmanifest reality, forever unmanifest.[34]

कर्मणः फलमाप्नोति सुखदुःखे भवाभवौ।
विद्यया तदवाप्नोति यत्र गत्वा न शोचति।। शान्ति २४१.११।।

Pleasure and pain, suffering and happiness, life and death, are the fruits of one's acts. Knowledge brings one into a state where there is no sorrow.[35]

यत्र गत्वा न म्रियते यत्र गत्वा न जायते ।।
न पुनर्जायते यत्र यत्र गत्वा न वर्तते ।। शान्ति २४१.१२ ।।
On reaching there, there is neither death nor birth. There is no rebirth; reaching there, one does not return to this world.[36]

That is also the position of practically the whole of Indian philosophy, excepting of course the materialist part of it, concerning *mokṣha*.[37] Even the materialists did not deny a certain link between acts and their consequences; neither did they deny, although they were accused of doing precisely that, the need for self-control.

That one should be troubled about the consequences of one's *acts* is both natural and right. But why should one be so deeply troubled by the cycle of birth and rebirth, of which one is not conscious anyway, of which one has no memory, that one should want to obtain *mokṣha* from it as the highest human aspiration? The answer to this question is provided in the *Mahābhārata*. Human experience is eventually repetitive. It is the same thing over and over again; only the names and the faces are different. *Mokṣha* is simply the human cry for release from the toil and fatigue of repetitive experience. That poignant cry is best expressed in the *Āshvamedhika-parva*.[38]

न क्वचित् सुखमत्यन्तं न क्वचिच्छाश्वती स्थितिः ।
स्थानाच्च महतो भ्रंशो दुःखलब्धात् पुनः पुनः ।। आश्वमेधिक १६.३० ।।
Nowhere is there too much happiness, nor does one remain in any state too long; obtaining the highest place, one still falls; and suffering comes again and again.[39]

अशुभा गतयः प्राप्ताः कष्टा मे पापसेवनात् ।
काममन्युपरीतेन तृष्णया मोहितेन च ।। आश्वमेधिक १६.३१ ।।
Confused by desire and 'thirst', I have known sinful deeds and, owing to them, unwholesome states.[40]

पुनः पुनश्च मरणं जन्म चैव पुनः पुनः ।
आहारा विविधा भुक्ताः पीता नानाविधाः स्तनाः ।। आश्वमेधिक १६.३२ ।।

I have died several times, and several times I have been born; I have fed upon various foods, and have suckled at many breasts.[41]

मातरो विविधा दृष्टाः पितरश्च पृथग्विधाः ।
सुखानि च विचित्राणि दुःखानि च मयानघ ।। आश्वमेधिक १६.३३ ।।
I have known all kinds of mothers, and I have known many fathers; I have known pleasures of strange kinds, and strange sufferings, too.[42]

प्रियैर्विवासो बहुशः संवासश्चाप्रियैः सह ।
धननाशश्च सम्प्राप्तो लब्ध्वा दुःखेन तद् धनम् ।। आश्वमेधिक १६.३४ ।।
I have many times known the loss of the ones I loved, and I have kept company with those not dear to me; I have known the pain of losing wealth obtained with much trouble.[43]

अवमानाः सुकष्टाश्च राजतः स्वजनात् तथा ।
शारीरा मानसा वापि वेदना भृशदारुणाः ।। आश्वमेधिक १६.३५ ।।
Insult and pain have come to me from others and also from those who were my own. I have known awful pains of the body and the suffering of the mind.[44]

प्राप्ता विमाननाश्चोग्रा वधबन्धाश्च दारुणाः ।
पतनं निरये चैव यातनाश्च यमक्षये ।। आश्वमेधिक १६.३६ ।।
I have received severe punishments, and I have known bondage that was dreadful. I have several times fallen into darkness, and I have known the pain of repeated dying.[45]

जरा रोगाश्च सततं व्यसनानि च भूरिशः ।
लोकेऽस्मिन्ननुभूतानि द्वन्द्वजानि भृशं मया ।। आश्वमेधिक १६.३७ ।।
Again and again I have suffered old age, disease, and afflictions of many kinds; and I have known the pain of conflicts inherent in this world.[46]

From this weariness of '*I have seen it all*' arose that ultimate aspiration: neither for grace nor for bliss, but simply for *release from the toil and fatigue of experience*. But one can say 'I have seen it all', even in *this* lifetime, not necessarily from one's own life, but from observing the lives of others as well, which, in being human, are also one's own. Weariness of repetitive experience can come from the collective experience of humankind, from collective human history. It does not in itself require a cycle of birth and rebirth, an individual history, to produce it. One can live many lives in one lifetime alone, and have a sense of weariness from it all. In one lifetime one can die several times, and several times be reborn in one lifetime.

The radical shift in the *Mahābhārata*

The *Mahābhārata* has human life as its main concern, therefore, not *mokṣha* as understood in its classical form but *dharma*. *Dharma* is the foundation that sustains and supports life in its numerous forms. Undoubtedly, a large part of the *Mahābhārata* is devoted to discussing *mokṣha* as liberation from the ceaseless toil of birth and rebirth. But that is mostly to state, in different contexts, the prevalent views of *mokṣha*, each of them with a particular philosophic axe to grind, and each of them tied to the presupposition of rebirth.

Rising above them all, the *Mahābhārata* clearly does four things, which make it a truly universal philosophy of human freedom.

One, it quietly disconnects *mokṣha* from the cycle of birth and rebirth, so that *mokṣha is human freedom here and now*, in *this* life. The main question is not what will happen to one after death, which can only be speculation, but what one makes of one's self in this life, which is concrete and visible. *Mokṣha* is a meditation not of death but of life. Besides, what one has no memory of, is ethically irrelevant. History presupposes memory; if one has no memory, history has no meaning. In the voice of Yudhishṭhira, the *Mahābhārata* raises this plain question.

Yudhishṭhira (*to Bhīshma*)

On achieving the highest state of *mokṣha*, do those great people have the memory of dying and being born again? It is only *you* I can ask this question. Kindly tell me the truth of it.

To me, there seems to be a great defect in the state of *mokṣha*, which is this. If, in that state, one still retains the memory of one's particular past, then I should regard this life of particularities, with particular desires and particular aims, the best. If, on the other hand, one has no memory whatsoever of the particularities of the past, then what greater suffering can there be than that?[47]

Bhīshma (*to Yudhishṭhira*)

You have asked a very complex question. In thinking about it, many astute minds get confused.[48]

The long answer that Bhīshma gives[49] is derived, he says, from the Sāṁkhya philosophy as propounded by Kapila, which, moreover, he declares to be the greatest of all philosophical systems.[50] Manifestly it is the philosophy of Sāṁkhya, along with Yoga, or Sāṁkhya-Yoga, the earliest of all philosophical systems in the history of Indian thought, that the *Mahābhārata* propounds. The substance of the answer that Bhīshma gives to Yudhishṭhira's question concerning memory is as follows. It is through the physical senses that one has the sensation and knowledge of the particularities of the world. The mind is connected with the physical senses, and memory is a function of the mind. Indeed, it is through the agency of the mind that the Self, the innermost substance, becomes aware of the functioning of the senses. For, in themselves, the senses have no consciousness. They, with the mind, and the rest of human personality are creations of Nature, *prakriti*. And since the Self, the *purusa*, is *housed* in the edifice they build, it comes to acquire the false consciousness of its identity in their terms, when, in actual truth, it is an existence wholly separate from them. When that false consciousness ends, there is the dawn of *mokṣha*. But *mokṣha*, the last freedom of the Self, is in one's consciousness; the psychophysical apparatus continues to exist until the machine is worn out—and dies. Until then the knowledge of particularities exist; memory exists; but, at the dawn of *mokṣ ha*, when the Self returns to the Self as pure existence, it returns to the world no more. Actually, this response did not answer the question that Yudhishṭhira had raised, for, *mokṣha* apart, he was raising a question about the notion of rebirth itself, that is, rebirth would make sense if only there was the memory of the previous life, without which it has no ethical relevance to the present. But that is also a question that cannot be answered with definite assurance. The *Mahābhārata*, therefore, quietly, without engaging in speculative arguments about it, puts it aside. Of greater ethical relevance are the attributes, *lakṣaṇa*-s, or '*the signs*', of a person, man or woman, who has achieved the last freedom, *here*, and not whether he, or she, has also thereby stopped the grinding wheel of birth and dying and being born again.

Two, in contrast to other philosophical systems, including Sāṁkhya-Yoga, where *mokṣha* is conceived as being beyond all relations, and thus a denial of relationships, the *Mahābhārata* shows *mokṣha* to be quite as relational as truth and *dharma* are. Freedom is an affirmation, and not a denial, of relationships, except that those are now seen in a radically different light. For that reason, the *Mahābhārata* is concerned with the attributes, the *lakṣaṇa*-s, of a person, man or woman, who has inwardly achieved *mokṣha*, first in his, or her, relationship with his, or her, self, and at the same time in his, or her, relationship with the *other*. True freedom brings the self and the *other* into a joyous relationship. Just as it is certain that desire leads to acts, and acts lead to bondage, so it is certain that one's freedom from them would be only one's own, leaving others still in the grinding wheel of suffering. That one has seen the Light, to use another metaphor, and has taken wings towards it, does not deliver the world from darkness. The free man of the *Mahābhārata*, in being free, devotes himself to the *other*. This is said in the *Mahābhārata* again and again, and yet again.

The *third* thing that the *Mahābhārata* does is to show that it is not until one had truly understood one's self, and had mastered one's self, that there could be a true reaching towards the *other*. At the same time, the finding of one's self is primarily through relationships, personal and social. Paradoxically, self-knowledge and self-discovery require the existence of the *other*, or else even the awareness of the 'self' would be inconceivable. However, none of this was ever turned into some hard theory. Everywhere in the world, all the time, a great many men and women, who have not understood their self truly, much less have mastered themselves, do still reach out to the *other*, in love and in friendship. If self-knowledge were to be a prior condition of love, then there would be in the world very little love, for there is so little of self-knowledge.

Four. Recognising this, and consistent with its method of inquiry into the human condition, the *Mahābhārata* begins, above all, by stating those truths of human life that are manifest, are empirical, and are easily verifiable in the common experience of men and women. Those truths are wholly independent of any particular religious faith that one might have. That is to say, neither do they compromise the faith, whatever it might be, nor does the faith in any way affect them. They are independent, too, of any philosophical position that one might take concerning man and the world. Thus, for example, reject the belief in rebirth, and nothing for that reason will collapse in the relationship of the self with the *other*; its foundations will still have to be in *dharma*, truth, and not-violence. Reject, or put aside, those fine philosophical refinements to the *karma* theory, with which the philosophical texts are full, and the truth will remain intact that there is a psychological correspondence between our acts and thoughts *and* what we are. In other words, *dharma*, or the foundation of relationships, is not derived from any philosophical or religious belief. *Dharma consists of trust, caring, love, and truth.* These may be religious ideas also. They certainly are. But even before they are that, they are *dharma*. And they are equally the attributes of *mokṣha* as freedom in this life, *here and now*, to which every human being is a natural heir. Freedom is human inheritance.

The attributes of a free person

The relational nature of *mokṣha* is best brought out in answer to the question: what, in relation with himself and others, are the attributes, *lakṣaṇa*-s, of a person who has obtained *mokṣha*? At an earlier stage of life, the stage of enlightened self-interest, he learnt to enjoy his senses moderately, because indulgence was harmful. He learnt to face success and failure without being either too jubilant or too disheartened, because the first of these produces egoism and the second a loss of the will to exert. He learnt not to grieve too much at the death of relatives, because to do so is futile.[51] He learnt not to grieve for past things, because that is useless. He learnt to distinguish between friend and enemy, but believing, at the same time, that there is neither friendship nor enmity that is permanent, one changing into the other with shifting self-interest.[52] He lived a full life by devoting himself to material prosperity, to pleasure, and to *dharma*, together. The *Mahābhārata* states: 'He who is given to only one of them is low; he who is devoted to two of them is middling; and the best of all is he who pursues all three.'[53]

His life had hitherto been one of desired objectives, *sakāma karma* intentional acts. Those constituted the stuff of experience. In everything and in all circumstances his need was one of self-discipline and balance. Above all, he understood that in the domain of *karma* there is no reprieve.

The state of *mokṣha*, according to the theory, while folding within itself the most heightened forms of self-control and balance, goes a great deal beyond them. It is a state of complete desirelessness and, therefore, of acts done without motive or interest, *nishkāma karma*. The main premise of the *karma* theory, and therefore of *mokṣha* theory, has been that only the acts done with a desired objective bind their doer. Acts that are totally disinterested do not count as *acts* in the logic of *karma*.[54] In other words, it is *consciousness* and not *acts* that is the decisive factor in that logic. Where the consciousness is emptied of *interest*, there the acts strictly speaking have no value. Logically, therefore, *mokṣha* is the state of a radically different consciousness, illumined by knowledge, far greater than all the riches of the world.[55]

यद्यप्यस्य महीं दद्याद् रत्नपूर्णामिमां नरः ।
इदमेव ततः श्रेय इति मन्येत तत्त्ववित् ।। शान्ति २४६.२० ।।

If somebody were to offer such a person the whole earth with its splendid riches, he would consider even that as nothing compared to what he has acquired.[56]

Such a consciousness transcends the tension inherent in the material and ethical opposites. The man who has attained *mokṣha* has risen above the polarity of pleasure–pain, attraction–aversion, happiness–sorrow, love–hate, praise–denigration, gain–loss, success–failure, fear–courage, honour–insult, strength–weakness, virtue–vice, good–evil, victory–defeat, wealth–poverty, conflict–harmony, gentleness–aggression, freedom–bondage.[57] It is between these opposites, and several more, that the human drama takes place endlessly. And, therefore, it is upon these that the *Mahābhārata* places the greatest emphasis in its teachings concerning human freedom.

The attributes of a person, man or woman, who has attained the state of *mokṣha*, follow with perfect coherence from the proposition that all human acts take place within a pair of opposites. He, or she, who has transcended the workings of the duality of opposites has attained the last freedom, *mokṣha*.[58]

नैवेच्छति न चानिच्छो यात्रामात्रव्यवस्थितः ।। शान्ति २३६.३६ ।।
अलोलुपोऽव्यथो दान्तो न कृती न निराकृतिः ।
नास्येन्द्रियमनेकाग्रं न विक्षिप्तमनोरथः ।। शान्ति २३६.३७ ।।

सर्वभूतसदृङ्मैत्रः समलोष्टाश्मकाञ्चनः ।
तुल्यप्रियाप्रियो धीरस्तुल्यनिन्दात्मसंस्तुतिः ।। शान्ति २३६.३८ ।।

अस्पृहः सर्वकामेभ्यो ब्रह्मचर्यदृढव्रतः ।
अहिंस्त्रः सर्वभूतानामीदृक् सांख्यो विमुच्यते ।। शान्ति २३६.३९ ।।

Neither does he desire anything, nor does he not-desire anything.
Neither does he do anything with motive, nor does he not-do anything.

A lump of clay and a piece of gold are to him of equal value. For him there is no distinction between the pleasant and the unpleasant.
He is indifferent to whether he is denigrated or praised.
Aware of his unity with all beings, he has feelings of friendship for all, and violence towards none.[59]

निर्ममश्चानहङ्कारो निर्द्वन्द्वश्छिन्नसंशय: ।
नैव क्रुद्ध्यति न द्वेष्टि नानृता भाषते गिर: ।। शान्ति २३६.३४ ।।
आक्रुष्टस्ताडितश्चैव मैत्रण ध्याति नाशुभम् ।
वाग्दण्डकर्ममनसां त्रयाणां च निवर्तक: ।। शान्ति २३६.३५ ।।
सम: सर्वेषु भूतेषु ब्रह्माणमभिवर्तते ।

There is in him no trace of ego, anger, or malice.
Towards the one who is aggressive and full of hate, he bears no ill will, only friendship. And he does not ever take recourse to lies.
In his thoughts, or speech, or acts, he causes no hurt to any being. He sees all beings with the eyes of equality.
For him there is neither assertion nor denial. His doubts and conflicts have been resolved. And he has gone beyond the duality of the opposites.[60]
He fears nobody and nobody fears him. Because he sees all living beings in himself, and himself in all living beings, he causes pain to nobody in thought, speech or act, and he acts towards all beings with natural kindness and friendliness.

सर्वभूतेषु चात्मानं सर्वभूतानि चात्मनि ।
यदा पश्यति भूतात्मा ब्रह्म सम्पद्यते तदा ।। शान्ति २३९.२१ ।।
यावानात्मनि वेदात्मा तावानात्मा परात्मनि ।
य एवं सततं वेद सोऽमृतत्वाय कल्पते ।। शान्ति २३९.२२ ।।

सर्वभूतात्मभूतस्य विभोर्भूतहितस्य च ।
देवाऽपि मार्गे मुह्यन्ति उपदस्य पदैषिण: ।। शान्ति २३९.२३ ।।

On perceiving his self in all beings, and all beings in his self, he attains the highest consciousness.
Living in the knowledge that others have in them the same soul as he has in him, he lives in a consciousness that is beyond death.
In becoming the self of the others, he acts for the good of all, and yet, he has no aim for his own self. Even the gods cannot trace his footsteps. Like a bird in the sky, or a fish in the water, he leaves no traces behind.[61]

द्वन्द्वैर्न यत्र बाध्यन्ते मानसेन च कर्मणा ।
समा: सर्वत्र मैत्राश्च सर्वभूतहिते रता: ।। शान्ति २४१.१४ ।।

Those who have attained that state are assailed no more by the duality of opposites. Feeling equality and friendship for all, they are engaged in obtaining the good of all beings.[62]

In all the portraits that the *Mahābhārata* draws of the free man, or the free woman, three features are common. He, or she, has risen above the play of the opposites; and although some of them, of the purely physical kind, such as heat–cold, still affect the body, they have ceased to assail his, or her, consciousness. The free person fears no one, and creates conditions where others likewise obtain freedom from fear. And he, or she, perceiving the human oneness works ceaselessly for the good of the others. The '*good of the others*' is in terms of *dharma*, whereby the *other* is enhanced, enriched, sustained, held together. Thus, again, for example, this time in the voice of a teacher, the *Mahābhārata* says:

आत्मवत् सर्वभूतेषु यश्चरेन्नियत: शुचि: ।
अमानी निरभीमान: सर्वतो मुक्त एव स: ।। आश्व १९.३ ।।

सर्वमित्र: सर्वसह: शमे रक्तो जितेन्द्रिय: ।
व्यपेतभयमन्युश्च आत्मवान् मुच्यते नर: ।। आश्व १९.२ ।।

Perceiving his oneness with others, and thus their togetherness, who is a friend to all; has disciplined his senses; does not seek recognition and acclaim; is free of pride—such a person is always free.[63]

जीवितं मरणं चोभे सुखदु:खे तथैव च ।
लाभालाभे प्रियद्वेष्ये य: सम: स च मुच्यते ।। आश्व १९.४ ।।

Who has risen above the duality of life–death, suffering–happiness, gain–loss, love–hate—such a person is a free person.[64]

न कस्यचित् स्पृहयते नावजानाति किंचन ।
निर्द्वन्द्वो वीतरागात्मा सर्वथा मुक्त एव स: ।। आश्व १९.५ ।।

Who is never desirous of what others are; but neither does he disregard anyone; is free of the conflict of the opposites; and has no excessive attachments—such a person is always free.[65]

अनमित्रश्च निर्बन्धुरनपत्यश्च य: क्वचित् ।
त्यक्तधर्मार्थकामश्च निराकाङ्क्षी च मुच्यते ।। आश्व १९.६ ।।

नैव धर्मी न चाधर्मी पूर्वोपचितहायकः।
धातुक्षयप्रशान्तात्मा निर्द्वन्द्वः स विमुच्यते।। आश्व १९.७।।
Who does not perceive others in the opposites of friend–enemy; who has freed his mind from the categories of dharma, artha *and* kāma*; indeed, who has gone beyond the polarity even of* dharma–adharma*; who is free of the history of accumulated* karma-*s; and whose conflicts have ceased—such a person is always free.*[66]

नैनं शस्त्राणि विध्यन्ते न मृत्युश्चास्य विद्यते।
नातः सुखतरं किंचिल्लोके क्वचन दृश्यते।। आश्व १९.२९।।
No weapon can hurt him; neither can death touch him; no one in the world could be more at pace than such a person.[67]

Seen in this light, *mokṣha* is as relational as truth and *dharma* are. Freedom is necessarily freedom in relation to one's self, but equally in relation to the *other.* Since bondage is created, in the first place, by one's ignorance, and wrong understanding of who one *is*, freedom lies also within oneself. Self-understanding is the clearest path to human freedom. And self-understanding is not something esoteric. It is achieved, in perceptible degrees, and in stages, by reflecting upon one's relation to the given human realities. For example, it is true that man lives *in* history: but am I my history alone? It is undeniable that each person is located in his, or her, given contexts. But am I only that which my contexts permit me to be?

Since all human acts take place between the opposites, and the acts necessarily bind a person to their consequences, the *act–consequence–act* chain forming the *samsāra*, the experiential world; if that chain has to be snapped, it is logical to posit a state, in this life itself, where consciousness is emptied of all conceivable opposites. That state is *mokṣha*. It is neither 'positive', nor it is 'negative', neither 'good' nor 'evil', neither 'freedom' nor 'bondage'. Then, one more step: 'Go beyond the polarity even of *dharma–adharma*, and truth–untruth; that done, renounce the faculty with which you renounced them; and, finally, renounce even the awareness that anything has been renounced at all.' This farthest point in the conception of *mokṣha* was reached in the following verse in the *Mahābhārata*:

त्यज धर्ममधर्मं च तथा सत्यानृते त्यज।
उभे सत्यानृते त्यक्त्वा येन त्यजसि तं त्यज।। शान्ति ३२९.४०।।

त्यज धर्ममसंकल्पादधर्मं चाप्यलिप्सया।
उभे सत्यानृते बुद्ध्या बुद्धिं परमनिश्चयात्।। शान्ति ३२९.४१।।
Leave dharma *and* adharma, *leave truth and untruth; then renounce the faculty with which they were renounced; that done, renounce the awareness that anything has been renounced.*[68]

There are three questions that naturally arise here. First of all, since the opposites are inherent in human life, why should one seek freedom from *them*, for it would amount to seeking freedom from life itself? Can there ever be such a thing as freedom from inherent reality? Second, if one must, is that kind of freedom psychologically possible anyway? And third, could it not be that, given the Indian philosophic habit of exploring an idea to its farthest limits, the idea of freedom from the workings of *all* opposites as the last freedom was actually no more than a logical construct on some facts that are empirically true?

The answer to the first question is evident, and is provided by human experience itself. Putting aside *mokṣha* in its classical form, there is no doubt that going beyond the fluctuating and uncertain workings of the opposites is required even in one's self-interest. One's mental health demands it.

Today, I am a king, and I think that I own the universe; tomorrow, I turn into a pauper, with not a room that I can call my own. Today, I am honoured and greeted with cries of acclamation; tomorrow, I am despised and greeted with howls of desecration. Today, I am loved, to a degree that the *other* cannot even breathe without me, if only in a figurative sense. Tomorrow, I come to be hated, to a degree that the *other* just cannot breathe until I leave, and vanish. What is attraction today, changes into aversion tomorrow. Every success carries within itself also the seeds of its failure. And what appears to be a failure is a turning point for a greater success, followed by a greater failure. And so on.

Does life then condemn me to be a dangling man, or a dangling woman, dangling forever between the opposites of attraction and aversion, gain and loss, exultation and grief, where the one can quickly change into the other?

Just as this is a central question in human life, it is a central question in the *Mahābhārata*'s inquiry into the human condition. Among numerous other stories of the human condition, it narrates the story of Bali who was once Indra.[69] The story is in the form of a dialogue between Shakra, who has just become Indra, the king of gods, and Bali, the man who had ruled the three worlds as the previous Indra but is now vanquished by Shakra. The new Indra, accompanied by a procession of gods, on looking for Bali everywhere, at last finds him in a cave on the sea coast of Kerala. Seeing his conqueror with his glorious retinue, Bali feels neither grief nor nostalgia. Fearless and calm, he stands upright and looks at Shakra. The dialogue that took place between the two was narrated in a previous chapter on the question of causality, to which the reader should turn again.[70]

Every human story says many things at the same time. So does the story of Indra and Bali, the victor and the vanquished. It is in the very first place the story of a man who, in his consciousness, had risen above the play of the opposites—victory–defeat, gain–loss, honour–insult. Hence its importance here, for that is one of the main attributes of *mokṣha*. Undoubtedly, Bali was a free person. However, his views were not of human freedom. On the contrary, he was advocating man's absolute subjection to *kāla*, Time, as the all-pervading force that determines every human situation.

महाविद्योऽल्पविद्यश्च बलवान् दुर्बलश्च यः।
दर्शनीयो विरूपश्च सुभगो दुर्भगश्च।। शान्ति २२४.१८।।

सर्वं कालः समादत्ते गम्भीरः स्वेन तेजसा।
तस्मिन् कालवशं प्राप्ते का व्यथा मे विजानतः।। शान्ति २२४.१९।।

Greatly learned or of little learning; strong or weak; of good looks or not; fortunate or unfortunate—all are reduced alike in the effulgence of Time. Knowing that all are subject to Time, what pain can it cause me?[71]

न मातृपितृशुश्रूषा न च दैवतपूजनम्।
नान्यो गुणसमाचारः पूरुषस्य सुखावहः।। शान्ति २२७.३०।।

Neither loving devotion to the parents, nor the worship of gods, nor all the good qualities one may have, can bring happiness to a man.[72]

न विद्या न तपो दानं न मित्राणि न बान्धवाः।
शक्नुवन्ति परित्रातुं नरं कालेन पीडितम्।। शान्ति २२७.३१।।

Neither learning, nor burning oneself in austerity, nor giving, nor friends nor relatives, can save the man struck by Time.[73]

पर्यायैर्हन्यमानानां परित्राता न विद्यते।। शान्ति २२७.३३।।

The one struck by Time, no one can protect.[74]

And that is another subject of the *Mahābhārata*'s inquiry into the human condition.[75] However, absolutely subject to Time, according to his belief, Bali was still absolutely free, inwardly, and that freedom came from within that same belief.

न च कालेन कालज्ञ: स्पृष्ट: शोचितुमर्हति।। शान्ति २२७.८६।।
तेन शक्र न शोचामि नास्ति शोके सहायता।
The one who knows the power of Time, does not, even when reduced by Time, sorrow or grieve, for grief is of no help.[76]

But put aside this question as well, as we had put aside the question of rebirth and its connection with the idea of *mokṣha*. Whether we believe, in its absolute form, or we don't believe, that Time determines all things, and there is no such thing as human freedom, the truth will remain in either case that our emotional and spiritual well-being demands that we transcend the workings of the opposites. What also remains is the second question in that regard: is such a state psychologically possible to achieve?

So far as this is concerned, there seems to be no inherent psychological *impossibility*, or even improbability, in the conception of a man rising above the opposites. It is not impossible, psychologically or logically, for a person to remain unaffected, for example, both by praise and blame. Neither is it impossible for a man to remain inwardly untouched both by the pleasures and the sufferings that may come to him, or her. There are a great many ordinary people who manage to achieve this in greater or lesser degree at one time or another in their lives. Thus, what is psychologically possible in *some* measure at *one* time is also possible in *full* measure *all* the time. There is nothing to suggest the impossibility of a man achieving distance from the opposites of all conceivable kinds, although everything suggests the absolute rarity of such a person.

Mokṣha as freedom *from*

The word 'freedom' implies bondage, of whatever kind. Freedom is always freedom *from*. Freedom from that state of being, physical or emotional or intellectual, which confines me, limits me, does violence to me, degrades me, chokes me, makes me unhappy, which by my own acts and feelings and thoughts I have created for myself. Or the *other* has created it for me, in which I have played little or no part. Or both I and the *other* have together created it for ourselves. *Mokṣha* is freedom from those states. *Mokṣha* apart, in whatever way one defines freedom, or liberty, either in political philosophy, or in the philosophy of law, or in spiritual traditions, those states are what freedom is *from*.

The *Mahābhārata* shows all the time that human freedom is freedom of the self, from the self, unto the self. I may have a completely wrong understanding of who I am. This gets transferred, at the collective level, into the wrong understanding of who *we* are. Freedom is at the same time freedom from the *other,* of the *other,* and unto the *other.* I may have a wrong understanding of who the *other* is. And, at the collective level, this gets transferred into a wrong understanding of who *they* are. Freedom is freedom also from the wrong perceptions of the relationship between the two, between the self and the *other*—both in a personal and in a collective sense. *That* freedom is *mokṣha* on this earth. This is not to be interpreted as some esoteric saying. It is plainly the case in whatever is human.

Human life and relationships are lived through 'place' and 'time', *desha* and *kāla*, which keep changing. These are also the two coordinates of 'history'. What it then means is that life and relationships are lived *in* history. Everyone lives in his, or her, specific contexts. We live in those contexts that are *given,* like the circumstances of our birth, in a particular place, in a particular family, in a particular society, with their specific histories. And at the same time we live in those contexts, which we *choose or create* for ourselves.

The *Mahābhārata* emphasises, at every turn, that the context of a thing determines its meaning. And, then, at every turn, it raises the question, 'Is that all that there is to *meaning*?'

If it were, then the meaning of my life must forever lie in something that is external to me, which surrounds me from all sides, is over and above me, weaves itself into the fabric of my existence, conditions my life, over which I have neither power nor appeal. If context is the whole of man's existence, then there can be no such thing as abiding human meaning, except what is provided by the context itself. For, just as the contexts of life keep changing, its meaning must keep changing, too. And every person will then be many different persons in the perpetual flux of spaces and times and relationships. The underlying question is, thus, of man's relationship with the changing circumstances of his or her life, with the past and with the present.

Am I only what my contexts, personal and social, permit me to be? If the answer is 'yes', then all this talk of human freedom, and its accumulated weight, is nothing but a heap of noble-sounding nonsense. If the answer is: 'No, I am not my history *alone*', then I begin to walk, even if haltingly, on the path of *freedom from history*.

What in substance that means is freedom from the past, and freedom from memory. On the one hand, the logic of *karma* would deny that there can be any such freedom, for one's past was a creation of one's own acts, or of the acts of the *other,* or of the combined acts of oneself and the *other*. But that very logic also asserts that we are free to create new *karma*-s. That is to say, we are free to create our *present*—in some measure at any rate. And that we do, when we live in the present and not in the past.

In actual fact, our consciousness is almost always of the present, and rarely of the past. Freedom is freedom *from* some situation in which I am *now*, whether political or economic or emotional or spiritual. The tyranny of the past always resurrects itself as the tyranny of the present.

Above all, *mokṣha* is freedom from *tamas*. This word is mostly translated as 'darkness', which does not bring out its proper meaning. For example, the translation of that famous upanishadic human prayer *tamaso mā jyotir gamaya* as 'lead me from darkness into light' is vague and imprecise. The word *tamas* is derived from the root word *tam*, which means 'to gasp for breath, be suffocated, choke, be exhausted, perish, be distressed or disturbed'. So, whatever suffocates, chokes, exhausts, distresses, and disturbs us, is *tamas*, or *tāmasic*.

The Sāṃkhya philosophy is among the earliest philosophical schools of India, along with Yoga, both certainly pre-*Mahābhārata*. The clearest and the most lucid exposition of Sāṃkhya philosophy is to be found in the *Mahābhārata*, propounded there by Pañchashikha in the main,[77] but in many other voices as well. The entire creation, *prakriti*, is seen as the product of the three main forms of primordial energy, of which *tamas* is one; the other two being *sattva*, or the energy that creates a feeling of joy and peace, and *rajas*, which creates discontent, greed, intolerance, sorrow, and remorse. None of the three exists without the other two. According to the Sāṃkhya, the Self, the *purusha*, which is entirely a separate entity from *prakriti*, gets somehow entangled with the workings of *prakriti*, which means the experiential world, and *mokṣha* is when it becomes aware of its true nature, and says to *prakriti*: 'enough.'

It is true that, given this philosophical premise as its main element, the meaning of *mokṣha* in Sāṃkhya will be in the terms of what follows from that premise. But, so far as human freedom on this earth is concerned, it is immaterial whether, or not, we accept the dualistic view of the Self and Nature being two wholly separate entities. Nor will it matter if, on the contrary, we believe, with the Vedānta, that all perceptions of duality are mistaken, and what is required is the awareness of the unity of the Self, the *ātman*, with everything that exists. The Vedānta, given that premise, has naturally a different conception of *mokṣha*.

The *Mahābhārata* cuts across different ontological positions concerning the Self. It suggests that it will suffice if we see the evident truth, which the Sāṃkhya points to, that we carry within ourselves energies that take us towards love and joy and peace, energies that make for greed and discontent; and those energies that suffocate, choke, distress, and disturb. This is true in a collective sense as well.

The universal ground of *mokṣha* as human freedom is freedom from whatever is *tāmasic*. *Mokṣha* is freedom also from what is *rājasic*. Everyone can see, as the *Mahābhārata* points out, that since there is in the world no substance that can fill a person's greed, which is like an ocean that never gets filled, greed leads man to endless striving and confusion, from which arise untruth, fear, and aggression. There is an evident chain of causation here: one thing arising from the other. 'From greed arises every conceivable attitude and acts that cause harm to one's self and to the other: anger, confusion, egoism, intolerance, shamelessness, loss of prosperity and well-being.' The *Mahābhārata* suggests that ignorance is the root cause of greed, and greed feeds ignorance. They suffocate, choke, and distress a whole social system quite as much as they suffocate, choke, and distress one's own life and relationships. They are *tamas*. In that sense, freedom from *tamas* is freedom *of* the self *from* the self *unto* the self.

The paths to *mokṣha*

Let us next see what the paths to *mokṣha* are. That should help us begin by seeing clearly what those paths are *not*. In that, we are helped very greatly by those numerous women in the *Mahābhārata* who teach us what freedom truly is.

First, external renunciation is no path to *mokṣha* as human freedom, neither is an outward withdrawal from the world, and thus a renunciation of personal and social bonds, any part of *mokṣha*, *if properly understood*. It is particularly important to grasp this, for much of the *moksha* literature is full of the sound of renunciation, 'renounce this, renounce that', 'leave this, leave that', which leads to a completely wrong understanding of what *mokṣha* is. That sound is heard undoubtedly in the *Mahābhārata* as well, but only in places where the *vairagya*, or complete dissociation from the objects of the world, is being advocated as a logical culmination of desire analysed. The dominant sound of the *Mahābhārata* is not of renunciation but of the freedom of the mind. For it is in the *mind*, and not in the external *things* of the world, that both bondage and freedom lie. It repudiates all false notions of renunciation.

The *Mahābhārata* says to us:

आकिंचन्ये न मोक्षोऽस्ति किंचन्ये नास्ति बन्धनम् ।
किंचन्ये चेतरे चैव जन्तुर्ज्ञानेन मुच्यते ।। शान्ति ३२०.५० ।।

Neither is mokṣha *in lack of possessions, in not-having;*
Nor is bondage in possessions and prosperity, in having.
Whether one or the other, it is knowledge that sets a person free.[78]

It is a woman, Kausalyā, the wife of King Janaka, who says to us, as she had said to her husband who had suddenly decided to renounce everything and take to living in the forest in search of *mokṣha*:

त्यागान्न भिक्षुकं विद्यान्न मौढ्यान्न च याचनात् ।
ऋजुस्तु योऽर्थंत्यजति नसुखं विद्धि भिक्षुकम् ।। शान्ति १८.३० ।।

No one is a monk merely because he has renounced, and he begs, and keeps silence. He alone is a genuine monk who has naturally risen above one's narrow and petty self-interest and is not attached to pleasures.[79]

अनिष्कषाये काषायमीहार्थमिति विद्धि तम् ।
धर्मध्वजानां मुण्डानां वृत्त्यर्थमिति मे मितिः ।। शान्ति १८.३४ ।।

If passions, kashāya*, are not removed from one's heart, to take to the ochre-coloured robe,* kāshāya *is no more than a means to selfish ends. I think it is only a means to earn a livelihood, by those who shave their heads and insincerely wave the flag of* dharma.[80]

Wholly persuaded, the king would later, in a different context, repeat the truth his wife had spoken.

काषायधारणं मौण्ड्यं त्रिविष्टब्धं कमण्डलुम् ।
लिङ्गान्युत्पथभूतानि न मोक्षायेति मे मतिः ।। शान्ति ३२०.४७ ।।

To wear ochre robes, to shave one's head, to carry a trident and a begging bowl—these are mere signs of renunciation; in themselves they do not lead to mokṣha.[81]

यदि सत्यपि लिङ्गेऽस्मिन् ज्ञानमेवात्र कारणम् ।
निर्मोक्षायेह दुःखस्य लिङ्गमात्रं निरर्थकम् ।। शान्ति ३२०.४८ ।।

Since discriminating awareness is the only means to mokṣha, *freedom from pain and suffering, all external signs are irrelevant.'*[82]
Inwardly free, it is a matter of indifference whether he wears an ochre robe or the regalia of a king.

Queen Choodālā of the *Yoga-Vāsishṭha* would teach her husband likewise some three millennia later.

Excepting a certain part of it, that is, the *vairāgya* tradition, which included the monastic disciplines, Indian thought has never maintained that a denial of the natural bonds of love and affection is the way to spiritual freedom. The great seers and thinkers of the upanishadic age, most of them at any rate, were married people, living with their families. They had not turned away from the world. On the contrary, their profound inquiry into the nature of reality came from a sense of deep reverence for life and from an intense passion to understand it systematically. The same is true about the people who fill the pages of the *Mahābhārata*.

Second. Neither is *mokṣha* to be achieved by practising this ritual or that. Just as the *Upanishad*-s had radically shifted attention from *acts*, or vedic rituals, to the inwardness of one's being, the *Mahābhārata* does likewise.

And third. The *Mahābhārata* shows all the time that *mokṣha* is not a 'project' of some special kind of people. Freedom is an aspiration of ordinary human beings. A man, or a woman, who has achieved inner freedom does not wear a uniform. Among the most important discussions on the ordering of life and relationships *into* freedom is one that is attributed to a meatseller, Dharmavyādha,[83] another to a grocer, Tulādhāra,[84] and the third one to an ordinary housewife.[85] A great many discussions on *mokṣha* as the freedom of the mind take place between a husband and wife, ordinary people. The *Mahābhārata* says:

यमे च नियमे चैव कामे द्वेषे परिग्रहे ।
माने दम्भे तथा स्नेहे सदृशास्ते कुटुम्बिभिः ।। शान्ति ३२०.४१ ।।

A saṃnyāsī *and a householder are alike in exercising self-control; and they are alike in being subject to the logic of attraction and aversion, egoism, arrogance, and grasping.*[86]

In other words, if one has renounced the world but has not removed the disorders of the mind, even a *saṃnyāsī* will remain in bondage, and if a householder has done so, he, or she, has already gained *mokṣha* as inner freedom.

The paths to *mokṣha* are journies within. That is to say, they lie in self-understanding and self-control. It is clearly through them that I bring order in my relationship with my self and in my relationship with the *other.* What is suggested is self-control over one's sense organs and over one's desires, or rather control over desire as such. Now, while the word 'self-understanding' sounds good, the word 'self-control' sounds, to most people, frightening, for the way in which it is prescribed and talked about, in most discussions, suggests a denial of desire, and thereby a denial of all that is human. In any case, when the *Upanishad*-s had been saying that '*desire*' is the root of life', and had seen it as part of the Brahman, the ultimate reality, and therefore sacred, why then such feverish denial of *desire*, or struggle against it, on principle? It is one thing to say that one should control desires; but it is entirely a different thing to say that *desire* itself has to be rooted out from the mind. It is the first of these, and not the second, that the *Mahābhārata* advocates. And that has its clear rationality.

This '*renounce desire*' is only a manner of saying: '*Refuse to be a dangling man, or a dangling woman, dangling forever between the opposites of satisfaction and dissatisfaction.*' It is, above all, pointing to the truth that *desire and its satisfaction cannot be the foundation of a relationship with my self and with the other.* For, in relation to myself, desire will only drive me fiercely hither and thither, so that I am restless in seeking satisfaction, and full of anxiety in wanting to retain it, to the point that I can hardly ever enjoy what I desired and obtained. In relation to the *other,* I turn the *other* into a means of my satisfaction, into an object, to be grasped and retained, and then manipulated. But neither does it mean that *desire* is the enemy of the self.

A-parigraha is the path to *mokṣha* as human freedom. Jainism would place the greatest emphasis upon it. But the word *a-parigraha* is almost always translated, wrongly, as 'non-possession', which refers to '*things*'. The meaning of the word '*a-parigraha*' is clearly brought out if we see what the word *parigraha* means. *Parigraha* means 'to take hold of on both sides; to surround; to encircle; to grasp; to clutch; to take possession of; to overpower; to take prisoner, conquer'. That is what we mostly do in a great many of our relationships. We take hold of the *other*; we surround, encircle, grasp, and take possession of the *other*, we overpower the *other*, in wanting to conquer, we imprison the *other*.

The one truth that is repeatedly brought up in the *Mahābhārata*, is: 'Whatever I do to the *other*, I do that to myself at the same time.' This is the essence of *karma*, or 'acts', which are simultaneously mental and physical. So the plain truth is: in grasping, I am being grasped; imprisoning the *other*, I lock myself in the same prison, the prison of desire and *parigraha*.

And why should one have self-control over one's sense organs? The answer to this question, practically in the whole of Indian philosophy, but more especially in the *Kaṭhopanishad* and in the *Mahābhārata*, begins with some evident propositions. Stronger than the sense organs are their objects; stronger than the sense objects is the will; stronger than the will is the discriminating mind; and stronger than that is one's *ātman*, or the soul.[87] Desire being the starting point of all acts, and the sense organs naturally rushing towards objects that are agreeable, and recoiling from the ones that are disagreeable, the variety of human acts and experiences arising from the ground that lies between attraction and aversion, the sense organs must be kept under self-control.[88] That is because they, and under their influence the will, tend to run riot if not controlled, and become self-destructive. The favourite metaphor in this regard has been that of a chariot drawn by five horses; the body is the chariot, the five sense organs are its horses, the mind is the charioteer.[89] The person who holds firmly the reins of the five horses is a happy charioteer. And there is no heaven and there is no hell apart from what the sense organs, controlled or left wild, create for oneself.[90] Therefore, it follows:

आत्मानाऽऽत्मानमन्विच्छेन्मनोबुद्धिन्द्रियैर्यतैः ।
आत्मा ह्येवात्मनो बन्धुरात्मैव रिपुरात्मनः ।। उद्योग ३४.६४ ।।

Disciplining one's body, mind and intellect, let one conquer one's self with one's self; for one's self alone is one's friend, and one's self also one's enemy.

Indeed, *mokṣha* apart, even pleasure has self-control as its very first condition. Seen in this light, it would no longer appear as a frightening prescription, frightening, because somehow the talk of self-control appears to be a denial of pleasure. But the very reverse is the truth.

The steps to self-discipline as preparation to *moksha* are as follows. First, stated in brief:

> *Anger must be controlled by forgiveness; fear, by vigilance; inclination and aversion, by patience; confusion and doubt and laziness, by practice; greed, by contentment;* adharma, *by generosity;* dharma, *with careful thought; attachment to objects, by meditation on their passing nature; the tendency to talk too much, by periods of silence; pride, by compassion; and the ill effects of material prosperity and wealth, by sharing.*[91]

The *Mahābhārata* says:

> पूर्वे समुद्रे यः पन्थाः स न गच्छति पश्चिमम् ।
> एकः पन्था हि मोक्षस्य तन्मे विस्तरतः शृणु ।। शान्ति २७४.४ ।।
> *The path that goes to the sea in the east cannot also go to the sea in the west. There is only one path to* mokṣha, *of which I shall speak in detail.*[92]

> क्षमया क्रोधमुच्छिन्द्यात् कामं संकल्पवर्जनात् ।
> सत्त्वसंसेवनाद् धीरो निद्रां च च्छेत्तुमर्हति ।। शान्ति २७४.५ ।।
> *Control anger with forgiveness; desire for the pleasures, by giving up resolves to obtain this and obtain that; and control the sleep of the mind with truth and knowledge.*[93]

> अप्रमादाद् भयं रक्षेच्छ्वासं क्षेत्रज्ञशीलनात् ।
> इच्छां द्वेषं च कामं च धैर्येण विनिवर्तयेत् ।। शान्ति २७४.६ ।।
> *Remove fear with vigilance; with self-reflection, protect the breath of life. With patience, control aversion and attraction alike.*[94]

> भ्रमं सम्मोहमावर्तमभ्यासाद् विनिवर्तयेत् ।
> निद्रां च प्रतिभां चैव ज्ञानाभ्यासेन तत्त्ववित् ।। शान्ति २७४.७ ।।
> *By exercising the mind, and with its application, remove your illusions, confusions and doubts. And with the application of knowledge, control the stupor and the excessive brilliance of the mind alike.*[95]

उपद्रवांस्तथा रोगान् हितजीर्णमिताशनात्।
लोभं मोहं च संतोषाद् विषयांस्तत्त्वदर्शनात्।। शान्ति २७४.८।।

Control the disorders and illness of the body by eating wholesome food in limited measure. Control greed and confusion of perceptions, the disorders of the mind, with contentment; and with careful reflection, discipline the objects of pleasure.[96]

अनुक्रोशादधर्मं च जयेद् धर्ममवेक्षया।
आयत्या च जयेदाशामर्थं संगविवर्जनात्।। शान्ति २७४.९।।

Conquer adharma *with compassion, and protect* dharma, *with reflection and analysis. Conquer vain expectations with exerting one's self; having, by avoiding excessive attachment to it.*[97]

अनित्यत्वेन च स्नेहं क्षुधां योगेन पण्डितः।
कारुण्येनात्मनो मानं तृष्णां च परितोषतः।। शान्ति २७४.१०।।

Conquer excessive attachment with reflection on the transitory nature of all that is. Conquer 'the hungers' with bringing the body and the mind in their inherent unity. Conquer your pride and vanity with compassion for yourself. And subdue your 'thirsts' with inner contentment and peace.[98]

उत्थानेन जयेत् तन्द्री वितर्कं निश्चयाज्जयेत्।
मौनेन बहुभाष्यं च शौर्येण च भयं त्यजेत्।। शान्ति २७४.११।।

Conquer laziness with resolute effort; empty argument, by showing what is evident and beyond dispute; the tendency to speak too much, with periods of silence; and fear, with inner strength.[99]

यच्छेद् वाङ्मनसी बुद्ध्या तां यच्छेज्ज्ञानचक्षुषा।
ज्ञानमात्मावबोधेन यच्छेदात्मानमात्मना।। शान्ति २७४.१२।।
तदेतदुपशान्तेन बोद्धव्यं शुचिकर्मणा।

Conquer speech and the restless mind with intelligence; intelligence, with the discriminating eyes of awareness; that too, with the knowledge of the self; and thereafter, with inner peace, do what is cleansed of all blemish.[100]

योगदोषान् समुच्छिद्य पञ्च यान् कवयो विदुः।। शान्ति २७४.१३।।
कामं क्रोधं च लोभं च भयं स्वप्नं च पञ्चमम्।
परित्यज्य निषेवेत यतवाग् योगसाधनान्।। शान्ति २७४.१४।।

Of the body and the mind, there are five natural disorders: lust for the pleasures, anger and aggression, greed, fear, and stupor. These are to be conquered with the conquest of speech and, with practice, by bringing into their inherent unity the body and the mind.[101]

In brief, the *Mahābhārata* teaches us:

अमूढत्वमसंगित्वं कामक्रोधविवर्जनम् ।
अदैन्यमनुदीर्णत्वमनुद्वेगो व्यवस्थिति: ।। शान्ति २७४.१८ ।।

एष मार्गो हि मोक्षस्य प्रसन्नो विमल: शुचि: ।
तथा वाक्कायमनसां नियम: कामतोऽन्यथा ।। शान्ति २७४.१९ ।।

The conquest of ignorance, of entanglements, of the 'thirst' of desires, of anger, of arrogance and false humility alike; a stable mind; and self-discipline over one's speech and other faculties—this is the joyful, clear, and purest path to mokṣha, *the last human freedom.*[102]
Self-knowledge is the abiding light on that path. And greater than self-knowledge there is no knowledge.[103]

An outer withdrawal from the world, and thus a renunciation of social bonds, is no part of *mokṣha* theory in the *Mahābhārata*. It is particularly important to grasp this because it was on this point, more than on any other, that there was that bitter strife between Buddhism and the *varṇa-āshrama* order. The *Mahābhārata* repeatedly says to us that neither is *moksha* in *not-having* nor bondage in *having*; in both circumstances, in *having* and in *not-having*, it is the discriminating knowledge that alone counts.[104] To wear ochre robes, to shave one's head, to carry a trident and a begging bowl—these are mere signs of the path of renunciation; in themselves they do not lead to *mokṣha*.[105] Since discriminating knowledge is the only means to *moksha*, all external signs are irrelevant.[106] Many men leave their families, their duties, their professions; shave their heads; take a trident; wear an ochre robe.[107] But, the *Mahābhārata* says, if passions are not removed from one's heart, the ochre robe is no more than a means to selfish ends, a means to earning a livelihood.[108] No one is a monk merely because he has renounced and he begs; he alone is a genuine monk who has naturally risen above self-interest and is not obsessed with pleasures.[109] Free, it is a matter of indifference to him whether he wears the robe of a monk or the regalia of a king.[110]

Mokṣha as freedom *into*

When one achieves freedom from some state, the awareness then is not so much of what one has freed oneself *from*, but of the freedom one has come *into*. This is common experience. It may still be that I have freed myself from a prison but do not know where to go. But the deeper truth is that if I had not known where to go, I could not have freed myself. In any case, human freedom is not a *destination* but a state of *being*. The man, or the woman, who has achieved *mokṣha* in this life, lives in the fullness of his, or her being, and has no particular 'aim', or 'project', or 'agenda'. And this is manifest in his, or her, relation with the self and with the *other.* Like the attributes of truth, the attributes of *mokṣha* are divided equally between the two, that is, if we speak about them as two distinct things. In reality, they are one.

In relation with the self, the free person has risen above the play of the opposites; has risen above the given history and the given contexts; and is free from the restlessness of *rājas* and the suffocation of *tamas*. For him there is neither assertion nor denial. Such a person comes into a state of being in which he fears nobody, nor does anybody fear him. Because he sees all living beings in his self, and his self in all living beings, he causes pain to nobody, in thought or in speech or in act, and acts towards all beings with friendship. Knowing that others have the same self, or the *ātman*, which he has in himself, he acts for the good of all. And yet, he has no *aim*—like a bird in the sky, or a fish in the water, he leaves no traces behind.

There is nothing to 'renounce', and there is nothing to 'obtain.' There is only to understand the true place of everything. Thus, in the life of a *jīvana-mukta*, in this life a free person, there is no external change of a visible kind; the change is internal, in his, or her, consciousness. Outwardly there is nothing that sets him, or her, apart from any other person who is self-governed, and is gentle and friendly towards others; but inwardly the change is radical. This point is brought out with the utmost clarity in t' description of a *jīvana-mukta* in the *Yoga-Vāśishṭha.* In this context, the *Yoga-Vāśishṭha* offers the twin ideas of *mahā-kartā*, 'the great doer', and *mahā-bhoktā*, 'the great enjoyer'. A *jīvana-mukta* is in a state where there is neither 'willing' nor 'not-willing', neither 'desire' nor 'not-desire'. He, or she, does things, and enjoys everything, except that the *doing* and the *enjoying* on his, or her, part is from a special awareness, in which the words 'doing' and 'enjoying' do not have their ordinary meanings. And yet, their ordinary meanings are not dissolved. He, or she, may enjoy, for example, eating ice cream quite as heartily as any other person. *Mokṣha* has never maintained that spiritual freedom is incompatible with, say, a fondness for ice cream. Likewise, with love. Love as a simple human feeling of care and affection. In a letter to Mary Hale, Swami Vivekananda wrote: 'Ah! The madness of love, and yet in it no bondage. Why, this is the essence of our Vedānta.' And this is a sign of a *jīvana-mukta*, a sign of *mokṣha* as *mastī*—madness of love, and yet in it no bondage.

There is another sign. In a letter to Francis Leggett, Vivekananda wrote: 'At twenty years of age I was the most unsympathetic, uncompromising fanatic; I would not walk on the footpath on the theatre side of the streets in Calcutta. At thirty-three, I can live in the same house with prostitutes and never would think of saying a word of reproach to them. Is it degenerate? Or is it that I am broadening out into the Universal Love which is the Lord Himself?'[111]

The highest point in *mokṣha* as human freedom was reached in that verse in the *Mahābhārata* that says:

> *Leave* dharma, *leave* a-dharma*; leave both truth and untruth. After leaving both truth and untruth, leave that which enabled you to leave them. Then take one last step—leave the notion that you have left anything at all.*

The *Yoga-Vāśishṭha* expresses this idea, the profoundest mystical meaning of human freedom, in a different way:

> मोक्षमिच्छाम्यहं कस्माद्बद्धः केनास्मि वै पुरा ।
> अबद्धो मोक्षमिच्छामि केयं बालबिडम्बना ।। ५.२९.१० ।।
> *For what reason, or from what, do I seek liberation? By what am I bound? Not in bondage, I seek liberation. What childish mockery is this?*[112]

> न बन्धोऽस्ति न मोक्षोऽस्ति मौर्ख्यं मे क्षयमागतम् ।
> किं मे ध्यानविलासेन किं वाऽध्यानेन मे भवेत् ।। ५.२९.११ ।।
> *There is neither bondage nor liberation. My stupidity has come to an end. What is the use of my playing with meditation or with the anxiety as to what will happen to me if I don't meditate?*[113]

> ध्यानाध्यानभ्रमौ त्यक्त्वा पुंस्त्वं स्वमवलोकयत् ।
> यदायाति तदायातु न मे वृद्धिर्न वा क्षयः ।। ५.२९.१२ ।।

Having given up the delusion of meditation or not-meditation, and in full awareness of the Self, the essential nature of man, what comes, let it come. There is no growth or decay for me.[114]

नाहं मृतो न जीवामि न सन्नासन्न सन्मयः ।
नेदं मे नैव चान्यन्मे नमो मह्यमहं बृहत् ।। ५.२९.१५ ।।

I am not dead, nor do I live. I am neither being nor not-being, nor made of anything real. This world is not mine; neither is any other world mine. Salutations to me! I am infinite.[115]

न मे भोगस्थितौ वाञ्छा न च भोगविवर्जने ।
अस्ति सर्वत्र मे स्वर्गो नियतो न तु कुत्रचित् ।। ५.३५.३८ ।।

I have no desire for the continuance of enjoyments or for abandoning enjoyments. My heaven exists everywhere. It is not fixed somewhere.[116]

सुखदुःखान्युपायान्तु यान्तु वाऽप्यहमेषु कः ।
वासना विविधा देहे त्वस्तं चोदयमेव वा ।। ५.३५.४० ।।
प्रयान्तु नाहमेतासु न चैता मम काश्चन ।। ५.३५.४१ ।।

Let pleasures or pains arrive or let them depart. Who am I among these? Let various desires arise or vanish in the body. I am not in them; nor are any of these mine.[117]

यदायाति तदायातु यत्प्रयाति प्रयातु तत् ।
सुखेषु मम नापेक्षा नोपेक्षा दुःखवृत्तिषु ।। ५.३५.३९ ।।

What comes, let it come. What goes, let it go. I have no desire for pleasure, nor contempt for pain.[118]

Two more states of *being* follow from this, each of great importance, if we as human beings are to live in the spirit of joy, regardless of the circumstances of one's life. We saw that, in the classical view of *moksha*, man eventually wants freedom from the wheel of birth and rebirth because of the weariness of experience, the sameness of things over and over again. In that view, *moksha* is then the ultimate product of human weariness. The *Mahābhārata* and the *Yoga-Vāśishṭha* turn it around and see *moksha* as *freedom from weariness as well*. Were this freedom not a manifest part of human living, then there is nothing that one could say to the *other* that would sound convincing and fresh. For everybody expresses feelings and emotions that have been expressed, even in the same words, countless times before. Yet every time they are expressed, it is as if they were being felt and expressed *for the first time*. That is how it is with every child. For a child, everything is new, and he or she is not aware of history. In that state, a child is a saint. *Mokṣha*, properly understood, is an invitation to the *newness* of everything. Even the sun, and the moon, and the trees, and the blades of grass, appear bathed in a new light.

Similarly, *mokṣha* should be a freedom from the endless harangue of *nitya* and *a-nitya*, what is abiding, and what is transitory. There is no question that there are in human life things that are abiding, and there are things that are of the moment, transitory. Seen from one angle, man himself is transitory. Or rather, he is a being in transition. However, from this it does not follow that emotions and feelings that are transitory, are *for that reason* also worthless. It is this second conclusion, that the renunciation literature in India made its focus, which is false. For if that were true, then the thinkers of the *Upanishad*-s would not have spoken of every human attribute, physical, emotional, and of the mind, as sacred. *Mokṣha* is to see in the transitory the face of eternity.

Despite its plainly universal meaning, and its secular nature, the idea of *mokṣha* became obscured by the religiosity of theistic practices. Even though it had nothing to do in its essentials with asceticism, the two became hopelessly intertwined. Thus *mokṣha* has invariably been perceived as a religious idea, and that, too, of the Hindus. What is more, excepting materialism, it was taken up in every school of Indian philosophy. And, with the exception of Buddhism, with its view that nowhere is a permanent 'Self' to be found, there was much speculation as regards the state of the *ātman* after one had obtained *mokṣha* and had thereby stopped the wheel of *karma*. Different schools conceived that state in very different ways and called it by different names. That part of Indian philosophy was also the most speculative and, for that reason, the most open to dispute. Ironically, there were huge quarrels about *mokṣha*, when *mokṣha* is freedom from all quarrels—with one's self and with the *other*.

Let us put them aside. For, in the voice of the sage Vasishṭha to King Janaka, the *Mahābhārata* says that such quarrels arise among:

यो हि वेदे च शास्त्रे च ग्रन्थधारणतत्परः ।
न च ग्रन्थार्थतत्त्वज्ञस्तस्य तद्धारणं वृथा ।। शान्ति ३०५.१३ ।।

Those who are busy memorising the Veda, the shāstra-*s, and other texts, but do not understand their true meaning. Their memorising the text is then useless.*[119]

भारं स वहते तस्य ग्रन्थस्यार्थं न वेत्ति यः।
यस्तु ग्रन्थार्थतत्त्वज्ञो नास्य ग्रन्थागमो वृथा।। शान्ति ३०५.१४।।
The one who does not understand the true meaning of a text merely carries its burden. But the one who does, for him the study of texts is not useless.[120]

Finally, in the state of *mokṣha* something else happens. In the strongest of voices, the *Mahābhārata* states the belief in the absolute power of Time, *kāla*. Bali had expressed that belief in saying:

अनीशस्याप्रमत्तस्य भूतानि पचतः सदा।। शान्ति २२७.९४।।
अनिवृत्तस्य कालस्य क्षयं प्राप्तो न मुच्यते।
Time consumes and digests all that exists. There is no turning of Time. Reduced by Time, man has no refuge.[121]

But in the state of the ultimate human freedom, *mokṣha*, Time itself is digested.

कालः पचति भूतानि सर्वाण्येवात्मनात्मनि।
यस्मिंस्तु पच्यते कालस्तं वेदेह न कश्चन।। शान्ति २३९.२५।।
Time consumes and digests all beings. But there is a state where, seeing one's self in all beings, and all beings in one's self, Time itself is digested. Nobody knows about it.[122]

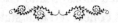

Notes

Chapter 1

1 *Ādi-parva*, 1.77–8.
2 Ibid., 1.79.
3 Ibid., 1.80–3.
4 Ibid., 63.68–84.
5 Ibid., 104.7–15.
6 Ibid., 1.85.

Chapter 2

1 *Anushāsana-parva*, 63.5–42; 66.55–60; 67.1–19; 112.10–2, 26, 28–30; *Vana-parva*, 200.23–3, 33–9. *Āshvamedhika-parva* (in the Kumbakonam edition (K) of the *Mahābhārata*, 101.17–32, the entire Ch. devoted to food and water as sustaining life and to their sharing), Ch. 92, pp. 6327–8, all the verses unnumbered in the Gorakhpur edition (G).
2 *Taittirīya Upanishad*, II. 1.
3 Ibid., II.2, III.2.
4 Ibid., II.3.
5 Ibid., II.3.
6 Ibid., II.4.
7 Ibid., II.5.
8 Ibid., II.6.
9 Ibid., II.6.
10 Ibid., III.1–6.
11 Ibid., III.7–10.
12 Ibid., III.7.
13 Ibid., III.8.
14 Ibid., III.9.
15 Ibid., III.10.
16 Ibid., I.11.
17 *Chāṇdogya*, I.11–2.
18 Ibid., II.3–7.
19 Ibid., III.13–8.
20 Ibid., VI.1–4.
21 Ibid., VI.8–16, VIII.14.
22 Ibid., VII.1–25.
23 Ibid., VI.5.1–4, VI.6.1–5.
24 Ibid., VI.7.1–6
25 I.3.5.
26 V. 12–3, VI.1.
27 Ibid., I.5.1.
28 Ibid., I.5.2.
29 Ibid., I.5.3–11.
30 Ibid., I.5.3.
31 Ibid., I.5.3.
32 Ibid., I.5.3.
33 Ibid., I.5.3.
34 Ibid., I.5.3.
35 Ibid., I.5.4–13.
36 Ibid., I.5.4–10.
37 *Kaushitaki*, 1.7.
38 Ibid., 2.2.
39 Ibid., 3.3–8.
40 Ibid., 3.3–4.
41 Ibid., 3.6–7.
42 Ibid., 3.8.
43 Ibid., 3.8.
44 *Aitareya*, I.2.1–4.
45 Ibid., I.2.5.
46 Ibid., I.3.1–2.
47 Ibid., I.3.3–9.
48 Ibid., I.3.3–8.
49 Ibid., I.3.10.
50 Ibid., III.1–4.
51 *Anushāsana-parva*, 63.5–42; 66.55–60; 67.1–19; 112.10–2, 26, 30–1. *Vana-parva*, 200.22–23, 33–9. *Āshvamedhika-*

parva, (in the Kumbakonam edition of the *Mahābhārata*, 101.17–32, the entire Ch. devoted to food and water as sustaining life and to their sharing); in the Gorakhpur edition., Ch. 92, pp. 6327–8, all the verses unnumbered. This is only a brief list. But the references listed here contain the fundamentals of the *Mahābhārata*'s discussion on food and water and their sharing.

52 *Anushāsana-parva*, 66.59; 67.6; 112.26.
53 Ibid., 63.31, 34.
54 Ibid., 63.7, 25–6; 67.5; 112.11.
55 Ibid., 63.8.
56 *Āshvamedhika-parva*, p. 6327 in (G), verse not numbered.
57 *Anushāsana-parva*, 63.30.
58 Ibid., 63.32.
59 Ibid., 112.11.
60 Ibid., 63.8, 19; 67.11–3; *Āshvamedhika-parva*, 101.9–15 (K).
61 *Anushāsana-parva*, Read Chs. 63, 67, and 112 in their entirety and in them, more specifically, 63.6; 67.4–5; 112.10–12, 23–5 and 31. Also *Āshvamedhika-parva*, 101.9 (K).
62 *Anushāsana-parva*, 63.25–6, 42; 67.8; 112.23–4. *Āshvamedhika-parva*, 101.77 (K).
63 Ibid., 63.6.
64 Ibid., 63.29.
65 Ibid., p. 6328 in (G), verse not numbered.
66 Ibid., p. 6328 in (G), verse not numbered. In (K), 101.48–9.
67 *Āshvamedhika-parva*, 101.9–13 (K).
68 *Āshvamedhika-parva*, p. 6327 in (G), Verse not numbered.
69 Ibid., p. 6327 in (G), verse not numbered.
70 Ibid., p. 6327 in (G), verse not numbered.
71 Ibid., p. 6327 in (G), verse not numbered. *Vana-parva*, 200.54, 57.8.
72 Ibid., p. 6327 in (G), verse not numbered.
73 Ibid., p. 6327 in (G), verse not numbered.
74 Ibid., p. 6329 in (G), verse not numbered. In (K), 101.66.
75 Ibid., p. 6329 in (G), verse not numbered.
76 Ibid., 101.32–4, 73–90 (K); *Anushāsana-parva*, 63, 21–7, 44–52; 66.60–4; 67.16–9.
77 For example, see *Anushāsana-parva*, 65.3–8; 67.11–9; 68.21–2;.1–22; and in (K) see 100.3–6; 102.2–19; 103.19–23.
78 Ibid., 93.13, 22, 33; 97.1–100; 101.31–5. All in (K).
79 *Anushāsana-parva*, 62.49.
80 Ibid., 62.50.
81 Ibid., see the whole Ch. 62.
82 Ibid., p. 6331 in (G), verse not numbered.
83 *Āshvamedhika-parva*, p. 6331 in (G), verse not numbered.
84 Ibid., p. 6332 in (G), verse not numbered
85 See *Āshvamedhika-parva*, pp. 6331–3 in (G).
86 See Ch. 13, 'Social Arrangements, *varṇa-dharma*, and Social Wealth, *loka-saṃgraha*', pp. 369-415.
87 This is discussed in Ch. 17 of this book, pp. 529–558.
88 *Āshvamedhika-parva*, p. 6329 in (G).
89 Ibid., p. 6329 in (G), verse not numbered.
90 Ibid., p. 6330 in (G), verse not numbered.
91 Ibid., p. 6330 in (G), verse not numbered.
92 Ibid., p. 6330 in (G), verse not numbered.
93 *Shānti-parva*, Chs. 143–8.
94 *Shānti-parva*, 146.5.
95 See *Vana-parva*, Chs. 2–3.
96 Ibid., 2.53.
97 Ibid., 2.54 and 55.
98 Ibid., 2.56.
99 Ibid., 3.2–3.
100 Ibid., 3.5–8.
101 Ibid., 3.9.
102 Ibid., 3.36–69.
103 Ibid., 3.67.
104 Ibid., 3.71–3, 81–5.
105 *Anushāsana-parva*, 98.18.
106 On this topic, the reader may want to have a look at the author's 'Max Weber's Wrong Understanding of Indian Civilisation', in *Dharma, India and the World Order: Twenty–one Essays* (Pahl–Rugenstein, Bonn; and Saint Andrew Press, Edinburgh; 1993), pp. 108–28.
107 *Vana-parva*, 2.62.

Chapter 3

1 *Taittirīya Upanishad*, I.7.

2 But this is generally missed in most writings on the *Upanishad*-s.

3 One of the most notable works in that literature is Bhartrihari's *Vairāgya-shatakam.* or 'One Hundred Verses of Disgust'. He was a prince of Ujjain; he married a princess from the kingdom of Magadha in Bihar; and it is said of him that he renounced the world and women five times, and returned to them every time. He was indeed a gifted poet; and before he wrote his 'Canto of Disgust', he had composed one hundred verses on the principles of governance, *Nīti-shatakam*, and another hundred verses on the 'Joy of Living'. The latter, *Shringāra-shatakam*, is a beautiful, lyrical work, in which he describes how the changing seasons produce different sensations in one's body and of feelings, and what a beautiful emotion sexual love is, different in different seasons. His third Canto clearly suggests that his disgust with the material world was only the reverse of his fascination with it. That is true, psychologically, of the entire *Vairāgya* literature, or 'Disgust literature'.

4 See, for examples, Chs. 5, 9, 12, and 18 of this book.

5 To those who may want to study, in greater detail than is necessary here, the various ideas of the *ātman*, the Self, that had prevailed at the time of the Buddha (563–483 B.C.), each contending with the other, I suggest the summary in K.N. Jayatilleke's *Early Buddhist Theory of Knowledge* (London, 1963), pp. 243–54; 264–6; and 268–70. Paul Deussen's (1845–1919) article on 'Ātman', in the *Encyclopaedia of Religion and Ethics*, vol. 2 (Edinburgh, 1919) may also be consulted. Although it speaks primarily of *ātman* as found in the *Upanishad*-s, and does not refer to other systems, it is valuable for the light it throws on the origins of the concept, with parallels in Greek philosophy.

6 For a brief discussion on this, see SuRāma Dasgupta (1907–1998), *Development of Moral Philosophy in India* (Calcutta, 1961), pp. 190–2.

7 See, for examples, *Vana-parva*, Chs. 211–3. *Shānti-parva*, Chs.125–6, 158–60, 183–7, 194, 202–3, 218–9.

8 See, for examples, *Shānti-parva*, 202.4, 16; 203.4–5, 14.

9 The same as above.

10 For example, *Shānti-parva*, 186.1–15.

11 *Shānti-parva*, 182.1–4. The sage Bharadvaj asks the same questions in the same words, 182.7–9.

12 Ibid., Chs. 182–7.

13 Ibid., 182.7–9.

14 Ibid., 186.1.

15 Ibid., 186.2.

16 Ibid., 186.3.

17 Ibid., 186.4.

18 Ibid., 186.6–9.

19 Ibid., 186.10.

20 Ibid., 186.11–2.

21 Ibid., 186.13.

22 Ibid., 186.14–5.

23 Ibid., 187.1–2.

24 Ibid., 187.3–4.

25 Ibid., 187.5–10.

26 Ibid., 187.11–9.

27 Because it has the brain as its physical basis.

28 *Shānti-parva*, 187.19–22.

29 Ibid., 187.23–8.

30 Ibid., Ch. 218–9.

31 Ibid., 218.4–5.

32 Ibid., 218.19.

33 Ibid., 218.9.

34 Ibid., 218.15–7.

35 Ibid., 218.23.

36 Ibid., 218.24.

37 Ibid., 218.25.

38 Ibid., 218.26.

39 Ibid., 218.27.

40 Ibid., 218.28.

41 Ibid., 218.31.

42 Ibid., 218.40.

43 Ibid., 218.41.

44 Ibid., 218.42.

45 Ibid., 219.2.
46 Ibid., 219.3.
47 Ibid., 219.4.
48 Ibid., Ch. 219.
49 Ibid., 219.7–8.
50 Ibid., 219.9–12.
51 Ibid., 219.33.
52 Ibid., 219.34.
53 Ibid., 219.25–31. Some explanation is required here for my translating the Sanskrit word '*guṇa*', as in the texts, as 'energy', and not as 'quality' or 'substance' customarily used for the word '*guṇa*' in the various histories of Indian philosophy. The debate in philosophical literature, in the West and in India, about 'quality' and 'substance' is a stock debate. That will be of no help in understanding what *sattva*, *rajas* and *tamas* are. Although using the word '*guṇa*' to denote them, without doubt the *Mahābhārata* is talking about them as three forms of *energy* that *flow* through the whole creation.
54 Ibid., 219.26; 247.20.
55 Ibid., 219.27; 247.21.
56 Ibid., 219.28; 247.22.
57 Ibid., 219.29; 247.23.
58 Ibid., 219.30; 247.24.
59 Ibid., 219.31; 247.25.
60 Ibid., 218.43.
61 *Shānti-parva*, Chs. 231–54.
62 Ibid., 240.1; also 236.28–9.
63 Ibid., 247.6. For Shukadeva's question concerning this, see 247.7.
64 Ibid., 236.30.
65 Ibid., 236.31.
66 Ibid., 236.32–3.
67 Ibid., 237.7–12.
68 Ibid., 237.3–6.
69 Ibid., 237.3–10.
70 Ibid., 237.11–4.
71 Ibid., 247.13–4.
72 Ibid., 247.15.
73 Ibid., 247.16.
74 Ibid., 247.17.
75 Ibid., 247.18.
76 *Āshrāmad*, 246.3; 248.2. See also *Kaṭhopanishad*, I.3.10; II,3.7.
77 *Shānti-parva*, 248.3–10.
78 Ibid., 255.9.
79 Ibid., 255.10.
80 Ibid., 248.3.
81 Ibid., 248.4.
82 Ibid., 248.5.
83 Ibid., 248.6.
84 Ibid., 248.7.
85 Ibid., 248.11.
86 Ibid., 248.20–1.
87 Ibid., 248.22, 24.
88 Ibid., 219.11.
89 Ibid., Chs. 236, 239, 240, 246, 248, 253, 254.
90 Ibid., 249.3–4.
91 Ibid., Chs. 232, 233, 235, 238, specifically, and implied in the rest.
92 See Ch. 13, 'The Question of Causality', in this book, pp. 369–415.
93 *Shānti-parva*, 232.19.
94 Ibid., 232.20.
95 Ibid., 232.21.
96 See Ch. 13 of this book, pp. 369–415.
97 *Shānti-parva*, 235.11.
98 Ibid., 235.11–2.
99 Ibid., 235.13.
100 Ibid., 235.14–7.
101 *Shānti-parva*, 242.8–12; also *Vana-parva*, 215.23–5. For greater details see *Shānti-parva*, where this metaphor appears at numerous places.
102 *Vana-parva*, 215.19–21.
103 *Vana-parva*, 216.46; *Shānti-parva*, 337.12.
104 See Ch. 13 of this book.
105 For an analysis of *sattva*, *rajas* and *tamas*, see also *Āsvamedhika-parva*, *Anu-Gītā*, Ch. 36–9.
106 And, centuries later, in the *Yoga–Vāsishtha*.
107 *Prashno-Upanishad*, 'The Third Question'.
108 *Ādi-parva*, 1.248–51.
109 *Shānti-parva*, 215.25–6.

Chapter 4

1 *Shānti-parva*, 260.12–3.
2 *Shānti-parva*, for the conversation between the two, see 287.3–11. This comes up again

in a longer conversation between a group of sages, *Āshvamedhika-parva*, 49.1–16.

3 Ibid., 287.10.

4 Surendranath Dasgupta, *A History of Indian Philosophy*, II, (Cambridge University Press, 1932), abbreviated hereafter as *HIP*, p. 486.

5 Ibid., p. 486n; also Macdonell's *Vedic Index*, p. 390.

6 Pandurang Vaman Kane, *History of the Dharmaśāstra,* Poona, 1930, hereafter abbreviated as HD, I–Part I, p. 1.

7 Ibid., p. 2.

8 Ibid., p. 3.

9 Ibid., pp. 3–4.

10 *HIP*, vol. IV (1949), pp. 2–11; also II, pp. 486–7, 502–3; and, for the meaning of *dharma* in the *Gītā*, pp. 504–7. For the use of *dharma* as a concept in philosophical texts, see, for examples, I, pp. 316–7, and II, pp. 479–84.

11 *HD*, I–Pt.I, pp. 5–6.

12 *Dharmanka*, the special number to commemorate the fortieth year of the monthly journal *Kalyāṇa*, in Hindi; edition, Hanuman Prasad Poddar and Chimmanlal Goswami; at the Gita Press, Gorakhpur, January 1966.

13 Dasgupta, *HIP*, II, p. 484.

14 *Bhāgvata-purāṇa*, VI.1.40.

15 Dasgupta, *HIP*, IV, p. 7.

16 Whichever *smrti* was in conflict with Manu's writings, was regarded as invalid, says Dasgupta, and cites Brhaspati quoted in *Vīramitrodaya-paribhaśāprakaśā*: see *HIP*, IV, p.6.

17 For a summary of different opinions on the date of the *Manu-smrti*, see Robert Lingat, *The Classical Law of India* (tr. J. Duncan M. Derrett, Thomson Press, Delhi), Ch. IV. Whereas William Jones, Chezy and Leiseleur-Deslongchampz put the date as far back as the thirteenth century B.C.; Buhler tried to show that the work was composed probably in the second century A.D.. Most indologists, influenced by Buhler, have taken the date to be between two centuries B.C. and A.D..

18 *Manu-smrti*, II.1 and II.6.

19 Ibid., II.12.

20 *HIP*, IV, p.8.

21 *Manu-smriti*, II.10 and II.12.

22 For the *Mahābhārata*'s radically different perception of *sadāchāra*, 'good conduct', see Ch. 17, 'From Ritual *Acts to Relationships*' pp. 529–558.

23 Manu-smriti, XII.88–9.

24 As in the *Brhad-āraṇyaka Upanishad*, I.4.226.

25 See *Vana-parva*, 151.22–3. *Shānti-parva*, 59.2, 8–56; Chs. 60–2; 64.5–6; 238.104–8; 244.14–6. And *Anushāsana-parva*, Chs. 208–54.

26 See, for unambiguous examples, *Vana-parva*, 152.26–38, 51–3; 298.26. *Shānti-parva*, 241.27; 244.14–7; 293.36–7; 299.12–6;300.1–4.*Āshvamedhika-parva*, 98.37; to be read with 98.35–6. The *Vishṇu-purāṇa* uses the word *sva-dharma* in the clear sense of *varṇa*-duties, I.6.7–8; III.8.11–2. The same is true of the other *purāṇa*-s as well. The *Bhāgvata-purāṇa*, besides the *Gītā*, the second most influential work, makes this point perfectly clear. 'It is to restore the social structure of *varṇa-āshrāma-dharma* that the last incarnation of God will appear.' XII.2.12, 16–7, and 38, read in that order.

27 Dasgupta, *HIP*, II, pp. 506–7; Surāma Dasgupta (1907–98), Development of Moral Philosophy in India (Orient Longmans, Calcutta, 1961), pp. 15, 21–2; Shrikant Sharan, essay entitled '*Sāmānya–dharma* aur *Viśesa–dharma tathā inake ādarṣa*', in *Dharmānk*, op. cit., p. 381.

28 For some instances of the different uses of the word *dharma*, see *Anushāsana-parva*, 174.28, 32–3 and 35; 175.8; and 254.8. Also the *Bhāgvata-purāṇa*, VI.10.9. Whenever an act was considered appropriate, its appeal was enhanced by saying: 'This, then, is *dharma*.'

29 For example, the discussion on *dharma*, in which gods and the sages took part, each

speaking of *dharma* in a different context, *Anushāsana-parva*, Chs. 188–97.

30 Sarvepalli Radhakrishnan, *The Hindu View of Life* (London, 1927), pp. 77–8, 80; *Eastern Religions and Western Thought* (Oxford, 1939), p. 353. V. Raghavan (1908–79), *The Concept of Culture* (The Indian Institute of World Culture, Bangalore; 1971), pp. 40–50. Bhagwan Das, *The Science of Social Organisation*, vol. I, pp. 49–50. *Sanatana-Dharma*: *An Advanced Text–Book of Hindu Religion and Ethics* (Adyar, 1940), published for the use of the students of Mrs Annie Besant's Central Hindu College at Benaras (now Varanasi), pp. 7, 13, 245, and p. 21, in that order. Swami Bharati Krishna Tirtha (1884–1960), the Shankaracharya of Dwaraka and then of Puri, *Sanatana Dharma* (Bombay, 1964), p.11, pp. 12–4, 36–7. For the diffused view of *dharma* by the other Shankaracharya-s, see the *Dharmank*, op. cit., pp. 4–7. Almost each one of the 285 essays there on *dharma* can be cited as an example. Rāmananda Sarasvati Swaminat (1867–1936), *The Hindu Ideal*, pp. 6–7, 118–25. D.S. Sarma, *Renascent Hinduism* (Bombay, 1966), pp. 54, 60, 61–3. Jadu Nath Sinha, *Foundations of Hinduism*, p. 70, and pp. 83–4. Benjamin Khan, *The Concept of Dharma in Valmiki Rāmāyaṇa* (Delhi, 1965), pp. 51–3. Mahamahopadhyaya Sadasiva Sastri Musalgadukar's *Introduction*, in Hindi, to the *Dharma-sindhu* (1790 A.D.) of Kasinath Upadhyaya with commentary by Pandit Vasishṭha Datta Misra (Chowkhamba Sanskrit Series, Varanasi, 1968). This brief list will suffice.

31 Radhakrishnan, *The Hindu View of Life*, p. 92; pp. 93–127; *Eastern Religions and Western Thought*, pp. 355–82. Sri Aurobindo, *Essays on the Gītā*, pp. 465–6. A full substantiation of this point, by referring even to some of the Hindu writers, or to the sayings of the Hindu holy men, will require a large volume.

32 *Education Gazette*, 8 May 1891.

33 On this subject, see my book, *Dharma, India and the World Order: Twenty–one Essays* (Saint Andrew Press, Edinburgh, and Pahl–Rugenstein Verlag, Bonn; 1993), pp. 3–16; 19–23; 24–8; 29–33; and the essays '*Dharma* is not 'Religion': Misconception has to be removed.' pp. 39–43, and 'Max Weber's Wrong Understanding of Indian Civilisation', pp. 108–28. See *his Finding Jesus in Dharma*: *Christianity in India* (Indian Society for Promoting Christian Knowledge, Delhi; 2000); and in that, see *dharma* in the very detailed 'Index' to the book. In the past three decades and more, through my public lectures, symposia, and writings other than those mentioned here, especially in *The Times of India*, I have been talking about *dharma*, not as 'religion', much less as the Hindu religion, but as the evident universal foundation of all human Relationships—of the self with the self, and of the self with the *other*, both in a personal and in a collective sense.

34 This is taken up in Ch. 13, 'Social Arrangements, *varṇa-dharma*, towards Social Wealth, *loka-saṃgraha*'.

35 The *Mahābhārata*'s perceptions of governance are discussed in Ch. 14, '*Dharma*: The Foundation of Law and Governance. *Rāja-dharma*', and Ch. 15, 'Sage Nārada's Questions to King Yudhishṭhira'.

36 Marco Pallis, *A Buddhist Spectrum* (London, 1980), p. 102.

37 *Shānti-parva*, 109.10.

38 Ibid., 109.11.

39 Ibid., 109.12.

40 *Vana-parva*, 207.77.

41 *Shānti-parva*, 21.7.

42 Ibid., 21.8.

43 Ibid., 21.9.

44 Ibid., 21.10.

45 *Vana-parva*,131.11.

46 Ibid., 131.12, and 13.

47 *Shānti-parva*, 193.31.

48 *Shānti-parva*, 259.20; see also Ch. 5 of

this book, pp. 113–168
49 *Anushāsana-parva*, 113.8. Also *Udyoga-parva*, 39.71. And repeated many times in the *Mahābhārata*.
50 See Ch. 10 of this book.
51 See Ch. 11 of this book.
52 See Chs. 14 and 15 of this book.
53 See Ch. 13 of this book.
54 *Shānti-parva*, 137.23. See the previous two verses, 137.21–2.
55 *Shānti-parva*, 137.24.
56 *Shānti-parva*, 137.22.
57 See p. 2 above.
58 See Ch. 7 of this book, pp. 239–52.
59 *Udyoga-parva*, 37.17, 128.50; also *Ādi-parva*, 74.24.
60 *Shānti-parva*, 137.21–4.
61 Even when the absolutist trends materialised and became an established force, in the form of theism, for example, and in its wake in the person of the guru, the relativistic character of dharmic thought was not ever dissolved. Rather, placed within the plurality of faith and philosophic opinion and custom, these trends eventually strengthened philosophical relativism.
62 *Shānti-parva*, 260.12–3.
63 Ibid., 260.7–8.
64 Ibid., 260.3.
65 Ibid., 260.4.
66 Ibid., 260.9–10.
67 Ibid., 260.5.
68 Ibid., 266.6.
69 Ibid., 260.18–9.
70 Ibid., 260.17.
61 *Udyoga-parva*, 28.2. *Vana-parva*, 152.28. *Shānti-parva*, 78.32; 142.8.
72 *Shānti-parva*, 309.16; also 78.32.
73 Ibid., 108.1–2, 158.2–4; *Vana-parva*, 213.2.
74 *Shānti-parva*, 109.2–3, also 160.1–2.
75 *Vana-parva*, 313.117.
76 *Shānti-parva*, 141.102.
77 Ibid., 142.23.
78 Ibid., 142.8.
79 Ibid., 142.5.
80 Ibid., 142.3–7.
81 Ibid., 287.10.
82 Ibid., 287.15.
83 See, for example, *Kena-Upanishad*, I.1.3–6; *Katha-Upanishad*, I.2.9, 23.
84 The reader may want to have a look at 'Two Methods of Understanding: Western and Dharmic', in my *Dharma, India and the World Order*, op cit., pp. 129–50.
85 *Anushāsana-parva*, 162.2.
86 Ibid., 162.3.
87 Ibid., 162.4.
88 Ibid., 162.5.
89 Ibid., 162.6–7.
90 Ibid., 162.8–9.
91 Ibid., 162.10.
92 Ibid., 162.11–6.
93 Ibid., 162, 17–8.
94 Ibid., 162.20.
95 Ibid., 162.21
96 Ibid., 162.23.
97 Ibid., 162.60.
98 Ibid., 162.61.
99 *Shānti-parva*, 259.25.
100 *Shānti-parva*, Ch. 124.
101 Ibid., 124.47.
102 Ibid., 124.50.
103 Ibid., 124.52, 54, 55.
104 Ibid., 124.56.57.
105 Ibid., 124.62.
106 Ibid., 124.66.
107 Ibid., 286.15.
108 *Strī-parva*, 7.22.
109 *Udyoga-parva*, 34.48.
110 *Vana-parva*, 33.23.
111 Ibid., 33.24.
112 Ibid., 33.26.
113 Ibid., 33.28. Read also *Shānti-parva*, Ch. 123, for a discussion on the three ends of life, *dharma*, *artha*, and *kāma*, and their interrelatedness. This will come up again in the context of the place of sexual happiness in life. See Ch. 11 of this book, 'Sexuality and Relationship, *kāma* and *saha-kāma*.
114 Ibid., 33.38–9.
115 *Vishṇu-Purāṇa*, I.7.23–4; also I.15.106–10. *Bhāgvata-purāna*, IV.I.49. However, *Ādi-parva*, 66.14–5, mentions only ten, adding that there are 'as many doors to *dharma*'.

116 *Vishṇu-Purāṇa*, I.7.28–30.
117 Ibid., I.7.32–35.
118 *Shānti-parva*, 158.2–3. These and the related verses will be repeated in Ch. 9 of this book, see pp. 312–14; 369–70.
119 Ibid., 158.4.
120 Ibid., 158.5.
121 Ibid., 158.6–7.
122 Ibid., 158.8–10.
123 Ibid., 158.12.
125 Ibid., 159.9–12.
125 Ibid., 159.9.
126 Ibid., 160.2–4.
127 Ibid., 160.6.
128 Ibid., 160.10.
129 Ibid., 160.12.
130 Ibid., 160.13.
131 Ibid., 160.15–6.
132 Ibid., 160.22–3.
133 Ibid., 160.26–7.
134 Ibid., 160.33.
135 Ibid., 259.15.
136 Ibid., 259.17.
137 See Ch. 17 of this book, 'From Ritual Acts to Relationships'.
138 Ibid., 160.36.
139 *Shānti-parva*, 259.25.
140 Ibid., 262.9.
141 *Anushāsana-parva*, 142.27–32.
142 Ibid., 142.27.
143 Ibid., 142.28.
144 Ibid., 142,29.
145 Ibid., 142.30.
146 Ibid., 142.31.
147 Ibid., 142.32.
148 Ibid., 287.20. For the *Mahābhārata*'s discussion on Truth, see Ch. 7 of this book.
149 *Vana-parva*, 213.31.
150 *Shānti-parva*, 259.26–7.
151 Ibid., 193.31.

Chapter 5

1 The reader should turn again to the 'Introduction' in this book; and in that, to 'The Method in the *Mahābhārata*'.
2 *Shānti-parva*, 297.28.
3 Ibid., 326.32.
4 *Anushāsana-parva*, 116.28–30.
5 Ibid., 115.23.
6 *Vana-parva*, 207.74.
7 *Anushāsana-parva*, 213.5 (K); p. 5955, unnumbered verse, (G).
8 Ibid., 213.6–7 (K); p. 5955, unnumbered verse, (G).
9 *Āshvamedhika-parva*, 28.16.
10 Ibid., 28.17.
11 Ibid., 28.18.
12 *Shānti-parva*, 294.24.
13 *Shānti-parva*, 272.20.
14 Ibid., 109.12.
15 *Karṇa-parva*, 69.57, and 58.
16 *Anushāsana-parva*, 116.31.
17 Ibid., 116.32.
18 *Shānti-parva*, 340.88. Also see *Vana-parva*, 313.129; 314.8.
19 *Shānti-parva*, Ch. 265.
20 Ibid., 265.3.
21 Ibid., 265.4.
22 Ibid., 265.5.
23 Ibid., 265.6.
24 Ibid., Ch. 272; 272.20; see also 340.82.
25 *Āshvamedhika-parva*, Ch. 49.
26 Ibid., 36.25–9.
27 Ibid., 36.32–51, and Chs. 37–48.
28 Ibid., 49.1–17.
29 Ibid., 49.14.
30 Ibid., 49.13.
31 Ibid., 49.15–6.
32 *Āshvamedhika-parva*, 50.2.
33 Ibid., 50.2–3.
34 *Shānti-parva*, 109.4, 160.24.
35 Ibid., 109.5.
36 Ibid., 187.4, 13, 18.
37 *Vana-parva*, 208.14.
38 Ibid., 208.15.
39 Ibid., 208.16.
40 Ibid., 208.19.
41 Ibid., 208.18.
42 Ibid., 208.22.
43 Ibid., 208.23.
44 *Shānti-parva*, 15.20.
45 Ibid., 15.21–2.
46 Ibid., 15.24
47 Ibid., 15.25, 28.
48 Ibid., 15.15.

49 *Anushāsana-parva,* 116.8; *Strī-parva,* 7.27
50 *Anushāsana-parva,* 116.22.
51 Ibid., 116.17.
52 Ibid., 115.19.
53 *Shānti-parva,* 153.29.
54 *Anushāsana-parva,* 116.16, 28–9; 233.10.
55 Ibid., 116.22.
56 *Anushāsana-parva,* 113.8. And repeated many times in the *Mahābhārata.*
57 *Shānti-parva,* 259.20.
58 Ibid., 259.22.
59 *Anushāsana-parva,* 115.18.
60 Ibid., 116.12.
61 *Shānti-parva,* 167.9.
62 *Udyoga-parva,* 33.52.
63 *Vana-parva,* 314.16.
64 *Shānti-parva,* 15.50.
65 *Vana-parva,* 28.3.
66 *Ādi-parva,* Chs. 177–79.
67 Ibid., 179.2.
68 Ibid., 179.3.
69 Ibid., 179.4.
70 Ibid., 179.5–8.
71 Ibid., 179.9–11.
72 Ibid., 179.12–3.
73 Ibid., 179.15.
74 Ibid., 179.16.
75 Ibid., 179.17–20.
76 *Sauptika-parva,* Chs. 3–4.
77 See pp. 77-112.
78 *Droṇa-parva,* 195.4–13.
79 *Droṇa-parva,* 195.14–20.
80 *Sauptika-parva,* 1.36–45.
81 Ibid., 1.45.
82 Ibid., 1.57.
83 Ibid., Chs. 2–5, which I have abridged and rearranged. Kripāchārya first gives Ashvatthama a somewhat long lecture on why things happen the way they happen, and propounds his view of the combination of *daiva* and *purushārtha,* 'providence' and 'human effort', as determining factors in a person's achieving success. 2.2–20.That has been omitted here, and is discussed in a later chapter in this book on the problem of Causality.
84 Ibid., 2.24–33.
85 Ibid., 3.3–8, 11, 16–7.
86 Ibid., 4.1–16.
87 Ibid., 1.53–5.
88 Ibid., 4.22–34.
89 Ibid., 5.1–17.
90 Ibid., 5.18–29.
91 Ibid., 5.31–2.
92 Ibid., 5.34–6.
93 Ibid., 6.7–9.
94 Ibid., 6.11–17.
95 Ibid., 6.30–1.
96 Ibid., 6.19–20, also 21–3.
97 Ibid., 6.32–3; 7.1–12, 59–61.
98 Ibid., 7.63–5.
99 Ibid., 7.66.
100 Ibid.
101 *Bhīshma-parva,* the *Bhāgvad-Gītā.*
102 *Sauptika-parva,* 8.6–8.
103 See Ch. 8 of this book, on the *Mahābhārata*'s analysis of self–interest, s*vartha.*
104 *Sauptika-parva,* 8.14–27.
105 Ibid., 8.47–62.
106 Ibid., 8.42–4.
107 Ibid., 8.67–8, 110–17.
108 Ibid., 8.118.
109 Ibid., 8.69–75.
110 Ibid., 8.109–10; 106–7; 131.
111 Ibid., 8.127–8.
112 Ibid., 8.146.
113 *Sauptika-parva,* 10.1–6.
114 Ibid., 10.10, 12.
115 Ibid., 10.14.
116 Ibid., 10.15–8, 20–1.
117 Ibid., 10.19.
118 Ibid., 10.24–6.
119 Ibid., 11.5–7.
120 Ibid., 11.8.
121 Ibid., 11.9–10.
122 Ibid., 11.11.
123 Ibid., 11.12.
124 Ibid., 11.13.
125 Ibid., 11.14–5.
126 Ibid., 11.18.
127 Ibid., 11.21–6.
128 Ibid., 12.1–3.
129 Ibid., 12.1–6.

130 For details see *Sauptika-parva*, Chs. 13–6.
131 Ibid., 14.5–6.
132 Ibid., 14.7–11.
133 Ibid., 14.16.
134 Ibid., 15.15.
135 Ibid., 15.16–7.
136 Ibid., 15.18.
137 Ibid., 15.13–4.
138 Ibid., 15.25–7.
139 Ibid., 15.28.33.
140 Ibid., 15.34.
141 Ibid., 16.1–4.
142 Ibid., 16.5–7.
143 Ibid., 16.8, 14–6.
144 Ibid., 16.9–11.
145 Ibid., 16.28–33.
146 Ibid., 16.34–7.
147 Ibid., 12.8.
148 Ibid., 12.60.
149 Ibid., 12.61–9.
150 *Vana-parva*, 12.126.
151 Ibid., 12.125.
152 *Udyoga-parva*, Ch. 71.
153 *Vana-parva*, 12.78; also *Udyoga-parva*, 82.31.
154 *Udyoga-parva*, 82.32–41.
155 *Vana-parva*, 27.7–9.
156 Ibid., 27.26–39.
157 Ibid., 29.1, also 30.
158 Ibid., 29.25.
159 Ibid., 29.27–8.
160 Ibid., 29.29.
161 Ibid., 29.40.
162 Ibid., 29.3–5.
163 Ibid., 29.6.
164 Ibid., 29.8.
165 Ibid., 29.7, 9, 22.
166 Ibid., 29.21.
167 Ibid., 29.28.
168 Ibid., 29.30.
169 Ibid., 29.32.
170 Ibid., 29.10–1, 16–7, 19–20, 36–7.
171 Ibid., 29.47.
172 *Anushāsana-parva*, 113.10.
173 *Vana-parva*, 29.31–52.
174 *Vana-parva*, 29.36–7, 40. For similar praise of forgiveness, see also *Udyoga-parva*, 33.55–9; 39.59–60; *Āshvamedhika-parva*, 115.41–7.
175 *Āshvamedhika-parva*, 114.37–44 (Kumbakonam ed.)
176 Ibid., 114.47.
177 Ibid., see p. 6375 in (G).
178 Ibid., p. 6375 as above.
179 Ibid., p.6375 as above. Also see Vidura on *forgiveness*: *Udyoga-parva*, 39.58–9.
180 *Vana-parva*, 28.36.
181 *Vana-parva*, 28.1–38.
182 Ibid., 28.6.
183 Ibid., 28.7–8.
184 Ibid., 28.17.
185 Ibid., 28.18–23.
186 Ibid., 28.24–5.
187 Ibid., 28.26–31.
188 Ibid., 28.27.
189 Ibid., 28.28.
190 Ibid., 28.29–30.
191 Ibid., 28.31.
192 Ibid., 28.32–4, 35, 38.
193 Ibid., 28.34.
194 Ibid., 140.65.
195 Ibid., 56.40.
196 Ibid., 56.37.
197 Ibid., 56.21.
198 *Shānti-parva*, 94.1.
199 *Udyoga-parva*, 72.63.
200 Ibid., 72.62.
201 Ibid., 272.64.
202 Ibid., 72.55.
203 Ibid., 72.58.
204 See *Sauptika-parva*.
205 *Udyoga-parva*, 72.52.
206 Ibid., 72.53.
207 Ibid., 72.54.
208 Ibid., 72.70.
209 Ibid., 72.71.
210 Ibid., 72.72.
211 *Shānti-parva*, 139.46.
212 Ibid., 139.72.
213 Ibid., 139.73.
214 Ibid., 69.1.
215 Ibid., 69.23.
216 Ibid., 69.4.
217 Ibid., 96.1, 24.
218 *Udyoga-parva*, 129.40.
219 *Shānti-parva*, 140.58–9.

220 *Shānti-parva*, 303.4; also *Karṇa-parva*, 72.26–7; 97.103–4. *Pañchatantra*, III.104.
221 *Anushāsana-parva*, 178.26.
222 *Shānti-parva*, 95.13.
223 Ibid., 133.15–20.
224 Ibid., 133.15.
225 Ibid., 133.16–7.
226 Ibid., Ch. 135.
227 Ibid. 135.2–5, 7–9.
228 Ibid., 135.11–2.
229 Ibid., 135.13.
230 Ibid., 135.14.
231 Ibid., 135.15.
232 Ibid., 135.19.
233 Ibid., 135.20.
234 Ibid., 135.22.
235 Ibid., 135.23.
236 Ibid., 215.12.
237 Ibid., 215.10.
238 *Udyoga-parva*, 34.78–80; 36.7–8; *Sabhā-parva*, 66.6–8; 89.6–7. *Anushāsana-parva*, 104.31–4; 161.31–5. *Shānti-parva*, 299.8–12.
239 *Udyoga-parva*, 34.80; 36.7. *Sabhā-parva*, 66.7; 89.6. *Anushāsana-parva*, 104.32. *Shānti-parva*, 299.9.
240 *Anushāsana-parva*, 104.33.
241 Ibid., 104.34.
242 Ibid. 104.31. *Shānti-parva*, 299.8.
243 *Udyoga-parva*, 36.8.
244 *Shukraniti*, III.233.
245 *Pañchatantra*, III.236.
246 Ibid., III.112; *Mahābhārata*, *Udyoga-parva*, 34.76–80; *Anushāsana-parva*, 161.34–5. *Tirukkural*, 13.9.
247 *Pañchatantra*, III.113.
248 *Shānti-parva*, 139.42.
249 *Shānti-parva*, 191.14.
250 *Udyoga-parva*, 34.77.
251 *Shānti-parva*, 287.18.
252 *Tirukkural*, 19.1–10. See Chs. 111 and 114; 132,12–3. Also *Vana-parva*, 208.50. These are few examples of what is being said, in different contexts, throughout the *Mahābhārata*.
253 *Shānti-parva*, 132.12.
254 *Shānti-parva*, 132.12.
255 Ibid., 287.26.
256 Ibid., 287.28.
257 Ibid., 287.28.
258 Ibid., 287.29.
259 Ibid., 287.30.
260 Ibid., 287.31.
261 Ibid., 287.32.
262 Ibid., 36.71.
263 *Pañchatantra*, III.115. *Manu-smriti*, IV.138. Gautama *Dharmashāstra*, IX.68. *Vishṇusmriti*, 71.73–4. *Yājñavalkya Dharmashāstra*, I.132.
264 *Shānti-parva*, 287.20; 337.13; an identical saying, in the parable of the dharmic butcher and the arrogant ascetic Kaushika, in *Vana-parva*, 213.4; 216.47.
265 *Udyoga-parva*, 37–40; and generally, Chs. 33–40, which constitute the *Vidura-nīti*, the prudence maxims of Vidura.
266 Ibid., 37.15. *Sabhā-parva*, 87.16. *Shānti-parva*, 168.4. Also *Pañchatantra*, II.174–5, III.4–5.
267 *Udyoga-parva*, 37.16. *Sabhā-parva*, 87.17.
268 *Udyoga-parva*, 36.12. *Shānti-parva*, 305.38.
269 *Manu-smriti*, IV.138.
270 *Udyoga-parva*, 36.19.
271 Ibid., 36.37.
272 See *The Rebel*, Albert Camus. In one of the most important works of our time, Camus laid bare the moral nihilism of communist philosophy and its practice. He shows how ideology became a metaphysical justification of organised murder. For it shows how a person can conceal his, or her, delight in violence by taking recourse to a philosophy of revolutionary violence. See also Denis de Rougemont, *Passion and Society* (tr. Montgomery Belgion; Faber & Faber, London, 1956), where he demonstrates how the love of pain pervades the Western consciousness.
273 *Shānti-parva* ,18.34–5.
274 *Anushāsana-parva*, 115.18.
275 Ibid., 115.19.
276 Ibid., 116.13.
277 *Shānti-parva*, 262.28.
278 Ibid., 262.29.
279 Ibid., 262.30.
280 Ibid., 262.33.

281 Ibid., 262.32. See also, in the same *parva*, 160.26–7, 326.33.
282 *Anushāsana-parva*, 142.27.
283 Ibid., 142.28.
284 See Ch. 14, '*Dharma*. The Foundation of Law and Governance'; pp. 417–464.
285 *Anushāsana-parva*, 212.40 (K); unnumbered verse, p. 5950 in (G).
286 See Ch. 14 of this book, pp. 417–464.
287 We will travel that ground in Ch. 18, '*Moksha* as Human Freedom: Freedom *from*, and Freedom *into*', p. 764.
288 *Shānti-parva*, 330.2, and 173.42. Also *Vana-parva*, 2.16. *Anushāsana-parva*, 244.3. *Strī-parva*, 2.22.
289 *Shānti-parva*, 330.16, 203.6, 217.2.
290 Ibid., 330.9.
291 Ibid., 330.12.
292 *Shānti-parva*, 203.1–3; 233.5–6; 235.86–7; 330.7–12. *Udyoga-parva*, 36.44–7.
293 *Shānti-parva*, 330.11.
294 Ibid., 245.18–9.
295 Ibid., 245.20.
296 Ibid., 245.21.

Chapter 6

1 *Droṇa-parva*, 51.21.
2 Ibid., 52.12, 16.
3 Ibid., 52.18.
4 Ibid., 53.22–3.
5 Ibid., 54.3–4.
6 Ibid., 54.9.
7 Ibid., 54.30–1.
8 Ibid., 54.37–8.
9 Ibid., 54.45.
10 Ibid., 54.50.
11 Ibid., 54.40.
12 Ibid., 54.42.
13 *Udyoga-parva*, 37.10–11.
14 *Strī-parva*, 4.15–8.
15 Ibid., 4.15–8.
16 *Vana-parva*, 184.18.
17 Ibid., 184.19–20.
18 Ibid., 184.21.
19 *Udyoga-parva*, Ch. 42.
20 Ibid., 42.3.
21 Ibid., 42.4.
22 Ibid., 42.5.
23 Ibid., 42.7.
24 Ibid., 42.11.
25 Ibid., 42.16.
26 *Shānti-parva*, 175.1.
27 Ibid., 175.5.
28 Ibid., 175.6.
29 Ibid., 175.7.
30 Ibid., 175.8.
31 Ibid., 175.9.
32 Ibid., 175.15; also 277.14–5, 29; 298.17; 321.73.
33 Ibid., 175.14.
34 Ibid., 175, unnumbered verse after verse 15.
35 Ibid., 175.13.
36 Ibid., 175.18.
37 Ibid., 175.11.
38 Ibid., 175.22.
39 Ibid., 175.20.
40 Ibid., 175.24.
41 Ibid., 175.31.
42 *Shānti-parva*, 175.30; 277.29.
43 Ibid., 175.29.
44 See Ch. 7 of this book, 'The Question of Truth', pp. 181–197.

Chapter 7

1 *Vana-parva*, 313.116.
2 *Anushāsana-parva*, 232.17 (K); p. 5988 in (G), verse unnumbered.
3 Ibid., 232.18 (K); p. 5988 in (G), verse unnumbered.
4 On this question, see *Shānti-parva*, 109.1–24, and *Karṇa-parva*, 69.23, 29–66, with many of the verses almost identical in the two chapters.
5 *Shānti-parva*, 199.63.
6 Ibid., 199.64, also 160.3–5.
7 Ibid., 199.65; *Anushāsana-parva*, 110.28–33. A complete list of the references to the importance attached to truth, *satya*, in the philosophical as well as in the other dharmic literature, particularly the Jain and the Buddhist, will require very considerable space.
8 *Shānti-parva*, 199.67.
9 Ibid., 199.68.
10 Ibid., 199.69.

11 Ibid., 199.70.
12 Ibid., 190.1.
13 *Shānti-parva*, 190.2.
14 Ibid., 190.5.
15 *Shānti-parva*, 162.24.
16 *Anushāsana-parva*, Shiva to his wife Umā, p. 5988 in (G).
17 *Shānti-parva*, 259.10.
18 Ibid., 162.4.
19 *Tirukkural*, 30.9. On 'truthfulness', see the remaining verses in Ch. 30.
20 *Shānti-parva*, 15.50.
21 Ibid., 109.2.
22 Ibid., 109.3.
23 Ibid., 109.4.
24 Ibid., 109.4–5.
25 Ibid., 109.6.
26 Bhīshma in the *Shānti-parva*, 109.4–24; and Krishna in the *Karṇa-parva*, 69.31–5; 54–65.
27 *Shānti-parva*, 109.4; *Karṇa-parva*, 69.31.
28 Krishna in the *Karṇa-parva*, 69.54–6; Bhīshma in the *Shānti-parva*, 109.13.
29 *Karṇa-parva*, 69.57; *Shānti-parva*, 109.15.
30 *Karṇa-parva*, 69.58; *Shānti-parva*, 109.10.
31 *Shānti-parva*, 259.25; also 262.9, which says: '*He alone knows Dharma who, in his acts and thought and speech, is a friend of all and is working forever for their good.*'
32 Ibid., 259.4, 26.
33 *Karṇa-parva*, 69.35; *Shānti-parva*, 109.6.
34 *Karṇa-parva*, 69.23.
35 *Karṇa-parva*, 69.34; *Shānti-parva*, 109.5
36 *Karṇa-parva*, 69.32.
37 This is explained at another place. *For example, if a father portrays his daughter having more qualities than she actually has, it is not to be treated as a lie.*
38 *Karṇa-parva*, 69.62–3, and 69.33; *Shānti-parva*, 109.24.
39 *Bhāgvata-purāṇa*, VIII.19.43
40 *Karṇa-parva*, 69.63.
41 *Karṇa-parva*, 69.46–53.
42 *Tirukkural*, 30.2
43 *Karṇa-parva*, 69.65; *Shānti-parva*, 109.24.
44 See, for examples, *Shānti-parva*, 110.11, 23; 111.6. *Vana-parva*, 207.74.
45 *Taittirīya Upanishad*, I.11.
46 *Droṇa-parva*, Ch. 190; and re–narrated in Ch. 193 of the same *parva*.
47 Ibid., 190.9–12; 193.48–51.
48 Ibid., 190.16; 193. 53.
49 Ibid., 190.14–5, 17; 193. 53.
50 Ibid., 190.19–20; 193.53–4.
51 Ibid., 190.42–4; 193.54.
52 Ibid., 190.43–4.
53 Ibid., 190.54–5.
54 Ibid., 192.62.
55 Ibid., 196.34–9.
56 Ibid., 196.43–53.
57 Ibid., 197.2–23.
58 Ibid., 197.24–44.
59 Ibid., 198.7–43.
60 Ibid., 190.56.
61 See Ch. 5, '*Ahiṃsā*, Not–violence, Foundation of Life, pp. 113–168.
62 *Anushāsana-parva*, 167.49.
63 *Shānti-parva*, 329.12; also *Ādi-parva*, 74.105; *Vana-parva*, 216.46 (K).
64 *Shānti-parva*, 329.13.
65 *Shānti-parva*, 162.1–2.
66 Ibid., 162.8–22.
67 Ibid., 162.8–9.
68 Ibid., 162.10.
69 Ibid., 162.11.
70 Ibid., 162.12.
71 Ibid., 162.13.
72 Ibid., 162.14.
73 Ibid., 162.15.
74 Ibid., 162.16.
75 Ibid., 162.17.
76 Ibid., 162.17.
77 Ibid., 162.18.
78 Ibid., 162.18.
79 Ibid., 162.19–20.
80 Ibid., 162.21.
81 Ibid., 162.22.
82 For instance, *dama*, self–control, as the highest *dharma*, leads to the other attributes of truth. Ibid., Ch. 160, particularly 160.14–8.
83 *Shānti-parva*, 162.23.
84 Ibid., 158.16.
85 Ibid., 158.17–8.
86 *Vana-parva*, 209.4. Dharmavyādha

the meat seller to Kaushika the learned brāhmaṇa.
87 Ibid., 213.31. Dharmavyādha to Kaushika.
88 *Shānti-parva*, 251.11–2. *Vana-parva*, 207.67.
89 Ibid.,299.13.
90 Ibid., 175.28; 277.24.
91 Ibid., 175.30; 277.29.
92 Ibid., 175.31.

Chapter 8

1 *Shānti-parva*, 320.43.
2 Ibid., 138.1–3.
3 Ibid., 138.4–6.
4 Ibid., 138.8.
5 Ibid., 138.9.
6 Ibid., 138.10–11.
7 Ibid., 138.13.
8 Ibid., 138.16.
9 *Shānti-parva*, specifically 138.13–7; 201–2; 207; 214–5.
10 Ibid., Ch. 138; 138.19–202.
11 Ibid., 138.136–84; 191–8.
12 Ibid., 138.139; 138.13.
13 Ibid., 138.141.
14 Ibid., 138.142.
15 Ibid., 138.140.
16 Ibid., 138.145.
17 Ibid., 138.152–3; 154–6; 304.38.
18 Ibid., 138.155.
19 Ibid., 138.158.
20 Ibid., 138.159.
21 Ibid., 138.160.
22 Ibid., 138.166.
23 Ibid., 138.146.
24 For this episode, see *Bhīshma-parva*, 43.11–83.
25 Ibid., 43.41.
26 Ibid., 43.42.
27 Ibid., Droṇāchārya: 43.56–7. Kripāchārya: 43.71–2. Shalya: 43.82–3.
28 *Strī-parva*, 2.35; and repeated at numerous other places in the *Mahābhārata*.
29 *Udyoga-parva*, 34.64–5
30 *Strī-parva*, 7.22.
31 *Āshvamedhika-parva*, 26.1.
32 Ibid., 26.2.
33 Ibid., 26.3.
34 Ibid., 26.4.
35 Ibid., 26.5.
36 Ibid., 26.13.
37 *Shānti-parva*, 139.65–6.
38 See *Ādi-parva*, Chs.156–63.
39 Ibid., 155.17–9.
40 Ibid., 156.3–4.
41 Ibid., 156.10–15.
42 Ibid., 156.16.
43 Ibid., 156.20–1. He enumerates the causes of pain and suffering in human life, 156.22–4.
44 Ibid., 156.26–9.
45 Ibid., 156.31–4.
46 Ibid., 156.37.
47 Ibid., 156.38.
48 Ibid., 156.39–41.
49 Ibid., 157.1–5. For what the Brāhmaṇī said to her husband, see the whole of Ch. 157. *Ādi-parva*, 157.1–38. Abridged and rearranged here.
50 Ibid., 157.7–10.
51 Ibid., 157.12–3.
52 Ibid., 157.14–7.
53 Ibid., 157.15,18–9.
54 Ibid., 157.33–4.
55 Ibid., 157.31–2, 37.
56 Ibid., 157.38.
57 For what she says to her father, see the whole of Ch. 158 of the *Ādi-parva*. Abridged and rearranged here.
58 Ibid., 158.1–2.
59 Ibid., 158.3.
60 Ibid., 158.7–14, 15–7.
61 Ibid., 158.21–4.
62 For the conversation between Kuntī and her host, the Brāhmaṇa, see Chs. 159–60, *Ādi-parva*.
63 Ibid., 159.2–7.
64 Ibid., 159.9–10.
65 Ibid., 159.12.
66 Ibid., 159.13, 16.
67 Ibid., 160.1–3.
68 Ibid., 160.4–5.
69 Ibid., 160.9–10.
70 Ibid., 160.11–2.
71 Ibid., 160.13–7.
72 Ibid., 161.1–4.

73 Ibid., 161.5–11.
74 Ibid., 161.12, 20.
74 Ibid., 161.13–5.
76 Ibid., 161.14 and 15.
77 Ibid., 161.22.
78 Ibid., 161.23.
79 Ibid., 161.24.
80 Ibid., 161.25.
81 Ibid., 161.26.
82 Ibid., 161.16–8.
83 Ibid., Ch. 162.
84 Ibid., 163.4.
85 Ibid., 163.10–19.
86 *Shānti-parva*, 259.20
87 Ch. 17, 'From Ritual *Acts to Relationships*'.
88 *Udyoga-parva*, 217.16.
89 Ibid., 217.14.
90 *Udyoga-parva*, 34.77–80; 36.6–9. *Sabhā-parva*, 89.6–7. *Anushāsana-parva*, 161.31–5. The Sanskrit text for this and the following five were provided in Ch. 5, '*Ahiṃsā*, Not–violence, Foundation of Life', section (viii) Violence in Speech and Words'.
91 *Udyoga-parva*, 34.76–80. *Anushāsana-parva*, 161.34–5. *Tirukkural*, 13.9. *Pañchatantra*, III.112.
92 *Pañchatantra*, III.113.
93 *Udyoga-parva*, 36.8.
94 III.233.
95 III.236.
96 *Shānti-parva*, 191.14.
97 *Udyoga-parva*, 34.77.
98 *Tirukkural*, 19.1–10. *Shānti-parva*, more than any other work, analysed this problem with objectivity and understanding and severely condemned the habit of speaking ill of others in their absence. See Chs. 111 and 114.
99 *Udyoga-parva*, 36.71.
100 *Pañchatantra*, III.115. *Manu-smriti*, IV.138. Gautama *Dharmashāstra*, IX.68. *Vishṇusmriti*, 71.73–4. *Yājñavalkya Dharmashāstra*, I.132.
101 As we saw in Ch. 7 of this book, 'The question of Truth', pp. 181–197.
102 *Shānti-parva*, 329.13, 337.13; an identical saying, in the parable of the meat seller Dharmavyādha and the arrogant ascetic Kaushika, in *Vana-parva*, 213.4; 216.47.
103 *Udyoga-parva*, 37–40; and generally, Chs. 33–40, which constitute the *Vidura-nīti*, 'the prudence maxims of Vidura'.
104 This maxim is repeated at numerous places: *Shānti-parva*, 138.144, 194, 196–7; 139.28–9, 47; 140.43, 45. Also *Udyoga-parva*, 38.9. *Anushāsana-parva*, 215.24–5. See *Pañchatantra*, II.41–8.
105 *Shānti-parva*, specifically 138.13, 17, 201–2; 207; 214–5.
106 Ibid., 140.17–8. Also *Ādi-parva*, 153.31–3.
107 *Shānti-parva*, 140.58–60.
108 *Shānti-parva*, 138.177–80.
109 Ibid., 138.179.
110 Ibid., 138.180.
111 *Shānti-parva*, 157.8–9, *vide* the parable of the mighty shalmali tree and the wind god, Chs. 153–7; also 139.112. *Pañchatantra*, III. 14, 18, 22, 43; III. 131–2.
112 Ibid., 138.181–2.
113 Ibid., vide the parable of the three fishes, Ch. 136.
114 Ibid., 37.15. *Sabhā-parva*, 87.16. Also *Pañchatantra*, II.174–5; III.4–5.
115 *Udyoga-parva*, 37.16. *Sabhā-parva*, 87.17.
116 Manu*smrti*, IV.138.
117 *Shānti-parva*, 139.75.
118 *Shānti-parva*, 138.59.
119 *Udyoga-parva*, 36.19.
120 *Udyoga-parva*, 36.37.
121 *Shānti-parva*, 303.4. Also *Karṇa-parva*, 90.111–2. *Pañchatantra*, III.104.
122 *Anushāsana-parva*, 178.26.
123 Ibid., 116.8, 16, 22.
124 Ibid., 116.8.
125 III.220; against excess generally, see also III.217–9, 21.
126 References to this are countless and repetitive. The full argument is stated, with brevity, in *Udyoga-parva*, 34.55–65.
127 Ibid., 34.64–5; *Gītā*, VI.5–6. Also *Anushāsana-parva*, 9.29.

Chapter 9

1 For a detailed study of this subject, see *Vana-parva*, Chs. 2, 186, 193, 213, 216, 260–1, 314. *Shānti-parva*, chs, 25, 27, 28, 139, 152, 171, 175–8, 190, 201, 220, 226, 239 276, 286 288, 295, 329–30. *Anushāsana-parva*, Chs. 179, 218–20, 225, and 244 (all in K) *Āshvamedhika-parva*, Ch. 16.

2 *Shānti-parva*, 201.10; also 295.27.

3 Ibid., 139.62; 201.12.

4 Ibid., 190.9.The objection to it, for dialectical purposes, is provided in the next passage, 190.10.; also 199.10. See also the *Bhāgvad–purāṇa*, XI.3.18.

5 *Shānti-parva*, 269.46.

6 Ibid., 269.48.

7 Ibid., 174.21.

8 Ibid., 174.22; 201.22; 224.7.

9 Ibid., 16.8–9; 188.6. *Vana-parva*, 2.25–6. *Āshvamedhika-parva*, 12.1–2.

10 *Shānti-parva*, 16.9.

11 *Vana-parva*, 2.25.

12 *Vana-parva*, 2.22.

13 *Shānti-parva*, 139.63–4; see also *Vana-parva*, 196.17–24.

14 *Shānti-parva*, 339.3.

15 *Shānti-parva*, 174.19. *Anushāsana-parva*, 182.22.

16 Ibid., 174.19. *Vana-parva*, 261.49.

17 *Shānti-parva*, 174.48.

18 Ibid., 25.23.

19 *Shānti-parva*, 25.23–5; 153.88; 174.20, 49; 175.4; 286.12; 330.8. *Vana-parva*, 260.13–5; 262.51. *Anushāsana-parva*, 182.22; 244.14–5 (K). *Āshvamedhika-parva*, 44.18.

20 *Shānti-parva*, 330.16.

21 Ibid., 174.13

22 *Vana-parva*, 2.21. *Shānti-parva*, 173.14; 188.6; 217.2. *Anushāsana-parva*, 178.30

23 *Shānti-parva*, 25.20; 174.40; 330.2. *Vana-parva*, 2.16. *Anushāsana-parva*, 244.3. *Strī-parva*, 2.22.

24 *Vana-parva*, 2.47. *Shānti-parva*, 201.4; 330.14. *Strī-parva*, 2.25.

25 *Shānti-parva*, 330.20; also 177.12 and 234.100–1. *Anushāsana-parva*, 244.15 (K). *Āshvamedhika-parva*, 44.19. *Strī-parva*, 2.3. *Rāmāyaṇa*, II.105.16. *Vishṇu –purāṇa*, V.38.87.

26 *Vana-parva*, 79.12. *Bhāgvad–purāṇa*, XI.7.7.

27 *Shānti-parva*, 330.22.

28 *Shānti-parva*, 330.22.

29 Ibid., 331.5; *Anushāsana-parva*, 244.58

30 *Shānti-parva*, 331.7.

31 Ibid., 331.8.

32 Bhartrihari's *Vairāgya-shataka*, 50, tr. A.B. Keith, *A History of Sanskrit Literature* (Oxford, 1920), p. 179.

33 *Shānti-parva*, 104.44.

34 *Vana-parva*, 2.37.

35 *Ādi-parva*, 75.50; 85.12. *Vana-parva*, 2.38. See also *Manu-smrti*, 2.94. *Vishṇu-Purāṇa*, IV.10.23. *Bhāgvad–purāṇa*, IX.19.14.

36 *Bhāgvad–purāṇa*, VII.15.20.

37 *Shānti-parva*, 180.24.

38 *Shānti-parva*, 180.25.

39 *Shānti-parva*, 180.26.

40 *Ādi-parva*, 85.13. *Anushāsana-parva*, 93.40. Also *Vishṇu-Purāṇa*, IV.10.27.

41 *Shānti-parva*, 174.63. See also *Bhāgvad–purāṇa*, XI.8.44.Mahat *Upanishad*, 5.85–8.

42 Ibid., 174.45.

43 *Vishṇu-Purāṇa*, VI.5.55, also I.17.65–6.

44 Ibid., VI.5.56.

45 *Bhāgvad–purāṇa*, XI.9.1.

46 *Shānti-parva*, 177.48.

47 *Shānti-parva*, 330.18–9; *Anushāsana-parva*, 244.17 (K), p. 6010 in (G), verse unnumbered. *Pañchatantra*, II.127.

48 *Vana-parva*, 2.39. *Anushāsana-parva*, 244.18 (K), p.6010 in (G) verse unnumbered.

49 *Vana-parva*, 2.40; *Pañchatantra*, II.125. Furthermore, on this see Ch. 10 of this book, 'Material Prosperity and Wealth, *artha*', pp. 357–86.

50 *Vana-parva*, 210.2–3.

51 *Vana-parva*, 210.3–5. For the same idea, in slightly different words, see *Bhāgvad Gītā*, 2.62–3.

52 *Vana-parva*, 2.34, 36. *Anushāsana-parva*, 7.21, 24 (G); 141.31–5; 244.31–2, 34 (K). *Shānti-parva*, 173.57; 178.26; 276.12: and entire Ch. 276.
53 Ibid., 158.12–13; *Anushāsana-parva*, 141.33.
54 *Shānti-parva*, see entire Ch. 158.
55 *Shānti-parva*, 159.3.
56 Ibid., 159.4–5.
57 Ibid., 159.6–7.
58 Ibid., 159.9.
59 Ibid., 159–11.
60 Ibid., 159.12.
61 Ibid., 158.4.
62 Ibid., 158.6–7.
63 Ibid., 158.8–10.
64 Ibid., 158.15.
65 See *Shānti-parva*, Ch. 81.
66 Ibid., 81.4.
67 Ibid., 81.5–6.
68 Ibid., 81.7.
69 Ibid., 81.9–11.
70 Ibid., 81.12.
71 See *Anushāsana-parva*, Ch. 124.
72 Ibid., 124.9.
73 Ibid., 124.10.
74 Ibid., 124.11.
75 Ibid., 124.12.
76 Ibid., 124.13.
77 Ibid., 124.14.
78 Ibid., 124.16.
79 Ibid., 124.17.
80 Ibid., 124.18.
81 Ibid., 124.19.
82 Ibid., 124.20.
83 Ibid., 124.21. The following five verses are unnumbered in the Gorakhpur edition. of the *Mahābhārata*. I have numbered them as '21a', '21b', '21c', '21d', and '21e'.
84 Ibid., 124.21a.
85 Ibid., 124.21b.
86 Ibid., 124.21c.
87 Ibid., 124.21d.
88 Ibid., 124.21e.
89 Ibid., 124.22.
90 Ibid., 124.23.
91 Ibid., 124.24.
92 Ibid., 124.25.
93 Ibid., 124.26.
94 Ibid., 124.27.
95 Ibid., 124.28.
96 Ibid., 124.29.
97 Ibid., 124.31.
98 Ibid., 124.30.
99 Ibid., 124.34.
100 Ibid., 124.33.
101 Ibid., 124.15.
102 Ibid., 124.32.
103 Ibid., 124.36.
104 Ibid., 124.38.
105 Ibid., 124.39.
106 *Shānti-parva*, 174.33; also 25.28. The *Bhāgvad–purāṇa*, III.7.17.
107 *Shānti-parva*, 174.34.
108 Ibid., 173.39 (K).
109 Ibid., 174.35.
110 Ibid., 174.36.
111 *Shānti-parva*, 250.3.
112 *Udyoga-parva*, 34.59–60. *Vana-parva*, 211.23. For details see *Shānti-parva*, where this metaphor appears at several places: for example, see 236.8–12.
113 *Vana-parva*, 211.19.
114 *Vana-parva*, 211.20.
115 *Vana-parva*, 211.21.
116 *Udyoga-parva*, 34.60.
117 *Shānti-parva*, 246.3; 248.2. Also *Kathopanishad*, I.3.10; II.3.7.
118 *Udyoga-parva*, 32.25.
119 See *Shānti-parva*, Chs. 160 and 220.
120 Ibid., 160.2.
121 Ibid., 160.6.
122 Ibid., 160.7.
123 Ibid., 160.9.
124 Ibid., 160.12.
125 Ibid., 160.13.
126 Ibid., 160.14.
127 Ibid., 160.15–6. Vidura speaks of the same attributes, and more of a person who has disciplined his self. See *Udyoga-parva*, 63.14–15.
128 Ibid., 110.1.
129 Ibid., the whole Ch. 110
130 *Shānti-parva*, 295.25.
131 Ibid., 330.21; *Vana-parva*, 2.46; 216.24.

See also *Pañchatantra*, II.164–71.

132 Bhagwad-*purāṇa*, VIII.19.21. See VIII.19.21–5.

133 *Vana-parva*, 2.45.

134 *Shānti-parva*, 330.21. *Pañchatantra*, II.164–71.

135 *Vishṇu–purāṇa*, VIII.19.24.

136 *Shānti-parva*, 298.20, 37.

137 *Udyoga-parva*, 34.63.

138 Ibid., 34.64.

139 *Shānti-parva*, 174.4.

140 There is a considerable body of literature on *Vairāgya*, most of it repetitive. For the basic argument, see *Shānti-parva*, chs.173–8, 330–1; *Anushāsana-parva*, Ch. 244 (K), pp. 6010–11 in (G) where all verses unnumbered; and *Āshvamedhika-parva*, 17.29–41. See also Bhartrihari's *Vairāgya-shataka*.

141 Ibid., 174.18.

142 Ibid., 174.23, and also 25–7.

143 Ibid., 175.19.

144 Ibid., 175.12–5; 16–9.

145 Ibid., 175.11–2.

146 Ibid., 175.22; also 337.6.

147 Ibid., 177.33.

148 Ibid., 177.49.

149 Ibid., 177.48; also 174.45. For a full indictment of Desire, *Kāma*, by Manki, who seemed to have grievously suffered on account of it, see Ibid., 177.1–54.

150 *Shānti-parva*, 28.36; 174.15; 262.22–3; 321.86. See also *Anushāsana-parva*, the same verse, but unnumbered, p. 6010 (G).

151 Ibid., 28.39; also 319.9–10.

152 Ibid., 28.41.

153 Ibid., 319.14.

154 *Anushāsana-parva*, 1'1.11.

155 Ibid., 111.12.

156 Ibid., 111.13.

157 *Shānti-parva*, 321.86; also 275.36.

158 Ibid., 175.35; also *Anushāsana-parva*, 244.30 (K).

159 Bhartrihari's, *Vairāgya-shataka*, 33. tr. A.B. Keith, op. cit., p. 179.

160 Ibid., 32.

161 Ch. 18, '*Mokṣha* as Human Freedom', pp. 559–592.

162 *Kaṭhopanishad*, I.2.1.

163 Ibid., I.2.2.

164 Ibid., I.2.23–8.

165 See Ch. 18, pp. 581–583

166 Ibid.

167 Ibid.

168 See p. 337 above.

169 See *Shānti-parva*, Ch. 174.

170 *Āshvamedhika-parva*, *Anu-Gītā*, Ch. 30

171 Ibid., 30.5–6.

172 Ibid., 30.7.

173 Ibid., 30.9–22.

174 Ibid., 30.24–5.

175 Ibid., 30.27–31.

176 *Shānti-parva*, 81.13.

177 That will be taken up in a later chapter of this work, Ch. 14.

178 *Vana-parva*, 216.10.

179 *Shānti-parva*, 25.23.

180 Ibid., 174.19.

181 *Shānti-parva*, 163.13.

182 Ibid., 330.27.

183 Ibid., 205.2; 330.12.

184 Ibid., 205.3; 330.13.*Vana-parva*, 216.17.

185 *Shānti-parva*, 205.1; 330.11.

186 Ibid., 174.39; also 25.26.

187 *Shānti-parva*,174.40; 330.2. *Vana-parva*, 2.16. *Anushāsana-parva*, 244.3. *Strī-parva*, 2.22.

188 *Vana-parva*, 216.27.

189 Ibid., 216.21.

190 Ibid., 216.23.

191 Ibid., 216.22. Although, as far as I know, the *Mahābhārata* does not ever mention a creature called '*a happy fool*', I know that such a creature does exist—*a happy fool!*

192 *Udyoga-parva*, 36.44.

193 *Vana-parva*, 216.24.

194 *Shānti-parva*, 174.40.

195 Ibid., 301.49, 50.

196 Ibid., 301.52.

197 Ibid., 330.7.

198 Ibid., 330.8.

199 *Shānti-parva*, 330.9.

200 Ibid., 16.10.

201 *Āshvamedhika-parva*, 44.18.

202 Ibid., 44.20.

203 Ibid., 47.7.
204 *Shānti-parva*, 279.6.
205 Ibid., 215.6; see also 290.20.
206 Ibid., 215.7.
207 *Shānti-parva*, 174.35.
208 *Shānti-parva*, 174.53; 276.11.

Chapter 10

1 *Shānti-parva*, 320.50.
2 *Shānti-parva*, Ch. 8; also 167.11–9; and 167.22–3, 25.
3 Ibid., 8.12.
4 Ibid., 8.11.
5 Ibid., 8.14.
6 Ibid., 8.15.
7 Ibid., 8.19.
8 Ibid., 8.18.
9 Ibid., 8.16.
10 Ibid., 8.22.
11 Ibid., 8.23.
12 Ibid., 8.24.
13 Ibid., 8.17.
14 Ibid., 167.14.
15 Ibid., 167.19.
16 Ibid., 167.15.
17 *Vana-parva*, 33.48.
18 Ibid., 33.49.
19 Ibid., 33.58.
20 Ibid., 33.50–1, 64.
21 See Ch. 11 of this book, pp. 295–333.
22 *Vana-parva*, 33.43–4.
23 *Shānti-parva*, 130.36; *Shukranīti*, IV.2.14.
24 Ibid., 133.4.
25 Ibid., 133.6.
26 Ibid., 133.7.
27 Ibid., 133.1–2.
28 Ibid., 133.3; also *Udyoga-parva*, 39.64–5.
29 *Shānti-parva*, 71.7, 13–4; 130.51.
30 Ibid., 132.18.
31 Ibid., 71.15.
32 II.81; V.22.
33 II.93–100; 103–11.
34 I.2.
35 V.23.
36 V.24.
37 V.25.
38 V.26. See also Bhartrihari's *Nīti-shataka*, 40.
39 I.10, also I.4–9.
40 I.7.
41 *Shānti-parva*, 26.2.
42 Ibid., 26.3.
43 Ibid., 26.5–10.
44 Ibid., 26.11–2.
45 Ibid., 26.17–8.
46 Ibid., 26.20.
47 Ibid., 26.22.
48 Ibid., 26.23.
49 Ibid., 26.27.
50 *Shānti-parva*, Chs. 175 and 176. See also *Bhāgvata-purāṇa*, V, Ch. 14.
51 *Shānti-parva*, 180.24.
52 Ibid., 180.25.
53 VII.15.20.
54 *Shānti-parva*, 180.26; *Anushāsana-parva*, 141.31–5, 244.32; *Vana-parva*, 2.38.
55 *Anushāsana-parva*, 244.32.
56 *Shānti-parva*, 177.1.
57 Ibid., 177.2.
58 Ibid., 177.3.
59 Not to be confused with the English word 'monkey', although they sound dangerously similar.
60 See *Shānti-parva*, Ch. 177.
61 Ibid., 177.26.
62 Ibid., 177.34.
63 Ibid., 177.35.
64 Ibid., 177.17, 22.
65 Ibid., 177.28.
66 Ibid., 177.37.
67 Ibid., 177.38.
68 Ibid., 177.39 and 40–6.
69 Ibid., 177.52. For the state of the mind that conquest will lead to, see 177.40–4; 45–8.
70 Ibid., 177.42.
71 *Vana-parva*, 2.40–8. *Shānti-parva*, 338.14, 18–9. *Anushāsana-parva*, 244.17; *Pañchatantra*, II.127.
72 *Vana-parva*, 2.40. *Pañchatantra*, II.125.
73 *Vana-parva*, 2.40. *Anushāsana-parva*, 244.18.
74 *Vana-parva*, 2.47. *Shānti-parva*, 203.4; 338.14. *Strī-parva*, 2.25.
75 *Shānti-parva*, 338.20; also 177.12 and 234.100–1. *Anushāsana-parva*, 244.15. *Āshvamedhika-parva*, 44.19. *Strī-parva*,

2.3. The *Rāmāyaṇa*, II.105.16.

76 *Shānti-parva*, 330.21. *Vana-parva*, 2.45–6. *Pañchatantra*, II.164–71.

77 Bhartrihari's *Nīti-shataka*, 40.

78 *Shānti-parva*, 104.42; also 179.12; 330.20.

79 *Udyoga-parva*, 72.18–20.

80 *Shānti-parva*, 104.44; also 179.12; 330.20.

81 Ibid., 104.45.

82 Ibid., 104.8.

83 *Udyoga-parva*, 72.22.

84 Ibid., 72.23.

85 Ibid., 72.25.

86 Ibid., 72.26.

87 Ibid., 72.32.

88 Ibid., 72.27.

89 *Shānti-parva*, 130.43.

90 Ibid., 130.49.

91 *Vana-parva*, 236.26.

92 Ibid., 236.27.

93 *Shānti-parva*, 292.1,

94 *Shānti-parva*, *Parāshara-Gītā*, 292.19.

95 Ibid., 292.5.

96 Ibid., 292.4.

97 *Udyoga-parva*, 36.21.

98 Ibid., 39.71. *Anushāsana-parva*, 175.8–9. *Shānti-parva*, 265.20, 22, 25–6.

99 *Udyoga-parva*, 39.72. *Vana-parva*, 197.6.

100 III.220; against excess generally, see also III.217–9, 21.

101 References to this are countless and repetitive. The full argument is stated, with brevity, in *Udyoga-parva*, 34.55–65.

102 Ibid., 34.64–5; *Bhāgvad-Gītā*, VI.5–6; also *Anushāsana-parva*, 9.29.

103 *Shānti-parva*, 294.24–5.

104 See 'Fines' in the index to *Arthashāstra*, tr. R. Shamasastry (1915).

105 *Svargārohaṇa-parva*, 5.62.

106 *Shānti-parva*, 321.46.

Chapter 11

1 *Vana-parva*, 33.37.

2 John Dowson, *A Classical Dictionary of Hindu Mythology and Religion*, etc. (Routledge & Kegan Paul, London, 1961), pp. 146–7.

3 *Mahābhārata*, *Shānti-parva*, 254.1–7.

4 Ibid., 254.1–3.

5 Ibid., 254.5, 7.

6 I have derived the information contained in this paragraph from the late Dr S. Sanjeevi, of the Department of Tamil, University of Madras.

7 See Radhakrishnan, *Religion and Society* (George Allen & Unwin, London, 1947), pp. 191, 194–5.

8 For its most scholastic interpretation in modern times, see Gopinath Kaviraj, *Bhāratīya Saṅskṛti aur Sādhanā*, op cit I, pp. 23–43, 302–15, 316–22, particularly the two essays 'Tantric Bauddha-Sadhana', pp. 513–47 and 548–58.

9 Ibid., I, p.558, translated from the Hindi by the author.

10 Ibid., I, p. 547.

11 See *Mahābhārata*, *Shānti-parva*, 144.5–6, 12–7.

12 *Bhāgvata-purāṇa*, XI.8.7–8.

13 The references are to *Pañchatantra* in the Varanasi edition (Pandita Pustakalaya, ed., Pandeya Rāmatej Sastri)

14 Translated by the author.

15 Ch. 38, also chs. 50–2 for the episode involving Ashṭāvakra and Uttara Dishā, in the form of an old woman who puts the ascetic to the test; particularly 50.83–4, 90–1, 98–101; 52.3, 5, and Ch. 75.

16 Ibid., 38.7.

17 I. 146–7.

18 I. 148. *Anushāsana-parva*, 38.25.

19 I.149.

20 I.153. *Anushāsana-parva*, 38.16.

21 I. 154. *Anushāsana-parva*, 38.17.

22 I.184.

23 I.207.

24 III.203.

25 IV.56.

26 *Anushāsana-parva*, 39.8

27 See again, as examples, *Anushāsana-parva*, 50.83; 90–1; 98–101; 52.5; 73.11–31; 74.5–6; 75.4, 9–10, 15–6; 78.27.

28 *Anushāsana-parva*, 43.1–2.

29 Ibid., 43.15.

30 Ibid., 45.9.

31 Ibid., 39.5–13; 40. 4–5, 10, 12–4.
32 Ibid., Chs. 40–3, which narrate the parable of Vipula protecting a willing Ruchi, the beautiful wife of his teacher Devasharmā, from being seduced by Indra, but by a method on Vipula's part which in its externals was open to objection, for he had filled the mind and body of Ruchi by his own subtle presence.
33 Ibid., 43.20–1.
34 Ibid., 43.22.
35 Ibid., 43.25.
36 Ibid., 23.64.
37 Ibid., 43.19.
38 Ibid., 46.14; also 20.21.
39 Ibid., 19.6–7.
40 Ibid., 19.7.
41 Ibid., 81.3–15.
42 *Anushāsana-parva*, 105.14–5.
43 Ibid., 47.25–6.
44 See *Ādi-parva*, 172,12–3.
45 *Shānti-parva*, 269.58.
46 *Anushāsana-parva*, 12.1.
47 *Anushāsana-parva*, Ch. 12.
48 Ibid., 12.52–3.
49 Ibid., 12.47.
50 *Shānti-parva*, Ch. 167.
51 Ibid., 167.2.
52 Ibid., 167.5–9.
53 Ibid., 167.9.
54 See Ch. 10 of this book, '*Material Prosperity and Wealth: artha*', pp. 271–293.
55 *Shānti-parva*, 167.11–19.
56 Ibid., 167.19.
57 Ibid., 167. 22–27.
58 Ibid., 167.23.
59 Ibid., 167.25–6.
60 Ibid., 167.26–7.
61 Ibid., 167.29–40.
62 Ibid., 167.29.
63 Ibid., 167.30–3.
64 Ibid. 167.33–4.
65 Ibid.,167.35–7.
66 Ibid., 167.38.
67 Ibid., 167.40.
68 *Ādi-parva*, chs.78–86.
69 Ibid., 82.18.
70 Ibid., 82.16. This, and the following, will come up again in the *Mahābhārata*'s discussion on 'what is truth?' Ch 7 of this book.
71 Ibid., 82.17.
72 Ibid., 82.22.
73 Ibid., 85.2.
74 Ibid., 85.3–5.
75 Ibid., 85.7–8.
76 Ibid., 85.12; also 75.50. This and the following verse will be repeated several times in the *Mahābhārata*, particularly during the discussion on 'pleasure' and 'pain', for which see Ch. 9 of this book.
77 Ibid., 85.13; also 75.51.
78 Ibid., 85.14.
79 Ibid., 85.15.
80 Ibid., 85.16.
81 This decision is questioned by some brāhmaṇa-s as a matter of principle. They were concerned that the principle of primogeniture, the eldest son of the king having the right to the throne on the king's death or abdication, ought not to have been violated. And it was Yadu, the eldest, born of Devayānī, and not Puru, the youngest, born of Sharmishṭhā, who ought to have been anointed king on Yayāti's abdication. Ibid., 85.18–22. Yayāti answers them by saying: 'You and others among the people, listen to me. On no account will I pass the kingdom to my eldest son. In the true meaning of the word, a son is one who obeys his father; is at all times desirous of his well–being; and is a person of good qualities. Yadu wasn't; nor was Turvasu, both born of Devayānī. Neither were Druhyu and Anu, born of Sharmistha. They always disregarded me and were somewhat contemptuous of me. It was Puru, the youngest, who, like a friend, sacrificed his youth for the sake of his father. It is he who is a son in the true meaning and he is a man of qualities, too. I humbly request you to respect my decision to anoint him king.' 85.23–9. The people in one voice gave their consent to Yayāti's decision as the right one, against which nothing could

be said. 85.30–1.

82 Ibid., Ch. 86. 86.4–13. See Ch. 14 of this book, '*Dharma*: Foundations of Law and Governance', pp. 417–464.

83 *Anushāsana-parva*, Chs. 19–21.

84 Ibid., 19.1–8.

85 Ibid., 19.14.

86 Ibid., 19.16–25.

87 Ibid., 19.80–6.

88 Ibid., 19.88–90.

89 Ibid., 19.13, 15.

90 Ibid., 19.98–100.

91 Ibid., 19.80–1, 83–4.

92 Ibid., 19.87.

93 Ibid., 19.91–2.

94 Ibid., 19.94.

95 Ibid., 21.5.

96 Ibid., 21.2–11.

97 *Ādi-parva*, 98.22–7, 38–41. *Vishṇu-Purāṇa*, IV. 10.23–7. The *Mahābhārata*'s teachings on life-in-family, *gṛihastha-āshrāma*, will be taken up in Ch. 12 of this book.

98 *Ādi-parva*, 98.41–2.

99 *Anushāsana-parva*, ch. 40–3.

100 Ibid., 40.18–9.

101 Ibid., 40.28–38.

102 Ibid., 40.39.

103 Ibid., 40.42–53.

104 Ibid., 40.57–8.

105 Ibid., 40.59.

106 Ibid., 41.8.

107 Ibid., 41.10–18.

108 Ibid., 41.19–26.

109 Ibid., 41.23, 25.

110 Ibid., 43.8–9, 11–2.

111 Ibid., 42.1–3.

112 Ibid., 42.17–21.

113 Ibid., 42.22–4.

114 Ibid., 42.25–7.

115 Ibid., 42.30–1.

116 Ibid., 42.32.

117 Ibid., 43.2–10.

118 Ibid., 43.6.

119 Ibid., 43.7.

120 Ibid., 43.8, 11.

121 Ibid., 43.13.

122 Ibid., 43.13–6.

123 Ch. 4 of this book.

124 *Anushāsana-parva*, 45.18–19.

125 Ibid., 45.23.

126 See the author's *Introduction to Kāma Sutra* (Rolli Books and Lustre Press, New Delhi, 1999; the German edition by Parkland Verlag, Koln, 1999; and the French edition by Guy Tredaniel Editeur, Paris, 1999).

127 Shalya-*parva*, 60.21–2.

Chapter 12

1 Bhandarkar Oriental Research Institute, Pune. See Vol. II–Part I (1941): pp. 649–52 on how one should answer the call of nature; pp. 653–6 on the rules concerning the cleaning of one's teeth; pp. 656–67 on the rules about the bath; pp. 672–75 on the rituals after the bath; pp. 677–89 on the rituals regarding the performance of *homa*, the ritual sacrifices, and *japa*, the recital of *mantras*; pp. 689–95 on the rituals surrounding the second bath in the middle of the day; Vol. II–Part II, pp. 757–99 on the prescribed rituals before, during, and after eating one's food; and pp. 800–02 on the rules regarding sleeping. In these pages of his *History of Dharmaśāstra*, Kane only summarises the rituals prescribed in the greatest of details in the *Dharmasūtra*-s of Baudhānaya, Gautama, Āpastamba, Vasishṭha, and Vishṇu, to mention here only a few.

2 See Ch. 17 of this book.

3 *Shānti-parva*, 193.18. This is repeated at numerous places throughout the *Mahābhārata*.

4 *Shānti-parva*, 12.12–3; 240.6–7; 275.5–17.

5 Gautama *Dharmasūtra*, III.1.35; *Baudhānaya Dharmasūtra*, II.6.29, 42–3; quoted in Kane, op. cit., Vol.II–Part I, pp. 424–5.

6 *Brahma-sūtra*, III.4.19–20.

7 *Manu*, VI.89–90, III.77–80. *Vasishṭha*, III.14–7. *Vishṇu*, 59.29. *Dakṣha*, II.57–60.

8 Kane, op.cit, Vol. II–Part I, p. 424.

9 *Shānti-parva*, Ch. 9.

10 Ibid., 9.30–1.

11 Ibid., 9.32.
12 Ibid., 9.33.
13 Ibid., 9.34.
14 Ibid., Chs. 10–3.
15 Ibid., 10.1–2, 4–5, 11–4.
16 Ibid., 10.22.
17 Ibid., 10.21.
18 Ibid., 10.23–4.
19 Ibid., 12.7–8.
20 Ibid., 12.14.
21 Ibid., 12.9.
22 Ibid., 12.35.
23 Ibid., 12.12–3.
24 Ibid., 13.1.
25 Ibid., 13.4–5.
26 Ibid., 13.10–11.
27 To be discussed in greater detail in Ch. 18 of this book, pp. 559–592. Also see the author's '*Mokṣha* as Human Freedom. Freedom *From*, and Freedom *Into*'; his two inaugural lectures at the Foundation for Universal Responsibility of His Holiness the Dalai Lama, New Delhi, and later published in their *Creeds of Our Time* (Full Circle Publishing, New Delhi, 2000), pp. 1–40.
28 *Shānti-parva*, 320.50.
29 Ibid., see also Ch. 320. See Ch. 18 of this book.
30 Ibid., 18.30–2, 34.
31 *Vana-parva*, 200.96–7; also 104–7.
32 *Shānti-parva*, 18.28–9.
33 Ibid., 12.13–4.
34 Ibid., Chs. 268–70.
35 Ibid., 268.2.
36 Ibid., 268.12–4.
37 Ibid., 269.1–4.
38 Ibid., 269.5.
39 Ibid., 269.6–8.
40 Ibid., 269.10–11, 17.
41 *Anushāsana-parva*, Ch. 141, p. 5924 in G.
42 *Anushāsana-parva*, Ch. 141, p. 5924 in G.
43 Ibid., 240.7; 275.16.
44 Ibid., *Parāshara-Gītā*, 292.9
45 Which is a part of the *Mahābhārata* text; *Bhīshma-parva*, Chs. 25–42.
46 *Āshvamedhika-parva*, 16.5–7.
47 Ibid., 16.10–11.
48 Ibid., 16.11–2.
49 Ibid., Chs. 16–51.
50 *Shānti-parva*, 109.10–12.
51 Ibid., 144.6.
52 Ibid., 144.5.
53 Ibid., 144.12.
54 Ibid., 144.14.
55 Ibid., 144.16; also 144.15.
56 *Ādi-parva*, 74. 41, 51.
57 We will meet her in a later part of this work, 'The Women of the *Mahābhārata*'.
58 *Ādi-parva*, 74. 41.
59 Ibid., 74.42.
60 Ibid., 74.43.
61 Ibid., 74.51.
62 *Shānti-parva*, 144.17.
63 See, as examples, *Anushāsana-parva*, 78.24–5; 81.14; and also 51.21.
64 See Ch. 14 of this book, '*Dharma*: The Foundation of Law and Governance, *Rāja-dharma*'.
65 The reader may want to have a look at Chaturvedi Badrinath's *Introduction* in *Kama Sutra* (Lustre Press/Roli Books, New Delhi, 1999); translated into German, *Kama Sutra* (Parkland Verlag, Koln, 1999); into French, *Kama* Sutra (Guy Tredaniel Editeur, Paris, 1999); and into Italian and Dutch.
66 *Anushāsana-parva*, Ch. 46.
67 Ibid., 46.5.
68 Ibid., 46.6–7.
69 Ibid., 46.9–10.
70 Ibid., 46.4.
71 Ibid., 46.11.
72 Ibid., 46.15.
73 *Anushāsana-parva*, Ch. 22, verse unnumbered in (G), p. 5546.
74 Ibid., Ch. 22, verse unnumbered in (G), p. 5546.
75 Ibid., the following verse.
76 *Anushāsana-parva*, Chs. 19–21.
77 Ibid., 62.20.
78 Ibid., 105.14–5; also *Shānti-parva*, 108.16–7.
79 *Shānti-parva*, 266.26.
80 Ibid., 266.27.
81 Ibid., 266.28.

82 Ibid., 266.32–3.
83 Ibid., 266.31, also 29–30.
84 See *Shānti-parva*, 108.13, 28–30.
85 *Vana-parva*, Chs. 307–9.
86 *Udyoga-parva*, 144.25–31; and Ch. 145.
87 Ibid., 145.1–3.
88 Ibid., 146.5–8, 20.
89 See *Shānti-parva*, Ch. 266.
90 Ibid., 266.38, 40, 51–2.
91 Ibid., 266.51.
92 Narrated elsewhere in this book. See Ch. 4.
93 *Vana-parva*, Ch. 214.
94 Ibid., 214.18, and 19–22.
95 Ibid., 214.23.
96 Ibid., 214.25.
97 Ibid., 214.26.
98 Ibid., 214.27.
99 Ibid., 214.28.
100 Ibid., 215.7–8.
101 Ibid., 215.9–13.
102 See *Āshvamedhika-parva*, 20.2–4.
103 Ibid., Chs. 20–34.
104 See *Anushāsana-parva*, Chs. 142–6.
105 *Vana-parva*, 146.2–4, 7, 9; 155.13–5.
106 Ibid., chs.152–4.
107 *Virata-parva*, 20.30–1. See entire Ch. 20.
108 *Ṛg-veda*, 10th *Mandala*.
109 *Katha-Upanishad*, the very first verse.

Chapter 13

1 See, for example, *Shānti-parva*, Chs. 188; 189; 293–6.
2 X.90.12.
3 XXXI.1.11.
4 VII.1.1.
5 1.4.11–3.
6 IV.13.
7 *Shānti-parva*, 186.1–4; 302.5–6. *Anushāsana-parva*, 208.4–5.
8 Ibid., 206.35–7.
9 Ibid., 290.146.
10 There is a difference of opinion on the question whether the Dasyu and the Dasa are identical. Whereas that is the view Pandurang Vaman Kane holds, *History of Dharmaśāstra* (Pune, 1941), Vol. II–Part I, p. 26; Ram Sharan Sharma, *Sudras in Ancient India* (Delhi, 1958), argues that the Dasyu were different from the Dasa (pp. 8–14, 23–4), and that 'the Aryans followed a policy of ruthless extermination towards the Dasyus, which, in the case of the Dasa, was tempered with moderation.' (p. 9).
11 Kane, op. cit, II–Part I, pp. 48–9; Ram Sharan Sharma, op. cit., pp. 8–13.
12 For example, *Shānti-parva*, 186.13; 286.33–4, 38, 45.
13 *Ṛg-veda*, X.83.1, identical with *Atharva-veda*, IV.32.1. RV, X.38.3; cf. AV, XX.36.10; RV, VII.83.1; VI.60.6; VI.33.3; VII.33—all quoted in Ram Sharan Sharma, op. cit, pp. 14–7.
14 *Shānti-parva*, 188.5, 11–3.
14a Ibid. 188.4.
14b Ibid. 188.5.
15 Ibid., 188.8.
16 Ibid., 188.7.
17 Pandurang Vaman Kane, History of *Dharmaśāstra*, Vol. II, Part I (Bhandarkar Oriental Research Institute, Pune, 1941), pp. 49–50.
18 For details, see Kane, op. cit., Vol. II–Part I, pp. 69–100.
19 This point is repeated in the *Mahābhārata*. The following references will suffice. *Vana-parva*, 182.20–1, 23, 25–6, 30–7; 183.42–3; 206.32–8; 219.13–5; 314.109–13. *Udyoga-parva*, 43.21–3, 48–9, 57; 45.5–8.
Shānti-parva, 244.13; 269.22–33; 275.23–33; Ch. 296; 302.27–30, 31–4; 323.88–92; *Anushāsana-parva*, 143.42–52; 164.11–5; 270.12–6 (K).
Bhāgvad-Gītā, IV.13; XVIII.41–5.
20 *Vana-parva*, 180.31.
21 Ibid., 180.32.
22 Ibid., 180.32–3.
23 Ibid., 180.21.
24 Ibid., 180.23.
25 Ibid., 180.25; also 219.13–4.
26 Ibid., 180.26; *Āshvamedhika-parva*, 116.6.
27 *Vana-parva*, 181.42–3.

27a Ibid., 313.107, and 313.108–11.
28 Ibid., 313.100. *Anushāsana-parva*, 143.50; also 111–3. *Āshvamedhika-parva*, 116.8.
29 *Shānti-parva*, 318.89, also 90–2.
30 Ibid., 318.88.
31 *Āshvamedhika-parva*, Ch. 92, p. 6377, verse unnumbered.
32 Ibid., Ch. 92, p. 6377, verse unnumbered.
33 *Majjhima-Nikāya*, ii. 128–30.
34 For a dialogue on this point which the Buddha had with Āssalayana, a young brāhmaṇa, who was despatched to contend with him, see Ibid., ii, 148–58.
35 1.38–44.
36 Ibid., 1.38.
37 Ibid., 1.40.
38 Ibid., 1.41.
39 Ibid., 1.42.
40 Ibid., 1.43.
41 Ibid., 1.39, 44.
42 *Anushāsana-parva*, p. 5921 in (G); 208.33–6 (K).
43 Ibid., 208.34.
44 See, for example, *Āshvamedhika-parva*, 97.10–37.
45 Ibid., 97.35–7.
46 Ibid., p. 6317 (G); 98.76. This view is repeated in 256.20–3. It is maintained that, devoid of learning or given to harmful deeds, a brāhmaṇa is a 'great god' still, *daivatam mahat*.
47 Ibid., 98.77–98. See also *Anushāsana-parva*, Chs. 33, 34, 35, and 36.
48 *Āshvamedhika-parva*, p. 6317 (G); 98.89–90.
49 Ibid., p. 6317 (G); 98.85, also 98.82.
50 Ibid., p. 6321 (G); 99.41, 59.
51 Ibid., p. 6321 (G); 99.42, 46. On the full identification of 'god' with the brāhmaṇa, and on the punishments for insulting him, see more fully 99.38–61. On the eulogy of the brāhmaṇa, also see *Anushāsana-parva*, chs.12, 30, 68–71; 208.6–11; Chs. 256–62, 264.
52 *Anushāsana-parva*, 35.14.
53 Ibid., 35.15.
54 Ibid., 35.16.
55 For this story, see *Vana-parva*, Ch. 185.
56 Ibid., 185.4.
57 Ibid., 185.5–7.
58 Ibid., 185.9–11.
59 Ibid., 185.13–4.
60 Ibid., 185.15, 17–8.
61 Ibid., 185.16.
62 Ibid., 185.20–1.
63 Ibid., 185.19–23.
64 Ibid., 185.25–30.
65 Ibid., 185.32–5.
66 Ibid., 36–7.
67 *Shānti-parva*, Chs. 168–9, 170–3.
67 Ibid. 172.26.
68 *Āshvamedhika-parva*, 118.113.
69 Ibid., p. 6379 (G); 118.12.
70 Ibid., p. 6377 (G); 116.16–8.
71 Ibid., p. 6377 (G); 116.19.
72 The literature on this is considerable. See, for example, *Āshvamedhika-parva*, 97.17, 98.14, 64, 102.77–8, 82, 110.16–8, 24.
73 *Anushāsana-parva*, 31.4, 65–8: vide the parable of the sage who incurred demerit for having instructed a *shudra* ascetic on a minor ritual detail, Ch. 31.
74 *Chāṇdogya Upanishad* IV.4, vide the parable of Satyakāma Jābāl.
75 *Shānti-parva*, Chs. 290–8.
76 Ibid., 296.27.
77 Ibid., 296.28.
78 Ibid., 284.122.
79 Ibid., 296.5–7; 20–1.
80 Ibid., 296.23–4.
81 Ibid., 296.31.
82 Ibid., 296.32.
83 Ibid., 296.33.
84 Ibid., 296.34.
85 *Shānti-parva*, Chs. 267–70.
86 *Vana-parva*, Chs. 206–16.
87 *Vana-parva*, 209.20–1.
88 Ibid., 209.25.
89 Ibid., 209.33.
90 Ibid., 209.27.
91 Ibid., 206.33.
92 Ibid., 206.34.
93 Ibid., 206.35.
94 Ibid., 206.36.
95 Ibid., 206.37.

96 Ibid., 209.43.
97 Ibid., 206.46.
98 *Shānti-parva*, 239, 28–32, especially 239–32.
99 Ibid., 206.47.
100 *Anushāsana-parva*, 104.77. See also. *Āshvamedhika-parva*, p. 6317 (G), verse unnumbered.
101 See *Vana-parva*, Chs. 207–14.
102 On this, see Chs. 4 and 5 of this book, on the meaning of *dharma*, and not–violence, *ahiṃsā*.
103 Ibid., 215.14.
104 Ibid., 215.15.
105 Ibid., 215.16.
106 *Ādi-parva*, Chs. 40–44; 49–50.
107 Ibid., 40.21–2.
108 Ibid., 40.23.
109 Ibid., 41.5–9.
110 Ibid., 40.32.
111 Ibid., 41.12–4.
112 Ibid., 41.15–9.
113 Ibid., 41.20–2.
114 Ibid., 41.23–4.
115 Ibid., 41.26, 32.
116 Ibid., 41.33.
117 Ibid., 42.1–2.
118 Ibid., 42.5–6.
110 Ibid., 42.8.
120 Ibid., 42.9.
121 Ibid., 42.10.
122 Ibid., 42.11–2, 13–22.
123 Ibid., 42.20–1.
124 Ibid., 42.33–41; 43.1–21.
125 Ibid., 43.22–36.
126 See Surendranath Dasgupta, *History of Indian Philosophy* (Cambridge, 1922), vol. I, pp. 31, 33–5. He rejects the view of Garbe and Winternitz that the philosophy of the *Upanishad*-s did not at all originate with the brāhmaṇas but arose in the ranks of the warrior class. Rather, in his opinion, 'the kshattriyas and even some women took interest in the religio=philosophical quest manifested in the *Upanishads*. The enquiries were so eager that either in receiving the instruction of Brahman or in imparting it to others, they had no considerations of sex and birth.' And this is all that is relevant to the discussion here.
127 For details, see R.S. Sharma, *Indian Feudalism* (Macmillan, Delhi, 1965; second ed., 1980).
128 *Ādi-parva*, Chs. 175–6.
129 Ibid., 175.1–5.
130 Ibid., 175. 7–9.
131 Ibid., 175. 10–11.
132 Ibid., 175. 13–4.
133 Ibid., 175. 20–3.
134 *Ādi-parva*, Ch. 173.
135 Ibid., Ch. 174.
136 Ibid., 174. 9–14.
137 Ibid., 174.15–6.
138 Ibid., 174.17.
139 Ibid., 174.18–9.
140 Ibid., 174.20.
141 Ibid., 174.24–5.
142 Ibid., 174.29.
143 Ibid., 174.30–2.
144 Ibid., 174.45.
145 *Anushāsana-parva*, 3.6–7, 9, 12–3.
146 Ibid., 3.3, 4, 11.
147 Invariably referred to only as 'Rāma', but not to be mistaken for the Rāma of the *Rāmāyaṇa*.
148 This story is narrated also in *Vana-parva*, Chs. 115–17. See also *Shānti-parva*, Chs. 48–9.
149 *Ādi-parva*, Chs. 177–9.
150 Ibid., 177.11–5.
151 Ibid., 177.16.
152 Ibid., 177.18–21.
153 Ibid., 177.22–3.
154 Ibid., 177.24–5.
155 Ibid., 178.8.
156 Ibid., 177.25–9.
157 Ibid., 178.1–6.
158 Ibid., 178.7.
159 Ibid., 178.9–12.
160 *Udyoga-parva*, 40.6.
161 For this, see Ch. 9 of this book.
162 *Vana-parva*, Chs. 97–9.
163 Ibid., 97.2–4.
164 Ibid., 97.5.
165 Ibid., 97.8.
166 Ibid., 97.9–10.

167 Ibid., 97.15–9.
168 Ibid., 97.20.
169 Ibid., 97.21–4.
170 Ibid., 97.25.
171 Ibid., 98.1–3.
172 Ibid., 98.4.
173 Ibid., 98.5.
174 Ibid., 98.6.
175 Ibid., 98.7–17.
176 Ibid., 99.2.
177 Ibid., 99.4–6.
178 Ibid., 99.6–7.
179 Ibid., 99.9.
180 Ibid., 99.10–12.
181 Ibid., 99.13–5.
182 Ibid., 99.16–8.
183 Spread over the *Mahābhārata*, and repeated in one context after another. At one place, in a concentrated form, see *Shānti-parva*, Ch. 235, which I have abbreviated.
184 *Shānti-parva*, 235.25–6.
185 Ibid., 235.27.
186 Ibid., 235.28–9.
187 Ibid., 235.30 and also 10.
188 Ibid., 251.1.
189 Ibid., 251.3, 5.
190 Ibid., 251.3–4.
191 See again *Vana-parva*, Ch. 180, where this very question is raised in the clearest of words, and, in the clearest of words, answered.
192 Ibid., see the entire Ch. 251.
193 On this again, see *Anushāsana-parva*, 33.8–10, 18–20; 34.27–8; 35.3, 13.
194 When I brought to the notice of my friend Dr Margrit Pernau–Reifeld, a historian, this tradition of feeding a brāhmaṇa as a sure means of earning 'merit', she promptly wrote back, 'When are you coming home for dinner, to give me an opportunity of feeding my favourite Brāhmaṇa and earning merit thereby?'
195 *Vana-parva*, 195.1–3.
196 Ibid., 195.4–6.
197 To be discussed separately. See Ch. 17 of this book.
198 *Vana-parva*, 193.27–8.
199 Ibid., 193.29.
200 Ibid., 193.30.
201 See Ch. 5 of this book.
202 *Anushāsana-parva*, 164.11–2.
203 Ibid., 164.14.
204 Ibid., 164.15.
205 Ibid., 164.10.
206 See pp. 31–2 above.
207 *Shānti-parva*, 73.28.
208 Ibid., 73.32.
209 For this, turn to Ch. 14, on '*Dharma* as the Foundation of Law and Governance, *Rāja-dharma*'.
210 *Shānti-parva*, 57.38.
211 *Anushāsana-parva*, 35.21.
212 *Shānti-parva*, 74.1.
213 See pp. 500–2 of this chapter.
214 *Shānti-parva*, 74.13.
215 Ibid., 74.14.
216 A great many of view's sayings have been brought together in another part of this work.
217 *Udyoga-parva*, 41.5.

Chapter 14

1 *Shānti-parva*, 109.10–12.
2 *Shānti-parva*, 121.5.
3 Ibid., 121.6.
4 Ibid., 59.14.
5 Ibid., 68.19–35.
6 Ibid., 67.16.
7 Ibid., 15.30; see also 32–42.
8 Ibid.
9 Ibid., 15.10.
10 Ibid., 68.8.
11 Ibid., 63.27.
12 Ibid., 63.29.
13 *Shānti-parva*, 63.26.
14 As we will hear in this chapter.
15 *Shānti-parva*, Ibid., 57.42.
16 Ibid., 71.26.
17 Ibid., 71.27.
18 *Anushāsana-parva*, p. 5950 in (G), verse unnumbered.
19 *Shānti-parva*, 67.16–7.
20 Ibid., 57.33.
21 *Shānti-parva*, 91.12.
22 Ibid., 91.15.

23 Ibid., 91.16.
24 Ibid., 91.17.
25 Ibid., 91.18.
26 Ibid., 91.20.
27 Ibid., 91.22.
28 Ibid., 91.38.
29 Ibid., 91.26.
30 *Arthashāstra*, Book I, Ch. XIX, 39.
31 See *Shānti-parva*, Ch. 122.
32 *Shānti-parva*, 122.36–50.
33 Ibid., 122.51.
34 Ibid., 122.52.
35 Ibid., 122.54.
36 *Anushāsana-parva*, 212.12 (K); 5948 in (G), verse unnumbered.
37 Ibid., 212.13 (K); 5948 in (G), verse unnumbered.
38 Ibid., 212.25 (K); 5949 in (G), verse unnumbered.
39 Ibid., 212.26 (K); 5949 in (G), verse unnumbered.
40 Ibid.,212.40 (K); 5950 in (G), verse unnumbered.
41 Ibid., 134.3–11.
42 Ibid., 134.6.
43 Ibid., 134.7.
44 Ibid., 122.40.
45 *Shānti-parva*, 93.23.
46 Ibid., 134.5.
47 Ibid., Ch. 70.
48 Ibid., 93.9–10.
48 Ibid., 93.10.
50 Book I, Ch. IV, 9.
51 Book I, Ch. IV, 9. These passages are from the translation of the *Arthashāstra* by R. Shamasastry, whose discovery in 1905 of that work, which until then had remained unknown, had created great excitement; for, until then, it was being made out that the Indians had had no political thought and knew nothing about governance.
52 *Shānti-parva*, 93.1.
53 Ibid., 93.2.
54 *Shānti-parva*, 90.27–8.
55 Ibid., 91.9.
56 Ibid., 69.4.
57 Ibid., 79.21; 93.10; Ch. 96; 100.5; and 103.7.
58 Ibid., 100.5.
59 Ibid., 79.21.
60 *Ādi-parva*, Ch. 87.
51 Ibid., 87.5.
62 Ibid., 87.6.
63 Ibid., 87.8–9.
64 Ibid., 87.12–3.
65 *Shānti-parva*, 91.49.
66 Ibid., 91.48.
67 Ibid., 91.47.
68 Ibid., 69.30.
69 *Shānti-parva*, 91.35.
70 Ibid., 57.7.
71 Ibid., 121.60.
72 Ibid., 69.27–8.
73 *Anushāsana-parva*, 212.27–9 (K), see p. 5949, the verses unnumbered.
74 *Shānti-parva*, 91.44.
75 Ibid., 57.11.
76 *Shānti-parva*, 56.17–8; 57.11.
77 Ibid., 56.17–8.
78 Ibid., 59.104.
79 *Anushāsana-parva*, 214 (K); p. 5953 in (G) verses unnumbered.
80 *Udyoga-parva*, 35.58.
81 *Shānti-parva*, 91.32.
82 Ibid., 91.33.
83 Ibid., 91.34.
84 Ibid., 91.35.
85 Ibid., 91.36.
86 Ibid., 91.37.
87 Ibid., 91.38.
88 Ibid., 91.39.
89 Ibid., 91.40.
90 Ibid., Ch. 107.
91 Ibid., 107.8, 14.
92 Ibid., 107.10.
93 Ibid., 107.16–7, 21.
94 Ibid., 107.28.
95 Ibid., 107.29. See the entire Ch. 107.
96 *Mahābhārata, Shānti-parva,* 71.10; 87.13–7; and repeated at numerous places in that *parva.*
97 See U.N. Ghoshal, *A History of Indian Public Life*, II. pp. 85–120, 254–9; *Contributions to the History of the Hindu Revenue System* (Calcutta, 1929); *The Agrarian System in Ancient India*

(Calcutta, 1930); D.D. Kosambi, *An Introduction to the Study of Indian History* (Bombay, 1956), pp. 213–16; 241–3; 279; 281.
98 *Shānti-parva*, 87.35.
99 Ibid., 88.30.
100 Ibid., 87.26–34.
101 Ibid., 71.7, 14.
102 Ibid., 87.18–9.
103 Ibid., 71.13–8.
104 Ibid., 87.15–6, 36; 88.12; 120.44.
105 Ibid., 87.36.
106 Ibid., 87.19–20.
107 Ibid., 139.100; also *Pañchatantra*, I.376.
108 *Shānti-parva*, 87.13–4.
109 Ibid., 120.44.
110 Ibid., 119.16; 133.1–2, 4–8.
111 Ibid., 134.3–9.
112 Ibid., 58.57, 86.24, 91.38.
113 Ibid., Chs. 156–7, 161.
114 A large part of the *Arthashāstra* deals with these matters. A long list of fines for all kinds of fraudulent dealings indicates the awareness of the various ways in which traders, merchants and artisans could, and did, cheat.
115 *Pañchatantra*, II.6; Shanti *parva*, 161–2.
116 Shanti *parva*, 298.4–5; 300.24–5.
117 Ibid., 71.16–20.
118 Ibid., 71.8.
119 Ibid., 71.9.
120 Ibid., 71.7, 13–5.
121 *Shānti-parva*, Ch. 15.
122 Ibid., 15.43.
123 Ibid., 15.38.
124 Ibid., 15.30.
125 Ibid., 15.5–6.
126 Ibid., 15.7.
127 Ibid., 15.34; for its elaboration, see 15.12–3, 32–3.
128 Ibid., 72.23–4.
129 *Udyoga-parva*, 34.25.
130 Ibid., 34.26.
131 Ibid., 34.27.
132 Anushashan-*parva*, 212 (K), in (G), p. 5950, verse unnumbered.
133 *Vana-parva*, 28.3.
134 *Āshvamedhika-parva*.
135 *Vana-parva*, 29.3–5.
136 Ibid., 29.6.
137 Ibid., 29.8.
138 Ibid., 29.7, 9, 22.
139 Ibid., 29.21.
140 Ibid., 29.28.
141 Ibid., 29.30.
142 Ibid., 29.32.
143 Ibid., 29.10–1, 16–7, 19–20, 36–7.
144 Ibid., 29.47.
145 Ibid., 29.39, 40, 43; for similar praise of forgiveness, see also *Udyoga-parva*, 33.55–9; 39.59–60; *Āshvamedhika-parva*, 115.41–7.
146 *Vana-parva*, 29.36–7, 40.
147 Ibid., 29.9.
148 *Vana-parva*, 28.1–38.
149 Ibid., 28.6.
150 Ibid., 28.7–8.
151 Ibid., 28.17.
152 *Vana-parva*, 28.18–23.
153 Ibid., 28.24–5.
154 Ibid., 28.26–31.
155 Ibid., 28.27.
155 Ibid., 28.28.
157 Ibid., 28.29–30.
158 Ibid., 28.31.
159 Ibid., 28.32–4, 35, 38.
160 Ibid., 28.34; and 140.65.
161 *Shānti-parva*, 56.40.
162 Ibid., 56.37.
163 Ibid., 56.21.
164 Ibid., 58.21.
165 *Udyoga-parva*, 33.48.
166 Ibid., 33.49.
167 Ibid., 33.52.
168 Ibid., See the entire *Āpaddharma-parva*, Chs. 130–173, in *Shānti-parva*.
169 *Shānti-parva*, 141.65 read with 63.
170 Ibid., 130.15.
171 Ibid., 130.36;133.1–2.
172 Ibid., 130.37.
173 Ibid., 130.27, 37–9; 132.4–5.
174 Ibid., 130.23.
175 Ibid., 130.30.
176 Ibid., 78.29.
177 Ibid., 78.18, 35.7.
178 Ibid., 78.38.

179 Ibid., 78.39–40.
180 Ibid., 78.44.
181 Ibid., 78.42–3.
182 *Shānti-parva*, 100.5.
183 *Shānti-parva*, 267.1.
184 Ibid., 267.2–36.
185 Ibid., 267.4.
186 Ibid., 267.5.
187 Ibid., 267.6.
188 Ibid., 267.9–16.
189 Ibid., 267.17–22.
190 Ibid., 267.23, 25.
191 Ibid., 267.25–9.
192 Ibid., 267.26.
193 Ibid., 267.27.
194 *Shānti-parva*, 69.79; 80–98; 103–5.
195 Ibid., 69.79.
196 See, for example, *Shānti-parva*, Ch. 69.
197 *Shānti-parva*, 69.80.
198 Ibid., 69.91.
199 Ibid., 69.98.
200 Ibid., 69.97.
201 Ibid., 69.103.
202 Ibid., 69.104.
203 Ibid., 69.105.
204 Ibid., 71.28–9.
205 *Udyoga-parva*, 34.31.
206 *Shānti-parva*, 90.5.
207 Ibid., 90.17, 19.
208 Ibid., 90.20–21.
200 *Anushāsana-parva*, 61.25.
210 Ibid., 61.26.
211 Ibid., 61.29.
212 Ibid., 61.31.
213 Ibid., 61.32.
214 *Shānti-parva*, 94.1.
215 Ibid., 96.1.
216 Ibid., 96.2.
217 Ibid., 96.24.
218 Ibid., 92.6.
219 Ibid., 57.38.
220 Ibid., 57.37.
221 *Vana-parva*, 25.11–6. Each of these verses ending with नेशे बलस्येति चरेदधर्मम् । See also 191.24–5.
222 *Nīti-shataka*, 83.

Chapter 15

1 *Sabhā-parva*, Ch. 5.
2 Ibid., 5.17.
3 Ibid., 5.19–20.
4 Ibid., 5.61.
5 Ibid., 5.126.
6 Ibid., 5.108–10.
7 Ibid., 5.90.
8 Ibid., 5.117.
9 Ibid., 5.111.
10 Ibid., 5.112.
11 Ibid., 5.113.
12 Ibid., 5.25.
13 Ibid., 5.26–7.
14 Ibid., 5.28.
15 Ibid., 5.24.
16 Ibid., 5.30.
17 Ibid., 5.52.
18 Ibid., 5.43, 75.
19 Ibid., 5.44.
20 Ibid., 5.37.
21 Ibid., 5.76.
22 Ibid., 5.34.
23 Ibid., 5.35.
24 Ibid., 5.74.
25 Ibid., 5.92.
26 Ibid., 5.93.
27 Ibid., 5.105.
28 Ibid., 5.106.
29 Ibid., 5.107.
30 Ibid., 5.115.
31 Ibid., 5.116.
32 Ibid., 5.48.
33 Ibid., 5.53.
34 Ibid., 5.54.
35 Ibid., 5.55.
36 Ibid., 5.120.
37 Ibid., 5.49, 50.
38 Ibid., 5.78.
39 Ibid., 5.79.
40 Ibid., 5.80.
41 Ibid., 5.32.
42 Ibid., 5.72.
43 Ibid., 5.119.
44 Ibid., 5.21, 22, 28, 36, 38–9, 59, 62–4, 66, 83, 122 and 123.
45 Ibid., 5.82.

46 Ibid., 5.94.
47 Ibid., 5.56.
48 Ibid., 5.81.
49 Ibid., 5.18.
50 Ibid., 5.45.
51 Ibid., 5.77.
52 Ibid., 5.89.
53 Ibid., 5.102.
54 Ibid., 5.124.
55 Ibid., 5.57.

Chapter 16

1 *Shānti-parva*, 329.49–52, 73, 84–8; 337.32–5. *Āshvamedhika-parva*, 107.34–5.
2 *Ādi-parva*, 83.7–12. *Vana-parva*, Chs. 30–2; 213.5–23. *Shānti-parva*, 139.82–5; 233.11–4, 21–3; 234.24–87, 93–104; 238.85–90; 244.1–6; 339.9–42. *Anushāsana-parva*, Ch. 9; 228.1–25; Ch. 269.
3 *Vana-parva*, 32.32–5. *Shānti-parva*, 227.6–8; 229.1–2, 20–33; 238.88–90; 244.4–6.
4 For endeavour, I.391–2; II.138–43, 147–51; III.254; for fate, I.352; II.10, 22–3, 114–5; the parable of 'Prāptavyamartha', 134, V.45, 91.
5 I.45–60.
6 *Shānti-parva*, 331.38. *Anushāsana-parva*, 163.1–9.
7 *Shānti-parva*, 331.9.
8 Ibid., 331.37.
9 Ibid., 331.15–43.
10 Ibid., 331.10.
11 Ibid., 331.11.
12 Ibid., 331.12.
13 Ibid., 331.13.
14 Ibid., 331.15.
15 Ibid., 331.16, 18.
16 Ibid., 331.30.
17 Ibid., 331.31.
18 Ibid., 331.39.
19 Ibid., 331.40.
20 *Ādi-parva*, 83.7–12.
21 *Shānti-parva*, 226.10; 165.48. *Pañchatantra*, II.10, II.114–5; and the parable of '*Praptavyamartha*'. That was the nickname given to a youth who was driven out of his home by his father, who thought him to be a fool, because the son had paid a hundred coins for a book that contained only one couplet: 'A man must get what he is destined to get, and not even Providence can stop that; I neither grieve nor am I astonished, for what belongs to one cannot belong to any other'. The young man through a series of fortuitous circumstances, ends up by marrying the king's daughter.
22 *Shānti-parva*, 226.20.
23 Ibid., Ch. 226.
24 Ibid., 226.8.
25 Ibid., 226.2–3 G.
26 Ibid., 226.4–5.
27 Ibid., 226.23.
28 Ibid., 226.22.
29 Ibid., 226, 20–2.
30 Ibid., 226.18.
31 *Anushāsana-parva*, 6.19. Read the whole Ch. 6.
32 *Vana-parva*, 32.11.
33 *Anushāsana-parva*, 6.1.
34 Ibid., Ch. 6.
35 Ibid., 6.5.
36 *Anushāsana-parva*, 6.7, 9.
37 Ibid., 6.12.
38 Ibid., 6.22.
39 Ibid., 6.43.
40 Ibid., 6.44.
41 Ibid., 6.47.
42 *Anushāsana-parva*, 6.11–7; *Pañchatantra*, II.147–52.
43 *Vana-parva*, 32.13–5.
44 *Shānti-parva*, 139.82. See also *Pañchatantra*, I.392; II.140, 142. *Shukranīti*, I.48.
45 *Shānti-parva*, 139.83.
46 Ibid., 139.84.
47 Ibid., 139.85.
48 *Pañchatantra*, III.254.
49 *Shukranīti*, I.53.
50 *Vana-parva*, 32.1–60.
51 The supremacy of human effort is propounded with vigour in the *Yoga-Vāsishṭha*, chs.4–9 of Part II. Its views are summarised in Dasgupta, *HIP*, II

(1932), pp. 252–6, and in B.L. Atreya, op. cit, pp. 127–34, 193–4. The material in this paragraph is derived from them.

52 *Yoga-Vāsishtha*, II.5.18; II.8.11; II.8.13; II.8.16; II.9.3.

53 II.6.4 35; II.9.4–6; II.9.16.

54 II.6.2; III.6.14; III.92.8; III.92.19.

55 Ibid., II.7.19.

56 Ibid., II.8.16.

57 Ibid., VI.b.157.29.

58 Ibid., II.6.18–19.

59 Ibid., II.5.9–10.

60 Ibid., II.5.12.

61 Ibid., II.8.17.

62 *Udyoga-parva*, 78.1–5. Also, *Anushāsana-parva*, 6.9–10.

63 *Anushāsana-parva*, 228.1–25. See (K). In (G), p. 5978, verses unnumbered.

64 Ibid., 228.1 (K); in (G), see pp. 5978–9, unnumbered verses.

65 Ibid., 228.2 (K); p.5978 in (G).

66 Ibid., 228.22 (K); p.5979 in (G).

67 Ibid., Ch. 228 (K); p. 5979 in (G), verse unnumbered.

68 Ibid., Ch. 228 (K); p. 5979 in (G), verse unnumbered.

69 Ibid., 228.20–1.

70 Ibid., Ch. 228 (K); p. 5979 in (G), verse unnumbered.

71 See again Ch. 5 of this book, '*Ahiṃsā*, Not–violence, as the Foundation of Life'.

72 *Sauptika-parva*, 2.2.

73 Ibid., 2.3.

74 Ibid., 2.5.

75 Ibid., 2.7.

76 Ibid., 2.6.

77 Ibid., 2.11.

78 Ibid., 2.19.

79 Ibid., 2.13.

80 Ibid., 2.15.

81 Ibid., 2.14.

82 Ibid., 2.16–7.

83 Ibid., 2.34–5.

84 On this, see *Anushāsana-parva*, Ch. 1, particularly 1.50–7.

85 *Ādi-parva*, 1.248–51.

85a *Ādi-parva*, 1.248–47.

86 *Shānti-parva*, 25.31.

87 Ibid., 25.5–12.

88 Ibid., 25.5.

89 Ibid., 25.6.

90 Ibid., 25.7.

91 Ibid., 25.8.

92 Ibid., 25.9.

93 Ibid., 25.11–2.

94 *Shānti-parva*, Chs. 227 G.

95 Which I have abridged and rearranged.

96 *Mausala-parva*, Chs. 7–8.

97 Ibid., 7.66.

98 Ibid., 8.12–8.

99 Ibid., 8.32.

100 Ibid., 8.33.

101 Ibid., 8.34.

102 Ibid., 8.31.

103 *Strī-parva*, Ch. 2.

104 Ibid., 2.8; also 9.14.

105 Ibid., 2.23.

106 Ibid., 2.9; also 9.15.

107 Ibid., 2.10; also 9.16.

108 Ibid., 2.24.

109 *Anushāsana-parva*, Ch. 164.

110 Ibid., 164.6.

111 Ibid., 164.7.

112 Ibid., 164.8.

113 *Shānti-parva*, 56.14–5.

114 Ibid., 56.16.

115 *Anushāsana-parva*, 164.4.

116 *Shānti-parva*, Ch. 139.

117 Ibid., 139.49.

118 Ibid., 139.52.

119 Ibid., 139.53.

120 They were discussed in Ch. 8 of this book, on self–interest and prudence.

121 *Shānti-parva*, 139.54.

122 Ibid., 139.55.

123 Ibid., 139.56.

124 Ibid., 139.57.

125 Ibid., 139.58.

126 Ibid., 139.82.

127 Ibid., 139.83.

128 Ibid., 139.84.

129 Ibid., 139.85.

130 Ibid., 139.97–111.

131 *Shānti-parva*, 229.20–33.

132 Ibid., 229.23.

133 Ibid., 229.24–6.

134 Ibid., 229.27–9.
135 Ibid., 229.27, 29, 33–7.
136 Ibid., Chs. 192, 200–1, 213–5, 219–21, 229, 242, 245, 253–61, 281, 306–12; also *Anushāsana-parva*, 245.12–20.
137 *Shānti-parva*, 222.25.
138 Ibid., 194.34–36; 214.31–5; 253.19–25; and 254.6–7.
139 *Shānti-parva*, 194.31–2; *Anushāsana-parva*, 245.12–20.
140 *Shānti-parva*, 194.36.
141 Ibid., 194.38–9; 253.19.
142 Ibid., 194.40–2; 253.21–3.
143 Surendranath Dasgupta, *A History of Indian Philosophy*, vol. II (1952), p. 328n.
144 Ibid., II, p. 329n.
145 Ibid., II, p.410.
146 Ibid., II, p.410.
147 *Shānti-parva*, 222.11–2.
148 Ibid., 222.15.
149 Ibid., 222.16.
150 Ibid., 222.17.
151 Ibid., 222.18.
152 Ibid., 222.19.
153 Ibid., 222.20, 22.
154 Ibid., 222.23.
155 Ibid., 222.27.
156 *Vide* his essays 'Theism in Ancient India', 'The View–Point of Nyaya–Vaiśeṣika Philosophy', and 'The problem of Causality—Sankhya–Yoga View', in his *Aspects of Indian Thought*, op. cit., pp. 45–71, 72–89, and 90–114, respectively. These essays constitute a comprehensive discussion, at one place, on the various Indian theories of causation, with which the problem of the human condition was intimately connected.
157 Ibid., p. 55.
158 *Anushāsana-parva*, Ch. 1.
159 Ibid., 1.21, 23.
160 Ibid., 1.24–5.
161 Ibid., 1.26–7, 29, 31.
162 Ibid., 1.28, 30.
163 Ibid., 1.35–6.
164 Ibid., 1.37–9.
165 Ibid., 1.40–2.
166 Ibid., 1.43–4.
167 Ibid., 1.45–6.
168 Ibid., 1.51.
169 Ibid., 1.52.
170 Ibid., 1.53.
171 Ibid., 1.54.
172 Ibid., 1.55–6.
173 Ibid., 1.57.
174 Ibid., 1.58–60.
175 Ibid., 1.61.
176 Ibid., 1.62–4.
177 Ibid., 1.65, 67–8.
178 Ibid., 1.66.
179 Ibid., 1.70.
180 Ibid., 1.72–3.
181 Ibid., 1.74.
182 Ibid., 1.75.
183 Ibid., 1.77–80.
184 *Shānti-parva*, Ch. 27.
185 Ibid., 27.11–8.
186 Ibid., 32.11.
187 Ibid., 27.23–6.
188 Ibid., 32.12.
189 Ibid., 32.13–6.
190 Ibid., 32.17–18.
191 Ibid., 32.19.
192 Ibid., 32.20.
193 Ibid., 32.23.
194 Ibid., 32.24.
195 Ibid., 32.25.
196 *Droṇa-parva*, 85.21–38.
197 Ibid., 85.53–4.
198 Ibid., 86.1–2.
199 Ibid., 86.14–17.
200 Ibid., 86.4–13.
201 Ibid., 86.10.
202 *Strī-parva*, Chs. 16–25.
203 Ibid., 25.40–1.
204 Ibid., 25.42.
205 Ibid., 25.44–5.
206 Ibid., 25.47–8.
207 Ibid., 26.1–3.
208 See *Karṇa-parva*, 91.1–12.
209 See *Shalya-parva*, 61–18–22.
210 Ibid., 61.61–8.
211 Ibid., 61.61–2, 65–6.
212 Ibid., 61.63.
213 Ibid., 61.63–4.

214 Ibid., 61.67.
215 Ibid., 61.68.
216 Ibid., 61.67–8.
217 Ibid., 61.69.
218 *Āshramavāsika-parva*, 8.20, 19, 21, 22.
219 Ibid., 8.23.
220 Ibid., 9.2–10.
221 Ibid., 9.18; 10.1–2.
222 Ibid., 10.3–5.
223 Ibid., 10.10–12.
224 Ibid., 10. 14–5, 18, 20, 25.
225 Ibid., 10.26–7, 34.
226 Ibid., 10.28.
227 Ibid., 10.29–32.
228 Ibid., 10.35.
229 Ibid., 10.19–20.
230 Ibid., 10.21.
231 Ibid., 10.16.
232 Ibid., 10.36–7.
233 *Shvetāshvatara Upanishad*, I.1.
234 Ibid., I.2.
235 Ibid., VI.1.
236 Ibid., VI.2, and 3–8.
237 This is done at two places in the *Shānti-parva*, Chs. 232 and 238.
238 *Shānti-parva*, 232.19 and 238.4.
239 Ibid., 232.20 and 238.5.
240 Ibid., 232.21 and 238.6.
241 Ibid., 232.42. Read this with the previous verse, 232.41.
242 Ibid., 238.19.
243 Ibid., 238.20.
244 *Shānti-parva*, 227.9–10.
245 Ibid., 227.11.
246 II.5.25.
247 *Shānti-parva*, 174.19.
248 Ibid., 174.39.
249 *Vana-parva*, 32.53.
250 Ibid., 32.58.
251 *Yoga-Vāsishtha*, 6/1–26–33.

Chapter 17

1 *Vana-parva*, 200.81.
2 Ibid., 200.82.
3 Ibid., 200.96–7, 104–6.
4 Ibid., 200.98.
5 Ibid., 200.99.
6 Ibid., 200.100.
7 Ibid., 200.102.
8 *Anushāsana-parva*, 93.4.
9 *Vana-parva*, 200.101.
10 Ibid., 260.25.
11 *Shānti-parva*, 193.18.
12 *Anushāsana-parva*, 108.1.
13 Ibid., 108.12.
14 Ibid., 108.14.
15 Ibid., 108.9.
16 Ibid., 108.10.
17 Ibid., 108.11.
18 *Āshvamedhika-parva*, Ch. 92, p. 6377 in (G).
19 *Shānti-parva*, 193.18.
20 *Āshvamedhika-parva*, Ch. 92, unnumbered verses in (G), p. 6379.
21 Ibid.
22 Ibid.
23 Ibid.
24 *Āshvamedhika-parva*, p. 6374 in (G), unnumbered verse.
25 Ibid., the following verse.
26 Ibid.
27 Ibid., p. 6374 in (G), unnumbered verse.
28 Ibid., p. 6374 in (G), unnumbered verse.
29 Ibid., p. 6374 in (G), unnumbered verse.
30 Ibid., p. 6374 in (G), unnumbered verse.
31 Ibid., p. 6375 in (G), unnumbered verse.
32 Ibid., p. 6375 in (G), unnumbered verse.
33 Ibid., p. 6374 in (G), unnumbered verse.
34 *Anushāsana-parva*, 108.3.
35 Ibid., 108.4.
36 Ibid., 108.5; also 6–7.
37 *Vana-parva*, 82.6–7.
38 Ibid., 82.7.
39 Ibid., 82.9.
40 Ibid., 82.10.
41 Ibid., 82.11.
42 Ibid., 82.12.
43 *Vana-parva*, Ch. 90.
44 Ibid., Ch. 88.
45 Ibid., Ch. 87.
46 Ibid., Ch. 89.
47 Ibid., Ch. 85.
48 Ibid., 84.156; 85.69–75, 81.
49 For a description of the many other places of pilgrimage mentioned the *Mahābhārata*, see Shalya-*parva*, Chs.

35–64; *Anushāsana-parva*, Chs.25–6.

50 *Vana-parva*, 94.1–2.

51 Ibid., 93.22–3.

52 *Shānti-parva*, 12.8.

53 Ibid., 12.35.

54 Ibid., 12.11.

55 Ibid., 12.14. See also 12.9–10.

56 Ibid., 13.1. For the opposite argument, and its rationality, that *tyāga* is in *not possessing things*, or having them, in giving them up, advanced in a conversation that the ascetic Shampāka once had with Bhīshma, see *Shānti-parva*, Ch. 176.

57 Ibid., 12.15.

58 Ibid., 12.16.

59 See *Vana-parva*, Ch. 259.

60 *Vana-parva*, 259.28.

61 Ibid., 259.29–30.

62 Ibid., 259.31.

63 Ibid., 259.32. This suggestion is made many times, at many other places.

64 Ibid., 259.33.

65 *Anushāsana-parva*, 120.1.

66 Ibid., 120.3–5.

67 Ibid., 120.6–7.

68 Ibid., 120.8.

69 Ibid., 120.12–15.

70 Ibid., 122.5.

71 Ibid., 122.6.

72 Ibid., 122.10–11.

73 Ibid., 120.10.

74 Ibid., 120.17.

75 Ibid., 120.18; and the rest of the chapter, 120.19–27.

76 *Anushāsana-parva*, 138.5–11.

77 Ibid., 138.5.

78 Ibid., 138.6.

79 Ibid., 138.7.

80 Ibid., 138.8.

81 Ibid., 138.10.

82 Ibid., 138.9.

83 Ibid., 138.11.

84 *Anushāsana-parva*, 60.4.

85 Ibid., Ch. 60. 60.1–6.

86 Ibid., 60.3.

87 Ibid., 60.10–14.

88 Ibid., 60, 6.

89 Ibid., 59.11.

90 Ibid., 59.12.

91 For more on this subject, see Ch. , pp.

92 On the importance of *anna-dāna*, 'the offering of food', see *Anushāsana-parva*, 63.5–42; 66.55–64; and Chs. 67,112, 121. In the conversation between Shiva and his wife *Umā*, Shiva holds 'the offering of food and water, *anna-dāna* and *jala-dāna*, as the most highly valued. See the same *parva*, Ch. 195, pp. 5995–6 in (G)

93 On the importance of 'sharing the earth', *bhūmi-dāna*, see *Anushāsana-parva*, 62.1–7; 9–13; 22–4; 26–31; 33–5; 45–50. And also in the conversation between Shiva and *Umā*, mentioned in the footnote above. *Anushāsana-parva*, Ch. 195 (p.5998).

94 Ibid., 98.46.

95 Ibid., 98.48

96 Ibid., 98.50

97 Ibid., 98.51

98 *Shānti-parva*, 251.11–2.

99 *Vana-parva*, 207.63.

100 And what does *śīla* mean? For that, turn to Ch. 4 of this book, pp. 77–112.

101 *Vana-parva*, 207.64.

102 Ibid., 207.65.

103 Ibid., 207.66.

104 Ibid., 207.67.

105 Ibid., 207.69.

106 Ibid., 207.70.

107 Ibid., 207.78.

108 Ibid., 207.84.

109 Ibid., 207.96.

110 Ibid., 207.94–5.

111 Ibid., 207.74.

112 Ibid., 207.75.

113 Ibid., 207.99.

114 Ibid., 207.77.

115 *Anushāsana-parva*, 104.2.

116 Ibid., 104.6.

117 Ibid., 104.8.

118 Ibid., 104.9.

119 Ibid., 104.10.

120 Ibid., 104.14.

121 Ibid.,104.13.

122 Ibid., 104.154–5.

123 *Anushāsana-parva*, 143.50. On this

subject more fully, turn to Ch. 13 of this book.

124 Ibid., 143.51.

125 *Udyoga-parva*, 33.16.

126 Ibid., 33.17.

127 Ibid., 33.29.

128 *Udyoga-parva*, 33.18–28, 40.

129 Ibid., 33.18.

130 Ibid., 33.19.

131 Ibid., 33.20.

132 *Udyoga-parva*, 33.21.

133 Ibid., 33.22.

134 Ibid., 33.23.

135 Ibid., 33.24.

136 *Udyoga-parva*, 33.25.

137 Ibid., 33.26.

138 Ibid., 33.27.

139 Ibid., 33.40. See also *Shānti-parva*, 330.29–30.

140 Ibid., 33.30–9.

141 Ibid., 33.30.

142 *Udyoga-parva*, 33.31.

143 Ibid., 33.32.

144 Ibid., 33.33.

145 Ibid., 33.34.

146 Ibid., 33.35.

147 *Udyoga-parva*, 33.36.

148 Ibid., 33.37.

149 'The Women of the *Mahābhārata*', forthcoming.

150 *Vana-parva*, 297.47.

151 Ibid., 297.42.

152 Ibid., 297.43.

153 Ibid., 297.50.

154 Ibid., 297.49.

155 Ibid., 297.48.

Chapter 18

1 *Shānti-parva*, 329.32–3.

2 *BhāgvadGītā*, 5.14–15.

3 See Chaturvedi Badrinath, '*Mokṣha* as Human Freedom: Two Lectures. Freedom *From*, and Freedom *Into*', being the inaugural lectures delivered at The Foundation for Universal Responsibility of His Holiness the Ḍalai Lama, New Delhi, on 27 and 28 March 1998; published in *Creeds of Our Time* (Full Circle Publishing, New Delhi, 2000), pp. 1–40.

4 They are set out in Ch. 9 of this book, 'Human Attributes: Pleasure and Pain, *sukha* and *duḥkha*', pp. 225–269. The Sanskrit text for each is provided there and hence omitted here.

5 *Vana-parva*, 2.21. *Shānti-parva*, 173.14; 188.6; 217.2. *Anushāsana-parva*, 178.30.

6 *Shānti-parva*, 25.20; 174.40; 205.6; 330.16.

7 Ibid., 25.20; 174.40; 330.2. *Vana-parva*, 2.16. *Anushāsana-parva*, 244.3. *Strī-parva*, 2.22.

8 *Shānti-parva*, 174.21–2; 201.22; 224.7.

9 Ibid., 16.8–9, 188.6. *Vana-parva*, 2.25–6. *Āshvamedhika-parva*, 12.1–2

10 *Vana-parva*, 2.22.

11 *Shānti-parva*, 139.63–4. *Vana-parva*, 2.22; 196.17–24.

12 *Vana-parva*, 2.28–31. *Shānti-parva*, 139.63–4; Ch. 174–8.

13 *Shānti-parva*, 25.23–4. Also Chs. *Anushāsana-parva*, 182.22.

14 *Vana-parva*, 260.13–5, 262.51. *Shānti-parva*, 25.23–5; 153.88; 174.20, 49; 175.4, 330.8. *Anushāsana-parva*, 182.22, 244.14–5 (K); *Āshvamedhika-parva*, 44.18.

15 *Shānti-parva*, Chs. 205, 233, 235, 330. *Udyoga-parva*, 36.44–7.

16 *Shānti-parva*, 296.16; *Anushāsana-parva*, Ch. 35.

17 *Vana-parva*, 210.2–3.

18 *Shānti-parva*, 273. 3–10. *Vana parva*, 210.3–5.

19 *Vana-parva*, 2.34–7, 46. *Anushāsana-parva*, 7.21, 24; 141.31–5; 244.31–2, 34 (K). *Shānti-parva*, 173.57, 178.26, 276.12 and the entire Ch. 276.

20 *Shānti-parva*, 93.40–3; 158.12–3. *Anushāsana-parva*, 141.33.

21 *Shānti-parva*, 158.2–21.

22 Ibid., 159.9–14.

23 Ibid., 139.62; 199.12; 251.25.

24 Ibid., 190.9; the objection to it, for dialectical purpose, is given in the next passage, 190.10; see also 199.10.

25 *Bhāgvata-purāna*, VIII.15.20.
26 *Shānti-parva*, 179.15; 199.22–4; 200.22; 285.20; 296.16–9, 22; Ch. 297; 304.30–1, 41; 309.44; Ch. 330. *Vana-parva*, 186.24–7; 213.5–6, 14, 28–9, 33. *Anushāsana-parva*, 9.5–12; 10.3–5; 152.5–6; 178.39; 213.48. Also *Pañchatantra*, II.20, II.3.83.
27 *Shānti-parva*, 181.8–9; 322.8–9; (the two Chapters are nearly identical except verse 2 which is omitted in Ch. 322.). Also *Pañchatantra*, II.5, 136–7.
28 *Shānti-parva*, 181.11; 322.11.
29 Ibid., 181.12; 322.12; and also 179.14, 16–17; 322.13, 15–16. *Anushāsana-parva*, 10.24.
30 Ibid., 181.13; 322.13.
31 Ibid., 181.14; 322.14.
32 Ibid., 181.16; 322.16.
33 See *Shānti-parva*, and in that *moksha-dharma-parva*, Chs. 158; 167.44–8; 174–7; 179; 180–1; 194–5; 199–205, 212–7; 219; 239; 241; 274–5; 279; 288; 290; 326; 329–30.
34 Ibid., 241.8.
35 Ibid., 241, 11.
36 Ibid., 241.12.
37 For a fair presentation of the argument against the existence of any substance apart from the psychophysical self, and therefore against the theory of rebirth, see *Shānti-parva*, chs.186–7, 218, and 237. See Ch. 3 of this book, 'The Spiritual and the Material in the *Mahābhārata*', pp. 41-75.
38 *Āshvamedhika-parva*, 16.30–7.
39 Ibid., 16.30.
40 Ibid., 16.31.
41 Ibid., 16.32.
42 Ibid., 16.33.
43 Ibid., 16.34.
44 Ibid., 16.35.
45 Ibid., 16.36.
46 Ibid., 16.37.
47 *Shānti-parva*, 301.80–3.
48 Ibid., 301.84.
49 Ibid., 301.85–116.
50 Ibid., 301.85, 100–6, 108, 109–114.
51 For the full argument see, for example, *Shānti-parva*, Ch. 174, particularly 174.6–12, 15–7. For other references in this regard, turn to Ch. 9 of this book, 'Human Attributes: Pleasure and Pain, *sukha and duhkha*', pp. 225–269.
52 See Ch. 8 of this book, 'Human Attributes, Self–interest and Prudence: *svārtha* and *nīti*'.
53 *Shānti-parva*, 167.40. *Vana-parva*, 33.38–40, 42–4; reasons in support of this view are provided in 33.21–37. For more details, turn to Ch. 11 of this book.
54 *Shānti-parva*, 192.73; the full argument is contained in the rest of the chapter, particularly 192.63–73; also 255.14.
55 See *Shānti-parva*, Ch. 246; particularly 246.1–3, 6–18; and 325.38–42, 47–50. Also *Vana-parva*, 203.96–112.
56 *Shānti-parva*, 246.20
57 *Shānti-parva*, 158.34–5; 167.44; 174.53; 236.36–9; 245.36; 276.11; 326.35–8. *Anushāsana-parva*, 243.36–40. *Vana-parva*, 216.10, 55. The *Bhāgvad– Gītā*, 14.21–5. *Āshvamedhika-parva*, the *Anu-Gītā*, 19.4–14; 46.39–46; 47.6–11.
58 *Shānti-parva*, 238.98.
59 Ibid., 236.36–9.
60 Ibid., 236.34–5.
61 Ibid., 239.20–2. Also 236.34–40; 239.19–24; 251.3–24; 286.13–20; 288.29–37; 326.33–4; 36–8; 329; 40–1; 331.43–4 Ch. 338; 339.44. *Anushāsana-parva*, 243.37–9. *Āshvamedhika-parva*, Anu-*Gītā*, 20.2–14; 46.39–46; 47.6–11.
62 Ibid., 241.14
63 *Āshvamedhika-parva*, 19.3, 2.
64 Ibid., 19.4.
65 Ibid., 19–5.
66 Ibid., 19.6–7. Also see, 19.8–30.
67 Ibid., 19.29.
68 *Shānti-parva*, 329.40–1; 331.44.
69 *Shānti-parva*, Chs. 223, 224, 227.
70 Ch. 16 of this book, 'The Question of Causality', pp. 477–528.
71 *Shānti-parva*, 224.18–9.
72 Ibid., 227.30.
73 Ibid., 227.31.
74 Ibid., 227.33.

75 Discussed in Ch. 16 of this book.
76 *Shānti-parva*, 227.86.
77 For instance, see *Shānti-parva*, Chs. 218–19.
78 *Shānti-parva*, 320.50.
79 Ibid., 18.30. For the full argument in this regard, which she advances and her husband would repeat later, see *Shānti-parva*, Chs. 18 and 320.
80 Ibid., 18.34.
81 Ibid., 320.47.
82 *Shānti-parva*, 320.48.
83 *Vana-parva*, Chs. 207–16.
84 *Shānti-parva*, Ch. 261–3.
85 *Vana-parva*, Ch. 206.
86 *Shānti-parva*, 320.41.
87 Ibid., 202,11, 246.3, 248.2. See also *Kathopanishad*, I.3.10; II.3.7.
88 Ibid., 250.3–4.
89 *Udyoga-parva*, 34.59–60. *Vana-parva*, 211.23–5. For greater details, see *Shānti-parva*, where this metaphor appears at numerous places, 236.8–12.
90 *Vana-parva*, 211.19–21.
91 See *Shānti-parva*, Ch. 274. For a more detailed but compact discussion on the origin, the support, and the conquest of each of the defects mentioned here, see 161.1–20.
92 Ibid., 274.4.
93 Ibid., 274.5.
94 Ibid., 274.6.
95 Ibid., 274.7.
96 Ibid., 274.8.
97 Ibid., 274.9.
98 Ibid., 274.10.
99 Ibid., 274.11.
100 Ibid., 274.12. For the radically different meaning that the *Mahābhārata* gives to *shuchi*, 'purity,' see the preceding chapter, Ch. 17, 'From Ritual *Acts to Relationships*', pp. 529–558.
101 *Shānti-parva*, 274.13–14.
102 Ibid., 274.18–9. See also Ch. 158.
103 Ibid., 357.12. *Vana-parva*, 216.46.
104 *Shānti-parva*, 325.50.
105 Ibid., 325.47.
106 Ibid., 325.48.
107 Ibid., 18.32–3.
108 Ibid., 18.34.
109 Ibid., 18.30.
110 For the full argument see ibid., Chs. 18 and 325.
111 Letter dated 6th July 1896, from London; Letters of Swami Vivekananda (Advaita *Āshrama*). See also *Shānti-parva*, 320.41
112 *Yoga-Vāsishtha*, V.29.10. I have used the edition of this work published by the Indian Heritage Trust, Madras (now Chennai) (1993), which is based on the well–known work on *Yoga-Vāsishtha* by B.L. Atreya (1936). Translations used here are by Samvid, but I have taken the liberty of making one or two changes.
113 Ibid., V.29.11.
114 Ibid., V.29.12.
115 Ibid., V.29.15.
116 Ibid., V.35.38.
117 Ibid., V.35.40–1.
118 Ibid., V.35.39.
119 *Shānti-parva*, 305.13.
120 Ibid., 305.14.
121 Ibid., 227.94.
122 Ibid., 239.25.

Index and Concordance

This index is a detailed road map to what is in this book and where, but only that. A road map is no substitute for travelling on the road.

Index and Concordance

accountability, the question of
intimately connected with that of causality and runs through the whole of *MhBh*, because it runs through the whole of human life, 508, 513–14; the story of Gautamī, and the issues the characters in it raise concerning, 508–13; when Yudhishṭhira holds himself accountable for the war and resolves to kill himself, Vyāsa recounts four different views on, 513–15; Dhritarāshṭra holds his son Duryodhana accountable for the war, 516–17, but is himself held accountable for not disciplining his son, 516–17; Gāndhārī holds Krishna wholly accountable, and curses him, 517–18; in equally bitter words, Krishna accuses her of transferring to *him* the accountability that actually belonged to *her*, 518; the accountability being transferred from one to another, a familiar human habit *MhBh* recounts, 508–14 and 517; Krishna on his accountability but not his culpability for the manner in which the war was fought and won, 518–19; accountability only if there is free will, 64–65, 520 (on which see under ***causality***); on Dhritarāshṭra seeking the forgiveness of the people, their representative Sāmba absolves them all, '*Human will cannot undo what the Providence has writ*', 522.

adharma*, the negation of *dharma
whatever is unjust and oppressive is, 86; whatever has the characteristic of depriving, starving, diminishing, separating, uprooting, hurting, doing violence, debasing and degrading is, 86, 89, 353; personified, with Violence as wife, Untruth as son, and Dishonesty as daughter, 105; its roots in ignorance and greed, 106–7; may be mistaken for *dharma*; the reverse too is possible, 93–94; the Mīmāṃsā view of, not as unethical but as vedicly prohibited, which view discarded by *MhBh*, 79–80; injustice, tyranny and anarchy the attributes of, 419–20, 550.

***adhyātma*, usually translated as 'spiritual' / 'spirituality'**
only infrequently used in the various traditions of Indian thought, 43; its root meaning: 'inquiry into the nature of the Self', 43; *Taittirīya Upanishad* relates it to the human body and attributes, 43–44; *MhBh* points to the inseparable relation between the material and the spiritual, 43; the false notion, with its harmful results, that spirituality consists in negating and renouncing the material, traced to the *vairāgya* tradition (see under ***vairāgya***), which *MhBh* sets out to correct, 44–45; if separated from the material attributes of life, such spirituality turns into violence to one's self and to the *other*, 45; elegance in thought and speech and conduct an essential element of true spirituality, 45; what is suffused with life, *prāṇa-maya*, is suffused also with joy, *ānanda-maya*, 45; *MhBh* teaches: 'true spirituality is to be found in the ordinary', 45.

***ahaṃkarā*, the individual will**
part of the psychophysical self, 56; in his account of the self/Self, Pañchashikha the Sāṃkhya philosopher on, 55. See under ***Pañchashikha***.

***ahiṃsā*, not-violence**
see Ch.5, 113–68; a foundation of life: discussed side by side with its opposite, *hiṃsā*, violence, 17, 114; the whole of *MhBh* is about this pair of the opposites, 114, Arjuna voicing the opposite reality, '*I do not see a single person who lives by not-violence*', 122–23; discussed in the midst of every kind of violence taking place, and this as a method, 17, 114–15;

- *ahiṃsā paramo dharmo*, 'not to do violence is the highest *dharma*', resound throughout *MhBh*, 114; the highest *dharma*, 100, 115–19, 126; Brahmā tells this to the contending sages asking him: 'What *is* the good?', 120;
- not just 'not-killing', but 'to do no violence to one's own being or to the *other*', 116–17; violence to the *other*, is also violence to one's self, 126; the main root of violence traced to ignorance about one's relationship with one's self and with the *other*, 115;
- one of the three main attributes of *dharma*, 86, 99–100, 117, 188;
- the killing of animals in the vedic sacrifice condemned, 118–19;

- and the opposite reality that '*life preys upon life*' stated and taken into account, 119–23;
- the rationality of, derived from life and not from *a priori* suppositions, 123–26;
- and the problem of relativity in regard to, 127–48, 'Nothing ever is absolutely good nor anything ever absolutely bad, and the same act is good or harmful depending upon place, time and the character of the person concerned', 127;
- and the question, honestly asked, honestly answered, whether, in certain circumstances, anger is justified, and revenge almost a duty: the stories of Aurva, 127–9: 'Whoever controls his just anger, can protect nothing', 128; of Ashvatthāmā, 129–42; and of Draupadī, 142–45: conclusions drawn from the Ashvatthāmā story of revenge, 141;
- Yudhishṭhira's reasoning with his wife Draupadī burning with the spirit of revenge, 144–6, 'It is forgiveness that keeps the world together', 145, 146, and Draupadī's response, 'Neither force nor reconciliation is good always', 147;
- the evident rationality of forgiveness and reconciliation, 144–6, and the rationality of the equally evident limits to it, 147–8; in the voices of the hurt and the wronged, for they alone have the moral right to pronounce upon forgiveness, 142, *MhBh* takes us through the logic both of anger and revenge and of forgiveness and reconciliation, 127, 142, 144–6, 147–8, 392–3, 451–3;
- Krishna on forgiveness and reconciliation as the highest pilgrimage, *tirtha*, of all, 146–7;
- the rationality of the argument against enmity and war, 149–52: Yudhishṭhira reasons with Krishna, 149–51; the bird Pūjanīya's advice to King Brahmadatta on the avoidance of enmity and war, 151–52; Gāndhārī to her son Duryodhana, 152;
- if war unavoidable, then the *dharma* of war to be observed, 152–3; the story of Kāyavya, a kindly robber, 153–5, '*Even among robbers there is a sense of limits*', 153;
- violence in words and speech: *MhBh* evokes the effects the hurtful and dry words must produce in the *other*, 155–61, 216–7; *Shukranīti* on harsh words, 156; Pañchatantra on hurtful speech, 156–7; a corresponding teaching in *MhBh* against speaking ill of others and self-praise, 157–8; no real conflict between strength and gentleness or between pleasant speech and truth, 159–60; (see also under ***speech***);
- 'trust' and 'distrust' related with *ahiṃsā* and with violence, 160–61;
- violence to one's self, the many ways of: 101, 160–63, 165–8;
- as freedom from fear, to which greatest importance attached, 114, (see under ***dāna***, under ***fear*** and under ***rāja-dharma***);
- as freedom from the violence of history, which is freedom from the violence of memory, personal and collective, 163–8;
- the greatest *dharma* of all, and it is upon truth that it is based, these three forming a unity, 549. (See also under ***dharma*** and ***satya***).

Alarka, the king
wanting to conquer the inner domain of his self, with the only weapons he knew, declares war against his physical sense organs, intellect and the mind, each of which in turn tells him that he would thereby hurt only his self, 261–63;

- *to be at war with one's self, is to be at war with everyone else, 263.*

***anna*, food**
Ch 2, 24–39; and medicine in the *Ayurveda*, 24; in the *Upanishad*-s, 24–30; as god to be propitiated, 27; in the *MhBh*, 30–39: *MhBh* attaches utmost importance to *anna* and its sharing, 30–2;

- water the essential basis of life, 31; *anna-dāna*, 'sharing food', and *jala-dāna*, 'sharing water', the greatest of all sharing, *dāna*, 31–34; the blessings of this life and the next attend upon him who readily gifts food to others; Krishna pronounces on the

inexhaustible merit, *punya*, earned by giving and sharing of food, with great emphasis upon feeding a brāhmaṇa, 34–6;
- along with sharing food and water, *MhBh* enjoins *bhūmi-dāna*, 'sharing land', and *vrikṣha-dāna*, 'sharing vegetation', 34–5;
- giving food and water not ritual acts, nor charity, but *sharing* in the awareness that one's life is connected with other beings, 35–7;
- Yudhishṭhira recalls the obligation of a householder in offering food to those who come to him which, being in exile, he will be unable to meet, and the sage Dhaumya's advice that he appeals to the Sun god who sustains vegetation and life, for the gift of inexhaustible food, 37–9;
- the 'always-full cooking pot' as metaphor, '*Where there is concern for others, and not for oneself alone, there the cooking pot is never empty*', 37;
- four *dosha*-s (defects) in the cooked food: *kāla dosha*, 'which has been kept too long and has turned stale', rasa *dosha*, 'which has lost its taste', samsarga *dosha*, 'which has been touched with unclean hands', and *bhāva dosha*, 'offered with ill grace', being the worst, the other three only hygienic, 39;
- one portion of the food one eats to be set aside for *the unknown guest*, 39.

***apad-dharma*, the law of abnormal times**
453–55; and its rationality: 'It is better to be alive than be dead; alive, a person can order his life again', 453; the king in distress may raise funds by force if necessary: this sanction based on three grounds, Bhīshma on: '*What door is barred to a man in distress?*', 453–54; no sooner is this said than *MhBh* also adds that, compulsions of distressful times notwithstanding, it should be remembered what is against *dharma* must eventually produce resentment and violence, 454; distressful times are the products of the logic of *adharma*, 455, created by the cumulative logic of one's own acts or of the *other*, or of the two together, 455;
- not to become an alibi for doing things that are wrong anyway, 454.

***aparigraha*, not-grasping**
as the single most important element in genuine happiness, all schools of Indian philosophy pointed to, 252; Vidura on, 253; the necessity of physical and mental discipline, 253; its meaning as 'not-encircling', 'not-engulfing', 'not-imprisoning', but wrongly translated as 'non-possession', which refers to *things*, 332; a path to *mokṣha*, to human freedom, 583.

***ārjavam*, straightforwardness, simplicity, lack of deviousness**
one of the signs by which *dharma* is known, 108, 111; and truth, 438, and thus a foundation of all relationships;
- as the first element in the king's right relationship with himself, 433–34; freedom from deviousness and cunning not only in his conduct towards those it is his *dharma* to protect but also towards an enemy, 433; the strongest statement of *MhBh* on, 'All deviousness is the place of death: simplicity and straightforwardness, the place of highest reality. This alone is the subject of knowledge; all the rest are empty words", 434;
- of the two kinds of intelligence, *kuṭila*, 'the devious', and *sarala*, 'the straightforward', the king must cultivate the latter, 455–6.

Arjuna
the third of the five-Pān ḍ ava brothers, and a husband of Draupadī, questions not-violence as a foundation of life, stating the opposite reality, 'I do not see a single person who lives by not-violence', 122–23; during a bitter conversation with Krishna, Draupadī mocks at, 143; fires at Ashvatthāmā a weapon of most destructive force, but withdraws it, having the power of self-control to do so, 139 (see also under ***Ashvatthāmā***); rushes to save Dron ̣āchārya, his archery-guru, from being killed in a manner most foul according to a clever plan, 190–91, but unable to save him, 191; in the context of

Dron.a's killing, calls Yudhisht.hira, his eldest brother, 'a mean despicable liar', 191; dwells upon the pre-eminence of wealth, 272–5, 314; his deep moral dilemma at the beginning of the war, 'to fight or not to fight?, which Krishna resolves, 351–2; but, after the war is won, he forgets Krishna's teachings and says to him: 'What was it that you had said? I have forgotten it Will you tell me again?', 352–3; on the fear of *dan.d.a* in the sense of both rule and punishment as the basis of social order, 445–6; but this, the fear of *adharma*, not of the ruler, 446; tries to protect from robbers the women of Krishna's household after Krishna's death but unable to, himself reduced by *kāla*, 'the turn of time', and throws away his weapons, saying '*the knowledge of weapons is not forever*', 496–8; is consoled by Vyāsa, who talks of man's subjection to Time, 497–8.

***artha*, material prosperity**
Ch.10, 271–93; one of the four ends of human life, 4; the questions raised in *MhBh* regarding, 4–5;

- two different attitudes towards: as the first condition of a dignified life and stable social order, and as profoundly destructive of inner peace and spiritual life, 272–3; *MhBh* examines both, 273–9, 280–93, and concludes: 'Neither is bondage in wealth, nor is freedom in *moksha*. Whether it is one or the *other*, will depend upon one's attitude to having and not-having', 272;
- the importance of: Yudhishthira decides, after he had become emperor, to renounce everything and live the life of a mendicant, 273; the views of Arjuna, Bhīma and the dying Bhīshma that *artha* is the basis of all that is good and desirable in life, specially for a king, 272–73; Pañchatantra puts great store by, 278–9;
- the other truth concerning, 280–88; and the paradox that the more one has the more is one dissatisfied, and is possessed by greed, 234–35, 282 (see also under ***greed***); and criticism of the view that *artha* is the source of everything desirable in life: in the voice of Yudhishthira, 280–82 and 286–87, 'I sorrow for those who regard money as everything', 287; the sage Manki on, *kāma* (desire) and pain, 284–5;
- drawing a picture of the ills coming from striving for wealth, *MhBh* draws a picture also of the ills that come from unsought poverty, 286, 287, 288–9; the dharmic balance: acknowledgement that human beings are diverse in their capacities, 288; '*Fulfillment is possible only within the wholeness of human attributes—in neither their neglect, nor in their idolatry*', 289, and 200;
- the proper distribution of wealth to be the principle, 289: 'The wealth, *artha*, not put to good use, becomes a source of *anartha*, disaster', 289;
- and the ways of *dharma*, 289–90; the influence of wealth to be subordinated to *sadāchāra*, nobility of conduct, 290–1; 'By all means endeavour towards material prosperity, but give up aggression towards others', 292;
- the avoidance of *ati* (excess): of virtue, of learning, of pursuit of wealth, of sexual pleasure and of royal power, 222, 291–93, in relationship with one's self: Nārada's questions to Yudhisht hira concerning, 466–8;
- public wealth to be under the control of *dharma*, and the principles to which the state earnings subject, 441–44; and their secular character, invoking only what is just and right in creating social good, 444;
- and its hoarding: '*Wealth that is hoarded, invites only plunder*', one of the principles of good governance, 442;
- only wealth earned through *dharma* is legitimate, and its rationality, 89, 278, 290, 442–3.

asceticism
see under ***vairāgya***

Ashtāvakra
322–27: wants to marry Suprabhā, and is

tested for his worthiness by her father, the sage Vadānya, 323; and his encounter with Uttarā-Dishā, 'North Direction', the woman Vadānya had asked him to visit, and the events that follow, 323–26; and his self-control in being neither distracted by physical proximity of another woman nor discouraged by stupid notions about women, mounted by Uttarā-Dishā only to test him, 326; returns, marries Suprabhā, and establishes man–woman relationship as a state of *saha-dharma*, '*togetherness with a sense of direction*', 326–27; in order to be worthy of a woman, the man has to have control over himself first, 360.

Ashvatthāmā

son of Droṇāchārya, 129–42: his resolve to avenge the ignoble manner in which his father was killed, 129; his story raises the question: are acts of revenge in certain circumstances ethically wrong? 129: his conversation with Kripāchārya and Kritavarma on the question of revenge, and on the rightness of what he proposed to do: to attack in the middle of night the camp of the winning and sleeping army, and find Dhrishṭadyumna, the killer of his father, 130–33; his encounter with a shadow he thinks is the shadow of (his own) *adharma*, 134; his prayer to Shiva, 135; kills Dhrishṭadyumna and all the five sons of Draupadī, 135–37, 150; next morning, is chased by the Pāṇḍava-s, found, and the events that follow, 138–39; is asked by the sages to withdraw the deadly weapon he had directed on to Arjuna,, but he couldn't, because lacking self-control, 139; directs it on to the womb of Uttarā instead, whose child will be born dead as a result but will be brought to life by Krishna, 139–40 (see ***Uttarā***), and 393; and his conversation with Vyāsa and Krishna, 139–40; his life spared because the son of the guru, but divested of the magic jewel he carried on his forehead, 139; is cursed by Krishna, 140;

- lessons from this story of the endless cycle of hurt-revenge-another hurt-another revenge, 141;

See also under ***weapons***.

***ātman*, the self**

MhBh recounts two opposite views concerning: there is *ātman*, the Self, eternal and with no attributes, distinct from the psycho-physical self, and that there is no such entity, and states equally the reasoning advanced in support of both: Ch.3, 42–75;

- is the same as the brahman, the Ultimate Reality, 46; doubts about: and the Buddha's doctrine of *anatta* (no-self), 46; the Jaina view of *jīva* and *ajīva*, 46; *MhBh* view of, based on Sāṃkhya philosophy: its three main aspects: 48;
- the doubts, with their reasoning, about any permanent Self apart from the psycho-physical self, expressed notably in: the dialogues between Yudhishṭhira and Bhīshma, 47–52, between the sages Bharadvāj and Bhrigu as recounted by Bhīshma, 48–52;
- the conversation between Pañchashikha, the Sāṃkhya philosopher, and King Janaka on the nature of the permanent Self, 52–57, and the former's views on the nature of the psycho-physical apparatus of the self: the three primordial energies (see ***guṇa-s***): *sattva*, *rājas*, and *tamas*: the distinct personality of a person results from these existing together in different proportions, 55–57;
- the manifest 'self' and the unmanifest 'Self': Vyāsa, in a discussion with his son Shukadeva concerning the self and the universe, feels obliged first to answer those who disputed the existence of the Self, 57–64; Vyāsa on causality and Time, *kāla*, the questions related with all discussions on the Self, 64–67;
- the radical shift in *MhBh* in the perceptions of the Self and the self: (see also under ***Mahābhārata***), 67–70:
- no final decision on the validity of one metaphysical position or another concerning the Self, the *ātman*, required; for, belief in a permanent Self of no particular help, nor disbelief in any such entity any particular

hindrance, in ordering one's energies in the fullest worth of being human, 67–69;

- from the metaphysics of the *ātman* to *dharma*, from the big 'Self' to the 'self' as experienced, one no pre-requisite for the *other*, 68;
- from the abstract concepts of *ātman* to human experience, to relationships with one's self and with the *other*, 68–69;
- mainly concerned not with the knowledge of *ātman*, but with the living in *dharma*, one not a pre-supposition for the *other*, 70;
- the ordering of energy, individual and social, as its main concern: the self, energy and relationships, 70–75, 579 (see under ***energy***);
- 'One's self alone is one's friend, and also one's enemy', repeated throughout, 205–6, 253 (see also under ***self-interest, svārtha***).
- cuts across different ontological positions concerning the Self, 579–80.

ātma-jñāna, self-knowledge
The big 'Self' of Indian philosophy swallowed the small 'self' of the individual, 13; knowledge of 'the Self', the *ātman*, does not necessarily lead to self-knowledge, *ātma-jñāna*, 13; the quality of relationships is decided by self-knowledge and knowledge of the *other*, 43; presupposes freedom of the will, 64; repeatedly said that '*Greater than self-knowledge there is no knowledge*', 69;

- radical shift in the meaning of, in the *MhBh*: 68
- takes up self-knowledge, not in the shadow of the big 'Self', but in relation to concrete situations through which one lives one's life', 13;
- not limited to the knowledge of *ātman* as the eternal reality of all beings, 69; which, moreover, considered neither sufficient nor even necessary for living in the full worth of being human, 69;
- self-knowledge is through the contexts and situations in which one finds oneself, and also creates for one's self, 69–70, through the concrete realties of experience and the complexities they give rise to, 530;
- all the areas of human living, and examined by *MhBh*, move towards self-knowledge, in none of them belief in the existence of eternal *ātman* a fundamental requisite, 69;
- to court pain and suffering as a source of self-knowledge a source of violence to one's self and to the *other*, 162: 'To starve and oppress one's body is no *tapas*, or austerity', 531; egotism keeps man from self-knowledge, 176;
- *MhBh*'s concerns are not with prescriptions but with self-knowledge, 388, not with ritual rites, 339, 530; the revolution of the *Upanishad*-s, in moving the mind from ritual acts to understanding, from rituals to inquiry: that of the *MhBh*, in uniting self-knowledge with the knowledge of the *other*, uniting one's life with the life of the *other*, 530;
- Sage Parāshara's statement concerning the requirements of ethical conduct includes self-knowledge, 385; Vidura's statements as leading to self-knowledge, 414; self-knowledge brings freedom from fear, 108–09, and is the abiding path to *mokṣha*, 587.

***ātmanas-tushṭih*, the assent of the heart**
one of the several conflicting criteria of *dharma*, offered by Manu, 80–81, but rejected by Medhātithi, 80–81.

Aurva
the story of his birth, and of the blinding of the princes who, in their greed for the money already gifted, had killed the Bhārgava brāhmaṇas including his father; begins a revengeful killing of *all* the *kṣhattriya*-s, to rid the earth of cruel and unjust men, 128, 142, 400–1;

- resolves to destroy that very world where drunkenness of power could destroy men and women and many an unborn child, 401; and his argument, addressed to his forefathers, concerning anger that is justified, and punishment as justice equally so, 127–29: "Whoever controls his just anger, can protect nothing", "It is only so long as there is someone to prevent the cruel deeds of the wicked, that the wicked will be restrained. Having strength, if he still does not restrain them, then surely he participates, too, in their wicked acts", 128;

- and the psychological aspect of the story: "If my anger remains unfulfilled, it will turn upon me, and will destroy me as fire does a piece of wood", 128–29; and asks his forefathers to suggest a way "that the world is not destroyed, but nor am I destroyed by the fire of a just anger suddenly quietened", which they do, 128;
- *MhBh* suggests: anger not always insanity; but the logic of anger always destructive of the self; hence the conquest of anger the greatest conquest of all, 129. See also under ***ahiṃsā*** and ***brāhmaṇa***.

Bakāsura
the *rākṣhasa*-king who oppressed the people grievously, the story of, 211–15: and his slaying by Bhīma at the behest of mother Kuntī, 213–15.

***bala*, force, power**
one of the elements in a hierarchy of increasing generality, permeated by brahman: an Upanishadic view, 26–27; along with *kṣhamā*, forgiveness, woven into every human relationship, 127; and the question, 'which is superior, bala or *kṣhamā*, power or forgiveness?', 127, 147 and 448–53; power the chief concern of dharmic political thought, 421; on becoming a justification of itself, power turns into tyranny,; therefore as subordinate to *dharma*, 429–30 (see also under ***desha and kāla*** and under ***ahiṃsā*** for arguments for and against the use of force and when); and, in the voice of sage Mārkaṇḍeya, *MhBh* to those who govern: "*Because you have power, do not do what is unjust, oppressive, full of violence, adharma*", 464 (see also under ***rāja-dharma***).

Bali
formerly Indra, king of gods, advances one particular view of causality, that Time, *kāla*, and not man, determines every thing, 494–96; his dialogue with Shakra who has just become Indra defeating him and wants to know the source of his equanimity even in adversity, 494; and his advocacy of man's absolute subjection to Time, 494–96, 575–77;

- 'Time is no respecter of persons. All are in the grip of Time—to be bent or broken', 496;
- 'Time preserves, and Time destroys; for life and death are in Time. There is no island in the ocean of Time', 496;
- There is no defying Time, only submission: not the submission of the coward, but of the wise, and wisdom is given to man', 496;
- advocates therefore also freedom from grief over what is past, 496, 575–77, (see also under ***causality***, under ***Time***, and under ***pleasure and pain***);
- and his question to Prahlāda: 'Between force and forgiveness, which is superior?' and the latter's answer, 147.

Bhagvad-Gita
A long discourse by Krishna to Arjuna, delivered at the beginning of the war, on the battlefield, to resolve Arjuna's moral dilemma: to fight or not to fight?, 351–52.

Bhāgvata-purāṇa
on whatever action is based on the Veda-s being *dharma*, 80; in the context of the pursuit both of wealth and sexual pleasure, points to the 'ever-thirsty' nature of desire, *trishṇā*, 232–33; on the causes of pain, *duḥkha*, 'The grasping of the things most desired by man is the cause of pain', 234; on pleasure and pain, *sukha* and *duḥ kha*, quoted at 160 4n, 231 26n, 232 35n, 233 36n, 233 41n, 234 45n, 247 106n, 252 132n; and its advocacy of 'giving up', 'renouncing', desire as such as a means to happiness, which as an absolute theory *MhBh* teaches against, (see also under ***desire***)

Bhangāsvana
the king, is transformed into a woman, and would not want to become a man again: the story of, concerning the question as to who enjoys sexual pleasure more, man or woman?, 312–13.

Bharadvāja
the sage, in conversation with the sage Bhrigu, advances his doubts about the existence of any permanent eternal Self apart from the psychophysical self, 48–52; his reply to Bhrigu on the latter's understanding of the origin of the four main social divisions, *varṇa*: and his rejection of the colour-theory of *varṇa*, 373.

Bhartrihari and his *Vairāgya-shataka* (tr. A.B. Keith)
in the context of pleasure and pain, quoted at 254 140n, 257 159n; and his Nīti-*shataka*: "Let those learned in the state craft praise or blame: let the goddess of wealth come or go as she pleases: let death come today or ages later: persons who are steadfast, do not ever swerve from the path of justice", 464.

Bhīma, also Bhīmasena
the second of the five-Pāṇḍava brothers: his conversation with Yudhishthira, his eldest brother, on the interrelatedness of human attributes within the self, where exclusive concern with any one of them, to the neglect or denial of the rest, harmful, 103–05, 276;

- in pursuance of a foul but clever plan to stun Droṇāchārya into abandoning the fight and then quickly killed, kills a war-elephant called Ashvatthāmā, and makes an announcement loudly, 'Ashvatthāmā is killed', creating an impression in Droṇa that it was his son Ashvatthāmā who was killed, 190–91 (see under ***Droṇāchārya***);
- his slaying of the *rākṣhasa*-king Bakāsura when, learning the cause of laments in the family of the brahamana who had given the Pāṇḍava-s shelter at the beginning of their exile, mother Kuntī orders him to relieve the family of their anguish, illustrating not gratitude alone for kindness received but risking one's life to secure 'good of the others', *para-hita*, 211–15 (see also under ***Bakāsura***); reassures Bakāsura's petrified attendants but makes them take a vow not to do violence: 'Those who will do violence, will by violence die', 215;
- on the prime importance of money, specially for a king, 275–76; on the true meaning of 'giving up', 'renouncing', *tyāga*, and 'austerity', *tapas*, from ritual acts to their ethical relational meaning, speaking of the life-in-family and not retiring to the forest as of great import, 342–44; his definition of *kāma*, the sexual impulse, 297; upholds the primacy of *kāma* in the sense of desire as the motivating force of all acts, 315–6; his advocacy of the equal importance of *dharma*, *artha* and *kāma*, 103–4, 276 and 316;
- at the end of the war, on Ashvatthāmā's revenge-killing of all the sons of Pāṇḍava-s from Draupadī, rushes alone to find him, and Krishna's anxiety on his account, 138;
- his devotion to their wife Draupadī, who turned to *him* whenever she felt troubled, 138, 140–41, and his tenderness to her, 366–7;
- kills Duryodhana in the last battle-by-mace between the two, but in a way that completely violated a cardinal rule of such contest, 518.

Bhīshma
the patriarch of the Kuru family: a dominant figure in *MhBh*'s inquiry in the human condition: the dialogues of Yudhishṭhira and Bhīshma, the latter lying on his bed of arrows, dying, forming in the main the philosophical part of *MhBh*; each subject carrying its own reasoning, and all brought together in a unity, Bhīshma on:

- *dharma* and *adharma*, and on the question of relativity concerning them, 90–103;
- the conquest of the self as the highest good, 107–09;

- not-violence, *ahiṃsā*, and violence, and on the question of relativity concerning them, 117–18, 123–26;
- forgiveness and the use of force, 148;
- 'friends' and 'enemies' and self-interest, 201–204; on Yudhishṭhira seeking his blessings at the beginning of the war, his candid confession that he is tied to the Kaurava-s with the bond of his self-interest, 204–05;
- truth, and on the question of relativity concerning it, 217–18;
- the causal chain of greed, 236–38;
- on *indriya-nigraha*, 'controlling one's sense organs and their corresponding faculties': relates it to *dama*, self-discipline, 250; on *aparigraha*, 'not-grasping', 252;
- the necessity of wealth for a king, 275–78;
- who truly is a happy person, 283;
- and his perception of women as sexually lawless, hence particularly in need of protection, 307–08; narrates the story of Ashṭāvakra's self-control in reply to Yudhishthira's question on *saha-dharma*, '*togetherness in living in dharma*', 322–26;
- narrates to Yudhishṭhira the dialogue between two sages, Kapila and Syūmarashmi, on the relative merits of the life of one who has renounced the world, *sannyāsī*, and that of a householder, *grihastha*, 348–50;
- his perception of the brāhmana-s as being of many kinds, 381–82; on the foundations of harmonious social arrangements towards social wealth, 410–11;
- the greatest part of *MhBh*'s philosophy of governance, *rāja-dharma*, unfolds in a long dialogue on that subject between Yudhishṭhira and, 422–64;
- propounds thirty-six self-disciplines of the king, 430–32; on trust as the foundation of republics, 440, but fear an essential part of social regulation, 446; 'the king should be neither too forceful nor too gentle', 452; on the law of abnormal times, *apad-dharma*, 454; the king creates historical conditions, the *yuga*-s, not they him, 460–62;
- his view that *kāla*, Time, is no force, only a mental construct to explain sequence, the real force lying in the human heart and the mind, 499; on the preeminence of human effort, 499–500;
- on purity, *shaucha*: being of four kinds: 'the purity of conduct, of the mind, of pilgrimage and that born of knowledge', 532–33, 536; on the mind and heart as pilgrimage, *manas-tirtha*, 536; on the nobility of conduct, *sadāchāra*, 551–2; on memory after *mokṣha*, 567–69.
- (See also under related entries in this index.)

Bhrigu, the sage

his conversation with Bharadvāja, in which he expresses his view that the Self, *ātman*, never dies but remains the innermost of all beings, 48–51; on the colour-theory of the origin of the *varṇa*-s, which the sage Bharadvāj dismisses completely, 372–74;

birth and rebirth

in Indian philosophy the perennial question of, and the anguished cry for freedom from the cycle of, which is a human cry for release from the toil and fatigue of repetitive experience, 565–67; and *MhBh*'s radical shift on, 567–70.

Brahmā, the Primeval Being

his answer to the seven sages questioning him on the agonising problem of relativity and of the plurality of faiths, 119–20; pronounces *ahiṃ sā*, not-violence, as the very first foundation of life, and thus the highest *dharma*, 120; creates *Mrityu*, Death, in the form of a woman and his conversation with her on death, 171–73; as the creator of the four *varṇa*-s, *brāhmaṇa* from his head, *kshattriya* from his arms, *vaishya* from his thighs, and *shūdra* from his feet, 372–73, 377 and 378 and 444; this idea taken too literally, 396; on forgiveness, 449–50; and his irrefutable reasoning for human effort, 483–6.

Brahmadatta, the king

his conversation with the bird Pūjanī after a

most distressful event between them, 500–501: on trust and trusting, for what kind of world will it be where nobody trusted anybody?, 221, 'Always fearing the *other*, will be like being dead', 221; and his belief that 'Time alone is the prime mover, and all events are owing to Time. Who is then guilty to whom?', 501; and Pūjanī questioning Time as the causal ground of every event, 500–502, and leaving him after giving him some sound advice on good governance, 502–3.

brāhmaṇa, the

as a social calling: who is a *brāhmaṇa*? 375ff; the true marks of, 378–79; eulogy of, 380–81–3; other perceptions: Bhīshma on *brāhmaṇa* being of many kinds, 381–82; the story of the sage Atri who, on the urging of his wife, goes in search of money, 382–3; the story of Gautama the cruel and greedy brāhmaṇa, 383; the arrogant brāhmaṇa and his humbling: several parables including those of *Jājali* and of Kaushika, 386–90; antagonism with *kshattriya*-s, between the thinker and the ruler, expressed through the metaphor of 'the right of way', as in the story of Shakti and Kalmashpāda the king, 397–400 (see also under ***Kalmashpāda*** and ***varṇa-dharma***);

- why is *brāhmaṇa* portrayed in *MhBh* as a perpetually angry man, quick to take offence and quicker to pronounce a curse?, 401–410; 'to please a brāhmaṇa and keep away from his ready anger became gradually not only a duty but also an art', which *MhBh* describes with a hidden sense of laughter, 403.

Buddha, the

his questioning the belief in a permanent eternal *ātman*, 'the Self', and his doctrine of *anatta*, 'no-self', had already had a long history before him, and recounted in *MhBh*, 46–53, 57–64, 57–64 (see again under ***ātman***);

- the main concern of, 67; struck by disease, death and decay, at first took to the path of harsh penance, only to discover that it was a wrong path; that salvation was not in punishing the body, but in knowing the causal chain of suffering and decay, and in destroying that chain, 67–68, 303; before him, in the *Upanishad*-s a similar turning away from senseless asceticism, 303 (see under ***vairāgya***);
- and his teaching as regards the 'twelve-fold chain of causation' of suffering, *bhāva-chakra*, 67, which will remain indisputable even if one rejects his rejection of the *ātman*, 67; neither was his own rejection of the *ātman* as a permanent entity any part of his perception of the causal chain of suffering, 68;
- his consistent refusal to fall into the bottomless pit of metaphysical questions and the wrangling over them, 68;
- his immense appeal, and that of his teachings, due more to the freedom they offered from the yoke of *varna* and *jati* that had become oppressive already in his times, 378; later, his voice, 'I do not say that there is any difference in freedom as against freedom', would only add force to the voice of *MhBh* against distinctions of the castes, and against the assumed purity of *brāhmana* by virtue of birth alone, 377–78; his teachings on social questions, a restatement of the original principle: '*varṇa* is a function and not the status of a person', 378 (for details, see under ***varṇa-dharma***, ***Social Arrangements***).

capital punishment

455–58 in the voice of Satyavān, *MhBh*'s argument against capital punishment, 556–58, "*The purpose of governance is, not to kill the wicked, but to create conditions in which the people can be good*", 458 (see also under ***rāja-dharma***).

causality, the question of

Ch. 16, 477–528: is connected with the question of the self and free will, 64–65; in *MhBh*, five different views on: providence (*daiva*) alone; human effort (purush*ārtha*) alone; neither the one nor the other alone but the two together; Time (*kāla*); and the innate nature of things (*svabhāva*); each argued with its own reasoning:

- discussion on providence vs human endeavour starts with the empirical fact that not always does effort bring the desired result, 478–79; hence arguments for *daiva*, 'fate', 'providence', 478–83 (see under ***daiva***);
- Brahmā's irrefutable reasoning for human effort having greater force than *daiva*, 483–85; Pañchatantra on human effort, 485–86; Draupadī's argument for human endeavour, 486–87; Yoga Vāsishṭha dismisses *daiva*, argues that efforts in this life can annul the dismal effects of the previous one, 486–87 and 486, 51n;
- the third position propounded by Krishna: human effort and providence go *together*, 487–91; Shiva in dialogue with his wife Uma on every act being tied to human effort and providence together, 488–89; Kripāchārya to Ashvatthāmā: all human beings are bound by two factors alone, providence and effort, 489–91;
- to bring providence within rational categories of thought, providence identified with *kāla*, Time, 491 (see under ***Time***); that Time determines every event, expressed in different voices, in different circumstances, 491–99, 500–501; the opposite view: if Time determines in advance every happening, then no accountability for what one is, 499, 500–502; 'There is no dialogue with Time', 499;
- the theory of *svabhāva*, 'innate disposition of things', another way of explaining the diversity of creation and events, 503–508, (see under ***svabhāva***);
- Gopinath Kaviraj on the subject of causality in Indian thought holds that *daiva*, *kāla*, *niyati* and *svabhāva* were collateral and had a common origin, all of them of determinist cast, 507–8;
- the question of accountability intimately connected with that of, 508–23 (also see under ***accountability***);
- the question examined in *Upanishad*-s in abstract terms, 523–24; in *MhBh*, always linked with concrete realities, 523–24;
- Vyāsa summarizes incompatible views concerning the cause of events, 525–6; the contending sages appeal to Vāsishtha to settle the problem, and his reply, '*I have little knowledge of this subject*', 526;
- the problem caused much conflict between philosophers and lawgivers, the shastri-s, 526;
- the conflict between *santosha*, 'contentment', and *purushārtha*, 'effort': the latter having its origin in *asantosha*, 'dissatisfaction with things as they are', 526; *purushārtha*, 'endeavour', quietly incorporated into ritualism, 526; Yoga Vāsishṭha on *purushārtha*, 526;
- the question of causality remains unresolved, 523–27; but, *MhBh* teaches, that need not produce moral paralysis of the will, 527–8;
- the radical shift in *MhBh* characterised by going beyond causality, 523, 527–8;
- whichever view one takes of causality, transcend self-reproach and blaming the other alike, both useless, doing no good, 523;
- to chart the progress of one's right relationship with one's self and with the *other*, no definite answer required whether determinism or free will?, but 'Happiness or suffering, the pleasant or the unpleasant, whatever comes, receive it with respect: and never feel defeated in your heart.', 527;
- Yoga-Vāsishṭha on going beyond causality, and the attitude towards the happenings of one's life, 528.

Chattopadhyaya, Debiprasad
the Marxist philosopher, maintains that Indian civilisation is essentially materialistic, 42.

Chirakārī
son of the sage Gautama, given that name because of his habit of reflecting on a thing long, and taking even longer to act upon it, not a bad habit at all as it turned out in his particular case, saving his mother thereby from being killed, 362–63. (See also under ***Gautama, the sage***)

***daiva*, providence, fate**
a fundamental concern of *MhBh* in exploring the question of causality, 8; belief in *daiva*, fate, as a force over and above human endeavour, and its reasoning, 478–83: the unevenness of human situations, 479–81, point to the existence of some other factor than human effort, "Were the fruits of one's acts not dependent upon another, paradhina, then one might obtain what one wished"; 479 Namuchi, once king but now in adverse circumstances, advocates 'fate' as the ruler of all beings, "A man gets what he is destined to get; and what is destined to happen must happen", "What he is not destined to get, that even his strength, intelligence, endeavour, humility, blameless conduct, and wealth, are powerless to secure for him", 482–83; and therefore also freedom from grief over what is past, 481–83; Yoga-Vāsishṭha dismisses 'fate' as a piece of imagination, just a word coined by fools, 488–89; in dialogue with his wife Umā, Shiva on *daiva* and endeavour going together: 488–89; Kripāchārya argues that all human beings are bound by providence and effort together, 489–91; since the human situation can be explained by *svabhāva*, 'the innate disposition of things', Sāṃkhya rejects, 505; Gopinath Kaviraj on, 507, 156n; *Sāmba* on, 522–23; the question, one of causality, remains unresolved, 527–28.

***dama*, self-discipline**
comes up repeatedly in *MhBh* in all contexts: as the basis of all answers to the question of the Good, 107; no *dharma* greater than,107; one who has self-discipline walks with a feeling of happiness, 108; a host of other results from *dama* 108; he who has *dama* has no need to take to the forest, 109; *dama* as an attribute of *dharma*, 109; and 110–11; self-control related with self-interest, as self-interest related with one's good, man himself the ultimate source of the rationality of *dama*, 222–23: "conquered, one's self is the best friend one has; uncontrolled, one's only enemy", 223;

- in the voice of Bhīshma, *MhBh* provides indisputable reasoning for *dama* as the way to happiness, 250–53; and the 'signs' which constitute the meaning of, which relate to one's happy relationship with one's self and with the *other*, and thus freedom from pain and suffering, as the conquest of the self, 353–54; in *MhBh* self-control is not a withdrawal from pleasures as such, but to avoid obsessive attachment to them, 249; *dama* not a denial of desire, for that would be a denial of all that is human, 583.

dāna
not almsgiving or charity, not ritual acts, 35; but sharing in the awareness that one's life is connected with other beings, 35–6; as 'sharing', 'communicating', 'imparting', 'paying back' (as in a debt), 'restoring', 'adding to', 39; *anna-dāna* and *jala-dāna*, 'sharing of food and water', are the greatest of all sharing, 31–34; *bhūmi-dāna* and *vrikṣha-dāna*, 'sharing land and vegetation', 34–5; as an attribute of *dharma*, 109;

- ***abhaya-dāna***, 'creating conditions of freedom from fear', is the greatest gift of all, 114;
- one of the three self-related disciplines, 216; the importance of giving to a brāhmaṇa, 408; one of the principles to which state earnings are to be subject, 442; the question: which is greater, *dāna* or *tapas*, sharing or austerities? and Vyāsa's answer that *dāna* as sharing is superior, 540–47;
- five motives behind all acts of giving and sharing, 544: but 'No matter what the motive be, one should always give and share according to one's capacities', 545;
- the psychology of 'asking' and 'giving' examined in *MhBh*: the one humiliating

and reducing inwardly, and the other often an instrument of power over the *other*, the psychologically difficult relationship between the giver and the receiver, the giving which has a price is no giving, 408–10, 545–46; the man who does not ask valued higher than the one who does, and the one who gives without the other having to ask valued higher than the one who gives only on asking, 409–10, 545;

- the radical shift in the *MhBh* on the meaning of *dāna*: from ritual acts to relationships: Ch. 17:
- not primarily a giving of things; other forms of: *prīti-dāna*, 'sharing love and affection'; *vidya-dāna*, 'sharing learning and scholarship'; *jñāna-dāna*, 'sharing knowledge', *abhaya-dāna*, 'creating conditions of freedom from fear', and *dīpa-dāna* and *aloka-dāna*, 'lighting a lamp' and 'spreading light', 546–47; above all, *dāna as a giving of one's self*, 547;
- *MhBh* brings in a mystic unity *dāna* with knowledge, truth, self-discipline, self-sacrifice, happiness and heaven and peace, 547.

***daṇḍa*, governance**
see under ***rāja-dharma***.

daṇḍa: saṃyaga
'impartiality in governance': see under ***rāja-dharma***.

Dasgupta, Surama
author of Development of Moral Philosophy in India (1961), discusses the Jaina view of self, 46 6n;

Dasgupta, Surendranath
author of History of Indian Philosophy and other works; on the term '*dharma*': gives an account of its different meanings, 79 4n, 81; on the question whether the philosophy of *Upanishad*-s originated only in the ranks of *kshattriyas*, 394; on the *Ayurveda*, 505.

death
Ch.6, 169–80; as relational as life is, 168; the story of young Abhīmanyu's death on the battlefield deals with the question Yudhishṭhira asks: 'What is death?', 170ff;

- Vyāsa narrates the story of Brahmā the Primeval Being creating *Mrityu*, Death, in the form of a woman, to relieve the Earth of the burden of ever-increasing population, 171–73;
- and her tears, which Brahmā takes in the palms of his hands but some fall on the earth, 171; and Death giving her creator reasons why she must not do what she was created for, 171–72; eventually submits, but says to him: "*Greed; anger; talking ill of others; envy and jealousy; ill-will; confusion of perceptions; shamelessness; and harsh words spoken to each other—these will devour the bodies of those who are embodied*", 172;
- "*All living beings cause their own death. Death does not kill them with a stick in her hand*", 173; Vidura on 'six deadly swords': "These kill human beings—not death", 173;
- all are equal in death, 173–74;
- in the voice of sage Arishtanemi, *MhBh* on the conquest of the fear of death, in one's right relationship with one's self and with the *other*, 174–75;
- conversation between the sage Sanatsujāta and King Dhritarāshṭra exploring the question whether there is or is not death, 175–76;
- Bhīshma narrates a conversation between Medhāvī and his father exploring the question how, given the reality of death, should one order one's life, 176–81 and 180; *MhBh* concerned with life and not with biological death: "Death is connected with life from the moment one is born"; one should free oneself of the fear of death, or else it would become the fear of life as well, 179; hence the concern of *MhBh* more with psychological death that takes place every moment, the death of the mind

and of feelings, 179–80; biological death alone is not death, 179;

- both death and the deathless reside in the body, 180, the conquest of death through truth, 179–80, 197;
- the tears of Death are asking, '*given death, why don't you learn to live?*', 180; by death is life assailed, one is alone in death, 255–57.

***desha* and *kāla*, the given place and the given time**

spoken together, 'the given place' and 'the given time': the two co-ordinates of history which keep changing with the flow of time, 20; self-understanding and the knowledge of the *other* linked with, 20; the value of an act depends upon one's motives but also upon, 90–91; 'place' can be seen but not 'time', the drama of human life enacted between these two co-ordinates, one seen and the other unseen, 90;

- and the question of relativism, 91, 94–95: all human attributes, *dharma* and truth most of all, examined in that light by *MhBh*, 90–101, 183–92: in the voice of Yudhishṭhira, 'The same act is *dharma* or *adharma* for different people, depending on 'time', 'place' and 'the person concerned', 94; 'None could see anywhere conduct that would be uniformly good for all', 93; *MhBh* on the problem coming up again and again in human living, leading to dilemmas, 94–95; whatever criterion one might adopt, it related above all with the idea of history, of which *desha* and *kāla* the two co-ordinates, 420; acknowledging them as indisputable, *MhBh* on how *dharma* in its essence, and truth likewise, always and everywhere necessarily the basic conditions of human living, not subject to *desha* and *kāla*, engaging at three different levels, all inter-related in a deep inner coherence, 97–98, 183–84, 192–97, 420–21 (see also under ***dharma and truth***); as one of the six elements of good governance, one's grasp of, 452; Vyāsa on, 540–41.

desire, *kāma*, in the non-sexual sense

MhBh's inquiry in the human condition, an inquiry in the workings of desire, of which many different forms, every act suffused with, 3, 7, 315–16; described by Vyāsa as 'the water' of 'the River of Time', 66; the starting point of all acts, 68; *MhBh* acknowledges its evident psychological force, 7, 69; then proceeds to discuss the logic of desire and what it leads to, which it does mainly in its discussion on pleasure and pain, *sukha* and *duhkha*, ch. 9, on *artha*, 'desire for material prosperity', ch.10, and *kāma*, 'desire for sexual pleasure', ch.11;

- can lead to tyranny and violence, 'the tyranny of desire', 7, 12–3; the contrary nature of, 17–18; Bhīma on the error of fragmenting *dharma* from, 104; destroys people before death does, 176; equality lies in destroying the feelings of, 193, 197; desire and, arising from it, thirst are seen in Buddhism as the two primary causes of human suffering, 226;
- because no one is completely free from, 228; but the nature of desire is such that it remains forever unquenched, 230ff; *therefore*, the argument runs, '*Whichever desire is given up, that brings happiness in that measure*', 234, 255; '*The one who pursues desire, is by desire destroyed*', 234 and 235–36, '*under the power of desire one remains forever unhappy*', 255;
- Bhīshma on the right relationship with one's self and thus with the *other*, in the awareness that there is no end to, each desire on its fulfillment creating a new one, leading to a perpetual sense of want, which is pain, 251, also 562;
- the *vairāgya* argument: 'The thirst of Desire is pain', 254–5,
- Bhīma's advocacy of the equal importance of *dharma*, *artha*, 'desire for material prosperity', and *kāma*, 'desire for pleasure', 276;
- the paradox of desire, 282;
- the sage Maṇki addresses *Kāma*, Desire, 283–85: '*Leave me alone!*', 284; desire the

strongest of the seven enemies of the self, '*conquering Desire, I will be happy like a king*', 285, 69n;

- *MhBh* advocates the disciplining of desire and not its rooting out, the latter unnatural and thus a source of violence to one's self, 251–52; 582–84; related to self-interest, 251; self-discipline is not a denial of desire, for that would be a denial of all that is human, 583;
- the *jīVana-mukta*, 'the one who has obtained freedom here and now', has risen above the polarity of desire and not-desire, 588–89. (See also under ***dama, 'self-discipline'***)

Deussen, Paul
author of the article on '*Ātman*' in the *Encyclopaedia of Religion and Ethics*, vol.2, in which he throws light on the origin of the concept of self with parallels in Greek philosophy, 46 5n;

Devasharmā
and the attempted seduction of his beautiful young wife Ruchi by Indra, and her protection by his pupil Vipula by possessing her mind that seemed open to the advances of Indra, 330–31;

- through this story *MhBh* conveys the truth—that sexuality is not of the body alone but of the mind even more; hence the possession of the *other*'s mind as much a 'sexual' act as the possession of the *other*'s body, and a greater offence, 327;
- and the question whether that would still be so, regardless of the purity of intention, 329–31. (See also under ***Vipula***)

Devayānī
wife of King Yayāti; and Sharmishṭha, herself a princess but obliged to act as her maid, and Yayāti who takes Sharmishṭha as her second lawful wife but in secrecy: their story, 317–22,

- through which *MhBh* teaches, among other things, that there is something inherent in *kāma*, sexual desire, which, even after its longest duration, keeps it unsatisfied, 320–21; and that desire alone cannot be the basis of man-woman relationship, 322. (See also under ***Yayāti***)

***dharma*, foundation of all relationships, individual and social**
Ch.4, 78–112; the main concern of the *MhBh*: one of the four ends of human life, 4; questions raised regarding, 4–5;

- a brief tour in the history of the different meanings of: in the Veda-s, the *Upanishad*-s and the *dharma-shāstra* literature, 78–85: as 'the old customary order', in *Atharvaveda*, 79; as 'religious ordinance'; 'the whole body of religious duties', in Aitareya brāhmaṇa, 79; as 'an end reached by obeying vedic commands', in Mīmaṃsā, 79–80; as *abhyudaya*, 'happiness', and *nihsh reyasa*, 'beatitude', in Nyāya Vaisheshika, 80; in Manusmriti, Manu's definition of, 80–81, on Veda and *dharma-shāstra* as the chief sources of, 81;
- varieties of: *pravritti–dharma*,' the works that are of this world' 81; *nivritti-dharma*, 'works that are not of this world', 81; '*kula-dharma*, 'the specific character of a family', 81; '*rāshtra-dharma*, 'the specific character of a nation', 81; *yuga-dharma*, 'the specific character of an age', 81; defined in the *Amarakosha* as *punya*, *vedic vidhi*, *nyāya*, *svabhāva*, *āchāra*, and so forth, 81, was certainly not regarded as universal, 81; *vishesha-dharma*, 'specific to a particular social calling', and *sādhāraṇa-dharma*, 'common ethical', and the classic problem as to their relative precedence when a conflict between the two, 82; in one view ethics subordinated to *varṇa-āshrama-dharma*, the demands of social structure, 82 and 83;
- modern apologists of, and their refusal to give a clear boundary to, when in *MhBh* it had a clear boundary all the time, 82;
- wrongly translated as 'religion', 83 33n, and wrongly identified with a given social structure, 84–85, leading to a completely wrong understanding of *dharma*, as the

- *Dharmavyādha*, the meat seller, on: 'What has its beginnings in what is just, and fair, and reasonable, is *dharma*. Whatever is oppressive, unjust, and unfair is *adharma*', 550;
- *dharma* consists of trust, caring, love, and truth, 570.

Dharmāńka
a special number of the journal *Kalyana* devoted to discussing *dharma* by many authors, 79, (their names not listed in this index).

***Dharmavyādha*, a meatseller**
his conversation with Kaushika, an arrogant ascetic-scholar brāhmaṇa, on the true meaning of *dharma*, which includes the question of violence and not-violence, 121–22; his admonition to Kaushika to return to his old parents he had neglected in the wrongly perceived pursuit of knowledge, and serve them, 364; on the great significance of *MhBh* making a brāhmaṇa learn about *dharma* and life from a meat seller, low in social standing and hardly expected to be a thinker,; and his teachings on *sadāchāra*, good conduct, and *shishtāchāra*, cultured conduct, 547–52.

Dhaumya
a sage and Yudhishṭhira's preceptor: his advice to Yudhishṭhira to appeal to the Sun god for the blessing of inexhaustible food, 40.

Dhrishṭadyumna
son of Drupada and brother of Draupadī; his revenge-killing by Ashvatthāmā, 135–37, whose father, Droṇāchārya, was killed by him in a manner most despicable, 191.

Dhritarāshṭra
the old blind king of the Kuru domain, and father of the Kaurava-s slain in the war: a troubled man at the beginning, and even more troubled at the end, of the war, all his sons killed, 516;
- his conversation with sage Sanatsujāta on what is death, 175–76;
- his companion Sanjaya holds him wholly accountable in not disciplining his son Duryodhana, and in treating the Pāṇḍava-s, his dead elder brother's sons, unjustly, 516–17; seeks forgiveness from the people for the war, and seeks their permission to retire with his wife Gāndhārī to the forest, and addresses them, 520–21: people's forgiveness for the past, and people's consent to what a king proposed to do with his personal life, 521–22; is absolved by *Sāmba* chosen by the people to represent them, 522–23–2; and his conversation with Vidura, his half-brother, on who is truly wise, pandita, 552–53.

Draupadī
the wife of the five Pāṇḍava-brothers, and a dominant presence in *MhBh*: mocks at Yudhishṭhira, her eldest husband, who engages her in long conversations about forgiveness, and her response: 'neither is forgiveness always a virtue, nor is force always the best means', 137; 148–9, 368;
- after the war is won, all her five sons along with her brother Dhrishṭadyumna killed by Ashvatthāmā in a revenge-killing (see also under ***Ashvatthāmā***), 129, 136–37, 150; on the news reaching her, she falls on the ground, 'looking like the sun totally eclipsed', 137: is lifted by Bhīma in his arms and consoled, 137: mocks at Yudhishṭhira, and vows to end her life if Ashvatthāmā is not killed in retribution, 138; in conversation with Bhīma after the humbling defeat of Ashvatthāmā, whose life spared because the son of the guru but the charmed jewel on his head removed and presented to her, 140–41;
- recalls her humiliation at the hands of Duhshasana, 143–45, 366; her rejection of the proposed reconciliation with the Kaurava-s, 143–45;
- on the importance of *desha* and *kāla*, 'right place' and 'right time', in human affairs, 147–48, 366 and 450–51;

- her relationship with Yudhishṭhira and Bhīma, 366–67; Bhīma's tenderness to her, 366–67; known also as Krishna, 'the one of dark complexion', 372–73;
- in discussion with Yudhishṭhira on causality, her reasoning for human effort, 'Taking into consideration time and place and by judging through intelligence one's capacities and strength, let a man, with untroubled mind, make effort and increase in blessings', 486.

Droṇāchārya
teacher of archery to the Pāṇḍava-s and the Kaurva-s and father of Ashvatthāmā, the story of, raising the question primarily concerning truth; 128–29; 190–92; abandons the fight when he hears Yudhishṭhira, the 'truth-speaking' man, say to him: "Ashvatthāmā is killed", when it was not his son who was killed but a war-elephant by that name, according to a carefully drawn plan to stun him by that devise, 190–91; and his death at the hands of Dhrishṭadyumna while sitting in grief in his chariot, disarmed, 191;
- that the nature of truth is exceedingly subtle and difficult to grasp, is still no freedom to speak lies that have the appearance of being outwardly true, 192;
- on Yudhishṭhira seeking his blessings at the beginning of the war, his candid confession that he is tied to the Kaurava-s with the bond of his self-interest, 204–5. (See also under ***truth*** and under ***Yudhishṭhira***.)

***duḥkha*, pain**
see under ***pleasure and pain***.

Duryodhana
the main antagonist in the story of the war between his clan the Kaurava-s and his first-cousins the five Pāṇdava-brothers: makes an obscene gesture to Draupadī dragged into the assembly when Yudhishṭhira loses the game of the dice after putting her also on the stake, 142; his mother Gāndhārī reasons with him against war, 152; is killed by Bhīma in a straight battle-by-mace between them, but by Bhīma violating a cardinal rule of such contest, 518, also 141;
- that he could never have been conquered by fighting in a way the *dharma* of the war would demand one ought, Krishna acknowledges, 518–19; and Krishna shows neither compassion nor grace to the dying, 519;
- Dhritarāshṭra, his father, on the character of, 520–21: and Kripāchārya on, as 'greedy and thoughtless', 130;
- that 'he had never behaved towards the people in any way offensive', and neither did he do 'even the smallest injustice to us ever', and that he was not the cause of the war, testified by *Sāmba* representing the people, 520, 522–23;
- in *Sāmba*'s voice, *MhBh* saying two things: one must transcend self-reproach and blaming the other alike, for both useless; and no one is an unredeemed villain, nor anyone an absolute hero, 523.

enemy and enmity, friend and friendship
MhBh on, in its discussions regarding not-violence and violence, 108, 115, 127–42, 149–51, 157, 173; and self-interest, 201–204, 205–7, 219–20, 221–23; and pleasure and pain, 241, 254, 261; and the importance of wealth but also the trap of desire and greed, 278–79, 284, 286, 291; and marriage, 355–56, 367–68; and the betrayal of a friend, 173, 383; and governance and those who govern, 433, 453, 467, 468; and in its discussion regarding the last freedom, *moksha*, 571–72,
- and all of them inter-related with a common thread running through them, the main teachings of *MhBh* regarding one's relationship with one's self, the conquest of the self: 115, 205, 206, 223, 253, 291, 584;
- and the argument against enmity, 149, also 150; the bird Pūjanīya's advice to King Brahmadatta on the avoidance of enmity and war, 151–52;
- beside the worldly wisdom, how a debt left unpaid, an illness ignored, a fire not wholly

extinguished, and a defeated enemy left alive, would be a cause of great fear always, 152, 219–20; *MhBh* enjions humane and honorable conduct towards enemy, 152–53, 221–22;

- *MhBh* on harsh words making instant enemy of friends, even those of long standing, 217 (see also under ***speech***); and "one should not begin enmity with anybody stronger and more powerful than oneself", 220;
- on the true test of a friend: "he who speaks for the good of the *other*, even if what is spoken be unpleasant is a true friend to the king", 221; "He whose anger one must fear, and in whose company one must remain distrustful, is not a friend: a friend is one who can be trusted like a father, others are mere companions", 221; and the strongest condemnation of betrayal of a friend, 173, 383 (see under ***Gautama, the ungrateful brāhmaṇa***);
- and 'marriage as friendship, not the theatre of power', 367–68; and the necessity of friendship between philosophy and power—for the good of the people, loka-hita, 414;
- and *mokṣha*, the ultimate liberation, is liberation from the workings of the opposites, friend-enemy polarity included, 570–71; and the attributes of a free person: "Aware of his unity with all beings, he has feelings of friendship for all, and violence towards none", 572, "Who does not perceive others in the opposites of friend-enemy—such a person is always free", 573.

energy
the Upanishadic emphasis on *prāṇa*, life-energy, is the emphasis on, 30, 70–71 (see under ***Upanishad*-s**); questions concerning *prāṇa* central to the Indian inquiry into the human condition, 71–75;

- nowhere is life-energy and its manifold workings examined in greater detail than in *MhBh*, proceeding through the complexity of relationships, 71;
- Bhrigu describes three forms of energy: of consciousness, *sattva*; of action, *rājas*; and that which suffocates and depresses, *tamas*, as the three main constituents of the Self as person, 52 (for details see under ***sattva, rājas*** and ***tamas***);
- Pañchashikha on, the whole creation suffused with the three energies of *sattva, rājas*, and *tamas*, 56–57; none of the three exists without the other two, 74 and 579; their combination in different proportions determines the *svabhāva*, 'the given disposition', of a thing, and gives each individual his and her specific temperament, 57, 503–504;
- in a radical shift in the knowing of the self, *MhBh* demonstrates that life being energy, and life a complex system of relationships, it is in relationships that the workings of energy are most manifest, in one's relationships with one's self and with the *other*, the self a complex field of energy, 71;
- *MhBh* has the ordering of energy, individual and social, as its main concern, 70; love is energy, hatred is energy too, 70;
- the paradox of energy: the highest form of energy arises from complete inner stillness, 70–71; this paradox comprises the paradox of time and that of memory, 72–73; the paradox of energy as the paradox of *kāla*, time, 72–74; the paradox of memory: *sattva, rājas* and *tamas* again, 73–75; divine energy united with human energy in the story of Ashvatthāmā, 134–35;
- sexual energy and relationships, see Ch.9: the tantric view of sexual energy, 299: that sex can be transmuted into highest spiritual energy by submission to it, 299; woman as divine energy (shakti), 304–52; the energy of self-knowledge, when the self is not separated from the social, can be subversive, 338; *MhBh* releases the immense mental and spiritual energy of asking questions concerning the self and the other as persons, 337–38.

family
see under ***grihastha and grihiṇī***

fear
a theme that runs through *MhBh*, as it runs through life; discussed in its opposite aspects: freedom from fear as the very first foundation of life and relationships, personal and collective, 108, 164–68: true wealth, individual and social, is that which secures for all living beings freedom from violence, freedom from fear, 89; and Fear a progeny of *Adharma* personified, 104; and the one who has conquered his self, "Himself free from fear, above all, he brings others freedom from fear", 108, 110; "The man with wisdom securing for others freedom from fear, becomes a giver of life—this is beyond doubt", 164; "Believe in what I am saying to you, for it is true: there is no greater gift in life than the gift of freedom from fear", a grocer to an ascetic, 165; and one should free oneself of the fear of death, or else it would become the fear of life as well, 179;

- freedom from fear the very first condition of social peace and human dignity: "Human beings take delight in sounds, touch, tastes, beauty, and in fragrance. But the one who is full of fear can derive from them no happiness whatever", 166, 446;
- in governance most of all, for nothing more degrading than living in fear, Shiva to his wife Uma on that subject: "Let the king protect his subjects from their fear of him; from their fear of others; from their fear of each other; and from their fear of things that are not human", 165, 425, 427, 429, 447; "The king should free the fearful from fear", 438, "The demerit a king invites by not protecting the people from fear, lasts a thousand years", 461; hence the question to a king: "Do you protect your nation from fear—of fire, poisonous snakes, diseases, and from the fear of the wicked?", 476;
- and the opposite reality, too: fear as the basis of social order: 423, 425, 427, 431, 438, 440, 444–47, 461; but this, as the fear of law and governance, *daṇḍa*, to prevent 'the big fish from swallowing the small fish': "It is without doubt the fear of rule that alone keeps the people on the path of proper conduct towards each other. In its absence, just as in the waters the big fish swallow the small fish, those who are powerful would feed on those who are weak", 445 and 446: "Only rarely is a person found who is good and clean by nature: only out of fear, and not out of goodness, do most people keep within bounds", 446; and the paradox this creates: 'fear is the basis of governance, and the purpose of governance is to secure for the people freedom from fear', and how *MhBh* resolves it, 445–46;
- and the distinguishing mark of a person who has obtained ultimate liberation, *mokṣha*: the free person fears no one, and creates conditions where others likewise obtain freedom from fear, 572–73.

freedom
see under ***mokṣha***

friend and friendship
see under ***enemy and enmity***

Gālava
the sage, on the many meanings of *shreya*, 'the Good', 80.

game of the dice, the
played between Yudhishṭhira, the Pāṇdava, and the rightful heir to the Kuru Kingdom and Shakuni from the side of Kaurava-s, with a mutually agreed condition that whoever loses will remain in exile for thirteen years, of which the last year will have to be incognito; fraudulently played, the dice loaded, and Yudhishṭhira loses after putting everything on stake, 142, 538.

Gāndhārī
mother of Kaurava-s; reasons with her son Duryodhana against war, 152; holds Krishna accountable for the war, 517; pronounces a curse upon Krishna, which comes true, 517–18.

Gaṇesha
god, agrees to be a stenographer to Vyāsa, the

author of the *Mahābhārata*, on a condition though: the story relating to, 2; his appearance, 3, and the benevolent god to be propitiated whenever anything is begun, as in the writing of this book, 3.

Gautama
the sage, 336; on finding that his wife was seduced by god Indra, commands his son Chirakārī to kill his mother and goes away, but soon feels horrified at what he had done, and hopes his son would be true to his name, taking long to reflect on a thing and taking even longer to act upon it; acknowledges to himself that it was out of a sense of jealousy that he behaved in the dreadful way he did: "Jealousy is the root of all that is painful", "In situations such as these, the fault is not of the woman but only of the man", 362–63. (See also under ***Chirakārī***)

Gautama
the ungrateful brāhmaṇa, kills his benefactor and friend, is seized and cut up into pieces on royal command, and fed to animals; but even the animals would not eat the meat of an ungrateful wretch, 383; his story narrated in the context of social callings and social divisions (for which see under ***varṇa-dharma***); not by birth alone is one a brāhmaṇa, 383.

Gautamī
through her story, *MhBh* explores the intimate but highly complex question of accountability, 508–09. Her only son is bitten by a snake and dies; Arjunaka, a hunter, catches the snake, brings it to her, and resolves to kill it, 508–09, and she asks him not to, "What was destined to happen, happened", "By killing it, my son will not come back to life. Then why destroy another life?", 509; and the conversation between them, the hunter insistent on killing the snake, and Gautamī refusing to be persuaded, 509–10. Then follows the argument between Arjunaka and the snake, the latter pleading not accountable, Death having prompted him to bite the boy and cause his death, and thus not a free agent, 510. Death appears, only to transfer the accountability to Time, *kāla*, 510–11, raising an ontological, moral, and even a legal, issue, 512, and the conversation between Death and Arjunaka. Now Time also appears and pronounces: "It is what the boy did, his own *karma*, that caused his death; none other was the cause of his death. The living being himself causes his death" "Just as from the clay, a potter makes what he wishes; a person makes everything from his own *karma*", 513; on hearing Time say this, Gautamī is reconciled and free from grief, 513: "Arjunaka! Let the Snake go.", 513. (See also under ***causality and karma***)

Gopinath Kaviraj
on tantra and on causality: on how the tantric practices were polluted, but defends the idea itself, and the problem with that, 302; on causality: holds that *daiva*, *kāla*, *niyati* and *svabhāva* were collateral and had a common origin, all of them of determinist cast, 507–8. (See also under ***causality***)

governance
see under ***rāja-dharma***.

greed, lobha
is a feeling, 18; one of the signs of the energy of *rājas*,56, 70, 71, 74 and 504; check on, in conflict with manly effort: a dilemma, 94–95; the psychological causal chain of, and the underlying logic of its working, 105–7, 236–8; comes up in *MhBh* repeatedly as the main cause of human disorder, 106; ignorance is the root cause of greed, and greed feeds ignorance, 106, 237, 562, 579–80; Death takes the form of hatred and anger and greed, 176; ati, 'excess', and, 222; no end to one's, 233; leads man to endless striving and confusion, 236; the products of, 238, 252, 281, 562; self-discipline, *dama*, and the end of, 'Who has conquered greed and its deluding confusion, has conquered his self', 238;

- Vidura on, 'too much greed brings ruin and too little brings nothing, 250; the Panchantantra's position on, 278; and

greater value on sharing and giving, *dāna*, to Maitreya advocating *tapas*, austerities: 'with affectionate heart you offered food and water to one hungry and thirsty, your guest', 542.

guṇa, energy
according to Sāṃkhya, the three primordial, 56; translated by the author as 'energy' rather than as 'substance', 53*n*; (see also under ***sattva, rājas*** and ***tamas***) all human relationships a combination of the three, 74; the ordering of energy, individual and social, the main concern of *MhBh*, 72. (See under ***energy***)

history, the question of
explored in *MhBh* at many levels, 9; meaning and Time and, 9; the Enlightenment idea of, 10–11; the *MhBh*'s concern with the evident paradox of, the paradox of memory, 166; freedom from history, is freedom from memory, freedom from what is past, 166; the crucible in which political ideas mature and human decisions arise, 420; *desha* and *kāla*, 'the given place' and 'the given time' the two coordinates of, 420; a free person as one who is free of the history of accumulated *karma*-s, 574; man lives in history: but 'am I my history alone?' 574, 578–9, 588 and 591. (See also under ***desha and kāla*** and under time and under *moksha*).

indriya-nigraha
controlling one's sense organs: one of the three different paths to happiness, 246–7, 248–53, 254; the metaphor of the chariot drawn by five horses (the five sense organs) and the skilful charioteer (the self) who keeps them under control, 'Just as the untrained and uncontrolled horses can hurt a bad charioteer, so do the physical organs of a man if they are not disciplined', 248–9, 252;

- the radical shift in *MhBh* in the perception of: not as withdrawal from the pleasures as such but avoiding obsessive attachment to, and its reasoning, 250;
- Vidura on, 249–50; Bhīshma on, relating it with *dama*, 'self-discipline', 250–53; and *aparigraha*, 'not-grasping', 252; not an ethical imperative but an evident psychological necessity in self-interest, and its reasoning, Vidura on, 249; because self-preservation, 253. (See also under ***dama*** and under ***pleasure and pain***).

Janaka
the king, his conversations with: Panchshikha on the nature of the Self, 52–57; and with his wife Kausalyā, who teaches him what renunciation is not, and the importance of the life-in-family, 345–7; with the sage Parāshara on *shūdra*: 'Is it by one's birth or by one's conduct that one invites impurity?' 384–5. (See also under ***Parāshara*** and under ***shūdra***).

jīvana-mukta
the one who has obtained liberation in this life, and his or her distinguishing attributes, 588: no external change, the change is in his or consciousness, which is radical; Yoga-Vāsishtha on, as *mahā-kartā* and *mahā-bhoktā*, 'great doer' and 'great enjoyer', except that 'doing' and 'enjoying' do not have their ordinary meaning but neither are their ordinary meanings dissolved, 588–89. See also under ***moksha***.

kāla
see under ***time***.

Kalmashpāda
the king: and the sage Shakti, the story of, illustrating the conflict between the *kshattriya*-s and the brāhmaṇa-s, as to which of the two has precedence over the *other*, 397, in this story in a physical sense, but a metaphor for 'the right of way' between a thinker and the state; whips Shakti brutally when he would not move out of the king's way, and the sage cursing him to turn into a demon, aware only of his demonic power, another metaphor, 397.

***kāma*, sexuality, sexual happiness**
Ch.11, 296–335: one of the four ends of human life, 4; the questions explored relating to, 6–7; quest of pleasure and happiness acknowledged

Kane

Pandurang Vaman: author of The History of the *Dharmashāstra* (1930); on different meanings of *dharma*, 79 6*n*, 80 11*n*; on *varṇa*, 372 11*n*, 373–74 17*n*, 374 18*n*; on the daily rituals prescribed for the householder, 337 1*n*; on the various law-givers attaching utmost importance to the 'life-in-family', 340 5*n* and 8*n*.

Kapila

the sage: in conversation with the sage Syūmarashmi on the *grihastha āshrama*, 'the life-in-family', and *sannyāsa*, 'life-alone', in which he extols the transformation of a *sannyāsī*, understood as the one who has renounced the world, 350–9 (see also under ***grihastha and gribiṇī***)

karma

acts, the theory of: and rebirth, 9; causality and *karma* examined in Ch.16; three major shifts in the theory of *karma*: belief in *daiva*, providence; second, providence identified with Time, then with God; finally *karma* came to mean ritual acts, 478; the essence of the *karma*-theory in two propositions, 562–63; 'just as a calf reaches its mother among a hundred cows, one's previous *karma* reaches its doer', 564; *mokṣha*, 'ultimate liberation', the ultimate point in the logic of, and its rationality, 564; this logic is not of the *a priori* kind, 564.

Karṇa

perhaps the most tragic, and also the most noble, figure of *MhBh*, whose tragedy began with his birth, born a prince but reared in humble circumstances elsewhere, 362; cast away by his mother, Kuntī, soon after his birth, and nurtured and brought up by another woman, Rādhā, who found him in a basket floating on the river, 362; Kuntī visits him at the beginning of the war, if only to ask for a favour, and addresses him as 'Kaunteya', 'son of Kuntī': still polite to her, Karṇa says: "I am not *Kaunteya*, I am *Rādheya*", 'son of Rādhā', 362, and the brief conversation between them, 362.

Kausalyā

wife of King Janaka; teaches her husband the true meaning of 'renunciation', 345–7: 'If passions are not removed from one's heart, then wearing the ochre robe should be regarded as nothing more than a means to selfish ends', 345.

Kaushika

the brāhmaṇa scholar and ascetic, the story of:

- had mastered the Veda but not his anger, had mastered knowledge but not his self, 387; the humbling of his arrogance by an unnamed ordinary housewife, 387–9, who tells him what it is to be a brāhmaṇa truly, which she thinks he is not, 387–8;
- is advised by her to travel to Mithilā and meet Dharmavyādha, a meat seller, to learn from him, 388; (see also under ***Dharmavyādha***)
- is instructed by a meat seller in the true meaning of *dharma* and violence and not-violence and life, 121–22, 363–65 (see also under ***ahiṃsā***),
- is advised to return to his old parents he had grievously neglected in his quest of knowledge wrongly perceived, 364; expresses his gratitude to the meat seller, "I was descending into a hell; but you have liberated me. In the future, too; now that I have seen you", 390.

Kauṭilya

and his *Arthashāstra* assigned 323 B.C. in the reign of Chandragupta Maurya: speaks of one supreme maxim to which the king is subject: 'In the happiness of his subjects lies his happiness; in their welfare, his welfare', 427;
on governance, 427; the long list of fines for offences mentioned in A indicates that cheating and deception were prevalent, 292.

Kāyavya

an elderly robber by profession, who insists that his fellow robbers strictly observe certain limits he specifies, the story of, 153–4.

Kripāchārya

a venerable figure of the realm, and one of

the only three survivors of the war from the Kaurava side; accompanies Ashvatthāmā on the latter's journey of revenge in the night: on hearing from Ashvatthāmā his plan to attack the sleeping Panchala army where he would find Dhrishṭadyumna, advises him against it, for such an act would be *adharma*, for one warrior to attack another warrior while the latter was disarmed and asleep, and the dialogue between them, 130–33; but after giving that lecture, quickly abandons that scruple, and is himself ready for ignoble killings, 135; torches the army camp from the three sides, and many died in the fire thus started, 136; on the question: providence or effort? 489–91.

Krishna

on the inexhaustible merit earned by gifting land, 34–5; on respect to be shown to the guest, 35–6;

- visits the Pāṇḍava-s in their exile, Draupadī engaging his attention the most, she speaking to him of her sorrow, 142–3: 'For me, there is neither husband, nor son, nor friend, nor brother, nor father—not even you, Krishna', 143; agrees to go to the Kaurava-s as ambassador of peace, and Draupadī's strong protest against any such move, for reasons she gives, 143–4;
- on speaking the truth, 187; on *dharma* and truth, 187; urges Yuddhishthira to say 'Ashvatthāmā is killed', a lie, with a view to stunning Droṇāchārya, Ashvatthāmā's father, when what was killed as part of the plan was a war-elephant by that name, 187;
- confides in sage Nārada his troubles with his relatives and seeks his counsel, 263;
- resolves Arjuna's paralysing moral dilemma, 'to fight or not to fight?', by means of a long discourse known as the Bhagvad-Gita, 352; which Arjuna forgets after the war is won and asks him to say it all again, and he says it is beyond his capacity to say it all again, but gives another discourse, known as Anu-Gita, 352, which by design in *MhBh* lacks the grandeur and philosophic depth of the original: the meaning in this, 352;
- on brāhmaṇa: "there is no god greater than brāhmaṇa" etc., 380–81; and on *shūdra*, "*shūdra* is forever a *shūdra*", 383–84: the dog, the *shūdra* and the chandala are forever impure", 384;
- on providence and human effort going together, 487;
- admits his accountability for the unfair and unjust means adopted to win the war, and his justification, 518–20; advocates that the ends justify the means, 519; but the whole of *MhBh* is about not only that the ends do not justify the means, but about the nature of the ends themselves in relation to one's self and with the *other*, 519;
- is cursed by the deeply grieving Gāndhārī for not preventing the war and its enormous destruction and suffering when he had the power to do so if he had so wished, 517–18: "You will drift in the deep woods, unseen, unknown, alone, helpless. And you will die a mean death", 518; and his response: 'You are only pronouncing in advance what I know is going to happen', but in equally bitter words turns upon her for transferring to him the accountability that belonged to her for not restraining her wicked-hearted son Duryodhana, 518;
- shows neither compassion nor grace to the dying Karṇa or to the dying Duryodhana, both killed by means unfair and unjust, 518;
- and the dialogue between him and Ashvatthāmā at the end of the revenge wrought by the latter,138–40; pronounces a curse upon Ashvatthāmā, 140;
- on purity being of five kinds: of the heart, of the acts, of lineage, of one's body, and of speech: of these, purity of the heart the most special, 533; on the true meaning of *tirtha*, 'pilgrimage, 534–36.

kṣhamā

forgiveness and reconciliation examined

in *MhBh* in the context of *ahiṃsā* as a foundation of life and the opposite reality: the rationality and the limits of, 142–48; Yudhishṭhira to his wife Draupadī on, 144–47; Vidura on, 147, 179*n*, 452–53; Draupadī on the limits of, 147–48; Bhīshma on, 148; through the story of a forgiving sage, Vāsishṭha, and an arrogant and nasty king, Vishwamitra, *MhBh* shows the moral power of, 398–400. See also under ***ahiṃsā***, and under ***Vāsishṭha*** and under ***rāja-dharma***.

kshattriya
the: one of the four social divisions, *varṇa*. See under ***varṇa-dharma***.

Kuntī
the mother of the Pāṇḍava-s: hears without their seeing her the loud laments of her host and his family, who had sheltered her and her sons, what they were saying to each *other*, 208–10; asks the man what the cause of their distress was, and the conversation between them, 211–13; decides to send Bhīma to Bakāsura as his 'food', knowing her son would bring to an end Bakāsura's oppression of the people, 211 (see also under ***Bhīma***); on Yudhishṭhira saying to her that she had been rash and unthinking, says: 'The good that the other did to one, should be repaid by doing good to the other in even a greater measure', 213, and her conversation with him, 213–4;

- casts away her first-born, Karṇa, soon after his birth, and floats him on the river in a carefully prepared basket to keep him alive, 362; visits him at the beginning of the war, if only to ask him for a favour, and the brief conversation between them, 362 (see under ***Karṇa***);
- the war won, and her son Yudhisht ̣hira the emperor, decides to turn her back on the world, and spend her last days in the forest with Dhritarāshṭra and Gāndhārī, changing with them the context of her life as well, 520.

lobha
see under ***greed***.

loka-saṃgraha
social wealth: 370; *MhBh* reiterates that all social arrangements have one common goal, of creating social wealth, of creating conditions in which each person can fulfill his and her human worth, 385; the way to, Bhishma on, 410–14: "All persons belonging to them are created alike by the five elements of Nature. They all have in them a similar Self. Even so, each has a different worldly function to fulfill. Fulfilling different social functions they come again into a unity", 411.

Lopamudra
wife of sage Agastya: and their story, 403–405.

***Mahābhārata*, the**
arranged in 18 *parva*-s, 'Books', in the following order: 1 *Ādi-parva*, 2 Sabha-*parva*, 3 *Vana-parva*, 4 *Virāṭa-parva*, 5 Udyoga-*parva*, 6 Bhīshma-*parva*, 7 Droṇa-*parva*, 8 *Karṇa-parva*, 9 *Shalya-parva*, 10 *Sauptika-parva*, 11 *Strī-parva*, 12 *Shanti-parva*, 13 *Anushasana-parva*, 14 *Ashvamedhika-parva*, 15 *Āshramavasika-parva*, 16 *Mausala-parva*, 17 *Mahāprasthāna-parva*, 18 *Svargārohaṇa-parva*;

- and its author, Vyāsa, and his divine stenographer, Gaṇesha, and their story, 2–3; a most systematic inquiry in the human condition, the subjects of the inquiry and their universality, 3–10;
- as the second of the two revolutions in Indian thought, the first that of the *Upanishad*-s, showing the physical, the mental and the spiritual attributes of the Self as a unity, the Self as a being in relation with itself and with the *other*, the two inseparable, 530;
- and its central concerns, the concerns of everyday life everywhere; and its inquiry into the human condition, and the questions that arise from it, questions related to the right ordering of one's relationship with one's self and with the *other*, both in the individual and the collective sense, 3–10, 530;

- and its method in the inquiry (see under ***method***): takes up all questions with the complexities of human life and relationships as their natural material, 44–5; confronts one reality with another reality, when both each other's opposites but both evident parts of life, and discusses both throughout;
- and its radical shifts in the perceptions of :
- the self, 66–70; of self-knowledge, 13, 68–70, 71, 530, 569; of *dharma*, 85–90; of violence and not-violence, 114; of truth and untruth, 192–7; of the place of wealth in human affairs,; of human attributes: self-interest, 200–223, sexual impulse, 316–33, and pleasure and pain, 260–63; in the' *because-therefore*' reasoning in the different perceptions of pleasure and pain: '*because* it is true that—it does not necessarily follow that *therefore*', 260–63; of birth and rebirth, 566–9; of *dāna*, 'giving and sharing', and *tapas*, 'austerity', and *tirtha*, 'pilgrimage', and *sadāchāra* and *shishtāchāra*, 'good conduct' and 'cultured conduct', 530; of causality, and going beyond causality, 527–8; and in its understanding of *mokṣha*, the human freedom, freedom from and freedom into, 567–70. (See also under entries relating to these subjects);
- a joyful affirmation of life and not its violent negation, 261.

Mahāvīra
a *kshattriya*: founded a system of thought pluralistic and atheistic in metaphysics, empirical in method, and immeasurably more systematic in ethical outlook than *Upanishad*-s; among the greatest teachers of all times, 394.

Maṇki
the sage: addresses Desire, *Kāma*, 283–5. See under ***desire***.

Manu
ancient Indian lawgiver: to be distinguished from the Manu of mythology, 80–81, 17*n*;

Marco Pallis
on *dharma*, 84; see his A Buddhist Spectrum (1980).

Mārkaṇḍeya
the sage: on what true renunciation is not, 346; on the subject of what 'purity', *shaucha*, truly is, 530–31; on the abuse of bala, of power, in his address to those who govern: "Because you have power, do not do what is unjust, oppressive, full of violence, *adharma*", 464. (See also under ***bala*** and under ***rāja-dharma***.)

Medhātithi
Mīmaṃsā philosopher, 9th century A.D: on *dharma* as that custom or practice that is based on the teachings of the *Veda*, 80; and his rejection of ātmanas tushtih, 'consent of the heart', as any criterion of *dharma*, 81.

Memory
human life impossible without, 73; as history, 73–4; the paradox of, memory which sustains life must also destroy life, that without which a person is nothing, and a society no society, also builds a prison in which the illusion of freedom, 73–4; collective memories as a fertile ground of hatred and violence, 74 freedom from the past is freedom from grief (see under ***pleasure and pain*** and under ***mokṣha***); and the energies of, that bring joy and happiness, and that are *tamasic*, disturb, distress, exhaust, and suffocate, 74; and transcending, beyond the tyranny of the past and also the tyranny of the present, reaching out to the *other*, 75;
- and Yudhishthira's question regarding, "there seems to be a great defect in the state of *moksha*" "If, in that state, one still retains the memory of one's particular past, then I should regard this life of particularities, with particular desires, and particular aims, the best. If, on the other hand, one has no memory whatsoever of the particularities of the past, then what greater suffering can there be than that?", 568; and Bhīshma's reply, which derived, he says, from the

philosophy of Sāṃkhya as propounded by Kapila, which does not quite answer Yudhishṭhira's question, 567–8 (see under ***birth and rebirth*** and under ***mokṣha***).

Method of *MhBh*'s inquiry in the human condition

10; distinguished from western method in going beyond the logic of either/or, 10–1, 12; inherent in life itself, and not an artificial construct of the mind, 12; and its eighteen main characteristics, 12–21, 444:

1. takes up self-understanding in relation to concrete situations, contexts, 13;

2. no dichotomy between the particular and the universal, 13;

3. not *a priori* definitions but lakshana-s, attributes, are sought, 13–4;

4. human life being relational, all ideas and concepts are relational, 14;

5. human attributes form a unity and meaningful only in relation with the rest, 14–5;

6. human attributes form a natural unity, hence neither their neglect nor their idolatry, 14–5;

7. *dharma* the foundation of life, 15; radical change in the meaning of *tapas*, 'austerity', *yajna*, 'sacrificial rite', *karma*, 'acts', *dāna*, until then understood as 'almsgiving', and *tirtha*, 'pilgrimage': all given relational meaning, the relation of the self with the self and of the self with the *other*, 15;

8. the 'neti' of the *Upanishad*-s, always wrongly translated as 'it is not this', but actually meaning 'it is not this alone', *na+iti*, 'the statement is not yet complete', 16, and thus as ethical discipline in all judgments, 16, applied systematically;

9. human life being paradoxical, is to be understood paradoxically, but some paradoxes only apparent paradoxes, 16;

10. the opposites are manifest in life simultaneously, and therefore both are to be stated together, 17;

11. the contrary nature of human desires to be understood, 17;

12. there are conflicts not only between 'right' and 'wrong', but also between 'right and right': hence the moral dilemmas that arise, 18;

13. every philosophical question concerning the human condition begins with a personal question, but goes beyond the personal, 18;

14. human life based on feelings and not on thoughts alone, 18–9;

15. the conversational nature of the inquiry, 19–20;

16. the intellectual and spiritual presence of women, 20;

17. the understanding of order and truth revolves around *vānī*, speech; in all relationships speech being central, 20;

18. the importance of history, *desha* and *kāla*, 'the appropriate place' and 'the appropriate time', the two coordinates of history, acknowledged fully, 20–1; that done, *MhBh* raises the question: 'am I my history alone?'

- *MhBh* develops a method of instructing in the form of asking questions, gentle and friendly; see, for example, Nārada's questions to Yudhishṭhira, 468–76.

***mokṣha*, freedom, liberation**

ch.18, 540–92: one of the four ends of human life, 4; questions raised regarding, 8ff; related to the question of the free will, 8; *MhBh* raises self-interest to the highest level in the ideal of, 560–61; the rationality of, 560–67; linked to the empirical propositions about *sukha* and *duḥkha*, pleasure and pain, 561–62; from these follow two general propositions of the *karma* theory: a) *sukha* and *duḥkha* the results of ones own acts and b) one suffers the fruits of acts done in one's previous lives as well, 562; the *karma* of a man never leaves him, 562–63; as the ultimate point in the logic of *karma*, 564–7;

- radical shift in *MhBh* in its teaching concerning *mokṣha*, in terms of four things it does, making it a truly universal philosophy of human freedom, 567–70:

- *one*, disconnects it from belief in the birth-rebirth cycle and its metaphysics: *moksha* is human freedom here and now, in this life: the question is not what happens to one after death, but what one makes of oneself in this life, 566–67; as meditation not of death but of life, 567; Bhīshma's reply to Yudhishṭhira's question on, 567–68;
- *two*, in contrast to other philosophical systems, *MhBh* shows *moksha* to be quite as relational as truth and *dharma* are, 569; freedom an affirmation and not a denial of relationships, but relationships seen in a radically different light, 569; the free man, in being free, devotes himself to the *other*, 569;
- *three*, not until one has mastered one's self can there be a true reaching towards the *other*, 569, but this not turned into a hard theory; *MhBh* states truths that are manifest, are empirical, e.g. *dharma* consists of trust, caring, love and truth, 570;
- *four*, not the definition of *moksha*, but the attributes of the person who has attained that freedom, all of them relational, 570–77; *mokṣha* as the state of a radically altered consciousness, 571–74, 'On perceiving his self in all beings, and all beings in his self, he attains the highest consciousness', 572;
- as a going beyond the play of the opposites, and its rationality, even a psychological necessity, so that man does not remain a dangling man, dangling between the opposites, 269, 571–77, 588;
- self-knowledge the clearest path to, 574; three questions that arise, 575; the story of Bali and his dialogue with Shakra, and its teaching, 575–77;
- as freedom from: from that which confines, limits, does violence, degrades, 577–80: as freedom from the past, 579; as freedom from *tamas*, what 'suffocates', 'depresses' and 'chokes', 579; freedom from the endless striving and confusion of greed, the *rājasic*, 582;
- and the paths to, 580–87: *MhBh* first shows what those paths are not, 580–83; first, neither is *moksha* in lack of possessions, in not-having: repudiation of all false notions of 'renunciation', *vairāgya*, in the voice of Kausalyā, wife of King Janaka, 581–82; second, nor is *mokṣha* to be achieved by practicing this ritual or that, attention shifted from vedic rituals to the inwardness of being, as in *Upanishad*-s so in *MhBh*, 582; third, *mokṣha* not a project only of some special kind of people but aspiration of ordinary human beings, 582; the one who has attained *moksha* does not wear a uniform, 582;:
- the paths to *moksha* a journey within, 582–87; nothing to 'renounce', nor any thing to 'obtain', only to understand the true place of everything, 588;
- as freedom into, 588–92.

mother
assigned the most exalted status in the life-in-family, 360–65; 'Greater than ten teachers, the preceptor: greater than ten preceptors, the father: greater than ten fathers, the mother. The mother greater than even the earth, and no guru greater than the mother", 360; her place in the life of a man, 360–61; nothing more reprehensible than to disregard one's mother, 361; motherhood, a biological fact, not biological alone: the story of Kuntī, Karṇa, and Rādhā, 362; the story of Chirakārī, and its lessons, 362–63; not *duties* alone towards the parents, but also *feelings* highly emphasised, 363–65.

Mrityu
see under ***death***.

Nakula and Sahadeva
the twins, and the youngest of the five-Pāṇḍava brothers: on *artha*, wealth and material prosperity, in relation to *dharma*, in a discussion on that subject, 314–15; point to the unity between the two, and do not grade one over the *other*, 314: in their voice, *MhBh* saying 'Therefore what one

should aim at is to earn wealth combined with the right ordering of relationships, and have the right ordering of relationships combined with material prosperity', 315.

Nandinī
the cow of the sage Vāsishṭha: the story of King Vishvāmitra's visit to Vāsishṭha's hermitage, his trying forcefully to take her away and the miracle that follows, 398–99. See also under ***Vāsishṭha***.

Nārada
the sage: on freedom from fear, 166; engages Pañchachūdā the nymph on her perceptions of the nature of women, 304–06; Krishna confides in him his troubles with his relatives and seeks his counsel, and N says to Krishna: 'Troubles are of two kinds, external and those within', 263–64;

- for the questions he puts to Yudhishṭhira, now the emperor, concerning governance in his domain, see Ch.15, 465–76, where *MhBh* develops the method of 'instructions in the form of questions':
- on the emperor's relationship with his own self first, 466–68;
- on the principles of sound statecraft, 468–70;
- on the principles of good administration, 470–73;
- on the security of the realm, 474
- and about his relationship as a king with the people, 466–76.
- Nārada's Questions form an integral part of *MhBh*'s philosophy of law and good governance, to be read with Ch.14; see also under ***rāja-dharma***.

Narasimha Kavirāja
author of *Vivaraṇa-siddhānta-cintāmaṇi*, on disease according to Sāṃkhya, 505.

***nīti*, prudence**
intimately related with the acquisition of wealth, and with self-interest, *svārtha*, 5; the questions explored relating to, 5–6; 'Whatever serves self-interest is prudence', 216; all *nīti*-maxims in *MhBh* focus on the need for self-control, of which the control on one's tongue the most essential, 5–6, 216–17; emphasis upon speaking gently and pleasingly, 217, and the problem concerning its likely conflict with truth, 217, 220 (see under ***speech***); in abnormal circumstances, 6, 218; in *MhBh*, in order to prevent prudence from turning into a lack of principles, and the talk of 'time' and 'place' into lack of scruple, every prudence-maxim balanced by the qualification attached to it, 6, 220–22; as related to trust and trusting: the danger of trust wrongly placed, and the greater danger of nobody trusting anybody, 5–6, 221–22; and the avoidance of ati, 'excess', and on the logic of excess leading to self-destruction, 222.

- obligations, duties and debts: see under ***grihastha and grihiṇī***.

opposites, the
material and ethical, and the tension inherent in, and the human drama enacted endlessly between, from the one to the *other*, listed in *MhBh*: pleasure-pain, attraction-aversion, happiness-sorrow, love-hate, praise-denigration, gain-loss, success-failure, fear-courage, honour-insult, virtue-vice, good-evil, victory-defeat, freedom-bondage, and several more, 571; *MhBh* placing greatest emphasis upon, in its teachings concerning human freedom, *moksha*, 571; and the going beyond, and its rationality, 571, 573–75; he, or she, who has transcended the workings of the opposites has attained the last freedom, *mokṣha*, 571.

other, the
both in individual and collective sense: one of the two main dramatis personae of the ***Mahābhārata***; the other one, 'the self'; and their unity. Both present in every context throughout this book.

Pañchachūdā
the nymph: questioned by sage Nārada, pronounces upon the nature of women after

saying: "I am a woman and I cannot denigrate women", that is what she does, 304–06; narrated in *MhBh* in its inquiry in the sexual energy and relationships, where the prevalent conflicting attitudes towards woman are recounted, 304–312, and put aside as mindless. (See also under ***women***)

Pañchashikha
the Sāṃkhya philosopher: grew up in the love and affection of his mother Kapila, and in grateful acknowledgement of what she meant to him, came to be known as Kapileya, 'son of Kapila', 53; arrives in the court of King Janaka who had a taste for philosophical discussions, his current inquiry being: after death, does the Self, the *ātman*, exist or not?, 52; and their conversation, 53–55;

- and his reasoning for the existence of the Self that is beyond birth and death, 55–57; but feels obliged to answer first an invisible audience, that disputed that there is any such entity independent of the body-mind apparatus. He does not abuse them, nor does he caricature their reasoning, and honestly states both, 53–54; which means *MhBh* states both with honesty, 53; in answer to Janaka's questions, 54–55, draws a picture of the physical and psychological apparatus of human personality, 55–56;
- talks about the three primordial energies with which the whole creation suffused: *sattva*, *rājas*, and *tamas* (for which see under them, and also under ***Sāṃkhya***).

Pañchatantra
on violence through vānī, speech, 157;

- puts great store by wealth, 278–79: 'There is nothing in the world that cannot be obtained through wealth', 279;
- on the nature of women, portraying them as sexually lawless, 304–06;
- on *daiva*, fate: a man gets what he is destined to get, 481; the parable of *Praptavyamartha*, 481–82, 21*n*; even so, advocates effort and endeavour, 485–86.

pandita
the wise: who is truly a, ? *MhBh* raises this question, and raises the naturally related question, 'who is a fool?, and answers them in the voice of Vidura, 552–55.

Parāshara
the sage: father of the author of *MhBh*, Vyāsa, and the story of his siring him from Satyavatī, a fisher girl, 2 (see under ***Satyavatī***); on *shūdra*, in the *Parāshara-gītā*, a part of *MhBh*, in complete contrast to Krishna's view, 384; on the origin of *varṇa* in a natural division of labour, 384–85; on *dharma*-s common to all *varna*-s, 385; on the impurities invited by birth and by conduct, 385–86. (See also under ***varṇa-dharma.***)

Parāshurāma
referred to only as 'Rama', but not to be mistaken for the *Rāma* of *Rāmāyaṇa*: the extreme and dramatic expression of antagonism between brāhmaṇa-s and *kshattriya*-s, in his emptying the earth of the latter twenty-one times in a continuing bloody massacre. When the arrogant son of an equally arrogant king burnt down the hermitage of his father, sage Jamadagni, and killed him. The story to be read metaphorically and not literally, 400.

Parikṣhit
meaning 'the last of the line', the king, son of ABhīmanyu, and grandson of Arjuna: born still when Ashvatthāmā directed his deadly weapon on to the womb of Uttarā, but brought to life by Krishna, 139–40, 390–93; in many respects a good king, behaves towards the sage Shamīka insultingly, picking up a dead snake and placing it round his neck when he would not speak to the king, that day being his day of silence, 390; and the son of the sage, Shringī, pronouncing a curse upon Parikshit, 391, whereupon on the seventh day thence, stung by a deadly cobra, dies, 391–93;

- this story also of a sage, Shamīka, refusing to feel insulted when a king behaves towards him insultingly; and in his admonition to his son, against anger because anger thoughtless: "Anger destroys what the seekers would have with great difficulty achieved in *dharma*", 392; and on forgiveness: "Self-restraint and forgiveness is the path of all true seekers", 390–93.

Patañjali
the author of *Yoga-sūtra*-s: demonstrates the innate unity of the body and the mind, of the physical and the spiritual, 43; his philosophy incorporated in *MhBh*, but with a radical difference, 44, for which see under ***Mahābhārata***.

pleasure and pain, *sukha and duḥkha*
Ch. 9, 226–69; how do they affect man? and what is their nature? central concerns of Indian thought, 226, because central concerns of human life; desire for pleasure and avoiding pain, acknowledged as given natural facts, 226–27, 402–403, but analysed in each philosophical school in its particular framework, 226–27, becoming increasingly technical, 227;

- in *MhBh* as experienced facts, sensations and feelings, and not abstract concepts, 227–28, 1n, 2n and 3n; and both defined in simple observable terms: "Whatever is agreeable to one is 'pleasure', whatever is disagreeable is 'pain', 227; everybody, at whatever stage of life, is dependent on pleasure, and has pleasure as his goal, 228;
- in Sāṃkhya: consciousness acquires three different characteristics: the one beyond pleasure and pain, or feels both pleasure and pain, or feels neither clearly pleasure nor pain, just confused, 63;
- of two kinds: physical and mental, 228, one arising from the *other*, 229; the body their basis, 228–29; four causes of physical pain, and of mental pain, 229–30; and the psycho-somatic link: "There is no doubt that mental illness arises from physical illness. And it is certain that when the mind is sick, the body will be sick too"; "When there is pain in the mind, the body burns too", 229; the psycho-somatic link conveyed through the story of the Rakṣhāsa and the brāhmaṇa, the former askng: "Why am I so weak and pale?' and the latter listing the familiar reasons why, 239–46: 'Maybe that is why you look pale and weak'; "Sorrow destroys one's form; sorrow destroys one's strength. Sorrow destroys knowledge and awareness; and sorrow leads to illness", 266;
- the reasons why in the world more pain than pleasure, when the abiding human wish for the very opposite, 231–35: i) because all objects of pleasure transitory, 231–32; ii) even if they were never-ending, desire itself will create more pain than pleasure by turning into unending 'thirst', *trishṇā*, which is pain, 232–34 (see under ***desire*** and under ***trishṇā***); iii) those very things that bring pleasure, "Whatever things are desired by men, those things become the seed from which grows the tree of pain, 234–35; iv) physical senses and faculties and their natural tendencies, and what they equally naturally lead to, 235–36;
- lobha and *duḥkha*, greed and pain and suffering, the causal chain of, 235–36: and the causal chain of ignorance-greed, and what they lead to, a wrong relationship with one's self and, therefore, with the *other*, bringing pain and suffering, 236–38, 252; 'Who has conquered greed and its deluding confusion, has conquered his self', 238 (see under ***greed***).
- to hear only a discourse on the four root causes of pain, does little to remove one's unhappiness: there are more immediate and ordinary causes of pain as well, 239; Krishna feels hurt hearing bitter words from his relatives, complains to Nārada, 239–40; and such as those listed by the brāhmaṇa to the Rākṣhasa in the story above, 240–46;
- from the same indisputable facts concerning, three different paths to the avoidance of pain and to happiness, each a separate journey, and each with its own reasoning, 246, *MhBh*

Prahlāda

the Asura emperor, possessing the immense power of benevolence, and Indra, the crafty god: their story illustrates the natural unity of human attributes, each with its own place and value but meaningful only in their relatedness with each *other*, 101–102, and all brought together in *sīla*, inner coherence, in relation to one's self and the *other*, 101–103;

• and the meaning of *sīla*: "Freedom from malice towards any being, in act, in thought, and speech; benevolence towards all; and sharing—this is *sīla*, 102, "Neither friends nor relatives, nor wealth, nor superior lineage, nor learning, nor the chanting of some mantra, nor one's strength, put together, can deliver a man from sorrow. It is only *sīla* that brings peace", 103;

- answers Bali's question on force and forgiveness: the answer being that neither force nor reconciliation is good always, 147.

prakriti
Nature: see under ***Sāṃkhya***

protection, rakshā
in *MhBh* the wider meaning of, 427: and the weak, the poor, the exploited, the helpless, for whose protection from the strong the king created, 425–26; and *MhBh* stern warning to the king if he is neglectful of them, 425–26;

- in *MhBh* the wider meaning of, 427.

Pūjanī
the bird: her story in relation with king Brahmadatta, 500–503, through which *MhBh* explores many questions concerning life and relationships: on self-interest and, in that context, on trust and trusting, 221, whether they could trust each after what had happened, 502–503; her questioning his advocacy of Time, *kāla*, being the causal ground of every event, 500–503; fate and human effort depend on each *other*, 502; on the principles of good governance, as her parting gift to the king, 503. (See also under ***Brahmadatta***)

purohita
preceptor to the king: the meaning of the word, 'what leads', 'what goes before', 414; not an individual, much less a brāhmana necessarily, but a symbol of detached, unselfish, friendly, and wise counsel as to how the power of the state to be exercised and towards what end, a symbol of *dharma*, truth and justice, 414; and only in that measure, a true preceptor, 414–15; marks of great respect to, an acknowledgement that it is *dharma* and truth and justice that should 'lead' and 'go before' and not the power of the state, 414; in this, the awareness of the necessity of friendship between philosophy and power—for the good of the people, *loka-hita*, 414; Vidura in *MhBh* the greatest purohita, who was neither brāhmaṇa nor *kshattriya*, but a *shūdra*, 414–15. (See also under ***Vidura***)

purusha
'the Self': see under ***Sāṃkhya***.

purushārtha
human endeavour: arguments for, and the questions concerning, 483–91: see under ***causality***.

***rāja-dharma, daṇḍa*, the foundation of law and governance**
Ch. 14, 418–64: when *dharma* wrongly translated as 'religion', quickly interpreted to mean that foundation to be 'religious' in character, which it is not, 418–19; and the questions concerning, 420–21;

- no good governance possible without *prabhāva*, *dhāraṇa* and *ahiṃsā* as attributes of *dharma* (for their meanings see 419 and also 85–6), 419;
- governance and law essential parts of political theory of which the elements are: the individual placed in a system of social relations, 420; on law and the exercise of power, 420; ends and means; freedom and justice, 420; power the chief concern of dharmic political thought, its sources, purpose and the legitimacy of revolt when power becomes *adharma*, 421; fundamental place of the philosophy of *rāja-dharma*: 'every human limit is inherent in it, all aspects of knowledge are united in it', 423–24;
- in all acts of governance, the protection of the people, rakṣhā, the goal, 424–27 and 428–29, derived from the evident truth 'protection supports the world', 424; and the protection of the weak, the poor, the exploited, the helpless, 425–27 (see also under ***protection***); and the wider meaning of 'protection' in *MhBh*, that of creating conditions of personal and social bonding, 427;

one's conduct towards one's self and towards the other in times that are abnormal?', *MhBh* develops a whole rationality of abnormal times, 451, equally importantly, shows distressful times arise from the cumulative logic of *adharma*, created by one's own self or by the other or the two together, 455–56 (see under ***āpad-dharma***);

- an argument against capital punishment: Bhīshma narrates a conversation between Satyavān and his father Dhyumatsena, a king, Satyavān bringing forceful arguments against capital punishment, 455–58; 'The purpose of governance is, not to kill the wicked, but to create conditions in which the people can be good', 458;
- 'the king creates historical conditions, not they him', 458–64; Bhīshma on this question, 459; division of the *yuga*-s, see under ***yuga-s***.
- See Ch. 15, for instructions to the king in the form of questions.
- Nārada's questions to Yudhishṭhira: on the principles of sound statecraft, of sound administration, on the security of the realm and above all on the foundations of good governance, 468–76. (See under ***Nārada***).

rājas
one of the three *guṇa*-s, 'energies', according to Sāṃkhya: defined, 56; in Panchshikha's account, as related to the other two energies, *sattva* and *tamas*, 56–57; Vyāsa on, and the other energies, 64; discontent, greed, intolerance, sorrow and remorse are the natural products of *rājas*, 74.

sadāchāra
'good conduct': a source of *dharma*, 81; 'what is *sadāchāra*?', this question answered in the voice of *Dharmavyādha*, the meat seller, 547–52; *sadāchāra* is to bring oneself in right relationship with one's self and with the *other*, 550; pertains not to outward acts alone, but to *feelings and attitudes as well*, 550–51; Bhīshma on, 551–52; as a determinant of being a brāhmaṇa, 552; and the santa, the saint, 557.

sādhāraṇa-dharma
see under ***dharma***.

saha
'togetherness': the foundation of all relationships, 364.

saha-dharma
'togetherness in observing *dharma*': 354; in the *dharmashāstra*-s the wife is called *saha-dharminī*, 354; *MhBh* sees the wife with altogether different eyes, 354; hence, *saha-kāma*, the feeling of togetherness as the foundation of sexual happiness, 357; as the foundation of family everywhere, 367; and the essence of *saha*, 'togetherness', 367, in which no exercise of power of one over the *other*, nor a swallowing of one by the *other*, nor an abolition of individuality and its distinct colours, 367.

Sāṃkhya
MhBh's philosophy of the self manifestly on the lines of, 46, 64; *Panchshikha* explains the Sāṃ khya view of the psycho-physical apparatus of the self, 55–57; the relation between *purusha*, 'the Self', and *prakriti* 'Nature', 63ff; the three energies, *guṇa*-s, *sattva*, *rājas* and *tamas*, flowing through life in their different proportion, 70; all human relationships a combination of these three, 74; general account of, 71–72; *svabhāva*, 'the innate disposition', in, 55, 57, 59, 503–506; rejects *daiva*, fate, as any explanation of causation, 505; the two schools of, that of Kapila and of Patañjali, 506; Bhīshma expounds Sāṃkhya philosophy as propounded by the sage Kapila, 568–69; meaning of *mokṣha* in, 579–80.

santosha
'contentment': and its rationality: since there is no end to desire, what is required is contentment, 251–52, regarded by the wise as the greatest wealth, 286; for discontent is lack of happiness, 252 and 266; conflict between contentment and human effort, for the latter has its origin in a-*santosha*, dissatisfaction with things as they are, 526.

returns a person to the *other*, 206–07; the story of Kuntī repaying hospitality and kindness received by putting her own son to great risk, 207–15 (see under ***Kuntī***);
- and the other: *MhBh* relates self-interest with 'one's own good', sva-hita, and then unites it with 'the good of others', *para-hita*, 215, 223, and initiates into a mantra: 'In the good of the others lies one's own good', 215–16;
- *MhBh* on the self-related and the other-related disciplines of *dama*, 'self-discipline', *dāna*, 'sharing', *vānī*, 'speech', *ārjava*m, simplicity and lack of deviousness', and *ahiṃ sā*, 'not-violence', to be cultivated even in one's self-interest, 216 (see entries under them, and under *dharma*, and under truth);
- self-interest and nīti, 'prudence', 216–23, (for which see under ***nīti***);
- in *MhBh*'s teaching against every kind of excess, of virtue, of learning, of wealth and royal power, self-control is identified with self-interest, 291; but *MhBh* painfully familiar with the unscrupulous pursuit of wealth and power against one's self-interest and the interests of others, 292;
- King Janaka's wife on going beyond one's petty self-interests as a mark of being a genuine monk, 345–46;
- and self-interest raised to its highest level in *MhBh*'s teachings on *mokṣha*, the ultimate liberation, 560, 570.

Shakra
the god Indra: and *Prahlāda*, the Asura emperor, and the inter-relatedness of human attributes, 101–102; transforms king Bhangās*Vana* into a woman who would not want to become a man again, 312–13; tries to seduce a willing Ruchi, the beautiful wife of sage Devasharmā, but prevented by the sage's student, Vipula, using his psychic powers, 327–28 (see also under ***Vipula***); seduces sage Gautama's wife, 362 (see under ***Chirakārī*** and under ***Gautama***); and his dialogue with Bali, wanting to know the source of the latter's self-possession and equanimity even in grave adversity, 494–96 (See under ***Bali***).

Shāntanu, king
married Satyavatī, the mother of Vyāsa, even though she was of lower station, a fisher woman, 2.

Sharma, Ram Sharan
and his *Sudras in Ancient India* (1958): quoted at 372 10n, 372 13n.

Sharmishṭha
see under ***Yayāti***

shāstra
MhBh on what is, 312: "Whatever is just and fair, is *shāstra*; whatever is unjust and unfair, is a*shāstra*", 312: and this applied to what the later *dharmashāstra*-s and shastri-s did to women who had become widows; and what they did, a complete negation of *dharma*, 311–12; hence they were *adharma-shāstra*s, the codes of injustice, inequality and violence to such women, 312.

sīla
'inner coherence'; in the parable of Prahalada, 101; defined as 'benevolence…and sharing … and freedom from malice', 102; not a material object but the center of the inter-relatedness of human attributes, 102–03; as the right relation with one's self and with the *other*, 103.

shishtāchāra
'cultured conduct': *Dharmavyādha*, the meat seller, teaches Kaushika, the brāhmana ascetic and scholar, about, 547–50: "The truly cultured have manifest in them forgiveness and reconciliation, peace and contentment. Free from wanting and anger and the habit of finding fault in others, they are of loving speech; abiding in cultured conduct", 549; and truth, of the greatest weight in, 550; the attributes of a person truly cultured, shishta, relate to a person in relationship with himself or herself and with the *other*, 550; the seeming circularity

in the definition of, 550; included in being wise, pandita, 553.

Shiva
his long conversation with his wife Umā who raises several questions concerning human life:
- on the attributes of a person who truly is in unity with *dharma*, 110–11;
- on *ahimsā*, not-violence, being the greatest *dharma*, 116; on freedom from violence, 165–66;
- on truth, 182–83;
- his declaration that all *varna*-s are *shūdra-mūlaka*, 'founded on *shūdra*';
- on the question of causality: that neither human effort nor providence effective by itself; every act tied to effort and providence together, 488–89;
- on the *dharma* of the king in protecting the people from fear,

shaucha
'purity','cleanliness': the question, 'what is shuchi?', 'purity', 'cleanliness', is answered by *MhBh* by turning away from ritual purity to the purity of the heart and mind, 109;
- *MhBh* gives a deeply relational meaning to, away from rituality, 340; purity of the heart is the greatest, 340;
- five kinds of, 377 (see under ***Krishna***); sage Mārkandeya on, purity of three kinds :of speech, of conduct and of the body, 530–33;
- most difficult is control of one's mind, 531–34; fasting does not remove demerit, 531–32; Bhīshma on, purity of four kinds: (see under ***Bhīshma***).

shreya
'the Good': sage Gālava on the many meanings of, 78; seven sages, themselves confused, state different philosophical positions regarding, each claiming '*this is shreya*', '*this is shreya*', and ask Brahmā for a definitive answer to the question, 'What is *shreya*, 'the Good'?', 'What paths lead to *shreya*?', 119–20, and his answer, 118; *Kathopanishad* makes a distinction between 'the pleasurable', *preya*, and 'the Good', *shreya*,: the logic of the one distinct from that of the *other*, 258–59. In *MhBh*, the question of *shreya* comes up throughout, and throughout relational, not an abstract concept in metaphysics, 176.

shūdra
one of the four social divisions, *varna*: the purely economic functions assigned to *vaishya* and to, 370–71; in the theory of colours, is black, 373; by conduct not by birth, 375–79;
- Shiva declares: '*shūdra* is the basis of all *dharma*-s': all social functions are '*shūdramulaka*', 'based on services', 379. (For details see under ***varna-dharma, social arrangements***)
- and Krishna on: 'I always fear when the Veda is recited by the *shūdra*', and, 'the dog, the *shūdra* and the chandala are impure', 383; sage Parāshara counters Krishna's view: 'the *shūdra* is not a lowly being', 384–5. (See for details also under *varna-dharma*, social arrangements.)

Shukrāchārya
guru of the Asura-s, father of Devayānī: on hearing Devayānī complain that Yayāti, her husband, had cheated her with Sharmishtha, curses Yayāti to fall instantly into old age, 317–20: after Yayāti's explanation, relents, but unable to annul the curse, gives him a boon instead, 320. (See under ***Yayāti***.)

Shukranīti
on harsh words, 156; on ati, 'excess', 291; *varna* is a social function, 378–9; almost wholly for human effort, in the debate between *daiva* and *purushārtha*: '*with effort it is possible to protect the lamp against the wind*', 486.

speech, *vānī, vac*
its centrality to order, 20; in the *Upanishad*-s: *Brihādaranyaka* assigns the physical world to: is the *Rig Veda* and is the gods, 27; Aitareya sees Fire in the mouth as the faculty of, 30; *Kausītaki* says seeing is more general than, 28; *MhBh* on

the onslaught of forceful speech as a link in the chain of greed, 106; violence in thought and in speech and in act, is the embodiment of *adharma*, 152;

- violence in speech and words, 155–61; hurtful words are like dry arrows that burn the bones and the heart, 155–6, 217; "The wound caused by an arrow is healed, and so is the wound caused by a sword; but the wound of hurtful speech is never healed", 216–7; hence repeated warnings against harshness of speech, 156–7, 216–7; "What is spoken without regard to place and time; is bitter in result; is unpleasant; displays one's meanness; and is spoken without cause—that is not speech but poison", 217, "He whose speech is dry and whose heart hard; who by his speech hurts and causes pain to others; should among men be regarded as the poorest of all, carrying in his mouth poverty and death", 217;
- and against speaking ill of others, 157–9, 217; no real conflict between strength and gentleness, between pleasant speech and truth, 159;
- prudence-maxims center on the need for self-control, of which self-control on one's language the most essential: 'all functions of the world are tied to speech, *vānī*, 216–7; the need to cultivate proper, 216; Krishna complains of the bitter words spoken to him by his relatives, 239; and endearing speech a sign of self-discipline, 251; one of the thirty-six self-disciplines of the king Bhīshma propounds: 'speak pleasingly without being pitiable', 430–11; Yayāti's advises his son Puru on self-control over one's speech: 'out of anger don't speak in a way that is hurtful', 501; 'with the looks, the heart, the speech and the deeds – the king makes the people happy': Vidura on happy speech as an element of good governance, 447;
- sage Mārkaṇḍeya counts purity of speech as one of the three purities, 531; Krishna counts purity of speech as one of the five purities, 533; *Dharmavyādha* the meat seller on a loving speech as a sign of the truly cultured, 548, and on the nobility of conduct, they hurt no one by speaking bitter and wounding words, 548–9; of the attributes of a person who has attained *mokṣha*, one is: 'in his thoughts, or speech or acts, he causes no hurt to any being', 572.

spirituality
offered as translation of adhyatma, 42; related to the material, and the spiritual to be found in the ordinary, see Ch. 3, 52–75, specially the 'Introduction' to that chapter, 42–5; the wrong understanding that spirituality consists in renouncing and negating the material, due to *vairāgya* literature, 44. (See also under ***vairāgya***)

sukha
'pleasure', 'happiness': see under ***pleasure and pain.***

svabhāva
'innate disposition', 'one's nature': the philosophical theory that explains the diversity of creation and events, 453–508; as a theory of causation, the theory of inner teleology of Nature, 453; its adherents in Indian philosophical systems include Sāmkhya, the Lokayata and the *Ayurveda*, 503; faith in, gives rise to the cool detachment of a scientist, 527.

sva-*dharma*
see under ***dharma***

svahita
'one's good': inseparable from parahita, 'the good of others', 207, and from s*vartha*, 'self-interest', 218; *MhBh* radically changes the perceptions of, by linking it logically with self-interest, and these two with the good of others.

Syūmarashmi
the sage: in conversation with sage Kapila, assigns a prominent place to the life-in-family, and his reasoning, 348–9.

tamas
one of the three primordial energies according to Sāṃkhya, defined, 56–7; in Panchshikha's account of the self, 56–7; Vyāsa on, in relation to the other *guṇa*-s, 64; the word '*tamas*' derived from 'tam' which means 'to gasp for breath, be suffocated, choke, be exhausted, perish, be distressed or disturbed', 579.

tantra
its philosophy and practice in relation to sexual energy, the discussion on: 299–302.

Time, *kāla*
explored in *MhBh* at three different levels, 9:

i. *kāla* not the historical time, nor the time physically measured, but the determining cause of all that is and all that is not, akin to God, 9, 65–6;
ii. in a combination of 'the proper place' and 'the proper time' and 'the person concerned', *desha* and *kāla* and patra, as a measure of appropriateness of an act, and thus of its meaning, 9 (see under ***desha and kāla***);
iii. as history, 'past' 'present' and 'future' its forms, and one's relation to them in one's relationships with one's self, 9;

- Vyāsa's strong advocacy of Time as the determining cause of all that is and all that is not, 65–7, 491–93; this is also his view on causality, see Ch.13 (see further under Vyāsa); the paradox of Time as primordial energy or force, 72–3;
- the Yoga-Vāsishṭha view of Time as wholly a creation of the mind, 73; providence, *daiva*, identified with Time, 491–103;
- Bali, formerly Indra but defeated by Shakra, on the power of Time, 494–6, 575–7 (see also under ***Bali***);
- forceful advocacy of Time in the story of Arjuna, the great hero, unable to protect women from a bunch of robbers, and Vyāsa consoling him, 496–8 (see under ***Arjuna***);
- Vidura, consoling Dhritarāshṭra, propounds the belief that every event is pre-determined by *kāla*, Time, 498;
- Bhīshma on Time as only a mental construct and no real force, 499–500; objection to belief in Time as the causal ground of every event, mounted in a conversation between Pūjanī the bird and King Brahmadatta, 500–3;
- Time digests everything, but there is a state of being where Time itself is 'digested', 592.

tirtha
'pilgrimage': of all the places of pilgrimage, the heart the highest, 340, 534; what is true *tirtha*?, *MhBh* makes it, like everything else, relational, 530, 534–9; answering a question, 'what does a person on pilgrimage really gain'? sage Pulatsya on, 537; is not a ' geographical place' one goes to, to remove one's sins, 530, 537; saying this, *MhBh* describes the sacred places of India, in the east, the west, the north, and the south, their sacredness because associated with the sacredness of life, relational and not ritualistic, 538; Pāṇḍava-s, on being exiled, go to numerous sacred places where many discussions take place concerning, 538–9; knowledge, truth, self-discipline, compassion, and a good woman are *tirtha*, 534; Krishna on, 534–5; two kinds of : the stationary and the living, of the mind, 535; *manas-tirtha*, 'pilgrimage of the mind', in the voice of Bhīshma, 536–7: 'The deep unsullied pure waters of truth that holds the heart, in that pilgrimage of the mind bathe: with faith in what is abiding', 536; true *tirtha* a journey within, which takes one at the same time on another pilgrimage: the journey to the *other*, 537.

Tirukkuraḷ
the ancient Tamil classic: on speaking ill of others which pollutes one's own mind and does injury to others (19.1-10), 252n; on truth: "Not all lamps are lamps; the lamp of truth is the lamp of the wise" (30,9; on 'truthfulness', see the remaining verses in the same ch.of T) 186, 19n; on the relativity of 'truth speaking': "Even falsehood has the nature of truth, if it confers a benefit that is free from fault" (30.2), 190, 42n.

Tolkāppiyam
the ancient Tamil classic, 300.

transitory, *anitya*, the
as one of the reasons why more pain in the world than pleasure, more unhappiness than happiness, 231–32 (see under ***pleasure and pain***); and, one line of thinking concluded, because this, it follows that withdrawal from the world, *vairāgya*, is the way to happiness, 253–7 (see under ***vairāgya***);

- and the radical shift in *MhBh* concerning the because-therefore chain of reasoning, 260–63; because it is true that all things of the wold are transitory, it does not follow that, for that reason, they are worthless: human life itself is transitory, but it does not follow that, therefore, it is worthless, 261;
- *MhBh* teaches that the worth of a thing is not derived from its duration but from the quality of what it creates, 261.

***trishṇā*, 'thirst', 'burning desire'**
see Ch.9, 225–69; happiness is in renouncing, 236; the reasoning why one must overcome, 232, 233–4, 236, 564; (See also under ***desire and greed***)

truth, *satya*
Ch.7, 181–98; that conflicting perceptions of truth have caused more violence and killing than almost anything else in human history, the most astonishing paradox, 182;

- *MhBh*'s definition of satya undoubtedly as correspondence with facts as heard, seen, and done, 182; but truth in Indian thought a great deal more than 'correspondence with facts', which subjected to a deeper view of, 182–3, 192; motives and feelings leading to acts pertain to truth as much as the acts, 182–3; what is factually true, separated from the motives, may yet be a lie: in the voice of Shiva: "What is externally true, but contains clever distortion, is in fact a lie", 183;
- *MhBh* discusses truth at three levels, all inter-related in a deep inner coherence: a) the relativity of truth, b) truth is relational, c) truth is not knowing alone, but living quite as much, 183; unites knowing and living, 183, 192;

a. and the problem of relativism that naturally arises, and Yudhishṭhira's questions concerning, 183–92; the seeming contradiction between the absolute value placed upon truth, 183–86, and truth being relative, 186; and how the 'truth is relative'-argument may easily degenerate into opportunism, and used in bad faith, 190; acknowledging both, *MhBh* resolves the problem: truth as that which is conducive to the greatest good of all beings, 193, 196–7;

b. the thirteen attributes of, 193–5, half of them in relation to one's self, and the other half in relation to the *other*, both inseparable; truth is indivisible, as *dharma* is, 195; the limits of truth's attributes cannot be stated, 195;

c. as not knowing alone, but living quite as much, 183, 192; the conquest of death through truth, 180, 197–8; the centrality of truth in human life indicated by the word 'samāhita', 'held together', 'united', 195–6, and also 'for the good together' as a view of truth,195–8;

- and the story of Droṇāchārya's killing on the battlefield, how what may have the appearance of truth may still be a complete lie, 129, 190–92 (see also under ***Droṇāchārya*** and ***Yudhishṭhira***);
- and the conflict between speaking pleasantly but speaking truthfully, both essential to life, "Men who always speak pleasantly are easily met; rare are the people who speak and listen to words that are unpleasant but to one's good", 220–11; Bhīshma on, "It is best to speak the truth: and speak the truth for the good. I call only that truth, that serves universal good", 193, 197, 218;
- as the foundation of governance, creating trust among the people, 437–8; impartiality in governance related to truth, because

equality one of the attributes of truth, 436–8; required particularly of those who constitute an assembly that legislates, 438; and *ārjavam*, 'straightforwardness', 'lack of deviousness', 438;
- as forgiveness and reconciliation, 449–50; as pilgrimage, *tirtha*: "Truth is what makes all pilgrimage sacred. To speak the truth, and do no violence to any being, are called pilgrimage", 534, 537; as a sign of being truly cultured, of *shishtāchāra*: "*Ahiṃsā* and speaking truthfully—these are for the greatest good of all beings. *ahiṃsā* is the greatest *dharma* of all; and it is upon truth that *ahiṃsā* is based. In whatever they do, those who are truly cultured begin with truth", 549;
- and transcending the opposites of truth-untruth, *dharma-adharma*, as the last freedom, *mokṣha*, 574.

Tulādhāra
a grocer, who instructs Jājali, a brāhmaṇa ascetic, in the meaning of *dharma*; and the significance of their story, 110 and 386. (See also under ***varṇa-dharma, social arrangements***)

***tyāga*, giving up, renouncing**
see under ***vairāgya***

Uddalaka
father of Shvetaketu: his conversation with his son in Chandogya *Upanishad*, 27–8.

Umā
wife of Shiva: in conversation with him on the many questions concerning life, for which see under ***Shiva***.

***Upanishad*-s**
revolve around the nature of *prāṇa*, life energy, 71; the method of inquiry in,; which contrasted with the method of inquiry in *MhBh*,; food and water in, 24–30;

- ***Aitareya***
holds that brahman, the Ultimate Reality, is to be understood from a close reflection on the material world; each god assigned a place in the human body, 29–30;

- ***Brihādaraṇyaka***
on the importance of *anna*, 'food', 27–8 and 42; its method, 27; food is of seven kinds, 28; divides all existence into three primary categories, 28; establishes a hierarchy of generality 28; three main motives behind human acts, 226;

- ***Chandogya***
its chief concern is to show that reality is a composite of material and spiritual events, 26; mind is a material substance nourished with food, 27; the ultimate basis of all is brāhman, 27; the parable of Usasti and the three priests, 26; everything is of relative value in a hierarchy of generality, 26–7; Uddalaka's conversation with Shvetaketu, 27; inquires into the intimate relation of the energy in Nature and in the human personality, 71; the parable of *Satyakāma* Jābāl and his mother: on his asking his mother: 'What is my gotra?', in other words asking: 'Who is my father?', and her reply, with the dignity of truth, 'I don't know what your gotra is. I conceived you when I was working as a maid in different households. I know only this, my name is *Jābāla* and yours *Satyakāma*, call yourself *Satyakāma Jābāla*'; and the significance of the story of, 384, 74n.

- ***Kaṭha***
on the relationship of the senses and the *buddhi*, 'the intellect', 61, 76n; on the distinction between 'the pleasurable', *preya*, and 'the Good', *shreya*;

- ***Kaushitaki***
demonstrates the preeminence of *prāṇa*, life, 28; its method both empirical and deductive, 29; its major conclusions, 29;

- ***Prashna***
of the six questions asked in this *Upanishad*, the third relates to *prāna*, life-energy: 'How does life-energy hold the outside material world?

How does it hold the inner world of man's mind?', 71.

• ***Shvetāshvatara***
on the causal ground of this world, 523; on Time, 524; on *svabhāva*, 'the innate disposition', 524; concludes that it is the Divine Being through whose power all that there is, exists and moves, 524.

• ***Taittirīya***
on food, 24–5; the material body, vital breath and mind are suffused with intelligence, 25; on hospitality, 26.

Uttarā
mother of Parikshit, 140, 393 (see under ***Parikṣhit***).

vairāgya
'disgust at', 'renunciation', 'asceticism': *vairāgya-literature*, also 'disgust'-literature, 44, 258; as the source of the wrong understanding that the spiritual consists in negating and renouncing the material, 43–4;

- stating strongly the reasoning of *vairāgya* as the path to happiness, 254–8, in the form of because...therefore', derived from a common stock of facts concerning 'pleasure and pain', *sukha* and *duḥkha*, (for which see under ***pleasure and pain***), *MhBh* shows how it ended in denying the body and the mind, 254, 303, and, in different voices, shows that reasoning to be false, 258, 580–82;
- the path of total withdrawal from the world, fraught with danger, 254, 580;
- relationships seen in *vairāgya* as only full of pain, because "Just as two pieces of wood floating in the ocean touch each other for a while, and then separate, so do the human beings", 255; "No one belongs to me, and I belong to no one. Just as the travellers on a road become companions for a while; so do the wife, brother, and good-hearted friends", "One is alone in birth; one is alone in death. One is alone in one's pain; and one is alone in crossing over. Father, mother, brother, son, guru, relatives and friends are of no help", 256; therefore, let one travel beyond them, 257: "I am in my being alone"; 257;
- *MhBh* a radical break from the path of *vairāgya*: from the same stock of undeniable human facts, draws different conclusions which are a joyful affirmation of life and not its violent negation, 261; the strongest affirmation of relationships, and not their denial, but relationships seen in a different light, 261;
- struck by disease, death and decay, the Buddha at first took to the path of harsh asceticism, only to discover that it was a wrong path; that salvation was not in punishing the body, but in knowing the causal chain of suffering and decay, and in destroying that chain, 303; earlier, in the *Upanishad*-s, a turning away from senseless asceticism, 303;
- the functional view of sex, one of balance, threatened by asceticism, 301; asceticism probably older than the Veda, and its many faces, 303; their common feature, their view of sex as cosmic snare, 304; the figure of the ascetic one of immense attraction—to women, 304; the ascetic denial, a sexual denial, and hence the denial of woman, 304; seduction of the ascetic an abiding theme of Indian mythology and literature, 304;
- critique of the *vairāgya*-literature: the ascetic denial of the body must lead to a hatred of all that is human, 258;
- in the voices of King Janaka's wife, Kausalyā, the sage Mārkaṇḍeya, and Vyāsa, and in several other voices, in *MhBh* the teaching away from the mistaken notions of renunciation, 342–47, 539–42; conquest of the mind and cleansing of feelings, not giving up of things, is what renunciation truly is, 344–47, 539, 580–81; Vyāsa on *tyāga*, 'renunciation', as 'sharing', 541–45;
- excepting *vairāgya*-literature, Indian thought never maintained withdrawal from the world, and renunciation of personal bonds,

behaved in the manner he did, and therefore took no offence, 387–93;

- the influence of *kshattriya*-s in breaking the vedic world-view: the Buddha and *Mahāvīra*, 394–5; the subsequent history of the complicated caste system and the reversal of the relativistic direction of Dharmic thought and life, 394ff;
- antagonism between brāhmaṇa and ksattriya, the thinker and the ruler: *MhBh* depicts that antagonism through the metaphor of 'the right of way': the story of King Kalmashpāda and sage Shakti, son of sage Vāsishṭha, 398–9; the story of King Vishvāmitra and Vāsishṭha, 527–9; the story of King Kritavirya and the birth of Aurva, 400–401; (for which see under ***respective entries***);
- why is brāhmaṇa portrayed in *MhBh* a perpetually 'angry man', quick to take offence and quicker to pronounce a curse, 402–410: the path of knowledge a difficult path, and brāhmaṇa excluded from seeking pleasure, 402; and where no joy, there the ground fertile for anger, 402; brāhmaṇa excluded from the power and the glory of the ruling class, and the affluence of the trading class, 402–3; discipline required of him, impossibly high, 405–7; and also turned into a perpetual yachaka, 'the one who has to ask', which humiliating, and reducing, 407–10;
- harmony among various social callings essential to social wealth, loka-saṃgraha, 410–15;
- in the person of Vidura, of *Dharmavyādha* the meat seller, of *Tulādhāra* the grocer, and in the person of the unnamed housewife, *MhBh* saying: "on the path of truth and knowledge there are no distinctions between one person and another except what he makes of himself, or she makes of herself", 414–5.

Vāsishṭha

the sage: through the story of king Vishvāmitra trying to take away by force his very remarkable cow Nandinī, and the events that take place, 398–9, *MhBh* teaches that a simple twig of a tree in the hands of a forgiving sage has greater power than all the weapons of a king, Vishvāmitra declaring: "The force of a *kshattriya* be damned. The true force is the force that comes from a life lived in knowledge, truth and peace", 399;

- agitated over the incompatible theories of causality, and unable to come to any definite conclusion, 526, several sages approach Vāsishṭha, the wisest of them all, and his cryptic reply to them: "I have little knowledge of this subject", 526.

Vichakhnu

the king: in his voice, *MhBh* strongly condemns the killing of animals as sacrificial offering in a *yajna*, propounds *ahiṃsā*, not-violence, 118–9; on seeing the head of a killed bull rolling, and many cows waiting to be sacrificed, says a prayer for the welfare of all the animals of the world, turns to the priests, and says: "Only those will approve of violence that are disordered, are fools, are men of no faith, are doubtful about the self, and are not highly regarded either", 118.

Vidura

the half-brother of King Dhritarāshṭra, and the detached observer in the unfolding drama of complex motives and relationships:

- in his voice, *MhBh* says: "In human beings, it is *sīla* that has the chief place. If that is lost, a person's life, wealth, and friends, all are meaningless", 103; on forgiveness and reconciliation, *kṣhamā*, 147, 179n, 453;
- on 'the six deadly swords': "These kill human beings—not death", 173;
- on the conflict between pleasant speech, to which great value attached, and truth, to which attached even greater value, 220–21: "Men who always speak pleasantly are easily met; rare are the people who speak and listen to words that are unpleasant but to one's good", 220;
- on *indriya-nigraha*, 'self-discipline, 249; on *aparigraha*, 'not-grasping', 'not-engulfing', 252–3;

- "Neither the both sides are seen anywhere to be victorious; nor are both sides seen defeated. What is seen, though, is the destruction of their prosperity alike", 150:
- War always is deceitful and wicked. In killing another, who is not himself killed also? And to the one killed in the war, victory and defeat are just the same": "I believe that death is no worse than defeat, but the victorious suffer as well", 150:
- The king wanting the welfare of his kingdom should avoid war always", 151; and, in the voice of a mother to her son, Gāndhārī to Duryodhana: There is no good in war, dear son, nor any holding together in the foundations of life. Where can there be in war any happiness? Nor is there any certainty of victory in every war. Therefore do not put in it your thought and expectations", 152;
- *MhBh* dwells at length, at the same time, on what should be done for internal security in times of war, should war become inevitable; but the foundations, the *dharma*, repeatedly emphasised: there is a *dharma*, too, of how a war to be conducted in human terms, 152;
  - and the attitude towards the enemy (see under ***enemy and enmity***): there is honour even amongst thieves, and the story of Kāyavya, 153–5 (see also under ***Kāyavya***);
  - after narrating a dreadful war and its suffering, *MhBh* shows that nothing that is of enduring worth was ever achieved by war, 463.

weapons

in the story of King Alarka, different kinds of weapons required in the conquest of the self than those used in expanding a kingdom, 261–63 (see also under ***Alarka***);

- and the lessons from the story of Ashvatthāmā's revenge at the end of the war (see also under ***Ashvatthāmā***), 141:
- Hatred and the spirit of revenge are the weapons that destroy the world.
- The power of physical weapons is increased beyond description by the power of anger and hatred and revenge breathed into them.
- Even a piece of straw becomes a weapon of greatest force when touched with great hatred and the greater resolve to revenge.
- Once fired, the weapons of hatred and revenge cannot be withdrawn—except by those who have the greater power of self-control, forgiveness and reconciliation.
- Therefore, the physical weapons of most destructive power shall never be in the hands of those with no control over their mind and over their judgment even less.
- No matter how great the danger to you, never use the weapons of ultimate force, especially over human lives.
- and Arjuna's conclusion: "The knowledge of weapons is not for ever".

woman

see Ch.11, 304–335; perceived both as divine energy, shakti, and as *maya*, 'the deluder', a source at once of fascination and fear, 304, 307;

- the figure of the ascetic one of immense attraction—to women, 304; the ascetic denial a sexual denial, and hence the denial of woman, 304; in the logic of which she became the eternal seducer, 304; seduction of the ascetic an abiding theme of Indian mythology and literature, 304;
- Pañchachūdā, the nymph, on the innate disposition of, as sexually lawless, 304–305, but this only a method of *MhBh* narrating also what must have been a prevalent view of, 306, and then discarding it as mindless; will be wrong to muddle the perception of woman as *māyā*, which had the grandeur of at least a principle, with woman as sexually lawless, leaving her neither sense nor dignity: the latter view discarded by *MhBh* no sooner than stated, 307;
- "there is in the ***Mahābhārata*** not a single woman who answers, even remotely, Pañchachūdā's description of women", 309;

- dismisses *daiva*, 'fate', 486–87, 51n;
- on *purushārtha*, 'human effort, 526–87; but effort to be in consonance with the *shāstra* and the approval of 'good men', 526;
- 'What is worn out, broken...consider that a new beginning', 526;
- narrates the story of Queen Choodala teaching her husband what freedom truly is, 582;
- on the signs of *jīVana-mukta*, 'the free man', 588–89; as the mahakarta, 'the great doer' and the mahabhokta, 'the great enjoyer', 588; there is neither bondage nor liberation, 589–90; see 589, 112n.

Yudhishṭhira

the eldest of the five-Pāṇḍava brothers, and a husband of Draupadī: the main interlocutor, in whose voice, in his many dialogues with Bhīshma and others, *MhBh* raises the questions (not listed here again), that arise universally about life and human living, in its inquiry in the human condition. Present throughout the book, his voice heard in most of the entries in this index.

yuga-s

the division of 'times': in *krita, tretā, dvaparā* and *kaliyuga*-s, 459; *krita* also called *satya-yuga*, 'the golden age', and *kali-yuga*, the worst of all times, 459; in the voice of Yudhishṭhira, *MhBh* asks: "Do historical conditions (*kāla*) create the character of the state, or does the character of the state create historical conditions?", 459, and in the voice of Bhīshma says, "Entertain no doubt whether it is Time that creates the king or the King that creates the Times. It is the king that creates the Times", 459;

- progress or decline, no mysterious teleology at work, only the consequences of collective *karma* of a society which determine its collective times, which can be changed for better or worse, 459.